BILL
GRAHAM
PRESENTS

Doubleday

New York London Toronto Sydney Auckland

BILL GRAHAM PRESENTS

My Life
Inside
Rock
and Out

BILL GRAHAM
and
ROBERT GREENFIELD

PUBLISHED BY DOUBLEDAY
a division of
Bantam Doubleday Dell Publishing Group, Inc.
666 Fifth Avenue, New York, New York 10103

DOUBLEDAY and the portrayal of an anchor
with a dolphin are trademarks of Doubleday,
a division of Bantam Doubleday Dell Publishing Group, Inc.

Library of Congress Cataloging-in-Publication Data
Graham, Bill. 1931–1991.
    Bill Graham presents: my life inside rock and out/Bill Graham
and Robert Greenfield.—1st ed.
       p.   cm.
    Includes index.
    1. Graham, Bill, 1931–1991. 2. Impresarios—United States—
Biography. I. Greenfield, Robert. II. Title.
ML429.G69A3   1992
781.66'092—dc20
[B]   91–8108
                                                  CIP
                                                  MN

ISBN 0-385-24077-5

DESIGNED BY GUENET ABRAHAM

For all my sons
B. G.

For Bill Graham, Melissa Gold, and Steve "Killer" Kahn:
May they rest forever in eternal peace.
R. G.

Contents

Part Three

Making It a Business

Part Four

Out of the Fire

Part One

In the Beginning

Chapter One

From War to War

1.

BILL: I don't mind hearing about what happened to me as a kid. But I've never been inquisitive. I have never once in my life said to any one of my sisters, "Tell me about this." I've asked very little about my mother and very little about my father. I have no recollection of either of them. None whatsoever. No memory. I was two days old when my father died. I never saw him and he never saw me.

I have no answers as to why I'm this way. Maybe there is a right and a wrong—that I should've wanted or I shouldn't have wanted. But that was another life. You could say I should want to know who I was. *No.* Because what's it gonna do for me? Fill in some space? I don't have those questions. *Who was my father? What was my mother like?* They're gone. I'm not saying it's right. But I've never tried to dig up pictures of my past.

EVELYN UDRY: The firstborn is Rita. I am the second. Then comes Sonja, then comes Ester. And then Bill. And we had a fifth sister. Tolla. Tanya. Who died. Now, I would have been between four and five years old. In Menel or Sopot. In Ostfriesen. The border between the north of Germany and Poland. And there I remember with my mommy, we had visited my father. But I couldn't tell you where. Was he working on some project? I couldn't tell you. But I remember we took the train. I even remember that I had a very big umbrella. Strange the things a kid can imagine. I remember it was so big, the umbrella. "I'm going to close it," I said. And my mommy said to me, "No, you will be all wet and you will not be nice-looking." I was between four and five. So this was 1928 or '29.

3

ESTER CHICHINSKY: From what I've been told by my grandmother, my father was something like a civil engineer. His name was Jacob *Grajonza*, which was the way I always had my name signed or written. At home, he was called "Yankel," but his name was Jacob. Grajonza is a Russian-Polish name. I look much like my father. My late son looked a bit like him. He was a big man. Broad-chested. With a prominent forehead and a V-shaped head of hair. On all the pictures, very well dressed. Extremely well dressed in suits. Very distinguished appearance. I think I have pictures that I gave to Bill.

EVELYN UDRY: My mommy had completely black hair. But really *dark* black. My daddy's was a little big lighter than dirty blond. Light brown, really. The same color as me and Sonja. Before getting white. He died in 1931. Because Bill is born in 1931. Eight of January, 1931.

ESTER CHICHINSKY: From what I have been told by my grandmother, in 1931 my father worked on a project and got hurt or fell or had some sort of injury. Maybe he broke his leg. After his fall, it is my understanding that he had a blood infection. He died of sepsis, which is a blood infection. I was six at the time. Five or six.

EVELYN UDRY: He's buried I think in Menel. In a Jewish cemetery. None of the children went to the funeral. We were all too small.

ESTER CHICHINSKY: On my mother's side, they were all Russian. From what has since become Lithuania. My mother always considered herself Russian. She spoke fluent Russian but hardly any German and no Yiddish. My father's side, yes. But not her.

From what I heard from my grandmother, on my mother's side, they were military people. Officers. Which unless you were real superior, they would never let you be. There was a drastic distinction between my mother's side and my father's side. Hers were from a higher class. But my father was always looked up to by his relatives because he helped his whole family come out from the Eastern Bloc to Germany.

My mother's name was Frieda. Her maiden name was Sass. She was a very, very, extremely beautiful woman. Very intelligent. Very bright. Very courageous. Loved by everybody. A very generous woman. She was a woman without fear. In the beginning after my father died, there was sufficient money for my mother and us to live on. Then she took over a stand in a mall. A huge mall.

EVELYN UDRY: Of course as children, we all went to the syngogue in Berlin. We kept all the Jewish holidays but my mommy did not wear a *shaytl* or a "false hair," as I call it. *Shabbat* was kept. Not that she was Orthodox. No no no. But *frum*.

ESTER CHICHINSKY: We were members of the Linden Temple. Not just for the holidays. We were all-year-round members. We had our private seats. Not that we necessarily went each and every *shabbos*. But our seats were there all year round. Which an average family could not afford or would not have done.

EVELYN UDRY: We lived on the Lindenstrasse, which was not a boulevard really but a big street. There was no Judengasse in Berlin where only Jews lived. Everywhere, it was very mixed. Our synagogue was about three or four minutes from home. A big one. A very beautiful one. I remember that my mommy took Rita and myself along with her, because Ester and Bill were too small. I used to go with her on Yom Kippur and Chanukkah and sit in the women's section. Even if I would have had a father, my daddy couldn't have been with us or we couldn't be with my daddy because upstairs was for ladies only.

The building we lived in was five or six floors high. You walked into it and behind the entrance, there was an empty place. You could then walk up to the right or left to your apartment. Ours was on the left side. On the first floor. Not big. I think it was something like two and a half rooms. A tiny room and then two others. When you walked in, the kitchen was the first.

ESTER CHICHINSKY: According to how we lived, according to our education, the schools we went to, according to the environment we were brought up in, according to the friends that came to our house, people of music and arts, you would never have known how hard my mother had to work to keep us going. We all loved theater. From what I have been told by my grandmother, Mama had a great love for the harp. She did play at times. But not so I can recall.

You have to remember one thing. I was a small girl. You know how children are. You see your mother cry and you wonder why. You see your grandmother telling you why or the family telling you but you are still a child. My father's death might have affected me then but not that I can remember to any great extent. If I had been the only child and felt my mother giving up because she had to moan all the time or it had affected me physically, it would be one thing. But we were part of a large, large family. My grandmother also lived in the same building as well. There was always a lot of people at the dining room table. I remember that if it came to a holiday, preparations were made two weeks ahead of time.

EVELYN UDRY: You know how we slept? *Badly.* As a matter of fact, *very* badly. In one bedroom, what you can call the bedroom, the biggest of the two and a half rooms, there were three beds. There we all slept. Changing partners a lot. My mother slept in the tiny room. I don't even know how. Because my mommy was a very tall person. One meter seven-five or eight, I no longer remember which. Very tall and very beautiful and she had to sleep on something shorter than a bed, similar to a couch you might say. And I remember when she came home sometimes, very tired from the market, she lied down in one of the kids' beds because they were big. Bill I think had something a little bit separate like a crib. But really he was sleeping with five girls.

My mother would go off to sell things in the market. Wednesday it was in one place and Thursday in another. Artificial flowers, some of which we made at home, twisting up the stems until midnight. Also jewelries. Not real but costume. Because at that time, fine ladies liked to have on themselves a big pin here and a brooch there.

Two or three years after she started selling, the wife of an old man named Horowitz who had a cellar very close to the Lindenstrasse where he made ladies' skirts said to my mother, "Frieda, why don't you try selling *skirts?* You will earn more than with those little flowers." So that is what she did. And it went quite fine.

I remember very early going to the market with Mama because my older sister Rita was already off to Shanghai. Which made me the oldest in the family. This is 1936.

RITA ROSEN: I was eighteen years old and I went to China. By myself— 1938. And I cried of course. A lot. Because I have never been away from home. But since I am the oldest one, I thought, "If I go, maybe I can bring over somebody. Maybe my mother." But it wasn't easy. First of all, you had to have money. I went by air. I went by train and by boat. But I cried all the way. If I could have swum back, I would have swum back. Because everybody else had a husband or mother or father. But I didn't have anybody.

EVELYN UDRY: Rita was in love with Freddy. He went to Shanghai to leave Germany, because he was a Jew. He got out early. I can still see how Freddy was. Very good-looking. Today, we would say like a playboy, you know? I was very young and I was impressed by two young men. One was Freddy and the other was my cousin Norbert. *Pppppf!* He was like Marlon Brando in his best days! You understand?

I was thirteen and going to the gymnasium at the time. From the gymnasium, I would go right to the market because my mommy couldn't bring home all the stuff. Some markets started in the morning, so I would go with Mommy to help carry all the cartons. And then to school. Then I would go back in the afternoon because she could never get home with all the stuff. I remember things that are absolutely crazy. Standing in the market with the artificial flowers. I would say, "Oh, the yellow one looks nice on your coat. The brown is better on your hat." A thirteen-year-old girl.

When you are that age, you help your mother as much as you can. Not that the cartons were so heavy. Because those flowers, they're very light. But each carton was big around like a table. So you had to carry them with both arms. On the Hochbahn and the U-bahn. And when you are thirteen, you just *do* it. You never even think just how tired your mother must be.

ESTER CHICHINSKY: The public school I went to was right across the street from where we lived. After we were no longer allowed to go to the public schools, I went to the Jewish *Madchen Schule,* the girls' school. I remember that the principal of the public school adored my mother. I believe it was 1938, I came home one day very unhappy. It was required in the morning when you came to the class and the teacher enters to raise your hand and say, *"Heil Hitler,"* and I was very unhappy about it. Because I remember she allowed me to enter the class a little later so I did not have to say it.

In those days, you had kids in the class who belonged to the Hitler Youth. I had a taste of fighting against them. After school and at night, boys and girls beating up on me. But I think that I was lucky. Not brave but lucky. I've never shown fear. But then it came to the point where the principal couldn't protect us anymore. This is when we were enrolled in a Jewish girls' school on the Auguststrasse next to a Jewish old age home. There we had fights every day. They waited for the Jews to come out. This is 1938.

EVELYN UDRY: I remember Kristallnacht. What a night. It started quite late. Eight or eight-thirty. Trucks. We didn't know what it was. Not normal noises but voices speaking through loudspeakers and screaming. As I told you, we had to walk through that empty space to get to our apartment so we couldn't see the street. We couldn't see the street, but we did hear the noises. After all, we were on the first floor. We heard screaming but we didn't know from where.

There was one family in the building who had a boy, a little bit older than me. Fifteen or sixteen. But he had troubles with one leg. And the father wasn't home. They came and got the boy. Of course we knew them, the mother and this boy, because they also went to the same synagogue. The mother of course was hysterical.

My mother said to us, "Don't move. Don't you go nowhere. Don't you open the door. I'm going to see if I can help this lady." And she went. When she didn't come back, we were afraid that they took Mama.

If they would have taken my mother, so help me God, I would have killed the guy. Take me, do whatever you want to do with me. It would not have mattered what they did to me. If anything would have happened to my mother. But finally, my mama came back. But for us it was too long. She went away too long.

You see, they denounced people as Jews. That's how all this happened. But my mommy was somebody. People liked her. They saw her always going and coming and *schlepping* and she didn't do anything to anybody, she was always nice, saying hello to everybody. And the people in the neighborhood knew that there's no man in the house. So we were all right for a while. But these were all important steps.

After *Kristallnacht*, they could do anything they liked to you. I had an identity card with the Star of David on it. In the middle of the *Mogen Duvid*, it was written *"Juden."* I had to carry the card with me all the time. They were checking for it even on the Hochbahn and the U-bahn.

I remember my mommy was very worried about Bill. As you know, in Berlin, there was *Hitlerjugend*, Hitler Youth. She received letters. People passed by, men and sometimes women, to ask about her son. "What age has he got? Is he in the Hitler movement?" Not everybody knew we were Jewish. They came around knocking on doors. Collecting these young kids. From one floor to the other. We saw them coming and my mommy said, *"No.* He's too small. He's too young." Because they took them from six on. Now, Bill, he was already five or six. But my mama said, "Oh no, he's *four."* But from that day on, my mommy was scared.

ESTER CHICHINSKY: When I hear or read in the paper that "Bill Graham was put in an orphanage," I never understand what they mean. He was not put there as an orphan. I think my mother had a certain foresight. She finally realized she had made a mistake by not getting out of Germany. A very good friend, Mrs. Mueller, gave certain ideas to my mother. To protect the young ones. Bill and Tolla, the youngest sister.

So my mother placed them both in a *kinderheim*, a place where kids were extremely well taken care of, with good education. All Jewish children, as far as I know. I saw Bill every day practically. I saw Tolla practically every day. But they did not sleep at home anymore. Fridays they came home. Saturdays they were home. Sunday, they were not home. Unless there was a holiday. Then they stayed with us.

My mother feared for the youngest children because the Germans had a certain satisfaction to tear families apart by not allowing them to leave as a whole.

BILL: I remember one time at the *kinderheim* when they made us stand out in the street for hours and hours and the streets were just lined with people. I remember this because I couldn't understand why we were being made to stand out there for so long. Then they asked us to raise our arms in the "Sieg Heil" salute. The Führer was passing by. I didn't see him because I was so short and there were so many people standing in front of me. But I did see the car.

I've been told by my sisters that at the *kinderheim*, I was taught to play the violin *and* the piano. Concerning the violin, I'm not sure. But I must've learned piano because I can still sit down now and play two or three tunes that anybody my age from Germany would recognize. My sisters have also told me that whenever I visited my mother's house, my biggest joy was to throw silverware out the window. As to whether I was more favored by her because I was the only boy, they've never said.

EVELYN UDRY: I couldn't go on with the college because I was Jewish. And so I was home. From where she took the courage, my mother, I don't know. But every morning, we went to the market. Sometimes, we did one market in the morning and we had to travel with all our cartons to another market in the afternoon. There were episodes that were unbelievable. She would say to me, "Go ask Mr. So-and-So because they bought a skirt from us or some flowers, could he keep for us from the smoked salmon the heads?" So I went and I got that for free. Because my mommy always did feed us. We didn't have turkeys but if there were potatoes, they were well made. If it was rice, it was good.

ESTER CHICHINSKY: I don't exactly remember the date when Bill left Berlin. But I do remember they had to close up this particular *kinderheim*. So there were two choices. Either you take your child home or let them take him on a transport. And I think my mother made the right choice. It was, I think, 1939. We were all at the train station. I remember this like Bill is standing in front of me now and I'll tell you why.

A week or two before, we had to prepare his luggage. We had a list of what he could take. With his sweaters and all his clothing and everything. Sewing on name tags, and such. I remember Momma explaining that she was going to send Bill and Tolla away. She had tears in her eyes. I remember her standing with Tolla and Bill at the train station with a big card hanging over them with all the information on it. Parent's name and everything. But a lot of children. A *lot* of children. I think it was good foresight on my mother's part to send him away on that transport. Otherwise, he would never have been alive.

EVELYN UDRY: It was a *tough* day. The day before, I went with my mommy, Bill was with us, to a place where we received the papers. To send him out. It was a Jewish agency. A big form. Two or three pages with Bill's picture on it, which we put into a hard plastic case with a band that went around his neck. I remember my mommy when we went home from the station. Crying and uhh . . . it was *terrible*.

If you ask me if he had any idea what was going on, my answer would be: *No. None at all.*

ESTER CHICHINSKY: Tolla when she left was about a year or a year and a half younger than I was. She was born in 1928. So she was eleven or twelve. Very pretty. Bill, I think, was nine. Eight and a half, or nine. We knew this transport was going to France. Then we received notes from France through the Red Cross. So we knew they had arrived okay.

BILL: My life began in Chaumont at the château. My life, hard as it may have been, stabilized there. Since I had no real memory of what had come before, it was the only home I had ever known. Home to me wasn't my family. Home to me was all these other kids. I was part of something there. Same kids every day. Same teachers. It was my first permanent space. It was my base. It was my *home.* I don't know how I got to Chaumont. Château de Chaumont. Located southeast of Paris, mid to the right of central France. A French officer in the Resistance who came from a wealthy family had turned his château over to an organization that housed, among others, German orphans. We were part of this exchange program but we got caught in France. Just like French students who got caught in Germany when the war started. The occupation and the overrun were not completed until 1941.

I was nine when I got to France. I was eleven when I left there. I have memories but not full ones. I have memories of huge tapestries on the walls of this castle. I spoke only German when I got there but I learned French very quickly. I do remember the one steady meal we had at the château was lunch. It was always the same. We practically lived on rabbit. Various types of rabbit, cooked any way they could.

I keep a box somewhere of things from my childhood. A poetry book given to me by other people in the château. Things from the orphanage in Berlin. I have my original *yarmulkah* and my original prayer book. Postcards that I got through the Red Cross from my sisters when they were still in Germany before the war started and there was still mail going.

The château itself was very beautiful. Far beyond anything I'd ever seen before. See, I came from orphanage life, not a home. On weekends, Ester told me, I'd go visit our mother's home. But I don't remember that at all. I only remember going from an orphanage in Berlin to a *castle*.

There were no dormitories. Just lots of us sleeping in a large room. Again, I remember very little in terms of specific things. I have a terrifying, terrifying fear of snakes and worms and the eeriness of them, which I attribute to my life there. Because once the war started, we went out with two or three of the teachers and some townspeople and we built air raid shelters outside the château in the ground. Then they came and put wooden planks in and hauled the earth up and we were able to get into these trenches. Covered with wood and dirt.

I remember going into the trenches once the bombing raids started. They weren't looking to bomb us directly but they were probably missing their assigned targets. And I remember being in these trenches and being terrified from the onset because invariably they were flooded to various levels with water from the rains. And then the sounds. The frogs and little eel-shaped things that moved in the water. I was terrified of them. The strongest recollection I have of that place are those trenches.

2.

ESTER CHICHINSKY: Until about 1940, we still went to school on Auguststrasse. Then tension started. Schools for Jewish children were closed completely. And forced labor came into the focus. You had to register for it. At least one out of every family. So my mother was forced to work for the army in a factory where they made parts for electronic devices. I was forced too. I believe I was fourteen.

The point was one of your family had to go. Otherwise, you could not get your food ration ticket, on which it said "J" for "Jew." So if my mother or older sister was sick and could not go, I did. Until the point in 1941 when they started taking transports right to the concentration camps.

See, in the beginning of the war, Russia and Germany had peace. The

Non-Aggression Pact. Russian Jews were not affected right in the beginning. My mother was a Russian national. My mother had a lot of Russian friends. Non-Jewish Russian friends from the theater. Many, many. So any time there was a call by letter that all the Jews had to come to some meeting place like a hospital or a Jewish center, we never answered the call.

You had to come there by yourself. But then you never saw those people again. They kept them maybe for a day or two and then they were told they were going to go on forced labor. But the truth was that they were shipped out to Auschwitz.

EVELYN UDRY: I had a friend who was Hungarian. A Jewish boy named Yuri Teichner. Yuri Teichner was my first man, my first love, my first everything. Yuri's parents were smart. They sold off all the machines, left Berlin, and went to live in Budapest. They got out early. But Yuri stayed behind. He came very often to our apartment.

I became pregnant with Yuri right away. I had my child when I was sixteen, working practically till the very last day. My mommy knew a lady so in the hospital, I was not Jewish. I had another name. Otherwise, they would not have taken me. Afterward, I come home with the baby. Yuri kept saying, "I have to do something and I'm going to do something. You come with me. Then I will bring out to Budapest one by one your entire family." So we left Berlin. You can imagine me leaving all my family.

My mommy was against that I take the baby. But my mommy was also against to keep the baby in the flat. So the baby stayed but one minute from our house with people where the lady was Jewish but not the name. Yuri and I made our way to Vienna on a train in a car filled with pigs. Nobody checked us at the border. Who is going to check on carload of pigs?

The next day, we got up very early. Yuri had an address of somebody who was not Jewish who lived five kilometers from the Hungarian border. So we went to see these people. The man was a farmer. A peasant. His fields of corn or potatoes was mostly in Austria, but a little part also in Hungaria.

All the time, we were seeing the snow getting bigger bigger bigger. So at midnight the farmer brings us out and leaves us at the end of his field. We were kissing each other. We were kissing because we were so excited and full of emotion. The farmer showed us the way with a lantern, saying, "In two minutes, we are going to wish each other "Happy New Year." And we did. Maybe quarter of an hour later, we separated. "You've got three more kilometers to do," he told us. "One moment, you will not see a church but only the point of the church. The spire. And when you see it, keep going. Because that point is already in Hungary."

I can't tell you how cold we got. We just couldn't walk anymore. But we were young. We knew what we were doing. So we did it. But the worst comes now. We arrived in the middle of the night where people were celebrating, looking for the train station in a place called Sopron, which in Germany they call Ödenburg. It took us three hours to find the station. Here we were, waiting for the train. And instead of the train, two policemen walk up. "Papers?" they ask. What can I show them? I have no visas. No passport. No nothing. Okay. "You have to come with us," they say. They took us both to jail. But not together. Yuri on one side, me on the other.

Thank God, it was the *Hungarian* police. With the German police, it would have been straight to Buchenwald or Dachau. So they put us in jail. Me with the women and Yuri with the men. We don't see one another for twelve days. Altogether, I was twenty-two days in jail. In a cell with three other women. One was completely crazy, hysterical, screaming at night. *"Don't touch me! Don't touch me!"* Crazy. Talking and singing and screaming all night. What I heard in jail was that it depended on which policeman arrested you and which one took down all your information when you came to the jail. Because some of them were Nazis, and some not.

One day, they come for me. I heard the keys rattling as the guard put them in the door. They took me to a place to sign a paper. I said, "I can't read Hungarian. I'm not signing. How do I know you're not putting me in the electric chair?" They said, "We cannot give you back your clothes unless you sign." But I didn't understand. So somebody came who spoke German. And I said, "Okay, I trust you." But I still didn't know where I was going. I was shaking. As young as I was back then, I was shaking. "Where are they going to take me?" I asked. Because until I saw Yuri again, I could not believe it was true. They believed what he told them. They got the address of his parents and checked them out.

From the jail, they took us right to the train. Three and a half hours later, we arrived in Budapest. It was still snowing. My first real look at Hungary was snow, with snow and still more snow, right until the end. Of course, his parents were overjoyed to see us.

ESTER CHICHINSKY: In 1941, Russia entered the war against Germany. Within days, I came home from the factory and all the doors were blocked. The lower apartment in our building was occupied by a couple that took care of the building. Like a concierge. And when I entered, the woman tried to avoid me. This still stays with me even now. She was not a person who liked Jewish people at all. I think she might be partially responsible for having reported my mother to the SS. Because she knew we were of Russian descent.

I think it was early in the morning and I'll tell you why. There was shift work at the factory, it was twenty-four hours around the clock. So I had just come off working all night and part of this woman's duty was to clean up the courtyard of our building. It had to be morning because she was doing it with something in her hands. First she tried to avoid me. On my way out, she made an anti-Semitic remark. Ironically, she said, "I don't know who did it."

Now when I left the apartment, my mother was there. And when I came back, nobody was there. It could have happened the night before or during the time I was working or the very same morning. Evelyn was not there anymore. She had gone to Hungary with her boyfriend. It was just Sonja and myself. And this was the last time I have seen my mother.

BILL: Paris had fallen and the enemy was coming. It got to the point where the Nazis advanced at will and things depended on what the retreat was like. In any defeat, some people stay and some leave. The enemy is coming. One man may say, "Well, I'll just keep my store going. Because where am I going to go?" And somebody else says, "I'm a bus driver and they may take my beautiful wife." So they pack up and leave. If a town is shelled, people are going to leave. If it's a munitions town, if they're gonna level it. Whatever the reasons are, people *move*.

I remember when they sent someone from the International Red Cross. All of a sudden, this man appeared. In his late thirties or early forties. With long curly brown hair and sort of a long lantern face. He was assigned to take us south. We couldn't stay at the château because we were Jews. German Jews and French Jews. So it was his responsibility to move us out. You have to remember, the country was being invaded. Whenever people move in great numbers, it's chaotic. People aren't thinking about which road to use, or what's the better highway. There are no store hours.

It's like when you swat an anthill. The ants just *run*. They scatter for survival. And invariably, it's in the direction *away* from the enemy. I remember leaving the château on a bus. They put us all on two buses. I remember a series of marches and staying in people's homes. There would be walking periods, getting on buses, and getting on trains. We started with sixty-four kids.

I remember getting to Lyon. Tolla was sick. She had pneumonia. I remember her coughing on the bus. For some reason while we were moving, we only had oranges but nothing else. There were always oranges all through this whole trip. We had almost nothing else to eat but there were *always* oranges. I remember she always needed more to drink and more to eat. I remember how she looked. Very frail. Round-faced. Brown hair. She was very concerned about me. At the château, I would see her all the time. Even though the girls lived in a separate wing.

We were close. We were brother and sister and we were close. What I remember is that because of where we found ourselves, we both gradually learned French. And then we began to talk to one another in a totally different language than we had before. That became part of growing up there.

What happened to her on the walk was the same thing that happened to me and to everybody. Malnutrition. There was very little to eat. Sometimes it was cold, sometimes warm. It rained a lot. We did a lot of walking because we were competing for transportation space along with everybody else. Kreitzer did his best to keep us all together but in Lyon, they told me, "She has to stay in the hospital here. You have to keep moving. If you're caught, you'll go to the camps along with all the other children." I remember going to the hospital when she was admitted. Then somehow I was back with the gang again.

They said, "We have to move on. She will get better and join us." At the time, I just didn't place much importance on it. I was convinced that when things got better, she *would* get well. She'd be okay. At the time, I was ten.

I do remember a moment outside Lyon, when we were walking and looking for shelter in the early evening. I wonder sometimes if I imagined this but I'm quite certain it happened because I mentioned it to my friend Sammy Schtuck who came with me from the château to America. A couple of parachutes appeared. Later I was told that the Germans regularly sent fanatics into areas where their troops were advancing. Volunteers. Like kamikazes. They'd parachute into an area and throw hand grenades to incite rioting. They were like psychological grenades.

We heard some machine-gunning and we were told afterward that the French Resistance got to them and put them against the wall. They had riddled them with bullets. These were two fifth columnists who never became prisoners of war.

It was August or September, I think. I remember trains. My memories from that time are not strong. I don't know now how much I once knew. But I know it was *more*. Also, how much do I *want* to remember?

I remember certain images. I remember the convent in Madrid. How quiet it was. The colors I saw. The light. The convent was right in the heart of the city. Dark brown and shades of tan. I remember the way the light hit it.

I also remember that as time went along, there were fewer children. One by one, they dropped off. I guess they were thinking, "My chances are going to be better here—I'm not gonna just follow this one man." Either that or they got sick or, as in Tolla's case, they were tired and couldn't keep up. It *was* difficult.

From Lyon, we walked to Marseilles. We stayed there for a while and then all of us were put on a train to go to Toulouse. Across the Pyrenees to Barcelona but I don't think we stayed there. My next stop seems to be Madrid where I stayed for two months in the convent. For some reason, we got stuck there. For two months. Through August and September. From the château to Madrid took probably three, four weeks.

It's amazing how undetailed all that is but I don't have that much significant memory of the time.

ESTER CHICHINSKY: I never went back to the apartment after I came home that morning. I went into hiding. My number one move was that we had very good friends on Lindenstrasse. Lindenstrasse was about a block and a half away with a big covered market, tons of vegetable stores, and a fish market alongside. Right next door was a shoe store. The name of the family who owned it was Hahn. I think on *Kristallnacht* my mother had done something for them. Matter of fact, I think Mr. Hahn was killed that night. But they had a friend who befriended my mother. Mrs. Mueller. She was not a Jewess.

From the apartment, I went to the shoe store and then to Mrs. Mueller, who kept me at her place on the Ansbacherstrasse, near Wittenberg Platz. I only ever left her apartment in the darkness. Mostly I got out at night or she went with me. She was not a married lady. She was very dedicated to show her friendship for me and risk her life for me. I was fourteen at the time.

One time Mrs. Mueller took me to Moabit. This was a political prison. I could not give my real name. Mrs. Mueller must have found out that my mother was taken there, not as a Jewess but as a Russian. A foreign national. Mrs. Mueller tried to get her put into a hospital for people that cannot be transported. She wasn't sick. It was specially done, you know? It's so difficult to make people understand. To realize what one did in order to survive and save one's life. People just cannot imagine. People cannot understand.

My mother was at that prison. Then she was transferred because of Mrs. Mueller, who kept me away because she kept saying to me, "If you go there, they'll get you too." One time I do recall, I went there on my own. I saw my mother once from a distance. In a prison yard. Wearing regular clothes. Also, I had met the person responsible for getting her into that hospital through Mrs. Mueller. I spoke to him for five minutes.

You had to be very careful in Germany at that time not to get involved in any of those "protected" cases, so called. That you're helping a Jew. Because that was the last thing to do at that time. In order to be safe, you had to be in a certain mental hospital, unable to be transported. But when the hospitals filled up, the Germans took you anyway and killed you. Through Mrs. Mueller, I was told that my mother was taken out and transported. From that hospital.

From what I understand, her transport never made it to Auschwitz. It was gassed out. The train itself. They injected gas into the cars of the train and they died. Her transport, along with many others, never made it to the camps. I only found out about it after the war. When I worked for HIAS, the Hebrew Immigrant Aid Society.

3.

EVELYN UDRY: So now I am in Budapest. I don't speak one word of Hungarian. I can't even say "Thank you." Not "How do you do?" Nothing. I said, "The only thing I can do is try to dance." Perhaps in an operetta, as my base was classical. I mean, I could dance on point and everything. I thought that it would be best because I could not speak Hungarian.

So I went to a theatrical agency and did several auditions. There was a certain Mrs. Rosznay who owned a theater. Her daughter saw me dance and by her, I was accepted. After six months, I had a one-year contract. So they say to me, "You need a stage name."

She picked "Evelyn Barnett." From a book maybe. I don't know. I didn't know anybody called by that name. So I became Evelyn Barnett. After several months, they made me the second soloist, the first was Mrs. Rosznay's daughter. A wonderful dancer. But the second soloist had to sing. "Can you sing?" Mrs. Rosznay asked me. I said, "Yes. In my bathroom." But I learned. I stayed there for *years*, always working. Yuri went back to Berlin on a false passport. He checked on my family for me. My mama was gone, he couldn't find Ester. He couldn't find these friends where the baby was. A girl. Then Yuri was taken to the camp. By the Romanian border. Bohr was the name. When it was liberated in 1945, six were left alive from fifty-nine hundred. One was Yuri.

SONJA SZOBEL: By chance, Yuri, Evelyn's boyfriend, came to Berlin to look for me. He was friends with Rudy Svoboda, a Czechoslovakian young man. They took me to Budapest in 1943. The night of St. Sylvester, New Year's Eve, from 1942 to 1943, we went out from the train. Rudy, Yuri, and me in snow up to my chest. And we walk. Whenever we heard something, I must go down. Crouching in the snow. I was very afraid. I was fifteen at the time.

We passed over the border with no papers, nothing. Everyone was drunk and celebrating Sylvester night. Yuri took us to his father and mother's house and they were very nice to me. Evelyn came but I didn't stay too long there because they said to me, "Sonja, it's better that you go in the *lager* where all strangers to Budapest go." It was a camp. Because you could not be more than thirteen years old without legal papers. So I put on a little, little dress and I made braids with my hair. I went there and say how old I am and I helped them in the kitchen and everything. Just to be legal and have papers.

BILL: We went from Madrid to Lisbon. In Lisbon, they put us on this liner, the *Serpa Pinto*. I went to Casablanca where I remember they would not let us off the boat. I have no idea why. It was very hot. We docked in Casablanca and sat there for days. It fascinated me to see men on the dock selling water out of bags. I'd never seen that before. To me, that was *staggering*. To sell water out of gunny sacks on their backs. Others kept diving into the water as performers. "First you throw the money, *then* I'll dive." This was not exactly fun time in Jamaica. This was . . . *I want your coins*.

From there, we went to Dakar. We all slept on deck and we practically lived on cookies and oranges. Cookies and oranges all the way across the Atlantic to Bermuda. The crossing took nineteen days. It was a very slow boat and there were problems. They kept changing course and they didn't know where they were going to land. We got stopped by a U-boat. Three days later, by a British submarine. I was frightened because I thought we could be torpedoed.

There weren't only children on the boat but also cargo and some regular passengers. I remember chess players on the boat. And people arguing, a lot of arguing, but not by the chess players. It was very emotional. A group of people who on a regular basis every day would argue and fight about things none of us understood, having to do with their private lives.

I remember the deck very well. We had some blankets and some clothing but we had to go down to the lower level to wash and go to the bathrooms. They told us we were going to America but that didn't mean much to me.

I know this was a long, traumatic experience. France, some memory. Then going through the south of France into North Africa to Bermuda, vague moments. I don't remember much specifically. You know, it's all,

"Then we got on the train, then we got off the train, then we ate in that restaurant, then we stayed overnight in that church." I can remember doorways and hotels and hospitals that we slept in but I couldn't give you much detail except that everything was commonplace. We stayed here, we stayed there, we slept on buses. And on the boat, people were arguing a lot.

EVELYN UDRY: In 1941, the Germans walked into Budapest. The Germans I had left behind in Berlin. I went to a rehearsal one afternoon and there were guys I've never seen before in leather coats. I said to myself, "This *must* be the Nazis." And sure enough they were. I had to smile and keep saying to myself, *"Dimanovich Roszy. Dimanovich Rozsy. Dimanovich Roszy."* Which was my new name. Along with Evelyn Barnett for the stage. That is what it said on my Hungarian papers.

So for two weeks I didn't sleep, saying to myself, "If they come in and I am sleeping and they ask me my name, I'm not sure I will say *'Roszy Dimanovich.'* " For two weeks I did this. And a good thing because they came at three-thirty in the morning to the hotel, checking on everyone. Eleven times I passed. Not only in the hotel. By now, I spoke Hungarian. I spoke only Hungarian whenever they checked. If this had happened after only six months in Hungary I would have been caught.

Always I smelled the German on them. They could all speak Hungarian and this was what they spoke. But they were Germans all the same.

ESTER CHICHINSKY: If Mrs. Mueller would not have had the connection to put me in a convent I would not be alive today. I was not saved by the Jews. I went to Heart of Jesus, a convent in the center of Vienna. In the beginning, I thought I was the only Jewish child there. In the end, I found it was not so. Mrs. Mueller I never saw again. I was told she was bombed out in the bombardment. She died in the middle of the street. If ever I could know where to find the grave of that woman, I would definitely go to see it. Because she saved my life. She knew my mother could not be saved but she demonstrated that she was a *mensch.* Do you know what I am saying? She demonstrated that she was a *mensch.* Even though she was not able to see or speak with my mother, whatever she couldn't do for my mother, at least she did for her children.

Mrs. Mueller got me to the convent. There, Sister Benedicta, who knew I was a Jewess, she asked only once if I would feel more at ease changing my religion. Then I could participate in receiving holy communion and the whole *schmeer.* Simply, I did tell her that I lived due to respect for myself and my family. That is who I am. If I am going to survive, I'm willing to fight. That is who I am. If I have to die, I'd rather die who I am. And she respected that.

I was there when Hitler gave the order that all the churches had to turn in their bells. They were having trouble in Poland and they needed the metal in them to melt down for guns and bullets. I remember one nun, Sister Manuela, had a slight heart attack because of this.

They protected me till the beginning of 1943. Then Sister Benedicta came to me and said I should not leave the building. She didn't say if somebody was coming after me but that building was under some kind of surveillance. What made me feel very itchy was that every place I went, there were suddenly nuns around me. On each side, without being told for two or three days in a row. So I knew somebody was watching.

One of the nuns took me to her brother, who was an Austrian officer and he took charge and told me where to go. I've had my difficulties many times with people who put all the Germans or all the Austrians as equal. And I have spoken up about it many times. It is just not so. I'm here to testify to that. If not for quite a few good Germans, there would not be one single Jew left alive today. The church *did* help. I am here to attest to that. Many, many German people risked their lives and this should not be forgotten.

That nun took me, not in her nun's clothing but in civilian clothes, to the border. Her brother brought me very close to Hungary. I stayed in Borgenlund overnight, got up in the morning, melted into the working people, and started to walk. They had given me a long skirt. I put up my hair, made myself up with a little dirt on my face, and I marched along until we came to a wagon where you sat on top, everybody saying, "How are you? How are you?" I didn't speak because I had a German accent.

I went as far as I could. When everybody sat down to eat, I didn't. I ran into the fields where the corn grew so high. I just went and went and went and I had to say to myself, "You live or you die. If they catch you, you're finished." Then I sat down, waited until it got dark, and climbed to where I could see the train. The frontier patrol was going back and forth so I sat there counting how often. I counted out that they changed patrol every twenty minutes.

The next morning I came in right to the train station. Thousands of people about, maybe six in the morning, people going to Budapest to work or across the border to work. They announced on the intercom in Hungarian and in German, "Train so-and-so is coming. Please have your tickets ready." I had nothing. All I had was two sets of underwear under my dress and some addresses rolled into a seam. I had Austrian money, which was of no use to purchase a ticket there.

So when they called the people to pass through, I squeezed myself into the biggest crowd. I got on the train and ducked into the rest room. But I couldn't stay there because people wanted to use it. So I came out and sat in a seat, just like a *bubeleh*.

Shortly before we came to Budapest, the train stopped and the conductor came through. If I got up and moved they would catch me somewhere else. So I had to make up a *spiel*. This was a key in any situation during the war. Don't lose your cool. I bent down and said, "Oh, my hat is gone." The conductor took me and said, "You sit over there." I came into Budapest riding between the trains in the passage. If I jumped, I wouldn't have known where I was running.

When we got out at the station, the conductor was right in front of me on the stairs. I'm right in back of him and he looks at me and says, "You follow me." But there were thousands about. You couldn't even drop a pin, so many people. So we start walking but people were shoving. "Make room," he kept saying. *"Make room!"* I know I cannot allow myself to get where he was taking me. So what I did, I stepped on somebody's foot and that person falls down and I pushed him over, one falls over another, and I got myself out.

I went to the Jewish community in Budapest and found a man who looked Jewish. He told me to go to a certain street where there's a Jewish committee where they help young girls. Stupid me. I went to the Jewish committee and there was a director. The *worst*. He should be hung. Not just for me but for a hundred others. Girls like myself he sent to a community camp in Budapest. Where they promised us we were going to be sent to Israel. Only he kept us there until the Germans came. I was on the first transport to Auschwitz.

EVELYN UDRY: For three years, I danced and sang for Mrs. Rosznay. Until one day when the biggest band leader, but when I say the biggest, it's like Glenn Miller was in America, came to see me.

I kept singing with Chappy until the day the Germans came. Chappy wouldn't play for the Germans. Not that he was Jewish. But five out of his eighteen musicians were. Unfortunately, all were taken away. The others just didn't want to play anymore. Chappy said, "For those bastards, we're not going to make any performances." And Mrs. Rosznay was Jewish. Mr. Rosznay wasn't. But they closed their theater. They killed her son. Jula Rosznay. One of the nicest young men I have ever met. He was twenty-eight.

Then came the Russians into Budapest. They were different from the Germans. I mean, they were not funny. That is the minimum I can say. They were *not* funny.

BILL: We got to New York on September 24, 1941. I remember seeing the Statue of Liberty but I remember much more thinking that this was gonna be the beginning. I remember we'd all been told that the one thing that would to happen was that we'd all be separated. We were going to go to this place in Pleasantville, New York, to be put in dormitories. Then we would be put out for adoption or to live in private homes. We were told that people would come visit us on weekends. But we were told that we would not be together.

I went through Ellis Island but I have very little memory of that. Space. Lines. Lots of luggage. I had my *yarmulkah* and my prayer book. Some pictures of my parents and my sisters. I don't recall having anything else. I had no attachments to anything I can think of. No toys. To this day, I've never knowingly enjoyed a toy.

I knew I was again going to be pulled away from something I'd gotten used to. Living and traveling with this bunch of people. I guess I got used to the orphanage in Berlin and then I got used to the château at Chaumont. It wasn't my real family. It wasn't my sisters. But it was these same people, you know? And now I was in America, where they told me that somebody was going to take me in their house. Who, I didn't know. People *they* didn't even know. I was going to be with people *no one* knew. So I guess the question I kept asking myself was, "Who *are* these people going to be?" But it was an answer no one knew.

Of the sixty-four kids who set out from the château in France three months earlier, eleven made it to New York.

4.

BILL: They put us on a bus up to Pleasantville, which is a couple of hours' drive from the city in upstate New York. There were army barracks up there, with double bunks. I remember them because when I was drafted years later, it was the same thing. I had the top bed. This is my first real beginning of ongoing memory, very strong and detailed, that never left.

Families and couples would come up there on weekends and look to see if they wanted any of us in their homes. Whether they were good people or bad people or whatever their reasons might have been, there was another factor that went along with it. At that time, there was a great drive within the Jewish community in the Greater New York area to be involved with these Jewish orphans. Immigrants from Europe who were parentless.

The Jewish Foster Home Bureau offered forty-eight dollars a month to these families so it would not be limited to only people with money. Some people I know did it because of humanitarian reasons. Others did it because . . . "Hey, maybe I can net six dollars a month out of this."

It first entered my mind that it was a business venture when I saw the way some of the people who came there talked to me. At the time, I didn't even know what business was. But people were thinking about taking me in their homes—judging me. You got to understand. One of the most important factors of my life, something that set it off in a certain way, was that they came there with this attitude. As though they were going to a pet shop. You know, what will *we* have to do? What are the positives and negatives of having this stranger in our house? Now I look at it much more analytically. But at the time, I thought, "Why don't they want *me?*" Because I was rejected from September twenty-fourth until the twelfth of November. Every weekend, and also sometimes during the week.

ESTER CHICHINSKY: We arrived at Auschwitz after three weeks in open wagons. Wintertime, snow falling on us, we were maybe originally five hundred when we started out, first girls only. But after we drove a little while, then they connected more cars, more and more. The train was so long by the time we passed the Czechoslovakian border that it was impossible to look and see the end. That's how many cars there were. There was always a selection being made. We saw people being taken off the train, but from a distance. And then we could hear the shooting.

People at that point, it's not that they don't care. You know that you might be next. So you lose your fear. You just try to live from minute to minute. Afterward, we found out the selection was mostly men.

From the first day on, it was snowing and all the cars were open. We had been given one blanket for three people, and everybody had something like a metal cap. When the cars were in motion, we picked up snow. That is what we lived off. No food. We just rubbed the snow on our lips. At first, we still had some manners and decency. People had to go, they stepped across the corner of the car at night. But then people just went *everywhere.* That's what we sat on, what we stood on. All you touched was *that.* People died on it, and people sat on dead people. You become emotionless, you become heartless, you become an animal. You lost touch with reality in life.

We would try to make a human chain for people to go out of the side of the car. But the Germans would shoot at them. At night, in the dark where nobody sees, people would take little strips from the blankets, double them up, and choke themselves. A sister or a brother or a mother. I dream a lot about it even now. Especially if I read something or see a certain movie. The slightest thing will remind me, and everything comes back. I am sure a lot of people went through a lot more than I did. But it's not something where I can say to myself, "Forget it."

In the camp, it was much worse than on the train. See, there's Birkenau, there's Auschwitz. When you arrive, there is a circle. The incoming train circles out. When you arrive, there's a left and there's a right. S.S. stand there, they say, *"Left, right, left, right."* People holding onto a child or onto a husband or onto a sister or onto a brother, they split them up. People don't think what's left or right. Their main concern is wanting to be with their loved one. With somebody from the family.

There are four or five very very tough situations that I live with even now from morning till night. No matter how shiny the sun shines outside and how much music and joy and laughter there is inside. One moment is not because of the left or the right. The moment for me is, there was a woman maybe two or three ahead of me with her family, a little tiny kid, and the mother didn't want to give up her little child. She was expecting too. Pregnant, so all could see.

She went down on her knees begging for that little child. Nazis with their boots on, they took that child, they smacked her on the floor, then they stomped with their boots straight at the pregnant mother as well. This is something one cannot forget. This is something that cannot be shown in the movies or on TV. And if it's shown, it's not real. It's a retake that nobody believes could be so.

Once I got into Birkenau, I was in a selected area where they did not cut off my hair. I did not have a number at that point, either. And it didn't dawn on me because, who knows? Early in the morning on the fifth day, the S.S. says, *"Jews out!"* We still had no numbers. We had to march to what looked like an old brick building. We come in, we take off all our clothes. I was with maybe three hundred others, in very long lines, fifty or sixty of us in a group. So I stand there and they give me a piece of cloth, it looked like a towel, with a piece of square thing like soap. I stand. Next one in, next one in. Down the line I see the tank-like things with gasoline in them. I came to a point where it was like a crossing.

I was young and strong. Beautifully built and naked. We all stood naked. All of a sudden, out of nowhere, somebody grabbed me by the head and pulled me out, put me in a big woolen cloak a mile too big for me, and shot me out back into the camp. It was a woman who grabbed me, one I never saw before. What I understood later is that maybe they needed strong women who could help them for the underground. Because that very same day is when I got the number tattooed on my arm: *8082.*

Maybe I had a guardian angel. Somebody who looks down on me. I don't have the answer. But it is something that I have been asking myself. Why *me?*

ROBERT HELLER: Do you know anything about the Hebrew Shelter and Guardian Society of the New York Association for Jewish Children? It's only like an hour and a half up in the country. It's changed considerably because now it's become more for kids from broken homes. Instead of sending them to reform school, they send them up there. The Rosenberg kids were up there. Before their parents were executed. They were up there in the middle fifties. I started there in about 1940. When the immigrant kids came, I was already like a big kid.

It was a big, sprawling place halfway between Pleasantville and Thornwood. It went for miles. You could get lost in the woods around it. The Cottage School itself was a small little area made up of about twenty cottages around a square with an administration building, all made of brick. I took my kids there some years later and my son said, "This is summer camp." It looked like a Levittown community.

Each cottage had two dormitories with about ten to twelve kids. There were small groupers and big groupers. The small groupers were like from nine to twelve, the big groupers were like thirteen. At fourteen, you left there. There were iron frame beds and each dorm had its own kind of big leader or monitor. The cottages were individually self-run. Each one had a cottage mother and a cottage father. We had our own farm with chickens, and milk from a dairy right next door. We could go into town, which was solid-rock anti-Semitic Christian.

I remember the auditorium, one of those get-together meetings on a Friday, where we were introduced to maybe a dozen or so kids. We were told they were refugees who didn't speak English and that it would be up to us to take care of them. Now for some strange reason, I became Billy's big brother. I don't know why or how because I wasn't that kind of guy. I was a troublemaker and a comedian.

In terms of the way he looked back then, I seem to see all eyes. I mean, he looked like those posters CARE used to put up. It's very, very distinct in my mind. His face was exactly the same as it is now. I mean a little old man's face. A Capuchin monkey. There were a dozen others. But with them I had nothing to do. With Billy, I was connected. Of all the kids there, he stood out. I can't say why. Maybe he was lonelier than most. Maybe he was more needy than most. He touched something in me. For some strange reason, I took on the role of big brother, and I was *nobody's* big brother.

BILL: Nine weeks I waited for someone to pick me out. I would clean myself up special for each and every visit because I didn't want to stay

there with a lot of other strangers. It was a revolving door. Every one of
the others I had come with had already been taken out. I was the last of
the eleven. I'd stand by my bunk, which I'd made up very tight and
clean. I wanted someone to go with—to choose me. I hated—*hated*—
being up for sale. The few weeks I spent in Pleasantville were far more
painful to me than anything that had happened before.

Some of the people who came spoke German, some Yiddish. But all
of them spoke English, which of course I didn't yet understand. They
knew the kids they were talking to had just come over on the boat. Any
couple who wanted to take in a child, they would let them do so. Because
if they screened them closely, how many would have been perfect?

Usually, the questions they asked were the same. "Where did you
come from? How was your trip?" It was very, *very* limited. Usually it was
me watching them talk about me in a language I didn't understand. It
could be very much the way an animal looks at humans or humans look
at an animal. "Well, what's *that* snake saying to *that* snake?" I didn't
understand any of them. But I knew my presence was being judged and
a decision was going to be made based on what kind of a feeling they got
from me. You know. Like people pick out flowers or to go a pet shop, or
select a dress.

ESTER CHICHINSKY: Although I came with a Hungarian transport,
because I was pushed to freedom from the showers, I was put in with
Hungarians and Romanians and Czechs. No Germans. At first they were
afraid of me. I didn't speak Hungarian, I didn't speak Czech. They were
skeptical. In each bunk, we were eight at first. Two blankets. So we took
turns. Anyone who sleeps at the end has to hold onto the corner. If one
turns, everybody turns. You look like monkeys. I was on the upper bunk,
which was lucky because at least I had some air.

There's one thing I can with a clear conscience say. I never hurt
anybody in camp. I never took advantage of anybody in camp. I never
said anything about anybody in camp. I helped anyone I could in camp.
Sometimes, we had girls in a lower bunk that couldn't stand up anymore.
At the roll call in the morning, I would go from one end of the line to the
other just to take their place.

After a few days, I got my feelers. I got friendly with people who
worked in the underground who were friendly with people who worked in
the metal areas, who knew exactly what was going on. I risked my life for
other people because they also had a right to live. Like myself, they were
only there because they were Jewish. There was no other reason. I did
not give in to the pressure of the *capos* or the intimidations of the
Germans. I didn't run. I stood still when they would loose the dogs on

us. If you ran, *then* they got a hold of you. I can honestly say that if you fought, you made it. If you let go little by little, it caught up with you.

I got to Auschwitz at the end of 1943. I was liberated on the nineteenth or twentieth of April in 1945. If I'm not mistaken, it was Hitler's birthday. I think it was.

EVELYN UDRY: You must understand the situation in Budapest. This is Buda, my right arm, and that is Pest, my left, and the Danube runs between, down the middle of the city. I was right near the river on the Promenade in Pest, where all the big hotels are lined up facing the Danube. The Russians came from the Pest side. As the Russians came, the Germans retreated across the river to Buda. Then started the most terrible time. The Russian planes took off in Pest, made a one and a half minute flight, and bombed Buda. The Germans took off from Pest. And I was in between.

We were in a bunker under the hotel. You couldn't get out. Ninety-one days I was there. Ninety-one days without seeing the sky. Ninety-one days in the same clothes. I didn't have another pair of stockings, another pair of panties, nothing. The hotels had their own food reserves. But by the last week, we ran out. We were eating soap. Soap to wash clothes with. The little pieces. The flakes.

Then the Russians came. They were not human beings. They were not human beings because they did such things. They raped all the women right in the bunker. There was a Romanian writer with his wife in the hotel who spoke Russian. And he said to me, "Evelyn, when they come close to you, do not speak one word of Russian." To me, they did not even look human. They were Mongols, with necks that went straight down from the ears. When I saw the first, I said to myself, "Look down or they will see I am afraid of them."

When they came, the Romanian man said to them, "That one, she has syphilis." This is how I got away. But not an old lady of seventy-two with her daughter sitting next to her, they put a gun on the chest of the daughter and told the old woman, "You better watch because you will be next." If you have lived through that, for certain things you are cured for life.

BILL: I don't really remember any of the people who didn't pick me. What I do remember is the rejection. It was, "You didn't buy me that weekend," times twenty-five or thirty couples.

Nine weeks. Having all kinds of doubts and the language barrier. Ironically, that was what finally got me out of there. My great uncle and his wife, Mr. and Mrs. Ehrenreich, came to the orphanage. They got interested in me right away because their son Roy had just started going to the Bronx High School of Science. The foreign language he was taking was French.

5.

BILL: Alfred and Pearl Ehrenreich. He sold insurance. They lived at 1635 Montgomery Avenue in the Bronx. She was a very good woman. He belonged to the Knights of Pythias. I think they came up to the home to do some good for both their son and me.

If she were to be portrayed in a film, it would someone like Anna Magnani or Katina Paxinou. My sister Ester has that same kind of face and character. Very, very warm. A good, decent woman with a need to help. She took me in. I have pictures of me when I came here. I was suffering from malnutrition. I was emaciated. Almost eleven years old and I weighed fifty-five pounds. I had rickets and a bone marrow problem. She took me in and got me healthy. She rubbed olive oil into my skin every day and treated me very fairly and decently.

A few weeks after I came to live with them it was December 7, 1941, Pearl Harbor day. I kept trying to figure it out. Because now Japan and America were at war. And then Germany came into it as well.

ROY EHRENREICH: He was eleven years old and looked about seven. He was thin and a little bit scared. He looked almost like a little old man in a sense. Terribly eager to please. Very, very shy. Clearly bewildered and not really understanding what was happening to him and sort of hoping that he was coming to a place that was going to be home. I think he was sort of delighted that at least somebody could speak to him, however haltingly, in a language that he knew.

Before his English became too good, you know, really fluent, some of the local neighborhood kids tended to be unpleasant, making fun of the accent. You know, kids can be very cruel to one another and here was a little kid with a funny accent who didn't really know how everything worked yet. The only time in my life that I ever got into a street fight was when Bill and I took on two of these kids in front of our building, which startled *everybody*. Everybody was shocked. Except my father, who was *delighted*. Bill was fighting a blond kid named Arthur Spierer, known as Whitey. I can almost see the kid I was fighting but I can't bring the name back. Nobody got hurt. But I think it made a difference.

I remember one thing Bill did say on Pearl Harbor day. He said, "Why is it that wherever I go, there is trouble? It follows me."

BILL: They put me in a class with seven-year-olds in P.S. 104, an old red brick elementary school down Featherbed Lane and Macombs Road. The first teacher I had in the library was Mrs. Leibel and she wore a toupee. I remember her only because within a few days after I came there, I was told by her through a student who spoke German that in America, it's against the law to write with your left hand. That I would be deported if I didn't stop and switch to the right hand.

I was left-handed. In a subsequent class, Mrs. Leibel caught me switching again. She ripped the pencil out of my hand and she said, "You *have* to write with your *right* hand." I kicked her and her toupee came off. I was expelled from school.

Once Germany and America were at war, I became the enemy. I had a lot of trouble coming home from school. Kids would throw rocks at me. Sometimes, a group of kids would beat up on me. I remember one fight on a rooftop. I wasn't by myself. There were three of us and about five guys hitting on us. They kicked the shit out of us and that was it. A number of times, a kid would say, "Hey, *fuckin' Jew!*" or "Yid *bastard!*" or "Go back where you came from— *Kraut!*" and knock my books out of my hand. Sometimes, I would stand there. Sometimes, I'd fight back. Other times, it was three guys and my senses said, "What am I gonna do? *Blindly* fight three guys?" Within a very short period of time, about a year, it stopped.

I was thrown out of school once 'cause I had a fight. A guy spit on me and I hit him. It was about a year after I came to the Bronx. Two guys got me in P.T. playing ball. They hurt me bad—in the body. They yelled, "You're a *German* Jew—you're a *Nazi! You're the enemy!* Go *home!*" There was *always* that. "Get outta here, get back to Germany." By then, I'd started to speak English fluently. I was *never* German. I was *born* in Germany. My parents weren't Germans. The point I was always trying to make even then was . . . I'm *not* who you think I am. And even if I was . . . *what* then?

What my brother Roy did, besides being my friend and then my brother eventually, because he became my brother, he was wise enough to say, "Learning English isn't enough. You'll always be a foreigner if you don't drop the accent." And he was the one who worked with me on the "TH's" and the "R's." I always think of "TH's" and "R's." "*Srow zee* ball." "I can't remember *zis*." The TH's and the R's are the giveaways. Those are the two that stay *wiz ze* foreign*ehs* who come to America. *Zay* always speak like *zis*. Around *za* corn*ah*. Roy and I would practice after school, over and over and over. I'd write things out in a notebook with black and white spots on the cover. The headlines. Rommel and Eisenhower and Montgomery. Tojo and Yamamoto. I'd copy them off the front pages. I'd write and then read them aloud and he would correct me. In our room on the floor between the two beds.

ROY EHRENREICH: There was a time during his first winter with us when he still had a very, *very* strong accent. He had picked up a fair amount of vocabulary but not the grammar. He had taken the family sled to a nearby street that was on a hill. There had been a very heavy snowfall and there weren't any cars about or anything.

Bill came back with a big gash. Of course, my mother got hysterical. It became clear he wasn't really hurt. "What happened, Billy? What happened?" And I can still break him up by doing this. "Me *here*. Boy *here*. Hill *here*. Big *white!* Big *white!* Me go *down* hill. Me yell, 'Watch out, crazy! Watch out, crazy!' Him no hear. Then *POW!*"

BILL: I remember seeing their apartment for the first time. It wasn't so much the apartment that impressed me as people living on top of one another in the building. Six floors, with an elevator. I'd never seen an elevator before. Their apartment was a living room, kitchen, bedroom, and another room, their son's room. I shared his room. You had to go through our bedroom to get to theirs.

They had the front view, we had the yard view, with the other houses facing ours. Montgomery Avenue was two streets away from the thoroughfare. University Avenue. Two, three blocks down was Tremont Avenue. University and Tremont. Andrews Avenue, Montgomery Avenue, Popham Avenue, Undercliff Avenue, then the river.

The living room was where my parents socialized. The women played Mah-jongg in the living room and the men played pinochle in the kitchen. About eleven, they'd break to have food. There was no television but we had a radio in our room and another one in the kitchen. The radio was our route to the other world. "Gangbusters" and "The Hit Parade" was in that room. "FBI in Peace and War" was in that room. "The Shadow" was in that room. Coming home at lunch to listen to "My Sister Ruth," a soap opera on at twelve-fifteen. That was *big*. It was a *great* room.

ROY EHRENREICH: I was never a very outgoing kid. My parents were unhappy about the fact that I didn't have any siblings. When I was about eleven, there was a kid who had a father and I think either two or three brothers and sisters and they were in a bad kind of financial situation and needed a place. They couldn't afford to have Stanley living with them. So he came to live with us. And we became very, very close very, very quickly. He was a foster child at the house he came from.

After about a year, the financial situation with his family changed for the better and they wanted him back. Of course, off he went. I guess that had a pretty strong impact on me. This was something that I had never had before that I liked. All of a sudden, it was removed. It was just about this time that the Foster Home Bureau was starting to get involved with refugee kids. I was too young to really be aware of what kind of negotiations took place. But my parents wanted somebody else for the same reason. So I would have a companion. The difference here though was that in the first situation, I had been sort of a little brother. All of a sudden now, I was now a big brother instead.

ISAAC AMATO: I was in an orphanage and an institution *plus* foster homes from the time I was one and a half or thereabouts. Being a foster child is *very* different from being adopted. Bill was a foster child, where you don't have the full legal and personal standing. You're always really an outsider. You're not really part of the home. You learn to be on your own. You *never* invite people over to your place. You didn't raid the refrigerator. You didn't get allowance. You could never argue. You never got into the normal situation where you would get into an argument and fight with your parents like normal kids do.

You were polite. You had a polite, orderly relationship with them. I remember as a foster child, the foster parent would ask me advice about their natural child. You become inhibited. At least that's my own background as a foster child. Although I never spoke to Bill about these things, here was a kid who lived the same way I did. When you were in a foster home, the social workers would come and they would measure your room. The room you lived in *had* to be a certain size. It was incredible. He bore this cross. Or whatever you want to call it. Of sadness. The tragedy there was something that helped in giving me an intuitive feeling about him.

I know the particular foster parents that Bill was with, they took a very keen interest in him. I think he was maybe more fortunate than myself. Some of the common things a foster child learns is that you are on your own. You learn very early in life to depend upon your own resources. You're on the defensive. I don't care how close Bill was to his foster family, I don't get that he had the feeling of *real* closeness with them.

BILL: Were they my parents? She was my mother. He was never my father because I'd never had one. Also partly because of who he was. He was an okay guy but I can't say I loved him or cared deeply about him. I think he was married to a wonderful woman.

ROY EHRENREICH: I think basically that my father was very happily married and my mother wasn't. I think it's as simple as that. Not so much that she married beneath herself. At the time she married, her parents were not terribly in favor of it. Because her father was a lawyer. I think perhaps not a very reputable one in Manhattan. And his father was a butcher. There was never a good relationship between my father and his father-in-law.

I think one of the big problems was that my father must have been pretty well crushed by losing this very good job he had as a buyer with Burdine's, a large Miami department store, in the early 1930s. It was certainly a Depression thing. And I think the problem that my mother had with him was that there was never any real resurgence of ambition. He just drifted along with it and he made do and he always worked. It was never a question of a shiftless husband or anything like that.

BILL: My foster father didn't know that he didn't have it beyond a certain point. He was one of the many millions who wanted to be more but wasn't. But he wasn't angry at the world. He just worked hard. He's not that important in my life. He never was. She was. My brother was.

Back then, the only thing I went by was what I knew last. My mother was in Germany, my sisters were in Germany, except that one of my sisters left before I did, Rita, to points unknown with someone. I knew my father was dead. I knew Tolla and I had been sent to France.

Within a year, I caught up. When I was twelve, they put me in with the twelve-year-olds. The language I got in six months. The accent was gone within a year or less. Because it was a way out. Somehow, when the accent was lost, the kids in the neighborhood accepted me. Then I switched over from P.S. 104 to Macombs Junior High School, P.S. 82, on University Avenue right next to the Park Plaza theater. That was a big break. Within the year, I was a New Yorker.

Al's Candy Store. It was right down the hill from Montgomery Avenue at University and 176th Street. There was a Chinese laundry on the hill and at the corner, there was a drugstore and next to the drugstore, there was the candy store. Everything in America in my mind relates to three things. Back then, the cost of the *Daily News* was two cents, a roll was two cents, and a container of milk was sixteen cents. That's the foundation of the American economy in my mind.

My job in the morning was to get up and go to the store. It was one of the things I didn't mind doing. I go out. And Roy didn't wanna to do that. I just loved it. Hey, snowstorm? *Far out*. Rain? *Yeah*. I'll go outside. I'll meet somebody, I'll come back two hours later. "Where are the rolls?" they'd ask. "I met Sam and we got into a little stickball game and . . ."

Religiously, this was what I was sent to get. Four rolls, a container of milk, and the paper. Sometimes, we ran out of butter. I'd get butter. It was rationed so I'd get the little stickers. Meat, I never bought. Candy store for the paper. Dairy two doors down. Container of milk, rolls, paper. Every day. Like a *clock*.

ROBERT HELLER: Now I went to 82, which is Macombs Junior High School. Billy and I came in contact at 82 again and this must be where I know Ike Amato from too. I had a most remarkable teacher there named Elizabeth Sheridan. She was a math teacher, which was not my favorite subject, but for some strange reason, she gravitated toward a certain kind of youngster. I had trouble there because of the head provost, the guy in charge of the monitors, who was a fuckin' Nazi. And I got into some trouble with him. Mrs. Sheridan adopted me. She gave me the first book I ever read, which was *The Education of H*y*m*a*n* K*a*p*l*a*n** by Leo Rosten. Which kind of opened up reading for me.

BILL: Mrs. Sheridan had this beautiful clear face. She wore her hair pulled back into a bun and she was totally dedicated to her students. In a movie, she'd have been played by Maggie Smith. When I saw that movie *The Prime of Miss Jean Brodie* I thought of her. I used to get into trouble *all* the time. For fighting in the school yard. Twice I got caught wheeling and dealing in the school yard, selling baseball cards and shooting crap. The principal couldn't deal with me. So he sent for Mrs. Sheridan to talk to me. She reminded me of my foster mother because she was there for the *right* reasons. She really wanted to teach and she really cared about the kids. She made every one of us feel like individuals. She was some fine lady.

ISAAC AMATO: Bill was vice president of the General Organization. His name then was Billy Grajonca. Even at that time, I can remember very vividly a tremendous presence. There's no two ways about it. He was a very forceful person. He struck me that way as a kid.

   In junior high school, he wrote some beautiful stories that were typed out and illustrated. A story about his pet dog, either real or imaginary. One time, our French teacher, Miss Redmond, a real formidable woman, asked for Bill's name and Billy said, "My name is Billy Grajonca."

   And she said, "There'll be no pet diminutives in this classroom as long as I'm your teacher." And Bill burst out into tears. Which showed you the feeling he had for his name. You know. *Billy.* My name is *Billy.* It gave you a sense of his character.

BILL: Early on, I *knew.* I don't know when I found out but I found out early on that when you take these children in, you get forty-eight dollars a month. Then it was raised. It got up to fifty-four dollars a month. I didn't want somebody to pay for my keep. I wanted the money to come from me—I wanted to earn it—pay my own way. The reason I sold baseball cards and played craps in the school yard and went looking for any after-school and weekend job I could find was to earn money. In terms of paying my foster parents, it was like, "You're good to me but I'm not yours. I don't want somebody else to pay for what you do for me. I'm gonna do it." It wasn't something that I suddenly thought of one day. It started with the nine weeks of nobody wanting me.

First there was delivering *The Bronx Home News*. Then groceries. There was another kid who delivered for a butcher store next door. Sometimes, he got sick. In time, I delivered both groceries and meat.

A dime tip was standard. Sometimes from a real shithead, I'd get "Thank you" and the door would slam in my face. Sometimes a nickel but the dime was the standard tip. For years and *years*.

Happiness then was when I got a sixth-floor walk-up. I'd be carrying a box with bottles of apple juice in it, vegetables, potatoes, all kinds of heavy cans, weighing *tons*, or maybe two or three bags. Six flights straight up and I'd be making all those turns on the stairs. I would hit that last step and I'd have all these bags and I'd give them to the lady and it was *serious time*. She'd say, "Hold on, sonny." Then I had to wait. Every grocery boy, everybody who first started earning money this way, the orgasm was in the slap of a quarter as compared to a dime.

When I got hit with a quarter, it was like someone saying *"Right on!"* to all my labors. A wise decision. In other words, somehow you're aware of what I just went through. A *quarter!* Usually, I got them on Undercliff Avenue because on Undercliff Avenue they had *money*. Those were the big buildings where people lived who had gone from taking orders to *giving* orders. The *bosses*. Accountants, or people who owned stores. They could afford to live in those apartments. Whoever made it then lived on Undercliff Avenue or on the sixth floor on Popham Avenue overlooking the river. The sixth floor in an elevator building with a view of the river? And you had groceries *delivered?* You know when I had groceries delivered to my house? *Never*.

Starting I think in 1944, I paid my foster parents every month the forty-eight dollars for my keep. I also bought a U.S. War Bond every month for eighteen dollars and seventy-five cents, which was what a twenty-five-dollar bond cost. *Every month*. To help make ends meet, my mother also delivered telegrams. I sometimes helped her and Roy do that. Every day I'd cross the street from school, put my books down, and go deliver groceries for the Eagle Market. I had a bike with a box on it. A three-wheel tricycle with an old green wooden box mounted on the front held in place by steel braces. I'd get home, eat, con the homework in any way I could, and then the school yard. Back to P.S. 82 from seven-thirty to ten at night. Half-court basketball indoors in the night center. Twelve-basket games and the winning team stayed on the court.

On weekends when I was delivering groceries, I used to cut out and get into a game. Just lock the wheels and go play. By the time I was sixteen, Jack Molinas was playing. Eddie Roman from Taft. Fatso Roth. Ed Warner from Clinton. Floyd Lane. The New York City high school all-star team, they were my heroes.

In the school yard, it was always playing for the sport of it but also playing for *something*. Like softball games there on the weekends. Heavy cement softball games. Fast pitch. *Serious.* Quarter a man. I played but not great. My favorite game then and now was street touch football. I *love* touch football. Anywhere from two to seven guys on a side.

Stickball was sewer-to-sewer. Hit by yourself and then run bases. Second base way at the next sewer. Car, sewer, car, sewer. Off-the-wall catch, *out.* Catch off any building, *out.* Guys playing stoop ball and "Captain" with a Spaldeen. One block away, that was the heavy marble block. Against the curb. Down between 175th and 174th, that was all marbles.

From the middle of the street to where the coin would be put up, leaning against the curb, it would be a nickel if you hit it. You'd pitch or throw the marble. If you didn't hit it, the other guy kept your marble. So what? If you hit, you got the nickel. For a nickel you could buy thirty or forty marbles. A nickel was a *nickel.*

From the opposite sidewalk, against the other curb, was a quarter. It would be like a hole in one. Guys would throw *missiles* toward this quarter. Five at a time. They would go bing! bing! bing! All of a sudden, one would hit. The real heavies would say, "*A-ha,* he figgered out the curve." But if you're a street marble player, you *know* the curve. A quarter back then meant a hundred or a hundred and fifty marbles. It was a quarter and three. Three tries. And on the second or third one— *BANG!* That was a *major* score.

ISAAC AMATO: He was always a big sports fanatic. We could always talk about sports because he loved sports. That was part of his New York heritage. Since we were both foster children, we were not the kind of close friends you might think. That was just not the way foster kids were. I think I had a good feeling of friendship. But there wasn't either of us saying, "Come on over." Just the fact that in neighborhoods in The Bronx, you can be living three blocks away and it's like another world. Each street had its own people.

BILL: At that time in the neighborhood, we already had at least 60 to 70 percent ethnics and some blacks. The blacks were the service people. The municipal labor force working with the city. In garages and repair shops. Labor jobs. There were a lot of Italians. A lot of Eastern Europeans. Summertime, all streets, all languages. Lots of German, Romanian, Bulgarian, Russian, and Polish.

University Avenue was a very wide street. The Champs-Élysées West. Like the Grand Concourse, it had an island in the middle with two rows of benches on which people sat in the summertime. There, they played *serious* chess and checkers. It was the ultimate pit stop. If I went even from my house to the house next door, I had to go there first to check it out. A block and a half down University to the park. Even on my way next door.

"Ma, these old sneakers don't fit. I left my others at Angie's."

Boom! I'm down to University for two hours. I get back, "Hey, I'm sorry, Ma. I got in a game." I'm not making this up. It happened *hundreds* of times. My house was here. Two blocks down, University Avenue, Percy's Pool Room was *here*. Big A&P where we shopped, *here*. You cross the street, right next to the school yard, the Park Plaza theater, *THE* social location. This was the *church*. This was the center of boys and girls. For me, it was boys boys boys. On Saturday afternoons, you'd go to the movies with the guys.

One year later, you go to the movies with the guys, you look at the girls.

Two years later, "Look, he's sittin' with her. He's sittin' with *her!*"

Right across the street was Ruschmeyer's where they made their own ice cream. Next to Ruschmeyer's, the Eagle Market and the butcher shop. Across University Avenue, my junior high school right next to the Park Plaza Theater. Even when I went to Clinton, that's where I played ball. The school yard never closed. I could come out of the movie house and walk right into a game. From thirteen through sixteen, half-court hoops, touch football, and softball were like my switchblade and my colors. I used to play with Alan Bernstein, who now runs the Maxwell Lumber Company in The Bronx. Paul LeNoble. Stanley Turnower. Irving Levine. And the girls. What *names*. My first girlfriend, Joyce Fliegler. Dolcie Ginsberg. Ursula Blum. Marjorie Holtag.

ROBERT HELLER: They called it the Silk Stocking District of The Bronx. It was mostly Jewish and the teachers were all Jewish except for a couple of Irish. And there was like one Negro to every two hundred Jews but they were in there. The Irish were the people *we* beat up.

BILL: I never was *bar mitzvahed*. I started going to school and then I had a fight with the rabbi about paying attention. I didn't have any patience. The Hebrew school was right across the street from my house. I was into it, I was reading Hebrew. But I just wasn't studious enough. The family was not religious. My father could not read Hebrew. I never thought twice about it really. Religion wasn't important to me. Other than for the facts of my life.

ISAAC AMATO: We went to summer camp together. Camp Wakitan, which was under the administration of the Jewish Child Care Association. In the Bear Mountain region by Lake Stahe. I guess we were fourteen or fifteen. It was a boys' camp and the head of it was Murray "Pop" Sprung, a prominent Jewish lawyer, who I think in 1948 prosecuted Tojo.

BILL: I remember going to Camp Wakitan in upstate New York. While I was there, the atom bomb went off. At the breakfast table, someone had the *Daily News*. The atom bomb had gone off. I became aware that if someone somewhere wanted me dead, I'd be dead. I was blown away by the power of it. Not, "How's somebody going to do it here?" But that it was now possible. I remember thinking, "My days are numbered. I'm at the mercy of someone." Sitting at this long table in Camp Wakitan, I remember thinking that someone now had a weapon that could annihilate us all.

They didn't have to come over the hill. They didn't have to punch a knife in me. It happened through the air. Direct combat was now not necessarily what war was all about. The article mentioned buildings *miles* away that were destroyed. *Miles* and *miles* away. Someone could be sitting in a palace and die. Not from shrapnel, but the heat.

I had followed the European war closely. *Very closely.* On a map in my bedroom with pins. The European war was something I wanted to have over for much more practical reasons than the one in the Pacific. I didn't really understand either war. But once the war in Europe was over, I thought I would find out where my family and friends were.

6.

BILL: My Russian name was Volodia. In Germany, I was "Wolfgang." My sisters called me "Wolfy." In France I became "Guillaume." My friend Sammy Schtuck in the château called me "Gui." William is Wolfgang. "Bill" is the slang name. It's just a nothing name. It doesn't say anything at all. It never has.

I never took the last name "Ehrenreich" because I never knew about my real family. The adoption thing came up early on. Then the idea was dropped and not really discussed again. How can you be adopted when you don't even know if you have a real family or not? Early on, there was some talk of it with the Foster Home Bureau. The reason it wasn't discussed again was that I thought that after the war, I'd be reunited with my real family.

The war ended in '45. Just before it did, the Jewish Foster Home Bureau contacted me with the news that HIAS, the Hebrew Immigrant Aid Society, was planning on sending teams of special investigators into the concentration camps and internment centers once the war ended. I went to a large building down in lower Manhattan with all the photographs and papers that I'd kept from my early days. Family pictures and letters. They made copies of everything, which were then sent on to Europe with these investigators. I knew full well that millions had been slaughtered. Then the miracle. They found my sister, Ester. I was fourteen at the time.

ESTER CHICHINSKY: Immediately after I was liberated from Spandau by the American army, I tried to get into Berlin. I was nineteen years old by then. I was in Berlin three weeks after the liberation. Earlier, I couldn't get through. It was impossible. The building we had lived in last was bombed out. The whole side of the street was completely bombed out. The whole section, the whole area was gone.

I was also in Bergen-Belsen looking if somebody heard about my family. Because it's hard to understand how people found one another. The Hungarians kept together, the Romanians kept together, people from different *shtetlach* kept together. So when I walked into Bergen-Belsen or a camp nearby where people stayed until they knew where they were going to move, I would ask, "Are there some Berliners here?" And then when I found them, I would go to the district and then the block.

I told some people I met that I had sisters in Hungary. I found out these people were going to Hungary but nobody had papers. I was someone without an identity. I asked them please to take me. And they did. I kept going back and forth on the train so no one would have a chance to ask me for documents. Any time the train stopped, I got down. So I was not caught. When we came to Budapest, I was on my own. I found an old lady, an aunt of the man to whom Evelyn was engaged. She helped me find Evelyn, who was living an entirely different life from mine. She had escaped the war, she was very unhappy about herself. She did not have much thoughts of family, let's put it that way. I did my best as a sister. But I had my certain goal. The *family*. There's one thing I'm very proud of. I did everything to the extreme to bring the family back together. The best that I knew how.

I went back again to that old lady and she told me where I can get information about Sonja. She was engaged at the time and dancing in a ballet troupe in Vienna. So now I have to get to Vienna. No papers, no documents. On the train before the border, here comes the Hungarian border patrol. They put me in jail with smugglers and all and whatnot. Two, three days I sit there.

One afternoon they make me go out and work on the fields. So I escape across the border. I went straight to the Austrian authorities and gave myself up. They had more heart than the Hungarians. One very nice officer said to me, "You have no ID?" And I said, "Yes, I have an ID. My number. That is all I have." And I show them the number on my arm. So they gave me a free pass to go on the train.

After a day or two, I found Sonja. She was with a whole group, a theatrical review, comedians and dancers and whatnot. I stayed over but they had their own lifestyle as artists and dancers. It was not a life for me.

For me, every hour was too valuable to waste. So I went back to Germany and stopped at every camp I could think of or find. One Friday night, I stumbled into Hanover and I sat down at an *oneg shabbat* with a man who I found out had come to open up HIAS, the Hebrew Immigrant Aid Society. I told him my story about how I had been going from place to place. He took me to the office and asked if I would be willing to help him out there. He understood that I also was looking for relatives and family but he said he could help me too. So I started working for Mr. Kreitzer of HIAS.

The first thing he promised me was that on his first trip to the U.S., he would help me locate where Bill's transport went from France. Finally, my boss went to this big conference in New York. Two or three days later, I get a telegram. It says, *"I found your brother."* We started corresponding.

BILL: At first, Ester wasn't certain what happened to my mother. I wasn't told through her. I was told through the records of HIAS. They notified me. What I think happened to me early on was that a subconscious wall went up. "I'm out here on my own. I don't have *anybody*." An island that I've lived on all my life. I knew I had to fend for myself and be careful not to let anything too close for fear of losing it again. There went my father, my mother, my sisters. What's the sense of opening that door? What's the sense of getting off the deck? I'd only get knocked down again. Before I do get up again, I'm going to make sure to look around really slowly. First, I'm going to make some moves. At least, that's a theory.

Early on, this coat was formed. I mean, I never remember being truly lost or emotionally sapped by the loss of anyone. That doesn't mean I don't care. Or that someone else loves deeper than I do. Or that I don't know how to grieve. But I do know I've always been prepared for loss. And therefore was never left totally naked.

I often ask people, "How old were you when your father died?" Or "How old were you when your mother died?" "Eight," they might say. *Oh.* You grew up without a mother through your formative years? You never had a father? I understand something about you that I could never really put into words. It's like we share something others can't comprehend.

ROY EHRENREICH: Not only did Bill seize upon the street culture but he saw the street kids as being the *real* kids. The ones that he could relate to most easily. The ones that provided in some sense role models. I did not present a role model, I don't think. Nor did my father. He didn't want to be either of us. He wanted to do things for himself. That was always a strong, strong motivation. To figure out how to do it himself. And I think that goes right back to the very beginning.

He got a lot of credit in the family for being able to earn money on his own. But I think he lost most of the credit for squandering the money on things that weren't considered worthwhile. On things the family saw as frivolous. At the very beginning, it was probably movies.

BILL: The Park Plaza theater had a little round box office in front. It was Art Deco. Loew's Paradise-type deco. One balcony. Loew's Paradise had *two*. There were two movie houses that I used to go to besides the Park Plaza. The Zenith at 170th Street and the Mount Eden. If I went before 10 A.M., it was eleven cents to get in and the first five hundred kids got comic books. It was always two movies and a serial and I was a big Phantom fan. Some kids' favorite was Dick Tracy or Terry and the Pirates. Mine was *the Phantom*. Like a weekly TV show. I'd go every Saturday morning to keep up with *The Adventures of The Phantom.*

The first movie I ever saw in America was the greatest movie I ever saw. I think I went with my foster mother. *Four Feathers* with Ralph Richardson. An *amazing* film. And *King Kong*. Every year, at least once a year, the Zenith would bring back *King Kong* and *Gunga Din* on the same bill. With the Phantom, of course. There was a time when I could have played *all* the parts in *Gunga Din*, including Sam Jaffee as Gunga,

Cary Grant, Douglas Fairbanks, Jr., *and* Victor McLaglen. I always went for dramas or adventures. Never comedies or musicals.

I had great heroes and I was very much influenced by the kinds of roles some actors played and how they played them. Paul Muni. *Big* fan of Paul Muni. Charles Laughton. Best of all by far, John Garfield. *The Fallen Sparrow, Sea Wolf, Body and Soul,* and *Gentleman's Agreement.* Garfield for me was Everyman. He always played the role of the guy that was fucked by the fickle finger of fate. He was never totally a bad guy. Even when he was a bad guy, I knew *why.* I believed society did it to him.

Whether it's the actor or the person watching him, I don't know. What impressed me about Garfield was the way he always expressed just what he thought his rights were. He had street class. Who am I to say how he influenced me? What have any of my heroes done for me? I don't know. But I do know I hated Joan Crawford.

Even when Garfield made a movie called *Destination Tokyo,* with Cary Grant, where he did sort of a number as an actor, "Okay, you want me to play this part? Okay, I'll talk Brooklyn," he still pulled it off. I just believed him. In *Body and Soul,* when he fell for the wrong actress, it just tore me apart. I used to sit there and say to him on the screen, "You dumb fuck, don't you see what she's going to do to you?" In my life, I came to see men totally controlled by women and women totally controlled by men. Just the way that Garfield in that movie got caught.

I was never studious. I was never inquisitive, other than about basic survival things. I worked hard after school and I loved sports. My grades were good because when I had a test, I would cram. For two days, I'd have a photographic memory. Sometimes, I'd write things down on the inside of my hand. Not too often. The worst was in physics and chemistry.

"What's the first color inside a frog's neck?"

Who *knows* what a frog's neck looks like or *should* look like?

"And the pubation period of an owl in Egypt is *what?*"

Whenever something made no sense to me, I gave up. Whenever I thought, "Why should I know this?" I didn't.

I was good at math and geography and history. English too. What I wasn't good at was biology and chemistry. Explaining how internal combustion works so the car moves. Or what batteries are all about. I have no idea. To this day, it is inconceivable to me that when I push a button, the TV goes on.

I made the swimming team in DeWitt Clinton High School. The breaststroke. But I didn't stay with it. I never went to practice enough. Although I really wanted to be part of it, I had set myself up to work. That I *had* to work.

ROY EHRENREICH: The main problem from my parents' standpoint was that he just went in too many directions at once. None of which were proper behavior for a young man of his age. This was obviously because he was running around with the *wrong* kids. That was the big thing, I think. The rap in the family was that sooner or later he was going to get into trouble for hanging with these kids.

BILL: We were the Pirates. The Pirates Social Athletic Club. Pirates S.A.C., yellow and green jackets. We had a clubhouse on Andrews Avenue, a basement with two rooms. During the week, without a girl, Okay. On the weekend, a *must*. You *must* have a girl. I was sixteen when I got into the Pirates. I was accepted young.

ROY EHRENREICH: The dinner table would pretty much be the discussion place. The sort of thing that got them upset was that he'd come in fifteen or twenty minutes late for dinner. That was a constant problem, over and over again. The major punishment was that he would be confined. You know, you can't go out. My mother was sterner on that standpoint. My father was the one who would say after a while, "All right, let him go. Let him go."

I think it was also seen as a bit of a problem in that DeWitt Clinton was the natural high school for anybody in the neighborhood to be going to. But I think the difference between Clinton and Bronx High School of Science was a significant one. For what it was worth, I was associating with brighter and more responsible kids and he was of necessity associating with wilder and less responsible kids.

I was the studious one and Bill was the wild one. Not a bad kid. They might have thought of it more as irresponsible or not serious enough. I mean, very typical American Jewish attitudes. They didn't terribly like his friends. He very rarely brought friends to the house. He tended to stay out late. All of these things. And it was not a question of him being a bad kid because he certainly never got into any *serious* trouble. But they wanted somebody else like me.

BILL: I became very good friends with a guy named Jerry Sontag, who to the best of my knowledge drives a truck now. In our gang, he *was* John Garfield. Big and tough with a great sense of humor, and he was the best street ball player I ever saw. Whatever the sport. To this day if I saw him, I'd look at him in awe. He was the first guy I ever met who could naturally go either way in hoops. Great hands.

When I was seventeen, I started going to Latin dances. I needed seven hundred and fifty dollars for a car. It became a big thing.

ROY EHRENREICH: I think at various times it was made clear that there just wasn't any money for him to go to an out-of-town college. I think they probably felt less badly about it because they didn't really think he was a candidate for that. At the time he graduated from high school, I was off at Penn. I got all the advantages. There's *no* question about that. I have always felt a certain amount of guilt about simply having had all the advantages throughout that period.

I mean, I was the little tin Jesus who would very rarely do anything wrong. And Bill was the one who kept hitting his thumb with a hammer.

BILL: During a pickup game while I was at DeWitt Clinton High School, I broke a bone in my right wrist. It didn't set right and they sent me for treatment to Montefiore Hospital. I had to continue to go for treatment for four or five months afterward. Then it was okay but I never told anybody at school that I didn't have to go anymore. So I spent the next three years of my life going downtown every Tuesday to the Strand or the Capitol or the Paramount Theater. That's when I began my great escape into that downtown world.

I'd get downtown at maybe ten in the morning for the first show. Stage show, movie, stage show, movie. I'd see Xavier Cugat with Abbe Lane. The Ritz Brothers. The Count Basie Band with Billy Eckstine. Always a juggler, a comedian, and then the headliner. Phil Spitalny and His All-Girl Orchestra, Featuring Evelyn and Her Magic Violin. I'd stay for three or four shows especially when it was Billy Eckstine. To me, he was like Charlton Heston coming down from the mountain with the clay tablets in his hands.

Dean Martin and Jerry Lewis, although that was later on. Sinatra, a few times. The Dorsey band. The Nicholas Brothers, two amazing tap dancers. Also Rudy Cardenas, a juggler. The worst. The *worst*. I always hoped that someday I'd actually see him hold those nine plates up in the air. You know? Just once. Sometimes, I'd bring my lunch.

I'd go by subway or just walk. I was an outrageous walker. Go from The Bronx all the way to downtown Manhattan. Take maybe three, four hours and sometimes walk back up. I got like Sabu, the Elephant Boy. Instead of running, I walked. I just went and went and went. I walked through any neighborhood. I got to be like a blotter. I would just absorb. I would look at anything and everything. I was a lot less inquisitive about what was in a book than what was out there around me.

I'd go down to the Battery. I was fascinated by Manhattan. I'd hit Harlem. Spanish Harlem *fascinated* me. Walking through it, I was a minority. It was a world much different than mine. Lenox Avenue, Seventh

Avenue, Amsterdam. Back then, I probably knew the streets of The Bronx and Manhattan as well as any cabdriver. Bar none.

7.

BILL: I was never able to get down with my father. I never really talked to him about anything important. Schoolwork or my problems in the streets. He was an insurance man, he played his cards, bridge and gin. Pinochle. He was a heavy, heavy cardplayer. Nickel and dime. He had a house game. Tenants in the same building. Irv Lustgarten and Al LeNoble, who lived across the street. A couple of people upstairs. Arthur, the guy downstairs.

I didn't confess things to my mother either but I knew I could talk to her whenever I needed to. If it wasn't my brother, I'd talk to her. It was me inside with my mother or my brother, and then on the other side was my father. Yet, my brother and I never ran together. But we were tight. Home was like a neutral zone for all of us.

Then I met this girl from Brooklyn at a dance. I was seventeen going on eighteen and a senior at Clinton. I had started going down to Manhattan and out to Queens with friends. None of us had a car yet, so we'd take the subway. In those days, you could pick up the *Post* or *The Bronx Home News* to find out about Latin dances. In the late forties and early fifties, the Jews and the Latins were very close. The headline bans in all the hotels in the Catskills were always Latin, with the society orchestra second on the bill. On Friday and Saturday nights, there would be dances in the Jewish sectors of Queens like Rego Park or at the St. George Hotel in Brooklyn or the Starlight Ballroom in the Bronx.

My first heart throb had been Joyce Fliegler but I lost her to another guy. Back when I was in the Pirates, S.A.C. It was the first serious emotional problem I had relative to ladies. One Saturday afternoon, Joyce said she couldn't make it to the movies with me. Sure enough, I was sitting there in the Park Plaza theater and a few rows down, there was this guy. He was in our club. He had his arms around a lady and it was Joyce. He didn't see me but I saw them. They left the theater and walked down the hill. She lived right down the hill from the movie house. It was pouring rain.

I stood across the street and I watched where they were going. They went into the two-story house she lived in. Inside these glass doors. The thick glass that you can't really see through all that clearly. I stood across the street and he kissed her inside that door, behind that thick, wet glass and I was fucking soaked. I thought he had good taste. I thought she was a shithead.

But time passed. Anyway, I met this girl at one of those dances, who lived in Brooklyn, and I liked her. I decided to cash in my years of war bonds to buy a car. Seven hundred and fifty dollars. I was certain that if I'd asked, my father wouldn't have let me buy one. I think my mother would've accepted it because it would've given me pleasure. My feeling was that he would have felt I was too young to have a car. He was pretty much a by-the-books kind of guy.

It was a light green Oldsmobile convertible, seven years old, with Hydramatic, and the shift on the column. Radio, heater. Leather seats. Two-door with a light-colored top. Even then, I never wanted to close the top. I got the car for seven fifty, and I decided not to tell anybody. I made sure to have the license and all that addressed to a friend of mine, Jerry Sontag, who also taught me how to drive.

I always left the car on Undercliff Avenue. There was University, then Andrews Avenue, Montgomery, Popham, and then you have to go down these long steps to where the rich people lived next to the river. I knew my father never, *never* went to Undercliff Avenue to park his car. Undercliff wasn't even part of the Jewish area. It was where the *goyim* execs lived. People who read a lot.

I *never* used it for school. Only to go see Alice, who lived in the Brighton Beach section of Brooklyn. I used to make all kinds of excuses to get there. I would never just leave the house and go around to Popham Avenue and then down to the car. It was like foreign intrigue. I would leave the house, walk down the hill to Andrews Avenue, and then to University, in a complete square. Down University to 174th, back up to Andrews to Montgomery to Popham, down the steps to the car. Even when I parked it there. I would put it behind a tree. To camouflage it. I mean, I was *insane.* I used to think about my father driving down there. He wouldn't know it was my car anyway. But what if he saw me getting out of it? Or something or other. So I never, never took chances.

To the best of my knowledge, no person older than twenty knew about this car. Six or seven months passed. Then one day I came home from school and my father was in the apartment, which was very unusual. Pearl must have called him at work or something. The minute I walked in, there was a look on his face I'd never seen before. It seemed for the first time that he was really paying attention to me. He stepped into the kitchen and he pointed at the table and he said, "Explain this."

On the table was a letter from the Veterans of Foreign Wars. They would send you metal dog tags with your license on it and these little slots for coins in the letter to send back to them. I said, "Well, Pa." And I told him the truth.

"Why didn't you tell me about this?" he said.

"I didn't think you'd let me have the car."

He really got incensed and he whipped off his belt and he held the buckle in his hand and said in so many words that I had to take my pants down and I said, "No. You're not gonna do that."

"Get over and bend down," he said.

My mother was in the other room and he wouldn't let her interfere. He yelled, *"You'll do what I say."* I remember grabbing his arm with the belt in it. He had never put a hand on me before. He'd yell at me sometimes for being late. But there was never anything physical. No violence.

He was stocky, maybe five eight or five nine. I must have been two or three inches taller but pretty slim. He was a *man*. Whether he could have beaten me up or not, I had no idea. I just couldn't let him use that belt on me. I remember putting up my hand to stop him and he pulled away. I remember taking the belt with both hands and just holding it. At that moment, he knew that physically, he could not back it up anymore. He realized that I could stop him.

It wasn't something either of us understood right then. But I know now. What that meant was that we were *never* going to be angry at one another again. He knew not only could he not do that then but he could *never* do it again. He could *never* have that hold over me. It was very sad. There was nothing more said. I remember apologizing to him later on.

"I'm sorry about the car."

"You should have told me," he said.

"You're right. But I didn't think you'd let me."

"Probably not," he said.

I remember wishing that it had never happened. Why was that necessary? I wanted him to give me an example of what fathers were all about but he just did not have it in him to do so. What I wanted was someone who would go out in the street and play some ball with me. My father? *Never.*

ROY EHRENREICH: There were lots of little incidents. But never any bullying or even anything physical. I think it was that Bill was sort of simply like a second-class member of the household and that was primarily because of the way they looked at me. I was the cause of it, however innocently.

In those days, a car was the *ultimate* status symbol. It was terribly important to Bill to have a car. I never particularly wanted a car. Because I have a peculiar form of color blindness, they told me in the Army that I would be a dangerous driver. And as a result I have never learned to drive. I have never driven a car.

BILL: I got a financial scholarship, I think it was called the Carl Wallach Foundation Scholarship. X number of dollars to go to school. I decided to take some liberal arts classes at Brooklyn College. I got a job working in Barron's Bookstore. Stocking and filing and running errands. For them and the music store next door. I took the subway to school every day because the car conked out on me. Within a year it died and I sold it for a couple hundred dollars.

I stopped seeing Alice because her father didn't like me. She was an Italian Christian and I was a Bronx Jew. It was a very strange period for me. I was very restless. I stayed at Brooklyn College all the way through 1950 and into '51. For some dumb reason, I went out for the football team. I was going to make it as either an end or a defensive safety but I broke my arm in a scrimmage.

I started going to the Apollo Theater with Jerry Sontag, who always stayed in my life. Jerry *was* New York. If you said to him, "I'm going to New Hampshire to go skiing" or "I'm going to California," he'd look at you with a completely straight face and say, "For? *For?*" Not even "*What* for?" Just "*For?*" Why bother *ever* leaving the island of New York? At the Apollo, we saw Arthur Prysock and Cab Calloway and Al Hibbler. As far back as I can remember, my big favorites in terms of records were early seventy-eights by Latin musicians like Pupi Campo, Xavier Cugat, Esy Morales. My feeling for Latin music grew I think along with my developing interest in women. Looking at them and seeing them move. The rhythmic stuff of how music relates to sensuality.

I started going to the Palladium at Fifty-third and Broadway during my senior year in high school. It cost a buck-fifty to get in. The real night to be there was Wednesday. I'd leave home, go to Brooklyn College, and come back into Manhattan at eight or nine at night. Go to the Palladium, throw my books into the checkroom, and dance for hours on end. Till three or four in the morning. Sometimes, I'd go right back to Brooklyn to go to school the next day.

I never looked for or sensed any trouble there. I never went to pick anyone up. I never felt threatened. Although I knew there were a lot of wild dealings going on. All the guys with their spats and canes and funny hats. It was a Latino crowd and a black crowd. Big bar action. A lot of rum and a lot of straight whiskey.

This was before Brando used to go there all the time. I remember Van Johnson came up one night. Esther Williams came there. One night, the king of the universe came. *Cesar Romero.* One of my all-time heroes because of his name but a terrible actor. It was a major, major event. A woman I desperately wanted to sleep with came with a man whom all the women wanted. Maria Montez and Turhan Bey. That was a *buzz* in Manhattan. Turhan Bey and Maria Montez.

The great thing about the Palladium was that people went there to dance and have a good time. It was the music that made them feel good. The *music*. It was upstairs in the middle of the block at Fifty-third and Broadway. You'd come up this long narrow flight of stairs to dirty velour walls. *Dark*. One huge room with overlapping velour and a wooden floor. Coatroom to the right, big bar to the left, stage straight ahead. Held about three thousand people. *Big*. Wednesday nights, it would be jammed. That was dance contest night. They had these great security guards. Always wearing white shirts with the top two buttons open and the collars *spread*, like wings. That was the look. All with mustaches.

I went week after week after week. Like a clock. Then I got to know Sardelle, a little black lady who checked the coats. She must have started working there in like 1803. Coats and coats and yelling and screaming and music. Mr. Hyman was the owner, a twitchy white-haired man in his fifties who loved Latin music. He twitched a lot and he was loved by everybody. They loved him because he was bringing them Latin music and he was revered when he walked through the hall. But he was always twitching. Looking over his shoulder and twitching. But he *was* Napoleon. They all answered to him. Immaculately dressed. Like Adolphe Menjou.

There were tables in the corner that people claimed by putting down their pocketbook or a cigarette pack or a coat. The most significant thing about the place was that there was a big ballroom with a mirror ball in the middle, low lighting, and the stage. Early in the night, people would just come swarming in there, they would run out on the dance floor and start to dance.

Sometimes, heavy-duty VIP's would sit in the section with the tables. To me, it was a section where you had to buy a bottle to sit down. You don't buy? The waiter's nose became nine feet long. In that section, three-drink minimum. So it was hipper to buy a bottle. That was the *heavy* section.

The people who danced in front of that section, which was stage right, they had people watching. So the only people who even danced in that corner were *dancers*. Serious dancers. I didn't dance there. I was relatively new. I enjoyed dancing very much but I wasn't a great dancer with a lot of fancy steps. I looked for women who *felt* the music. Who weren't exhibitionists. Dancing is movement—sensuality—passion. You don't always have to get to sex, you can just be holding someone and moving with that person in rhythm. Just kissing. Nine times out of ten when I'd find a woman sitting or standing somewhere who was attractive and I'd ask her to dance, she would say no. She'd be thinking, "Does this *schmuck* know how to dance? Why should I waste my time with him?"

Then sometimes I'd find a woman who *would*. And then one who had said "No" to me before might even ask *me* to dance. Because she might say to herself, "Hey, he's a good dancer." The songs themselves would go on for fifteen or twenty minutes at a time. The band would extend them, solo after solo. First the piano and then the percussion and then the brass and then more vocals. Machito, Tito Puente, Tito Rodriguez. Everybody dancing and dancing and dancing and the entire ballroom would get off. We weren't all making love at once but we were in the eye of this wonderful storm. Dancing inside this great groove. Time out, world.

In the middle of a song, the whole orchestra would suddenly stop playing except for the bass line. But nobody would stop dancing. We'd all clap our hands and keep the clave beat and everybody simply surrendered to the passion of the music—thousands of us. We'd keep perfect time till the solo was over and the entire band would come back in and take it on home. *Thousands* of us. And everybody felt good. Everybody felt *so* good.

I remember the *guahira*, the *dansons*, the way Latin women moved and how that just put me away. I remember Celia Cruz and La Lupe. I'd stay until three o'clock in the morning most of the time. The simplest way to explain the Palladium is that it was where I went to recharge my battery. Just take it and stick it in the wall. I'd come out hours later, feeling great. Get into the subway and get home maybe at four or four-thirty in the morning.

The Palladium eventually changed my entire life. I met a couple other white kids who loved Latin music like me. They became the people I spent time with. I sort of left The Bronx scene. I still knew Jerry Sontag and I played ball there sometimes but my life became Latin dancing and going to the mountains to work on the weekends. The mountains for money, and the Palladium for pleasure.

My biggest ambition at the time was to someday dance in the corner at the Palladium where people sat at those tables and watched. I mean, *that* was it. After I got out of the service, I went to the Palladium the first Wednesday night. When they had exhibitions by people like Augie and Margo and the Mambo Aces and it was also "Contest Night" when anyone from the audience could enter.

That night, I not only danced in the corner, but I also entered the amateur contest and *won*. I won a Wednesday Night Dance Contest. You understand what this means? It means, "Why should I ever want to be president of the United States?" Because I've accomplished something better. It was great. God, it was *so* great.

8.

BILL: In 1950, the Korean War started but I really didn't pay that much attention to it. I was still going to college and working this part-time job with a jewelry company on West Forty-seventh Street in the diamond district. Davidson and Sons, 20 West Forty-seventh Street. They manufactured rings. I worked there from ten to four every day and then I went to school at Brooklyn College. I filled orders and I helped with shipping, repackaging synthetic stones coming in from Europe and sizing them. Eventually I ended up in inventory control. Amethysts and garnets.

By this time, I'd begun to think seriously about what I was going to do for a living. Then I got my draft notice, telling me to report in two weeks. My brother Roy had already graduated from college and been drafted into the Army. He was doing Army public relations work in Anniston, Alabama. I told the people at Davidson and Sons that I got my notice. I worked there another week and then I took off the week before I went in.

Guys in the neighborhood were doing whatever they could to get out. Walking around all day long with soap in their armpits so their body temperature would go up. But I never thought about anything like that. Before I reported for my physical, they gave me a going-away party at the jewelers'. I had gotten really friendly with some of the old European men who worked there. I would talk to them on my break and at lunch.

Not only did they give me a going-away party but also the most cherished material thing I still own. A gold ring with my initials, "BG." The old guys, the jewelers, the ones who had to be weighed out every day when they worked with gold to make sure they weren't stealing it, they made it for me. They all stole a little bit of gold dust every day from the filings that came into the office. All the jewelers had pinched a little gold dust every day so they could make that ring for me. The only ring I still wear to this day.

I was eighteen at the time. I wanted very much to become an American citizen so my sisters would be put on the preferred quota list. If you have a blood relative living in America, then it's a lot easier to get in. At seventeen and a half, I applied for citizenship. But the process could not be completed until I was twenty-one. I decided then to change my last name. Because people were making fun of me all the time. Grajonca. "Hey, Junka." "Hey, Junkie." No one even said it right. "Pichunky." "Kachonky." "Kajotsky." "Conuncky." So I legally changed my name from Wolfgang Grajonca to William Graham.

I got Graham from the phone book. All I did was look at G-R-A-J. I looked to see what was closest to it. G-R-A-K or G-R-A-H. The first name I came to was "Graham" and there were hundreds of them in the book. I wanted a simple name. I've felt very badly about doing it ever since because I don't really like the name. I've never liked it. I liked Grajonca. I just didn't like what people did to it.

A week later, I reported for my physical. I was drafted and I had to report to Fort Dix in New Jersey. I was assigned to Camp Chaffee in Arkansas for basic training. I can't say my mother was upset. Her attitude was "What you got to do, you got to do." She hoped I wouldn't go into combat. It seemed pretty sure Roy wouldn't because he was in public information work.

Basic training was a shock. Early on when you're with your family, you take orders from your mom and pop. Then you have your first job. Somebody snaps their fingers and tells you what to do. I had some experience in menial jobs like delivering groceries. But the grocer was a good man. He was nice to me. The butcher, he was a good man. They weren't tyrants. They treated me well. But the Army was the real thing. Blindly, I was told to follow orders.

I remember going in to speak to the battalion commander at Camp Chaffee. At Fort Dix, they'd said, "Wait till you get to your post." I said, "I'm going to do it in basic training." I went to my captain in basic at Chaffee and I pleaded with him to process my citizenship papers. Because I wasn't going to be twenty-one until January 1952. This was the summer of '51. I'd been drafted and my family had been put into the camps and now Ester and Rita were in Israel on this long quota list to come over. If only I could have become a citizen, I could've brought them over immediately. I remember thinking that a man had to have the right to expect automatic citizenship in a nation that had asked him to fight and go to war.

The captain said, "We have no time for this, soldier." I started to argue and I think I was fingered right then and there. I was a New York Jew in Camp Chaffee, Arkansas.

Both the corporal and sergeant in charge of my platoon had been in combat. Their feet did not ever touch the ground. The corporal did not like me or anyone from the city. He was from Nebraska. The local hero, with his "Rifleman" thing on here and his pistol thing on there, plus whatever else he could legally put on his chest. And he ran my ass.

During basic training, I repeatedly asked for permission to see the captain. I kept on insisting that they had to do something about this. Because I'd been informed very clearly that once I became a citizen, my sisters' names would go right to the top of the quota list. I kept on saying,

"How can I be a soldier in the United States Army unless I'm a citizen of the United States?"

Anyway, one day I tried to put on my backpack and I just couldn't. I had this pinched nerve in my back. If I stood a certain way, my neck locked and I couldn't lift anything. I couldn't lift the pack. The corporal said, "Soldier, I'm giving you a direct order." We were leaving to go on one of those ten-mile steambath hikes. In Arkansas in the summer, it was freezing when we'd get up. Then by 10 A.M. it would be a hundred and ten. Lovely weather. *Lovely.* Just take a small bag, you'll be prepared for everything.

The corporal, he told me I was disobeying a direct order. Finally, I said, "I can't put the pack on. I can't. I *can't.*" And he said, "You put that on, *boy!* You get that up, *soldier!* You're in the Army *now!*"

I said to him, "Look, don't you understand? I have this pinched nerve in my back. I can't lift it."

"You think I want to hear your shit?" he said.

Finally, I told him, *"Fuck you, Jack!"*

He broke me out of ranks and made me go back to the barracks. He wrote the whole thing up. Summary court-martial for insubordination, which was the least serious of court-martials. Because they had nothing to take away from me. I mean, I wasn't going to even get my first stripe for another three months and my pay was like a dollar four a month. So they put me on KP and I scrubbed bunks for the 5th Armored Division.

During the rest of basic, I got to be buddies with a couple of other guys from New York. We went into town *once*, I think. We played lots of touch football and basketball in our time off. I hated the regimentation. I hated what we had to do. That the coin *had* to bounce off the sheet. That the shoes *had* to be polished for no good reason.

Shooting, I stayed away from. There was very little of it until we went out on bivouac for the last few weeks. We had to take rifle practice but that didn't really faze me. I got through the rest of basic without confronting anyone. I was assigned to learn how to call in fire missions. To direct the cannons. I was an artillery spotter. What they called a forward observer. Back then, I knew nothing about being a conscientious objector. But if I had, I would have been one.

I also knew nothing about Korea. I was drafted because they told me I had no choice. There was no indoctrination whatsoever about communism or what we were fighting for or against over there. Once basic was over, I was assigned to Fort Lawton, Washington. Fort Lawton was the first stop on the way to overseas reassignment. I got to go back home for a two-week leave. Roy wasn't there, he was stationed in Alabama. It felt odd being in uniform and it was very hard for Pearl because both of her kids were gone from home.

I wasn't really scared. By this time, I'd built up a feeling about myself. I had the capability to make it work for me. Whatever "it" happened to be. I figured that even if I went into combat, I'd find some way to be the master of my destiny. From New York, I went by plane to the state of Washington. It took sixteen hours. We stayed at Fort Lawton for a couple of days. Then we were shipped to Japan on this huge troop ship. *Thousands* of troops. Two weeks, the trip took. Some guy on board told me he had heard from somebody else that when they call out for volunteers for certain jobs, hold off until they ask for people to cook. Then yell out your name and volunteer. Administrator, deck work, inventory, everybody wanted those jobs so they could avoid KP, washing dishes and stuff like that. They called out, "Anyone here with kitchen experience?"

"Here," I told them.

So I got assigned to the kitchen. My job on the boat for two weeks was transporting food from the kitchen to sick bay. I really lucked out on this job. There were so many guys on board—we were sleeping in nets below deck. Five nets one on top of the other and I was one guy up from the bottom. The second night out, somebody started a crap game and I got into it.

Everybody had brought food from home when they got on the boat. But by the third or fourth night, it was all gone. Somebody at the game said, "I wish I had a sandwich." I said, "Hey, I work in the kitchen. I can get you a sandwich. Gimme a buck." A buck for a sandwich and a quarter for an orange. No one seemed to mind that it wasn't free. It was my job and my ass that I was risking. By the next night, more guys were asking for food. It became a movie. I had to get *another* guy to help me. Of course, I cut him in for a piece. Sandwiches, vegetables, fruit, and candy. All kinds of food. I think the sandwiches leveled off at a buck and a half. The fruit was still a quarter. By the end I was doing over a hundred sandwiches a night and maybe twenty pounds of fruit.

We were shipping everything through the boat. Guys carrying it in boxes. The guy I cut in got totally possessed. At first, he said, "You know, we could get caught." I said, "It's not just for the money. Everybody's gonna eat, we'll have a good time, and we'll both do all right." Which was part of this odd attitude I began to have. That if anyone had an endless amount of anything which did not get shared, I would be part of getting it to others.

Here was the United States Army with *tons* and *tons* of food. Guys gambling all night got hungry. They wanted to eat. Why shouldn't they?

What was a hundred sandwiches? Mayonnaise or mustard? Guys would line up at the beginning of the game. "Cheese? Ham? Roast beef?" It was never like in that movie *King Rat* where the guy who had everything, George Segal, made everyone pay *his* price. The guy I cut in for a piece of the action made four hundred bucks working with me.

Remember, I was also betting on the crap game. As the wrong bettor. Playing it safe, never going for the big kill. I was always the wrong bettor, betting *against* the shooter. In Las Vegas, if eight or six is your point in craps, you get odds of six-to-five. But in a regular game, it's even money. So there's a little edge. On nines and fives, you get three-to-two. On tens and fours, it's two-to-one. But on eights and sixes, it's even. Over a long stretch, sometimes but not always, it gives you a little edge.

When I got on board, I had eighty dollars in my pocket. When the boat got to Japan, I had three thousand seven hundred dollars in my pocket. More money than I had ever made anywhere before, by *far*. Three thousand seven hundred. I was twenty years old. Now, we were coming in to dock in Tokyo. Here was the new world waiting for us. Hundreds of guys were involved in card or crap games all over the deck. Some guys were completely tapped so they had to stop.

But there were six or seven guys who had won big money. All of a sudden, we're pulling into the bay when the game starts. The *big* game. It was a shootout. The big winners from all the other games that had been going on for the past two weeks started to play. I didn't want to be part of it. I was tired from making sandwiches and carrying bags of fruit back and forth.

But somehow, I got into the game as one of the wrong guys, betting against. A guy dropped out. Another guy stopped. Another guy dropped out. He lost maybe ten grand. I wanted to stop then and there but the guy with the dice said, "Come on, Bill. Come on. Let me roll and then you can stop." And *he* tapped out.

I started with thirty-seven hundred dollars. By this time, I don't know how much I had. All I know is that my pockets were full of money. A couple of the other guys had guys protecting them and their money. There were camps of supporters and I had about fifteen or twenty guys there who knew me. It got down to three guys left. I wanted to quit. They said to me, "What are you? Chickening out?"

"Okay," I said, "Let's go."

I figured I'd play just a bit more, lose a little money back, and then say forget it. A guy said, "C'mon, Bill. Why don't *you* shoot? Now there were only three of us."

I picked up the dice. Now, I *never* shot. *Never*. I only bet against. People were huddled around us on every side. This was like the focal point of the entire *ship*. This game as we came pulling into the harbor. I picked up the dice. I threw a number. I made it. I threw, then I passed. Then I rolled a four. When I rolled a four, I said, "Five hundred I four. Anybody who wants it."

Guys started to bet against me. Whatever the bets, no matter how many, I covered them. People who were there said they'd never seen anything like it. That it was history. People coming off this boat talked of nothing else.

I had rolled a four. If I rolled a four again, I would win. If I rolled a seven, I would lose. It had to be a four or a seven. If any other point came up, all the money would ride. What were the odds of a four or a seven? A seven could come up six-one, one-six, five-two, two-five, four-three, three-four. Six ways. A four could only come up three ways. Three-one, one-three, two-two. Therefore, the odds were two-to-one.

After the first roll, I rolled at least twenty more times. It may have been fifty. I rolled and I rolled and I rolled. No four, no sevens. I kept rolling. Twelve. Two. Five. Eight. Nine. Ten. Six. Eleven. Twelve. Two. Three. No four. No seven. I rolled a nine. "Twenty no four," someone yelled out. Guys were betting against me like crazy. Cover, cover, cover. Understand what twenty rolls was. And twenty stops in between. I know it was more but let's just say it was twenty.

I was rolling and I was rolling and every time I rolled, I had to cover more bets. I was down to two or three hundred bucks. That was all I had in my hand. I was sweating, I was insane. I was totally, totally, totally convinced that I had willed these dice to do what I wanted. "Why should you fuck with me?" I was saying to them in my mind. "I work hard. I'm gonna get this four. And I don't know what I'm gonna do with the money. I don't even *care* about the money."

I said to myself, "Why would I *not* make this four?" And I was covering every side bet. Into the pocket for money on this side of my pants. Into the pocket on the other side. The one in back. Finally, it got to the point where I had no more money and I just said, "No more bets." Then there were *more* rolls. No sevens and no fours. I shook the dice. Then I got superstitious about blowing on them. I blew on them last time, I was not going to blow on them for this roll.

Then came the final roll. The first dice stopped on a one, which was a good sign. The second one spun and spun and spun like one of those ivory tops on very hard wood. It has been proven that there is a split second when anything in motion that is a perfect square spins before it stops. What I'm about to tell you, you *have* to believe. The second dice for a split second hit on three. Then it kicked over into a six and I crapped out.

Not only was I tapped out. Try three thousand four hundred sandwiches spinning around in my brain. *Schlepping* oranges and bananas up and down the dumbwaiter while timing the guard as he made his rounds. All for *nothing*. In terms of gambling, this was *it* for me. It was the *end*. I *never* forgot this moment. Whatever compulsive need I had to gamble was finished in me at the age of twenty.

All of a sudden, I had no money. I was not covered. When I got off that boat in Japan, I was *naked*. I had no money and no control over my destiny. For all I knew, I was going to have to *steal* in order to survive.

9.

BILL: I was reassigned to stay in Japan for a couple of weeks. But I had a major shouting match with this administrative officer there who I kept pestering about citizenship papers so I could bring my sisters to America. He said, "I don't like *you* and I don't like what you stand for." Not my religion. He was a country guy and we were all city boys, a bunch of us waiting for reassignment. He said, "You better ship out, you're not gonna make it here." And I believed him. I didn't want to fight him physically. So I volunteered to ship out. It was the only way. I figured if I went into combat, I could get back home faster.

In order to rotate back to the United States at that time, you needed thirty-six points. If you were stationed in Japan, you were gone from America for a year and a half. Two points a month. If you were at Division Rear, which meant in Korea but not in combat, you got three points a month and you were there for a year. But if you were in combat, you got *four* points a month. Four times nine is thirty-six.

They flew me to Taegu where I was a forward observer in the 7th Infantry Division, which was what I had been trained to do back at Camp Chaffee. The basic job of a forward observer is very simple. You go out into no-man's land with a radio phone, and sometimes with a forty-five-caliber pistol as well, along with another guy who has the wire. Or you have the wire, and he has the phone. Your main job is to find the enemy emplacement and call in their position, either by phone or by crawling back on your ass and giving it to them in person. Seek out the enemy prior to mass movement of infantry so artillery can bomb the area and kill anything that lives so the infantry can then move through. You're the first one who goes out beyond where the infantry is. And that was my job.

I realized that I'd made a mistake. I didn't want to be there. I had always said to myself, "I'll be okay. I'll make it. What's going to happen to *me*?" I realized I had never thought about what it would be like when

I got to the front where it was real and it was my life. At Division Rear, the enemy could not really reach me unless it was by an air strike. They were not going to waste their bombs because they were looking to hit the ammo dumps first. At the front, the fear of dying really entered my mind for the first time.

What I remember most about Korea is Martin, the guy who brought us the mail on a motorbike. I also remember I was afraid a good deal of the time. So was everybody who did what I did. In that, I wasn't alone. After two weeks out, we'd come back to Division Rear. How different that was. I remember being back there reading magazines in a tent where it was warm and comfortable and thinking how crazy I had been to volunteer for combat just to save three months. *Three months.* Is that so important? Now that I was at the front, I would've rather stayed away from America for a year or eighteen months. For no other reason than to avoid getting hurt or dying or seeing death or fighting. The sheer simplicity of self-preservation.

Most of the time it was too hot. Rain and muck, living in foxholes and sometimes bunkers. Every once in a while I'd go back to the Division Rear to sleep in a tent. Food was something I ate in order not to go hungry. I didn't get close to too many people. What for? People I was out in the field with during the first seven months had been wounded or shot and eventually died. Then they were replaced. Friendships were difficult because there was constant change.

Mack and Jimmy were two relatively new guys. Jimmy was black and a real actor. From East Islip, Long Island. The real-life Eddie Murphy. In the hip world, a *master.* Mack was white. Short and squat from California. For a while, they were the only two guys with whom I went out on missions regularly.

All this time you have to remember that I was still not a citizen. In Japan, I had hammered that guy in the Administrative Office to help me and that had started the friction between us. I got to Korea, I busted the chops of the lieutenant in charge of our platoon. That was how my relationship started with the captain. He was the one who said, "We're fighting a war here, soldier. I can't be bothered with this." He was the one who had to allow me to hand in papers so I could bring my sisters over to America. But he wouldn't do it. He was too busy.

To this day, no one I know has ever figured out why we even got into that war. It was all a stalemate. We weren't going anywhere with it. Every once in a while, the feeling was that somebody back home wanted things to change. So a general would say, "Okay, let's take *that* hill. Get the troops." We got overrun in Kumwha. It was part of a thing called the Battle of Triangle Hill.

The irony of my Bronze Star citation is that it represents an example of what we did on a *routine* basis, laying communication lines and maintaining them. I only received the citation because what I did happened during a *big* battle.

The most significant part of that day for me happened earlier. D Patrol, another platoon on the same mission, got overrun on the other side of the bridge. They were overrun and we were being outflanked. I looked over there through my binoculars and to me, all war is still personified by what I saw. The four-man patrol had all been killed. A North Korean soldier was going through the belongings of the dead guys. He tried to get a ring off one of their fingers. Within ten seconds, the horror part of the movie came on the screen. He couldn't get the ring off the finger so he took out this heavy-duty knife, hacked off the finger, and took the ring.

I went out on something like sixty or seventy missions, many of them just like that one. Some nights when we were out, we never heard or saw a thing. Other times, there was shooting. A few times, there were killings.

One day, we went up at five in the morning in advance of what was supposed to be an attack. I had the wire in a heavy pack on my back from which it spooled out. Earlier, our troops had overrun an enemy position. By the time we got there, all of the enemy soldiers but one was dead. He started getting up so Mack had to kill him.

That morning, we were going out on the side of a plateau in order to get a better angle on the mountainside we wanted to attack. From their side, a recon team was doing the same thing. We saw each other's movements and began shooting at one another. Jimmy got hit in the groin. He caught a bullet in his body and he couldn't move and he was yelling. There were four North Koreans shooting at us and we returned fire until I had no more bullets left in my gun. So I took Jimmy's gun and used it. We ran out of ammunition but they kept shooting.

It was five o'clock in the morning and so foggy that we could barely see. Division knew what was going on but there was no way they could do anything to help us because at the time, their position was all the way back down at the bottom of the hill.

Maybe the North Koreans wanted to take us prisoner. Maybe they also only had a couple of bullets left. Because we were hiding and suddenly, they were *there*. They didn't yell. They were just *there*. Three of them. Two went for Mack and I started wrestling with the other one. He had a gun in his hand but he didn't use it so maybe he had no bullets left. Mack killed both of the men who attacked him. It was very quick. The guy jumped me and we both fell down. We got turned over in the brush. We rolled and stopped and somehow I got hold of his gun. I got up and hit him. I hit him and hit him. By now, the North Koreans were sending mortar fire into the area. At one point, they sent up a flare and we were all in totally white light. It was as if they could see us in their binoculars but we were too far away to shoot at with small arms. I picked Jimmy up and carried him over my shoulder. He was screaming in agony all the way.

We had to go over this ridge that was very mountainous. I'd say about three hundred yards back to our lines, through a ravine and then up the other side. By now, it was nearly daylight. We made it back and they took Jimmy to the hospital and he recovered. Mack got hurt too and also wound up in the hospital.

Shooting at someone or being shot at is one thing. Being confronted all of a sudden with the reality that all you're doing is defending your right to live is another. I mean, you *have* to defend yourself. But having done that, how do you feel? You're alive. So you must feel better than the other guy, right? But what do you do with that? Can you talk about it?

This is not something I'm proud of. I'm not certain I killed that soldier but I hit him as hard as I could in the back of the neck with the gun. He rolled off me and stayed down. It had nothing to do with my strength. I think I just got lucky because of the way he hit the ground. To the best of my knowledge, he wasn't my enemy. Yet he would have taken my life.

Up to that point, I always thought I was perceptive. I thought I had a good idea of right and wrong. That I could stand back and look at something and know what was going on. But when you take somebody's life or you hit somebody hard enough to take their life, everything changes. It all becomes different. For the first time, you see how it all comes down not just to human rights but the right to *live*. That simple, basic thing.

After all this happened, I was ordered to go out on another mission. By then I was a corporal. But really, rank meant so little. If the corporal died, you became the corporal. If the sergeant died, you were the sergeant. The big thing in those days was sewing kits. That was how you knew if you were doing well. Putting another stripe on the sleeve of your uniform.

It was no more than three or four days after Jimmy got hurt. Mack was no longer around. So I was with this new guy who was a great map reader. He had been transferred from somewhere else. We were always told of the plans in the afternoon so we could study them for that night. The sergeant explained the mission to us. It was going to be a brightly lit night with lots of moon and the area itself had very little brush. The enemy was above us and we would have been very visible because there was no camouflage. We would have been moving targets. It seemed to me that what we were being asked to do was suicide. Sheer suicide. I told the sergeant I would not go.

The sergeant said, "Well, these are the orders."

I said, "I can't follow these orders."

He said, "If you don't, I have no choice. I have to go to the captain. These are orders from the captain."

That same afternoon, I had to go back to Division Rear to the captain's tent. Because this was a *very* serious issue. A soldier who had refused to go out. The captain had that Howard Keel look. Very clean and stylish. He was from Missouri and he always wondered why he had never made major. A guy who always went by the book. Regular Army of course, a career soldier. In wartime. It's odd how people from the city cling to city people and small-town people to one another. He was a small-town guy. An officer, while I was an enlisted man who had been *drafted* to do my job.

Inside his tent, the captain told me he had studied what we were supposed to do that night and he didn't see why I wouldn't go. It was refusing a direct order under battle conditions which meant a general court-martial. In so many words, I explained to him that after being out there for seven months and doing this day in and day out, I was quite certain that if I went out there tonight, they would kill me. He kept saying, "This is a *direct* order, soldier." I kept saying, "But you don't understand. The risk is too great." It was basically an open field with very little shrubbery and we were on an incline with the enemy holding the high positions. I had only just been through something pretty bad and I didn't want to go through it again. I felt that on this mission, I would have even less of a chance than before.

Simply, he read the book to me. Which was that under battle conditions, what I was doing was punishable by *death*. I said, "If I survive long enough to stand trial on this, the jury will have to decide whether or not you sent me on a suicide mission." Not whether he had the *right* to give me the order but whether under certain circumstances, disobeying the order was valid. I told him I felt I would have a better chance with a jury than out in that field that night.

He said, "You're a good soldier and you have a good record and there's no reason you won't do this."

I told him that I would not go and that if he pressed charges against me, I would take him on in court in order to save my life. That night, we did not go out into that field. That particular mission *never* got done.

A couple of days later, I bumped into the captain outside my bunker. I saw him and I didn't say anything but just kept going instead. He came after me and said, "You're on *report*, soldier." He got me for not wearing a helmet, insubordination to an officer, and failing to salute. Because he had not pressed charges on the other thing, he wanted to bust my hump any way he could.

The only problem was that we had the Bronze Star ceremony coming up. The four-star general couldn't come to it so they sent a lieutenant general instead, a guy with three stars, and it was all right out of a movie.

Here I was about to get the Bronze Star. A helicopter came in, a jeep rolled up to meet it, a red rug got rolled down from the steps, twelve feet of rug, and out came the general. They read about what I did, holding the lines under enemy fire and so forth, and he pinned the medal on me. I got a salute, he got back in the helicopter, they rolled up the rug, and we were left standing there with our sergeant, with the enemy ten miles away. The general was on the ground for maybe fifteen minutes, give or take thirty seconds. Pins, salutes, he shook my hand. "Well done, Corporal Graham." And he was gone.

Because of the medal ceremony, I had the captain by the balls. He had to back off the general court-martial and leave me alone. I only had another month to go on the front lines so that may have been another reason. Before I could finish my nine months, I got a telegram from the Red Cross saying that my foster mother was ill and a request had been made by my foster father for emergency leave. Then the Red Cross requested emergency leave for me, which the Army denied, feeling that she would recover.

A few days later, a second telegram came. It said, "Mother *severely* ill. Leave granted." So I packed my duffel bag and got on a plane. The captain was still there when I left. Later on, I was told that he got it on the hill. He got himself killed on that very same hill.

The theory was that it happened because he was such a spit-and-polish fanatic. Always polishing his helmet so it would glisten and shine. He went into battle looking like he was going to be marching in some parade. It was daytime battle and he was like a moving mirror in the light. The enemy saw him shining brightly and they riddled him with bullets.

He had wanted to court-martial me for the way I'd looked. Because I didn't have my spit shine on. I wasn't glaring and bright and polished. I wasn't ready for a parade. I was ready for combat. He wasn't and I think it got him killed.

10.

BILL: I went from Kumwha to Taegu to Japan to Wake Island to the air force base in Honolulu. Honolulu was the first place where I was able to get to a phone to call the apartment back in The Bronx. My brother Roy picked up the phone. I said, "How is she?" He said, "She's gone. She died yesterday." I would have made it there in time if they had let me go when the initial request was made.

ROY EHRENREICH: It was an immense trauma for me. I was getting out of the Army in November. I was down in Alabama and I was going to meet them in Jacksonville to go down to Miami for a couple weeks of vacation. I got a call about four or five days before I was discharged from my father who said that Mom wasn't feeling too well and she might have to go into the hospital for a little while. They didn't think it was anything serious but I should come back to New York and then we would go down to Florida later.

I went back to New York by train, not thinking that anything serious was happening. I was kind of surprised that there was nobody there to meet me. I got home and learned she was in the hospital and in an oxygen tent. My father had been waiting to take me there. We went to the hospital and the doctors let me into the room. She was in the oxygen tent. She opened her eyes and said, "Thank God you're home." She closed her eyes and died about six hours later.

She had been operated on for something like a twisted intestine. She died of internal gangrene. It was clear at the time that she had simply waited for me to get back. She was hanging on until she was satisfied that I was okay. She was fifty-three.

FRANK EHRENREICH: They held up the funeral for a couple of days in order to notify the Army so Bill would get the information. He made every effort to get there in time. I'll never forget that. He flew in from Korea with no stop-offs anywhere. He would get off one plane and then get on another one. You know how it is when they transport soldiers in cargo planes. You can get on any plane that's going your way. But he never saw her.

BILL: I got to the apartment and I was in uniform and my brother Roy was in uniform. Now you have to understand that during all the growing up years, I was absolutely convinced that Roy was favored by them. He always got the leaner piece of meat. They never yelled at him as much. They never had to go to school to get him back into class. They never had to bring him another pair of pants because he'd ripped his in the school yard. My father never had to hold up a belt to him in the kitchen because of a car.

When I got home, my father was sitting in the living room. I'd never seen him so low. What followed was one of the few really cataclysmic moments in my life. My father started talking about his wife. What a wonderful woman she was. Why did she have to die so young? All the life she still had left to live. Someone who did so much for other people. He kept on saying, "Taking in these children and giving them a family and giving them a life."

Finally I said, "Pop, this is Roy and this is Bill here. What are you talking about?"

And he said, "You don't know. What do you know? What do you know? You just don't know."

Roy took me into the other room and said, "You may as well know now. I'm not their son either."

They had legally adopted him through a private agency when he was about six months old because Pearl couldn't have children. At that moment, ten years of mad reasoning swam through my mind. Trillions of thoughts over the years of "I'm not theirs, I'm not theirs." That's why I get the corner piece of cake and he gets the *middle.* That's why I get the chicken leg and he gets the other wing, the one I wanted. Because it was always there when we were together but no one ever talked it out. That feeling that *Roy* was their son, not me.

Perhaps I would have felt differently about my father if I had known. Because I always loved her and my father did give lovingly to Roy, who gave lovingly to me.

ROY EHRENREICH: I was legally adopted by them when I was six months old. They told me about it when I was about eight. I had been going to an experimental school at Teacher's College at Columbia run by a woman psychologist named Leta Hollingsworth. They went to her and asked for her advice. Very clearly, she gave them spectacular advice, which they must have followed right to the letter. With all these years behind me, I look back and I see I never really wanted to know my natural parents. In terms of why they never told Bill, my guess is that it was probably my mother's decision.

BILL: When I left Korea, I was in the middle of my thirty-second point month. They gave me a thirty-day emergency leave to go home. Once that was over, they wanted to send me back for my last four points. They wanted me to do another six weeks in combat before I could rotate back to the States for good. Then in the middle of everything, my father had a heart attack. But they were still going to ship me back.

That was when my brother stepped in. He contacted the *New York Post* and *The Bronx Home News* and senators Lehman and Ives. He wrote them letters saying, "This is my foster brother. He came from Europe and he is *still* not a citizen even though he fought in the Army, won a Bronze Star, and was wounded by shrapnel. All he wants is to bring his sisters over here from Europe and now the Army is sending him back to combat again."

Roy wrote that they should station me in New York City on Governors Island. He asked them to let me complete my service there. Because my father needed me. He told them I had already been through enough, what with hand-to-hand combat and all the rest.

First, the Inspector General, the IG, gave me another sixty days of emergency medical leave. Because of the pressure, they let me stay on Governors Island. Eventually, I got a hardship discharge. Instead of twenty-four months, I got out in twenty-two. Only because of my brother Roy.

When I turned twenty-one, I finally became a citizen. My oldest sister Rita came over from Israel.

She had spent the war in Shanghai in the white ghetto where it was pretty bad. She and her husband Eric told me stories about eating lice to survive and dead bodies in the streets. I was still in uniform when Rita came. It was 1953. She and Eric stayed in New York for a while. A friend of theirs from Shanghai offered Eric a job in San Francisco, so they moved there.

Two years later, Ester came. It took a while because she had a problem with the medical requirement. She had to pay off some doctor to say that she didn't have a spot on her lungs. I remember going to greet Ester when she first came to New York. I had no memory of what she looked like, other than the pictures from our childhood and she was just a girl then. She was coming down all these steps with her seven-year-old Avi by her side. As soon as she saw me, she got very emotional and her face started to go.

My sister was an awesome sight to behold. About five foot ten, a striking robust earth mother. I saw her coming toward me and I just froze. Ester was possessed. All of a sudden instead of joy, I was thinking about what might happen to me next. It was *"Oh, Ester! Oh, Ester!"* and she was coming down the steps. This runaway diesel with her son, Avi at her side was coming toward me and I was backing off but she wouldn't let me get away. She grabbed me and gave me this love crunch of death. She hugged me and hugged me and grabbed me and touched me and squeezed me. This moment I will never forget as long as I live. It was *amazing*.

Chapter Two

Mountain Rat

1.

BILL: I found this old magazine the other day. In it is a full-page picture of me and Eddie Fisher. The caption reads "EDDIE NEVER FORGETS—NOW OUT OF THE ARMY, EDDIE REMEMBERS THE WAITER HE MET WAY BACK WHEN AT GROSSINGER'S." Of course, I was that waiter. On the cover of the magazine is Arthur Godfrey. I think it's called *TV HITS* or something. Open it up to page fifteen and there is a big story about how Eddie Fisher is now a star again after entertaining all the troops in Korea on USO tours. In the picture, I'm standing next to Eddie and we're both looking full face into the camera. Underneath it says, "Eddie's back on the old circuit at Grossinger's but he always has time to greet an old friend."

He and I knew each other in 1950 when I worked there as a waiter and he was the band boy, trying to become the band singer. Not well, but we knew each other. By the time he came to entertain the troops in Korea, I was already out of there. But that picture has us both in a single frame. He came out of Korea. I came out of Korea, and look at who we both were then.

I first started working up in the mountains when I was fifteen and a half. It was at Goldberg's Hotel and I remember peeling thousands of radishes and potatoes. I remember just sitting there *forever,* peeling. I was the kitchen boy. It was like my *sentence,* rather than a job. I got fired from there and went to the Flagler Hotel in South Fallsburg, which has since become a mental institution. It always was one but they never knew it. They just changed the name on the sign and converted it right over.

At the Flagler, I was the pot washer. I stood inside this huge cauldron with a whipper, cleaning the pots. I would also grease the pots and empty out the coffeepot. From six-thirty in the morning until nine-thirty at night with no breaks except right at the start of each meal. Because by then I would be nearly clean. I had almost caught up.

The chef there took a liking to me so I went back the next summer. I was one of the few geniuses on the planet able to break eggs while talking to someone. Two eggs in one hand, *break*. I was a *piston. Piston Bill*. So I did that and they got someone *else* to clean pans. In the middle of the summer, there was an argument and Charlie, the chef, a great *great* guy, he made me the breakfast cook. I was sixteen and a half and the dining room held four or five hundred people.

Now Charlie was very good-looking. El *Stud*. Great uncle to Victor Mature. And he was having an affair with the owner's wife, who was older than him. She liked me because he liked me and he kind of took me under his wing and showed me the kitchen. The waiters would come charging in to place their orders. Omelets over easy, whatever. I had another guy to help me because at breakfast, it got *real* busy. But I had the chef's hat on and I got the substantial raise in pay from sixteen to twenty-two bucks a week.

The waiters would all come in at once and start shouting at me while arguing with one another over whose was what. But they couldn't order me around. I was able to establish guidelines. You don't fuck with me, I don't fuck with you. You want something I have? You want over easy, hold the onions? You *ask* me. You yell at me, you don't get *shit*.

Now I was just a kid and these guys were *men*. Did I say *men?* They were male *barracudas*. Professional mountain rats who worked wintertime in Florida or Vegas and summer in the mountains. They didn't respect me because they'd seen me as the kitchen boy. It was "Look at that *schmuck* with the funny hat on." I hardened rather quickly there. Not that I was soft before. But it got to be, "*Hey. Hold* it. Just hold on. Don't put your finger in *my* face."

I had to get up at four-thirty and be in the kitchen by five-fifteen. I cooked on a big range with gas burners and I was a good short-order man. Pancakes and waffles. By three o'clock in the afternoon, I was off. I could go swimming and do what I wanted. I had a room in the staff quarters. It wasn't a room. It was a *space*. With a cot in it. But I liked the mountains from the very beginning. I'd walk a great deal. I'd go into Fallsburg to the Wonder Bar where B. S. Pully was performing. I lived near the basketball court and I used to watch people go into the nightclub at night. I never could because I didn't have a suit yet. I was fascinated by that whole world. People going to a place where they would eat and eat and eat and eat and eat, and then rest. So they could eat some more.

The Flagler back then was garment center people and light manufacturing. People who had come into money. What got me about being up there was the irony that in the middle of nowhere were these *huge* hotels. You'd be driving along, there was nothing but trees and farms, all of a sudden there was a building that holds a *thousand* people. There was Grossinger's, it was *huge*. The Flagler. Gilbert's. Brickman's. Brown's, where Jerry Lewis started. The Nevele.

Ninety-two miles up Route 17 from New York, there was this whole other world. Twenty-eight miles from the city was the Red Apple Rest. This was a pit stop that *you* didn't make. Your car went in there by *itself*. It stopped whether or not you put on the brakes. Then through the Wurtsboro hills, where all the cars got overheated and had to pull over to the side of the road. It was also a place I got stuck a lot when I hitchhiked up there. Back then, I was heavy into *willing* cars to stop. I became excellent at reverse magnetism. "You *will* stop, you slimy motherfucker Studebaker." Wurtsboro was also the shooting-off point. You got to Wurtsboro and you could go to Ellenville one way or direct to Monticello another. Many times at night someone would have picked me up right outside the George Washington Bridge and I'd feel safe because they were going all the way up to the mountains. So I'd fall asleep in the car. Four in the morning, the guy would wake me up, it would be pouring buckets out there, and he'd say, *"Wurtsboro!"* Meaning he was going another way from there.

So I'd get out and of course I'd think, "Instant pickup again." I'd be standing there looking at *zilch*. There was nothing moving on the road. My mind started *willing* cars to appear. Something was coming over the hill. That man *knows* I'm here. He *will* see me. Then he was gone. I was splattered, instant *hate*.

Tuxedo Park and Harriman were the fancy-schmancy areas where I never wanted to get stopped because I probably would have been arrested. They were *money*. They were all-powerful and I was their servant. There had to be another street I could use other than the one they were on.

There was a time when I could rattle off the distance and the mileage town by town, just like a clock. It used to be a three- or a three-and-a-half-hour ride from the city to the Catskills, depending on the traffic. Friday afternoon was *death* going up and Sunday after lunch was *death* coming back. From two in the afternoon on Sunday all the way until two in the morning was *murder*.

People would go up there for the season with boxes and ropes and mattresses on top of their cars. They trekked and they *schlepped* and anything they were not sure about, they took with them anyway. "I don't know . . . I'm only going up for two days . . . better pack the *large*, *unabbreviated* version of the World Atlas. Just in case. There *has* to be a use for it." Also, the little box refrigerator *filled* with food. Because Jews *must* play safe. Why take a chance on all the stores being closed once they got up there?

It took me a long, long time to get over the degree to which humans were able to consume food up there. It must have been all the fresh air. The art of eating was a constant contest. Not that I got to work in the dining room for a while. I lost the job at the Flagler for the following summer because Charlie got caught sleeping with the boss's wife and he got fired. It was the talk of the house.

He asked me to go work with him down in Florida for the winter but I said no. Among other things, I think I would have been dead by the age of eighteen because of all my arguments across the counter with waiters in the mountains who migrated South for winter work. Because they would argue with *any* head cook, not to mention a seventeen-year-old kid like me. "I'll take *that*," one would say. "Well, no," I would say, "that belongs to so-and-so, he ordered over-easy with mushrooms on the plate." They would grab for the plate anyway and then I would hit with the stick and then the scenes would start. "You touched me! You touched my *flesh!*"

Really, it was all self-defense. There was this Rumanian waitress named Anna, who waddled through the kitchen and grabbed everything that moved. She hated me, she hated the place, all she wanted was money. She hated everything she put down on her table. *"ANNA, GET BACK!"* I'd scream at her. "We don't have any more. *What?* I'm lying to you? *ALL RIGHT! ALL RIGHT!* I *GOT* KIPPERS! BUT I *AIN'T* GIVIN' 'EM TO YOU!" And then the kitchen would go totally silent.

Arguments would go on till Charlie spoke. Charlie was Buddha. He was the real life Charles Bronson. He looked at you, your potatoes were mashed. Once he was gone from the Flagler, I moved up the hill to Grossinger's. At the time, that was *the* one. The top place. Liberty, New York. I was seventeen and working as a busboy out in the dining room. As they used to say, it was a five and three house. Five-dollar tip for the waiter on Sunday after lunch, three for the busboy. The assistant maître d' there was Joseph Goebbels. As a busboy, I'd have anywhere from thirty-five to forty people to take care of for each meal. A good waiter carried twenty-four to twenty-eight people, and I would carry two waiters.

I worked on the upper terrace, which was real nice. Split level, with a view. A lot of famous people came up there. Milton Berle and Sophie Tucker and the Ritz Brothers. Rocky Marciano trained there. Tony Zale came up. Downstairs, they had dancing in the Terrace Room, a nightclub where I saw Pupi Campo play. Every summer in the mountains, they brought up heavy-duty bands. Tito Puente was at the Swan Lake Hotel. Rodriguez was at the Stevensville. Machito was at the Concord. Latin music was *the* music of the day, especially for Jews.

It was hard money working as a busboy. I took a lot of crap. After the meal was over, I had to sweep up, dust, clean the silverware and the lamps. Once a week we had to take all our silverware and the water pitcher and anything that was metallic and burnish it by putting it into this machine with rocks and greasy pink stuff. On Sunday afternoon, which was supposed to be a day off, I'd have to stand in line and burnish my silver. I was supposed to carry it in on a tray, clean it off, and bring it back to my drawer so the captain in my area could inspect it.

One Sunday, I didn't have the time to put it all on a tray because I wanted to go watch a game. I was in the kitchen burnishing all my stuff. I got it polished off but if I put it on my tray, it would have been three or four trips back and forth to get it all put away. So I stuck all my big stuff inside a towel which I then put inside another towel which I then put on my back. I tied a pail filled with all my silver to my belt. I was bent over with this *huge* sack on my back. As I carried it back into the dining room I was literally jackknifed in two under the weight. I finally dumped it all out on my table where it laid like a metallic *mountain*.

The captain came running over to me. He was this nervous little refugee from Yugoslavia or Bulgaria. Whenever he got excited, he would stutter. He came running over to me in his white suit and he said, "V-v-v-v-v-v-vat you think this is? A a-a-a-a-ardvare store?" That became like the national anthem of nervousness up there. For years afterward, whenever anybody left more than two things in one place, guys would look at one another and say, "What do you think this is? A *hardware* store?"

I had my first real girlfriend up there that summer. Her name was Ruth. She was a waitress and a very nice lady. We lived in a staff bungalow halfway down the hill. I remember it was her birthday and I didn't know what to do for her. It turned out that Harry Belafonte was going to be in the playhouse that night, out behind the pool. That same night, a guest at my table had a big birthday party. What the hotel did was see that the guest automatically gets a big cake. They *shpritzed* on "Happy Birthday, Thelma" with whipped cream. I put the cake down on the table for this girl Thelma and, as they sometimes would do back then, Thelma's parents said, "Listen, we don't want to eat this here. Send it down to the nightclub. Because after we see Harry Belafonte in the playhouse, we're going to the nightclub and we'll have it there with coffee.

So I took the cake and stuck it under the table. Now there was another table in the dining room up at the front, in the fancy section, where all the entertainers and boxers and sports people could come in fifteen or twenty minutes early to eat in order to get a jump on the rest of the guests. When Belafonte came in to eat, I got this idea. I went over to him and introduced myself and said, "I know you're here to do a show tonight but one of the most popular waitresses on the floor is having a birthday party tonight. I know it's asking a lot but it would give her such a thrill because she really loves you and your music. Would you join us?"

He just looked at me and said, "Where are you?" I showed him where we were on the hill and he said, "I'll think about it."

"Thank you very much," I said. "Good luck with your show."

I still had the cake stuck under the table. Once the meal ended, I took the cake out through the side door down the hill covered up by my waiter's jacket. I got some drinks and paper plates and stuff to eat. I told Ruth's girlfriend to go take her for a ride somewhere. In the bungalow, I took a knife and operated on "Thelma" and made it into "Ruth." We were all sitting around eating cake at around one in the morning when there was a knock on the door. *Harry Belafonte.* He came in with his guitar. Now this cabin was *tiny.* A little bathroom with a shower and a big bed and that was *it.* There must have been twenty-five people squinched into the room. Belafonte talked to us and then he started to play and he sang us every calypso song known to man. "Day-O," and "Island in the Sun" and "House." It was just a great party and it went on till early in the morning.

He left and Ruth and I went to sleep. The next morning, I came into the dining room and Thelma's parents were not happy. The captain got us all together, the same guy as with the hardware line, and he said, "Aw-rite. Vat happened vit the cake?" Because the people asked for it in the nightclub and it wasn't in the big walk-in refrigerator in the kitchen so they went to the maître d' in the nightclub who called the dining room maître d' who then called the captain. The captain was home putting things in his hair, three in the morning. He came to the dining room *before* breakfast. This was *Stalag 17,* he *was* going to get an answer. "Vere is zee cake?" Of course, nobody said anything and everybody knew.

After breakfast, they went into the kitchen to interrogate the kitchen staff. The kitchen staff got together but they had no idea who took the cake. So the investigation took a more scientific turn. "Aw-rite, Billy. You took the cake *from* the dining room *to* the kitchen, yes?"

"Yes," I said. "I put it in the freezer."

The captain said, "You cannot put it into the free-zaire, you *must* give it to somebody first. To who you gave it?"

"I don't *know,*" I yelled. "I put it in the freezer."

The investigation was never completed and the culprit never found. It became the high point of the season. I was really scared while it was going on. Everyone told Ruth that no matter *what* happened from that point on in her life, nothing would ever top that birthday party.

The next season, I got moved up and I started to serve the table in the front where all the celebrities ate. I remember serving Milton Berle, Henny Youngman many times, and Sammy Davis, Jr., when he was starting out with his father in the Will Mastin Trio. Jerry Lewis came over once from Brown's. He was sitting there at the table and I was serving him and he said, "I'll show you guys." He made me take off my jacket and sit down at the table and eat while *he* served everybody and it was very very funny. He really had talent when he was young. Doing pratfalls in the dining room and driving everybody insane.

Serving this table, I usually did better than the other waiters in terms of tips. I helped myself out by doing things like going and getting half a dozen copies of the *Daily News* and half a dozen copies of the *New York Times* before breakfast so I would have them ready for the guests.

If I knew a guest was into golf or baseball or overseas news, whatever it was, I'd read up on it. Then whenever they wanted to talk to me during the meal, I was ready. I was conscious of the fact that these people thought they were a different class than me. I think I treated them the way they wanted to be treated. Most of the entertainers were very nice. Some were finger-snappers. Soon, I got to be very professional even about dealing with that.

When I finally got out of the army in June, I went back up to Grossinger's to work for the summer. Ruth was no longer there. I kept seeing this one waitress around the dining room but I never really got to talk to her because she worked all the way on the other side. I was quite certain that she had boyfriend and later on, I found out that she did. But I just *loved* the way she moved. Like a gazelle. Like Ava Gardner. Late in the summer, we finally got together. Her name was Patricia and she had her own place in Liberty on a hill.

She was two years older than me, my first experience with an older woman. Early on, she told me she was separated from her husband. She had two small children who were being taken care of by her mother in upstate New York. She was working as a waitress at the hotel in order to support them. We liked each other a lot and we made each other happy in every way.

Eventually at the end of the summer, I had to make that decision. She lived in the mountains. I was a city guy who didn't really know what he wanted to do. I had only just gotten out of the Army. The little picture she had of her two children was all I could see. Like a dot at the end of a tunnel that just kept getting bigger and bigger.

I went up to see her a few times during the fall and winter but the trips got farther and farther apart. I finally realized that it wasn't going to work. Even though I cared very deeply for her and didn't want to lose her, I didn't think I could hack it with the children. There was nothing about her that I didn't like except for the responsibility that came along with them. So I had to break it off. She was still working at Grossinger's the following summer and that was one of the reasons that I couldn't go back.

For me, the first daily challenge that was even more fascinating than living in the city was working in the mountains. It was the first time I ever had one-on-one communication with strangers on a regular basis. *Instant* communication. It was the beginning of living theater with real dialogue and characters no one would have ever believed on stage. I still feel that in many ways, the mountains taught me *everything* I know.

2.

BILL: The dining room at the Concord held four thousand people. The dining room staff alone was four hundred. The kitchen was huge, much bigger than Grossinger's. It wasn't as family. It wasn't as *haimish*. It was more business. It wasn't as family-oriented even though they had a lot of families going there. It was more contemporary, as opposed to old line. If Grossinger's was still thirties and forties, then the Concord was *all* fifties.

It was a better house than at Grossinger's. Six and four tip for the waiter and the busboy when I first got there and then seven and five as time passed and the cost of everything went up.

JOE DEROSE: To really understand the setting at the Concord, you have to appreciate that there were basically two factions working in the dining room. You had the college kids, of which I was one, and you had the professionals. They came basically from Pennsylvania, the coal mining sections. It was a coveted job because you could make a lot of money. You worked your tail off but the dollars were there.

It was a great job for someone who came out of those coal mining areas because they didn't need an education. All they needed was a strong back. Sam Freiberg came from there.

BILL: Sam Freiberg had already been there a long time when I got there. Sam had one of the funniest, greatest senses of humor *ever*. He was amazing. A mountain rat who gambled a lot and could never get out of the mountains. He went up there for a weekend ninety years ago and he stayed forever. In the morning, he was never really awake. He had been up all night gambling, fooling around, who knows what?

Now, in the kitchen, there was a place where you got your hard-boiled eggs out of this big bin. If you wanted soft-boiled, you took this timer they had, spun it to three minutes, and then dunked this metal container with the eggs into boiling water. It would come up two and a half or three minutes later, and you took your eggs. Of course, there was highway thievery going on all the time. "Those are *my* eggs!" "No, they're *mine*." Sometimes waiters would mark their names on the eggs. "Mine are three and a half. No, *mine* are! Mine, mine, *MINE!* I was here before you! I saw you go open prune juice!" Waiters would literally *kill* for those eggs.

There was a little waitress there who had a mouth like a toilet. If you messed with her, she'd kill you. She used to gamble with us, with her money stuck in her bra. One morning she was there and there was this big commotion in the kitchen. "*Fuck you!* You took *my* eggs? I'll *kill* you.*" On and on. I was standing about twenty feet away when Sam Freiberg came walking by, with his eyes half closed, still asleep. Sam was kind of our leader in the kitchen, the guy to whom everyone could turn to when there was a beef.

The waitress saw Sam. She said, "Sam, they're taking my eggs and I want you to take them to court. I have my rights. Those are *my* eggs!" At first, Sam did not listen. Then he stopped and looked at her. By now she was yelling like mad. He looked at her and she finished up by screaming, "What *are* you gonna do? What are *you* gonna do?"

Sam looked at her through a haze and he said, "Names and addresses—I need names and addresses."

JOE DEROSE: Sam Freiberg had a sideline. He was a shylock. Now at that time, the Concord had one of the largest kitchens in the world. On Sunday mornings, all the waiters and waitresses who borrowed money from Sam would line up to pay Sam back ten dollars, which was the vigorish on the hundred dollars they had borrowed from him. The gig was ten a week. They never paid the principal because they didn't have a hundred. And the line would stretch for the length of the entire kitchen.

Because he went way back, Sam also had one of the premier stations in the dining room. You didn't fool around with Sam. Sam was a very, very big hitter. He was imposing physically. Probably five ten or five eleven but built very broadly. And he literally had no neck. His head just sat on his shoulders. And he was tough-looking. He created an atmosphere of fear.

In any case, Bill owed Sam money. Billy and I were walking up the famous Concord Hill. As we get to the crest of the hill, who was walking the opposite way? None other than Sam Freiberg. And you have to understand that at that moment, Sam was the *last* person in the world that Billy wanted to see. But there was no getting away from him.

We converge on each other. And Sam says to Bill, "How you doing, Billy?"

Bill says, "Ah—I'm living."

And Sam says, "You're *lucky*."

BILL: Irving Cohen ran the dining room then, as he does to this very day. Gradually, I got to know that he was Edward G. Robinson. He had his clique of waiters, most of whom came from Scranton and Reading in Pennsylvania. Because they could make a better living in the dining room than in the coal mines, they were *very* loyal to him. The whole pecking order in the dining room was set.

Irving Cohen, the maître d', would stand at the front wall next to a board. On this board would be a circle for each table. Around each circle would be a little spot in which he put a pin. In a drawer, he had all these different colored pins. An orange pin could mean a middle-aged couple. A blue pin might be a young single person. Another color could mean an ugly single person. Irving could look at this board and see exactly where to seat you and in what category you'd go. When you got to the front door, there was this split second when he'd let you know. "You want something from me?? I want something from *you*." And then you took care of him.

Five was okay. Ten would get you the table you wanted. Twenty was the *room*. He would seat you according to how you looked to him. He would analyze your entire situation in a second. Like he had X-ray eyes. He also had a very strong condescending attitude toward anybody who addressed him. In that dining room, he was the *king*. The *emperor*.

JOE DEROSE: Irving ruled the dining room like a dictator. I mean, without question. He had absolute authority over it. He could make or break you economically. For instance, if Irving Cohen wanted to give you a station in Siberia, way across the other side of the room, you had real problems. Your guests would always be angry at you because of how long it would take to get from the kitchen to the table. By the time you reached them with food, everything would be cold.

JACK LEVIN: Irving hated *all* of us. He hated me more than anybody. Because every day, I had a fistfight in the dining room. I ran a month and a half straight without missing a day of getting into a fight. In those days, I was an *animal*. When I walked into the dining room in the morning, nobody dared even say "Good morning" to me. Because I couldn't *stand* it in the morning. I hated the idea of getting up. Some of those kids would go back to the room after lunch to get some sleep. I would never do it. I couldn't stand the thought of waking up *twice* in one day. So I was always operating on no sleep. Absolutely none whatsoever.

We used to play cards all night long or shoot craps all night long and then come in here and *schlep* trays. Let me tell you. I've loaded tractor trailers. I've loaded boxcars. I've done a lot of tough work in my life. This is the *toughest*. Forget just physically. To deal with the public, especially when it comes to food, is difficult. People are hard to please.

BILL: Irving would do a favor for a friend even if it meant firing somebody on the floor. He didn't care who you were or what you name was. If a season guest had somebody they wanted to work and they said, "Hey, give him a job, Irving," he would just get rid of someone like a sacrificial lamb. His assistant, Chick Kaiser, was the people's man. Him, everybody loved. Chick was a gambler and always in trouble but he fell right in with Sammy Freiberg, Jack Levin, myself, and the others.

In time, I came to hate Irving as much I had hated that captain in the Army and for many of the same reasons. Because the Army had not let me go after the first telegram, I had missed seeing my mother by a day. Then they pushed another button to send me back to Korea again. Then they shuffled papers while trying to decide what to do about me. Finally it was, "All right. Your father's sick. Your mother died. You were wounded in Korea and won this medal. We're going to throw you a bone and release you." What I had to go through to get my freedom just didn't sit too well with me.

SAM FREIBERG: We lived in a world of strictly gambling and drinking and dancing and parties, of which Bill was a part. There was no thinking about what was going to happen ten years from today. It was all strictly day-to-day. What's happening next? Where are we going tonight? It was *action*.

At that time, I used to lend a lot of money. The guys would pay me back and give me a gratuity on the side. You know, for lending them money. It was six for five, yeah. When Bill came on the scene, he fit right in. It was like a piece of the puzzle that had been missing. The circle was broken but he made a circle there. Because he was strictly a "Yes, I'm for it. Let's go do it" kind of guy. Nothing bad, you understand. He never did nothing dishonest.

JACK LEVIN: When I first came up to the mountains, there were over three hundred hotels up there. Wherever we went back then, it was *action*. Action was all over. It was Action, Jackson. There were also nightclubs. Guests would leave the hotels to go see Belle Barth work at the old Fifty-Two Club not far from Brown's. Her last show started at maybe two-thirty or three in the morning. There was a rhumba place in Liberty where everybody used to go that was really fantastic. Another club, a fag hangout, was unbelievable.

In Parksville, there was the Cherry Hill, owned and operated by black people but only white people were ever there. The music was fantastic. The girls, you would flip over them. It was an automatic turnaround. Whenever a guy walked in the front door, all the woman sitting at the bar would turn around.

BILL: I look at a waiter like I look at a woman. Let me see you take ten steps with a tray. I can tell how good you are. On my tray, I could go four times around five high with "mains," the main dishes. A metal cover went on top of every plate and I would pile them up five high. That was as high as I could go. Jack Levin could go *six* high. Carrying the tray on his *fingertips*.

I think Jack Levin was born with that tray on his fingers and they all grew together, the fingers *and* the tray. Because a waiter would never just carry mains. I had to put the little vegetable plates on the side and stick some soup in there and also carry the bread tray over here. So I might only be five high but when I came into the dining room, I had a whole restaurant in my arms. The worst meal was "Au Jus Night." The night they served roast beef au jus. As in "Oh, *Jew*." Or "Oh, *you!*" Or "Oh, *juice!*" It was which cut they wanted that always drove me wild.

"Pink," they would say. But not *pink* pink. *Light* pink. *Sort* of pink, but *done*. But *pink* done. On the side, I want the au jus. Not *on* the plate. *In* a little plate. Also, they always wanted the end cut. In order to impress everyone with their order. Back then in the mountains, it was all make-believe. People would save their money to come up to the Concord for two weeks in the summer. A girl who worked as a secretary, as soon as she sat down at her table, she became an interior decorator. A guy who was stock clerk, he became a lawyer or dentist-to-be. For two weeks, it was dreamland.

On Friday nights, people came up from the city to check in. At a quarter to nine at night, they would still be wandering into the dining room asking if they could get something to eat. If someone sat down at my station, I was stuck. I *had* to serve them. One Friday night, I had the singles table. This woman came in very late, sat down, and snapped her fingers at me. She said, "I want half a melon and some Chinese noodle appetizer and I'll have an end cut."

"Please, do me a favor," I said, "don't snap your fingers at me." I brought her out the melon. By this time, it was like almost a quarter to ten. I said, "The truth is, we're out of end cut."

"How can you be out of end cut?" she asked me.

"It's very late," I explained. "We're hardly even serving anymore. Since you came in late, I'll be glad to serve you. But we're out of end cut."

"I don't believe you," she said to me. "You just don't want to go back to the kitchen and get one for me."

"You want to come in the kitchen with me?"

"Now you're trying to insult me?" she said.

"Miss," I said. *"Please.* Don't do this to me."

By this time, it was really getting unpleasant. People were starting to get up from the table and leave. It was that tense. She was really going for it. She had saved her money to come up here for two weeks and she was going for it.

"Listen," I told her. "You're welcome to come to the kitchen with me and look. There's really no one even back there anymore."

"I *insist* you go in there and find me one," she said.

So I went back into the kitchen and I looked around but there weren't any more. I went back to the table and I said, "Would you like something else?"

"I suggest you find me an end cut," she said.

And I broke. "THERE ARE *NO END CUTS!*" I screamed. "Let me tell you something, lady. I work very hard. You come in here and you snap your fingers at me and try to make me look bad in front of the other guests. At the end of the meal, when I'm finished working, I always get myself something to eat. I sit down and I have a peaceful meal with my friend. I want to show you what I have that you can't have."

I went over to my side stand, reached underneath, and took out a plate. I showed her my end cut. "That's *mine,*" I told her. "I would've given it to you if you had been even a *little* bit nicer. But you didn't ask the right way."

She went wild. She reported me to Chick Kaiser, the assistant maître d'. Chick yelled out in the dining room, "Billy Graham? Billy Graham? You're *fired!*" Now the girl felt good. She had gotten me fired. She left the dining room. As soon as she was gone, Chick yelled, "Billy Graham? Billy Graham!"

"Yeah, Chick," I yelled.

"Only kidding," he yelled. "Only kidding."

The next day she came back for her breakfast, she was like a lamb. Like a *lamb*.

JOE DEROSE: It was a great place to be at that stage of your life. I would heartily recommend it to any young man. Females were there in abundance. A whole slew of college girls from Boston. Then you had the guests. And the married women whose husbands would go home during the week. You worked like a dog. But you were so young and so alive that you endured.

Still, it really was a brutal grind. You worked three meals a day, seven days a week. You got up very early and went down to the dining room where they never had enough cups and saucers or silverware. So you had to fight to get your share. First thing in the morning, you had to fight like hell to get your stuff. Put it out, work the meal, and deal with people who had the attitude, "Look, I *paid* for this. I'm going to eat myself into oblivion if I want." They were difficult people to serve. You finished breakfast maybe ten-thirty, you had to be back in the dining room at eleven to set up for lunch. If you were lucky, you had time to walk home and wash up.

Come back and work your ass off right through lunch. Finish by two-thirty and then you had about two and a half hours off in the afternoon. In the afternoon, I would play softball. We had a team and we played different hotels. Afterward, I had to drag my tail back to the room. I had to walk up this hill and I would barely make it. I couldn't lay down because if I laid down, I would never get up again. I had to make it to a shower. If I could make the shower, then I could work the evening meal. Five o'clock, you're back in there for dinner. Work till nine-thirty or ten. Then you would go out dancing somewhere all night long, and it was *great*.

BILL: By the time I started working at the Concord, I had really gotten into dancing. I was one of the few waiters at the Concord who was allowed into the nightclub because there were never enough good dancers around to dance with the women guests. The Cotillion Room was a huge place. It held like eight thousand Jews. You could have your three hundredth wedding anniversary there and still not fill the place, it was that big.

Right next to it was this long snaking bar with a jukebox at the end. The Erskine Hawkins Trio plays there now. They played there *then*. Whenever they took a break, people would push buttons on the jukebox to keep music playing in the bar.

One night I finished working the last meal, I went down the hill and I put on my suit. I went back up into the bar and I sat down right next to the jukebox. Sitting two or three seats away from me at the bar I saw a woman in her late twenties with reddish auburn hair, poured into this gold lamé dress and really *stacked*. Music was playing from the jukebox. She came over and said, "Would you care to dance?"

We moved into this little area right in front of the jukebox doing a nice slow bolero and started to talk. She told me she was Audrey from Philadelphia. I told her I was Bill from D.C. I had just finished law school but as yet, I had no definite plans. She happened to be an interior decorator. Just like every other girl I ever met up there from Philadelphia. All of them were nothing *but*.

As we danced, I got that thing in my neck where it stiffened up and then my back locked so I could barely move. "Jeez, I'm sorry," I told her.

"What's wrong?" she asked.

"I've got a bad back," I said. "I can't dance anymore."

Without missing a beat, she said, "Are you in the main building?"

"No," I said. What was I going to tell her? I was in the waiter's quarters down the hill? "No," I said. "I'm in one of the bungalows off the grounds."

"Well," she said, "I'm in the main building."

She said it as if this was something that had happened to her a dozen times before. I mean, how many guys could have gotten stiff necks halfway through their first dance with her? But it didn't faze her for a second. Then she went over to the bar, picked up her little gold purse, and gave me the key to her room. "Why don't you go up there and relax," she said. "I'll go to the drugstore and get some liniment and lotion, and I'll rub it out for you."

I went upstairs and I sat down on her bed and I waited. A few minutes later, she came in and put this package down on the dresser. I started to get up from the bed and she came over and said, "I'll be back in a minute." Then she gave me a very seductive kiss right on the mouth. She went into the bathroom. I took off my jacket and rolled up my sleeves. A few minutes later, she came out in a nightgown and a negligee. A very shimmering, see-through, scintillating outfit, all light pink.

She came over to the bed and grabbed me and did a one-and-a-half gainer, whirling me down on the bed. Now we were rolling around together. One thing led to another. She helped me remove my shirt and pants, groaning and talking all the time. By this time, we had nothing on. She kept groaning. Then she wheeled me around and said, "Bill, just *fuck* me!" When she said this, my hot torpedo became a warm banana. It was instant *stop*. Like someone had pulled the plug yet turned on all the lights at the exact same time.

The crudeness of what she had said affected me. She reminded me at just the wrong time of who we were. Two animals. I realized I couldn't do this. Not that we shouldn't. I just couldn't. I sat up. "What's wrong?" she said. "I'm sorry, I just don't feel well. It's my back." I mean, what was I going to say?

"I'll fix your back," she said.

I started putting my clothes on and she said, "What are you doing? Where are you going? You're leaving? What's the matter? I'm not good enough for you?"

Then she went into this terribly sad monologue. "Who the fuck do you think you are? Bill the lawyer from D.C., huh? I don't need you. *Fuck you!* You fucking *lawyer.*" Really nasty, throwing pillows and ashtrays around while I was getting dressed as fast as I could. On and on and on, and it didn't stop until I left the room with my shoes and jacket in my hand. I felt very badly about the whole thing.

Lunch, the next day. I was coming through the dining room with a full tray. Three tables straight ahead of me, there she was. Standing like an aircraft carrier in my way. "Oh, my *God,*" I say. I walked past her to my station and I could feel her right behind me, trailing me across the entire dining room. I turned around at my station and she was staring at me and breathing hard and she started in right away. "A lawyer from D.C., huh?" she said.

"Do me a favor," I said. "This is hot food. Let me serve these people. We'll talk about this later."

I went toward the table and she followed me. "Who the *hell* do you think you are?"

By now I was whispering to her out of the side of my mouth while I set plates down in front of my guests. "Look, I'm sorry, I'm sorry. But you *have* to let me serve these people."

"How *dare* you? Who the *hell* do you think you are? I'm not good enough for you? Why did you take me upstairs? To torture me?"

On and on and on. Finally, I got her to agree to back off. We'd talk after the meal. The meal ended and the dining room emptied out. I did my silver and cleaned off my table and then I went to eat my lunch with all the other waiters. She came over to us, so I got up and went to sit down at another table with her. "Look," I said, "Something happened to me last night and I don't know how to explain it to you." Finally I told her, "It was what you said. It made me feel like I was supposed to be some kind of machine."

This got to her. Suddenly she became very young again. She said she didn't mean it that way. Then she said, "Okay. So you want to get

together again tonight?" It was like everything was now back to "reset."
We could start all over from square one.

"I really don't think so," I told her.

"You *son of a bitch!*" she screamed at me. "Who the *fuck* do you think
you are? Bill the lawyer from D.C.? What is it? You think you're too good
for me?

3.

JACK LEVIN: Did we gamble? *Whoa,* did we gamble. God almighty, did
we gamble. Card games, crap games, you name it. If there was a
cockroach that I thought was faster than another one, we would bet on
cockroach races. There was this little waitress who worked up here then.
We were kids but not her. She had to be forty or forty-five and a
grandmother already. They had a crap game at the staff house. She used
to come in wearing a slip and a bra, pick up the dice and roll them, and
you'd swear it was a truck driver, the way she used to talk. She was a
wonder drug, that one.

Guys made three, four, five, or six hundred a week, it all depended on
the week, which was good money. The only problem was that check-out
day was on Sunday. Like around three o'clock. By maybe eight o'clock at
night we were broke. All of us. We were all chemists back then. We
turned money into shit.

BILL: The first summer up at the Concord, I started to realize what the
dining room was really all about. *Action.* Heavy betting on sports, crap
games, and poker games. The first year, I just watched. I wasn't active.
Then I met this young lady named Patricia who was a waitress with the
station right next to mine. She was going to Penn State at the time. She
was the second important Patricia in my life.

In my room in the men's dorm, I laid a big piece of sheetrock across
my bed. I was the wrong bettor and I ran the crap game in there. Then I
got an idea that I proposed to Patricia. "Why don't we get a place together
up here? I'll run the crap game and you run the poker game." It turned
out there was a vacant bungalow off the grounds down at the bottom of
the hill in Kiamesha Lake. We rented it for August.

Once a week, on Tuesday night, we'd have a crap game and a poker
game. Just move the bed over and put the board down. Pay three-to-two
on the nine and the five, two-to-one on the four and the ten, even money
on the six and the eight. Waiters and busboys and sometimes a dishwasher
or somebody from the laundry would play. I would take a dollar out of

every pot but no one had to pay to get in the game. In the other room, they played cards.

That first summer, we just had some drinks and peanuts and stuff. Nothing fancy. My next summer up at the Concord was the real payoff. We decided we were going to run the game *right*. Tuesdays and Thursdays, Pat doing the poker game and me the crap game. Gradually, I got into this whole Robin Hood thing. "Look what I *could* be serving these people." Because in hotels like Grossinger's and the Concord, there is so much food that there is never a check in and a check out. You can go into the kitchen and say, "Twelve steaks, four of this, three of that . . ." put it on your tray, carry it into the dining room, and just load it all into your side stand.

Patricia and I would order stuff, put it in the side stands, wrap it up in aluminum foil, and carry it down to the game. We became like the Aluminum-Wrap King and Queen of the Western Hemisphere. Roast beef, apples, cookies, milk, whatever. Bags and bags of the stuff were going out side doors with winks and timing. It was incredible what we took out of there. Pickled lox and pickled herring. One night, we had more than the usual crowd for the game so I went into the dining room at ten o'clock at night, took one of the round tabletops that seated twelve people, and rolled it all the way down the hill. We played on it and in the morning it took both of us to roll it all the way back up.

We charged for nothing. But we served practically right off the dining room menu. We had two refrigerators so we could save whatever we brought down there. Cheese of every variety. Fruit, steak, pastrami, liquor, juices, anything you wanted. This soon became *the* game up there. A lot of people knew about it but nobody talked about it. From this game, we were taking out somewhere between fifteen hundred and two thousand a week. Net, net, net, *net*. This is 1955. Between fifteen hundred and two thousand a week.

Guys would order. "I'll have a pastrami rye with cream soda." Sometimes I would have a list of what was available that night. I would take whole cream pies out of the dining room. Trays of steaks. Meatloaf. Hamburgers. Chinese food. We would plan every day. Well, what do we need for tonight? Then we'd go shopping.

It became a big thing to play in the game. The in-guests, the wheeler-dealers, the meat and produce guys, the garment center guys, the heavies, they all wanted in. Waiters would come up to me in the dining room and say, "Bill, Mr. Levin wants in the game. What can you do for him?" I became like a broker. The son of Streit's Matzohs, he was a guest at my table, he insisted on getting into the game. I would see him all night in my room and then serve him breakfast in the dining room. It was such an honest game that while Patricia and I were servicing the players, they'd sometimes take our dollar out of the pot *for* us.

By this time I had really gotten to loathe Irving Cohen. With a passion. The way he treated people, the way he snapped his fingers at them, the way he made Chick Kaiser do all the dirty work. I was never sure if Irving Cohen knew about the game. But he knew I was doing something. It infuriated him that I would come into the dining room like a surgeon. Someone else would have already set up my station, someone else would have gotten my livestock. I would just come in and serve the people. Then I would say "Good night" and leave.

I had one guy cleaning up my tables and another guy doing my goblets and someone else cleaning my silver. But I never flaunted it in anyone's face. During the meal, I hustled and took care of my guests. But I never did silver. I never did goblets. I never did setup and it drove Irving crazy. At that time, unions were already coming into the mountains, trying to organize the waiters and busboys but hotel owners never wanted to let them in.

Over the years, I had worked some of the big conventions at the Concord. Like the Democratic party or Kodak Films or Seagram's Gin. Thousands of people. Instead of a guest who sat at your table at all meals, they could sit wherever they wanted and mingle. When they sat down to eat, they would give you a chit. Pink for breakfast. Blue for lunch. Yellow for supper. Out of a booklet they had. That piece of paper meant payment by the people sponsoring the convention to the hotel and then from the hotel to us. Our tips came out of the fee paid to the hotel for the convention.

There was already a rumble going around about someone taking a kickback off that but it was very hush-hush. Then in June 1955, the AFL-CIO got the legal right to address the staff. The announcement that they were coming in a couple of weeks went around the dining room. I remember that Irving Cohen had just fired a busboy to make room for the relative of a season guest and I really felt bad about it. He was like Captain Bligh in *Mutiny on the Bounty*.

Through a friend who worked in the accounting office at the Concord, I got the names of a dozen or more conventions that had been at the hotel in the past few years. I took some time off, put on my decent clothes, and went to New York. I went to the corporations and told them who I was and that this union meeting was about to take place. The reason it was taking place was that some of us felt we had not gotten a fair shake.

Within a matter of two weeks, three corporations had given me written testimony. First, each organization had met with hotel executives to discuss arrangements and fees. They would determine that at every meal, each waiter and busboy would get a specific amount for each chit handed in. Something like fifty cents for the waiter and twenty-five for the busboy. That was how they kept count and we got paid.

There was only one problem. When we were given the table assignments, the pay was something like *forty* cents for the waiter and *twenty* cents for the busboy. Ten cents per meal per person for the waiter and five cents per meal per person for the busboy was going somewhere else. If the convention only had a thousand people and each one was worth a dime, that would be a hundred dollars a meal plus a nickel from the busboy's tip. A hundred and fifty a meal, which came to four hundred and fifty a day. A two- or three-day convention and the pickup on the side would be two or three grand. A few conventions a year. Years and years and years of this. It added up.

They held the union meeting in the extension to the original dining room. It was before dinner one night. First the union man addressed the room. He said, "We want to protect you. If we come in and you do your job well, you can't just be fired for any reason. There *has* to be cause. We want you to have health benefits. I know you people here don't think you need things but you do."

The old guard, the Pennsylvania guys, none of them really wanted a union there. Their attitude was, "Hey, what are you gonna do for us? We already got a job and Irving Cohen protects us and you know, we're okay." The union guy was talking but no one cared.

He said to them, "I'm really talking about protecting your rights because we're going to have a shop steward here, and if you have a grievance and don't think you're being treated fair by the ownership, we'll represent you."

Then Irving Cohen stood up. He said, "Look, we've always been one big happy family here. I don't know why we need these people. Look at you. *You* raised your children here. *You* sent your boys through college with what you earned here. *You* bought your homes. We don't need this," he said. "If we have any grievances, we can handle them ourselves." He went on and on about love and sharing and how there was no need to have anybody else there because we could settle whatever differences we had together. Keep in mind. Nobody *ever* talked to him. They all went to Chick Kaiser, who was the in-between man.

At the end, he said, "All right, thank you very much. Now you've heard both sides and you're going to be voting. Thank you. Are there any questions?" I raised my hand in the back of the room. The minute he saw me, Irving knew that he was dead.

HY RANKELL: I myself never thought the union would come in. At the time, it didn't make a bit of difference to me. I was very happy with the whole arrangement the way it was. I was so accustomed to doing the work that I took it for granted everyone else would feel the way I did. I remember someone saying to me when the members of the NLRB took the votes out of the ballot box, "Any union is better than no union. At least you have some sort of protection." But I was so wrapped up with the hotel that I voted for the hotel. This was the only job I had ever had.

JACK LEVIN: Irving Cohen was telling us the pros and cons of a union which he really didn't want us to join because in those days, a union was . . . you know. He was talking and talking and talking and he was asking people to stand up and voice their opinion. Well, every five seconds Billy would jump up and ask him this and ask him that and ask him this. Now I started to get mad at Billy. I wanted to go home. Everybody wanted to go home. But he kept asking questions and questions.

BILL: I was standing there in my white jacket with the "C" on it for the Concord, black pants, with a black bow tie clipped to my collar of my white shirt, which was hanging open. I said, "I've worked very hard for this money and so have the other people here. I can't tell anybody else how to vote. I just want you to know the truth. You knew we get paid flat rates per chit for working conventions. I got proof here that last year on three separate conventions, we got beat bad. I got proof here, in *writing*. On two occasions when we were supposed to get fifty cents, we got forty instead. When we were supposed to get sixty-five, we got fifty-five." I held up the documents and said, "Here it is. Here's the *proof.*

"I'm not a union man," I said. "But something's got to be better than this. Something that would give us a chance to be treated fairly. So that we get what we're supposed to get. So that we get what we *earn.*"

The whole thing took maybe five minutes. When I finished, there was no sound. Not a *sound*. There were no cheers. It was very quiet and people just kind of mumbled to themselves and moved away. Nobody went up to anybody else to talk about it. No one responded to what I'd said. When everyone voted, it was like three hundred something to seventeen in favor of the union.

HY RANKELL: I was there when they counted the votes. It was overwhelming in favor of the union. Truly.

BILL: The next morning, there was a scene that could have come straight out of *On the Waterfront* where Lee J. Cobb says to Marlon Brando, "You don't work these docks! You don't work anywhere! You don't so much as lift a hook! You got that?" By the main door of the dining room, Irving Cohen called out *"Graham!"* Over the loudspeaker. Now many times before, I had asked him, "Please, Mr. Cohen. Don't call me Graham." I hated it. Either Billy or Mr. Graham but not just by my last name.

"Graham!" he called out over the loudspeaker.

We went into this walk-in closet where they kept all the extra supplies for the bar outside the dining room. In so many words, he said, "You want a piece of advice? Get your ass out of here. I don't like you. I don't like what you stand for. I don't like who you think you are." I never saw any man hate another man like that. Every time I tried to talk, he'd cut me off. When he got angry, he was like me. Never let the other guy talk.

He said, "I'm not going to fire you. You're going to leave on your own. You know why? 'Cause I'm going to freeze you out."

"Did I lie?" I kept saying. "Did I lie?" He didn't answer and he wouldn't let me talk. He was so angry that he just stormed out of the closet. Just like Lee J. Cobb.

Breakfast was extraordinary. All the waiters and waitresses were coming by to say, "Hey, Bill, thanks" or "Not easy, huh?" They all knew I was a marked man. That summer was one of the most extraordinary periods of my life. I had three tables at which eight people could sit and one that seated four. The most people I could have carried would have been twenty-eight. I think my high that summer was *eleven.* I would get three or nine or five. The only people I would get were people who said, "We *want* to sit with Bill. We're his season guests."

Sometimes, the place was overflowing. In the middle of the dining room, there would be this island of empty seats. Every day I'd walk in and if he was there I'd say, "Mr. Cohen, how are you today, sir?" The game was functioning, the aluminum wrap was rolling out of the dining room. Nobody ever talked about the game, so I was doing just fine. I think Irving thought I was just stubborn.

In the morning, Irving would come in early. His busboy would bring him coffee to his private table next to the kitchen. He'd sit there waiting for this guy to bring him his newspaper and look at me like he was the inspector and I was Fredric March in *Les Misérables.* At the end of that summer, I went home with a little over seven thousand dollars. At the time, it was a *lot* of money.

IRVING COHEN: You're talking about Bill Graham. A character like him. He was *anti.* He was anti-*everything.* Anti-establishment all the way but a *hell* of a guy to work with. Really great. When it came to the guests, they loved him. He had a way with people. The only problem I had with him, I had to understand his way of thinking. Which wasn't easy at the time. Now I do, you know. We're both much older.

He was a free thinker. And I wasn't accustomed to that. I was accustomed to going over to tell somebody, "Listen, you have to look clean." And Billy Graham says, "I know you have to look clean. But if we give them the service, why do we have to look clean?"

He always asked the question afterward. "Billy, you got people sitting at the station," I would say to him. "Why are you standing and talking to Sam?"

"Oh, they can wait a minute. You know, I'm waiting here for tomorrow morning." He used to tell me that. "Because when I go over there, you know I'm going to take care of them."

The only problem I had with him, I couldn't make him take a haircut. This is a true story. He told this on the Johnny Carson show. We have a rule here, and it's almost a health rule. Any waitress, normally it's the waitresses that have the long hair, the girls. They *must* wear hair nets while they're carrying a tray of food. It makes sense. Their hair could go on some of the food they're carrying in. And Billy Graham refused to take a haircut. He hated haircuts, he hated shaves. I had to fight with him to take a shave. One day, I brought him in a razor and I said, "Billy, I want you to use this. Go into the bathroom, you don't need soap, just *fitt*, clean it down a little."

He did that but he refused to take a haircut. And one day I called him over and I said to him, "Listen, Billy. If you don't take your haircut, you have to wear a hair net. Now that's going to look funny. Because then you're going to look like my sister." I told him, "Just tie your hair back."

He said, "No, I can't. Listen," he said, "this is my style. This is the way I am."

I said, "Well, I can't use you on the floor because we'll get other characters to come in that are going to be like you." I said, "They're going to say to me, 'Well, why is *he* walking around with long hair and I'm not walking around with long hair?'"

We had sort of an understanding with one another. I said, "If you can't take your haircut, I can't use you." Instead of waiting to be fired, he said to me, "I'm going to make it very simple. I'm going to leave." I just couldn't tolerate it, you know. He's a tall fellow and when he walked around the dining room, his hair flowed all over. It blew in the wind, you know?

4.

BILL: When I got back to the city, I started working as a waiter at Ben and Doris Maksik's Town and Country Nightclub in Brooklyn. On Flatbush Avenue and Avenue U. Friday and Saturday nights, it would be weddings. Saturday and Sunday afternoons, weddings, sweet sixteens, and *bar mitzvahs*. The cast of characters on the staff there was amazing. Like half a dozen Sam Freibergs. All of a sudden, a busboy would be missing, never to be seen again. In would come Tony D's nephew as his lifetime replacement.

Ben Maksik, the owner, was a wheeler-dealer. He had the intensity of Nehemiah Persoff. He would sit in a cage in the kitchen. Whenever I picked up my order, whether it was six soups and three chickens, two ribs, and one steak, or whatever, he would always check what was going out so no one could take more than they were supposed to. There was a checker standing there already. But that wasn't enough. Ben *himself* was on guard. He was the guy in the tollbooth at the Lincoln Tunnel taking your dollar before he let your car through. *Only* once he had checked was it all right to pass.

He was always immaculately dressed. A wiry guy with that intense Murder, Inc., face. In his face, it was written, "God forbid that there should be *more* than eleven string beans on that order." He always had six to eight half dollars in his hand. Like Captain Queeg's ball bearings in *The Caine Mutiny*. He would be in the cage whenever I went through with my order, shuffling those half dollars so I could hear them ringing in my ears. After a while, he would not even have to say anything. I would hear the half dollars, he would check out my tray, and then his mouth would move sideways. *Pass.* Out into the dining room I could go.

His wife Doris dressed like she was sixteen years old and the party they were having was for her. Like that year's version of a Barbie Doll. She was at least in her forties. Her hair was all done up in braids and then twisted around. She would move around all the tables and drive everybody crazy by saying, "This should be *here*, not there." The place had three levels and held twenty-five hundred people. The stage was huge. *Everybody* worked there. Xavier Cugat and Abbe Lane, Milton Berle, Tony Bennett, Sophie Tucker, the Ritz Brothers. All week long, they had shows and then on the weekends they would double up with afternoon weddings and *bar mitzvahs*. Within six months, I was a regular. I was making a couple of hundred bucks a week from the work and then I got involved in the game in the back. All told, I was making four or five hundred a week. Back then, that was large money. I had a DeSoto with strips of wood on the side, also a convertible. With about nine hundred parking tickets that I kept in the dash. I was never a fast driver. But if I was going somewhere and I wanted to go over there but there seemed to be a little grass in between with a sign that said "No U-Turn," I would go right over the grass.

I was also trying to go to school again but school didn't sit well with me. I tried because I thought it was the thing I should be doing. By this time, I was living with my brother Roy and a friend of his in an apartment on Eighty-sixth Street in Manhattan. My lifestyle was totally different than theirs. They had classical music and chess and bridge. I was *tummeling*, running, dancing, crap games, playing ball, coming home in sweatpants so wet that they were sticking to me. Three guys living in two rooms. It was tough going. So I moved to 145 Waverly Place, right off Sixth Avenue.

My apartment was seventy-one steps from the basketball courts on Waverly Place. I had it measured. Four steps down from my brownstone and from there, seventy-one steps to the courts. I *lived* on those courts. Great black guys played there all the time with silk stockings on their heads to keep their hair in place. Sometimes, Harlem would come down to play there. Sometimes, we would go up to Harlem to play. I wasn't big and I didn't have the moves that some of my friends did. But I always played great defense. Always. Like, "You want to score? First, you *kill* me."

My apartment was on the ground floor and the rent was forty-two dollars a month. Joe DeRose, who I already knew from the Concord, was also living down in the Village then. He sold me a record player for seventy-five bucks. When I opened it up, there were two parts that became the speakers and at the bottom was the turntable. When it comes to fixing or repairing things, I am one of those people who find it very hard to take a piece of paper out of an envelope. I'll tear up the letter first and then look at the envelope and say, "Why isn't anything written on this?" As far as I'm concerned, *God* makes everything work.

So now I was going to install my hi-fi in my apartment on a Sunday morning. In order for the turntable to turn, I had to take this thing with two prongs and stick it in the wall. For electricity. The two speakers had a thin single wire with a single thing at the end. To me, Jack was a guy's name. Each with a single jack. I decided I wanted one speaker in the front room and one speaker in the bedroom in back. Of course, there was not nearly enough wire. So I figured I would go get some extension cords and cut them up. After all, wire is wire.

Because it was Sunday, no stores were open. I walked for four or five blocks in every direction and by the time I got home, I was furious. It had turned into a bad day. I said to myself, "Well, I can set them up another time." Then I started going around the apartment. Whenever I saw a lamp or a wire leading to the toaster, I cut it off. I kept saying to myself, "I can fix all this later on." I figured I could use all these wires as links. Only I didn't have electrical tape to splice them together with.

So I used Band-Aids instead. I cut out the gauze part and used the tape. Tape is *tape*, right? Now I had a speaker in the front room with nine pieces of wire attached to it and one hooked up in the back with nine more amputated pieces of wire all patched together leading to it. It had taken me a few hours but now both speakers were connected to the turntable by wire.

I still had not plugged the turntable into the wall. By mistake I took a lead from one of the speakers and I stuck it into the wall and after all this time and work, all I got was *"POP! POP!"* I blew the speaker out because I had put the thing right into the wall. So then I did what those huge machines do to used cars that are then going to be dumped on to the scrap heap. I crushed the speakers and broke the turntable and I called up Joe DeRose and screamed down the phone at him, "Why didn't you tell me this thing didn't work *before* you sold it to me?"

JOE DEROSE: I had graduated from law school and taken a sublease on an apartment on 95 Christopher Street. The Village was a *spectacular* place to live then. There was always something happening and I'm taking twenty-four hours a day. There was a pulse that just kept on going.

BILL: I liked the life down there because nothing was set. There didn't seem to be any responsibilities yet. I could work the weekend or take it off and go somewhere instead. I could play ball or go dancing. But I wasn't really going anywhere with my life. So I decided to visit my sister Rita in California.

RITA ROSEN: I was in San Francisco and I wanted to be a mother to him. I used to write him and call him and tell him all the time to come. I said to him, "If Mama would know that you're coming, she would be very happy." But he didn't have the money to come and I didn't have it either. So I borrowed a hundred dollars from a girlfriend and he came.

BILL: The flying time was sixteen hours, with one stopover in Kansas City. Once I got out there, I couldn't believe how the Bay Area hit me. The Golden Gate Bridge and the cable cars and the boat ride to Alcatraz. What I liked was that the game was not always on the goal line out there. It wasn't always life and death. There were time-out signs. It was a *nicer* game. It amazed me how easy it was to escape the city and how beautiful it was when you did. I stayed two weeks and decided that I had to come back and try this. I went back to New York and got out of my lease in the Village. I found an ad in the newspaper for an agency that arranged for drive-away cars to the coast.

I went and sat in the car and looked at the dashboard. It was like a view of the inside of my stomach because somebody had taken off the meter. There was no gas gauge. There was no emergency brake. No heater. No radio. A steering wheel, a gas pedal, and the clutch. And that was it. Gutted. I mean, *gutted.* Zilch. I pulled out of the lot and drove into the tunnel. I was headed back to the city to the apartment so I could load my belongings, especially this Simmons mattress which I loved and had already decided I was going to take.

The car overheated in the tunnel. I had to pull over and put water in the radiator. Fine.

The next morning I loaded up the car. Clothing in the backseat and in the trunk. I had my Simmons mattress on the roof with a rope tied through the cracks at the top of the windows to keep it in place while I drove. I put this huge teddy bear I had bought for my nephew Avi next to me and took off.

The car had no low gear. When I was going up even a 10-percent grade, it sounded like a Sherman tank. The carburetor didn't work even *after* they fixed it. I had to stop for gas every two hours because with no gauge I had no idea how much gas was in the tank. It was October and I had no heat. One night, I would stay in the car, the next I would get myself a motel.

People would drive past me and do double-takes. The teddy bear's head was bigger than mine. It wasn't every day that you got to see a Yellow Cab with a mattress on the roof and a giant bear sitting next to the driver with clothing piled up in the back in the middle of Utah.

It was my very first trip across America and I wanted to see it all so I drove Highway 30 into Highway 50 across Ohio and Indiana and then up into the Rockies.

One afternoon, I hit one of those sudden typhoonlike storms, where one minute it was nice and clear and the next, there was a torrential downpour. Thank God, I had a plastic cover over the mattress. But some of the water got through the cracks and the mattress started to get really heavy.

As I kept driving along the wind picked up. The mattress slid three or four inches over the top of the car to one side. The car started to billow back and forth across the highway in the wind. I was scared. The rain was coming down so strong that it was spraying into the car where I had left the windows open so the rope holding the mattress in place could pass through. And of course, Teddy was getting wet. I saw all these trucks and cars pulled off the highway because the storm was getting so bad that they couldn't even drive anymore. It was raining like in movies set in the jungles of Brazil. Finally, I pulled over to the side where a truck was already parked next to a big cow field. I could feel the wind picking up the car. There was a ditch right next to the highway and I was sure the wind would blow the car over into it.

I was scared to death. "The weight," I thought. "It's got to be the weight of the mattress. I know what I'll do. I'll get my Swiss Army knife and cut the cord."

At the time, I was wearing a pair of cutoff shorts, no shoes, and a T-shirt. Because it was comfortable to drive like that. When I looked out in my rear window, I saw a VW bug parked a few feet behind me. Now, what if I cut the mattress and it went flying off the roof of my car and hit the VW?

I decided to get out of my car. Picture this. No socks. Shorts, T-shirt. Howling wind and pouring rain. I had this open knife in my hand and I proceeded to get out of my car and go over to the VW behind me, screaming, "DON'T WORRY! I'M GONNA CUT THE MATTRESS OFF MY ROOF!" I got out of a New York City Yellow Cab in Utah screaming, "I'M THE GUY WITH THE TEDDY BEAR IN THE CAB IN FRONT OF YOU. I'M GONNA CUT THE MATTRESS ROPE BECAUSE I THINK MY CAR MIGHT TURN OVER."

I looked at the woman sitting behind the wheel of the car. In a second, her face went from the size of a pin to that of a Samoan. She didn't say a word. Her eyes never left my face. She just kept me in view as she reversed the car fast as she could and left, preferring to face the thunder and the madness of the devil rather than me. Then I realized, "Oh. No wonder. I'm standing here on the highway in the pouring rain with a knife in my hand, no shoes, no socks, in a pair of shorts and a T-shirt." I walked to my car and I cut the back part of the rope. The mattress moved a little. I cut another part of the rope. *WHOOSH!* That mattress left the roof of my car like a piece of cardboard in a tornado. It *flew* so far off into the field that I knew I'd *never* get it back. About ten minutes later, the storm stopped and I drove away. As I did, I thought to myself, "Well, at least some cow got a nice new bed."

ERIC ROSEN: Bill came to visit me and Rita and we had for him a one-bedroom apartment in our building. The next morning, I went to work and we stopped by the dispatch office for Pacific Motor Trucking in San Francisco. I introduced him to the superintendent and they talked and he filled out papers. The superintendent asked, "When do you want to start?" He said, "I'm ready." The guy said, "That's your desk." And that's how he started.

BILL: I was restless, all the time. I remember one time taking a job with a trucking company in San Francisco and working there for over a year. I got into some acting stuff and went to read for a part in a play, but I didn't get the part. I went right back to New York and started working again at Ben Maksik's and driving a cab. I did that a lot. In those years, I drove the United States eight times, hitched twice, and even did it once on a Lambretta motor scooter. That took thirty-two days.

5.

JOE DEROSE: Billy was a vagabond who would commute from New York to San Francisco and back. Either by hitching or by witching or however he did it. All I know is that one day I heard a knock at my door and who was there but Billy with his sleeping bag. I'm not even sure how he found out where I was living. The only thing I do know was that Billy didn't have a dime in his pocket. I was delighted to see him. He asked if he could stay with me. I said, "Absolutely." For the next six or seven months, he lived with me at 95 Christopher Street.

BILL: We were sharing a place at 95 Christopher Street on the tenth floor. And the building on the other side must have had nine stories because we could always see people sitting on the roof sunbathing. Joe DeRose was sitting by the window one day when we saw these two ladies across the way. They were sunbathing. I got behind him, started rubbing his back, and said, "Joe, you're lying on a beach on your stomach and one of those women comes over and says, 'Do you mind?' And she sits down and starts to rub your back. And it gets more serious. She *really* gets involved with your rhythm and you're moving together. What do you say about *that*, Joe? *Huh?* What do you say?"

And he said, "I don't have much to say."

He kept looking at these two beautiful women across the way. I said, "Joe, now she's *sitting* on your back. She's sitting on your *back*, Joe. She's got her fingers on your neck and she's leaning forward and pressing her body against you. What do you say *now*, Joe? What do you say *now?*"

He let out this big sigh and he said, "Tell her to get off my back!"

We decided to try and pick them up. At the time, Joe had a convertible. An Oldsmobile Hydramatic. Joe yelled, *"Hey! You wanna go for a ride?"* They shook their heads, yes. He yelled, "We'll meet you *downstairs!*" So the two of us went downstairs. We sat and waited in the front seat of his car, Mr. and Mr. Joe New York. They didn't come down. We waited and waited and then we got out of the car and yelled up at them, *"Hey! Hey!"*

They were nine stories up and they looked down and Joe screamed, *"Hey!* You comin' down?"

And they said, *"No.* We changed our *minds."*

Joe said, "*Hey!* Come *on*. We been waitin' for you. What do you want us to do now?

This was broad daylight in the middle of the Village. Christopher Street. A lot of people in the street. One of the ladies on the roof looked down and yelled, "Well, why don't the two of you go in the backseat and fuck each *other?*" I never forget that.

JOE DEROSE: It was a studio apartment with like a half a bedroom. He slept on the couch, I slept on the bed. At the time, I was practicing law in the Bronx. I would buy these whole filet mignons which I got at an extraordinarily good price at the market. It cost me peanuts. Literally every night, I would live on filet mignon. I was into Bolla Soave wine, which at the time wasn't terribly well known. It had a real nice taste to it and it was about two dollars a gallon in those days. Billy of course was also living on filet mignon and the finest of salads and white wine. For six or seven months straight. He was doing this, he was doing that, he was running around. Maybe he was starting up at the Actors' Studio. But he wasn't working.

My sublease came up. So we decided to take another one on West Fourth Street, the hub of Greenwich Village. We had just finished moving our clothes from 95 Christopher to 241 West Fourth and again I want to emphasize that for six or seven months, the man had lived like a *king*. We were not in the new apartment fifteen minutes when he came back with some blueberries. On the bulletin board in the kitchen, he tacked up a piece of paper. He drew a line down the middle. On one side, he put "*Bill*." On the other one, "*Joe*." And next to Bill, he put, "A dollar thirty-five." I said, "What the hell is that?" He said, "You owe me half of a dollar thirty-five." I said, "You've *got* to be kidding." I could not believe it. It absolutely blew my mind.

Not only did he live with me for six or seven months for nothing, he also took half my wardrobe. To this day, I think Bill has my turtleneck sweater. He took my scale. In a way, Bill was like a beatnik but an organized one. Never out of control, never into booze or drugs. Even with females, he was very straight. In some respects, we *were* the odd couple. He would do the dishes, I would cook. I would cook, we would take turns trying to keep ourselves from being devoured by the garbage.

At one point, Bill and I started having words one day about something one of us was *not* doing which he was *supposed* to do. In the background, there was music playing. An Ahmad Jamal record or something like "Poinsietta" or "Bolero" that would build and build and build. Billy and I were head to head and toe to toe, yelling and screaming at each other.

Don't ask me why. But the music got to both of us. Before you knew it, we started to dance. It was the funniest thing. We both broke up laughing.

BILL: I had a regular driver's license and I took a stop-start test, a timing test to check on my reflexes, so I could get a hack license as well. I worked for Ace Cab on Eighteenth Street and Eleventh Avenue, driving either Plymouths or DeSotos. Hard shifts usually, mainly midnight to 8 A.M. Other times, I'd be going to school or working as a waiter at Ben Maksik's. Sometimes I'd do a *bar mitzvah* in the afternoon, a wedding in the evening, leaving the hall at eleven, and then go do the cab for eight hours, and catch three hours of sleep the next morning. Then I would start in all over again.

When I started driving a cab, I began to think that it might be the ultimate job. On the radio, I could listen to the ball games or the soap operas or the music I liked. I could quit whenever I wanted to, pull over when I felt like it. I was my own boss. Whenever I was driving, I thought I had something. "If nothing else works out, I can always do this for a living."

At night, I'd listen to Symphony Syd and Al "Jazzbo" Collins from the Purple Grotto. William B. Williams during the day. The best thing about driving a cab for me was that I would pass a school yard sometimes and see something interesting and pull over. A basketball game or a softball game or a stickball game that looked good. I'd get out of the car and watch for an hour. The simplicity of competition. Four on four in the school yard or guys playing stickball in the street. Sometimes, I'd stop the cab for two or three hours.

The great advantage of the cab was that I didn't make big money but I earned a living. I listened to music and talk shows on the radio. I ate in restaurants where there were great exchanges going on between other guys. I saw great, great stickball battles for a quarter a man. I saw cement softball games where the king of the universe was Freddie Schloss, a guy who stood five foot one. The best shortstop who ever lived. Babe Ruth wanted to meet Freddie Schloss. That's how good he was.

I thought a lot about what the king of the waiters could make. I could have been either the ultimate waiter or the ultimate cabdriver. That's what I was good at. In terms of crossing the country, I just drove back and forth in spurts. I wanna go to New York. I think I'll go to California. Back and forth and back and forth, again and again.

JOE DEROSE: The unique aspect of 241 West Fourth Street was that we were on the second floor and our windows overlooked the entrance of the building. In order to come to or leave 241 West Fourth, you had to pass right under our window. Whenever a young lady would visit us, we would say good-bye to them. Then we would get two pots of water. Bear in mind that West Fourth was probably the most traveled street in West Village. It was summertime and the place was teaming with hundreds of people. Whenever girls would leave our building, we would shower them with pots of water. They would get drenched. They would be mortified and embarrassed in front of hundreds of people. Then we would yell out, "And *don't* come back!" And slam the window shut. We got the greatest kick out of that. They wouldn't know what hit them. At the time of course we were going through a lot of girls.

BILL: I was in New York with Joe DeRose and I was ready to come back to California because I'd met a young lady out there who was an actress. She got me interested in acting. So I went to another of those car agencies. The guy said, "We have this brand-new Mercedes but it has to get to Los Angeles by next Wednesday."

"Great," I said, "I'll take it."

The guy said, "It belongs to a guy named Buddy Hackett."

I already knew Buddy Hackett from Ben Maksik's and the Concord. He didn't know me from Adam but I had actually worked as a waiter at his wedding at the Concord. Come to think of it, I also worked Eddie Fisher's wedding at Grossinger's when he married Debbie Reynolds. He didn't really know me either.

I had to have the car to Buddy Hackett by Wednesday and this was on the Saturday before. "There has to be two people driving," the guy at the agency said to me.

"No problem," I told him. "My brother's going with me. So it'll be okay."

Which was not true at all. Specifically, the guy said that Mr. Hackett's golf clubs were in the trunk and he needed them on Wednesday for a tournament starting on Thursday. So I had to drive nonstop. "No problem," I said. I was happy because to me this looked like an "in" to show business. I was supposed to take the car to Twentieth Century-Fox in Los Angeles where Buddy Hackett was filming on location. The instructions were to call him when I got there and if I made it by Wednesday, there would be a hundred-dollar bonus on top of all the gas and everything else. Ironically enough, Joe DeRose was going to be out there at the same time, staying at a friend's house.

I picked up the car and started to drive. No bennies, no nothing. I took Route 66, the southern route. I drove and I drove and I drove. Sometimes, I had to stop but I *never* got out of the car. Late Tuesday, I reached the Arizona desert and was looking for gas at five in the morning.

I pulled into a station and I remember sitting there, freezing. I looked to my left and there was the face of a full-blooded red Indian on the other side of the glass. It was so cold I did not even roll down the window. I just said, *"Fill it up,"* and then I slid the money to him through a crack at the top.

I wasn't a race car driver but in that Mercedes, I was going ninety miles an hour and it felt like nothing. I got to Needles, California, and I called the number they had given me for the studio. The secretary from the production company said, "Yes, Mr. Hackett's been waiting for the car. He's on location on a boat off Long Beach. We have the hundred-dollar bonus for you. Just leave the car here on the lot." I had gotten the car there in three days minus two hours.

I said, "No, I was given instructions to give the car *directly* to Buddy Hackett."

She was very nice. She said, "Look, Mr. Graham. These are the instructions. Just do it this way."

I hung up and then I called her back. I said, "Well, when will he be back from location?"

"I don't know," she said. "What's your number?"

She called me back and said, "One of our people just spoke to Mr. Hackett. He's very appreciative of you getting the car here but he doesn't have the time to discuss it with you now."

"Well, can't I talk to him?"

"No. Just bring us the car."

It got to be unpleasant. It was wrong of me to do what I did but I got mad. It was like I wanted a medal for driving this car cross-country nonstop in three days minus two hours. I went to visit Joe DeRose in some guy's apartment in Los Angeles. "Joe," I said. "C'mon. Get in the car." Joe got in the car. I told the guy, "If there's any trouble, here's my sister Ester's number in San Francisco." I drove Joe from Los Angeles to Carmel where we stayed in a hotel on Ocean Avenue for two or three days.

All the while, Joe kept saying, "Billy, this guy is going to *shoot* you." Buddy Hackett's golf tournament was going on but he had no clubs. We left Carmel and drove to San Francisco. I got to my sister Ester's house and she was hysterical. The guy from L.A. had called her because Buddy Hackett had called *him*. The police had gotten in touch. The car was *hot*. It was on the wire services. My sister kept telling me, "You're going to be *deported*. I'll never *see* you again. How could you *do* such a stupid thing?"

"They can't deport me," I told her. "I'm a *citizen*."

"I'm not!" she said. "Look what you're doing to *me!"*

"To *you?"* I said.

"You don't care about your sisters. You don't care about your family, you only care about yourself."

On and on and on. I was standing at the bottom of the steps and Ester just kept on punishing me. "Can I come inside?" I asked.

"No," she said.

"But it's raining."

"I don't care. How could you *take* that car?"

Joe was now really worried. He said, "You know, Billy, I'm a lawyer. And I really can't get involved with this. I'll see you later."

"Where are you going?" I said.

"To the airport." He took his bag. *Boom. Gone.*

I stayed at my sister's house that night but I knew she was wondering if she should let me. The next night, I got into the Mercedes and went right back down to Los Angeles. Not on 101. I drove on 99 through Bakersfield. I was really scared. I didn't go fast. Just nice and quiet and calm. I parked the car in an outside lot near Twentieth Century-Fox. I went to a phone booth and called a cab. When the cabbie got there, I said, "Hold on a second, willya?" I called the number I had at the studio. I said, "I'm calling on behalf of Mr. Graham. Mr. Hackett's car is now on the lot." I put down the phone, got into the cab, went to the airport, and flew back to San Francisco.

At the time, it was crucial for me to make contact with a person I thought was a heavy in the entertainment industry. Because I had decided to become a character actor and this was going to be my *in*. My first big break.

ROY EHRENREICH: I remember the Buddy Hackett car and the sense of accomplishment that he had in getting out there in two and a half days or something like that. Pulling over to the side of the road somewhere in Iowa and sleeping for an hour and then going on. He was the only person I knew who did that sort of thing. But if anybody was going to do it, he was the right one. He was the logical one.

BILL: Hitchhiking across the country, I always had great, great luck. A couple of times I froze and I got rained on because I never took a sleeping bag. Most of the time, I'd end up washing dishes at some country diner, doing the windows or washing a car for food. No begging. Someone would always let me work so I could eat a meal.

Usually, it took me between eight and ten days to get across. Sometimes, two weeks. Between 1956 and 1958, I did a lot of this. Six weeks to two months in New York and then back to San Francisco again. On one of those crossings when I hitched to New York, I just wanted to keep on going. I went down to this ship owned by the North American Steamship Company. One guy knew another guy who knew another guy who knew the steward who liked me so I got a work-away card.

I'm pretty sure it was illegal at the time but so long as I worked, I got my meals. The name of the ship was the *J. D. Olden Barneveldt*. It was a passenger ship filled with the wives of GI's going to Europe to join their husbands. I worked in the kitchen with the cooking pots. The cooking pots were bigger than the ones in the mountains. All the way from New York to Rotterdam, I scrubbed those pots with two little Brillo pads in my hands.

From Rotterdam, I took the train through Basel to La Chaux-de-Fonds where my sister Evelyn lived. From the time I left California to the time I got to her house, I spent a total of twenty-four dollars. That was it.

6.

EVELYN UDRY: When Bill came first to visit, it was in March 1957. The feeling of what it was like for me to see him after all those years, that nobody can explain. *Nobody.* I think we didn't talk for an hour. We just looked at one another. The last I have seen him, he was a little boy who was my brother, leaving us when he was seven and a half. And now all of a sudden, I see a *man.* I cannot tell you how it was. To see my brother then standing again in front of me.

At that time, he was searching for himself. I had married a man named Jean Pierre who was an architect. Bill was killing him with, "Find me something to do! Find me something to do!" So he did. Bill worked with a friend of Jean Pierre's, putting in the windows in bathrooms and staircases and everything. He stayed with us for about two and a half or three months but he could never live in Europe. He loves Europe. But he is too much American to ever stay here for good. He's got American in his *skin.*

BILL: I stayed with them for about three months in La Chaux-de-Fonds, the richest city per capita in the world. All the fancy watch factories are there. It's about a hundred and twenty kilometers north of Geneva. A beautiful area. I met a lovely lady there and they made me the unofficial assistant coach of the high school basketball team.

My brother-in-law was involved in the construction of a building and he got me a job putting window panes into the windows. Then I would do the putty. What I remember most about La Chaux-de-Fonds is how much I loved the life there. Twelve o'clock noon, everything stopped. People got on their bikes and rode home until two o'clock for lunch. The sauces, the bread.

Most of the other workers on the job were Italians. When the basic frame of this five-story building was completed, which in that small a town was a big to-do, they had a party on the top floor of this building that was still a frame. Wine and cheese and chocolate and two of these Italian workers with accordions, playing. It was probably the most emotional party I ever went to in my life. That in America—*never*.

Then I went to Vienna to see my other sister, Sonja. I took a train and Sonja said she would meet me at the station. The train slowed down coming into the station. The station was jammed with people waiting for it to arrive. Suddenly, I saw a woman jump into the air while throwing her arms up over her head. The window was open and I heard her scream. I realized that it was Sonja. She had recognized me. Now she was chasing the train. When I stepped onto the station, it was Ester all over again. Because there are times when Sonja can be like Ester times *two*. But it was nothing but pure love coming to me from her. Pure sisterly love. She was the last of my sisters that I was reunited with. It had taken me twelve years to see them all again.

Sonja and my sister Evelyn had danced together in Ballet Szobel, a troupe Sonja and her husband put together. They were the first dancers of that kind to go to Cairo and Lebanon and Casablanca. They played all the big hotels. Flamenco and tango and they were great. I stayed with her in Vienna and it was very special to be there with her.

One day, Sonja asked me if I wanted to go with her and a friend to a soccer game in Budapest. The friend was a woman named Gerda, who had been in the dance troupe with her and was now visiting Europe. Sonja told me all about Gerda. At the age of nineteen, Gerda had gone with the troupe to play the Kit Kat Club in Beirut. A man sent her flowers backstage and then came to see her. He told her up front, "I find you extremely fascinating and I would like to get to know you. I am the Minister of Construction in Iran and I have a wife and five children. But I would like to make you an offer."

After spending some time with him in Beirut, Gerda accepted the offer. She got her own home in Teheran. A seaplane. A stable of horses. Maids and valet service. Every day from noon to three, he would be with her. She had a membership at the very exclusive French club in Teheran. Everybody knew she was his mistress. Whenever he traveled outside of Iran, which was often, she would be his woman.

He told her there would be no pressure on her at all and that if she ever wanted to leave him, she was free to go. Until that time, he deposited two thousand dollars every month for her in an account in Switzerland.

She accepted the offer and then she really fell in love with him and the life. She traveled around Europe with him, wore great clothing, and went to fancy balls. When I met her she was twenty-five and she had been living with him for six years.

Gerda came to Sonja's house in Vienna. A beautiful woman with a great sense of humor, warm, jovial, and alive. She spoke English very well. We went to Budapest to see the soccer game. My sister, her husband, Gerda, and me. It wasn't so much love at first sight as, *"Oh, you like blue?* I like blue. *Three o'clock is your favorite time of day?* Me, too. *You eat carrots? You walk backward sometimes?"* It was just warm and charming. When we came back to Vienna from the game, she said, "It was so nice to be with you. What are you doing tomorrow?"

The next day, we took a walk. From the first moment I met her, she never stopped talking about her life and how wonderful her man was. We just fit together so well. For the first time in years, she saw that she could be with a man at two o'clock in the afternoon who would still be there with her at six and at nine. We even talked about it. She said, "You're *still* here." She was supposed to stay in Vienna for a week and then go meet her man in London. By this time, she had told me that she thought from time to time, he had other women. She told me that once in Teheran while he was gone, she had spent the night with another man. But that she had felt very badly about it because she was not that kind of woman.

She was there for a week and we were together day and night. But nothing intimate happened between us. No touching, no kissing, nothing. She had this beautiful apartment in Vienna. When I would leave there at three in the morning, I'd give her a formal good night kiss on the cheek, and that was it.

The night before she was supposed to leave for London, I went to her house to have dinner. She called her man in London and told him she would be staying on in Vienna a little while longer. She told him she had met someone that she found interesting and with whom she wanted to spend a little more time. She described me to him. He told her that he would meet her in Paris in a week. Then she put down the phone and turned to look at me as if to say, "Now, we're going to have an affair." It was a dream sequence that was just perfect. That night, we began the affair.

The next day, we went for a drive. She had a yellow Mercedes 220. We got into the car and drove to Lake Bismarck down to Zurich and Offenburg. She called her man again and told him that we were going away together. All along, she kept talking about how wonderful he was, how decent, how good, how bright, how charming.

We kept driving and a week later, we reached the Côte d'Azur. We drove through southern France to Toulouse and Avignon and Montpellier. We went across the Pyrenees into Barcelona and bought suede jackets. We came back and saw the Atlantic Coast. Normandy, the castles, and Mont-St.-Michel. We drove across Bordeaux. Anybody we met thought we were a young married couple.

We weren't making any plans. We were just walking through the grape fields and climbing trees. We were going to another soccer game or a mime class or to the theater. We were driving to Paris to see half a dozen films. We would be driving and stop at a hotel in the afternoon, make love, pay for the room, get back in the car, and keep on going. One day we were in St. Paul de Vence, north of Cannes, and we spent the afternoon drinking this incredible wine and watching the old men play bocce ball or *boule*, which is what they call it in France.

We had rented this little house for a couple of days that was right next to the bocce ball court. We went upstairs and kept on drinking this wine. We put two chairs by the window so we could look down at the bocce ball court and we continued to drink. It was late afternoon and very warm so we both just took off our clothes. We were totally naked. There were three empty bottles of wine standing between us. Out through the window, these seventy- and eighty-year-old guys were playing bocce. We just sat there for an hour, talking about who we were and how crazy it all was.

Then her man was going to be in Geneva. She said to me that it was time for us to meet one another. We were in Lille at the time, north of Paris, for the ballet, which she loved. We drove back to my sister Evelyn's house. Gerda came upstairs and said to Evelyn, "I love your brother. But I don't know what I'm going to do. I love this other man as well. I don't want to lose either one of them." She left me there with the understanding that I would meet her that night at the Hotel President in Geneva. First for a drink and then dinner with her man, who was visiting his sons, who were almost grown up and part of the international set.

I got all dressed up and I started to walk along the lake to the Hotel President, which took a good twenty minutes. As I was walking, I saw this scene in my mind. I was little Billy Grajonca in a suit going to the Hotel President to have dinner with my lover and her man and his three grown sons. I went to the front desk and asked for him. They called up and told me to go ahead. I got into the elevator, the guy had white gloves on. When I got off again, I realized that her man did not have a *suite* on the top floor. He had the top *floor*.

She opened the door in a yellow flare skirt, very simply cut. She kissed me on both cheeks. She was *his* woman. She wasn't mine anymore. It hit me like a bomb. She was talking away, very excited, and she got this butler to bring me a glass of sherry. I was standing by the window waiting to meet him. In perfect, perfect Oxford English, someone said, "Ah, you must be Bill." I turned around and you know who was standing there? *Yul Brynner*. A man built like a brick, in tailored pants and a shirt with no tie on. This was a guy who did like nine thousand push-ups a day. The Yul Brynner walk, the bearing. He gave me the classic line, "Gerda does not stop talking about you." Meaning of course, "It means nothing to me." He was charming, he was well educated and totally in control. I felt he was interested in me only because he wanted to see where her heart had gone.

The three of us went down in the elevator together. It felt strained. At least for me—I have to believe that they had never been through anything like this before and they were both being as charming and decent as they could. We got off the elevator and walked through the lobby to the restaurant. She was holding both of us by the arm. To myself, I thought, "This is your life, Bill Graham."

We went into the dining room. Of course, they already knew this guy. He was the big spender from Iran. At the table, the three sons are already sitting down. One was not any more handsome than the other or more dashing. They were *all* Jean-Claude Killy. they were all Robert Wagner, European-style. Immaculately dressed and regal. I was wearing a suit, so I qualified to play my part.

Then the meal began. The drinks and the aperitif and the croissant and the fondue with the dip and the fromage and the pêche and the da-da-da. The conversation went like this:

"Did you?"

"No, I have not skied in Graz this year, it's a little soft."

"I went racing. I took my two point eight to Torino but then I heard there was this new exhibition in London so I hoped to . . ."

What was I going to say? "I'm thinking of maybe going up to The Bronx to shoot some pool and then go back to my house on Eighty-sixth Street?" They weren't cutting me down. They were just really talking about *their* world. One went to school in Zurich, another in Geneva, another in Paris. They were nice kids, really. We finished eating and they had reserved a table for us in the room next door where there was music and dancing. Gerda was dying to dance. She turned to her man and said, "I would like to dance with Bill."

"Of course," he said. "Please do."

We danced. Then she danced with him and with the sons. We had a few drinks. When the night was over, I said good night to everybody. Her man said, "I hope we see you again soon, please. Do come visit us in Iran." He was most charming. Gerda said, "I'm going to walk you home."

I said, "No, no. That's okay." It was two-thirty in the morning. We left the hotel and decided to walk together.

In so many words, she said, "I can never imagine a greater, more enjoyable time with any man than we have had. You were what I was looking for before I settled for what I have."

I kept saying, "What can I give you?"

"I want to be with you," she said. "But I don't think I could live with struggle because I am now so used to this kind of life. But I *want* to be with you."

"I don't even know where I am yet," I told her.

It was a long walk and then we sat down and we talked for another half an hour. She asked me to live with her on the money he had given her, either in Paris or New York. I declined but she didn't really insist. I knew she could not live on my level. Besides that, I felt like I still had something I wanted to say. I didn't know what that was, but I *had* to say it. Not that I didn't love and care for her. I ended up walking her back to her hotel. It was about five o'clock in the morning by then. She cried. And then she resumed her role in his life.

She wrote to me many times through the years. I wrote to her. In 1968, I saw her in New York. She was still with her man. She was as beautiful as ever and still as special. She said that she still loved him and she still loved me but I never took the step. Even then, I think she would have done it and come with me. We went out and had dinner and went dancing but we did not spend the night together.

If you're asking me about the women in my life, she might have been *it*. I think she might have been the one.

Chapter Three

My Life in the Theater

1.

BILL: Whenever I'd come back to San Francisco back then, I'd stay in a guest house at 323 Locust Street. Twenty dollars a week. Pretty much three dollars a day for two meals *and* a room. I worked as a statistician and a timekeeper, going over payroll for Pacific Motor Trucking Company at 110 Market Street, right across from the Ferry Building. I had a job for a while with a division of Minnesota Mining called IWI, Insulation and Wires, Inc. For nearly a year, I was an office manager for them in San Bruno. I also had a job for a while with the Guy F. Atkinson Construction Company in Weaverville, California. I was the paymaster on a dam project.

Weaverville is west of Redding in the middle of nowhere. I lived there for about five months and it was the most insane job *ever*. It would be freezing cold in the middle of the night. By ten in the morning, it would be scorching hot. My job was to go out onto the construction site to make sure guys were really working so they could get paid. They were building the biggest earthen dam in the world. I had to go out in the field with my hard hat and climb over the hillsides and call out, "Pete here?" And some guy would answer, "Present, *asshole*." They *hated* me. They used to bribe me so they could get out of work and go into town. They'd take turns. There were supposed to be five drillers in the tunnel but one would always be gone. It was horrible work but very good money. Especially since I couldn't spend it on anything and all the meals were free.

I still had no direction. I even applied to sail around the world with Sterling Hayden. Not that I had even sailed before. It just seemed like an adventure.

I'd often see Lawrence Ferlinghetti in City Lights whenever I went in to buy books. In Washington Square, I'd see Kenneth Rexroth reading his poetry. But I didn't really know either of them well. I wasn't in the literary set. I didn't move in any circle at all. I belonged to the Jewish Community Center at California and Presidio and I used to play ball there three nights a week and go swimming. My passion at the time was a woman in her fifties named Blanche, who was the night lady five nights a week at Zim's on Eighteenth and Geary next to the Alexandria Theater.

Blanche loved my friend Bill Sample. We used to go in there after playing ball and tell her stories that were bullshit. She always gave us shakes right to the very top of the rim. Two Zimburgers, a side of fries, and a shake. With Blanche there to serve it. In those days, that was the orgasm. Especially after a winning night in the gym.

I had a girlfriend who was an actress. Through her, I started taking private acting classes from Maura Gilbert who was at the Actor's Workshop in San Francisco. It was all just relaxation and character and motivation. It wasn't until later on when I went back to New York again that I got, "The pail has water in it, you're in a hurry. No, the pail has water in it, you're in a hurry, and there's a guy behind you with a *gun!*" This was much more beginning stuff like what was the objective in a scene that had character relationships. Not so much sense memory at all.

In some ways, I had an advantage. If I wanted a facial expression, I could take one from a cabdriver I'd seen. Any time I did anything, even a small scene in class, I was very much encouraged by everyone. I played a small role in *Death of a Salesman* in Berkeley. I was the son of the guy that Willie Loman had worked for all those years. The one who tells him to go back out on the road and sell.

ISAAC AMATO: Indirectly, I think I may have gotten Bill involved with a guy called Henry Stein who was a friend in The Bronx too. Not that we knew each other all together. Henry Stein was involved in theater in San Francisco. The Improviso Theatrical Touring Company. I recall very vividly that one reason there was trouble with the company was that Bill already had his business sense and he wanted to get them organized on a sound business footing. There was a kind of competition or conflict between him and Henry Stein. It's very vivid in my mind. They didn't get along well together. They did Christopher Fry's play *A Phoenix Too Frequent.*

BILL: Henry Stein was a young director. He had a loft on Fillmore and Filbert in San Francisco in a Victorian house. He wanted to put on plays and most of the people there were students at San Francisco State. It was a struggling little company. Their hope was to play schools and maybe get an endowment. That was where I met Sandy Archer. I was working at the time and she was going to school. In the evenings and on the weekends, we rehearsed and performed. I was encouraged by her approval of me. I thought she was a huge talent.

It was a touring theater before the idea of touring theater really existed. An attempt to take plays into communities where there were no plays to be seen. We performed at the Daly City Rec Hall. A rule that was used later on in the Mime Troupe applied. If there were more people in the audience than the cast, we performed. Since we were doing small one-act plays with a very small troupe, we almost always went on with them.

RITA ROSEN: After all the good jobs he had in San Francisco, he comes to me and he says, "I don't think I want to do this."

I said, "Why?"

He said, "I want to be a movie star." Or, "I want to be in the entertainment business."

I said, "You want to be . . . ?"

I started to cry so badly that I could not even speak. I said to myself, "Here, I tried *so* hard." You know? Well, I couldn't do anything. So I had to give him the money to go to New York.

BILL: I went back to New York in '59 and took some classes with Uta Hagen. She was really decent to me and very much into the classes. I told her that my heroes were Eli Wallach and Lee J. Cobb and Nehemiah Persoff and that I wanted to work toward being a character actor. I had to audition to get into her class. I did a scene from a Christopher Fry play called *A Phoenix Too Frequent*, which I had done out in San Francisco. Then I auditioned for Paula Strasberg. I did a scene from *No Exit*. Paula said, "I would like Lee to see you." Lee Strasberg saw me and he said, "Very good. You should make a presentation for the Actors' Studio." At the time, the Studio was full up. So I never actually got in. But I did spend months going to his classes above Carnegie Hall.

In that class was Tina Louise and Richard Beymer, who later was in the movie *West Side Story*. One was worse than the other and they were both incredible. It was like watching Joan Crawford and I was the world's biggest hater of Joan Crawford's talents. Dustin Hoffman was there. I remember him being an extraordinary talent but I didn't know him.

The class was mostly improvisational and sense memory. Mr. Strasberg was very high on this. "All right. You're shaving. You're shaving. You have things on your mind. You're shaving, you have things on your mind, you're being nagged. You're shaving, you have things on your mind, you're being nagged, and you've got to scratch somewhere."

Eventually, I got fired from the class. One day, I was doing a scene sitting on a bus. That was my assignment in Improv. I was just sitting on a chair on stage, relaxed. Lee Strasberg said to me, "Relax your knee. Your right knee." So I did. "Relax your *right* knee," he said to me. I remember looking at him and saying, "How do you know my right knee is *not* relaxed?" He took great offense at this. He said, "Just relax your leg, I don't want to get in a conversation with you, Bill Graham, just relax your knee."

"It's relaxed," I told him.

We got into this whole thing and I remember standing up and saying, "Fuck you *and* your relaxed knee." Then I walked out of the room.

It was silly but it became a big stink in the class. Mr. Strasberg was an authoritarian, so talented and bright, and he adored the guru role he had at the Actors' Studio. Brando and Newman and all those people swore by him. He certainly had a talent for teaching because look at who came out of the Actors' Studio. I would also give great credit to the class itself and the other actors you met while you were there.

I went out looking for acting jobs. I did *Hatful of Rain* and *Born Yesterday*, the Broderick Crawford part, out on Long Island. I played Biff in *Death of a Salesman*. I loved the whole thing. I honestly believed I was believable onstage. I liked the interplay with the other performers. It was never just lines for me. I thought I was able to hold my own with other artists.

ROY EHRENREICH: At the time, Bill very much wanted to be successful as an actor. I saw him perform once or twice in *Hatful of Rain*. I went with some of my friends out to Long Island. I even went over lines with him at one point. He wasn't good. He was *Bill*. He wasn't the character that he was playing.

Once at the Actors' Studio, Marilyn Monroe was auditing a class that he was in. Bill nearly fell over when she came over to him at the end of the class and asked him if he would like to do a scene with her. She said, "Well, give me your phone number and I'll call you." He did and she was supposed to call at six and he waited until a quarter to seven. The phone rang and he picked it up and she said, "Bill? This is Marilyn. You know. Marilyn from *class*."

BILL: For a short time as an actor, my name was Anthony Graham. Because there was already a Bill or William Graham in the actor's book. I don't remember where I got "Anthony." It just sounded right to me. If my name had been "*Schmaltz* Graham," I still could have played certain parts.

I went looking for TV and movie roles but I didn't have the talent or whatever it was they were looking for. Rejection was very difficult for me to deal with then. It always has been. I went to see an agent with my pictures. I remember him telling me that I had a great face. I said to him, "Next you're going to tell me I should play gangsters, right?" His name was Al King. His office was on West Fifty-second Street. He was the one who first described to me the cycle of a show business career.

"Who's Rock Hudson? *Get* me Rock Hudson. Get me *a* Rock Hudson. Get me Rock Hudson. *Who's* Rock Hudson?"

I became a stand-in for Paul Burke on "Naked City," the television show. I got paid twenty-six dollars a day. Paul Burke played one cop and Horace McMahon played the other. They shot in Central Park, on the docks, and in Washington Square. In *Mad Dog Coll*, the movie, I got machine-gunned somewhere in the seventh second. They shot the movie in Brooklyn. That movie featured the only actor ever to be nominated for an Academy Award for a B-picture, Peter Falk. He played a gangster named Abe Reles.

I was also in *Breakfast at Tiffany's* but I don't think you could find me. I was an extra in that movie. And those are all my film credits from before I got started in rock and roll.

That same agent, Al King on West Fifty-second Street, said that I should go to L.A. because I had a great face and if I went to Hollywood and got a couple parts, maybe I could come back to New York and work. He said to me, "You'll work a lot in L.A. because of your face."

I said, "Well, that's not my talent."

"Yeah but that's the way it is. They want a New York cabdriver or a New York ball player, you'll get the part."

I moved to L.A. and lived on Fountain Avenue in Hollywood, right near the flea market. I got a great job in a restaurant on Rodeo Drive, thirty-five seats, a first-class French place where I delivered the greatest short performance of my life. It had just two waiters, a captain, and a maître d'. The captain, his name was Mario. He talkta like dees and he wasa vedy guuda luukinga man, he a loveda toa, how you say, fucka de weemen, he loveda life, he deed everythinga likea dat. He was the captain. But I had to be interviewed by Max.

Max was a sweat gland. He was fat and sleazy. A large moving mop inside a fat tight shirt. When I met him, he stood maybe five feet five inches tall and weighed three hundred pounds. Eugene Pallette. Remember Eugene Pallette? He *was* Eugene Pallette. Only uglier. I'd met Mario in the afternoon and he said, "You weela meet Mox, you weela nota bea friendsa."

Max sat me down. "Where have you worked before?" he asked. I told him the mountains. Of course, I had never before done *première classe*. Mario said he would cover me when it came to fileting fish and preparing chef's salads at the table. In that kind of place, the captain took the order. The waiter *schlepped*. The captain served. When he finished operating, the waiter threw away the medical instruments and moved the plate. So Mario, I could learn from.

Max asked me about the Concord. I made up that when I had visited my sister in Geneva, I had worked at the Hotel St. Moritz. I was afraid he was going to ask me what was in a *pêche flambé* or how to serve certain dishes or where you cut a duck first. But he didn't. He didn't because he didn't know himself. Of course, I didn't realize that at the time. But he did say, "Naturally, you have to speak French. I myself speak fourteen languages. Do you speak French?"

When he said that, I reared back, hit him with my glove backward, and said, *"Mais oui!"*

That delivery got me the job. You know. Like *"Shlemiel,* how could you even *ask?"*

All the stars of the day came to this place to eat. Tony Franciosa and Karl Malden and David Niven and Charles Laughton and John Cassavetes. Some of them I got to talk to. I told them I was an actor. I had a great conversation with Lee Marvin, who told me, "Hey, Billy. If I can find anything for you, I'll let you know." But nothing ever happened.

The place was closed on Saturdays and Sundays but I still pulled in somewhere between four and five hundred dollars a week. At that time, it was *very* good money. People would leave a twenty-dollar tip, which in those days was big stuff. Mario taught me everything. The guy was the *best.* A man and a woman would come in and order and he would be serving the woman but first he would look at the man and say, *"Permettez?"* Any time anyone who looked famous came in, Max would come running out of the kitchen to take their order.

One night, Trevor Howard and Marlon Brando and Eva Marie Saint were in there. Max was beside himself. This was his great moment. *Marlon Brando.* Max wrote up the order and then he decided to do all the serving. At one point, Mario turned to me and the other waiter and said, "You weel now see Mox work." They ordered roast duck. Two ducks came out. Max decided to carve. Mario would have done it like a jeweler working on a diamond. Max stabbed the duck and then started cutting it like a murderer. The knife got stuck in the breast and Max used too much strength to move it. The duck went flying off the tray onto the floor.

The table went crazy laughing. Mario had to go carve the other duck while Max hid out in the kitchen.

After Max recovered, he went back over to them again. "Sometimes, you get a duck like that," he told them. He was covering himself every way he could. "We should have used a plate with a little edge on it. They cooked the duck too well. The knife was not sharp enough." On and on and on. Through it all, they were in stitches.

For dessert, they decided to have *pêche flambé* and banana *flambé*. Max said, "I'll take it."

Mario and I set up the cart with a side tray on it for the Sterno can that provided the flame. We got the pan, the brown sugar, the caramel, the cognac, the orange twist, the peaches, and the bananas. Everything in separate plates. We wheeled out the cart so Max could do the service. Now the whole key to *pêche flambé* is that you have to put in the caramel and the sugar and the orange twist and let it simmer for a while. Then you put the cognac in and you tip the pan so that it *flambés*.

All of Max's glands were now wide open. He was sweating like mad. Mario was just standing in the corner looking like Otto Preminger at the premiere of one of his own movies. Max put everything in the pan. Not like Mario would have done it, gently against the side. With Max, it was *"Boom! Boom! Boom!"* Mario would have made a *pas de deux* out of it. Not Max. Finally, the whole thing was gurgling. But Max had put in too much sugar. He tipped the pan. No flame. It was mud. A stew. So far, so bad. Max took the cognac and poured some more in. It did not help. By now, huge pieces of peach were floating around in this bowl of mud. The pan was so full that he couldn't even tip it. He took a match and lit it and the whole thing exploded. It went up in a *huge* flame. Max crawled into the kitchen. Everyone at the table was sick from laughing. We gave them Jell-O for dessert.

An hour later, Trevor Howard asked Mario to do the dessert *right* for them. So he did. Max stayed in the kitchen. They left and gave us a *huge* amount of money. It was now two in the morning, a typical restaurant scene with the waiters sitting around, counting up their money. Max came back into the dining room. He could have gone right over to Mario and said, "Please. Teach me how to do that." Instead he said, "What a night, huh? Every once in a while, you get a duck where the knife sticks in the bone. From now on, we should make the main cut in the kitchen."

Mario did not say anything. Neither did I or the other waiter. Max went right on. "And that damn *flambé*, there's a certain balance that I *just* missed. Maybe I put in a little too much sugar, eh, Mario? What do you think?" Max was waiting on this answer like his whole life depended on it.

Mario said, "Uh, cud be, Mox. Cud be."

"The timing, eh, Mario? The timing was off from when I put in the caramel. Then I should put in the sugar and then I should have put in the cognac *before* it simmered down." Maybe. *Then* I should have. *The sugar. The caramel. The cognac.* On and on.

"May bee, Mox," Mario told him. "May bee."

Max broke. He ran over to Mario and screamed, "WHEN THE FUCK YOU GONNA TEACH ME HOW TO DO A GODDAMN FLAMBÉ?"

It was the end of Max. Mario had him forever. Just by saying, "Cud be, Mox" and "May bee, Mox." Max *never* recovered.

I worked in that restaurant for seven or eight months. I did a play in Venice to which only two reviewers came. I played Jerry in *Zoo Story* by Edward Albee. I was working and acting and taking modern dance classes. I had an agent at the Louis Scher Agency. Through Mario, I got into a poker game twice a week and I made a couple of grand and I bought myself an Oldsmobile. About five months after I got there, I got the call that ended my acting career.

They were shooting a pilot for a new TV series called "The Law and Mr. Jones" with James Whitmore. It was about a Southern attorney who decided to practice in New York City and take on a New York sidekick as his counterpart. When my agent told me about it, I said to myself, "I'm gonna get this part." When I went to read for it, there were sixty actors there. A week passed and I didn't hear anything. Another week passed and they called me back. Now there were fifteen or twenty guys there to read. Another couple of weeks passed. They cut it down to eight and I was one of them and I read again. Then they cut it down to four.

I was told that James Whitmore had final approval over who would play the part. So he read with all four of us separately and I was told that it was between me and this other guy. By this time, everybody knew I was going to get the part. But they couldn't make up their minds so they decided to film a scene with me and Whitmore, and one with Whitmore and the other guy. This was a network television job, full-time. I called my agent every day to find out what happened. One day, he called me and said, "Bill, come on down to the office."

I went there. I said, "You got news?"

He said, "I got to level with you. The other guy got the job."

"Good for him," I said. "But there *has* to be a reason. I know I read well."

"You did," he said.

"So what's the reason?"

"Let's go take a walk," he said.

"Just tell me now. What are you afraid of? I'm going to break furniture?"

And the guy said, "Yeah, I am. I know you're temperamental."

I said, "If you won't tell me till we get outside, let's go."

We went out in the parking lot and the guy said, "I know other times they told you that you were too tall or too thin or too New York. But this time you had it. You had the goods."

"So what was it?"

"I'll give it to you in the words of the people who made the decision. When they looked at footage of you and the lead actor, it was decided that your physiognomy played too strong."

"Excuse me?" I said. I had no idea what the word meant.

"Your face, Bill," he said. "Your face."

He was telling me that I'd been penalized for something over which I had no control. The way I *looked*. That was when I quit acting, right then and there. I handed in my notice to Mario. Maybe two days later, I left L.A.

I went back to New York and hooked up with a guy I'd known from The Bronx who wanted to go motorcycling through Europe. We went from New York to Lisbon and then to Gibraltar and then to Genoa. He bought a motorcycle there and I got to use one that belonged to his friend. It was an English bike, a Vincent Black Shadow. Together, we rode to Verona and Trieste, up to Lake Como and Locarno. The guy I was with just wanted to keep going but I stopped in Geneva to stay with my sister Evelyn and her husband.

Over the next year, I just bummed around Europe. I spent time in Valencia and Madrid and in Paris. It wasn't a good period. I was thirty years old and depressed. I knew I wanted to do something but it wasn't sitting behind a desk. If you paint or write or if you're a performer or an actor, at least you earn your way in this world doing what you're good at. You express your inner emotions through your talent. Your vocation and your avocation come together. It may not always be easy but when you do succeed at it, that's what you *chose* to do. But for me, it didn't work.

It was obvious to me what I could *not* do. I never thought of being a writer or trying to make it as an athlete. But I did want to be more than a waiter or a cabdriver. Doing that wasn't creative enough. It wasn't always enjoyable.

For a year and a half, I had been totally into acting and now I was lost. I really thought I had the ability. But what I didn't have was patience. Maybe I didn't have the talent either. But if you look at some famous actors, you wonder, "How did *they* ever get there?" In order to make it, I would have had to have been much more determined. Maybe it was just not my calling to begin with.

2.

BILL: I kind of drifted back through New York and then out to San Francisco where I got a job working as an office manager for Allis-Chalmers, a company that manufactured heavy equipment. For the time, I was getting paid a lot of money, twenty-one thousand dollars a year with a bonus. I was their regional office manager, responsible for San Francisco, Seattle, L.A., and Denver. They were an international concern that made hydraulic equipment, trucks, and conveyor belts.

One of my jobs at Allis-Chalmers was to hire and fire secretaries. An employment agency sent over a young lady named Bonnie Maclean that I interviewed. They called me up afterward and said, "What do you think?" I said, "No, no, she won't do." A few days later, Bonnie Maclean herself called me and said, "You told the agency you couldn't use my services. Could you tell me why? What qualifications *didn't* I have?"

I stopped and I thought about it. Then I said, "I'm sorry. I have to tell you the truth. You were wearing the ugliest chartreuse coat I ever saw in my whole life." She laughed. I said, "Would you mind coming in again?"

She did and I hired her. Then we started dating, which was taboo. A few months after that, I met a friend of mine in San Francisco down where we were both working on Market Street. He said, "What's new? Are you seeing anybody?"

I said, "I just got a lady."

"Oh yeah?" he said. "What's she like?"

Without batting an eyelash, I looked at him and I said, "She wears glasses."

That was my whole description of Bonnie. Where I came from, wearing glasses was like being a four-eyes. Like, Jesus, where was that at? For me to say that, it was like saying, "She's got something more. She's special. That's not *all* there is to it. *She wears glasses.*"

Bonnie was *awesome*. Our early social life together revolved around me keeping my motor scooter together. It was a 1956 Lambretta. An antique that just refused to die. But that was the way Bonnie and I got around for years. She was always on the back seat of that thing in the wind.

Even while I was at Allis-Chalmers, I was still going out all the time in San Francisco to see shows and I was still interested in the theater. Back in the Improviso troupe, I'd met Sandy Archer while doing Christopher Fry's *A Phoenix Too Frequent*. She was the link that got me to the Mime Troupe.

The Mime Troupe was tough going. Driving the truck down to Palo Alto and putting up the posters and selling the tickets. Taking the show down and then reloading the truck. I'd get home at 2 A.M. and bitch to Bonnie about the world and she would have something for me to eat. She was the ongoing receptacle for all the mania at the end of the day. Whatever was going on in my mind, I had to bounce it off somebody and Bonnie was always there.

RONNY DAVIS: We were getting bigger at the Mime Troupe and Sandy Archer said, "Why don't you try *this* guy?" I met him, we talked. We had this classic moment where we talked and talked and I ate all his chopped liver while he was in the back. I got along with him, no problem. And I needed a guy like him. I saw him dancing once. That's another connection we had. Which is we both dance Latin. It comes from the Borscht Belt. He worked in the same hotels I did. My brothers worked at Grossinger's, I worked at the Concord. As a busboy and as a waiter and a hotel clerk and all that shit. I mean, that's where you worked.

PETER BERG: What was incredible was that it wasn't the sixties yet. You know, 1965 wasn't the sixties yet. The day I walked into the low-rent space the Mime Troupe had rented in this church on Capp Street, which has long since been demolished, I had on a three-button suit. This play by Nina Serrano, Saul Landau's wife, was being rehearsed. I walked in raw, with no idea of what I was looking at.

I went into this tiny office that Ronny Davis had and there was Bill Graham. And if I looked funny in a three-*button* suit, this guy was wearing a three-*piece* suit. He was really just straight New York. New York fifties, not the sixties. The *fifties*. He was a very on-the-make organization man. Identifiable to me from people I would see on the train in New York. On the subway. He had the look and all the pauses and timing of a corporate junior officer.

Ronny I saw right away was a radical. A 100-percent full-bore, out-there, mad-and-frustrated art type. At the time, his résumé did not match with anything in the United States. Student of a mime master in France. Jewish and from Brooklyn. He was like a Cuisinart Special. I mean, a really bizarre case. But I liked him. And I did not like Graham. Graham reminded me of business people from New York. I thought he was Wall Street. A yuppie *before* there were yuppies. From his whole come-on. His whole thing.

Ronny said, "We're going to do a commedia in the park. Based on *Il Candelaio* by Giordano Bruno. It was a five-act play, either a fifteenth- or sixteenth-century piece of theater. "Can you transliterate it into a three-

act commedia?" It was like, "This will be your test." Ronny just handed
me the assignment and I went home and started writing.

3.

PETER BERG: The Mime Troupe moved into a loft at Fifth and Howard.
And I don't know what they looked like to Graham. But to me, it looked
like Wino Alley. It was an art group in Wino Alley. To me, it was
incredibly romantic and beautiful. I've just confessed something about
my own character that it appealed to me to have to wade through the
winos to go up to a place where people were talking about Artaud and
Brecht. This was pretty sensational. As good as the Lower East Side.
From my point of view.

Up the stairway was a large loft that was big enough for at least two
rehearsal spaces. Then a costume area behind it. Then you went left to
the offices of this New Left group. The second office was the Mime
Troupe. There was a desk by the door that became my desk and then
another desk farther along. Sandy Archer or Rob Hurwitt. And then the
desk in back was Graham's desk. Who carried out his role at the
telephone like he was Patton. As though it was blood and guts, you know?

JIM HAYNIE: I got hired by Ronny Davis to be technical director of the
Mime Troupe after a performance they did on the campus of UC-Davis. I
slept on a mattress in the back of their loft for the first week I was in San
Francisco and got crabs immediately. The loft was right behind the
Chronicle building. SDS shared the floor in a room next door. I discovered
Bill sitting three feet from Ronny. He had a nameplate on his desk that
said, "Sol Hurok." There was an aisle between their desks and they sat
at the back end of the office and yelled at each other all day long. At the
top of their lungs. And if you know Bill Graham, you know roughly how
loud that can get.

They yelled about anything. They disagreed about *everything*. In fact,
they are opposite signs in the Zodiac, Ronny being a Cancer and Bill a
Capricorn. Bill was also an entirely different sort of horse in that he
didn't take part in politics at all. He was just interested in getting the
shows on and so forth. In a way, I leaned more toward him. Because we
would have these meetings where guys would stand up and say, "What
are we? We're *Communists!* We're *fuckin'* Communists, *right?* We're
radicals!" It would go on for *hours*. Troupe meetings didn't have much to
do with shows or anything. They were like these ideological discussions.

One guy would just try to out-radical the other. One would say, "You
know, you're just a fuckin' bourgeoise *pig*." All the lingo of the day would

come out. They were Ronny's meetings, basically. Bill never went. If he did, he would leave early.

ROBERT SCHEER: It was important to Ronny to be radical. Whereas I never got the feeling that it was important to some of the others of us there. That was not the thing. We were radical in the sense that if you knew the government was full of *schmucks* and they did the wrong thing, then you took a radical position.

RONNY DAVIS: We operated as efficiently as we possibly could. First of all, you're doing three things at once. You're trying to survive with no money. You're trying to be antiestablishment and also you're trying to create something new artistically. Not just do crappo Left Culture or liberal culture. You're trying to invent new material. Art forms as well as new venues and not be capitalist. Not knowing what that is. So what is that but chaos?

PETER COYOTE: I went out to the Mime Troupe and they had the two most beautiful women I had ever seen in my life. Sandy Archer and Kay Hayward. In one place. And I said, "*This* is what I want to do with my life." I walked into the office and Sandy was behind a typewriter typing. It was like walking in and there's Kim Basinger. I was so self-conscious that I immediately turned all my attention to Ronny. He asked me some question about Marshall McLuhan. Well, I had been dating Marshall McLuhan's daughter along with reading him and I knew him *cold*. I just took off and Ronny and I got into one of these passionate, involved, intellectual conversations. Sandy just kept right on typing away. After it was over, Ronny turned to her and said, "What do you think of this guy?" She said, "He talks a lot."

The next time I came in there, I had on a suit. I met John Robb, who was their hot actor, and he was there in a pair of long red underwear with half a Pall Mall stuck behind his ear. He looked me up and down and said, "Pretty rich for the Mime Troupe."

Within a month I was performing. Within three months, I was directing. You could go as far and as fast in the Mime Troupe as you could. Peter Berg was there. Emmett Grogan was there. Kent Minault. Bill Linden. Jim Haynie. Ronny had a genius for being the nucleus of an amazing concatenation of people and events. He was a great inspiration and teacher to me.

I come from the same sort of thing as Ronny. Lefty Jewish intellectuals. My background is also Commie Jew Reds. But at a certain point, I didn't have any money coming from home and I'd come in an hour late to rehearsal because I was trying to save my pad and somehow pay the rent and I'd get a revolutionary speech, you know, because I was getting paid five bucks a day for a seventy-hour week in the Mime Troupe. It just didn't wash, you know? Eventually Ronnie burned everybody out.

PETER BERG: If I wrote something and it got produced and performed, I would get five dollars a day as the writer. Everybody got five dollars a day. We were all art slaves. Absolute art serfs.

JUDY GOLDHAFT: I taught dance classes, Sandy Archer did acting classes. I remember doing some kinds of classes with Bill. What I recall about them is that he was not real good at them. And he did less and less. He came as an actor and he found that there was no business manager, really. And that was something that needed to be done. And he spent more and more time in the office. I remember at one meeting his saying that nobody ever talked to him when they came into the office. He complained about it. I remember making an effort to make sure that I always said good morning to him when I went into the office because he just would have felt somewhat left out. But in fact, he was very quiet and not very outgoing toward people while at the same time feeling that people weren't relating to him very much.

ROBERT SCHEER: At the time, Bill was not slick. Bill was a *haimishe* guy. You did not think of him as some sharpie even though he knew about box offices and tickets and promotion. The way I was introduced to Bill Graham was that this was the guy who was going to do all the stuff for the Mime Troupe that no one else wanted to. Sell more tickets and promote the thing. Really, it was kind of a thankless shift.

PETER BERG: Bill was *very* worried. That's what I remember him as. Recently, I just came back from the East Coast. Someone asked me, "What were the people there like?" And I said, "Well, there's this certain bunch of them that practice worrying as a *way*." The *path* of worrying. And this had nothing to do with being Jewish or anything else. It just had to do with being anxious. Terribly anxious. When you looked in his eyes, all you saw were crossed paths. Just danger. It was like, "I don't know what I'm doing but I'm doing a *lot* of it." And he was also very subdued. I think he had made a life change that people around him didn't know about. They didn't know he had stepped out of the groove. But he still wore everything that belonged to the groove. As insurance, or whatever. He looked like he was worried about the stock prices that day.

At the beginning, he was a life preserver. Absolutely. Because who had any sense running the Mime Troupe? Nobody did. Bill acted as though he did. Other people talked, he listened. He was dutiful. An organization man. But he really looked desperate and incompetent. That was the Bill Graham I met the day I came into the Mime Troupe.

At any rate, I went home. I wrote this thing and brought it in. People began rehearsing it. I had never done this before. I mean, I had *never* done this. I mean, I just *walked* in. I really did. Just walked in the door and it was *go*. It was going to happen.

BILL: What was most obvious and what lured me to these people was that they were involved with an attempt at making changes in the society. They weren't just actors. They weren't just trying to earn their way as performers. They were expressing their problems with society through theater by taking *commedia del l'arte* and updating the dialogue to relate to the strife of the day, be it the Vietnam War or civil rights. They were really the first radicals I had ever met, in the sense of using theater as a public platform to make a statement about what was going on in the world.

It didn't take long for me to realize that we were all misfits in a sense. But they were misfits *and* activists as well. Social political activists. Ronny Davis was not looking so much for people with acting talent as those who could express their anger and their *angst* on the stage. I had great respect for him for that and great admiration as well. He looked for people who were involved and aware first of all. He felt he could teach them how to perform in time. But he couldn't teach them how to be involved from the *heart*. That had to already be there at the start.

I remember when they began doing *Il Candelaio*, The Candle Bearer," by Giordano Bruno, in masks and costumes that were outrageous. Everything was overplayed. The play had to be rewritten so they could reach out to the street people in their own language. Stuff like, "Hey, you can't piss on the cops, man," and *"Fuck you,* I can say what I want." They changed the original dialogue to suit the times.

RONNY DAVIS: We were opening *The Minstrel Show* at the same time as we were doing this arrest in the park. People didn't quite know who we were because we were doing this most radical production of *The Minstrel Show* and then we were doing the thing in the park. They said, "You're cursing a lot." "No, we are not cursing." We never cursed in the park. In fact, I had ACLU lawyers come in to look at the show that Peter Berg wrote to see if it was obscene. And they said, "Well, you know, it's a little vicious. But there's no obscene words."

I said, "We're never going to say any of those words." I mean, no way.

But somebody would pull their pants down or Luis Valdez would do a number. By no means did we say curse words. We knew that was too simple. That's another myth. That we were saying curse words in the park.

PETER BERG: Obscene. Lenore Kandell's book was obscene. Lenny Bruce was obscene. *The Beard* by Michael McClure was obscene. This was the new "obscene" thing. But Ronny said we were going to do it anyway. He said, "This will make a great political act even if we can't perform the show. It will say a lot. Besides, we're defiant. Let's see what happens. Let the thunder break." So we showed up in Lafayette Park by the Russian embassy. And we set things up and the police started coming. People got into costume and then Ronny told Luis Valdez, "Give me your costume." Ronny bumped him from the part so he could play it himself.

JUDY GOLDHAFT: We didn't want Luis to get arrested. Ronny wanted to take the bust.

CHET HELMS: I was in an apartment somewhere over in the Mission. I forget where but I remember Phil Lesh was there. All these guys had gone to a meeting of the Mime Troupe because the Mime Troupe was going down the tubes. A meeting about financial difficulties and what they were going to do about it. At Graham's instigation, they made a conscious decision to go into the park and get busted. I felt that it was wrong to provoke a political confrontation for purely financial reasons. But it did get attention.

JUDY GOLDHAFT: The thing is, yes, it was discussed beforehand that we would get busted. The media was invited. Ronny said, "Even if they bust me, we're going to do the play anyway. We'll have scripts there." A number of people had volunteered just in case they were going to bust us. They would then read the play to the audience.

PETER BERG: We all talked privately in meetings that it would be a good thing to have happen. Because it was provocative. It got attention.

BILL: The bust in Lafayette Park was my first taste of ultimate theater. Human, one-take, live confrontation with the cops. Ronny was actually onstage where he got arrested. We were banned from the park and the San Francisco Arts Festival.

I remember running around like a madman trying to raise money for

Bill's mother and father—the only known picture.

Bill at the age of eight—his first identification card, Nazi war eagle and swastika included.

Tolla and Bill standing in front of (left to right) Evelyn, Sonja, Ester, and their mother.

Roy, Alfred, and Pearl Ehrenreich with Bill and Fluffy, their dog, 1942.

HIAS Finds Refugee in Bronx

Through the efforts of HIAS, the Hebrew Sheltering and Immigrant Aid Society, William Grajonca, who escaped from Germany through France in 1939 and reached New York in 1941, will soon be reunited with two sisters still in Europe. William is a student at Macombs Jr. H.S. 82. He has been living with Mr. and Mrs. Alfred Ehrenrich, 1635 Montgomery Av.

A clipping from the *Bronx Home News*, dated October 28, 1946.

With the wonderfully named Joyce Fliegler,
The Bronx, 1948.

Getting ready to ship out to fight a war he
never really understood.

Bill and Alice in Brooklyn in a car with the top, as always, down.

With his great kitchen mentor, Charlie, who had only "to look at you and your potatoes were mashed."

The immortal picture (from a magazine called *TV Fan*)—Bill at Grossinger's (note the script *G* on his lapel) with Eddie Fisher, the greatest Jewish pop idol of the day.

Looking very suave, with Gerda in Europe.

In the Mime Troupe loft. Luis Valdez stands in the foreground, Ronny Davis behind him, Sandy Archer is seated at the table. [Erik Weber]

Bill with Mime Troupe members just before the arrest of Ronny Davis for performing in the park without a permit, Lafayette Park, August 7, 1965. [Erik Weber]

S.F. MIME TROUPE
WILL HOLD AN
'APPEAL' PARTY
924 HOWARD STREET (BETWEEN 5ᵗʰ & 6ᵗʰ STS.)
SAT. NIGHT — NOVEMBER 6
FROM 8 P.M. TILL DAWN

Entertainment, Music, Refreshments! **DONATION: AT LEAST $1⁰⁰** *Engagement, Commitment & Fresh Air!*

R. G. Davis, director of the San Francisco Mime Troupe, was found guilty on November 1 of performing in the public parks without a permit. The four-day trial was pointless because the court did not allow the only relevant issue, freedom of speech and assembly, to be considered.

The trial settled nothing. The Mime Troupe is determined to fight until the parks are returned to their only "owners," the people of San Francisco.

For this is what it is all about: Who owns the parks? Chairman Walter Haas and his fellow members of the Recreation and Parks Commission? They apparently think so, for they revoked the troupe's permit on the grounds the Mime Troupe's commedia dell'arte production of "Il Candelaio" was not in "good taste" or "suitable" for "their" parks. The troupe defied the ban to test a constitutional issue: the commission's power to interfere with free expression. Then Municipal Judge FitzGerald Ames ruled that the commission's revocation power was "a matter of law" and not for the jury to decide. Thus the commission's powers were not allowed to be contested, and Davis was found guilty.

The only legitimate purpose for issuing permits is to schedule events properly — preventing time or place conflicts. The contents of performances is not a matter for the commissioners to judge. And Walter A. Haas's idea of good taste is NOT a "matter of law"!

There are adequate laws to handle any crime committed in the parks. Was the Mime Troupe accused of being disorderly? No. Of creating a public nuisance? No. Of obscenity? No. It was banned because it did not conform to the commissioners' standard of "good taste" (whatever that may be). If the commissioners believe the troupe violated any law, then let them charge the troupe with a violation of that law.

WHO OWNS THE PARKS? The people of San Francisco. The parks are very large and there is room for us all -- room for any expression of any idea. Freedom of speech and freedom of assembly do not stop where Mr. Haas's good taste begins.

What is the effect of the commission's action and the court's failure to confront the issue? Our freedoms are lessened, for when one means of expression is cut off, who knows what will be next? The 20,000 persons who enjoyed the troupe's free park performances in the past four years will no longer have that opportunity, thanks to the "good taste" of six commissioners.

THE CREATIVE LIFE OF SAN FRANCISCO IS NOW DIMINISHED AND THE PARKS ARE CONSIDERABLY LESS JOYFUL.

The following artists will appear at the APPEAL PARTY on behalf of the San Francisco Mime Troupe:

JEANNE BRECHAN	THE FAMILY DOG	JOHN HANDY QUINTET	JIM SMITH
SANDY BULL	LAWRENCE FERLINGHETTI	JEFFERSON AIRPLANE	ULLETT & HENDRA
THE COMMITTEE	THE FUGS	SAM HANKS	& OTHERS WHO CARE

FOR FURTHER INFORMATION, CALL GA. 1-1984

The handbill for the first Mime Troupe benefit, November 6, 1965.

New Year's Eve 1966 at the Fillmore. From left to right: Phil Lesh, Marty Balin, Jerry Garcia, Pigpen, and John Cipollina. [BGP Archives]

The San Francisco rock establishment, circa 1966. From front to back: Danny Rifkin, manager of the Grateful Dead; Ron Polte, manager of the Quicksilver Messenger Service; Rock Scully, co-manager of the Dead; Julius Karpen, original manager of Big Brother and the Holding Company; Bill; and Bill Thompson of the Jefferson Airplane. [Jim Marshall]

At the top of the stairs in the original Fillmore. [Jim Marshall]

Bill and Janis, face to face, Speedway Meadows, Golden Gate Park, May 1967. [Grant Jacobs]

our defense. Marvin Stender was working for free, with Marshall Krause from the ACLU helping, but there were still court expenses. The benefit was my idea. Just out of desperation in order to raise some money.

4.

BILL: The first appeal party, November 6, 1965, was, is, and will always be by far the most significant evening of my life in the theater. We needed to raise funds. What I really wanted to do with the fund-raiser was keep it in the focus of the people downtown.

The bust had put us on the map with everyone. The man in the street and not just the small percentile of people who were in the political arena of life. We made up these handbills advertising the appeal for Saturday night. On the Friday before, I made arrangements to rent a Cadillac convertible.

We put an announcement for the event on a banner made of canvas on both sides of the car. We took the actors and actresses, Ronny, and Sandy Archer and all in costume from *Il Candelaio* and had them sit in the back end of the car while we had a parade downtown. On Market and Montgomery Street.

I'd told the police up front what we were doing and they said, "If you have that parade and you hand out papers, article nineteen, section forty-four, you cannot distribute leaflets unless you pick them up." "We'll pick them up," I told them. "If not, you bust us. You bust us downtown handing out leaflets for the bust benefit." We had three cars with the last car being the Cadillac filled with actors and actresses and we went down Market Street at noon, hitting everybody with pamphlets.

Sandy Archer and Ronny would get out of the car and stop on a corner for five minutes and talk to the public, most of whom were working people on their lunch break. It was very effective. Of course that night, we were on the five o'clock news.

The appeal itself represented the artistic community coming together. Before, they'd never really been under the same roof at once. If you went to a poetry reading, you'd see Lawrence Ferlinghetti. If you went to a jazz club, you'd hear John Handy. The Jefferson Airplane were working at a club called The Matrix. Not that I really knew any of these people then. I didn't. Because I wasn't in the scene yet. I didn't hang out with any of them. I certainly wasn't in the same circle.

For that night, we built a stage at the near end of the loft so we could play into the room. We put up some lights that we owned. I took a piece of four-by-eight sheetrock and I stood it up on the short end at the top of the stairs leading into the loft. I had one of the illustrators in the Mime

Troupe draw this up, and then I got it printed and I put the printed sheet on the sheet rock. It said, "If you earn $12 a week and you live within the city, a dollar's okay. If you earn more than $14 a week and you have less than one child, $1.93," and on and on. It was like a menu. Finally, it got to, "If you live outside the area and you have two cars, it should be $4.03." The highest amount we would take from anyone was $48. That was on the bottom. A couple of people actually gave us $48.

We also put the word out. Anything you want to bring, *bring*. Any statement or artistic expression you want to make, *fine*. A lot of people said, "Hey, I'm gonna come? I'm gonna bring a stalk of bananas. I'm gonna bring ten pounds of grapes." People brought things to us and we hung them in the loft. Although sometimes we would rent the loft out to light show artists, I had never before gotten involved with them. Guys said to me, "Can I hang my bed sheet ahead of time?"

"What are you talking about?" I asked.

"My bed sheet," they would say. "My screen." They called themselves "Liquid projectionists."

"Excuse me?" I would say.

"I have plates and I have liquids. And I travel."

Guys came up during the day of the benefit with loops of eight-millimeter film hanging around their necks. They had their bed sheets and their eight-millimeter cameras.

"Hello, I'm Louis B. Mayer."

They'd look around and say, "Can I have *that* corner?"

"Okay."

Then another guy would come up with slides. The only advertising we did was handbills. We got thousands of them printed for free. Maybe the total cost of the whole benefit going in was a thousand dollars. For the car rental and the banners and alcohol. I called all the "liberal" merchants who sold me cases of vodka for cost. We lined six huge steel drums with aluminum wrap and filled them with gallons and gallons of vodka and orange juice and threw in grapes and bananas and whatever. We offered it as punch. For a donation at the door. Once you got inside, no money. I didn't want anyone to use money. I always had this feeling about going to a hundred-dollar-a-plate dinner and then they would charge you for a drink. So I wanted it to be free once you were inside.

ROBERT SCHEER: The night of the first benefit, Bill and I went for a chopped liver sandwich at David's. We always ate at places like David's. I was on the back of his motor scooter. What was it, a Vespa or a Lambretta? We went to get this chopped liver sandwich and I remember talking at dinner because we were worried that *no* one would show up.

That was the main thing. We had absolutely *no* idea whether this thing would work and it was considered a very wild idea to have groups play in order to try and get a big crowd.

Anyway, we ate. Then we got back on the motor scooter and drove over to the loft on Howard Street. I had already been in Vietnam by this time and I had come back and done a series of lectures about it at the Presidio Hill School for the San Francisco Opposition and I had spoken to the Mime Troupe as well. I don't know if I was touring with them yet. I might have been. I remember very clearly that we did not know whether this thing would be a bust or if anyone would be there. We had put on things before that no one came to. It wasn't like anybody including Bill had the magic touch. Up to that point, I believe a number of his schemes for raising money for the operation of the Mime Troupe had in fact failed. I remember scenes where Bill would be saying, "I'm trying to sell this thing and get people into a theater and you bastards want to make it hard on me." So anyway, this was the big test for him, I think.

Anyway, we pull around there and the fucking line is going around the building. It wasn't just hot. It was *incredible*. It wasn't like five or six people. It was this fucking *line*. People were all around. We were saying things like, "*Wow! Wow!*" Then Bill turned around on the motor scooter and said to me, "*This* is the business of the future." I'll never forget that.

As we went in, there were people on line who were teenagers and they would shout, "Can you get me in?" People who never were interested before and didn't know what we were doing. Who were nonpolitical. A lot of clean-cut kids from Marin County whose fathers worked for the phone company and whose mother was the dean of a college. *They* were standing in that line. Suddenly, they were going to make a transition.

BILL: People lined up in the street for the party. Huge hoards of people. Thousands of them. Legally, the loft held maybe six or seven hundred. I'd say we had fifteen hundred in there at one time. It was this cross section of people who had *never* come together before. A mixed group. It was amazing. In San Francisco, you could turn over seventeen different parts of the city and the worms under each rock would represent one neighborhood. That night, all the worms got into one pot.

It wasn't psychedelic yet. There was a little weed but nothing heavy. But I saw things that were firsts all night long. I saw people come in and instantly start dancing with other people and only then did I realize that they didn't know each other. They just started dancing. I'd never seen that before. It was like instant cousin-ship. They became a one. It was like when you look under a microscope at protoplasm. All the cells were touching and bubbling at once. That night, they were *all* in the play. It was theater-in-the-round.

Sandy Bull played that night and he was *magnificent*. All by himself on a twelve-string guitar. The Fugs were great. So was John Handy. So was the Airplane. Ferlinghetti read in front of John Handy, and they were great.

Let me give you proof of my lack of knowledge about the scene. A couple of weeks before the event, a guy called and said, "I'm with a group called the Family Dog and we're into rock and roll. We're involved with music." But they weren't too specific. I said, "Well, you're welcome to come up. Do you want to be involved?" And the guy said yes. So that night, when Chet Helms showed up, I asked him, "Where are the dogs?" This is true. That was why I listed them on the program. I thought they were a dog act.

CHET HELMS: Bill never let the truth get in the way of a good story. He did not meet me until after the first Mime Troupe benefit. There were several early contacts between Luria Castell and Alton Kelley of the Family Dog Collective and those people at the Mime Troupe and Graham. The night of the Mime Troupe benefit, I was across town at Longshore-men's Hall seeing the Mothers of Invention and somebody or another, booked by the Family Dog. They were his competitors. Basically, they knew it was a fledgling little scene and they went to him well in advance of both dates. They were already locked into a contract and he was just beginning to say, "Well, maybe we're going to do this on this date." They asked him to take a date a week or so later so they wouldn't go head-to-head. Because everyone felt the market here was pretty limited. He refused to do that. At the time, they offered to produce a benefit for the Mime Troupe and suggested the old Fillmore as a cheap and available venue.

There were a lot of people at Longshoremen's Hall as well that night. But they had to pay performers and promotion costs and all that stuff. They either broke even or lost money. Lost money, I would guess.

PETER BERG: I think he was making a transition from the fifties to the sixties. And his epiphany was the first benefit we had. The man actually changed religions. I mean, he changed *identities*. I saw that Bill Graham melt. And a new Bill Graham be born at the first benefit. There were four thousand people trying to get in a space that held five hundred. So Graham writing signs like "No Inzy-Outzy" was a little bizarre. We were talking about a cultural revolution going on. Truly. Not minor. *Grand.*

Those Mime Troupe benefits were the towering cultural events leading to the Haight-Ashbury.

He ran around like, "Don't let him in, don't let *them* in. They don't have tickets? *Fuck* him." You know. Throw water on their heads. Keep them out. On the other hand, you would say, "Uh, Bill? What do you think is going on?" And he would say, *"Absolutely amazing!"* I think it was his LSD.

RONNY DAVIS: I was in Sausalito and I came back and I saw him collecting the money at the door. He had a green sack under his arm and he was collecting one-dollar bills and he was stuffing them in that green sack. Climbing over people, sort of in a little bit of a hysterical state. Slightly hysterical about collecting this money because there were *so* many coming.

BILL: I had my clipboard and I was rushing around checking on the back door and the front door and asking, "Is there enough ice?" And "Are the ashtrays clean?" The highlight of the night for me came when we literally couldn't get any more people in there. They were all lined up down the block, waiting to get in. At about eleven o'clock, a police sergeant came up the front stairs. Someone came up to me and said, "Bill, there are four cops here and they want to shut the place down."

The sergeant asked me if I was in charge. I told him I was. He said, "Where's your permit?" The next thing he said was, "You *have* to close it down."

I remember getting into a dialogue with this guy and I couldn't bend him. He said, "First of all, it's a fire trap."

"Jeez," I said. "I don't know about that. We're on the second floor here and we've got the elevator in the back and the stairs in the front." Then I started saying, "This is the Mime Troupe, Sergeant. They've been suppressing our rights and we're here to stop that."

"It's *much* too crowded here," he told me. "There's much too much smoking going on, and it's a hazard, and you got to close it down."

I remember saying, "The big problem is that Rudy Vallee's flying in from L.A. and Sinatra's coming in from Vegas. After they finish their regular gigs, they're coming in late to work for us. You *got* to let us stay open. Ask some of the people to leave. But don't shut it down."

I wasn't getting anywhere. He said, "Look, they're smoking and . . ."

"Hold on," I said. I went over to the microphone and I said, "The officer's here and what he says is right. We have to be concerned about one another. Please don't smoke anymore." I went back to him and I said, "Now, what else?"

"That's not good enough," he said.

"What else do you want me to tell them?" I asked.

I went through this whole game with him and I wasn't getting anywhere. Finally, I looked straight at him and I said, *"Captain . . ."* When I said "Captain" instead of "Sergeant," his chest expanded, his voice changed, and he said, "All right now, *son.* Let's see how we can work this out. They've got to stop smoking and some people have to leave. When they do, you can't let any more in. I'm going to put two men on the downstairs door. Since you're waiting for Mr. Vallee and Mr. Sinatra, I'm gonna trust you on this, *son."* And he left.

Soon as he left, we asked the two cops downstairs if they wanted to have a drink. We got them plastered in about twelve minutes. Meanwhile, we were directing people up through the freight elevator in the back. Forty at a time, *boom.* We ended the night at about 6:30 or 7 A.M. with Allen Ginsberg and Peter Orlovsky leading the crowd in changing their mantras. The place was still 90 percent full.

It was a revelation. Not just for me. For everybody.

That night, we *all* found each other.

5.

BILL: We had raised forty-two hundred dollars. When it ended, we just sat around for a while talking about this miracle. That morning when I left, I went to my regular pit stop. Mel's Drive-In on Geary and Arguello. It was open twenty-four hours a day. I had this Army pack with a strap that I would sling over my back so I could ride with it on my scooter. I put the forty-two hundred dollars in it so I could take the money home for safekeeping. That was when I first got into the habit of taking the sack and throwing it into what would be my seat from ten feet away. I didn't know that night was the beginning of anything. But I knew it was the most exciting experience of my life.

RONNY DAVIS: In the first benefit, we raised a certain amount of money. I don't remember what. We were supposed to pay Marvin Stender, our lawyer. We never paid Marvin Stender. Even though we had all this money. The first benefit was dancing, the art crowd. In the second benefit, we went even further.

PETER BERG: Graham started opposing the politics of the Mime Troupe. Because he knew there was a new market. And he dove into it. I don't blame him for this. He was a genius about it. Of all the Mime Troupe people at the time, history might say he was the most remarkable. I mean, the first benefit had been his acid experience. I saw his eyeballs. His eyes changed. And he softened in one regard and he hardened in another. He softened in regard to weirdness. Before it, he thought weird people were weird. Like *"On guard!"* He was the organization man about weirdness. He softened down immediately. Weird people were *good* all of a sudden. And he hardened in dropping the content of what we were doing. The content was *not* good.

There was a crucial meeting between the first and second benefit. Where he suddenly said, "All the political pretensions that you're involved with *suck*." He said, "Look, you're asking me as business manager to provide you with nickels and dimes. And I can do *thousands*. There's a funnel here. I saw it." And the second benefit was his. And he was into it. And that made him Fillmore Bill. He became Fillmore Bill at that benefit.

BILL: After the first one, we got hundreds of phone calls and letters from people who had been there or heard about it. They said, "We don't care if there's anymore need. There's a cause. Is there going to be another one?" I realized it would have to be in a larger place. Even though those two cops from downstairs were dancing and drinking and having a great time at the very end of the first one, we would still need a permit for another one.

A week or so prior to the first benefit, Ronny and I had already had a specific difference of opinion about the company. I felt we should sometimes do plays that had commercial appeal as well as creative and political content. Lighter stuff that people would come to see. By that I did not mean *Born Yesterday*. It was a *strong* discussion. It was his troupe and there was a decision made that I was going to leave it. My leaving had nothing to do with the benefit or the success of the benefit. It had started earlier in the year, even before the arrest.

We had a different definition of reality. One time I said to Ronny, "What does reality mean?" He said, "I can do whatever I like. No one tells me anything." I said, "When the light turns from green to red, Ronny, you stop. Just like we all do." I said this in a Mime Troupe meeting to him. Between us, there was a challenge. I found my worst traits in him and he found his worst traits in me. We were like two bulldogs on each other. And we were both right.

We had differences of opinion and I was in the process of eventually leaving. But there was no hurry. It was like "I can still sleep with you but we're not going to get married next year."

ROBERT SCHEER: Ronny always wanted to make it on *his* terms. That was his strength. It was the source of his strength and his failure as well.

You always had to be on *his* terms. Without that, the thing would have become just another cop-out.

His real cause was artistic purity. To shake people up and reach them. So they would end up thinking a different way. He was the Lenny Bruce of legitimate theater in a way. Ronny was a powerful presence and I think he educated Bill. They spent many hours together. He was kind of a guru to him.

BILL: I wrote up a handbill for the second benefit. It said, "The Mime Troupe is holding another appeal party Friday night, December 10th, at the Fillmore Auditorium. The first party last month at the Troupe's South-of-Market loft was so successful that hundreds of the Troupe's friends were turned away because there was no space for them. This time there is a larger hall to dance in and many of the same artists and entertainers will be there, as well as some new ones. The place is huge and like, it's there. We hope people in the business of entertaining people will be dropping in after completing their own commitments."

Ralph Gleason was the one who suggested the Fillmore to me. I said, "We've *got* to find a bigger place than the loft, Ralph." I had never before seen the Fillmore. I knew nothing about it.

The Fillmore Auditorium was located on Fillmore and Geary, which was like 125th Street and Lenox Avenue in Harlem. Everywhere I looked, it was just soot that had been washed into the walls. What I liked about it was the space. It was much bigger than the loft. There was a real stage. It was a theater, a real showplace. I loved the size of the floor and the height of the ceiling. In there, Charles Sullivan, a black businessman, had booked a lot of the best R&B acts. Usually they would play in Oakland because they could draw more people there. But Charles had put on James Brown and Duke Ellington. At the Fillmore, Bobby Bland and the Temptations had played on shows that Charles Sullivan produced.

I met Charles Sullivan by appointment the second time I saw the ballroom. Charles was a very big man. He stood about six five and weighed two hundred and seventy or eighty pounds. He always wore a suit and tie. Albert King, the blues musician, looked like him. That's why I always liked Albert King. Charles had cigarette vending machines in the hotels and the bars. He owned a liquor store as well. He also had other things going on. But he was legal. Straight, straight, *straight*.

We made some arrangements about the bar because he wanted to keep the concessions. I said, "Well, I'm gonna bring in our people and our food but I'll work something out with you." I insisted that he let me run the place that night. It was a one-shot deal. For maybe a couple of hundred bucks. He was very nice. We needed a dance permit but I didn't have one. Of course he had one because he operated the place. So he allowed us to use his permit and didn't charge me for it.

The second appeal was a "Dance Concert." What I remembered from the loft was that people who had never danced before were dancing. Middle-aged women and men who brought their kids, they found an area for the kids to sleep in, and they made circles with other people to dance. Like people who had been hidden but now had come into the light.

RONNY DAVIS: And then everybody claimed that *they* found the Fillmore. Graham claimed that he found the Fillmore. Then Ralph Gleason claimed that he found the Fillmore. *I* found the Fillmore. Because we wanted to do *The Minstrel Show* and we wanted to open it in the Fillmore Auditorium.

All right. Graham gets very excited about the dollars at the door. And he gets very excited about the success of the Fillmore Auditorium show. He gets a contract with the black guy who owned the Fillmore. He nails it. *Closed.* He came into the office one night sort of smirking with his briefcase and his suit on. And I thought, "Hmmm. The guy's nailed a contract or something." Something like that. Slowly but surely we were becoming more distant from each other.

Second benefit, we have less to do with it. He has more to do with it. He's doing less with us. Makes more money.

BILL: For the second benefit, we had this great black group called Sam and the Gentlemen's Band. Grace Slick and Darby Slick and the Great Society. The Mystery Trend, a group of visual artists, one of whom was Ron Nagle. Frank Zappa came by the second night. The Committee was there again. Scott Beach. Those kind of people.

The great break we got was that Bob Dylan came into town to play in Berkeley. He was being interviewed on KQED, the public television station in San Francisco. I was pushing the benefit. Bonnie and I got in there through a side door and we put our handbills on every seat. This man came over and said, "Who are you?" He was with Bob Dylan. It was Danny Weiner. We stopped what we were doing while he went to the stage where Dylan was rehearsing. Then he came back out and said, "It's okay with Bobby." So we finished papering the house.

I asked them to ask Dylan if he wouldn't mind holding up this large placard with all the groups on it who would be playing on it. I attended the press conference and asked him some questions from the audience. "Oh," he said. "*You're* the guy who gave me this." And he held the placard up on the screen. I think we got more out of that than anything else. "Oh, yeah, you're having this benefit for the Mime Troupe, with these acts, huh?" It's in the film, *Don't Look Back*.

In the hall, we put up huge bed sheets on wooden pipes all the way around as screens for the light shows. The Mime Troupe had to continue with plays and rehearsals and everything else so it was basically Bonnie and I doing all the work. The second one was a bigger success than the first. We had more people there and we made more money. Somewhere between fifty-five hundred and six thousand dollars. It went until two in the morning, which was the law.

One set of speakers, one set of monitors. One roadie for each band. We played records in between bands. Stuff I brought from my own house. Latin and Jazz. Miles Davis and Ravel's *Bolero*. My sister Ester came and ran the kitchen we set up upstairs. We had soup and salad. Downstairs on the Geary side was the bar. We had another benefit on January 14.

The handbill for that one reads, "This is our third thing. For the first two, all the entertainers that participated donated their talents for the sake of greener grass or whatever. From here on, we'd like to show our gratitude for the sound they provide. That's the reason for the two dollar tariff. Hope you can make it." That show was the Great Society, Mystery Trend, the Grateful Dead family, formerly the Warlocks, and the Gentlemen's Band, who headlined. There was a poster that went with this show. There was a blank space for the Dead, who were then still the Warlocks. They had no picture so it stayed blank. But I did give them a space.

BOB WEIR: I didn't know Bill *per se* at the time. Our drummer Billy Kreutzman got on the phone to him to get us on the bill. We had just changed our name from the Warlocks to the Grateful Dead. But Bill Graham didn't like the idea. He was going to put Warlocks on the poster. And we had a long hassle with him and he finally put "Grateful Dead—formerly the Warlocks."

Billy Kreutzman was more or less our manager at the time. Billy and Graham developed a dialogue at that point. Bill would call Kreutzman every now and again and I guess what happened was that Bill developed some sort of respect for Kreutzman's business acumen or something. I'm not sure how it goes but there were a couple of weeks there when Bill had decided that he was going to put together the Fillmore Auditorium. And he was on the phone to Kreutzman quite a lot, getting advice. Which if you knew Billy was like the halt leading the lame, I think.

BILL: Each band got scale. Two or three hundred dollars. For some reason I remember four guys, a hundred and fifty-eight dollars. That was scale back then. Maybe for five, it was two hundred. By this time, the

Mime Troupe had become like the orphan child of San Francisco. We had also gotten a lot of write-in checks and donations from people. But Ronny and I had agreed already that this would be the last benefit. I already knew I was going to keep on with this.

RONNY DAVIS: Third benefit. He calls me and he says, "We can do benefits. We can do a *lot* of benefits together." I said, "We're not in the business of doing benefits. We're in the business of doing plays. You do the benefits. Good-bye." And I went back to a rehearsal. I should have said, "Listen, you're under contract to us. We want two percent of the rest of your money for the rest of your life. We want one point oh percent of all the money you get in the Fillmore Auditorium. We'll make a deal for you. You could say, 'Bill Graham *and* the Mime Troupe Presents.' "

If I had made a deal with him at that time and if I had been a business person like him . . . because he *always* had secret money. You never knew what he had. It was always secret. But that's what you have to do as a businessman. You never quite tell what you've got in your hand. You play poker. Or if you're smart, you *don't* play poker. You own the *house* where they play poker. As he did in the hotel.

So he had extra money. He could put up ten thousand dollars to buy a contract which we didn't know about. Had I said to him at the moment, "Okay, we will go into business . . ."

But I told him, "*You* do benefits. *We're* not interested."

Righteous, radical, nonmaterialist point of view. Had I been more revolutionary and radical, I would have said, "That's an interesting proposal. I'll bring it up at the next meeting. Let's see if we want to do some more benefits."

We would have had a discussion. And somebody would have said . . . I'm sure somebody would have said . . . Kent Minault would have said, "What's the difference in getting foundation grants and getting money from Bill Graham?"

And I would have said and everybody would have said and eventually we would have arrived at the conclusion that we *should* have made a deal with Bill Graham and then we would have all become partially million-aires.

BILL: There was a meeting of the Mime Troupe where I got up and talked. I told the actors that they were being paid lousy wages for a lot of work. I said that we could all go into the business of regularly putting on events like the benefits. That we should do more of them on a regular basis. After I talked, they voted on the question. There were more than fifty people in the troupe at that time. *Two* voted to go ahead with the benefits. Myself and Jim Haynie. Everyone else was against it.

PETER BERG: He left the Mime Troupe for political reasons. He stated it that way. I wish it was tape-recorded. Because it's only my frail memory, you know. But it was something like, "You protest-art, art-as-protest people are wrong-headed. A work of art cannot be a political statement. Politics have to do with people and what their problems are. And what the problem is right now is that people want a new culture. . . . You can't do plays as though they're social weapons. They're not." What a social weapon would be to make a venue for a new culture. That would be a social weapon, and that would change society.

Just put yourself back in the sixties for a moment and listen to that. This sounds like somebody making large-scale compromises. "There are new markets, let's exploit them" is the same thing as saying, "Let's present a new culture as a venue." And I think he still hasn't resolved that. To this day. He's the Stewart Brand of rock and roll. Playing both sides of the street. It got attention. And Graham walked out. Graham walked out after he made this political statement. That as an entrepreneur he could purvey more new culture than we as political activists could conceive or commit. Do you know what I'm saying? I mean, he said that to *us*, though.

RONNY DAVIS: He saw the money was into doing the rock and roll and he took off with it. And we let him do it. Had we been smart and said, "No, you can't do it. You're contracted with us and you're going to work for us," we would have gotten some of that money. The trouble was that I didn't like rock and roll. I didn't like that music. And I *still* don't.

From the get-go, he was a businessman. Unfortunately, we never changed him. What we never did was convince Bill Graham that art and social change were more important than money. And what I never did with the Mime Troupe was ever convince them that liberalism was not good and radicalism was.

PETER COYOTE: The Mime Troupe was deliberating whether to take a lease on the Fillmore as kind of a source of income for the Troupe. And the story is that Bill saw his main chance and he signed the lease and the rest is history. Myself, do I harbor grudges about that? No, I don't. I always thought that Bill Graham was a *mensch*. I always liked him. I always thought that Ronny Davis was a *mensch*, I always liked him. I always thought that the two of them in the same room was like *plutonium*.

Five minutes, it's critical mass, and you leave.

Part Two

The Sacred Store

Chapter Four

The First Days

1.

BILL: I seemed to have a knack for it. The carrying out of the details of public assemblage. Working the room and hiring the right people to do security. Little by little after the first and second benefits, certain things began ticking me off. I realized that at two o'clock in the morning, these people who had been dancing all night long were not yet finished with their flight. Even though the music was over. They were coming in like a glider lands. You can't glide and glide and glide and then come right down *bang* on the ground.

At the third benefit, I remember asking, "Who turned the house lights on?" I told people not to do that again. When the music ended, I wanted the lights left soft. The next time, I rented a mirror ball. I started the mirror ball turning and put on slides of flowers and animals with soft, soft music going in the background so people could land without a crash.

Knowing that the participating extras in this movie were going to tell me whether I was doing the right thing or the wrong thing, I began to realize what could be done without being asked to make it better. I saw I could earn my living by trying to get closer and closer to the way something *should* be. With me, it was public assemblage.

Something called the Trips Festival was scheduled for the weekend of January 20, 1966. Somewhere along the way, it didn't seem to be coming together. So Ramon Sender called me and said, "Will you help us?" I had already met Stewart Brand through the Mime Troupe.

CHET HELMS: The original idea for the Trips Festival came from Zack Stewart. He and Stewart Brand put it together along with Ramon Sender

135

and they brought Kesey into it. Zack and Ramon and Morton Subotnick were all involved with the Tape Music Center and the Ann Halprin Dance Company and that whole orbit of people who in the past had also been connected with KPFA. I had not yet met Bill officially at this point. His reputation was that he was the big money guy involved with the Mime Troupe. The business guy.

ROCK SCULLY: We were actually the people who got the hall for Kesey because we already had an arrangement with the Longshoremen's Union. I knew all those people through my stepfather, Milton Mayer, and through the political stuff I had done at State College. Prior to the Trips Festival, we had already done a couple of shows in there.

It was a big union hall, modern construction, with cantilevered rafters that ran up and then dropped off so it was sort of like a tent inside. The windows were maybe seven feet high all the way around and the rest was all ceiling, which made it perfect for liquid light projections and movies and stuff. We moved the stage around but it didn't sound too good anywhere in there. We had to hang parachutes and banners from the balcony and ceiling to kill the rackety sound. The hall was only supposed to hold seventeen hundred. For the Trips Festival, we had anywhere from twenty-three hundred to thirty-two hundred people a night in there.

BILL: I remember the Merry Pranksters were there and they were pretty spaced out. Very decent people but just *out there*. I had not yet seen the acid thing in full force. That night, I did. It shocked me. They might as well have been offering hand grenades to people. When LSD exploded inside a body, how did they know how much damage the shrapnel could cause? They had ices spiked with acid, available to all, children as well. There were big tubs on the balcony and downstairs for anyone to consume. From the outset, that has always been my one ongoing argument with Ken Kesey. There *has* to be a warning. If people don't know, how can you assume that their body can take what yours can? How can you know that?

KEN BABBS: The Trips Festival was made up of all the diverse elements of the psychedelic groups around San Francisco at the time. The way we got to know Bill was that he came running up at one point saying, "Hey, people are trying to sneak over the fence and get in without paying." By then, there were thousands of people already in there who *had* paid. So I said, "Well, don't worry about it, Bill. People have made enough money." He looked at me like I was crazy and went running back out there and started kicking them back over the fence again.

OWSLEY STANLEY: Bill didn't have a clue. It was completely out of control and he was trying to control it and of course, you couldn't. It was that thing, the harder you tried to grab it, the more slippery it became. Which was the way we were thinking. We couldn't figure any way to hook him into LSD. Back in those days, we were really rough with it. A large dosage was really rough. It would have been a *hell* of a jolt for a guy in his late thirties to suddenly come face-to-face with the universe that way.

I was real stoned when I came in contact with him and I could see right through the bullshit. And I realized that he was half-terrified by what it was and was doing everything he could to control it and to suppress his realization that there was something special going on here. Besides something that was obviously making money.

CHET HELMS: Big Brother played at the Trips Festival. But only over Ken Babbs's dead body. Right before we came on, there had been a bunch of conga drummers playing. Babbs had this remote control microphone and he was on a tower they had built in the middle of the hall. "Okay," he said. "That's the end of that. We've heard enough of this jungle bunny music. Nobody wants to hear jungle bunny music." He was outrageous. For one thing, he was stoned on acid. But he was *outrageous*.

I announced Big Brother and they played one number. We were each supposed to be allowed to play four or five songs. They had played one and he was announcing them off. I grabbed the microphone and said, "*Goddamn it!* Big Brother was brought here to play four songs and goddamn it, they're going to play *four* songs. What do you say, audience?" And everybody said, "*Yeah!*" So they played their four songs. But if I hadn't stepped in, he would have cut them off. It was *immensely chaotic*.

KEN BABBS: We had this thing like a Moog synthesizer with sound coming out of like sixteen different speakers so we could whip sound all the way around that curved place. I was always kind of like the emcee, the Mr. Interlocutor kind of guy. I would get up there on the microphone and be talking and we could roam my voice all around and then Kesey had a thing over on the side where he could be talking and he had a projector that he could write on and it would put the words up on a big screen on the stage behind the band.

He would write stuff that he would just be writing and we'd be talking back and forth so it would be a lot of intermixed stuff. It wasn't just what you put together in the moment. You put stuff together and *then* used it in the moment.

The whole thing with the Acid Test was that the drama would start to come up and the thing was to let it go all night and not stop until it was worked out so when everybody went home, they would have that sense of completion and not feel frustrated or irritated. It had to have that sense of completion.

KEN KESEY: I've tried to think of the real origins of this phenomenon, which I consider myself to be a large part of. One of the people it goes back to, of whom you may not have heard, is George Stern. He was an artist and poet and he did happenings. He and Michael McClure and Allen Ginsberg would do these things in San Francisco. When I first saw them, I thought, "This is the new edge of the way entertainment's going to be done."

And when we started doing the Acid Tests in La Honda, the thing that made them exciting was the fact that they were entertaining but it wasn't a closed circle. We hadn't planned our entertainment to the point that everybody knew for sure how it was going to end up.

It had that acid edge to it. Which is, "This is something that might count." We might conjure up some eighty-foot demon that roars around. As Stewart Brand said, there was always a whiff of danger to it. Those Saturday nights got bigger and bigger until finally La Honda couldn't hold them and we started branching out with the Dead, who had just become the Dead. They'd been the Warlocks before until then.

When we started doing the performances elsewhere, we were carrying most of the equipment because *we* had the bus. We would set it up with the Dead at one end and the Pranksters at the other end and kind of rally back and forth with the sound. Each of the scenes got bigger.

Then we went to the Trips Festival. By then, we *really* knew what we were doing. The night before, I got busted. Which didn't hurt the crowd any. If I wanted to draw a crowd, all I ever had to do was get busted. I was busted up on the roof of Stewart Brand's apartment with Mountain Girl for her little stash of grass under her sleeping bag. I tried to swallow it, it like to choked me to death. This was while the cops had me. They let me out in time to go ahead and do the Test. I don't know who came up with it or from where. But somebody got me a gold lamé space suit with a helmet.

BILL: The most significant part of the whole weekend was that I had been there Friday night and all day Saturday and the Merry Pranksters came in to begin setting up. They set up their scaffolding thing in the middle of the floor, which was going to block some of the people in the back, and I didn't like it. "Well," they said. "You gotta talk to Ken."

I said, "Where's Ken?"

"He's not here right now," they said.

About fifteen minutes before we were supposed to open, I was making sure that all the garbage had been put in the dumpsters. Garbage cans should be *here*. Concession stand should be *there*. Lights at a certain level. I wanted everybody out of the hall because the first people who paid to come in, it should be *theirs*. I didn't want nineteen workers in front of the stage. When I said these things to them, they all looked at me like I was from Mars.

Just before the show started, I was standing in the hall when I saw bikers coming in for free through the back door. There was a guy standing there in a space suit. A full body space suit with a helmet on top and this big silver arm that was moving people around. I ran to him and I looked at him and I said, "Why are you letting these people in? Are they working here?"

This space helmet turned toward me with the visor up. Two eyes looked at me and then he turned back again without a word. I said, "Excuse me, *excuse* me." He looked at me again and he just kept on letting people in. I tried to get the door shut but I couldn't because people kept pushing through, all strangers coming in with no tickets. Then I started yelling.

I said, "WOULD YOU MIND ANSWERING ME? WHAT THE *HELL* ARE YOU DOING *HERE?*"

Even as I was talking to this guy, he was still letting bikers in. I had nothing against bikers at that point but they weren't working there. They were coming to see the show. Finally, I said, "Are you *Ken?*" I had seen his picture before. Inside the helmet, it was Kesey's face.

"Do you mind telling me what the *hell* you think you are doing?"

His way of setting the rules for the night was to finally turn to me. Without saying a single word, he flipped the visor of his space helmet down. That's how we met. To this day, my ongoing vision when someone says Trips Festival is *click*, visor down! *Off. Gone. Next?*

KEN KESEY: I didn't even have to touch it. It was one of those balanced-up helmets. I just nodded and it went *plop*.

BOB WEIR: When we had the Longshoremen's Hall Acid Test, Bill was trying to keep that running like a Swiss watch as well. And it was not possible. We were there with the Pranksters and the buzz was, "Who's this asshole with the clipboard?" And he got into it a couple of times with a couple of the Pranksters, most particularly Kesey and Ken Babbs.

A few months later, we were playing the Fillmore and he was running that show and I was coming up the steps right behind Ken Babbs. Bill sees Ken Babbs and he goes, *"Trips Festival. Trips Festival."* Banging his palm against his forehead every time he said it. Ken Babbs immediately starts banging his hand against his forehead, saying, *"Asshole. Asshole."* Needless to say, Ken got thrown right out.

KEN KESEY: Did you watch Jerry Lewis on that TV show "Wiseguy"? Made me think of Bill Graham a lot. If Bill Graham had gotten into the rag industry, that's what he would have been like. He wanted every nickel out of all these people coming in that night and there were lots of people who were part of this Acid Test retinue that didn't *need* to pay. They were *already* part of it. He really took issue with this, saying, "No, no, *everybody* pays." This is where he began to make his real Bill Graham reputation. Which was a cross he had to bear for many years. Until finally he crawled up on it and decided to rule from there.

PETER BERG: The feeling was significantly different than at the Mime Troupe benefit. I remember the Hell's Angels were punching people out in the hallways. Not just people but pseudo-Hell's Angels. These two-bit motorcycle clubs would actually walk up to these Angels to challenge them. The president of the San Francisco chapter told me, "They're masochists. Do you see the way this asshole is behaving in front of me? I'm just going to kick his teeth out."

JERRY GARCIA: The first time I ever saw Bill was when the Acid Test moved to the Trips Festival at Longshoremen's Hall. And here's this guy running around with a clipboard, you know. I mean, in the midst of total insanity. I mean, total, wall-to-wall, gonzo lunacy. Everybody in the place is high but Bill. And I was having the greatest time in the world. Theoretically, there was this program. With the Acid Test coming on at a certain time.

But in reality, everything was just happening. Everything was going on at once. There was no focus of attention. Everybody was just partying furiously. There were people jumping off balconies onto blankets and then bouncing up and down. I mean, there was just *incredible* shit going on. Plus, it was like old home week. I met and saw everybody I had ever known. Every beatnik, every hippie, every coffeehouse hangout person from all over the state was there, all freshly psychedelicized.

And it was just *great*. It was a great, incredible scene and I was wandering around. I had some sense that the Grateful Dead was supposed to play sometime maybe. But it really didn't matter. We were used to Acid Tests where sometimes we'd play and sometimes we wouldn't.

Sometimes we would get up on stage, play for about five minutes, and all freak out. And *leave*. You know?

That was the beauty of it. People weren't coming to see the Grateful Dead. So we didn't feel compelled to perform. If we wanted to, we got together and played. Sometimes, it was great. Sometimes, it was horrible. Sometimes, we freaked out and didn't go through with it. All the different possibilities were there.

Anyway, I was standing out there wandering around and my attention was drawn to this opaque projector projecting on to one of the many screens in the place. And the screen said, *"JERRY GARCIA, PLUG IN!"* I was looking at it and thinking, "Ah, this is an oddly personal thing for it to say. *'Jerry Garcia, plug in!'* Oh! It must be time to play."

So I head to the stage where our equipment is set up. My guitar was leaning more or less on an amplifier. I get up there on stage and I look at my guitar and somebody has knocked it over and the bridge is now broken off and it's completely sprung, the strings are sticking out everywhere, and it's a disaster, the thing is fucked. I'm looking at this electric guitar, thinking, "Well, I guess I'm not going to be playing tonight." Then all of a sudden, here's this guy with the little sweater and the clipboard. He says, "Well, are you the Grateful Dead? You're supposed to be playing now."

And I said, "Oh, *us?*" I was dumbfounded. *"We're* supposed to be playing now?"

Meanwhile, there are people curled up around the base of the microphones. They're all over and the stage is crowded with people. I'm sitting on the floor, looking down at the guitar in my lap. I'm holding it like a baby. I gesture to the guitar and I say, "It broke. *Broke*, you know?" And Bill looks down at it. Immediately, without saying a word, he falls down onto the ground and starts picking up pieces. He fumbles around with them trying to fix it for me. I thought, "Naw, what a nice guy." Here's this guy in the midst of all this chaos. Nobody cares whether I play or not, you know. But here's this guy trying to fix my guitar for me. I just thought it was the most touching thing I'd ever seen. It was a sweet display. It was incredible. Here's this guy who doesn't know anything about guitars and he's trying to fix mine.

Always loved him for that, you know. It's like I'll always have that image of him. No matter how much he screams or what kind of tantrums he throws or anything. With me, he's never been able to shake that first impression of, "Here is this helpful stranger." In the midst of hopeless odds, trying to help me with my guitar.

As a matter of fact, I *didn't* play that night. The band didn't play either. We had a great time, but we didn't play.

BILL: The majority of people were fine. But too many of them were having to cope with being wired. It wasn't easy if you didn't take the right amount. There were a lot of people who were having serious problems with where this drug was taking them. It was a new experience for me and I was worried about people getting hurt after they left. Driving somewhere, not in control of their senses. It seemed to me to be a high price to pay for a short trip. What was the pleasure in that?

It was an initiation rite. If I'd known more about it, I'd probably have said that I did not want to be involved. But once I was there, I thought that if I left, it would only make things worse. At least I could run the facility right. Because a man walking around naked, stoned on acid, not knowing who he is, what is funny or joyful about that?

From the Mime Troupe to the Trips Festival to my first show in February, I realized what I wanted to do. Living theater. Taking music and the newborn visual arts and making all of that available in a comfortable surrounding so it would be conducive to open expression. What I saw was that when all this truly worked, that space was *magic*. For me, the key element was the public. Their reaction was the payoff.

2.

BILL: Right after the Trips Festival, I began work on my first show. "Bill Graham Presents Three Dance Concerts, Friday, Saturday, Sunday, February 4th, 5th, 6th, 1967, The Jefferson Airplane. Sounds of the Trips Festival." That's what the handbill says. Peter Bailey did it and the thing is totally unpsychedelic in terms of art. Just a picture of an airplane with a horse.

This was the first time *we* put bed sheets on all the walls so the band was surrounded by slide shows, films, and glob-liquid projections. At the foot of the stage, we had all these lights facing up and we ran the wiring to the balcony at the rear of the hall. The wiring was attached to an accordion and the keys were marked orange, blue, and green and those were the footlights. The *first* attempt at special effects in the Fillmore. A guy tapping accordion keys in the balcony.

I put up maybe eight to ten rows of chairs in front of the stage so people could see even if they wanted to sit. People could stand and dance behind those chairs. It was not a concert as we know them now. People would run into the place, establish the fact that the band was on the stage, and they'd then go on about their business. Others would walk in, go upstairs, and never even see the stage.

There was a dance area under the black lights that I set up halfway under the balcony. We had people who volunteered to come in and paint faces. Before the next few shows, we started putting balloons on the floor so that as people walked in, they would just be there. I bought an industrial vacuum cleaner, added a reverse motor, and used it to blow up all the balloons.

In the side lobby, we put up glass cases. The staff then was me and Bonnie, Jim Haynie, and John Walker. Whenever we saw anything interesting in *Time* or *Life*, we would clip it out and put it into one of the glass cases. What we constantly worked on was how can we affect the inhibited person who was coming in? The one who maybe was straight and afraid he was going to be stared at?

When you got to the top of the steps, we'd take your ticket. There was a barrel filled with apples that said, *"Take One or Two."* Bite into an apple, read the things on the wall, a balloon may come your way, music may start, it's okay.

What I remember about the early shows is that I made notes. I made notes and I made notes and I made notes. Hundreds of notes about people coming in, access and egress. I spent a lot of money cleaning up the place. I had a kitchen built on the second floor.

I was always looking for ways to make the place more *haimish*. I wanted to ease people in and then back out again so the experience wouldn't be jarring. The balloons on the floor and the newspaper clips on the walls and the apples made it softer for people to come in. If you were shy, you didn't have to worry about other people looking at you.

Once I knew how long the band was going to play, usually it was forty or forty-five minutes, I could get my bar ready and put ice in the cups and get half a dozen hamburgers on so people would not be waiting.

After the break, I would go into the men's room and I would make some more notes. Notes and notes. Bonnie was in the box office. She kept track of the money. I was introducing the acts, moving the equipment, whatever. I would put the acts on, take the acts off, help with the equipment, then run downstairs to check on the ticket count. Everybody played two sets a night. The in-crowd would always catch the second show.

At the second Mime Troupe Benefit, John Carpenter and Chet Helms had more or less come to me and said, "We're the Family Dog and we don't have a facility and we're also looking for a place to put on shows." They did it in a very nice way. "We don't have one yet, so let's go into partnership. Because we know about this band and that band. You have the hall and we know the bands. Like the Butterfield Blues Band." So we made arrangements for three days of concerts, a fifty-fifty split. I ran the place and set things up. First show was the Great Society, Quicksilver, the Grateful Dead, and the Butterfield Blues Band.

CHET HELMS: John Carpenter, who at the time was managing Grace Slick and the Great Society, first formally introduced me to Graham at the Fillmore Auditorium at the second Mime Troupe benefit. At that point, he was just sort of thinking out loud and talking about trying to rent the place on a regular basis, saying, "You know, this hall is *so* cheap. Sixty-five dollars a night or five hundred a month. This thing looks like it's kind of happening and you know, maybe we ought to try it."

The first show we did there, the deal was Graham would put up all the money and the hall. He would take certain expenses off the top like security guards and hall rental and then take 50 percent of the proceeds. Essentially, John Carpenter and I brought the bands to Bill. They were *our* peers. They were the guys we hung out with and palled around with. While *he* was ten years older. But we weren't any kind of formalized booking agents or anything.

The first show was a fifty-fifty deal. I think he put up a total of two hundred dollars in expenses and got half the proceeds and it was an enormous success. We felt that he did almost nothing for his share. For the second show, we said, "No way, *José*. This is a *burn*." It came down to he was going to get 10 percent. And we said, "No, 7. Or that's *it*." The subsequent shows we did there, he was paid 7 percent of the proceeds. We had the leverage at the time because he needed us. He wouldn't have gone from 50 percent to 7 percent if there was not some utility to him at the time.

Technically, we were doing shows on alternate weekends with him but it didn't work out that way. A couple of times, he canceled us kind of at the last minute and we had to shift our show because something wasn't working out for him and he needed the date, or something. Because we didn't have a written agreement with him, we kind of got shuffled around several times.

BILL: Every night, Butterfield tore the town apart. He was *awesome*. With the original band. Jerome Arnold, Elvin Bishop, Sam Lay on drums, Bloomfield, and Mark Naftalin. The "East-West" band. Great, great band. Later, I would always introduce them as ". . . a heavy breeze from the Windy City . . . the Paul Butterfield Blues Band."

The song "East-West" itself was amazing for me to hear. Because at weddings, *bar mitzvahs*, and anniversaries, whenever it gets to a joyous occasion, they would play this certain music. And that was what Michael Bloomfield would play in "East-West." His desire to get that out of himself and let it transcend all else was incredible.

It was wedding music. I'm getting married. I love you. And you love me. We're going to share our life together. We'll celebrate with song and food. What is the song? The one Michael Bloomfield played in "East-West." That lick he had.

My God, it was every Middle Eastern couple walking down some little path somewhere. It was also the pied piper. It had a jaunt to it. It was sensual. But with all your clothes on. Flamenco music. Moorish. The music of Casablanca. That was what made Bloomfield and the Butterfield Band so great. They provoked moods and colors and shadings. They eliminated words.

MARK NAFTALIN: On one occasion after we had been provided with what was represented as being Leary acid on sugar cubes, Michael Bloomfield came and rejoined me at some point in the wee hours of the morning after a solo sojourn of some kind and he said that he had penetrated the mysteries of Indian music and he knew how it worked and what it was and that he'd had a revelation.

Right away after that, we started playing "East-West," which was constructed on the basis of a bass line which Mike said he had taken from a Nick Gravenites song called "It's About Time." I don't know if you'd even really call it a composed bass line. I mean, it's really just a scale. But it goes with a certain beat and that was the basis of it. And then we put it together in sections. So that each soloist would play his solo—and it would be quite extended, no chord changes, just the one chord—and then it would reach a peak and end with a break.

And then the new section would begin again at a much lower volume and build again. That was Mike's trip. You know. Ease on in, jack it up, break, and then ease on in again. It developed as an excursion in different modalities. He would fool around a lot with the minor second and modalities that included the minor second, which is not characteristic of Western music or pop music or blues that we were used to. He had been listening to Ravi Shankar.

Another area of the tune would be *very* major with major seconds and major sixths and almost a country-and-western or a Mexican flavor. Butterfield would have his section and that would be primarily his blues. But he would also wail on as the other sorts of feels would come up. He would be on those too. It wasn't always the same. It developed and it grew. The tune would take typically, I suppose, half an hour to perform. I'm sure many times it was even longer than that. Forty-five minutes or maybe even an hour.

It would get up there in length and there'd be more sections and the sections would be longer and the climax of the tune, sort of a resolution to the modal excursions and the modal questions that had come up, would be in the form of a very major concluding section, which would end with very loud guitar, drones and wailing, and I would play "Joy to the World" with all the stops out and both hands in octaves on the organ. I would just kind of mash down on top of this very loud wailing. I really don't know what else to call it. And that seemed to work pretty well and it was powerful.

BILL: Every night, we said, "My God. I'm going to bring them back." And John and Chet said, "You ought to try to bring them back." And I said, "I'm going to try to." But in a very open, very nice way. At the end of the third night, they took their money. I think we made eight hundred and they made eight hundred. Hey, that was good. Now before this, I remember something happened during the weekend. John Carpenter saw me go over to somebody at the bar and ask them to put out a joint. He asked me why I'd done that and I said, "Well, I can't have the police think I allow that openly because they'll close me down."

He said, "We don't run *our* business that way."

I said, "Well, I do. So long as we do shows in this building, that's the way it is."

Then it sort of became an issue with us every night. "Hey, Bill, you know you *gotta* relax."

"In my house," I would tell them. "I can't relax. We're working here and it's against the law and I can't let it look like we allow it. Of course, it's going on, but I can't let it be that open. I'm sorry. But that's the way it is."

So we disagreed. John Carpenter and I didn't get along too well. But Chet and I got along okay. Every night we'd sit upstairs with the apple box and we'd be filling it with ones and fives and tens and by the third night, we were all saying over and over again, "What a great band. Boy. We got to bring them back. We're *gonna* bring them back."

I went home that night and I said to Bonnie, "I'm going to set the alarm for 6 A.M."

"Why?" she said.

" 'Cause Albert Grossman, their manager, lives in New York and I want to talk to him first thing in the morning."

I got up at six, which is nine back East, and called the office. No answer. I called back at ten, Albert wasn't in yet. I got a call back from Danny Weiner, who was the booking guy for Albert at the time. He said, "Albert isn't in yet, I'll talk to him." I told him, "Hey, we had great success with Butterfield. I wanna have 'em back soon."

I went back to sleep. Half an hour later, the phone rang. It was Albert. We talked. Albert had been a club owner in Chicago, the Gate of Horn, and then he went to New York and found Bob Dylan and Peter, Paul, and Mary. Within a half hour, he said, "Okay, let Danny work things out." I got to the office a few hours later. By mid-morning on Monday, I made the deal for the next time Butterfield came to San Francisco.

Monday went by. Tuesday went by. Wednesday went by. Thursday afternoon, two or three o'clock, Chet walked into the building. I don't want to knock him but he was pretty wasted. "Hey, Bill," he said. "How you doing?"

"Okay," I told him.

"What's going on?" he said. "We just called New York and Dan told me what you did."

I said, "What'd I do?"

"That's not too cool, man."

"You want us to be partners, Chet?" I told him. "You can't run it the way you did last time. You can't have an open-door policy and load hundreds of friends in for free. We lost a lot of profit because of all the people you let in."

He said, "You booked Butterfield behind our backs."

Somehow, something came out of me and I said, "Chet, you're gonna be in this business and I'm gonna be in this business. And I'll tell you, there's only one suggestion I can make to you. *Get up early.*"

He never forgot that. I never forgot it. Chet *never* got up early. And what I really meant had nothing to do with *when* you got up. It really meant, no matter what time you get up, use your time to work.

CHET HELMS: One thing that still goes a bit deep with me is the whole incident that he's so fond of telling about Butterfield. In my personal view, he was in some technical sense a partner in our operation and he had a fiduciary responsibility to us. That fiduciary responsibility was not to cut our throat by calling Grossman.

He loves to tell the story of how I'm a late sleeper and he gets up early in the morning and the early bird gets the worm. He loves to tell how smart he is. But to me, that was just a breach of faith, basically. It was a breach of honor.

The first time Butterfield ever played in San Francisco, he had sold two hundred albums on the West Coast entirely at the time. John Carpenter and I went down to a jazz club in Huntington Beach, to see them a week before our gig here, and John and I were the only two people in the club. This was before the *East-West* album came out. *Nobody* knew Butterfield. Why people came to see him in San Francisco was that John and I had personal phone lists of people we knew. Two or three hundred. And we got on the phone and called every single one of them and said, "Are you going to be at the Butterfield concert?" We had been part of a big party circuit and that was sort of how we would organize the parties. Just get on the phone and call.

We had to fight Bill tooth and nail over having Butterfield play in the first place. We had the commitment but Graham didn't want to let us do it because he thought it was going to fall on its face. For the weekend up here, Butterfield got twenty-five hundred dollars. Which was astronomical money compared to what we were usually paying then. The first night was packed. We had like eighteen hundred people at two dollars each. We ran like seven thousand people through there that weekend.

But that was sort of the beginning of the end. We did four shows there together in all so I think there was just one more. After the thing with Butterfield, John Carpenter and Bill were not getting along at all. I felt betrayed by Bill but I was still cordial with him. Not John.

I tried to mediate things a bit and keep things going. We did one last show with Love and the Sons of Adam and the Charlatans in March and John and Bill had a big fight over Bill's allegation that we didn't bring our own thumb tacks and cellophane tape. To put up some kind of decoration inside. Crepe paper or something. Which resulted about a week later in Graham just saying, "You're out. You're *out*."

But we could feel it coming. We had been looking for another venue and shopping for halls. We brought our new landlord to our last show at the Fillmore. He owned the Avalon Ballroom, one of a thirties' chain of swing ballrooms in a building called the Puckett Academy of Dance. We always called it the "Fuck It Academy of Dance."

It had an L-shaped balcony, gilded booths, and columns. Red flocked wallpaper and a lot of mirrors, with the stage in the far diagonal from the door. Like a music hall with a sprung wooden dance floor. The best dance floor *ever*. Better than the old Fillmore. When seven or eight hundred people got dancing on it, the floor moved in sync. It helped you.

For the next five years, I went toe-to-toe with Graham with a smaller hall, no financial backing, and no real business experience. I worked eighteen-hour days, supported twenty to forty employees, and produced over five hundred evenings of entertainment at the Avalon. My lack of ultimate financial success was not the result of sloth or a compassionate admission policy. I was simply undercapitalized.

BILL: I would sometimes go for social reasons to the Avalon. To see a band like Sopwith Camel. The original Avalon was run much looser than the Fillmore. Chet's door policy was if you met him once or you could convince him that you met him, he would let you in. Then the band couldn't be paid and they couldn't get home. People loved Chet and he was a very nice man, but he didn't have a sense of responsibility. In that era, that fit. I didn't fit in their eyes. So the Avalon was looked upon with great favor by the Golden Gate Park crowd and the Haight-Ashbury crowd. Chet was in it for *righteous* reasons. Bill does a good job. But he's a *businessman*. The pure hippie of the day thought of the Avalon as the *real* church. Mine was the commercial church.

BONNIE SIMMONS: I worked for Chet for about the last six months of the Avalon's existence on Sutter Street. Chet was a fine person. He just hired too many people. His theory was, "I'll hire a hundred people and pay them each sixty dollars a week." In those days, you could potentially make a living on that. He always seemed like an okay person to me but very disorganized. I mean, we were *hippies*.

A couple of times, Chet sent me to the Fillmore to borrow cups. Either they did not have the money to pay for them or they had forgotten. The Avalon was never quite as together as it should have been. I don't think Bill ever knew my name. But he never yelled at me, or anything. He just gave me the cups.

RONNY DAVIS: I wish I could get it clearly what the difference is between Graham and Chet Helms. Because Chet Helms is a long-haired hippie, not progressive but reactionary, ultimately reactionary. He is the reactionary element of the hippie metaphysical side. He would *not* do a benefit for the Mime Troupe. He would *not* do a benefit for the Panthers. He would *not* do a benefit for the cripples or anybody. He was only doing it for the *art* of the music. I would argue the substance of the music is *trash*. I would argue it's absolutely reactionary.

3.

BILL: By now, Walter, the cop on the beat, wasn't too happy about these shows taking place. There was the December show and the January show and he sort of let the word out that he didn't like it. For the February show, I put up a notice on the wall stating that I was applying for my own dance hall permit downtown because Charles Sullivan had said I should. Just in case anything went wrong, in terms of insurance and so on.

Ten days later, I had to go downtown to get my license. When I went, I didn't go with a lawyer. I thought it was an automatic thing. Some woman before me wanted to fix up a beauty shop. Somebody else wanted to change around his lawn. We all had to go in front of the Board of Permit Appeals in the Hall of Justice on Howard Street. I came next.

Deputy Chief Scott was holding these hearings. He said, "Anyone in the room opposed to Mr. Graham getting a permit?"

These two men stood up. One was Police Lieutenant Leo Hayes from North Station. The other was a rabbi from the synagogue next door to the Fillmore. Rabbi Elliot M. Burstein from Congregation Beth Israel, 1939 Geary. A man in his late thirties or early forties. I was asking for my permit so I could put on a Batman Dance, March 18, 19, 20. The police lieutenant had a petition with twenty-seven names on it. All local merchants who were opposed to me doing business there.

Then the rabbi came up to testify. Deputy Chief Scott said to him, "Yes, Rabbi?" His very first lines were, "Your Honor, Mr. Graham's peoples, dey're urinating on mein holy valls."

I said, "You gotta be out of your mind. Those stains have been on your walls for at least *fifty* years."

There was a little alleyway that separated the Fillmore from the synagogue. They pissed against this wall, they pissed against that wall. I knew they did. But *way* before I ever got there. When people are stoned, they piss. Like when a dog sees a hydrant. When I saw the lieutenant come up and then the rabbi come up, I thought, "This *isn't* an automatic. This *isn't* just a formality that I'm going through here." Because of their objections, the permit was denied.

When I left there, I called Alan Myerson, a lawyer I knew from the Mime Troupe bust who founded and directed The Committee. Alan recommended Bill Coblentz. First I had to go to Charles Sullivan. I said, "Charles, for the next show, I need to use *your* permit again. Because the police want to put me away. I'm a white scene in a black neighborhood and it means work for them."

He said, "Yeah, I'm with you, Bill. Let's just see what happens."

Unbeknownst to me, the police had already begun very quietly suggesting to him, "Why let anybody else use your permit?" But he hadn't told me that.

We held the Batman Dance in March. On Friday, we had the Mystery Trend, Big Brother and the Holding Company, and Family Tree. Next night, Quicksilver, Family Tree, and the Gentlemen's Band. Next night, Great Society, Quicksilver, and the Skins. Also, I gave away a mynah bird. We raffled it off on the third night. Before that, the bird hung out over the stage. Somebody from the Animal Society came and objected and they were right. Because it became deaf. A month later, the guy who won it came back.

I said, "How's the bird?"

"Delicious," he said. But it was a joke.

BILL COBLENTZ: Bill came to see me and said that he had this dance auditorium. He was starting out, he didn't have any money, but he knew that occasionally I handled civil liberties cases and he thought that they were infringing on his basic rights. After I listened to him, I thought, well, that was probably true. I mean, why shouldn't he be able to operate a dance hall that was monitored and kept clean and sort of a safe haven on Geary Street? So I checked further and near there was a house of prostitution and they weren't bothering that place. So we went before the Board of Permit Appeals again.

BILL: After I got hold of Coblentz, I told Charles Sullivan my problem. Then I put on my suit and tie and went to see *every* merchant in the neighborhood. White, Oriental, and black. I went to the grocery store where I bought all my hot dogs. I said to the guy there, "You sell me your stuff and then you tell me, you don't want me here? It's not right." The Chinese people who ran the joint on the corner where I always ate, I wined and dined them socially. I became a waiter. I just put on my waiter's mind. "How are you today?" I would say to them.

Some guy would be standing in his store in the middle of the day. There'd be no business whatsoever. Every other second, I would keep saying to him, "I know you're a busy man. But do you mind? I don't want to take up *too* much of your time." The petitions had been taken around by Walter, the cop on the beat. He had collected all the signatures. In the next few weeks, I went from merchant to merchant and got twenty-four of them to say it was okay, they had no real objection to my running my business there.

I knew that in court no one can argue with religion or kids because you always lose. So I went to see the rabbi next door on my own. I walked in and he said, "Yes, Mr. Graham?" He had an office upstairs in the synagogue and he never once asked me to sit down. I stood in front of him and stated my case. I took the soft approach. Rather than say, "Why did you say those stains were from *my* clients?" I said, "Look, I'm trying to run my business here and what is it that you're objecting to?"

He started lecturing me right off the bat. "Do you know what life is all about?" Real pontification. "Do you know what I'm doing here? People of the Jewish faith come here to pray and read the Torah."

"Yes, I know. But what is it you're objecting to?"

Somehow, he finally got to, "You don't understand. What do you know from persecution? Do you know what happened to my people all these years?"

I realized that he thought he was talking to a *goy*.

He said, "You don't know, you don't understand, you don't have the suffering."

Before I blew up, I said, "Can I ask you a question, Rabbi? Have you *ever* been outside the United States?"

"What has that got to do with persecution?"

"*Have* you?"

"No."

"HOW *DARE* YOU TALK TO *ME* ABOUT PERSECUTION?"

In about thirty seconds, I let him have it. What happened to my mother and my sisters. I told him *everything*. At top volume. "Calm down, Mr. Graham, calm down," he said. This was his other classic line. "I didn't know. I didn't know. You're a Yid?" That was the one that killed me. That made me okay. I was a Yid. "Sit down, sit down," he said. "Have a chair."

"I've been here forty minutes. I don't want your chair."

I was livid. "WHAT DO YOU WANT FROM ME?" I kept yelling. "*LEAVE ME ALONE*."

He kept saying, "Relax, just relax. I didn't know who you were."

"*YOU* DIDN'T *KNOW?* WHY SHOULD I HAVE TO USE *THAT?*"

Finally, he said, "We have to talk about the holidays."

The whole *mishegass* was about the High Holy Days. On those days, he needed parking in the neighborhood or else the people would go to another synagogue. To end the whole thing, we agreed that he would write up a document where I volunteered out of my concern for him *not* to have shows on the High Holy Days. Then I had to go to his house a few days later and wait in the hallway for the signed documents.

What I would do was rent out the Scottish Rite Temple around the corner from the Avalon Ballroom. I would advertise, "This week's show, due to religious services at the synagogue, I'm moving." For the people who automatically showed up at the Fillmore no matter what, I had two trucks shuttling them to the show. *Holiday? Far out.* I would move them on a relay system to the right hall.

Then there was another hearing to which Bill Coblentz came. This time, we had testimony from teachers and criminologists and sociologists on our behalf from U.C.-Berkeley and from Santa Cruz, saying the shows had qualitative merits. They were an expression of the free will of the people, as was the way they dressed and danced. And we *still* didn't get the permit. Second hearing, permit *denied*.

One day after that, in the late afternoon, Charles Sullivan came to the Fillmore. This was late March or early April. He didn't look too good. "Bill," he said, "I have to talk to you." He sat me down and said, "I got to level with you. They're leaning on me hard and I got a business to run and I got a wife and kids and I have to pull my permit. I can't go no further, Bill. I gotta pull it."

I'd felt that this was coming. I'd even told Bonnie about it. I didn't know whether to go somewhere else, or what to do. I do remember going home that night and saying to her, "Well, we'll go in the morning and get our stuff." As far as I was concerned, it was *over*.

The next morning, I got to the Fillmore and there was Charles Sullivan sitting on the steps. Same suit, shirt, and tie from the day before. He was disheveled and it was obvious to me that he had been up all night. I went and put my hand on his shoulder and said, "You all right?"

And he said, "Bill, I want to talk to you."

So we went upstairs to my little cubbyhole office and he proceeded to tell me his life story. How he had been born in New Orleans and had to leave the South because he couldn't take always being challenged because he was such a big black man. How he had made his way up to Chicago and started working in the meat packing houses, met his wife, saved some money, and decided to come out to California, the land of promise. Along the way, the white man had messed with him. Every time he was due a promotion and some white guy got it instead, Charles would say, "I didn't cause no one no harm."

He said, "Bill, I came out here and I saved my money and I started getting into vending machines and I bought a little piece of property and opened a liquor store and I put my kids through school. I had some setbacks but I'm doin' okay now. Now these guys downtown are leanin' on me hard and they want me to take my permit away from you. Now I watched you start . . ."

He was shaking as he talked to me. "Yesterday, they really got to me," he said. "Sayin', 'You got vending machines, Mr. Sullivan, and you got liquor stores and you got your little business going and why don't you let us deal with that man and back off?'"

And he said, "Bill, it's my life. After I saw you last night, I started thinking about myself and what I been through and what they're making you do now." Then he just broke down. He said, "I can't do it. I can't. I just can't back off. I can't pull that permit away from you."

He leaned forward and got all choked up. His eyes were red from no sleep. He was angry inside and he said, "No, no, no. I just ain't going to let this happen now. You just go back downtown, man. And you beat those white motherfuckers."

He was the guy, Charles. He was *it*. I don't know if I could have *ever* found another place. Why would I have even tried? That *was* the place.

4.

BILL: It meant more work for the police, that was all. There was a potential problem. A thousand white kids were now going through a black neighborhood at two in the morning. I'm not saying the cops were wrong to be concerned. Their approach was wrong. But hey, if I was the cop on the beat and I wasn't looking for more work, if I had a choice of that building being closed every night, or every night I would have to work until two in the morning, what would I choose?

There *were* some problems. A car would be broken into every now and then. A ticket would be stolen. But we watched the streets. We patrolled them ourselves for a few blocks in every direction. We were out there and sometimes it did get bad. There was a mugging from time to time and fights outside after the show but my relationship with the neighborhood was strong from the beginning. Still, the Board of Permit Appeals refused by a vote of three to two to overrule the first denial. There was a police captain there and he said to me, "*We* don't want your element around here."

Then on April 21, 1966, a Thursday, the *Chronicle* ran an editorial called "The Fillmore Auditorium Case." Basically, they said the police were wrong. "The police," they wrote, "formerly besought by Graham to list their objections, have failed to respond and it must seem that they have no case against him. Usually, it's the police saying, 'Okay, this is what's wrong!' Now we're saying, 'What's wrong?' "

It was a *big* turning point for me. In more ways than one.

BILL THOMPSON: What happened was that the police tried to close Bill down. At that time, Bill used to blow up the balloons. Bill did *everything*. He would arrange the chairs early and he would sweep. You would see him sweeping the place. I mean, he had everything covered. He was a one-man ball of fire. You could get tired just watching the guy.

Anyway, this cop was talking to Bill while he was blowing up a balloon. The cop had a cigar, and they didn't like the hippies coming down there and all that stuff. So the cop took his cigar and exploded the balloon. There was like a second of hesitation before Bill gave him the Graham riot act.

"*You blew up my balloon!*" That was all he kept saying, no matter what the cop answered. "*You blew up my balloon!*"

I went to the editorial department of the *Chronicle*. I had Ralph Gleason on my side. I talked to them and they wrote an editorial. I was the one responsible for that editorial. Bill came in and thanked me. He gave me a fifty-dollar bill. Back then, that was as much money as I made in a *week*.

BILL: The night after the editorial appeared, two cops showed up at the Fillmore and handed me a copy of the editorial and a cartoon of kids going into the Fillmore and a cop crying with the caption, "They're dancing with tears in my eyes." That was what really pissed them off. Then they started arresting kids. Fourteen of them. It was a front-page story the next morning. They were busted for being under eighteen and at a public dance and I was charged with selling tickets to minors, a violation of Section 558 of the Municipal Code, which was passed I think in 1909. When I asked these cops what they thought they were doing, I was threatened with arrest for interfering with an officer in the performance of his duty.

I had a meeting with the mayor at the time, John F. Shelley. A *putz* but at least he listened. I said to him, "Where do you *want* the kids to be?" That was my whole thrust. First of all, we weren't promoting drugs, just good times. "*You* go to ball games?" I said to him. "Some of them may not like ball games. They like something else. What's wrong with that?" I told him there was also another thing. By choice, I had never sold alcohol or beer. I had never even thought about it or wanted it there. The mayor might have been listening when I spoke to him but I couldn't tell for sure. He just *sat* there.

The Avalon Ballroom was running at the same time and no one ever got busted there because they were in a good neighborhood. In the long run, did the busts help? It made us *media*. People said, "Wait a minute. I have kids. Oh, it affects *my* children?" Even the Hearst paper in town came out in support of us, calling the law outdated. By the end of May, all of the charges were dropped. By the first week in June, the board reversed their opinion and granted me the permit. The rabbi even testified on my behalf. As did the head of the local merchant group, an assistant to the Dean of Students at the University of California, and Ralph Gleason. Some guy on the board asked me how I had picked up so many supporters.

"With *pressure*," I yelled back at him. "Just like you."

I was very emotional at the time and angered by one simple reality. I had my rights. If the tables were reversed, how would the cops have felt? I was totally obsessed with what was going on. Like someone building their own house.

At the time, I was thirty-five years old. My generation had generally been passive. But the young people on the campuses and in the Haight, the painters and the musicians, were for the first time as a larger unit in our society saying, "We want to try something different. We don't want to follow in your footsteps." I was there at that time at my age. It was more than getting a chance to pitch in the major leagues. It was the theater of life. It was living theater. Everybody was *real*.

BILL COBLENTZ:　The case was won strictly on its merits. Because I had some credibility and I was straight and I had visited the Fillmore with my wife and I said it was fine. There was nothing wrong. I never particularly cared for the music. But what impressed me about the place was how orderly it was. People *were* smoking dope. But they were behaving themselves.

BILL:　A few months later, Charles Sullivan got himself killed. He had a bad habit of always carrying a roll of money with him. He was proud of his work and proud of the fact that he earned a good living and he always carried a roll. They jumped him and stabbed him to death. I went to his funeral in Colma, California. It was small, mostly family.

　　Had that not happened, I think I would have done anything Charles wanted. Just out of gratitude.

5.

BILL:　Bonnie and I were living together. The problem was that I gave no thought to anyone else, including Bonnie. My lack of awareness came from the fact that I was totally consumed with my work. Following a show, I would usually get up at eight o'clock in the morning. I hadn't gone to bed until three or four because after every show, I'd head for Mel's.

　　In the box office, we'd put the money into a heavy-duty wooden apple crate and then take it upstairs and stuff the money into that same green duffel bag. I'd put the duffel bag on my back and go home on the scooter. Some nights, there'd be four or five thousand in there. When I'd get home, we'd dump it out on the kitchen table. It became a ritual. Bonnie would take her shower and come out. I'd take my shower and she would start on the singles. I'd do the fives and twenties and pile them up. It would take an hour or two. The next morning, I'd get up, we'd have breakfast, and I'd take the money and go to work. Bonnie would then put the money in the bank.

　　In June, I put on Lenny Bruce with the Mothers of Invention. He had been appearing at Basin Street West in North Beach at the time of the Mime Troupe bust and I'd gone to see him. But I did not meet him or speak to him. I'd heard his records and I was not really a great fan. Although his stuff was very deep and perceptive, I thought he took too long to get to the point and that he milked his stories. Too much foreplay. I felt basically though that he was being deprived of his rights.

What I wanted to present was a combination of talent and a martyr. A man who truly was fighting for his sanity and fighting for his life. I got his phone number from I think Lawrence Ferlinghetti. No. Lawrence gave him *my* number. He wouldn't give me *his* number.

Lenny called me from L.A. During the conversation, we talked about the shows. I remember he made a big deal about, "I don't want your slide projector. I'll bring my own slide projector. I don't need your slide projector. Mine's as good as yours . . ." On and on. He made a whole big issue of the slide projector and how long the show would be and the Mothers of Invention, who were on the bill with him. What do *they* do? When are *they* going on? Why do we need *them?*

He negotiated his own deal and drew up a contract in his own handwriting for a thousand dollars cash per show plus half the gross of ticket sales over a thousand. Obviously, he was trusting no one at the time. He had said no to me a number of times about coming back up to San Francisco. I told him it was important for him to come back to the city so he could prove that he was standing up for his rights and his life and his work.

He told me that he'd be coming in from L.A. on a flight that got to the San Francisco airport at eleven or eleven-fifteen. I said, "Lenny, I'll have somebody pick you up."

He said, "No, no, Billy. It's got to be *you*. Why can't *you* do it?"

Fine. I drove out to the airport, I stood there, I waited, I looked at every person who got off the flight from L.A. No Lenny Bruce. I waited for the next flight. Same thing. No Lenny. I called his house in L.A. No answer. I went back to my house out in the Avenues. Bonnie and I had an argument. She said, "Why should *you* have to go down there to pick him up?"

I said, "It's *Lenny Bruce*. What're we going to do? He makes the rules, we play the game."

I went to sleep. The phone rang at about two in the morning. It was Lenny. He said, "Listen, Billy. I'm gonna make the three forty-five." It was a TWA plane. I remember that flight. It left L.A. at three forty-five in the morning.

I drove back out to the airport in this Karmann Ghia convertible with the top down, wearing about nineteen coats. He came off the plane, it must have been 5 A.M. It was a great meeting at the airport. Like a Kafka movie. I said, "Lenny?" He said, "Billy?" He was carrying all his stuff loose. Slides, the slide projector. He had these incredible circles under his eyes. He was wearing a Nehru jacket and he looked puffy. Everything about him was puffy.

We got to the car and he said, "Holy shit, I'm going to fucking freeze.

What are you, fucking crazy? You're outta your fucking mind. Driving an open car to the airport at night? Fucking insane."

That was the way he talked. It was all "fucking this" and "fucking that." We got on the highway. It was real quiet for a while. For a couple of minutes, he didn't say a thing. Then his first line was "You got anything in the icebox?"

I had asked him over the phone if I could make reservations for him to stay somewhere. But he had said, "It's all taken care of." As I drove him back to the city, I kept waiting for him to tell me where I was supposed to take him. Then he asked me about the icebox.

I said, "I don't know, Lenny. Some liverwurst, like that. Why? You wanna stay at the house?" No answer. We kept on driving. We were on Highway 101 and I said, "Geez, Lenny. I hope you know what this means to us. It's really good you're here and I hope it's good for you. Zappa's excited about the show, and the whole city's buzzing."

He just kept mumbling about the fucking car and how fucking crazy I was to be driving with the top down at this hour of the night. We got close to the city. He said, "Why don't you take the Broadway off-ramp?"

I said, "Lenny, that's not the way to my house."

"Take it," he said. "I'll stay with Albert. It's all right."

I didn't say anything. I took the Broadway ramp. He said, "You know that all-night magazine stand and bookstore?" The one on Columbus and Broadway which later came to be right next to Carol Doda's joint. "Okay. Drop me off there." We pulled up to the Swiss-American Hotel, which was the joint where he always stayed on Broadway right above Enrico's.

It was now well after 5 A.M. and we were driving up Broadway, which was completely empty. I mean, *totally* deserted. Nothing moving on the street but us. Lenny had his slides and his projector and his camera and all his stuff with him in the front seat. The only light on all of Broadway, the only store lit up was where they sold girlie magazines in that all-night newsstand. We pulled up to the curb. Lenny got out. There was one guy standing all the way at the very back of the place, reading a girlie magazine.

Lenny said, "Albert?"

The guy looked up, recognized Lenny, put the magazine down, and then they both just left. No hellos. No good-byes. I was in a silent movie.

The next afternoon, Lenny came in to set up his slides. He started talking about his mom. How he didn't do right by her. He came into the office and sat around for an hour, talking some about the cops but mainly about his mom. How good she'd been to him and how he'd messed around. He kept saying, "I gotta straighten out my life. I hope it goes different from now on." He was very nervous about his performance. At that point, it wasn't as though I could have told him what to do with his act. He was *Lenny Bruce*.

JIM HAYNIE: Bill would preach to people, business-wise, about what their obligations were. In fact, he made business people out of a lot of band managers who were dumbheads who wouldn't have been able to do it otherwise. He actually would *instruct* them. Particularly guys like Michael Bloomfield. He would be an hour and a half late and Bill would be across Geary Boulevard kicking his butt, making him come in screaming, "Where have you been? You sonofabitch, don't you realize your obligation here?"

Lenny Bruce, same deal. When it came time to do the show, Lenny was two hours late. He was in North Beach doing something. Doing the stuff or whatever. Bill would be screaming at Lenny Bruce. Well, for me, Lenny Bruce was the high priest. I held him in tremendous regard. I would never have screamed at the guy.

Now I had seen Lenny before in North Beach at some joint on Broadway and he was very funny. And I had seen him at a New Year's show in Los Angeles and he was very funny and incisive and witty and brilliant. And then when he came to the Fillmore, he was over. He had gone over. He had already been eaten up by all the shit. Society was bound to chew him up.

It wasn't funny, it wasn't entertaining, it was very sad. In the way that he was a defeated person at that point. You wondered, "Is he playing the victim? Is he playing into it?" But at the same time, you felt the force of society. You thought, "Maybe there *is* no way out." It was tragic. It was a fucking tragic night.

PETER BERG: I remember the horrified look on Graham's face when Lenny Bruce did that last pathetic performance, incredibly whacked out on amphetamine. *Shredded*. Bruce was shredded. And Graham was like, "I'm *not* responsible. I'm not responsible for this."

BILL: I can't say he was good. The performances were like eulogies to himself. What people saw from him was what had happened to a person who had been fucked with for a very long time. It was the living death of a genius. He took on the law and he lost.

That night, he was strictly doing stuff that controlled his mind, all about legalities and the criminal laws and Penal Code One Point Two Nine and he showed his slides. Really, the Mothers of Invention saved the shows. It was really sad. He was a beaten soul and he was naked on stage. About six weeks later, he was dead.

6.

BILL: Bonnie did all the books. The only time I ever dealt with the money was when I helped her do corners so we could stack it up for deposit. I had an account in my name in the bank and that was *it*. No insurance on the hall, no nothing. Just a checking account at the local bank. I was doing all the booking and the promotion and the advertising. As we got into the summer of '66, I started trying to work up shows five or six weeks in advance.

The staff was very small. I had John Walker on the door. Jim Haynie, whom I had met through the Mime Troupe, was the fix-it-all man, doing wiring, cleanup, and building the stage. He was a carpenter, actor, linguist, and just a real bright street guy. It was Bonnie, me, Johnny Walker, Jim Haynie, and Marushka Greene.

JOHN WALKER: When I met Bill, I must have been sixty-eight years old. Yeah. He give a dance down at Longshoremen's Hall. And I went down there to the dance. I paid my way in. Somebody I knew who used to put out posters for Sullivan introduced us. Bill said, "This guy's been tellin' me that the Fillmore is a white fish for Sullivan. So I'm gonna try to rent it."

I said, *"Yeah?"* I said, "You in the *dancin'* business, huh? If you rent it, I know I got a job with you there."

He said, *"Yeah. You got a job."*

So on Tuesday afternoon, I went up there. This was the spring of the year and he said, "We got a lot of straightenin' up to do around here. We got to hang curtains. We got to build a new stage." His sister had staked him to fifteen hundred dollars. His sister did. And so, that last about fifteen minutes. When we got through buying paint, he was broke again. *Yeah.*

So he asked me, "John, you got some money?"

I said, *"Yeah."*

He said, "You got two thousand dollars?"

I said, "Well, I ain't gonna get broke. But I could let you have two thousand."

So we go downtown and get it and he said, "Why don't you take the rest of the day off?"

JIM HAYNIE: One of the regular things that used to happen was that the fire inspectors would come around every weekend to see how many people we had in the joint. We were supposed to have something like 956. That was what it said on the wall. We always had 2,500 or more. Before the fire guys ever got up the steps, we would know they were coming through our grapevine. We had this guy named Lee Jones and he would always be smiling and talking with them and he'd start them on a little tour around the back.

We would have somebody get into the musician's place and have them put out all the reefers. Then I would lead them through there just to keep their eyes off the crowd. Meanwhile, the head fire guy would have left one of his men posted at the box office, shutting it down while he counted the tickets we had already sold.

There was a gate and an alleyway between the Fillmore and the synagogue next door where people stood in line waiting to get in. Bill would get to the line of people waiting to come in and sneak them up the back way. He would take a pasteboard box and just grab money and shove it in the box and slip them all in through the fire escape door on the side *while* we had the fire guys going through the back. While we were supposedly shut down, Bill was slipping them in through the side and making money.

He couldn't resist. That money was there. They had it in their hands. And it belonged to him. Yet if you ever tried to sneak someone in, he would freak out and vilify you tremendously for the heinous act that they were committing. Trying to sneak in maybe five people for the whole evening when there were already thousands inside.

JOHN WALKER: Here's what he did say. He said, "If the dance go over, you'll get your money. If it don't get over, we'll both be out there hustlin'." I said, "Okay." First night, we had better than three thousand in there. Band from Chicago. Butterfield Blues Band. *Yeah*. It was two and a half dollars to get in then.

Right from the beginning, I took tickets at the door. To the gentlemen, I would say, "Have a good day." And to the girls, I'd say, "What was the little boys made out of? Rice and spice and nothin' that ain't nice. Now, have a good day." And they'd be there laughin'. Used to also say, "What the young girls know, the old men want to find out." *Yeah*.

Now Bill, he called me in the office one day. I went in and he said, "Count that money stacked up there." I said, "Okay. What is this for?" He said, "That's your money." I said, "Yeah?" He went back in the safe again and he gave me four hundred more. He said, "This is interest on your money." He said, "If it don't be for you, I never would have made it." I said, "Well, you'd a made it. You'd a made it." But I thought that was awful sweet of him all the same. *Yeah*.

BILL: Again, within the first six months, I don't know exactly in what order, the balloons were there, the apples were there, the glass cases were up on the walls. I would have the artists do the posters for the shows in advance. Wes Wilson I was introduced to through the Trips Festival. He had medium long hair and a very soft, gentle face. I used him on the early posters and he would get a hundred and fifty or two hundred or two hundred and fifty for each one. He would draw them out and bring them to me for approval.

I made it very clear to him that he was the artist but that he was not totally free because he had to communicate information. It wasn't just *his* poster.

WES WILSON: With printing and everything, I got somewhere around seventy-five bucks for a poster. There were probably five hundred printed on fourteen-by-twenty paper, pretty much some kind of vellum-y stock that was cheap. The main thing was money because you couldn't really afford to do anything fancy. The inking was black and white or a single color. Of course, the washup took time and that was an additional factor. From the seventy-five, I would make about forty-five bucks. So about probably eight hours of work.

I remember the Batman poster had like a billion things on it. Bill came down with this incredible list of stuff. "Don't forget to put the dates on it," and of course, I always said yes. I was literally thinking, "Well, I can always write it all in somewhere."

He thought that was so great. He was really impressed. Here he had shelled out, I think it was like fifty or sixty bucks, and he got all these posters and it was just a real knockout. Everybody loved it. He got excited because it just really got his thing happening and I could tell he was going to call me for everything he needed after that. And I was happy about that. I only needed to do two a week to cover my expenses. Eighty-five to a hundred dollars a week.

BILL: I was *possessed.* I'd go out there totally speeded up on my scooter with my Army pack serving a dual purpose. Now it became a poster pack. I would stick a big pile of posters in there with my industrial stapler. And in my coat, my fiberglass 3M tape, so I could put posters up on steel or concrete, not just wood. I would leave the city at four in the morning and go to Berkeley. I plastered everything downtown, always looking for construction sites so I could cover the wooden walls.

When people woke up in the morning, *full.* Every wall. I knew then the posters were hitting home. Because as I went back down a block, I would see people taking them off the walls for their own.

In the early days, I had a tough time convincing people to put them in their stores. They'd look at me and say, "Get that shit out of here." So I started making deals. I would go into a grocery store or a record store and say, "If you put one in the window, I'll give you an extra one for free." When they became popular, store owners would say, "Can I have three? Can I have four?" Once it turned around, they *wanted* them in their stores. But only for a price. Which was I had to give them four extras on the cuff.

At the early stages, it cost like five or six cents a poster to have them printed. I'd print maybe five thousand. Later on, they got more and more expensive. Two color, three color, five color. Some were almost unreadable. I kept on saying to all the artists, "If you keep this design, the only thing I need from you is an asterisk. So we can explain it all on the bottom." But then that sort of became the big thing of the week, too. Trying to figure out what they said.

WES WILSON: The good thing about Bill was he wasn't really that up on what he wanted in terms of graphics and he trusted me more in what I would come up with. I enjoyed and appreciated that. After a while, I didn't do posters for Chet. Mainly because he stopped asking me. I think he felt I should be just *his* poster artist or else nobody's. So Kelly and Mouse kind of became the Family Dog artists. Stanley with the airbrush and Kelly, the two of them got into some great stuff, piecing together things. They'd go to the library and find images and make copies of them and they'd work with Frank Westlake at Fine Leaf Press and came up with competitively priced posters. So we had this kind of rivalry in a sense.

A kind of competitive graphic thing was happening. Each party would try to outdo the other. And it created a great deal of positive energy in the field.

BILL: Within the next few months, I put on all kinds of different shows at the Fillmore. I had Allen Ginsberg, Sopwith Camel, and the Mime Troupe in a benefit. I had *The Beard* by Michael McClure, a great play which some people wanted to ban because they thought it was obscene. I'd been to New York and seen two one-act plays by LeRoi Jones, one called *The Toilet* and the other *The Dutchman*. By themselves, they would have drawn twelve people. I put them on with the Byrds and we got a full house.

LeRoi Jones himself came out to direct the plays. We had all the people sit down on the dance floor *around* the show. The actors did one play, then they took a break, and then they did the next one. The people were blown out. Mesmerized. The lighting was very stark and it was blackness all around the show so people got the *experience* of being in a theater. For most of those kids, it was a first. They had never been to live theater before. And then the Byrds came out to play. They got the plays for one part of their brain and then the music, for the other.

7.

BILL:　Bill Thompson and I always got along. From the days when he was working as a copy boy at the *Chronicle* and I'd see him when I'd go in there trying to get the Mime Troupe listed in the theater section. Bill became the road manager for Jefferson Airplane, who had a manager named Matthew Katz, only he pronounced it "Cates." Bad, *bad* news bear. *Baaad* news. He invented the idea of having two or three groups go out under the same name to different parts of the country.

GRACE SLICK:　I was not in the band at the time but I was at some party with all the Jefferson Airplane and they were saying, "Ooh, you've got to meet our new manager. He's like going to do all the shit for us, and everything." They pointed to him across the room. He had on a black beard, a black mustache, and a black cape with a red lining, and white lace cuffs. *Okay?* He looked the way Hollywood says, *"Here's the devil."* The guy was *telling* them who he was. He was not even jacking them around. I looked from across the room and I went, *"That's* going to be your manager? You're *kidding."*

BILL THOMPSON:　The first time that Jefferson Airplane worked at the Fillmore, I think it was February 4, 5, 6, 1966, Matthew was out of town. We had just gotten this twenty-five-thousand-dollar advance from RCA Victor Records, which was unheard of at the time. *Nobody* got an advance. It was based on an article Ralph Gleason had written about something new that was happening here. Everybody jumped on a plane and came out to see the band and then there was a bidding war.

At the time of the Fillmore show, he was out of the country somewhere. The Bahamas, we heard. People were calling up and Marty Balin said, "Well, why don't *you* talk to people since Katz is gone." I actually booked the first show with Bill. At a thousand dollars a night. At the time, that was a *lot* of money. A lot of money.

Originally, we had another singer with the band. Signe Anderson. At four-thirty in the morning in Chicago in August 1966, the first time we had ever gone on a trip, she called me to say, "I'm quitting the band. I quit. I've had it." That was actually when I called Bill. I said, "Bill, please talk to her." Bill called and talked to Signe and soothed things over. But she told the band she was leaving. She was quitting. Which didn't make people feel happy.

JERRY GARCIA: When Grace joined them, it changed. Grace was already one of the big superstars of the Bay Area, even with the Great Society. It was obvious she was hot. Because she really had great presence. On stage, she had that scary magnetism, that *power.* You could tell she was happening.

GRACE SLICK: From an audience standpoint, at the time the Airplane was more accessible. It was easier to identify with the people in the Airplane than the Grateful Dead or Janis, because Janis was *so* powerful and *so* different, all the emotions right out there. The Grateful Dead looked like they were almost dead. They were only just twenty years old, you know. But they were a *bizarre*-looking group of people. The people in the Airplane were like two-years-of-college, white boys singing folk music. They were just more accessible on a pop-y kind of level.

BILL THOMPSON: Jack Casady stoned one night said, "Grace, I hear you're having problems in your band? Are you thinking about joining us?" We were the hot shit of the town. I think her marriage was not happening or something. She said, "Yeah." So I bought her for seven hundred and fifty dollars from a guy named Howard Wolfe, who was her manager at the time. Probably the greatest move since whoever bought Manhattan from the Indians. He was being a nice guy, really. He kept three songs, two of which were pretty good. "Somebody to Love," and "White Rabbit."

PAUL KANTNER: When Grace joined the band, people *wept.* It was as if Paul McCartney was leaving the Beatles or something. It didn't matter *who* was coming in. It was just Signe leaving. She had a whole coterie of idealistic fans.

BILL THOMPSON: Grace's first show, we had a date playing in Santa Barbara. And then we had one flight only to fly to Los Angeles to make a connecting flight to Des Moines to play at Grinnell College. The flight was at like 9 A.M. I roomed with Spencer Dryden and I had everybody up and ready to go. Only Jorma Kaukonen and Jack Casady had taken the equipment truck in order to go to some party in Aldous Huxley's ex-house. The plane was leaving in forty-five minutes and they had all the equipment.

Those guys showed up and they looked like they were dead. By now, the plane was on the runway. I went running out on the field and I stopped the plane. I just made up lies to the crew. I had seen Bill Graham work so I knew how to do it. I said, "We spend a million dollars a year flying with you people, you have to take us on *and* load all our stuff." So they did.

We flew to Grinnell College for the Homecoming. You should have seen it when we came out to play. We had a light show. But all the girls were in ruffled dresses all the way down to the ankles with corsages, and their *families* were there. We started the light show and we had three sets to do that night. The first set, it was like we were from Mars. Guys with their hair cut like Dobie Gillis were standing there and staring at us. The parents were all farmers. They were looking at one another and saying, "What the hell *is* this stuff? Too loud for me, Maude. Time to go home and milk the goat." So they all left.

The second set, people started dancing a little bit. They started getting into it. The third set, people went *nuts*. Off came the corsages. Shoes were coming off. Guys were ripping off their ties. They went *nuts*. It was one of the greatest feelings I ever had. It was like the turning of America in a way. We went out and played everywhere and did that. We were the first band to do that out of San Francisco. I always felt good about being part of that.

BILL: Katz did some dumb thing and I got them on a television show. "The Bell Telephone Hour." They filmed it at the Fillmore. Matthew came in wearing his cape and they had a big to-do and they didn't want to deal with him anymore. So I just started guiding them and giving them advice. They started having their paperwork done out of the Fillmore. In a room upstairs, we set up an office. Marushka Greene helped and I worked a lot with Bill Thompson.

BILL THOMPSON: I kept going to Bill for advice. I said, "Bill, look, man. Why don't you come in here and *manage* this band? Maybe I could help you out somehow but I don't know how to do it myself. If you don't come in here, there's going to be some crooks from L.A. that are going to come and grab the Airplane."

I had asked the band first and everybody loved Bill. He was the guy. He was *success*. They wanted him. Then we went down to L.A. and recorded *Surrealistic Pillow*.

BILL: Katz had a management contract with them. When the band worked for me, we *never* had a contract. We all agreed that I would take an equal share. I got the same as each one of them did. Bill Thompson did most of the work. I did it because they needed somebody. The one thing I knew about the bands in those days was that I was much more realistic about life than they were. Because I had lived through more of it.

BILL COBLENTZ: They had *lots* of legal problems at the time. Of their own doing. It was awful. Not only Katz but a couple of other claims too. In terms of who owned their music. I mean, I remember when Grace wanted to buy a car. I said, "Fine, we'll get you a letter of credit." No, she wanted cash. So I went with her and I noticed she had a brassiere on, which was something she did not wear very often. Because she wanted to stuff the cash in her bra. Which she did. Then we went and she bought a Mercedes, which was then about eighteen thousand dollars.

Three days later, she totaled it. Things like that just upset me. They shouldn't have but they did. Then I would talk to them about investments. I just thought they should put *some* money aside. They would say, "Well, if I don't get the right *vibes*, I don't want to do it."

BILL THOMPSON: Bill Graham and the group had lots of fights. *Horrible* fights. He didn't really understand the scene so much. He was the guy who made it happen and without him we wouldn't be here today. But he didn't understand *them.*

Around January 1967, Bill became the manager. That was another one of the fights between them. They didn't want to sign a contract with him. They had been burned before and he wanted a contract and that really led to a lot of trouble. I was trying to kind of be in the middle of it but it just wasn't working out.

PAUL KANTNER: Part of being in a band is accepting the other band members' dim areas in the hope that they'll accept yours. Bill never understood that. Not that we ever really gave a shit about it. It wasn't something that we considered. He had his way and we had ours. Sometimes we got along and sometimes we didn't.

GRACE SLICK: We liked him though. Because we were all characters back then and everybody looked different. That was perfectly acceptable. Pigpen didn't look anything like Marty Balin who didn't look anything like Jorma and I didn't look anything like Ginger Schuster. We all had our costumes on. Bill Graham had on a New York kind of costume. There was a consciousness of him being almost like the principal of a school. He liked us but he was the *straight* guy.

PAUL KANTNER: He didn't understand us, particularly as Jefferson Airplane. He liked *salsa* music better. And he would say things like, "Can't you play quiet? I can't hear the words." Or, "Can you play a song I can hum?"

GRACE SLICK: It was like the bands and the artists were *here* and then Bill Graham and the parents were *there*. He was a little better than the parents. We could talk to Bill Graham better than we could talk to the president of the Bank of America or even the president of RCA Victor. But he wasn't one of the hippies and he wasn't all the way over to where you just didn't want to have anything to do with him either. He had a real good business head.

BILL: We were ready to go on the road and the band was rehearsing in the Geary Temple down the street from the Fillmore. They had started to make some money and I realized there was a change coming about because now they could strut a little better financially. Jorma was not there. Finally he showed up, two hours late. I said, "Jorma, you know you held up the whole band. Where were you? What could have held you up?"

He looked at me like there was nothing to it. And he said, "I was at a *fitting*, man."

He had just had a leather outfit made and he had been at a *fitting*. I blew it. I went mad. *"WHAT DO YOU MEAN YOU WERE AT A FITTING?"* I screamed at him. "You couldn't even *SPELL* that word six months ago! *FITTING!"*

They came from the laissez-faire school of show business. I'll play the way I feel. To them, the stage was not a stage but their own living room where they could do whatever they pleased. I remember one night when they played everything that they knew. Like three hours. And the people went *bananas*. And it was *real*. Not phony, like even audience reactions became later on. But, *"Wow! Just great!"* I went back and I said to Paul Kantner, "Just from a moral point of view, why don't you go back out and take a bow?"

"What'd you say?" he said.

"Just go out and take a bow," I told him.

Paul said, "Fuck that. That's show business."

I turned to him and I said, *"Schmuck!* What do you think you're in?"

It was the first time he ever went out and took a bow. The public *loved* it.

8.

KEN KESEY: By the time I came back to San Francisco in October for the Acid Test at San Francisco State, things had changed. People had begun to sum it up just the way the Mafia would divide parts of Chicago. It happened *that* fast. We were planning to do this Acid Test Graduation with the Dead but people I had never heard of were in charge of the large halls. I had no intention of being a rock and roll entrepreneur, ever. But everybody thought that I was, coming back like Jake LaMotta to grab my share of the trade. It wasn't what I had in mind at all. I had other fish to fry.

KEN BABBS: We were talking about doing another Acid Test at the Fillmore. Neal Cassady wanted to get the hall for the gig. So he went there and pulled his car right up in front. Bill Graham was on the steps and Neal yelled at him. "Hey, *Bill!* We *need* the *hall*. Can we *get* the hall? We're going to do *another* gig."

Bill said, "Ah, Neal. It's Friday night. It's late. I'm going home. Let's talk about this on Monday."

"No, *no!*" Neal said. "We got to deal with it right *now!* We got to handle this thing right *now!*"

Bill said, "Neal. You'll be here on Monday and I'll be here on Monday. Let's do it on Monday."

Neal said, "*Bill.* I know you'll be here and I'll be here. But what about the *hall?*" It was like two people from different universes that came together in the same universe.

KEN KESEY: This was the avatar. Cassady. One of the great failures of all time. I mean, he failed *big*. But everyone who touched him was influenced by him. Allen Ginsberg and William Burroughs and Jack Kerouac and me and Bill Graham. Cassady was Bill's nemesis. I mean, Neal could eat three Bill Grahams with a small glass of sauterne on the side to wash him down. This was a guy who was off the scale.

I remember going to the Fillmore to see a concert that Bill was doing. We had our outfits on. We had just gotten off the bus. We were coming there in full Prankster power. It was about six-thirty in the afternoon, the sun was just going down, and it was pretty. Suddenly, Bill came out of the Fillmore. He was very busy. He looked up and there we were, coming toward him.

He didn't want to deal with us so he got out in the street and pretended to be looking for something. As he went by, Cassady said, "There's Bill Graham out there, checking the tire treads to see if one of them picked up a nickel." Bill heard him. He flushed. But he couldn't take Cassady on. No one could. He could run circles around anyone with words.

Bill came over and asked him why he had said this. Neal said, " 'Cause I'm concerned about your soul, Bill."

Bill said, "This is just show business, Neal."

Neal said, "This is *soul* business, Bill."

Not many people do what Cassady used to call the inside straight. He went for the inside straight *all* the time. Like Zarathustra or Lao-tzu, who was able to make that Zen koan maneuver and expose where you were.

BILL: At this point, Kesey had incredible power. I was afraid that he was going to run amok with it, which he did for a while. There was going to be an Acid Test Graduation in Winterland. I was going to run it the way I had the Trips Festival. But I got a tip that Kesey and Owsley were going to tap into the water system and just turn on everyone who came there.

CHET HELMS: In fairness to Kesey, I think he had a lot of faith in his abilities to transform people and in the ability of acid to transform them. He had some illusions that he was going to transform the Hell's Angels. Which to some extent he did. But I always felt there was a very military tone to Kesey's trips. When he was running from the cops, it was like Rommel in the desert or something. It even extended over to their affection for the Angels and wearing of colors and uniforms. A kind of militancy in collective action.

There had just been the Watts Acid Test down in L.A. and there had been a dosage error where they mixed the wrong proportions in the Kool-Aid so that people got eight *hundred* mikes instead of eighty mikes. So they had a lot of freak-outs and people who had serious problems. People who had been immensely loyal to Kesey quit after that, including the dose master. It was just too much for them.

Graham called me and said, "Chet, this is what people are telling me. That this guy intends to dose the oranges and the door handles and the food and *everything* is going to be dosed. What do you think?"

I said, "I don't know. I think he's probably serious. That he *will* do it." I had only met Kesey a couple of times and I wasn't an intimate of his. So I said, "I know people who will know. I'll call them and see what they think. Let them do a little asking around to see what's up."

So I called my friend who had been the dose master. He did a little checking around and he stated to me that Kesey's intent at the time was to dose *everybody*. I called Bill back and told him this and he said, "Well, that's the end of that."

Tom Wolfe gives me credit for pulling the plug on the Acid Test Graduation scheduled for Winterland. He makes me out to be the stick-in-the-mud prude who kind of killed the party. But I had no real control over the situation. Bill asked me what I thought was a very fair and ethical question. You know. "What is this guy going to do?"

KEN KESEY: The Acid Test Graduation finally happened in a warehouse on Sixth Street in the city. The Dead were supposed to play but because it all got too tacky, they didn't. We got a group called the Anonymous Artists. For the Acid Test Graduation. The *Graduation*. Which in its way was appropriate. Because it *was* the denouement of something.

BILL: I stopped it from happening. If you were going to get together with your friends and carefully let them experience something on a safe level, fine. But why should everyone be told to take great challenging steps with *their* psyche? Just because *you* had decided to do so with your own? Ken was never as disrespectful of human life as Timothy Leary, who sold it and flaunted it and pushed it. "Tune in, turn on, drop out." Get with it. Get down. Forget your parents. Forget your friends. Get only with your own kind. To this day, I *still* cannot tolerate him.

OWSLEY STANLEY: I thought it was dangerous for persons much over forty to get involved with psychedelics. Because of my experience with Tim Leary, who was maybe forty-four or forty-five when he first took acid. He was a very bizarre dude. I would try to tell him, "Hey, you know, Tim! You're talking bullshit, you know? I mean, *hey*. It's *me!* Don't give me that *shit*, man*!*" But he was constantly missing the *thing*, you know? Like it was going on in the next room. He was all hung up examining his own navel. Instead of like going with it.

KEN BABBS: Really, the most important thing about it was the fact that at the time, it was time not to do Acid Tests anymore. It was time to move on and do other stuff. So we did. We all moved up to Oregon.

Chapter Five

Doing Shows

1.

DAVID RUBINSON: I came out to San Francisco in December 1966, a month before the Human Be-In. The best band out here then was Moby Grape. Bar *none*. Moby Grape and then Steve Miller. Big Brother was terrible. The Airplane was terrible. The Warlocks who then became the Grateful Dead were terrible. All these people, they were horrible.

They couldn't play. They couldn't tune their guitars. And they were doing what to me was the ultimate injustice. They were doing Elmore James *badly*. It was like Lenny Bruce said to a policeman who arrested him. "You're going to get *me* busted by doing *my* act for the judge?"

These incredibly untalented, unmusical people were getting up and doing stuff they had learned off some old Kent or Chess record which I had loved since I was fifteen years old. They were doing "Baby, Please Don't Go" and "Gone Down New Orleans." They were doing the blues and the kids were loving it because they had never heard it before. Which was why I despised the Beatles until they developed their own stuff. It was laughable to me. I watched these San Francisco bands play blues that they couldn't play. But Steve Miller, Sons of Champlin, and Moby Grape were *staggering* bands. Because they completely had their own stuff.

BILL: From the very beginning, I accepted the fact that I had no real personal knowledge of the rock scene of that era. I had been into Latin music all of my life. I didn't listen to the radio so I didn't really know what was going. Even if I had, I wouldn't have heard the music that was being played at the Fillmore then. The earliest education I got about the scene came when Paul Butterfield first played for me and we began talking about the blues and Chicago and the Mississippi Delta. He just started throwing names at me. The Staple Singers and Otis Redding and Bobbie "Blue" Bland and James Brown and Chuck Berry.

There was an *ultimate* musician everyone wanted to see. Everybody said, *"This* is the guy." *Otis*. Otis Redding. He was *it*. For everybody that talked to me. To get Otis to come and play the Fillmore, I flew into Atlanta in order to go up to Macon, which was in the middle of nowhere. I think it impressed them that I would go all that way. But I thought, "How do you explain to somebody that I really would like them to come here and play for me?" I could have offered ten thousand dollars, which would have meant I would have been dead. Out of business. At the time, I couldn't afford it. Or I could've said that when I talked to artists I respected, Paul Butterfield, Michael Bloomfield, Jerry Garcia, when I asked, "Who's your guy? Who's number one on your list?" they all tell me it's *you*.

I tried to be humble with him. Not, "You *gotta* come play the *great* Fillmore," but the other way around. "Everybody tells me that it's not right unless I get you to do this. Myself, I'm a Latin music fan and I don't really know of you. I'm a Carmen MacRae fan."

His people asked me about the kids who went to the Fillmore and the drugs they took. They thought it was like voodoo rites out there. The lights, the paints, the crazy clothes. It was *strange* for them. Which was another reason that my going to Macon helped. Because I was a pretty straight guy and I didn't dress fancy.

Finally, he agreed to come with his band, called the Robert Hathaway Band. He played in December 1966. By *far*, Otis Redding was *the* single most extraordinary talent I had ever seen. There was no comparison. Then or *now*.

PHIL WALDEN: I was Otis's manager. I guess maybe Jon Landau told me about the Fillmore and it was not a problem to go there. Obviously, we thought it was something that would be to our advantage. Because in those days, our exposure to the white market, just to put it in very blunt terms, was very limited. Otis had worked to white audiences but at white colleges in the South because it was a tradition. Black people *always* entertained white people down there.

Within the business itself, the black record business, nearly all the managers were white. Back then, I was constantly being told, "Man, you can't treat these people like they're *white*. If you do, they'll eat you up. You give them a finger, they want the hand. Then the arm. They want everything. They're *never* satisfied."

Why *should* they be satisfied? Why shouldn't they want the same damn things? I never would be satisfied. Why shouldn't they want the same damn things? I never would be satisfied with just the finger. I wanted the hand too. The arm. The whole damn *body*.

BILL: Every artist in the city asked to open for Otis. The first night, it was the Grateful Dead. Janis Joplin came at three in the afternoon the day of the first show to make sure that she'd be in front. To this day, no musician ever got *everybody* out to see them the way he did. Every musician then into music came. He was THE *MAN*. THE *REAL* MAN. If you liked R&B or white rock and roll or black rock and roll or jazz, you came to see Otis.

With a huge band behind him. Eighteen pieces. The first night he wore a green suit, a black shirt, and a yellow tie, with a key chain hanging from his belt. Six foot three, a black Adonis. He moved like a serpent. A panther stalking his prey. Knowing he was the ruler of the universe. Beautiful and shining, black, sweaty, sensuous, and passionate. He was the predecessor to the one who finally broke through to playing before a mixed audience of black *and* white rock and rollers.

Not until Jimi Hendrix came along did I realize that Otis had been there before him. Jimi was the first one who had white women *openly* desiring him in public without even realizing that they were doing it. But Otis was the predecessor.

On stage, the man never stopped moving. He would do a number and at the end of the number, he would strut the stage. *"Yeah! Whew! Hey! Oh! Yeah! Party! Oh! Yeah! Whew!* One, *two . . ."* and right into the next number. Three, four songs into the set on the first night, I was standing on the side of the stage. I couldn't believe how great he was.

He started doing his strut, back and forth. *"Yeah! Oh! Damn! Whew!"* As he was doing this, there was this woman leaning against the front of the stage. A gorgeous young black lady in a low-cut dress. She started sighing like she just could not hold on. *"O-tis! Oh! Ah! Ah! Oooh!"* He saw her. He was going back and forth and he said, *"Yeah!"* He had the microphone in his hand and he saw her and she said, *"Unnh!"* He walked across the stage, leaned down, took the mike, and pulled a move that has never been equaled.

He leaned down and looked at her, and he was a big, good-looking guy, and she was going, *"Oh! Oh!"* And he said right into her face, "I'm gonna s-s-sock it to you, baby. One, *two . . ."* And the whole place went *"Hah!"* all together.

I had expected something special but not this. This sheer *animal*. He did something that night that nobody could do. He got them clapping as

he did "Fa-fa-fa-fa" all over the stage. When he finished, the people were
high, screaming *"Yeah! Yeah!"* and applauding like mad and just before
the applause died down, he hit them with "I been lovin' you too long . . ."
He hit it *every* time just before the fall. Just before the audience came
back down. You're high? You're gonna come down? I'm *still* here. I
haven't left *yet.* Nobody *ever* did that. To this day, I've *never* seen anybody
do that. When Richard Pryor was at his best, you could never turn off
the laughter. There was another laugh and another and it hurt. This
didn't hurt.

What he had was that he was calm. He was laid back. But he moved
at the same time. He was the *real* Tom Jones. The one Tom Jones always
wanted to be.

A shining hour. Otis finished. He was upstairs in his dressing room. I
was outside when he called me in. *"Bill! Bill!"* I walked in and he said,
"I *love* these people!" He was out of breath and sweating bullets because
he had just really rocked that house. The band was high. They knew
they'd burned. He was sitting there with towels all over him and I said,
"Otis, I can't tell you. Jesus . . ." And I started to go on and on.

The first thing he said to me was, "Very nice ladies here. *Very* nice
ladies."

PHIL WALDEN: Otis was quite fond of the women out there. He was
pretty fond of women *everywhere* he went. He left his mark, shall we say.
That great writer from the San Francisco paper, Ralph Gleason, he gave
Otis one of the best reviews he had ever gotten. I think he really captured
him. He said Otis Redding was just pure sex. Everything he did. Every
word he uttered. Every motion he made. It was all just the most
completely sexual thing he had ever witnessed in his life.

BILL: "My God," I said to Otis. "Two more nights. Is there anything I
can get for you?"

"No, no," he said.

As I was leaving, he said, "Yeah, Bill. Hold it. We just got back from
England and when you tour over there, you can't get no ice. Can I get me
a big thing with ice and some 7-Up?"

"No problem," I said.

I ran downstairs to Denise, who worked behind the counter. I said,
"Denise, I need two big containers with a lot of ice and some 7-Up."

She said, "The ice machine broke."

"What do you mean, it *broke?*"

"Well, we're serving drinks anyway but we don't have ice."

I left the building. I ran out of there, *possessed.* I ran down Geary to the market a block away. I bought a bag of ice. I ran back up Geary Street into the Fillmore. I broke up the ice on the counter. When I got back in there, I was breathing pretty hard. Then I put the ice in the cups and added the 7-Up. When I hit the double door to go upstairs, I started thinking, "How am I going to let Otis know what I just did for him?"

On purpose, I started breathing real heavy all over again. I started panting like I had just ran the four-minute mile. "7-Up," I said. "Enough ice for you?"

"What's the matter?" Otis asked.

"Nothing. I had to . . . *we* . . . never mind."

"Hey," he said. "What happened?"

"Well," I said, still trying to catch my breath. "It's no big thing. I . . . we . . . uh . . . the ice machine broke. I had to run down the street to get you the ice. Hey, no big deal . . ."

Then Otis made the great move. He grabbed my shirt. He said, "You did *what?* You went down the street for ice for *me?*"

"Yeah. So what?"

He gave me this big hug. Then he pulled away, and said, "Let me tell you something, man. When I play this town from now on, I play for *you.*"

If anybody ever wanted to know what the business was all about, I always thought that night was it. How do I tell you I want you to come back here? Just 7-Up, with ice.

That was the best gig I ever put on in my entire life. I knew it then. *No* maybe about it. Otis for three nights at the Fillmore. That was as good as it got. Good sex with somebody you really love is great stuff. So was that.

PHIL WALDEN: I think I've got two posters that I've saved in my life. One is Monterey Pop and the other was when Otis played at the Fillmore. Otis had a funny reaction to it, boy. He said, "Oh, these fucking hippies, man. They're smoking dope and shit like it's *legal* out here. See, *everybody's* high." This was a cultural revolution for these black guys from the South.

I think Otis set up what was going to happen in the seventies because for the first time, people found out that on a lot of these great black records, it was black *and* white people playing *together.*

Which was never a problem in the South. Visually, you didn't see it. But all the great stuff you were hearing came from the common ground that existed between blacks and whites in the South. A lot of people said later on, "Well, how did Gregg Allman learn how to sing *black?*" He didn't. It was part of his *culture.* Gregg don't know how to sing any way *but* black. That's not foreign to him. Singing like Donny Osmond would be hard for him. For the white have-nots and the black have-nots in the South, music was *the* common ground.

BILL: I realized then how great he was. With every passing year, those shows get better and better in terms of all the other people I've seen on stage since then. Otis didn't dance *per se*. The inner parts of his body moved. It was where his voice came from and how he put *everything* into a song. Otis was a first *every* time for me. Every show was new and different. There was the animal and physical intensity. He was sheer rhythm and he was *impassioned*. The key to a great artist is the ability to make the audience feel he is into it *every* night. Otis did that. He hasn't been equaled. There's nothing close.

I might love this person or that act or some band. But who's gonna do "GOTTA GOTTA GOTTA GOTTA . . . UH UH *UH!*" like him? There's just no one else who can.

2.

BILL: I was beginning to realize I could disregard whether the supporting acts on the bill would sell any tickets on their own. I could put on not only what I wanted to but what I *should*'ve been putting on.

I didn't have to worry that the top act would only sell so many tickets so I needed to find another act that would sell out the rest. The headliner *alone* was big enough to fill the Fillmore. Then I could say, "My God, I heard this *incredible* tape the other day." Or, "Butterfield told me about this guy named Otis Redding." Or, "So-and-So told me about Chuck Berry." Or "This band told me about the Staple Singers." Or "That guy told me about Freddie King."

Freddie King didn't mean *anything* in San Francisco at that time. But Quicksilver alone would sell out the hall. It was like a mother saying to her child, "You want the ice cream? You gotta eat the meat. You gotta eat the vegetables. The meat is good for you, the vegetables are good for you. Gotta eat your meat and veggies. *Then* you get your ice cream."

The ice cream was the Grateful Dead or Quicksilver or Jefferson Airplane. But the vegetables you had to go through to get to the ice cream might have been Lightning Hopkins or Junior Wells. It was like, "Go on. You'll *love* him. You don't think so now. But you will. When you *try* him."

The Staple Singers were another example of an act that most of the kids didn't know. Mavis Staples for me was in the same class as Aretha. They worked with Rahsaan Roland Kirk and Love. Rahsaan had finished and I could feel the audience starting to go to the concessions. Back then, I would always do the same thing. Introduce the act and walk to the corner of the stage so I could feel it and check out the first songs.

Mavis started snapping her fingers into the microphone as Pops took it all alone on the guitar. She sang, "You're gonna hear from the Lord . . ." and the entire room turned around and sat back down. No more selling at the concessions. The sign of a great talent to me? No one goes out to buy a *thing*. They sit and watch or stand and dance or whatever. Watching the room turn around for Mavis and leaving that night knowing the audience had all tasted a fresh new fruit and would want it again, that was the greatest for me.

Watching someone like Howlin' Wolf, who stood six feet five and was not all that young when he first came to play the Fillmore, do a total somersault on stage in a *suit*. It was amazing.

In 1966 and '67, the average seventeen-year-old kid did not know who Chuck Berry or B. B. King or Albert King were. The way I got hold of all these people was that one guy would give me the next guy's phone number. Howlin' Wolf gave me a number for Big Joe Williams. Because a lot of them didn't work out of agencies. They had some guy in Chicago or Detroit handling their business. So it was a chain reaction thing. One led to another. Because if it hadn't have been for Muddy Waters, there might never have been an Eric Clapton. Or Junior Wells or Luther Allison.

We had Muddy Waters at the Fillmore first with Butterfield and Jefferson Airplane. Every musician wanted to see Otis but they all wanted to *play* with Muddy Waters. He had Otis Spann with him and they did "Hoochie Coochie Man" and "I'm a Man." "I spell M-A-N." Muddy was awesome in that he had a great groove but he was like your uncle or your daddy, telling you things from his own experience. Whereas Otis Redding was still singing to an audience of his peers. To me, Muddy was a lot like John Walker. He was older. He had that regal presence. He had lived through a lot of shit but he didn't make the world pay for it. Butterfield revered him.

There are two or three names in the business that are on the top ten list of every musician I know. Muddy was one of those people.

3.

BILL: Michael Bloomfield and Jorma Kaukonen from Jefferson Airplane kept talking to me about Chuck Berry. They said, "He *has* to play the Fillmore." Because he was where all their licks came from. But he just wouldn't come out to play. It was always, "The Fillmore, man? I don't know." So I went to Wentzville, Missouri, to talk to him. Chuck wouldn't even come to the airport to meet me. I had to rent a car and drive out to his farm.

He said, "I don't bring no band. You supply the band. You supply the dual Showman Amp. You supply me a Cadillac at the airport."

I came back and we made the deal over the phone. Eight hundred dollars for two sets a night, three nights in March. The opening act was a band called the Loading Zone and they stayed on to play behind him. First night, we had a full house. Chuck Berry. His was the name that most white people *did* know but they'd never seen him before in this scene. That night, eight o'clock, he wasn't there. Nine o'clock, he wasn't there. Five minutes to ten, I was out of my mind. The Loading Zone had finished their set a long time ago. We reset the stage for Chuck and put his dual amp out there.

Ten P.M., I just happened to be in the office. In fact, I was on the phone calling the airport to see if his plane had landed. There was a knock on the door. I opened it and there was Chuck Berry. I shook his hand. I said, "How you doin', Chuck? You're a little late."

He didn't move or speak. He set his guitar case down on the floor and stood there staring at me. "Right," I said. "You want to get paid before you go on."

I went and got the checkbook. Some bands would take a check and deposit it. Others wanted the check cashed right then and there. I made the mistake of looking over at Chuck Berry and saying, "You want cash or a check?" The look he gave me was, "Are you out of your mind? Why do you ask such a stupid question? I won't even honor it with an answer."

"Okay," I said. I took the check, wrote it out, and moved it over to his side of the desk.

He signed the check on the back. Then he moved it halfway over toward me. Like into the medium, *neutral* zone of the desk. He still hadn't said a word. I pushed eight hundred dollars in cash over to his side of the desk. He counted it out in front of me. He took the money in one hand, slid the check all the way over to me, and put out his other hand for me to shake.

"Mellow," he said.

I took the signed check and stuck it in my pocket. He put down his coat and unpacked his guitar. I said, "Chuck, are you ready?" I thought he would say, "I gotta go to the bathroom. I gotta change my shoes or my shirt." He said, "Let's go." It was like, "You want me to fight ten rounds? I'll fight ten."

He walked onto the stage. I said, "Chuck, you want me to introduce you to the band?" He looked at them. He said, "Hello, hello, hello," to each one in turn. There was no set list, no nothing. They had no idea what he was going to play.

I went to the microphone and said, "It's a great honor, would you welcome please, the *Man*, Chuck Berry." One, two, one, two, *three*. They went right into it.

Chuck did his thing. He did his chicken dance back and forth across the stage. After forty-five minutes, he came over to my side of the stage. The kids were going crazy, screaming, *"More! More! More!"* Chuck put his guitar in the case. I said, "Chuck, what're you doing?"

"What is it?" he said. "What is it?"

I said, "Chuck, listen to that applause."

"No," he said, "I don't hear it. I don't hear it. They don't want me."

He was doing this jive Scatman Crothers routine on me. *"YEA!"* they were all screaming. *"MORE!"* He couldn't *HELP* but hear it. "They don't want me, boss," he said. "They don't want me, boss man."

I knew it was a number. But I figured I had to get into it, or else.

"Chuck," I said. "They *want* you. They *want* you."

"They don't *love* me," he said. "They don't *love* me."

By now, he was strapping on his case to leave.

"They *want* you, Chuck," I told him. "You can't leave. They *love* you."

He leaned over to me. "They *love* me?" he said. "They *want* me? I'm goin' out there." He opened up the case. "I'm comin'," he said. "I'm here. And I *love* you."

He went back out, got to the microphone, and said, "Yeah, you love me, you want me, yeah, and one, two, one, two, *three*."

What he was really saying to me was, "They want me, they love me, but *you're* not paying me enough money. Why aren't *you* paying me more money? Next time, *you're* gonna pay me more, right?"

And I was saying, *"Right."*

I realized he had been doing this number for like nine hundred and three years. That short thirty seconds was pure genius theater of the very first order. Somebody had to answer Gabriel. I'm blowing my horn but nobody hears me. They *hear* you, Gabe.

KEITH RICHARDS:　It was the strangest thing. In '64 and '65 and '66, it was only okay to tour in America with mixed acts in the *South*. In the North, it was much harder. In the big cities and the industrial centers, you just *couldn't*. Even though presumably they were more tolerant. Certain lines had been drawn.

Back then, it was a brave move to mix up soul acts with the most extreme of white music at the time. Bill was the first one to do it in a big city on a regular basis. Especially in a community joint like the Fillmore where people virtually *lived*. I mean, he had that same audience in there for *years*. Bill really did create an opportunity that changed a lot of things.

4.

BILL: The greatest compliment I was ever given came at the Fillmore. It was Cream and the Butterfield Blues Band. I just happened to go into the rest room during a break. I was standing at the middle urinal when two guys came in after me, one on either side. They were looking straight ahead, the way you do when you're taking a leak, and right out of the blue one said, "Oh, shit, man. I forgot. Who's playing here tonight?"

Without batting an eyelash, the other guy said, "I don't know, man. What's the difference? It's the *Fillmore.*"

Most people *did* know who was playing. My whole theory about promotion was that you may decide to go roller skating tonight. But if you do, you'll know what you missed at the Fillmore. That was my entire theory about advertising. Get the word out to everybody. This is what's here *this* weekend. You don't want to check it out? *Fine.* But you know what it is. You want to eat over there? Eat over there.

DAVID RUBINSON: He and Bonnie were running the whole thing. What did Bill bring to San Francisco? He brought delivery on promises. He brought a place where when the bands were told they would be paid three hundred dollars, it was three hundred. If you were told to show up at five o'clock, at five o'clock he was there. The band could come in, the electricity worked, there was good food backstage. That's what Bill brought.

And it was all in cash. Everything was in cash. *Cash!* Bill would go to all the head shops in the city and he would give them tickets for the coming week's show and pick up the money from last week's show. There was no distribution network. There was no BASS, no Ticketron. Tickets were sold from all the head shops and record stores. And Bill would have a brown paper bag and say, "How many tickets did I give you?"

The guy would say, "Three hundred."

Bill would say, "Okay. Three hundred, that's six hundred dollars. And here's three hundred more for next week."

It was the most remarkable blending together of the Catskill Mountains aggressive mentality, the refugee mentality where everything you owned had to be able to fit in a handkerchief on your back or on a stick or it didn't exist, and people who were totally stoned. Bill interfacing with these people was fabulous. It was *great*. The head shop would get 10 percent of whatever they sold plus a couple free tickets. He was always giving them gifts. Tickets, jackets, records, whatever it was. He developed an incredible alternative economy. Seen from an MBA's point of view, it made perfect sense. Seen from my point of view, it made perfect sense. Because how did he make his money at the Concord? Not waiting on tables. *Running the game.* To make it happen, everybody down the line had to get a piece.

What we had was Bill Graham going around with his Catskill Mountains mentality dealing with these space dogs and crazy people and acid freaks and musicians. He brought a certain incredible level of truth to it all. The people out here were all Gentiles and they thought like Gentiles and acted like Gentiles and it was all wrong. Somebody had to take care of the Catskill Mountains end of it. And that was what Bill did. First for the Mime Troupe and then at the Fillmore. He was like the *wife.*

BILL: Fridays and Saturdays we were always jammed, no matter what. But on Thursdays and Sundays, it was a little less. To balance things out, I would give out the handbill for free. I initiated a policy within the first year that if you came on Thursday or Sunday, instead of a handbill of next week's poster, which you then got every night for free, you got a poster of next week's show instead. This got people in on those nights. It was also a way to advertise the next show because they stuck them up in their homes and in their stores. It was the forerunner of merchandising.

5.

BILL: Before this time, there always were pockets of people in our society seeking alternate lifestyles. In the sixties, the funnel opened wide. For the first time in modern history, there was social upheaval among the young. The children. The world of people between fourteen and twenty-five. That didn't happen in the thirties. That was an economic upheaval. People may have rejected the existing order before but the difference this time was in the sheer strength of numbers. The vehicle was music. And millions of young people got on the bandwagon.

MICHAEL STEPANIAN: What happened basically was that Bill Graham stood up before a full house at the Fillmore and said, "Everyone in this hall can be represented by these two guys. These guys are going to take care of it and I'm going to take care of all the expenses." This was the HALO benefit in May 1967. He was talking about Brian Rohan and myself. We went to the Grateful Dead house on Ashbury and opened an office.

I would go to the office and there would be lines of kids waiting, lines of hippies. "What happened?" I would say. A draft thing. "What happened?" A *this* thing. "What happened?" A *drug* thing. And I would represent every single kid for nothing. No one ever went to prison. I appeared for all of them. I got jammed up but basically, the San Francisco courts didn't mind. They had a history of Barbary Coast stuff. These kids were clean. None of them ran away. They all showed up in court. They never tattled on each other. Those were the rules I had.

We would be there in court, the baby sucking on her mother's tit, the kids with long hair. At first, the bailiffs would look at us like we were ugly. Then the kids would testify about how the cops had knocked down the walls to bust them. We'd be fighting illegal search. We'd cross-examine the agents and we'd yell and scream. Pretty soon, there was a wave of sympathy for these people.

I would be saying, "These are doctors, these are lawyers, these are kids with parents who are rich." It would be a kid from Westchester, it would be a kid from Shaker Heights. It would be a kid from the fancy suburbs of Denver. And they were all *here*. The cops even related to us, they would call us to find lost kids. And the parents would come. "I lost my daughter." I'd put the word out, "Find the daughter." We'd find the daughter. We'd bring her to the parents. She'd say, "I'd rather stay here, Mom." "Okay, fine. I just wanted to know you were well." There would be this beautiful sense of togetherness. They were all emulsified into this culture where people were taking LSD and walking around and dancing and it was clean and it was beautiful and we had Brian Rohan doing the music stuff while I handled all the rest of it. And we both had short hair. We all had like short hair.

BILL: On May 25, 1967, there was a benefit for the Black Panthers at the Fillmore. Huey Newton, LeRoi Jones, and Stokely Carmichael were there. I remember Huey Newton sitting on top of the steps in one of those big straw fan-back chairs with two guys standing next to him with sticks in their hands. He really did that. I don't know if it was the same chair that he sat in for that poster that was everywhere during that time, but he did sit there like that, as people came up the stairs to greet him.

The second time I went up the stairs, they wanted to frisk *me*. I said, "You frisk me and I close this building." It was like I was being *held* in there by them. That they would give me back my building once they were through with it. Once I established that they could not take over the building but that I would be glad to do what they wanted within reason, they were very decent and the night ran very' well.

PETER BERG: There were riots in the Fillmore [September 27, 1967]. The next day was the first Digger picket. By the end of the week, we had twenty-five people dropping out of the Mime Troupe to form the Diggers.

PETER COYOTE: The Diggers were saying that anybody who used money was a fucking fascist pig. Everybody seems to have misunderstood the Diggers as a Salvation Army group. You know, be nice to people. It was far more dangerous than that. It was a radical anarchist group that was really about authenticity and autonomy. If you had an idea, you took responsibility for it and got it done. There was no sense waiting for tomorrow.

The kids were coming to San Francisco. They were being attracted by all the media hype and the city was pissing on them. Somebody said, "Hey, let's feed them." Somebody else said, "Hey, let's fuck around with the Free Frame of Reference." Everything was designed to jog conscious-ness. To break addiction to identity, to money, to job, to whatever. Because we knew that the real problem was the culture. The problem wasn't capitalism. The problem wasn't Communism. The problem was the *culture.*

The whole internally consistent ball of wax that had people enslaved. One of the things about the Diggers that was really radical, unlike the guys we taught like Jerry Rubin and Abbie Hoffman, was that free also meant identity was free. You didn't get your picture in the paper. You didn't take credit for what you did. You just did it because you wanted to and that's what made it free.

People thought we were just giving stuff away. But in Peter Berg's Free Store, not only the goods were free but the roles as well. Someone would come in and say, *"Who's* the manager?" And you'd say, *"You* are." What do we do today, you know? Ron Thelin and Arthur Lisch set up a table on the freeway during rush hour traffic. Four places. Crystal, linen, champagne. They sat out there reading the newspaper with two places empty. Anyone who wanted to get out of their car and eat with them, that was fine, you know?

You were responsible. Eternity was right now, and you were responsible for acting out your future. No Communist or capitalist forces intervening. *Do it.* You want to do it? You want to feed people? *Do it.* We had this incredible, inventive theatrical sense. The common denominator that made everything comprehensible—in other words, the reason that acts of extreme personal expression were comprehensible was because the sub-text of everything was revolution. *Change.* That's why it meant something when someone grew their hair. It was all the subtext.

Whether Bill knew that we could kill his audience as we did at one point when somebody tried to hold a Digger music festival, I can't say for sure. I'd like to give him the benefit of the doubt. Bill's loyalty to the people involved or his ability to see there was a commonality in attitude and posture between us may have figured into it. He was a businessman. But I think he wanted the buzz.

PETER BERG: At this point, the strongest memory I have of Graham is going to see him at the Fillmore Auditorium with a Digger partner named Sweet William. Sweet William was rather scary to people at the time. He was big and he wore black leather. He went with me and said, "I'm going to come just so this guy knows we're *serious*." And we went to ask for five hundred dollars for some Digger cost.

At this point, the gulf between Graham and I was a *chasm*. Enormous. We are talking about opposite ends of the planet. And he opened up this big, ledger-style checkbook and just paid. "Take the check. Do it." I don't know why he acquiesced on our request. Sweet William frightened him. He was making a lot of money off the hippie phenomenon. That was a point of resentment at that time. And he should have given some money back to the community. But he was certainly willing to.

We did an event for him in the Fillmore called, "Roll Your Own, Stone Your Neighbor." We had charcoal burning in braziers and we threw hashish down in them and blew smoke through tubes. You know, mailing tubes. He was *appalled* that this was going on.

PETER COYOTE: Imagine Bill Graham as we were coming out of smoke generated by buckets of burning marijuana. Bricks of marijuana that were laying on coals with big cardboard tubes to blow the smoke across the corridor. Bill was screaming, "THE FUCK IS GOING ON HERE? WHAT ARE YOU TRYING TO DO? GET ME *KILLED?* Oh, you *fucking guys!* You *fucking* guys . . ." But he didn't stop it.

I think we went too far in Bill's house. But I also think there were no recriminations from it. In the sense that I don't think Bill would give us another benefit. I don't think he would have done that. But he played. He played. And he had a lot to lose. You've got to take your hat off to that man.

JUDY GOLDHAFT: But everything was fine. No one got hurt. He was hysterical because he thought the Fire Department would close him down, with the braziers. I admit, it was dangerous. We asked people after they finished, after we had blown all this smoke everywhere, to roll from one line to the other and see who they could capture. It was very scary but no one got hurt. That was typical of Digger events. They were dangerous. Exciting, strange, and wonderful.

PETER COYOTE: Our parents came out of the Depression and built this permissive loony bin of a culture and the kids grew up knowing they were being shortchanged. They were not getting vital stuff. Part of the energy for the Haight was this hunger for real experience. I ran away at seventeen. I was in jail. It didn't matter where you came from. What mattered was, *"Would you play for keeps?"* I went to jail, I didn't call home. That was playing for keeps. That meant you do what you can. Same for Emmett Grogan.

MICHAEL STEPANIAN: We had Bill Graham who was saying, "This is where you're going to sing and this is where you're going to watch shows and I don't want you fucking around." *Yes, sir!* Emmett Grogan was saying, "All right, this is what you're going to eat. We're going to feed you, stop fucking around." You got arrested? You come to me. *Mike.* I was part of the establishment along with Bill Graham and Emmett Grogan. You got sick, go see David Smith at the Haight-Ashbury Clinic, he's going to take care of you. No bullshit. We love you but we will not tolerate evil. Evil is *not* allowed. In other words, we represented the establishment *within* the culture.

And we made deals. I made deals with the cops. Leave them alone, they'll surrender themselves. Bill Graham made his deals. Fucking Emmett Grogan, baby. He made his deals. And it was a structure. Every single day was absolute fun for me. I never got burned out. It was absolutely fantastic. I enjoyed it all. I had *wonderful* times.

BILL: Grogan and I got along because underneath it all, he knew that he was running another riff. He was a scammer but he had good in him. He was always playing a full court press on half-court. He had it *down*. He could ride with the bikers and he could be out there with the Diggers and hang with the musicians. He could get down and get high and he had a very strong street sense and he knew a lot. He was a mature street person at a time when there were so many novices. In that era, puppies were being born by the truckloads.

And they were so ready to overcome. *Which way do we go? Do we follow the yellow light or the green?* Emmett never had bucks but he had the inner code. It's that question of what do you know and then what do you do with what you know? There was such a big difference between someone like Emmett and Tim Leary. I'm totally convinced Timothy

Leary *knew* he was fucking with you. He *knew* but he just couldn't resist it.

Grogan was trying to do good. Did he give you an elbow sometimes to get the rebound? Yeah. But did he hit you between the eyes and then knee you in the balls when you were down? No. He told me right to my face what he thought of me and I liked that. We had some meeting about the Diggers putting on a free concert either in the street or the park. He said in so many words, "It hurts that we've got to come to you on this. But let's just get on with it and do it anyhow."

After that, he came to my office and said, "You know, you make bread from the scene and you should contribute to the Diggers and the street people and the homeless that we have."

I said, "I'm all for it." Because we had just done this benefit for HALO at the Fillmore at the end of May.

Of all the Diggers, I felt the closest to Grogan. Peter Coyote at least would always give me the benefit of the doubt. Peter Berg was Joseph Wiseman in *Viva Zapata,* declaring war on the world through Ronny Davis and the Mime Troupe.

As a group, they were extraordinarily resourceful and had some strong basic ideas about coexistence. But they only had a starting team—no bench.

PETER COYOTE: We were defining ourselves by how far from the majority culture we could run. Bill never pretended to be anything else but what he really was. If he had looked like Sonny Bono, I might have really pissed all over him. But he was always this *guy.* This guy who walked out of Auschwitz. So what the fuck did he care about shoulder-length hair? He really loved what he was doing. And what could you say about him if your model was autonomy and authenticity?

You going to penalize him because he got wealthy doing it? You can't reinvent the wheel, or singlehandedly make up a new culture. And the Diggers were *never* free. That's the irony. We always needed a Bill Graham or food stamps or a rich trick somewhere to help us run those theater pieces. Because they were just theater pieces. Subsidized by a host of invisible streams of currency. Bill was out *front.* He said, "I'm a capitalist. I want to make money." He did what he was going to do. I have a lot of respect for that.

6.

BILL: Lou Adler of the Mamas and the Papas and Dunhill Records called me a number of times concerning this festival they were putting

on in Monterey. But it was strictly about names and how could they
contact certain people in the Bay Area music community like Big Brother
and the Holding Company. I had the feeling they wanted to do their own
thing. At that time, my mind didn't work the way it does now concerning
the effect of competition. Meaning that if somebody does something close
by, it could affect me. I didn't really think anything of it except, "He's
gonna do that? *Fine*. Let him do it."

Derek Taylor was also involved. Him I knew from when Paul McCartney
had come to visit the Fillmore in April.

DEREK TAYLOR: My first contact with Bill came during the lobbying
period for the festival. He was one of the people we went to and I found
him utterly charming. He was engaging and a wide-awake kind of man.
If there was a heavy side to Bill, I didn't see it. He handed me a lot of
posters. "Look what I'm doing with them," he said. "I'm doing this and
this . . . Wes Wilson's my guy. He's better than any of them."

In the first phase of the festival, Alan Pariser raised fifty thousand
dollars, ten thousand of which came from Bill. Then Lou Adler and all
the rest came in, and Emmett Grogan and Peter Coyote of the Diggers
told us we were the scum of Hollywood. So then we had to go to Bill again
and ask for our cards back so he could mark our cards and say that we
were all right and get us in to the backstage sort of thing at which Bill is
so good.

Bill helped and also Ralph Gleason in terms of getting clearance with
the Diggers and Rock Scully and Danny Rifkin and all *those* heavies.
They all had to be told that we were okay.

PETE TOWNSHEND: The first time we came to America we played along
with Cream, supporting Mitch Ryder and the Detroit Wheels and Wilson
Pickett at Murray the K's show at the Academy of Music in New York. As
an institution, that sort of show was falling to pieces. It wasn't filling up.
The kids weren't coming. Smokey Robinson was billed to appear with
Wilson Pickett. Diana Ross was a guest at one point. In the end, it
turned out to be an opportunity for Murray himself to come out in his new
bimbo's wigs. I mean the guy was a tremendous indictment of the
American music industry. He had wonderful stories to tell. But they were
all of pathos as far as we could see.

What was interesting about going from that scenario was the contrast
with the way Bill was already working at the time on the West Coast. If
we had gone over to San Francisco then, we could have played at the
Fillmore. It's just that we didn't go. We *stayed* in New York but came
back very shortly after to play Monterey. We played Monterey on Sunday

night. We spent the Friday and Saturday night of the weekend at the Fillmore, the ground-floor one, the original, a very very nice place, near the water, on a hill.

Simon and Garfunkel had come to that Murray the K show. I think Neil Diamond might have done a guest thing. There were some big names for the time, American names. But Bill was just cutting through all that stuff and giving people time to play and perform and the audience time to sit down and relax.

What was happening at the Murray the K show, which should have been a lesson for the promoters to realize, was that the kids were coming in and they were staying *all* day. They were staying all day because they liked the music. They weren't staying all day because they wanted to get away from school. If that had been the case, they would have gotten bored. They stayed because they liked the music they were hearing and they wanted to hear it again and again and again.

There was a certain diffidence in the audience to this cavalcade approach. It didn't allow for any real involvement. I think Bill hit on the fact that people *did* want to listen. He certainly created what I came to know as the "electric ballroom syndrome" in America. Which actually changed the face of rock because it made it *listenable* music.

BILL: I drove down to Monterey by myself and I was there for a week. I don't know how or why but I had access to everywhere. They gave us some kind of pass. I do remember that early on, there were some financial problems. Something broke down or something fell out and they needed money, which I gave them. I guess that was why I had backstage access. That backstage pass cost me ten grand.

Eighty percent of my time I spent in the audience. Because it was like the Fillmore times *X*. There were people there who wanted to get in for free and also people who had no need or desire to get in at all. Thousands bought tickets and thousands didn't and they were all there together. There was no pressure to see the act. They were just there together. They were in the same space. It was also my first experience with instant trade fair. On occasion we had put some artwork up in the lobby at the Fillmore. But here it was on a much bigger scale.

So much of Monterey had *nothing* to do with logistics or planning. The bird just landed there. No rules, no instructions. It also said a lot to me about Northern California. So much of it could *never* have happened anywhere else.

GRACE SLICK: My idea of a good festival, the best festival of all time, was Monterey. They had these little booths where you could actually walk up if you wanted to buy something, with artists' stuff on display. You could get food. You could go to the bathroom. People could see things. It wasn't too big. When it was over and you wanted to go home, you could just get in your car and *drive* there.

PETE TOWNSHEND: Over in England, the LSD revolution was much more politicized at the time than it was in San Francisco. It was smaller and very cliquey. We were very surprised when we went to Monterey at how *wet* everybody appeared to be. Kind of *emotionally* wet. They were using those borrowed, secondhand catch-phrases. You know, "Peace and love." People were spray-canning it on the walls. But they were still beating the shit out of one another.

Over in England, there were people like Tariq Ali and Richard Neville of the *Oz* magazine and the *International Times.* So it was much harder. Monterey did change the way we thought because we didn't like the atmosphere there. All the same, my wife and I, who was then my girlfriend, we did meet a lot of people at Monterey who are still our friends today.

Some of it was a bit sad in a way. It was sad to go see the Haight-Ashbury, which was already very, very commercial. I'm not saying this just for the book, but Bill was extraordinary because he was like a *rock* in the middle of this. For us, coming from the outside, he was very important. Because you sort of felt that without him, all these airheads would fall to *bits.* He wasn't doing acid. He wasn't drinking. He didn't seem to be the kind of guy who would be interested in anything except keeping that ballroom going.

There was a feeling that he was a serious promoter and that he was making money. And that was important. Obviously, not lots of money. Because he was the only promoter known in the history of the music business to spend *any* money on a PA system. And he was obviously taking the ticket money that he earned from top bands like The Who and passing it on to people who weren't selling tickets at that time like Cannonball Adderly, with whom we played the Fillmore the next time through. Cannonball still had his brother Nat with him then and these guys were just great heroes to me. They both really liked The Who and it was interesting to feel that what we were doing was acceptable to people like that.

I remember feeling very secure when we worked for Bill. I didn't feel secure at Monterey.

PHIL WALDEN: Backstage, everybody was standing around. I said to Otis, "We don't have much time. You told Steve Cropper what songs we're going to do?"

He said, "No."

"We're going on in about ten fucking minutes," I said. "Don't you think we ought to?"

"Yeah," he said. "What do you want us to do?"

I got pencil and paper. I was trying to remember the things we had done well on the European tour. I said, "Why don't we open with 'Shake'?" Everybody had been calling the audience "the Love Crowd." So when we got to "I been loving you too long," I said to Otis, "You know, you ought to do a little recitation up front. Why don't you say something about this love crowd?"

"What do you want me to say?" he said.

So we came up with that little monologue thing. I got mad at Otis before the show because Booker T. and the MG's and the Marquees were mad at me. Because I said, "Okay, Booker. You can do one song and then the Marquees can come out and do one song, and then Otis is going to come on."

They said, "Oh, *man*. We flew all the way out here and we want to do a *set*."

And I said, "Well, you can't."

So everybody was pissed. They were out there playing and I turned around. Otis was behind me and I swear to God, he had a spliff about this big in his mouth. I said, "Don't smoke that shit *now*, man! Not before we go on."

"Ah, fuck," he said. "Don't worry about it. Everything is all right. Don't worry about it. It's just a fucking show."

This is with *no* rehearsal. I had to write down the keys we were going to do the songs in on a piece of paper. And he went out there and he said, *"Shake!"* and that place was *gone*. He did that little monologue thing and it fucking *killed* them.

PETE TOWNSHEND: Now, at Monterey, Owsley was introducing like Version 7 of his own acid, which up to that point had really only been available in Europe in its clinical variety from Sandoz Laboratories which is still used for psychotherapy in Europe and very finely controlled. So you knew exactly what you were getting when you took some of it. With Owsley, you had no clue at all. I took some of his after Monterey and I never touched a drug again for eighteen years. It was *extraordinarily* powerful. The thing about Owsley is that when he gave you something, he would take it too. Just to show you. He was like the man who used to eat the king's food. "Hmm, so you've had some of that? I'll have some, *too!*" And then he'd go over to somebody else and say, "Have some acid." He just must have had the most extraordinary liver.

OWSLEY STANLEY: When you're first born, everything's okay. You accept it all. As you grow, you erect walls and you start to filter out the mass of information that comes into you in order to make sense of it. The baby is processing everything. *Everything*, right? When you take acid, you see incredible patterns. The incredible patterns that you see is just the noise from your own nervous system which is normally filtered out so that you don't hear it. You selectively censor the data from your senses, including those we don't recognize like the telepathic ones. You see colors like the purple that comes out of mercury vapor lamps in the streets, which is a color you don't normally see. But all this information is always there.

When you take acid, all of a sudden you get all these inputs and you're processing the whole thing. People seem to be in trances when they get really high because there's just so much going on that they can't possibly make a decision. They see all of the wavelike propagation of probability going off into the future and it's almost impossible to make a choice. If you're absolutely cosmic and one with the creating entity, you cannot get up. You trip over your own two feet. That is just the way it is, you know?

CHIP MONCK: I was stage right at Monterey, that's where the dimmer boards were, until the acid hit. And then I looked at Laura Nyro and she was going, "Black . . . *out*." I was just staring at her thinking it was *wonderful*. *Instead* of blacking out the stage. It was the first time I had taken acid. I was getting very tired and I thought it was a purple heart. I thought it would be a good idea to get up. But it wasn't. It was Owsley purple.

That's why anywhere after Booker T. and the MG's, the Pennebaker film is *completely* red. I just said, "Go to frame six, guys—wow, this is fucking groovy." Pennebaker was *not* pleased. We were using telephone operator headsets at that time and a 101G power unit, which was stolen from the phone company. The thing that powers multibutton phones. It was a big clumsy unit that put out eighteen volt talk. I wired up all the headsets with twisted zipcord and that was our intercom. The moment anybody played loud, you couldn't hear a thing. During a break in the music, I said, "Frame six." Everybody went to frame six, we took off the headsets, and we sat there, just sort of gazing at it. *Right*.

ERIC BURDON: When The Who began smashing up the stage, which in America I suppose was a taste of brutal theatrics, Bill was right in the middle of the milieu, thinking it was a terrorist attack of some sort. I was standing right there and I could see the look of horror on everybody's faces. I think maybe that particular incident made Bill wake up and realize what he already knew. A little peace and brown rice may be all right, but there was still a monster running amok and it was still alive and kicking. That fascism was still bubbling under.

What brought it all together for me was the following act. After The Who. You had two expressions of violent action on that stage at Monterey. Although the actions were the same, they amounted to totally different statements. One was brutality, one was rape, and one was erotic. I saw Jimi Hendrix take the stage flashing to the max and almost transgress from male to female while the music still remained male.

PETE TOWNSHEND: Derek Taylor keeps telling me that all I ever say to him are very, very unkind things. On that particular occasion, I said, "You know, Derek. This whole thing is a load of shit. You know that, don't you?"

We went up on the stage and did the gig and then I came back and I said, "This is even more shit up on the stage than it is *off* the stage." I can't remember my exact words but I know he was upset. Then of course somebody ran off with the money and I went back to him and I said, "I *told* you so."

CHET HELMS: In a sense what happened at Monterey Pop *did* break Janis Joplin internationally. But really, she was gaining a major national reputation by word-of-mouth before Monterey Pop.

Basically, we all resisted Monterey Pop because we felt it was kind of slicko L.A. hype. We felt that they were coattailing a bunch of L.A. acts on the success of what was happening in San Francisco.

PHIL WALDEN: After it was over, Otis said, "Why don't we rent a car and drive down the coastline and go spend a couple days in L.A.?"

"Great idea," I said.

So we rented a car the next morning and it was a great, great drive. I mean, just a wonderful trip. I got down there and I bought the *L.A. Times*. Pete Johnson had written this review and he said, "The Festival really took off when Otis Redding got up on stage." Otis was sitting there having coffee and I said, "*Otis*. We fucking *killed* them up there!"

"You're shitting me," he said. "That little old show? You mean, we did it all right?"

"Yeah," I said. "It says so right here. We were the *best* thing there."

He said, "Oh, shit. You believe that?"

For him, it was just a little show. That he had sung in for free. We hadn't made a nickel on the motherfucker.

BILL: It's always an amazing experience for me when I go to something that is *not* my production. I am like the maître d' from the Catskills. I know I'm powerless so I'm forever pulling myself back. There's no water here. Why is it taking so long to move the equipment? You call *this* a hot dog? I'm always three-by-fiving on my little cards. But Monterey passed the test. In the sense that the majority of the people came there to enjoy themselves, and they did. What prevailed over everything was the meeting of unnamed tribes who didn't even know they were tribes.

"Where do you come from?" "Oh, I come from Marin." "Oh. *Where* in Marin?" "And where do *you* come from?"

The looseness of Monterey, I always attributed to Lou Adler. After a while, there *was* no control. But they didn't *need* control because of the audience. They were all already members of the same organization. *Before* they got to the grand meeting at Monterey.

7.

JIM HAYNIE: I quit the Fillmore just before the Summer of Love. I could see Bill wanted to be open six nights a week. I was already burning the candle at both ends just doing four nights. And I could see it was going to be *hell*. At some point, Bill had made a deal with Winterland. We would go over there Friday and Saturday nights, with the Fillmore open on Thursdays and maybe Sunday for the afternoon.

Bill and I would take all the screens off the walls of the Fillmore and truck them across Geary Boulevard in the middle of the night. Just the two of us, actually carrying them, rolling them, getting them in, and hanging them. All by ourselves. That was what wore me out. The back and forth and the back and forth in the middle of the night.

But not Bill. We had this huge old A-frame ladder that we used to hang lights. It reached up like eighteen feet. I got to be like a monkey on it. I could just run up and down it like it was nothing. One night I was hanging things up there and Bill was holding the bottom. He said, "I've got to go get something." When he got back, I was sleeping. On the ladder. Way up at the top with my arms and legs interlaced in the rungs. He called out my name and shook the ladder and said, "*Wake up.* We got work to do."

I said, "Bill, how can you do this?"

"How can you sleep like this?" he said. "We got work to do."

"Bill," I said. "We haven't slept for twenty-six hours! Not *one* minute, you know!"

But that was the way he was back then. *Totally driven.* I decided I didn't want to do it anymore. So I checked out.

BILL THOMPSON: When the Summer of Love happened, that was it. It had all started happening in the summer of 1965 and it was over by the summer of 1967. Basically, it was an *incredible* two-year movement of people and energy. But you know what? There are still a lot of people I talk to who were influenced so much by it that it has carried on in the rest of their lives. And I feel good about that.

BILL: For openers, they were all doves. Everybody said, "I'm against Vietnam." Every one of them said, "There is nothing wrong with being gay." They all said, "I'm willing to march and I'm also willing to go pick flowers if I feel like it. I want to be free to pray or dance and if I have to, I *might* get a job."

Today, everyone says, "I *have* to get a job and when I have the time, *maybe* I'll think about gay rights and black people and what's happening in Central America and Ethiopia." In the sixties, we didn't know as much as we do now. We weren't as jaded. The more we get, the smaller the dream seems to become. What occurred then was a general hope. A general hope by the mass as a *unit*. When you put them all together, it meant that millions openly and willingly joined forces for the first time ever. A growing army with so few qualified leaders.

GRACE SLICK: We were well educated. They told us, "Here's what you *ought* to be doing. You ought to be marrying a lawyer and getting two cars and da-da-da-da." On the other hand, we had gone to college and we had all this other information from literature about how you could live apart from what your parents had told you was just wonderful. What our parents had told us was just wonderful didn't sound awfully exciting. It may have been secure but it sounded really boring. The sixties was simply a bunch of well-educated kids going, I *don't* think so! I don't, I don't, I don't *think* so!"

DEREK TAYLOR: What was remarkable about that was that all these people were able to spontaneously combust and get themselves sitting down in the middle of the road. I thought it was a jolly good idea. It only went wrong because people always fuck up in the end. You know what the prayer book says. There is nothing by the wit of man so devised that does not in the fullness of time become corrupted. Because we *always* fuck up. All politics ends in tears.

JERRY GARCIA: It was inevitable. I mean, the media portrait of the innocent hippie flower children was a joke. Hey, everybody knew what was happening. It wasn't *that* innocent. Our own background was sort of that deeply cynical beatnik space which evolved into something nicer with the advent of psychedelics. Stuff like cops and politicians and the rest of the world, all those people just kept right on grinding along in the same old groove. So it was not as though any of this was surprising. It wasn't surprising to get busted. It was surprising if you *didn't* get busted.

MICHAEL STEPANIAN: In a strange way, the kids had a certain veneration for the law. Leave me alone. Hey, man, you've got your law, that's cool. But I just want to be in my own space. Into my own trip. I ain't bugging anybody, don't bug me.

That was kind of the strange relationship they had with the law until speed came in. Then they made Haight-Ashbury one way. The tourist buses started coming through. Then they left. The kids went out to the country. Bolinas, Santa Rosa, Healdsburg, Auburn, Santa Cruz. Basically, they all left the city and it became a very different situation. More drugs came in and it was an angrier crowd. There were some homicides in the Haight-Ashbury. A lot of rapes, many of them unreported, came down. Essentially, there was a dissipation of the environment. The idyllic time was over.

PETE TOWNSHEND: The most important thing about Bill was that he seemed to be free of hypocrisy. That was something of which there was an immense amount in that period. I'm not decrying the acid movement or that particular period, the flower power movement. I'm not saying that it was all hypocrisy. I think it's been done to death in this country, they've analyzed it and taken it apart and it's come up looking very shabby. It was a very important period. I don't think people realize how important it was to postwar baby boomers.

There was some detritus, as you would expect. There was some damage and some waste. But it was an absolutely definitive time. It was very important in that something was flaccid. It was very important in that something was nonachieval. As a generation both in Britain and America, we were discovering that we didn't want to attempt to achieve on the same level as our forebears because it obviously put them in such a position of danger. Somehow Bill managed to find the correct middle path.

PETER COYOTE: The sixties pushed so hard and so fast on so many fronts that it got the majority culture scared. It raised a number of questions for which there were no answers. What they did was throw the government to a housekeeper. They said, "This is scaring us, we don't know what to do. We don't have the answers. Let's at least give it to the conservatives." *Big* mistake. Let's give it to Walt Disney to run. We scared them so bad that they gave it to Reagan. And there's been like this little ten-year backwater. But if you actually look at the movements that were either incepted or came to fruition, I don't think the sixties did destroy itself.

A couple of things did happen. One was that drugs cut a big swath. You can't keep up twenty-four-hour-a-day inventiveness on the natch. So that was one thing. The second was getting out of the urban environment. A lot of us really wanted to make our acquaintanceship with the planet and with cycles that are more or less eternal. *Under* the inch of asphalt.

A lot of people just spread out and began trying to learn from the Indian people, from the woods, from the land. The urban scene kind of decentralized. What happened was that there were a series of way stations all up and down the coast from Happy Valley to the forks of the Salmon River to Briceland to Garberville to Arcata to Whitethorn.

I went to Olema out by Point Reyes Station. I ran a ranch. The commune there lasted for about three years. And then a bunch of us lived on the road in a truck caravan. I don't think it ended. I think it was just part of like an ongoing quest.

PETER BERG: Just for fun, play with this one. What's new since the sixties? Try it. Go through it. What's *new* since the sixties? Not computers. They were there before. To a lot of people, it must have seemed that the cultural revolution of the sixties was *too* much. Drugs were too much. Jimi Hendrix, Janis Joplin, and Emmett Grogan all died of heroin. But not during that period. And sex, right? The sexual thing went overboard because of herpes and now AIDS. Politics went overboard. Because of people waving Vietcong flags. Totally unnecessary. I mean, you didn't have to wave Vietcong flags.

My personal feeling about what's going to happen next is that the cold war is going to end finally. This idea of people together on the planet is going to have an emergence. As like a feeling of freedom. Planethood is coming. That's going to be like moving from the Middle Ages to the Renaissance. And the sixties were probably the first move toward the Renaissance.

Which is why I asked the question, *"What's new since the sixties?"*

You can't think of a lot, right? Running injuries. But what *else?*

Chapter Six

Summer of Love

1.

BILL: That summer, we were working all the time. I had my work and I was living with Bonnie and that was my whole life. We were at the Fillmore or Winterland six days and nights a week. Sometimes, it was one show Tuesday, Wednesday, Thursday, and then a different show Friday, Saturday, Sunday. Sometimes, it was the same show for all six nights. But every night we were doing very good business. There were so many quality acts that I couldn't get them all in at the time. So why not take advantage of it?

What happened was that we had a cancellation at the Fillmore. Bonnie and I lived in a little cottage off Twenty-first Avenue between some streets and the back alley. A great little house. I said something about having had a phone call and so-and-so had canceled and she said, "Good, we can get married." And I said, "All right." I think it was that simple.

BONNIE MACLEAN: I think things between us had already changed *before* we got married. We got married because we had come to a crisis. Bill insisted that we get married because we had come close to parting ways. It was probably not the way to go about it. We accomplished the marriage but then there was a resentment about difficulties between us. So it was bound to fail. Sadly.

BILL: The bands got paid more each time they played based on how they had done before but it was all still flat fees. We didn't do percentages. The opening act usually got scale. If you were responsible for some or any of the draw, then I would base what you got paid on what that might be. Most bands started at five hundred a night. The next time, they would go to seven-fifty or maybe a thousand. The heavier bands eventually got two thousand dollars a night.

In terms of draw, the heaviest local bands were the Airplane, the Dead, Quicksilver, and Big Brother. All strong enough to fill the Fillmore by themselves.

JERRY GARCIA: We were younger than most of the Pranksters. We were wilder. We weren't serious college people. We were on the street. We just got high and went crazy, you know? It was unstructured. Socially, our scene had a little bit of the kids of Stanford alumni and faculty. So it was with more of an intellectual bent than street kids in the present-day sense. It was in Palo Alto, which is more Bohemian than anything else. But we were definitely Dionysian as opposed to Apollonian. We were celebrating *life*. For us, psychedelics were what we'd always been looking for. Drugs were part of that continuous search for the explosion. The realization of something.

The Pranksters liked us because we were so out there. But our music scared them at first. Then as soon as they realized that it was not going to hurt them, they liked it. Like a scary roller coaster ride.

DENNIS McNALLY: They always did a lot more gigs with Bill. Whatever anybody will tell you, they did *many* more gigs with Bill than with Chet Helms. Even though they were supposedly the hippie band. Big Brother was the one that did enormous numbers of gigs with Chet. Bill would *pay*. To quote Rock Scully, Chet would go, "You know, I've got family. I can't pay right now." Rock would go, "Look, *I'm* the master of that rap. You can't get away with that with *me*. We *have* to have the money. We're just as poor as you are.

JERRY GARCIA: Chet was always a businessman. He was always a shrewd guy with an eye for a trend. I saw the gleam in his eye the first time we ever walked into one of the first Family Dog shows at Longshoremen's Hall. They had the Lovin' Spoonful on and we were all stoned on acid. Phil Lesh went up to Luria Castell and said, "Lady, what this little séance needs is *us*."

We saw it right away and we thought, "*Yeah*. We *should* be here. *Hell*, *yeah*. You kiddin'?" It was *obvious*. I mean, I could see Chet figuring. Every hippie in town was there that night and having a great time and he could see there was something happening. I could see him *figuring*.

He always was a nice guy. A great politician. Money was always a problem. Sometimes you didn't get it. Sometimes he didn't get you enough. Sometimes he got it to you real late. One thing or another. Doing business with him was like doing business with a hippie. With Bill, it was like being at the other end. Bill was a *New Yorker.*

A lot of us out here in California didn't have much experience with New Yorkers. It was like, "Relax, man. *Slow down.*" He couldn't stand that shit. *"Mellow out."* Oh, God. He'd go, *"Zaarrrrh!"* It's that energy. He was like the guy who taught us about that. A lot of us had never been out of California. You know, what else was going on anyplace else that you even wanted to know about? But to us . . . oh, boy. He was like a *Martian.*

BOB WEIR: As history has proven, Bill had some sort of acumen of his own. He has talents in that area. He was always asking us and other musicians, "Who should I get in here?" And that was a good move. Because it kept everything fertile and it made San Francisco sort of the hub for a while. Back when promoters were actually talking to musicians about what would make a good show. The scene here was pretty tight. It was pretty cozy. And we were an anomaly even then.

DENNIS MCNALLY: With Bill, the gigs were good. It wasn't quite the homey atmosphere of the Avalon. It wasn't as loose. A lot of it had to do with the Angels. The Grateful Dead played for Chocolate George's funeral in Golden Gate Park late in 1966. To this day, Grateful Dead crew members have friends in the Hell's Angels. And Grateful Dead crew is *part* of Grateful Dead.

BILL: My thing with the Hell's Angels pretty much started at the original Fillmore. Over at the Avalon, they had free reign. It was *their* turf. Chet let them come in and go out and pretty much do whatever they pleased. He pretty much left them alone. I told all my people at the Fillmore that if anybody ever challenged them, I did not want them to lay down their life. They were to come and get me instead.

And then I would get into it with the Angels for as long as it took to make them understand that *no* one came in without first buying a ticket.

BOB WEIR: This is just an insight into Bill's personality. Sometimes, I think he really is the cartoon character that people think he might be. I was going to see the Byrds play at the Fillmore. I think it was right near the end of 1967 and it was a big deal. Bill had gotten the Byrds to actually play there. And McGuinn was late. I just happened to be arriving then. I was standing out front about to go in when McGuinn came walking around the corner.

Really, the reason I was standing out in front and sort of backing off was that Graham was pacing up and down with this real big visible black cloud over his face. I didn't know what was in it or what was wrong but I was starting to put it together because I've been late to shows and I've seen him in that mood.

He was wearing a porkpie hat. When around the corner came Jim McGuinn. Graham turned around and he was facing McGuinn and I could see like the dots between their eyes. Graham saw McGuinn and he took off his hat and he threw it down and he *stomped* on it. He jumped up and down on it. He was just straight out of a thirties movie or Laurel and Hardy. But it was happening for real, right in front of my eyes. I couldn't believe it.

Then of course he laid into McGuinn, who never stopped. He just kept sliding past him. Through all the invective, Graham wouldn't do anything to hold up McGuinn's progress to get inside. Even as he was headed through the door. Because McGuinn knew that the only safe place for him was on stage.

BILL: The Byrds wanted to do one set instead of two. David Crosby was going through one of his histrionic life changes and he didn't want to *face* the audience. He was enjoying the light show very much and he couldn't be moved at that particular time. Jim McGuinn had just changed his name to Roger and I called him "Jim" by mistake. That was wrong. And I didn't bow, or whatever. We all just got off on the wrong foot. Their drummer was a lovely guy but quite frankly, he never knew what to do with the sticks. It was one of those weekends. *They* didn't want to play. *I* didn't want them to play. But we had a show to put on. So we had a few words with each other.

JOHN WASSERMAN: (KSAN "LAST DAYS OF THE FILLMORE" INTERVIEW)
Bill did a number on them. He said, "I'll *never* have these guys in here again. They will *buy* tickets to get in and if I know they are here, they will not even get to *buy* tickets. I will *never* book them again. I will go to *everybody*. They will be blacklisted in the Western *Hemisphere*." Yelling and screaming.

Two months later, the Byrds were back. I said, "Bill! You did fifteen minutes on how the Byrds were *never* going to set foot in San Francisco again. You were going to *block* the airport. Now you've got them booked and they're playing for you."

He said, "Well, I owe it to the *people*."

JERRY GARCIA: One time I came *real* late to a show. The Grateful Dead were on stage playing with this *other* guy on lead guitar. This guy who used to play with Aum. He was a pretty good blues guitar player. I thought, "Jesus, Bill's going to fuckin' *kill* me." But he didn't say anything. For some reason, Bill has never chosen to take me apart.

But him and Phil. Oh, boy. Phil used to just jump all over Bill and Bill would scream at him and I mean they would get into some *shit*. Because Phil has a little of that beatnik attitude. "Fuck *you*, man!" You know? *Fuck you!* He's got a little of that edge like he doesn't really care. It's just who he is. And when he was younger, he was a short-fuser. It didn't really matter what it was about. Usually, it was just personalities.

But Bill also did solids for us. That's the thing. He did *way* more solids. *We*'ve always had an adversarial relationship. We goof on Bill. That's the thing about it. It's like we know we can get him going. He's so easy.

Early on, I don't think Bill noticed our music much. But about that time Mickey Hart joined the band, we started doing things that had more exotic rhythmic flavors, and Bill started to get into it. He always loves it when the crowd gets off even if he doesn't personally understand or personally dig the music. He is also truly a New Yorker on the level of, "Here's the audience. Give 'em a show. Give 'em a *hell* of a show." Which also used to make him nuts with us. Because we didn't mind going from a huge, exciting peak to something really boring. That used to drive him *crazy*.

Because the way our shows used to work—well, they didn't work at all actually. He always had this whole rap about showbiz, how you've got to give them the sword swallower first and we'd say, "Right. Yeah, Bill. Sure." You know, *"Right."*

OWSLEY STANLEY: It used to be the price was a buck, right? *Everybody* went. It was cheaper than going to a movie. It wasn't that important and the bands didn't care because it wasn't a lot of money. Bill started running it as a business and offering bigger money and charging bigger money on the door. Now you can't be free because you get *schmucks*. They fuck up *everything*. Free concerts, they piss on the floor. It's got to be a certain amount of money but it can't be a *lot* of money.

As soon as it started being as much money as a movie, the whole character of the thing changed. Instead of people just having a good time and dancing and everything, they stood around mesmerized, staring at the stage as if they were going to miss a stroke of the guitar player's pick or something. It became like watching a movie. Eventually they even started sitting down and staring at 'em. Before, it was just this incredible crazy wonderful experience. It was the money that buggered it up.

JIM HAYNIE: I remember the first time I played the baby on New Year's Eve. The Dead, the Airplane, and Quicksilver were all playing. It was the Dead's turn at midnight and their big song was "In the Midnight Hour," the Wilson Pickett thing. I was really, really high. I had taken this acid about thirty-five minutes before. All these black guards in their little uniforms, which was what they wore in those days, put me on this litter, which Bill had rented from a theatrical supply house somewhere. Eventually I destroyed it.

Six of them hauled me up on this thing on their shoulders and someone put on a tape of this majestic horn playing. Like "Here Comes the King," or some kind of shit. I was lying down with all these flowers and this flowered wreath on me and I'd never been in such a garden before. I had this sash across the front of me saying, "1967." And a diaper.

I was lying there and we came through the hall and the spots hit us and everybody went "*ROOOOOOOAH!*" The whole place roared. Because they hadn't expected a thing like this. I was obviously wired. At some point, I sat up. As we approached the stage, about three quarters of the way through the house, I finally made it to my feet. I stood up and I began throwing flowers at them and they were eating it up. I was being carried right through the audience followed by spots with these loud trumpet fanfares.

We hit the stage and they put the litter down and I was still somehow maintaining my balance, incredibly. I was standing on this litter and as soon as we hit the stage, the Grateful Dead socked it to them with "In the Midnight Hour." I danced and I danced and I danced. After I got off stage, I noticed that I had torn up the litter and the plywood on top of it. I had torn up my feet on the nails and just *shredded* my feet. But I hadn't realized it because I was out there.

I was in a complete reverie. I was dreaming a fantastic renewal. That's what I was dreaming. I was dreaming that we were all being renewed. That I represented innocence. So whatever I did was cool and that we were all innocent and we were all fresh and reborn.

My diaper was soaking wet. That year I didn't take it off. In ensuing years, I did. I would take it off and throw it to the crowd at a certain point because that was a gesture of innocence. I didn't need that. I would be *completely* naked. Even at the Cow Palace. In front of fifteen thousand people. I did that I think for ten or twelve years. I wasn't working for Bill anymore but three weeks before New Year's Eve, he would always find me and say, "Jim, it's that time." And I would go and do it.

2.

BILL: Janis Joplin's talent was that you believed she was singing her guts out every night. In that sense, she was like Piaf. You were watching a candle burn, with no wax to replace what had already been used up.

Janis was a feel, an emotion, a spur. Janis was not a song. Janis was the first white singer of that era who sounded like she had come from the world of black blues. I don't think men found her that attractive. I think men found her an awesome female. Not necessarily sexually but sensually. She aroused something in men. She aroused desire but was not the object of that desire. And I think she was never able to deal with that reality.

At the beginning of the scene, there were no stars. The bands just played. But then it started to happen. The instant acceptance by so many other people as the goddess. It *had* to have an effect on her. She had no choice in the matter, really. She became an involuntary leader. People wanted to dress like her and wear their hair like her. It wasn't like it had been for Judy Garland or Billie Holiday. Because they played mostly clubs. Look at the scope of the audience that the sixties wound up creating. As a result of that era, a white girl from Port Arthur, Texas, became an international sociological queen. But still just that same person she had always been.

Janis was one of the few who really didn't want to make it just for the sake of making it. She wanted to be a star *on* the stage. Not a commercial asset star. Not, "I'll get bigger, I'll buy things, I'll be more respected in the world." She was a street blues singer who lived in fear of something. My guess would be that when she put all her talent, adulation, and financial security on one side of the scale, what did she have on the other? When she woke up at home on Sunday morning after being on the road, what did she really have to call her own and balance out her success?

In the case of Janis, the private side was *not* happy. The balance wasn't there.

CHET HELMS: I think the Albert Grossman organization tried to mold Janis in this white Billie Holiday role. The blues singer. Down and out and junked out. I think emotionally she got wrapped up in that image. She felt she *had* to pay her dues to sing the blues. She felt in some sense that she had *not* suffered enough. Therefore, she *had* to suffer. I think she had probably already suffered enough, as it was.

JOHN MORRIS: I remember a scene in the Pan Am Building in New York. Janis wanted Bill to manage her. We were in two pay phones and he was saying, "No, no, no, I can't do it" and I was standing there saying, "You're out of your mind!" And he was saying, "No, no, no. I'm going to give her to Albert. I'm going to give her to Albert." And I was saying, "You're crazy!"

We had this screaming, yelling argument and he *did* give her to Albert. When I say he gave her to Albert, I mean he convinced her to go with Albert. And he could have done it himself. Because at that time, Bill's respect for Albert was *immense*. Albert was like a *god*.

BILL: I remember saying that if they wanted somebody of strength, they should go with Albert. If he was shifty, it was justified because he always really tried to do the best for his artist. He maneuvered very well in the big game. I wasn't qualified to manage Janis at that time. I wasn't qualified because of time. I knew who Janis was. I knew she was not a sometime thing. She needed full-time management or she would go astray. She needed somebody to really lock into her career and her life. She would've been a whole life for someone. And I couldn't give my life over to her. Because I felt that what I was doing was bigger and more important than dealing with one single artist.

The two or three times that Janis and I spent a lot of time together were flukes. They were never planned. One night at Winterland when she was still with Big Brother but already a star, we got together after the show. She mumbled something to me about, "Do you want to get something to eat?" We went to her car, a psychedelic painted Porsche but she said she didn't feel like driving. She said, "Let's get something to eat somewhere we can sit outside." It was one of those nights that come so seldom to San Francisco and are so rare. When you can drive in an open car and sit outside. So I drove.

We went to Mel's on Geary and got a bunch of hamburgers and fries and milkshakes. She also had some booze with her. We went out by the bunkers across the Golden Gate Bridge on the Marin Headlands. We sat out there and ate and she started talking. She was a little loaded. Her life was not going so well. She had some personal problems. Mainly, she wanted a new relationship with a man. She talked about her life on the road. She said, "I go on the road and I'm in the Holiday Inn in Toronto. After the gig, all the guys go upstairs and freshen up. Then they come down and score chicks." There was this long pause. Then she said, "What does a woman do?" That always explained it for me.

Janis was among the very few who on a given night could be an erupting volcano on stage. She'd give the kind of a performance that you could *never* capture on record. Like the Dead. Very few artists have the talent and the hunger to *go* for it every night. To convince the audience that their performance is as important and meaningful to them as it is to those who watch them perform. For an entertainer, that's the ultimate challenge. To put it out there every night. The very best they can.

On certain nights when she paced herself on stage, Janis would get you feeling great through the middle section. Then she would go to the big finale and she would get onto a *higher* level. Otis had that. Then she would come back for an encore and say, "You think you've had it all? You're *wrong*."

On a personal level, what she said to me that night always stayed in my mind. I know a lot of happy men who can be on the road for weeks and be with women and then come home to a wife.

But what does a *woman* do?

3.

PAUL BARATTA: Going into the summer of 1967, I would hear Bill say, "When the Blues Project come here, we're *really* going to do good business." I didn't know who the fuck the Blues Project even was. When the Doors came to play Winterland a couple of weeks later, I looked around and said to myself, "What the *fuck* has my life come to? What am I doing here? I'm in this cockamamie broken-down, old roller skating rink with music I don't understand and people who are *so* bizarre."

I remember the Doors coming in. I saw them outside and it almost looked like a tableau, these four guys moving in unison. The spatial relationship between them changed yet they moved together as a unit as they came across Geary Boulevard and up those two steps into the Fillmore and through the doors. There was something very charismatic about these people and I hadn't yet had the opportunity to really feel like any of the people in this industry had what I would consider charisma.

They went on stage and it was the last set. I was standing alongside the stage and Jim Morrison went into what effectively was going to be their last number. Fittingly, he sang "The End." Maybe two thirds of the way through it, he went down on one knee in front of the audience, really in a passionate, spontaneous gesture. And it was responded to by the people in the audience.

At that point, I knew *this* was theater. At that moment, my whole being *learned* it. This was everything I ever understood about theater. Everything I knew about theater suddenly applied *instantly*. It was as if I'd had a crash course. In one blinding flash of light. From that point, I talked the business and I could do it. It was as simple as that. Like being on acid without having taken the drug.

Performer on stage interacting with the audience to form a unit. Not just somebody performing *at* an audience. If ever there was a unit like that it was the Fillmore Auditorium.

KEN KESEY: It could have been after I got out of jail. Anyway, a good deal of time had passed. The Doors were playing and it was *such* a different feeling than our scene with the Acid Test. Lots of Hell's Angels. Really very, very dark. Slickly put on.

The production quality had obviously been heavily planned. When they first came out, Bill started it off by projecting these great big pictures of the Doors. The Doors then came on and played and it sufficed so far as the audience went because they were kind of browbeat into acceptance of the thing. But so far as uplifting, it wasn't. The Doors never pretended to be uplifting.

I walked out into the lobby and there was Terry the Tramp standing there just loaded to the gills. As Mountain Girl used to say, Terry the Tramp was the most fop of all the Angels. He wore more stuff and had more stuff hanging off of him and he could just shake it all over. He was standing there confronting all these people and shaking around.

I said, "What do you think of the Doors, Tramp?"

And he said, "Gettin' smaller all the time. Gettin' smaller all the time."

And it was exactly right. Everything was getting tighter and stranger.

BILL: The Doors had three gigs to do at the original Fillmore. The night before, they were playing in Sacramento. They were just getting hot at the time and we were sold out. All the guys in the band showed up on time but there was no Jim Morrison. He never showed up at all and no one knew where he was. We had to ask all the people to keep their tickets and we refunded some money and asked the others to hold on to their tickets for another night.

The next afternoon, Jim walked into my little office at the Fillmore and apologized. He told me that as he was leaving Sacramento to drive to San Francisco, he went past this movie house. *Casablanca* was playing. He just couldn't help it. He went in to see *Casablanca* instead.

I kept telling him, "I'm a big Humphrey Bogart fan myself. I know *Casablanca* very well. But *Casablanca* in Sacramento was not exactly what was on my mind last night. You *should've* called."

He said, "Yeah, I *could* have called." Then he said, "I saw it *three* times. That was how much he liked the movie.

The next time the Doors came through, they were on top. It was a big event but Jim was late again. I wasn't too happy and we had a few words upstairs. He had been drinking again and began the show pretty looped.

I was in the back of the house and the place was full. Jim took the microphone and started doing what Roger Daltrey still does with it now. Lassoing it around and around but in much bigger circles. The microphone was way out there and then it was right back over the drummer's head. Then it was about ten rows out into the audience.

I decided to cut through the house to warn him to stop. I got about five or ten feet in front of the stage and of the three thousand people in the place, the microphone hit one person. *Me.* Right in my head. All of a sudden, I had this fucking bulb sticking out of my skull. I got hit and I was bleeding.

After the show was over, I went up the steps to the dressing room and asked the other guys in the band to leave the room. I said to Jim, "See this?" And I pointed to the knot on my head. "Thank God it was me because if it was somebody else, you'd have a big lawsuit on your hands now and you'd be in big trouble. You got to watch yourself." Actually, my opening line to him was, "Are you out of your fucking *mind?*"

He said, "Yeah, you're right. You know. I got to be careful. Wow. You know?"

When they played the Fillmore again a couple of months later, Jim brought this big box into the office. He said, "Hey, Bill, sorry about the last time. Hope your head's okay."

I said, "My head's okay. Just be careful this time."

"Here," he said, giving me the box. "At least you'll be protected."

He had brought me a pith helmet that he had painted with all these psychedelic colors. On the front of it, he had written, "The Morrison Special." I wore it all night long but somebody stole it out of my office a couple of days later.

I was a big fan of his. Obviously, fame got to him and it affected him to a point where he couldn't deal with it. Initially, Jim wanted to be a filmmaker and a writer and a poet. But all of a sudden, the whole world adored him.

He was the first real male sex symbol in rock. He and Hendrix. Jim once told me once about going to Cleveland. The Doors played and played and they wouldn't let them off the stage and they finally had to go back out and take a bow and they put all the house lights on. He said to me, "I realized then there were twelve thousand people out there and every woman in the house wanted to fuck me."

That kind of thing *has* to drive a person crazy because you become a mark. Want to listen to my tape? Want to fuck me? Can I carry your bag? He and Janis and Hendrix, they became involuntary leaders. And that was the pressure. What do you think of this? What do you think of that?

Can I wear what you're wearing? How do you part your hair? Do you piss like I do? They all become slaves to idolatry.

But Jim was more than that. Early on, I saw something special in him. The same experience I had from man-to-woman when I fell in love with Ava Gardner on the movie screen. He was her male counterpart. It was when he took a step. It was when he just went from one place to another on stage. It was the way his body moved. It had as much to do with him thinking about it as a panther climbing up a tree. Or a cobra twining around a limb. It was natural. And he had that *punim*.

What he began to do was literally tell the world, "You're driving me crazy. I can't deal with all this adulation." So he found things to hide behind. He got a little paunchy. He grew a beard. I think he went to Paris at the end to prove he was more than just a rock star. Poetry was very important to him. One night at Winterland in the middle of the set, he said, "I'd like to do some poetry." And the public wasn't that kind to him. Because they wanted to hear the music. They loved it when he sang. I would watch the audience and the women never took their eyes off him. They loved it when he *didn't* sing. Because then they could just concentrate on *him*.

Jim was James Dean and he was Marlon Brando. One day in San Francisco, I took him around to all the radio stations, four or five of them. We just drove around town in my old Karmann Ghia. He loved that day. He put on this big Western hat over his eyes and we did the radio stations and then we went up in the hills of Marin. We went over to Tiburon and up to Rancho Nicasio and had some food. Then we went up to Point Reyes and looked at the ocean. He said, "This will always be one of the real fine days for me and I thank you for it. I just don't get this in Southern California."

We talked a lot about our childhoods and it blew his mind when I told him where I was from and what I had gone through to get here. He was *it* for me in that he had that face and he had that voice and he wrote those songs.

4.

PAUL BARATTA: The first week of the 1967 six-night-a-week summer series, we had the Jefferson Airplane, Gabor Szabo, and a little cockamamie group that opened the show whom we paid seven hundred and fifty dollars for the six days, two shows a night. The Jimi Hendrix Experience. The people were jamming the place. Bill kept saying to me, "I *told* you the Airplane drew. I *told* you they drew." The people would come in and they were all there *long* before the opening act. Bill said, "They like to get here early so they can find a good seat." Hendrix played, Szabo played. The Airplane played. Hendrix played his second set. Half the joint left. That was all they were there for, really. *Jimi.* They knew more about the music than we did. Because we never had the time to listen to it.

BILL: Jimi first came to San Francisco right after Monterey Pop and played at the Fillmore with Gabor Szabo and Jefferson Airplane. He opened and then Gabor Szabo and then the Airplane. That was the first night. Afterward, the Airplane asked him if *they* could open the show. Jimi took the town by storm.

The second night I was walking through the house when he started to play. The main thing that night was that he seemed to *just* play guitar. Whenever his body *really* felt like moving, it moved. Most times when Jimi Hendrix performed, part of it was, "All right, I'm going to push my body around and *then* move the guitar. I'm going to move my tongue and I'm going to move my ass and I'll sock it to you." But they were preordained moves. When they weren't, there was nobody close. He was *supreme.*

It has always amazed me that no rock historian has ever dealt with the most significant aspect of who Jimi Hendrix was. After Otis Redding, he was the first black man in the history of this country who caused the mass of white females in the audience to disregard his race and want his body. They wanted to fuck him as a unit. After Otis, he was the first black sex symbol in White America.

Live, he was a combination of the ultimate trickster and the ultimate technician with great emotional ability. Some great artists I found mainly technically great, not emotionally balanced. When Hendrix gave bad performances, it was because he gave in to the visual. He gave in to performing. When he was doing a three-and-a-half gainer on stage, the fingers couldn't possibly have been as lucid as when he concentrated on playing. When he played and moved and didn't sell his body, he was an adagio dancer.

He was also a fashion leader. Jim Morrison was the first rock star ever to wear leather pants. Then Hendrix came to San Francisco with a scarf tied around his knee. When he left, there was one on the elbow and one around the head. All of a sudden, everyone else was doing just the same.

5.

BILL: Cream and the Butterfield Blues Band were playing the Fillmore. Pouring night. There was a marquee at the original Fillmore and my office was above it. I could open the door and step out and I would be standing on top of the marquee. I heard some noise outside my windows. Somebody was trying the doors. There was a haberdasher downstairs and a drainpipe you could climb up to get on top of the marquee. Once in a while, I'd find people outside the window on the second level. I looked out and there were two guys trying to get in. One was Carlos Santana. The other was Michael Carabello and Carlos had a harmonica in his pocket.

They were like seventeen years old. I'd been sound asleep at my desk and they woke me up. "Hello?" I said.

"Oh, jeez," they said. "You know. Like we wanna see the great Eric Clapton, man. But we don't have the bread."

They seemed so sincere that I let them in. They told me they were putting this band together. For me, the magic word was "conga y timbales." I said, "Conga y timbales?" Right away, I wanted to see them play.

CARLOS SANTANA: Everybody talks about the sneaking-in thing but I don't remember it. It could have happened to somebody else in my band and Bill thinks it was me. I know I was there a lot, trying to get in like everybody else. I was a kid right out of high school and nobody else was putting on shows like Bill did then.

I was supposed to be going to Mission High but I would only show up in the morning for homeroom. They would take attendance and then I'd split. Mainly what I did was pretty much just daydream. About playing with a lot of people I have played with, and getting involved I guess with Bill Graham. Music always was one of my obsessions. Before coming to San Francisco from Tijuana, I was already a musician. From 1959 to 1961, I worked in those strip joints on Revolucion Street in Tijuana. I would start at four in the afternoon. We played for one hour and the prostitutes undressed for an hour. Seven of them would do their thing and then we would play for another hour. Until six o'clock in the morning. Mainly blues. Black people would come over from San Jose or L.A. to spend the weekend. To cop some drugs and chicks and they would run out of money. They would come to play at the club to make some. We got an education from them.

In San Francisco I was washing dishes at Tick Tock's on Third Street. Between that and cutting school, I barely got out. They were very gracious to give me my diploma. Because all I knew in my heart was that I didn't belong in Vietnam and I didn't belong in school. So I quit Tick Tock's and started hanging around more at the Fillmore. That was how Bill and I got closer. He started seeing me *everywhere*.

PAUL BARATTA: I knew the kind of money that Carlos and his first
manager, Stan Markham, *weren't* making. At the Jefferson Airplane,
Gabor Szabo, Jimi Hendrix show in June, I saw them downstairs four
straight nights, plopping down their money. The fifth night they showed
up by the ticket booth and I was standing at the top of the stairs. I came
down and Stan said, "Any chance we can get in to see Hendrix? We
already paid our way in a few times. We just don't have any more money."

I couldn't say no. From that point on, Stan and Carlos and I started
having a relationship where I *always* let them in. They paid when they
could and when they couldn't, I let them in.

CARLOS SANTANA: That's how everybody learns. If you're a musician,
you cop an album and you wear it out, pretending you're *him*. Michael
Bloomfield or B. B. King. You fantasize playing on stage with him until
you learn to play *your* solo after they play their solo. You find your own
ways.

At the time, Butterfield was the most important blues band to me
because their music was so deeply rooted with Little Walter and Chicago
and the Delta. To me, they were the most important until Eric came
around with Cream and started playing infinitely more lyrically, and Jimi
Hendrix. But before that, Butterfield was my first.

I would watch Bloomfield's hands. Musicians that I love play from the
whole body. They play from the calves, the *cojones*, everything. A lot of
street musicians play like that. Studio musicians play from their fingers
out so they don't penetrate too much on the listener. You know, it sounds
pleasant but it's like plastic flowers in your room. If you want the *real*
flowers, you got to go see street musicians. Because they know how to get
inside themselves and inside the listener a little deeper.

JIM HAYNIE: It was my job to set up all the local bands who wanted to
audition and get them to come in on Sunday and play for nothing. The
most memorable one was the Carlos Santana Blues Band who came in
with Stan Markham, a friend of theirs from Mission High. Sunday
afternoon was a dollar to get in and Bill liked that. He liked mothers
bringing their kids. We would fill the floor with balloons and a lot of times
we would have popcorn for them. The kids would just run around and the
moms would dance like crazy and these tryout bands would be up there
trying out.

CARLOS SANTANA: Bill was having these matinee things on Sundays and
Paul Butterfield and Charles Lloyd were on the bill. My recollection is
that Paul Butterfield probably took some LSD because he showed up late

with no shoes on and he looked like he had just seen God and he was still watching and beholding Him in the ceiling. So they had a jam session. Jerry Garcia and people from the Grateful Dead and the Jefferson Airplane. Michael Bloomfield was playing keyboards. Stan Markham, who I had met in high school, was the guy who first introduced me to the hippie world. He went right up to Bill Graham and said, "Hey, you know. I know this Mexican kid from Tijuana. He loves playing blues and he loves B. B. King. Will you let him play?"

Bill went, "Go ask Michael Bloomfield."

Sure enough, Stan asked Michael Bloomfield. Michael Bloomfield looked at me and said, "Here it is. Go ahead."

Bloomfield lent me his guitar. I played a little bit and by the time I got to my solo, Bill heard me. He saw the reaction of the people and the musicians. It was good enough for him to give me a shot later on with my own band. He said, "Do you have your own band?" I told him I had two guys, a bass player and a drummer. At the time, we were playing mainly songs like the "Work Song," which Paul Butterfield had done but which was actually a Cannonball Adderly composition. And "Chim Chim Cher-ee," the way Oliver Nelson and Wes Montgomery did it.

About a month or two later, we auditioned for Bill. Whenever somebody wouldn't show up, Bill would say, "Okay. Come on in and play." Somebody would cancel or he would get into a fight with the artists or whatever. The first show we played, we opened for Paul Butterfield. And we played all his songs *before* he went on. It was really, really crazy. The second time somebody didn't show up was when the Loading Zone canceled, so we opened for The Who. The weekend of Monterey Pop.

Every time somebody would miss it, we would be there in a *second*, man. We were hanging around anyway. We didn't have no place else to go. That was how we got to headline. I'm very proud that Bill had us as the top name on the marquee before we ever had an album out. So thanks to Bill.

BILL: To this day, Santana is still the only band ever to headline the Fillmore *without* having made a record.

6.

PAUL BARATTA: In terms of finding new acts, we had our ears tuned to the ground. I started reading *Melody Maker* so I could know what was going on in England. People kept coming in and saying, "Have you heard this new group on KMPX? They are *sensational*." Who the hell even had time to listen to the radio? We were in there all day long, *working*. But we kept hearing so many things about this band called Cream. Bill, God bless him, he had the intuition to pick up on it. This was the difference between us. If it had been me, I would have booked Cream for a week. Bill booked them for *two* weeks. He called Robert Stigwood in London and paid Cream five thousand dollars for the two weeks. So they got twenty-five hundred a week.

They opened on a Tuesday night. On Wednesday morning in New York, everyone knew what a sensation they had been. Elmer Valentine called from the Whiskey-A-Go-Go in L.A. and said, "I understand Cream was sensational. I'd like to put them on." And we were saying, "How the *fuck* do these people know?"

BILL: They were the first power trio, blues-based but with that powerful rock and roll guitar. They played the Fillmore for five nights in a row second on the bill to Butterfield Blues Band and then I put them on for six nights headlining over the Electric Flag and Gary Burton.

ERIC CLAPTON: I remember a whole kind of circle of events that would surround us each time we were in San Francisco. Playing the Fillmore, the hippies in Sausalito, meeting the Grateful Dead, meeting Big Brother. All night long in Sausalito, where it was *very* hippie, these guys would be outside our window with bongos and congas. Over in England, we had been playing *clubs*. Clubs and concerts. Not really concerts as they are today but more like jazz festivals.

At that time, England was still into traditional jazz and pop music, really. There wasn't a fusion of rock or blues or anything like that. So there wasn't a serious audience as such. The only time we ever got a serious audience was when we played a jazz festival.

The first time I went to San Francisco, I experienced the kind of more introverted or serious or introspective attitude toward our music which seemed to go hand-in-hand with hallucinogenic drugs or grass or whatever. It was more into a "head" thing, you know? I was encouraged really to get outside of the format. I was encouraged to experiment.

When we played the Fillmore for the first time, the band was *in* the light show. If you were in the audience, you didn't know *who* was playing. Not at all. It was a sensory thing. They didn't want to dance, really. Most of the audience would sit on the floor and just stare at the light show. *Zonked*. If they weren't zonked, they would pick up on a contact high from the music and the people around them.

There was very much a whole kind of Fillmore energy coming off the audience that combined with the band. Which was not yet over in

England, though it did come for a while when they had concerts in Hyde Park which were quite psychedelic in their way, and very free.

BILL: He was the ultimate of all gentlemen. At all times. Eric Clapton, except for his fingers, never went from thirty-three to either forty-five or seventy-eight RPM. He was always thirty-three. His movements, his walk. If he was putting on a jacket or blowing his nose, whatever it might be, the center of Eric Clapton was always thirty-three. Except for the fingers.

He was very reserved when I first met him. He had that shortness of words that some of the English have. With their friends, they're very talkative. With others, they just answer. Eric was an answerer.

ERIC CLAPTON: I never really got to know Bill until I crossed him. Back then, you *never* got to talking to the promoters. I mean, you just *didn't*. It was a forbidden track. If you wanted to talk to anyone, you usually had to find some musician. In order to make contact. Normally, the promoter wasn't in your line of communication.

So I wasn't aware of Bill even being connected with the Fillmore in any way until one day I decided I was going to go out for a walk in between shows. I was forbidden by him to go outside. It was like school. He came down quite heavy, telling me, "Where do you think *you're* going? You're staying right *here* until it's over."

"Who *is* this guy?" I thought. "What *is* this?"

I saw a regime. From that point on, I assessed a lot of other things. If people were caught with dope inside the place, they *weren't* turned over to the police. They were dealt with inside the building. The drugs were taken away and they were given a reprimand and then they were turfed out. But they weren't dealt with as society dealt with them. Bill had his own rules inside the Fillmore and it all stayed in there. It was like a little family. Once I got to know that, once I got to know where the limitations were, then it was great. I felt very, very at home there.

BILL: I remember the first time I saw him. He wore a dark green, corduroy jacket. Like a racing green MG color. And he was a giraffe. You know how giraffes always look? Long-necked and regal? He was regal in his walk and the way he carried himself, on stage and off.

In his playing, the combination of technique and emotion was always high. The technique was always more for me than the emotion. With Hendrix and some of the others, I would judge them by saying, "He's really much more emotional than technical." Eric was not a pyrotechnics guy, with smoke bombs flying off his guitar. He didn't try to do those things. But he was a tight dancer. He never let go of the partner. He never went solo any other way. He was always in control and there were times when I wished that he would just let loose.

Pete Townshend of The Who would lose it the way that a fighter would lose it in a big bout. I never knew, "Did he lose it accidentally or was he going for it?" Eric never totally let go of it at any point. He kept to the point. There was nothing that was *not* Eric. He always knew his way back out. He would get into a pocket and look to discover all the colors in the world but he never forgot where he had come in. He might go on to a different place than the one he came in on. But he never dropped it completely. Not unless he knew there was another, different way out. He left *markers*.

ERIC CLAPTON: Once I realized that it was a little kingdom within a kingdom, then I was very happy to be there. I remember about a year before going to play there, I had read the Hunter Thompson book on the Hell's Angels. There was a little kind of hierarchy of people that he mentioned in the book. One was Terry the Tramp.

We were getting ready to play one night and this guy just walked into the dressing room. I thought, "What is this? You know, can *anyone* come in here?" The guy was really big and in a bad way. I mean, he was covered in grease and dirt and blood. Someone that worked for Bill said, "Is it all right if he comes in and sits down here? Because he just wrecked his bike."

I said, "Well, who is it?"

"Oh, it's Terry the Tramp."

I swallowed. You know, this was the big time. *Terry the Tramp.* You know? I was more impressed than if B. B. King had come walking in. The guy didn't say a word but he was a very impressive character. Very heavy. The real stuff. Don't forget, I had already kind of educated myself in what America would be like. The first books I ever bought were about America. The first records were American. I was just devoted to the American way of life without ever having been there. I was ready for it all. I wanted to learn about red Indians and the blues and everything. I was really an American fan.

BILL: Cream was the first of the English bands like Pink Floyd and Ten Years After who exemplified something much different than what was going on in the American scene. There was a deep respect and a great relationship between the manager and the group. Invariably, the manager would be with them in the early days. Not the road manager or someone from the office but the *manager*. With Pink Floyd, it was Steve O'Rourke.

For Jethro Tull and Ten Years After, it was Terry Ellis and Chris Wright who then went on to form Chrysalis. With Traffic, it was Chris Blackwell. With Cream, it was Robert Stigwood.

In England, they were allowed to be both agent *and* manager. Most of them took a much bigger percentage than American managers. English musicians considered themselves tied to their manager and you would never hear of English musicians trying to get out of their contracts because of dissatisfaction. There was a pact. They were in it together. There was much greater loyalty. Where they played was absolutely relative to the manager's wishes.

ERIC CLAPTON: There was a lot of bravery back then. There were a lot more risks taken and people out on a limb. There weren't many bands doing what Cream did. I don't know how we got the courage to do it in a way. We went out there and took on San Francisco and we didn't even know what we were in for or what we were up against. That time, we went round America and kind of took it by storm. Because what we were doing basically was bringing their music back home and showing it to them for the first time.

Even though there were the Grateful Dead and the Jefferson Airplane and Big Brother and all that, they were kind of playing pop music. They weren't relating to their own roots too well. They were trying to get away from it all. They weren't playing blues. There weren't many blues bands around at all, except for Butterfield. Butter and me and Mike Bloomfield, we all hit it off immediately. Now, none of them are left except for Elvin Bishop.

Bill's great point was that he had deep-seated feeling for what was right in the music. He was very instrumental in getting people together. He made sure I met the right musicians. He would keep certain people away and bring other people in. Through him, I met Carlos Santana and the Electric Flag. All through Bill.

BILL: With Cream, I had the deal with Robert Stigwood's office. Stigwood was one of the first giants of rock and roll who knew *nothing* about rock and roll. He couldn't keep the beat but he knew numbers and how to manipulate them. I don't think he himself had ears but he could tell what the public wanted. Dollar-wise, he was very, very difficult to deal with.

Six months after Cream destroyed everyone at the Fillmore, I had them back for four nights at Winterland and two at the Fillmore, where they played with James Cotton and Blood, Sweat, and Tears. Stigwood was the first guy ever to wear his full-length coat into Winterland *over* his shoulders. Nobody even wears a coat in San Francisco. Much less *over* the shoulders with the hat *and* the dickey scarf wrapped around his throat. Like he'd come in from Pluto and the natives on earth were alien to what he represented.

The night he came to catch the show was a great one. I had just given each guy in Cream one of those little tape recorders that were brand new and had just come on the market. Because we'd done very well with them there. This was the third night of the show and Stigwood had not been there either of the first two nights.

Sonja and Evelyn, both of my sisters from Europe, had just come to America for a visit and it was very important to me that the two of them, and Ester as well, be able to see the show from the stage which I had set up on the side of Winterland.

On stage, I put six chairs for my sisters and their husbands which nobody could see and I'd had it okayed by the band beforehand. Just before Cream went on, this man appeared with two other men. He asked who was going to sit in those chairs. Someone told him, "Those are for Mr. Graham's family."

He came over to me and said, "Excuse me, Bill. That's Robert Stigwood standing over there, the manager of the Cream. And *he* would like to sit in those seats. I know your sisters were going to be sitting there. Think you can make some other arrangements?"

I said, "Can we make some other arrangements for Mr. Stigwood?"

"No, no, no," he said. "He would like *you* to make some other arrangements for *your* family."

"Tell him that it's just not possible right now. It's a little late, and the show is about to go on." But I said it in a very nice way.

The guy went over to tell Stigwood the news. I watched him come all the way back again to complain to me about it. "My sisters are going to sit there," I told him. "What other arrangements does *he* want me to make?"

Back again, he went. The third time the guy came over, he said, "Look. Mr. Stigwood is rather insulted. Do you know who he is?"

I said, "Yes, I know who he is. I know who *he* is. I assume he knows who *I* am. Therefore I assume he *must* know who my sisters are. Would you let him know that my sisters *aren't* going to be moving?"

Stigwood was at the foot of the steps leading up to the stage. I was at the top. The band was about to come out. There were fifty-four hundred people in the house waiting to see them. Finally, the guy came back to me and said, "Bill, the Cream will *not* play tonight. Unless those seats are given to us."

By now, my sisters were standing at the foot of the stage. I led them up because I didn't want them to see what was going to happen. I got them in their seats and then I went back down to the bottom of the steps. I got four of my security guys. Willie and Jonesy and Pete and Stardust. Four good security guys.

I went over to Mr. Stigwood and I said, "Excuse me. I'd like to introduce myself." By this time, he was ready to receive me. I was looking at a Simonized version of Errol Flynn. He was wearing a suit and I looked the way I always did at a show. Like hired help. I said, "I'd like to introduce myself."

"Yes, I know who you are, Bill," he said in a very snippy, British condescending manner.

"Good," I said. "Let's make certain. I'm Bill Graham. You're Robert Stigwood. That's *your* band. Those three ladies on the stage, those are *my* sisters. You don't offend my sisters that way. Now, you've got to make a decision. You can walk out of the building right now or we can carry you."

"What do you mean?" he said.

"You're going to have to leave the building," I told him. "One way or the other. Take your pick."

"Well then," he said. "I'll tell the band *exactly* what's happening. We'll see about their playing."

There were two of my guys on either side of him. They walked him through the audience, out through the side door to the outside of the building. I decided I had to go tell the band what had just happened.

I said, "I want to tell you guys up front what just went down. This is the way it was." I told them the story.

Now they had just received these tape players from me. Ginger Baker put his gift down. In one sentence, he said it all. He said, *"Really? That's marvelous. That is marvelous."*

ERIC CLAPTON: We thought it was *hilarious.* Bill threw him out and then he came and told us. He said, "I have some bad news for you. We had to just throw out your manager." We thought it was *incredible.* Because we all knew what Robert Stigwood was. God bless his soul. I still think the world of him. But he did try to strong-arm it quite a lot and he had nothing, not a leg to stand on with us because we had too sharp a sense of humor. It was just Bill showing no respect. *Absolutely no respect.*

PAUL BARATTA: The legal capacity of the Fillmore was nine hundred. That was a big laugh. Any weekend that you would come in there during the Summer of Love, there was a minimum of fourteen or fifteen hundred people in there. On the very first Saturday night that Cream played, we put thirty-six hundred people in that joint. I figured it out once. How much Bill grossed in those two weeks. Eighty-three thousand dollars. We took the entire staff, the concessions people and everybody, on a ferry and kept them out all day and took them over to Sam's Boathouse in Tiburon and fed them that night. From what Cream made.

7.

PETE TOWNSHEND: We all grew in the Electric Ballroom. We grew extraordinarily. We were able to experiment. We were able to take chances. Before that, there was blues jamming. You were allowed to do blues solos, which was the kind of thing that Eric Clapton would do with John Mayall. I used to kind of wonder about that because to my knowledge, I didn't think that B. B. King or Bobby Bland or Albert King actually did that. They just played songs with short breaks in the middle. But Eric could flutter his eyelids and go *off*, you know. It was kind of a sexual experience for us all.

We hadn't done that because we were more of a pop group. Although we were an R&B band, we were more song-oriented and we found that we were able to experiment not just on the length of songs but also on song cycles. So we were taking a chunk of the act and saying, "Right, let's play 'Fortune Teller,' let's play 'Come On, Everybody,' let's play 'Summertime Blues.' Let's play an old Chuck Berry song."

The effect was of a cameo of music which might not actually elicit a response until it was quite clearly over and then everybody would go *"YEAHHHH!* Rock and roll!" Not for what you'd just done but kind of for the idea of it. That led very naturally to quite elaborate and drawn-out sets for us including stuff like *Tommy* and the mini-opera.

Also, going a bit further to the *way* we performed solos. It was very much a kind of physical thing between Keith Moon and me and John. Like throwing a ball around. Kind of a rhythmic thing rather than about musical dexterity. Like a *drumming* thing I suppose.

The reason we grew is because people were *really* listening. We grew in self-respect and self-esteem. We were stunned to realize that our audience was intelligent enough to know what was going on. Previously, we had really undervalued them.

GARY BROOKER: Procol Harum weren't like Cream, who were over there just a bit before us. They were in the same situation that The Who had been. The Fillmore was the absolute making of their whole style. They had only a few songs. They had their set. Which in England was all right. It did you fine for an evening. But once you got to America, it was a bit boring to play the same set twice in a night. So you would make variations and play something new or run through a quick one in the dressing room and say, "Well, let's try that." People had to extend themselves.

The year before, nobody would have sat down and listened ten minutes to a guitar solo. Nobody would have even *thought* of playing one.

ROBIN TROWER: Before I joined Procol Harum in 1966, I can remember going to see Cream at a dance. I remember about fifty people standing around the front of the stage watching the band. The rest were dancing. And that was typical, you know? There wasn't so much of the theater-type rock and roll show until America started to put that together. Bill Graham, really. I suppose.

GARY BROOKER: At Fillmore, you got a feedback the moment you were playing. If somebody played a good solo, that made the band rise up a bit more as a whole. Their effort increased and their intensity. You could actually feel that the audience felt that. Even within the number. Which again pushed you further. You could get to the end of the song and everybody, both band and the audience, would be in an extremely high state of excitement.

PAUL BARATTA: Bill and I were in that tiny office at the Fillmore a zillion hours a day. I'd get in at ten o'clock in the morning. We'd work the show until two-thirty at night. Then we would clean the place up and go for lunch and breakfast both at Mel's. Get to bed at five in the morning and then get up and be back at work by ten. We were calling England at the hour most appropriate for them, which was after we closed the Fillmore at night.

We were putting in enormous hours. Who the fuck had time to listen to the radio? What we did was keep our ears to the ground. We booked some bands by *osmosis.*

8.

JOHN MORRIS: Bill and I met in Toronto where he came in July 1967 with the Jefferson Airplane and the Grateful Dead to do a "Sounds of San Francisco" show at the O'Keefe Convention Center. After Toronto, he put me out with Jefferson Airplane on the road for about four or five months. They loved Bill and they hated Bill. He had the patience and he didn't have the patience. He didn't have the style and he did have the style. He had the instincts but . . .

BILL THOMPSON: They didn't like it. For a long time, the band would say, "Hey, man. I need to get a kilo of grass. We should go out and *work*, man." Bill had them working *all* the time. They wanted to play music and this got to be like a *job*. That's why all these people had dropped out anyway. They didn't want a job. Later on, bands learned that the way to *really* get rich was on the road.

We played Hunter College. Ron Delsener was the promoter. His first show. Grace refused to do an encore. Her line was, "Frank Sinatra doesn't do encores." Graham came back and said, "I quit. Fuck you people. You fucking people. Who do you think you fucking are?" And this was *between* shows. I went, "Bill, don't you think you could maybe wait till *after* the show?"

"No! I wait for *nobody!*"

Boom! After that was when the stuff *really* started.

PAUL KANTNER: There was one supreme example of him wanting us to work too much. We had a gig at the Fillmore one night. At the Fillmore, we usually played two or three sets. That night, we played one set and he hustled us down to the airport to fly to Sacramento to do a show. *Same night. With* our equipment. Then fly back and do the final shot at the Fillmore. We did it. It was amusing, sort of. But it was not the kind of thing I really liked to do regularly.

Because a show was not just a performance. In San Francisco, anyway, and particularly then. A show was a whole social something-or-other. Bonfire ceremony or something. After we played, we wanted to go out and hustle girls. Get drunk and party, come back and play another set, go out and party again, and pretty soon, dawn was there. To break that up was *business*. It was an amusing experiment to do it once. Just to see what you could do. But it was like work.

JOHN MORRIS: Paul and Grace were San Francisco with a capital "S" and artists as well. It was an amazing family. Spencer Dryden, who was the drummer, was a great guy. He was the most business-oriented. But Bill wanted to turn it *into* a business and Bill's version of business was a compulsion. They didn't work from that attitude and it was a big conflict. He put me out on the road with them because I was straighter. I was East Coast. Grace and I got along like a house on fire because she had gone to Finch. She had a whole collection of Chanel suits. A couple of times we went to the Trident in Sausalito together. She put her hair up in a bun and me wearing a suit. Nobody knew who the hell she was. It was hilarious.

On stage, she *killed* them. She was *so* beautiful. And totally real. But schizophrenia abounded. She could also be the toughest, most foul-mouthed rock and roll lady. By comparison, she could make Janis look pale.

BILL THOMPSON: At first, Marty Balin had been the power in the band. And then it became Grace. Marty kind of pulled back a little bit after she got all the publicity for "White Rabbit" and "Somebody to Love." Basically, it was an ultimatum from Grace that did it. That if Bill stayed, she and Spencer Dryden would leave. At the time, Spencer had a lot of influence with Grace. He was drilling her.

He and Bill didn't get along. Spencer wanted to take a fifth of bourbon in the dressing room. This was *before* people asked for things. Bill said, "Who the *hell* do you think you are, mister?"

JERRY GARCIA: Spencer Dryden came from the L.A. scene. See, now L.A.'s different again. It's like a whole 'nother trip down there. It's that thing of, "Watch out for the sharpies, man. Because them motherfuckers . . ." You know what I mean? *"Look out for the sharpies, man."* Down there, they've got that ultra-paranoia, especially if there's money involved. *"Watch out."* You know? They're really on that trip down there. It's the Hollywood background. I mean, they're *seriously* weird about that shit. Spencer was like a model of one of those guys who go, "They're going to *burn* you. Those fuckers will burn you *every* time." Which of course they then *always* do. You know?

BILL THOMPSON: We came as a bunch of hippies and all of a sudden, *boom!* We were like America's Beatles. This big story happened in *Life* magazine about San Francisco and here was this girl with this bunch of weird guys. How could she be with those guys? They all looked like child molesters. They made the Rolling Stones' hair look like crewcuts. "White Rabbit" really started the Summer of Love off. It made it happen.

All of a sudden, we were *superstars.* From being guys who had to figure out how we were going to pay our rent.

We rented a house in L.A. where the Beatles had been living and recorded "After Bathing at Baxter's." George Harrison wrote "Bluejay Way" in that house and they used it in that Lee Marvin film "Point Blank." Everybody swam naked in the pool. Little girls looking for the Beatles would wander in. Jim Haynie was our security guard. He was always nude and he had a dick like Secretariat. It was really wild and the album itself was pretty weird. Grace and Spencer would just stay up at night and drink. He really got her into drinking.

The band would go in and start recording and we would do takes.

Forty, fifty, sixty different takes of a song. Then Spencer would come in at one o'clock at night and want to listen to all the takes all over again. Jorma was there with his wife from Sweden and they didn't talk to each other for a while. Jorma got mad at a bunch of people swimming in the pool and he took a gun out and started shooting bullets in the water. Jack had been in prison for a couple of weeks because Owsley gave him too much STP. He was naked on the sand and he got busted by the police. He woke up naked in jail with his hands and feet on bars like some kind of caged animal.

Graham was around, glowering. Because he didn't understand it. *I* didn't understand it and I was *part* of it. And that made things worse. *Surrealistic Pillow* had done a million and a half and this album only sold like three hundred and fifty thousand copies. We just kind of went the opposite way on purpose and it actually helped us for a cult following.

BILL: Marty Balin had written this ballad called "Today" that I thought was a mindblower. I wanted them to release it as the single. Paul Kantner and I had a lot of words about it. Instead, they released "The Ballad of You and Me and Pooneil," which was more than six minutes long and just a very difficult song to hum. They said, "We already put out the commercial thing with 'White Rabbit.' Then we put out *another* commercial thing with 'Somebody to Love.' Now the public will eat up anything. Whatever we want to give them, they'll take."

We went on the road but the number Paul Kantner had insisted on releasing did not get much airplay. We continued to have big arguments about it. Marty Balin's song "Today" was *misty*. It was *magic*.

GRACE SLICK: Part of it was, and this is embarrassing to admit, I didn't want to work as much as Bill Graham wanted us to work. Because I would really rather fuck off more than work. I'm not a dedicated musician and I'm not striving to make eight million dollars in one year. I'd rather have a couple days when I could sleep off a hangover. Literally. And Spencer felt like that too.

PAUL KANTNER: That was one of the places where songs come from. That space of having something to write about other than being on the road. I think Spencer bullied Bill out of it and I think Grace went along with it beyond a reasonable point. I could have lived with Bill and we could have controlled him I thought with no problem, as we had all along. I mean, he would always yell and scream and I would always get quieter and then we would do everything just as we had wanted to do it. Spencer *was* a little nutty at the time. I put it on Spencer. More than Grace would.

BILL THOMPSON: January or February of 1968, Marty and I had to go tell Bill. It was kind of like going and telling Genghis Khan some bad news. He got mad. He was mad at me for a while. Because he didn't know what to think. After that, I became kind of the acting manager.

BILL: I never took a dime in commission from the Airplane in all that time. Never ten cents because they were trying to get out from under. Going through the whole East Coast and playing at the Fillmore, there was never a commission taken out by me for management. At the end when I got too busy to do it anymore, someone said, "Well, we really should settle this with Bill because he never took anything for all the work." The decision could be made only if they *all* agreed to do that. All of them agreed to do it except for one person. So there was never a financial settlement.

The way I always liked to introduce them on stage? "If you're going to fly first class . . . *Jefferson Airplane!*"

Chapter Seven

Bringing It All Back Home

1.

PAUL BARATTA: He was reluctant as hell to open Fillmore East. It would have been easy for me to do if I was in his position. In his position though, I probably wouldn't have done half the things he wound up doing. But in my position, I wanted him to do *everything*. Everything that seemed right. We turned down a lot of things that seemed *schlocky*. But I liked the idea of us being in New York. It seemed like something that was right for the company that was being built. I felt Bill had all the *chutzpah* in the world and the toughness to be able to go into New York and make a success out of that.

Someone had put on Cream at the Village Theater in New York and the place became available. Bill said, "I've got this guy John Morris who wants me to do it." John Morris came out. I really wasn't knocked out with him. But I was knocked out with the idea.

And Bill was being as hesitant as he could. He was really nervous. It was New York. It was big time. He didn't want to go in and fall on his ass.

JOHN MORRIS: I was sitting on my hands in New York and not working, waiting for Graham to do something. In the door walked Joshua White and Chip Monck, who said, "There's this theater downtown and this guy named Tony Lech"—which they pronounced "Leck"—"And these two guys from *Crawdaddy* magazine and they need somebody to come in and handle the ball game." They had come up with the idea and gotten the money.

Gary Kurfirst was running the Village Theater at the time across

226

Second Avenue and doing sporadic concerts. I went to see a Cream concert there and the first show was supposed to start at eight and it started at nine-thirty. The audience for the second show came in and there were like nine thousand people in the place at the same time. Tiny Tim was on stage and somebody threw a lock that almost hit him in the face. I saw the thing in the air and I just reached up and grabbed it and went and found Gary and goddamn near killed him. But that show was the seed because it was absolute chaos.

We went down to the Anderson Theater before doing any shows there and here was this guy Tony Lech who ran a bar with a gun and Jerry Pompili was his heavy. After we got to know Jerry and he started changing into the wonderful person he is now, we used to refer to him as "the *light* heavy." Tony didn't know what the fuck he was involved with. The great story about the Anderson Theater was that the play which closed it was called *"The Bride Got Farblundjet,"* with Menasha Skulnik and Molly Picon. I actually saw it. One of the great thrills of my life. "The Bride Got Confused." And from that, right into Moby Grape and Country Joe and the Fish.

BARRY MELTON: When Bill expanded into the Fillmore East in New York, I think in many ways Country Joe and the Fish were the spearhead. We were the first of the Bay Area bands with the exception of the Jefferson Airplane to really go out and tour the United States seriously and make serious money out there on the road.

Our first promotion of real consequence in New York where we were very successful was at the Anderson Yiddish Theater. With the Fugs and Pearls Before Swine. We were the headliners because we were the West Coast Unusuals. My grandmother went to the gig. My father comes from good redneck stock in Texas but my mother's a Russian Jew. This was my mother's mother. From Brooklyn. Came from Brooklyn to the Anderson Yiddish Theater and she was *so* proud of the fact that her grandson Barry was playing at the Yiddishe Theater.

Pearls Before Swine opened. That surprised her a bit. She had been born in the old country. In the last century, no doubt. Then the Fugs came on. My grandmother came back to the dressing room and she was visibly upset. She kept telling me, "I *vant* that singer! I *vant* that singer! I'm going to vash his mouth out with soap!" Fortunately, this was before our own "F-U-C-K" cheer was even conceptualized. Compared to the Fugs, we were *clean*. But my grandmother was upset for *weeks* after that show. She wanted to get hold of Ed Sanders and Tuli Kupferberg and wash out their mouths with soap. She was *livid*. That they would dare do that. In the *Yiddishe* theater, no less.

JOHN MORRIS: We had done a couple of shows at the Anderson and I got on the phone and called Bill and said, "You're out of your goddamn mind if you do not come to New York and take this over. We're making money. It works. You can either come take this operation over or the Village Theater across the street." I said, "You've *got* to come to New York." It took a week or two. Actually, I campaigned Bonnie like crazy, too. I said to Bill, "Look, you're a New York guy. You've *got* to do this. It's in your *blood.*"

"No, I don't want to expand. I don't want to do this."

And on and on and on. And he came in. That was when we sat down with Tony Lech. And Tony basically *did* tell him to fuck off.

JERRY POMPILI: Tony looked like a Damon Runyon character. Curly reddish hair, glasses, and he always wore these cheap leather car coats with shit stuffed in all the pockets. One day, Tony said to me, "There's this fucking guy coming here, this promoter from California. Bill Graham wants to talk to me. I want you to come along. I don't know what the fuck's gonna happen on this."

With Tony, I was like his henchman. I have no idea why. I don't even remember why I liked the guy. He was just a real character. Anyway, we set the meeting for the Tin Angel, which was up above the Bitter End. We went up there and we sat down. Tony ordered soup. Bill came in and introduced himself, very polite.

Tony said, "So, what's your deal? What's your proposition?"

Bill laid out this very sober proposition. He said, "Look, I've been promoting now in California on a regular basis for two or three years. I'm thinking about coming to New York. I've caught some of your shows, I'm very impressed with your operation. To tell you the truth, I think you're doing a good job here. I think we can work together. I can bring in the acts. I can get better prices than you because I have a relationship with them. We can make this a going deal."

Tony finished his soup. He looked up at Bill and he went, "Who the *fuck* are *you* to come in here?" It was like a scene from a cheap, third-rate gangster movie with some Jimmy Cagney impersonator playing Tony's part. "Who the fuck are you to come into *my* town and tell *me* anything. You think I need *you* to do what I'm *already* doing?"

Tony knew *nothing* about the business. He didn't book *any* of the acts. He had *no* idea who any of those people were. All he knew how to do was sell the tickets and count the money. I was sitting there as he did this thing and I was watching Graham during it and he didn't bat an eyelash. He was just cold. Tony finished his outburst.

Bill said, "Well, I'm sorry you feel that way and thank you for your time."

He got up and shook my hand very politely and said good-bye and walked out. I turned to Tony and I said, "Something tells me you just made the biggest mistake of your life."

JOSHUA WHITE: We knew it was not going to survive because Tony Lech was such a sleeze and the *Crawdaddy* people were not strong people. They were into the *scene*, not promoting. Yet they were *packing* the theater. There was a need for a venue.

So they brought Bill Graham back to New York. It was during the Big Brother concert. The light show used to have a trick we would do where we would put these blue lights across the front of the platform behind the screen. They were ultraviolet lights with blue filters on them, so really they were ultrablue lights. Not very powerful but a beautiful light. A physically beautiful light. When the screen was raised to reset the stage, all you saw when you looked at the stage was this line of blue lights. It provided illumination for the people on the stage to work but it didn't let the audience actually *see* what was going on. It was a light curtain.

The light show looked wonderfully mysterious behind it with all its lights kind of getting ready back there for the next scene. It was a wonderful feeling when that screen went up. The best part was that if you were standing on the stage, you could see the audience. They were all blue but you could see them all.

We took Bill and put him out on stage. Before we set up for Janis, the screen went up. He turned around and he took a look at the house. As only a great promoter can do, he just went *brrrrm!* And he *counted* the house. From that point on in his mind, he was convinced he could make a go of it. I was there. I saw the *click* in his eyes. I saw him realize this is *do-able*. Because here were these sleazebuckets promoting Janis Joplin with two thousand people in the house. So why wasn't *he* doing it?

BILL: Gary Kurfirst, who manages Talking Heads and David Byrne, had done some shows at the Village Theater. As a movie theater, it had been the Loew's Commodore East. The place held twenty-four hundred. It was on Second Avenue and Sixth Street. I went to see the theater and I saw it again and I saw it again and I saw it again and I saw it again.

At the time, I was not yet a professional theater-looker. It was more instinctive. How do the trucks come in and then get out? Where does the equipment come through? How high is the stage? Access, egress, dressing room areas, *space*. What do I have to build? What do I *not* have to build? I had a waiter's eye for space. The theater itself was okay. It was dirty and some of the seats needed to be painted but it was in pretty good repair. The boiler room worked. The wiring needed fixing. We needed major stage repairs.

In a lot of ways, it was like the movie theater I had gone to every Saturday as a kid in The Bronx. The Loew's Paradise. Soft red velvet on the walls. Carpets on the floor where you came in. Mirrored walls and a chandelier above the double balcony. A classic New York theater with great concessions upstairs and a great lobby. It had dressing rooms because in the twenties and thirties, it had housed the Yiddish Theater of New York. It had also been used as a meeting hall in the thirties and forties by Bolshevik groups on the Lower East Side. It was at least sixty years old when I first saw it.

It stood on a corner, three quarters of a block wide. The front was very small but then the building opened up behind the neighboring stores. Above us was NYU, the theater and technical wing.

I got in touch with Mike Rogers, the broker for the building, and we started negotiating to buy the building. It was big numbers. Four hundred thousand dollars. I talked to Mike many, many times about insurance and bringing it up to code and who pays for what once we started doing things. I brought in Bill Coblentz and a New York lawyer whom he knew. I'd been doing very well at the Fillmore in San Francisco but that kind of money I just did not have.

Mike Rogers and I finally agreed and I signed papers. An intent on my part to buy. As it turned out, Albert Grossman was also interested in it. Albert *had* the money to buy the building. He was wealthy. In the next couple of weeks, we talked. I said, "I'm going to run this place. I don't have partners. But if you want a piece of it, I'll let you in." Because Mike Rogers had also been negotiating with him. We talked and Albert and his partner Bert Block bought in for twenty points, ten and ten each. They put up eighty grand. Forty each.

I know I made the down payment but for the life of me, I cannot remember where the money came from that I used. Bonnie might know. But I don't. I never was a good businessman in that way. I knew I was taking a risk. But I never minded the risk factor. Because I hadn't yet started to live any higher. I still knew that if it all went down, I could go back to being a waiter. To being a waiter and playing craps. That was *always* there. It still is. To this day.

2.

BILL: I hired Kip Cohen to be the first house manager and Joshua White for the light show. I kept going back and forth from San Francisco to New

York so I took an apartment around the corner. Seventy-One East Seventh Street. The rent was ninety bucks a month. The East Village then was heavy. Heavy drugs and hippies and ethnic groups. The old people who lived there were all Poles and Romanians and Slavs and Italians. The Hell's Angels' office was on Fifth Street between First and Second, right around the corner, which became a great problem for me over the years.

Chip Monck was our technical director. We tore down some brick walls and changed the whole back of the theater so we could get the wiring through. We made a lot of changes in the stage area to make it effective so we could do a variety of productions.

CHIP MONCK: When Bill took over the place, it was in bad repair. There had been a lot of water damage. It had baby theatrical dressing rooms on five levels, which accessed from up stage left. I remember Barbara, my girlfriend, at the time sitting in a bosun's chair hanging halfway down from the proscenium, washing the rococo frieze which had been made by Motoma Amusement Company of Chicago, which went broke during the Depression.

Graham had already started his bit of brilliance. Which was, "I'll build the best sound system available. You don't bring your fucking sound in here and stack it on the side of the stage and make my theater look like a piece of trash. You leave your shit outside. Bring your monitor system if you absolutely have to, but *my* house system is what you use."

The speakers were all on the fly system and they would actually come up and down. We could bring them right down to the front of the apron to do repairs on them and then send them back up. It was all counter-weighted. As was the bridge. Langhart built the entire system. He was a professor. Chris Langhart made the crooked straight and the structurally ill well, in the unassuming manner of the genius with which he usually worked.

Bill would periodically come rushing in through the back door off Sixth Street, trying to steal tools. He didn't like the way I left my tools on stage. So he would rush in the door, grab anything he could, and rush back out. Just to prove that it *could* happen. One day, I got him in the back of the neck with a two-by-four. Then he didn't steal my tools anymore.

BILL: Did I do any physical work to get the Fillmore East ready? I *yelled*. I had some pretty amazing people in there doing the work. Chip Monck, who wore gold and maroon jumpsuits with zippers everywhere and pockets even on his toes. I once gave him the world's biggest zipper because of the way everything on him zipped in and out. I had Kip and Josh White and Chip. I felt blessed that these guys were there.

JOHN MORRIS: I remember Graham arriving for the opening night, and of course by then we had worked for like ninety-six straight hours. There was Chip Monck and myself, both absolutely filthy from the neck down. But we were sitting in my office, having our hair cut. We had washed our hair and managed to get a guy who had been at Sassoon to come down and cut it for us. Then we were going to put on nice clean shirts on top of all that filth with our newly cut hair.

Graham walked in just as our hair was being cut. He said, "What the *hell* is going on in this *fucking* place? You're sitting here getting your *hair* cut?

We said, "Go out and look at the goddamn theater and leave us alone."

The guy who was cutting our hair, his name was Jonathan. He came over to me and he said, "Who was that?"

"Ah, it's not important," we told him. "Just some guy from out of town."

JOSHUA WHITE: I repainted the box office. I cleaned up the marquee. One of the reasons I did that was so I could put the "Joshua Light Show" up there. It all took about two weeks. I had what's called a primary typewriter with very big letters. Kip typed up a set of flyers for the Village Theater. For the first show Bill put on there, which was Big Brother and the Holding Company, Tim Buckley, and Albert King. March 8, 1968.

Across the street at the Anderson, they had a Gladys Knight concert with Pablo's Lights. Kip was outside handing out brochures for our show and it said, "The Village Theater." What happened was that the people who had owned the theater before claimed the name. Overnight, it went from the "Village Theater" to "Fillmore East." It was supposed to be "Bill Graham Presents at the Village Theater" but the other guy was going to sue. So it was a snap decision. One that became famous.

BILL: I wanted a clean, well-run theater. We fixed the lobby and the concession area. We updated everything. We screwed everything down real tight. I wanted it to look classy. So that when people came in from off the street, they would rise up to a higher level. Like when someone walks into a spiffy restaurant. Automatically, their back gets straighter. They change to fit the room. That's what I wanted to happen to the people in that place.

Eventually, I had all the ushers in green and gold football shirts.

Green and gold. The colors of the Pirates S.A.C. From my old neighborhood in The Bronx.

3.

BILL: We fixed the marquee and put a message of welcome on it. Even though they had tickets, there were maybe a hundred people in line at about five in the afternoon on the night we opened. In San Francisco, I would always walk around the block three or four times before I opened the house. Just to see who was coming in and find out if there was anything out there that might be a problem. If so, I wanted the problem to know I saw it. I wanted them to see me seeing them.

I was walking down the side of the building when I saw four kids, maybe eleven or twelve years old, standing by the third set of doors next to the stage door, banging away with the back of their feet. Which is what I used to do when I was a kid in The Bronx. I'd bang and then wait for somebody inside to snap the door open. Only there was nobody inside but workers.

I was walking and I didn't even stop. As I went past them, I just said, *"You! Split!"* But I never stopped to make it a directive. I was on my way somewhere else. There was only one difference. I was in New York now. It was as if I'd said nothing at all. I kept hearing those feet against those doors. I turned in place and said, "You hear me?"

I kept walking. The other three had stopped and were just standing there. But this one kid with freckles and red hair was still banging away. I turned around and went back toward him. So here it was. John Wayne looking at Richard Conte. He was waiting for me, standing exactly the way a gunslinger does with his hand at his side. It was the showdown at the O.K. Corral. I went right up to him and I said, "You out of your mind?"

The kid looked at me and hitched up his pants. The timing and the way he did it was perfect. Just before he hitched them up again, he went, "Fuck you!" And he started kicking the door again. I was standing right in front of him. He was it. *New York.* Finally I said, *"Hey!"* He put his foot down.

"Yeah?" he said.

"I just bought this place. My name's Bill. What's your name?"

"Rusty."

"Rusty. Let's get something straight. That shit don't go down here."

I told him where I lived now and where I used to live. "You guys live here?" I asked them.

"Yeah!" they said.

Within fifteen minutes, we worked it out. I told them, "Whenever a new show comes in here, we unload the trucks at the side door. You guys want to help? We'll work out what you get. You want to see shows? You go through the office and do it straight. Nobody on this block fucks with the trucks or the building. Can you cover that?"

For the next three years, those kids covered that street for me. They loaded and unloaded trucks for four bucks an hour and came to almost every show. I never once had a problem with them again.

KIP COHEN: Somehow, we managed to ticket twenty-eight hundred people. There were a lot of heavies there. The vision I have is of the walls of the inner lobby and seeing Jac Holzman of Elektra Records and Judy Collins almost being crushed to death against those walls because of the surge of people pouring into that theater. I remember sitting in the aisles. I had never before felt that kind of intensity. Nor had I personally experienced the electrical charge that emanated back and forth from the stage to the audience. Gospel perhaps would be the closest thing to it.

It started high and got even higher. It was just an incredible, exhaustive evening.

JOSHUA WHITE: The opening night review in *Variety* said that the New York rock scene had made a great leap upward with the opening of the Fillmore East. Half the review was about how great the theater was and half the review was about how great the light show was. I didn't feel any embarrassment about that because I had been working for years to get to this point and do this sort of thing.

BILL: The crowd that night was different from San Francisco. The hair wasn't nearly as long. There was a lot of weed but not much acid or psychedelics. Janis could be a lot like the Dead. *So* magical on a good night. But Janis was a lot better about a year later when she played Fillmore East with Ten Years After and the Staple Singers.

That first night, we had to clear the entire house before we could start the second show. Usually if you've given somebody a good meal and you ask them to please leave because there are other people waiting outside, they'll go. We worked very hard to get everyone out. Twenty-three hundred out, clean the house, twenty-three hundred back in. Show times were either seven-thirty and eleven-thirty or eight and eleven-thirty. It varied. Usually, we had a half hour swing to turn the house around.

I remember that first night, we all just sat in the theater after the second show for a long, long time. For hours on end. Everybody just sat. When we left, it was light. I had made like nine pages of notes and we started talking about them and somebody said, "Well I'm hungry." So somebody went out to get something to eat and then we got hungry again and we went to Ratner's and then we came back inside. Fifteen or twenty of us stayed the night. The show was over at two-thirty and I got home at six. We all felt great about being right that the people would respect the house. The house itself felt good.

AHMET ERTEGUN: It was a great event when the Fillmore came to New York. It was in kind of a poetic area. Prior to the rock and roll explosion, Second Avenue had been the home of the Stuyvesant Casino where Bunk Johnson, who was Louie Armstrong's trumpet teacher, first came to play in New York. We bought him a set of teeth and a new horn and he had this original New Orleans band with George Lewis and Baby Dodds on drums. Baby Dodds was King Oliver's original drummer. It was an incredible event.

That area, the Lower East Side, was kind of a terrific place to have the Fillmore. There were elements of danger in going there. There were the motorcycle guys who would come wandering around whenever the Grateful Dead or the Jefferson Airplane played. But nothing fazed Bill Graham. Nothing. Nothing fazed him. Undaunted, like a champion warrior, he faced all calamity and walked through. Unions and tough guys and this and that. Because of his incredible vitality and force as a person, I consider him one of the great legends of rock and roll. An immigrant who came to America with a lot of ideas and hopes and who found an incredible niche. He built a place for himself.

JERRY POMPILI: For Bill's first show at the Fillmore East, Tony Lech printed up two thousand *counterfeit* tickets. Then he gave them out in Spanish Harlem. He really wanted to trash Bill's thing. I wouldn't have anything to do with it. I said, "You know, this is fuckin' lunacy." I just walked out on him right then. I walked out on him, his cousin walked out on him, we all walked out on him. So that was the end of Tony for me.

4.

JOSHUA WHITE: Fillmore East didn't do good business right away. It ran in the red for *months* before it began to turn the corner. Bill had a lot of cash flow from San Francisco so he could afford to keep it going. First of all, it was hard to book acts because you needed a lot of lead time. Then Martin Luther King was assassinated.

BILL: Opening night was packed but then there was a lull. I got scared. Because when you're waiting out the tide, how long do you have to wait? I couldn't have made the move into New York at a worse time. Because less than a month after we opened, Martin Luther King was killed. Problems between black and white in the streets created fear. People did not want to come down to the Village.

JOHN MORRIS: I was with Peter Townshend the night Martin Luther King was killed. We had a Who concert the next night at Fillmore East and we had to make the decision whether or not to go ahead with it. We went back and forth and back and forth. Being supposedly the politically aware one back then, I said, "Look. There are going to be thousands of people out on the street waiting to get in. We've *got* to play." And Pete agreed. He was sitting in the office, talking about violence and how he hated it. How he didn't understand what was going on in the world. I mean, we literally talked for two or three hours. Even then, he was one of the most eloquent, intelligent human beings. He was a *pleasure*. We decided to go ahead and do it. A lot of people were against it. But we did it.

Pete had been talking to me about peace and how he was *never* going to smash his amps again. He had been talking about how maybe he had been doing the wrong thing. Maybe *he* had been contributing to all this violence. He went on stage and he started to play.

About halfway through the set, I was up on stage and I looked at him and I knew everything was about to change. Because up to that point, he had played this whole subdued physical thing.

Then he turned around and went at the amps. We had a screen behind them. While Townshend stabbed them, beat the shit out of them, and then smashed his guitar over them. At one point, he looked over and he saw me. And I went, "*Whoops* . . ." because I thought he was going to come over the top with a guitar and get me.

He lost it. He had gotten so into it so much that he had lost it and reverted. There was so much boiling up in him that the only way he could get it out was to do it that way.

PETE TOWNSHEND: Even in New York, where you knew that Bill wasn't as in charge as he had been in San Francisco—it was in the papers all the time about local threats and stuff that was going on—you still felt you were going into his territory.

I remember Bill trying to persuade us to do two sets and we were sitting there trying to explain why we couldn't. This was in what had been called the Village Theater. We were in the stalls with the sound men running around and the roadies doing *"Test . . . Test . . . Test."* We were sitting there and it was just like we were rehearsing for a musical. Somebody came up and said, "Do you want some coffee, you guys?" And we said, "Yes, please." The guy went away and came back with some coffees. Then another guy said, "No. I'll get you some sandwiches." They got us some sandwiches. They brought us paper to write on.

There probably was an office we could have gone and sat in but really you felt like you were sort of half in Bill's living room and also half in that quite magical place of theater. Somehow, Bill had hit on it. He gave us dignity. We felt we weren't the pop plebes we had been when we went out with Herman's Hermits and we were told to shut up and get in the back of the bus. We were dignified people. We were *artists*.

JOSHUA WHITE: What they would do is still sell two shows. We would start the first show late, closer to nine p.m. so that when the second audience was arriving for the eleven-thirty show, the headliner was just going on. They managed to mix both audiences. The headliner would do a nice long show and then they would have the second act on and then close with the opening act. Nobody seemed to object to that. New York audiences having been so abused up to that point. Really, Fillmore East didn't come to life until the following fall. We even closed for a while during the summer.

Once Martin Luther King was assassinated, it was dangerous. There were riots, and people didn't want to go out.

5.

BILL: Martin Luther King's death forced me to start thinking seriously about moving out of the original Fillmore in San Francisco. The streets in that area were so tough anyway. After the assassination and the riots that followed, white kids were afraid to come into the area. I remember standing out in front of the Fillmore one night at about six o'clock. It was still light. This white guy was standing on the corner at Fillmore and Geary and this black guy just happened to be standing in front of the building.

The black guy crossed the street. The white guy said, "Got a light?" The black guy said, "Yeah." Then he leaned back and whaled him right in the face. *Whack!* The white guy went down. The black guy ran down Fillmore and into the park by Geary, across from Winterland. We ran after the guy, me and two of my uniformed cops. The guy cut across Geary and he was going down Post. He was running and running and running. At that time, I had speed and endurance. But this guy was *fast*.

He started running up toward Mount Zion and I realized I was losing him. When he started out, he was like fifty feet ahead of me and now he was sixty and I was losing him. I was running and panting and I shouted, *"Stop! Stop or I'll shoot!"* The guy stopped dead in the street. "Hey, okay, okay," he said. As he stopped, I realized I didn't have *shit*. I was standing with my finger pointing in the air like it was a gun. I turned around and one block away were my two cops, both of them having asthma attacks. I realized I had to do Cagney.

"You *move!*" I shouted. "You just *move* and I'll *kill* ya!"

I was insane. People were opening their windows. I was totally out of breath and screaming at the guy and if he had just tapped me, I would have fallen over. Finally, my two cops came up. Smitty took the handcuffs off his belt. Panting like crazy, he came up with one of the great lines in the history of rock and roll. *"You . . ."* he said, looking like he was going to die on the spot. "You . . . is under *arrest.*"

We took the guy back to the Fillmore and sat him down upstairs. He was a young tough street kid. I said, "Why'd you hit that guy?" He wouldn't answer. "Why'd you hit him?" I said. "All he did was ask you for a light. I was standing right there."

"You *know,*" he said. "You know *why,* man. *You know why.*"

"No, I don't. Tell me. Why?"

He looked at me and he said, "He killed my brother, man."

"What do you mean he killed your brother?" I said.

"He killed Martin Luther King. All you white bastard motherfuckers. You killed *Martin Luther,* man."

That was a pivotal moment for me. Afterward, there were more people getting jumped on the street, more ticket snatchings, more purses grabbed, more slurs. None of it against me. I never had a problem with the black neighborhood. Because when they needed things from me, they got them. Benefits for voter registration? Fine. Even if Huey Newton wasn't too pleasant. I always gave them the use of the hall.

Attendance was going down. There were some shows that should have been giants that weren't because people weren't coming. Out of fear of the neighborhood. Then they killed Bobby Kennedy in June. The word was out that the Carousel Ballroom at Market and Van Ness was closing. I knew I had to make my move.

Ron Rakow was a wheeler-dealer who had convinced the Dead and other Bay Area groups that he could run that hall for them. In terms of being my competition, he was mainly playing to their ego. If I would offer a band, say, seven hundred and fifty dollars, he would go to fifteen hundred. I would go to seventeen. He would go to two thousand. *Pass!* Because even at capacity, he would lose money paying that much.

The Carousel always had the same problem that Chet Helms did at the Avalon. I wouldn't let the scene come in for free. But they did. The band had so many guests? They *all* got in with no questions asked. And then the band would want to know *why* they hadn't gotten paid.

Ron Rakow found a way to convince the Dead that he was one step beyond me. That I knew the business world but that I was taking advantage of them. He would not do that. He'd been in the world where I came from but then he'd gotten hip and soulful. I am not saying that he actually said these things to them. But that was the attitude. One of the ways these kind of people *always* endeared themselves to the Dead was to say, "We can handle Bill." What they really meant was, "We're going to prove to you that we can be a bigger crook than him." And they always were.

The guy who owned the Carousel building was over in Ireland. I knew many other people were after the lease. From the sheer point of survival, I *had* to make a move. For me, the Carousel could become my lifesaver. So I called his representative and asked if there was any chance of my seeing him. The guy said, "Well, he's busy over in Ireland." I said, "I'll go over *there* to see him." He couldn't believe I would. But I always felt I had to take the extra step.

You don't want to travel? *I* will. You won't hold your breath? I'll hold mine. You don't want to walk backward? *I'll* walk backward. If it was for an act, I would make them scrambled eggs after the show so they would play for me the next time. I couldn't give them more money. What could I give them that was more than money? Everybody wanted to see this guy in Ireland and in terms of money offered, it was going to be "Can You Top This?" I didn't want to get into that. I wanted some private time with him instead.

I called the guy where he was working in Ireland on a construction site about eighty miles away from Shannon Airport. He was building a hotel. He said, "Don't you want to wait till I get there in a few months?" I said, "No, if it's all right with you, I really have to make a decision about my place now." I made arrangements and flew to New York. From New York, I got on Aer Lingus. There were seventy-one other people on the plane. Sixty-nine were nuns. The other two were a man and a woman who told me about Catholicism all the way across the Atlantic.

I got there at eight in the morning. There was a short, heavy-set, thick, red-necked man there to meet me. "Bill Graham? How are you? Bill Fuller."

"Good. How are you?"

"Have you had breakfast?"

We sat down in the airport for breakfast. Steak, eggs, and potatoes.

"Good now," he said. "Care for a drink?" He bought a bottle of bourbon and he told me his life story. Fascinating adventures all over the world. Shipping, mining, you name it. "I *love* to take risks!" he said. "Life is a risk." Finally, he got around to asking me what I wanted. I told him. "Oh, that place I have, yes," he said. "What's it called?" It was like one of nine hundred places he owned.

I told him about the Fillmore and what I did. His guy in San Francisco had said good things to him about me. He had also told him that a lot of other people wanted the place. I said, "Look, this is what I do and here's what I think your place is worth. Concessions and rent and . . . whatever you think is fair."

"Whatever *you* think is fair," he said.

"Mr. Fuller," I told him, "I'm in trouble. I *need* your place. It's the best one in San Francisco other than the one I have." Then I told him about Martin Luther King's death and the neighborhood around the Fillmore. I laid it right out for him and I said, "I wish you would consider me."

"Why should I consider you?" he said. "Why not just make a deal now and be done with it? Gene, my man in San Francisco, likes you and you'll be dealing with him."

We kept talking and drinking and talking and drinking. *Boom, boom, boom.* He just knocked that liquor down like it was nothing. There were maybe three shots left in the bottle. I'd had maybe seven or eight drinks and I was barely holding on. At a quarter after four in the afternoon, I still hadn't left the table or been to the bathroom. I was *plotzing*.

"Good then," he said. "I'll get back to work. Gene will draw up the papers."

He got up and I realized he was not asking me to come home with him or go do anything. He said, "Good, good," and he got up and left at about four-fifteen. At five o'clock, I was on a plane back to New York. I got off the plane and called Bonnie. I said, "We're *in* the Carousel." With a three-year lease. There were all kinds of stories going around in San Francisco that I bought the guy off or paid him under-the-table money. All I did was get up early. Anybody else in San Francisco who wanted that hall could have gone over there to see him. But I was the only one who did.

6.

BILL: The closing show at the Fillmore Auditorium was Creedence Clearwater Revival, Steppenwolf, and It's a Beautiful Day. The next night we opened at the Carousel, now renamed Fillmore West, with Butterfield

Blues Band and Ten Years After. I wanted a smooth transition from one place to the other. We'd been at the original Fillmore for two and a half years, from December 10, 1965 to the end of June 1968. There was a sadness at leaving but over time, the memories of that place and the things that happened there have become much more important to me than they were then.

The Carousel Ballroom was above a rug-selling place. It had been a car dealership and then it became a ballroom. There was a velour ceiling draping down over the stage area with a big parquet wooden dance floor that made it good for playing basketball in there on Tuesdays, which became Dollar Nights. I put the stage in the middle. There were pillars all around and people could sit on risers when they didn't dance in the back or on the sides. There was a big bar and a restaurant by my office. You came up two flights of stairs from the street and when you got to the top, you *really* came into a ballroom. It was all on one level with the dressing rooms behind the stage.

When I started there in 1968, we were still in an era where thank God the agent and the manager and the artist did not know that they could dictate who else should be on the show. So I was able to book the other acts the way I wanted to without being challenged about who else would be playing.

The Haight was still hanging on. But the kids there now were extras in a bigger movie. They were acting out roles. They had a bigger brother who had put on a headband or they had seen pictures of how it was *supposed* to be done. There were fewer originals but the cast was getting larger all the time. But the music was still good. It was still experimental. My musical education continued. As quickly as I was being educated by the musicians, I would share that with the audience.

I could get about twenty-eight hundred people into Fillmore West. It was a different sort of feeling than the original Fillmore but we were able to put up glass cases with cork bulletin boards inside where we would post news stories and special photographs and information. There were still balloons when people walked in and apples downstairs. It was a great laboratory. A place where people could let their hair down.

CHIP MONCK: I built all the electrics for Bill at the Carousel Ballroom. Unfortunately, I was also doing other things at the time. Which was my falling-out with him. In Bill's eyes, you had to eat, breathe, live, and shit Fillmore. That was it. I came out with John Morris and we looked at the place. It had been a dancing ballroom and all that was there was a sheet for a light show and a stage. Two sets of stairs and the answering machines for the telephones were under the stage because that was closest to the telephone wall jacks. When you wanted to record an announcement, you crawled under the stage and pushed the button before you left the building.

MARUSHKA GREENE: Once we took over the Carousel, it got real bad. If Bill heard a phone ring more than three times, he would go crazy. He would come out of his office, screaming, "Why isn't this phone fucking getting *answered?* What *is* this?" For some reason, we didn't have that many lines at the old Fillmore so it was not that much of a problem. When we moved to the Carousel, we got more.

I was the only one in the office at first. Every time the doorbell rang, I had to run down two flights of stairs to get the door. There were three or four more phone lines coming in by now so it was always a question about which one to do. I remember one time I was counting all these receipts. I probably had ten thousand dollars in cash on my desk and I was trying to count it. We had a phone man in working on the phone. The doorbell rang and I was worrying, "Should I run down and get the door? What do I do with this money with this strange man here? If I run down there, *for sure* the phones are going to ring."

I just covered my desk and ran down to get the door and sure enough, the phone rang. Bill was in his office with his attorney and he came out screaming because of the phone. Bill Coblentz took one look at my desk with all this money on it and he said, "Do you need some help, Marushka?" Then he went in and talked to Bill. About fifteen minutes later, Bill came back and said, "Do you need some help?" And I just went, *"Yes!"* Like it hadn't occurred to him before.

CHIP MONCK: Bill would stand at the top of the stairs at Fillmore West with a little basket in his hand, taking tickets. But he wouldn't *tear* the ticket. He would just *put* it in the basket. Then he would rush downstairs and hand them all to the box office person and they would sell the same little ticket again. He was brilliant. He knew how to handle a cash business.

RAY ETZLER: Fillmore West was where Bill *really* learned all the secrets. Like say it cost two and a half dollars for a fifty-pound bag of ice. He used to say, "Don't put too much ice in the cups." Then he did some cost analysis. He was a time and motion guy. His time and motion was how many people could he push through the doors in the shortest amount of time and then after they got in there, how many more could he *still* push in? And to hell with everything else.

Once the place was jammed, he started studying how much he could sell them *while* they were inside. By talking to the Coca-Cola guy, he discovered that when you're selling food, the per-unit cost is the key. First off, the cups shrunk. They went from ten ounces to eight. Then he found out that ice was cheaper than Coke syrup. We had a big meeting. From then on we loaded up the cups with ice.

BILL THOMPSON: I remember being at the Carousel one night just after it became Fillmore West. The Grateful Dead dosed Bill with acid and he played the congas or something until four or five in the morning. It may have been a spiritual revelation for him. It didn't *really* change him. But it did, in a way.

BILL: Starting in 1967, it got to be a thing with the Dead to get me high on acid. I'd never touch anything they gave me. I'd never hug them. Their ladies used to want to kiss me because they had first put a blotter of acid in their mouths. I used to say, "Kiss the back of my hair if you want." It became a big running thing. It got to the point that whenever I brought food from home, Bonnie would put it in a bag and I would put wax paper around it and seal it with tape. So they couldn't dose anything. The same for my Thermos.

On the job, *somebody* had to be in control and I decided that it should be me. On my off time, there wasn't much fear of it. I didn't have that much time off. I really never thought too much of it. Once in a while, I might smoke some reefer to relax. I had first seen it years before. In the Palladium, the Latinos would smoke very tiny joints. Long, tiny ones. I smoked them sometimes with other dancers, but not often. Also in the Army. But it didn't mean much to me. It never has.

By this time with the Dead, it had gotten *serious*. In that era, I was going through my 7-Up and Coca-Cola phase, where I would be drinking from a can of soda all day long. Just hyper, I guess. What I would do in the dressing room at Fillmore West was take garbage cans full of ice and fill them up with cans of 7-Up and Coke.

One night, they decided to go for it. What they did, unbeknownst to me, was warn all their people, "Don't touch any of the soda cans in our dressing room." Then they took hypodermic needles and shot acid through the top of every soda can.

OWSLEY STANLEY: Nobody injected anything. We knew he liked the soft drinks and the soft drinks were kept in a cooler. When you picked up a soft drink out of a cooler, it is always covered with beads of condensation. So a drop or two was put on the lip of every can in the room. They were all still sealed. No one had opened any of them. It was a perfectly normal-looking can of soda with a few drops of what you would expect to find on it. *Moisture*, right? The drop was in the little ridge around the outside. Take a sip and the drop went in with the first sip.

We had been trying for years to hit him and we knew he wouldn't touch anything that was opened or anything in a cup. He had to open his own. We saw what kind of soda he liked and made sure that every can he was likely to find was already fixed. But it wasn't me who did it. It was another guy. Our road manager at the time. He was very clever at that.

BILL: Early on, I went through the dressing room, took a can of 7-Up, and drank it. Twenty minutes later, *snap!* I started feeling weird. I looked in the mirror and all I saw was green and yellow and blue. I went backstage and I saw Mickey Hart. Mickey was the one.

MICKEY HART: I had the can. But he did it himself. He drank that soda down. He just like kicked it back. Three or four great wallops. Then he went off to just keep doing what he had been doing. I said, "I'll see you later, Bill. And the road you'll travel now will *not* be a familiar one."

BILL: He was thrilled, and I could have killed him. "You sonofabitch," I said. And he said, "We're going on, Bill. You want to play? Come with us." I said, *"Sure."* They gave me a drumstick and they said, "You just call off the songs and we'll play them."

I wanted to open with "Sugar Magnolia" because that was always my favorite song. But they said, "We don't open that high." So they wound up doing it later on. I was on stage for *four* hours. Playing the gong. To me, the stage always belonged to the artist. The audience never came to see me up there. I would introduce the band and then get off.

That night, I was fully aware that I was on stage and that I didn't belong but I didn't give a fuck. I was up there and I was going to do it. Because it was *fun*. It was a *gas*. I took the kettledrum and I took the gong and I had a ball.

MICKEY HART: The next thing I knew, he was hanging over the gong on stage. And he had no mercy. He was beating the gong *wildly*. He was smiling and just whacking that gong and foaming at the mouth. I mean, he was just *gone*. And I said, *"Bill!* This is a *ballad* song." Then he started playing the cowbell. He was *in* the band. He really was. He was right there. He became one with the universe. And we couldn't stop him. He was *possessed*. He kept hitting that cowbell like it was the last thing in his life.

It was *so* important to him that nobody could say no to him. He was right there in the rhythm too. He was really playing. We weren't kidding around. We weren't laughing. It wasn't fun. We were in for the groove and we were *flying*. And this guy was flying with us. Afterward, I gave him a gold-plated cowbell to commemorate the night.

He really lost himself and then I think he started to see what it was all about. Once he got high, he saw that we were seriously into this. This was not a lark. We were not just a bunch of hippies getting high and going *"Yahoo! Look at the colors!"* We were serious musicians exploring a new zone. That was something that made an impression on him and he saw that the Grateful Dead was basically good. He *likes* good. Bill likes good because he's seen enough horror. When he sees something good and friendly that takes care of its own, he likes that.

For him to present what we held most dear to us in the way that it should be presented was important. For that reason, we thought, "This guy has promise. This guy, he'll do for now." There *could* be a better version of him but we'll see what we can do. We'll *work* on him. Here is material to develop.

BILL: Acid is heavy stuff. It's *heavy* stuff. I know I have a strong constitution so I was able to deal with it. But what if I didn't? I found out later I could do some of these drugs, like organic mescaline, which I really liked. They were all right for me when I had some time to myself. I could eat a magic cookie and feel very good with no big after-effects and no big to-do. I'd just feel good for a few hours. Having so little time off, it was great sometimes to be like that.

I always thought the thing about getting high was overdone. Even at its height. I think I conditioned myself not to do it for a simple reason. *Somebody* had to be in control of their senses. *Somebody* had to touch base with reality at all times. And I decided that it had to be *me*.

PAUL KANTNER: I have to think that between us and the Dead, we sort of brought Bill into the New Age, as it were. Kicking and screaming. We didn't quite succeed. But we got him halfway there.

7.

PAUL BARATTA: We had all these groups that were hopping on my head. They were saying, "This sucks rocks. You're booking unknown groups that come from the outside. We're homegrown. Yet we don't even get a shot." They all wanted to play the Fillmore West but we just couldn't bring them in there unknown because the place was too big. So I invented the idea of Tuesday Dollar Nights when everybody got in for a buck and the local bands could play for minimal money. There were also basketball games on the floor of the Fillmore West before the show. I named the team the Fillmore Fingers in honor of Bill constantly giving everyone the finger. I broke my ankle playing basketball there and worked for the rest of the summer with it broken, not being able to put the thing down. For eight weeks, I went up and down those stairs at Fillmore West on crutches. Bill was gone most of the time. But it didn't bother me. Because it really was a labor of love. For me, it was all new. There was no format for anything.

Who decided that the shows would run from 8 to 2 A.M.? Who decided that you let everybody sit there and you threw nobody out? That you put apples in the barrel? The posters were new. The music was new. The sound delivery system was new. Light shows were new. The people who were now coming to see the music were new. How did you know three dollars for a ticket was enough? How did you deal with the fucking agencies? It was all new. That was an awful lot of information to process.

Unquestionably, Bill was the one who banged that format together. He made it work. He presented it in a professional way using his theatrical sense, his lunacy, his personal charisma, his need to be in the limelight. A lot of very talented people put bits and pieces of it there but they needed somebody to synthesize it. And then do battle to keep it going. And that was Bill.

The funny thing was that we actually did pop some acts out of those Tuesday Night sessions. Aum. Eddie Money. A band called Cold Blood.

BILL: Back in the original Fillmore, this guy named Raul came to my office and said he had a band named Cold Blood that he wanted me to see. I told him that I didn't have the time to go see them where they were playing. He said, "We'll bring them here." I had never gone through this before so I said, "Come on in." The guy said he would set up the stage for them in the middle of the day and when I was ready, I could come out and listen to a couple of songs.

A few days later, the guy came into my office and said, "We're ready." I walked out into an empty auditorium. Upstairs, downstairs, balcony, everything totally empty. They had put a chair for me in the middle of the auditorium. One chair for me to sit in. Usually, when you audition someone, you're in a room with other people. I sat down in the chair and they went on stage. It was the middle of the day. When I go to a show, I always think, "Soup, salad, *main course.*" But they just started right off playing rock and roll and R&B. Cold Blood had this lady in it named Lydia Pence, who had a big, booming voice.

The problem was that prior to the date, I don't think any of the musicians had ever met one another. I watched them for twenty-five minutes. They finished and they said, "Thank you," and they went off stage. I thought, "Oh, God. What am I going to tell them?"

The entire band came into my office. They said, "What did you think, Bill? Tell us the truth now, man. Be straight. No shuck-and-jive. Can you use us? What do you think?"

I knew I was *never* going to go through this again. To sit there like some buyer of meat. So I thought for a while and then I said, "I've got to tell you the truth. The way I really feel." Raul, the manager, was Lydia Pence's old man at the time. He looked at me and he said, *"Yeah? Tell us!"*

"You want to know what I think you should do?"

"Yeah, yeah," he said. "Tell us."

"I think you should disband."

There was a pause. Then Raul said, *"What?"*

"I think you should just disband and start all over again. Because the way it is now, it just doesn't fit."

The next line from Raul is what makes rock and roll great. He looked at me and said, "Who the *fuck* asked you, man?"

8.

BILL: In terms of Fillmore East, it got to a point with Bert Block and Albert Grossman where I felt they were not comfortable being involved. Either they weren't getting things done the way they wanted them done or they didn't see a long-term return on their money. I got the feeling that they wanted out. So I approached them and I said, "Would you feel better if you left? I don't know where this thing is going. I'm staying with it. I don't want to get out. But if you do, I'll give you back exactly what you put in. No more, no less. If you want to get out at a later time, it might not even be that." And they agreed.

Where I got the money to buy them out, I have no idea. I never really thought of them as partners. Even though I always got along with them, I still felt better on my own.

What I felt best about at the start with Fillmore East was not money. It was the staff. I had found some good New York people with brains. Of everything, I felt the best about that.

JOHN MORRIS: During this period, Bill and I got closer and closer. I knew all about Wolfgang Grajonca. Because we had sat night and day and talked and talked and he had told me the whole story. I was one of the very few people at that point who knew all of that. How he came on the boat and went to the Cottage School in Pleasantville, New York. He had told me about how the people would come and pick all the other kids and he was left standing there in line by his bed.

My parents lived in Pleasantville. We drove up there and had dinner with them and I said, "Bill, we're within two or three miles. Do you want to go see it?" There was a visible twitch. The shoulders did a twitch. And he said, "Yeah."

So we drove to the playground field. We drove all around it. He got out of the car and it really was like a movie. He walked across the field and I thought, "Dumb move." And I just sat there. When he came back, he had tears in his eyes and he didn't say a word. Not a word.

"Are you ready to get out of here?" I asked.

We drove away. It was one of the most moving experiences I ever had with Bill. I could just see all this stuff go into his mind and then come back out. The whole thing. We returned to New York and on the way back into town, he said, "You know, *thanks.*"

JOSHUA WHITE: John Morris got Fillmore East all up and running. His wife Annie was there, his friends were there, people were banging away.

During that summer when Fillmore East was pretty much closed, John had started promoting an outdoor festival in Philadelphia. It was just John doing a typical John. While at Fillmore East, he had already started working on something else. And Bill got pissed.

JOHN MORRIS: Bill came to New York and we went to Ratner's next door and we sat down. Bill said, "John, you're a diamond cutter. And right now, we don't need a diamond cutter." He said, "You made this place, you put it together, you brought in all these technical people. But right now, a diamond cutter is not what we need."

He said, "The business is running like a business now and Kip Cohen's got the managing thing down. I'm grateful for all of this, that, and the other. If I ever need a diamond cutter forever, anytime for the rest of my life, I'll always come back to you."

I knew while he was saying it that he and I were through.

JERRY POMPILI: Bill's analogy was, "When I want to hire a guy to drive dynamite across the desert, John is my guy." In other words, use him for the job you needed him to do and that was it. I don't think Kip Cohen engineered him out of a job. Kip Cohen *was* the guy to run the place. As he well proved.

BILL: I once said that the best way I can describe John Morris is that if I was ever asked to pick Natalie Wood up at the airport, I would send John.

In the early days of the Fillmore East, Kip ran the building. I was still there a lot. Then, I would come in periodically. Sometimes, every other week. Sometimes, every month. It depended. I had gone into a more expensive space in San Francisco. Business was going through the roof. What added to the mania was three thousand miles. The back-and-forth between Fillmore East and West.

Sometimes I'd have Janis on one coast and Hendrix would say to me, "You want to have a beer in New York?" I'd go to New York and then back to San Francisco for another show. Kip Cohen not only ran the building. He was my front man with the neighborhood and the Merchants Association and whatever problems we had with maintenance. He was the glue who kept it all together for me in New York. The guy was *organized*. That freed me to be me and do whatever it was that I do. Which for me was *gold*.

9.

BONNIE MACLEAN: Did I see Fillmore East before it opened? Gosh, I don't remember. I don't know. I was in the hospital having David and Bill was already in New York. David was born September 19, 1968.

PAUL BARATTA: Sometimes, Bill would stay in New York. I remember sometimes he would show up just in time for shows in San Francisco. He would come in just before and look around to make sure that the apples were in place and the pictures were on the walls and all that kind of thing.

The thing that really wound up being the severing point between us began with the birth of his son. If I'm close to somebody, I guess I want them to be perfect. And what happened then was so much less than perfect. The whole business of not being there. The only people that seemed to be there for her were my ex-wife and I. We weren't even together at the time but we were there in the hospital every day Bonnie was there. But not the night David was born.

JOSHUA WHITE: One of the people that had been with our show was living in San Francisco. So we sent him to the hospital and he took pictures of the mother and the baby. We had them air-expressed to New York, which was not something that one did in those days. Someone went to the airport and got them but we didn't get them in time for the first show. During the second show on a Saturday night, I think Kip called Bill out on stage and we put pictures of his son up on the screen. Whom he had never seen. It was wonderful. Then he came backstage and looked at the pictures.

BILL: Bonnie had a couple of false alarms and then I had to go to New York and then David was born. They airmailed his picture and showed it on the screen at Fillmore East. The first time I saw my son was on the screen at Fillmore East. If there was any blame, then it would have to be on me, not Bonnie. I knew then and I know now that I was totally possessed by making the Fillmores work. It was as if two babies had been born before him. One in New York and one in San Francisco. There were two other children who had come before. And I didn't make room. I just didn't make enough room. Bonnie was not the first to stray. I was. We had difficulties at home because I was not there much.

ISAAC AMATO: I remember visiting Bonnie in the hospital when David was born. It upset Bonnie very much that Bill wasn't there when David was born. That had a tremendous effect on the marriage. The only thing I could feel about Bill was that this was part of his background. On one hand, there was a close loyalty to his family. On the other hand, his ability to establish a close, intimate family bond was prevented by the very nature of his upbringing. The archetype itself just wasn't there.

BONNIE MACLEAN: Concerning the fact that Bill wasn't there when David was born, I was perfectly adjustable. What did I care? I had just had this wonderful little baby. It was mother time. I was *ecstatic*. I do remember Bill Coblentz chewing Bill out because he thought it was terrible that Bill wasn't there.
   It wasn't that. I didn't know it at the time. I didn't know it until somebody told me. Some two months later. *Why* he wasn't there. I mean, I was *so* dumb. I didn't pick up on it. I used to wonder about this and that. But I didn't get the drift. Until somebody told me. And then, well . . . *pfui!* That was the beginning of the end.

BILL: Even during the pregnancy, I was gone a good deal of the time and working very hard. There was no blame there. I don't mean by that to take away from what was really wrong. Mainly, it was the work. But then we were having trouble at home because it was hard on her, very hard, to be alone all the time. Then when I did get home, I was talking about business. Then I met a young lady who was just available. At the Carousel. Like you see in the movies, someone who asked no questions and was good to me and available whenever I wanted her there and there was no price. That became a problem. For a while, I hid it and it continued but she was certainly not the reason for the initial problem.

PAUL BARATTA: As the business became a big business, as we progressed from being Bohemian for lack of a better word, or let's say New Age and then we became mainstream, it was a different feeling. It just became big business. The groups were demanding more and the finances were getting expensive. Mike Wallace wanted to talk to Bill. People suddenly were coming to pay homage to somebody who before had to fight his way for everything. Bill was enjoying that. But suddenly, he was in a position of greater responsibility and he seemed more tense. The more success he achieved, the more tense he became. The more he started to be at odds with the Ralph Gleasons and the Jann Wenners and the whole *Rolling Stone* establishment, as it were.

There were groupies. He had never really had women in his life before. He was just so ambitious and always so focused. Bonnie mentioned to me that she hadn't any feeling or need to mistrust him because he didn't have time for women. Now all of a sudden, there were these temptresses who were laying out for him and he was feeling his oats.

Bonnie always seemed patient with the work. She was not patient with the extracurricular relationship. I was his ally in that. I tried to be, anyway. I understood what he was going through. I had been through it myself. There were a lot of similarities between Bill and me. It was just a question of degree. If I were to try and understand, if I were to put myself in Bill's place and I was working as hard as he was and had put in that much effort and built what I had built, and somebody came along and turned my head for whatever reasons—the flesh is weak. It's something I understand. And it was weak with him.

BILL: The initial problem was just that there were two lovers. There was Bonnie and the West Coast lover. Then there was the East Coast lover. East Coast lover, West Coast lover, and Bonnie. Then West Coast, East Coast, Bonnie, *and* David. Call it anything you want. The friction was created by my obsession of running both Fillmores correctly. There is no question that Bonnie had to share me with too much.

BONNIE MACLEAN: Around Christmastime, I learned that he was having this affair. Right after that, David and I moved to another place in San Francisco. It wasn't Bill's place although he did put his stuff in there and what not. But he got an apartment, too. I think I was a lot less aware then than I am now. I certainly had my faults in the matter too. I don't mean to put all the blame on him.

But I think he was as unable to commit as he had been all along. In that regard, he was a bad bargain from the beginning. The fact that he wanted so desperately to get married, *that* was the aberration. The rest was consistent. I wasn't capable of understanding him well enough or dealing with his problems well enough to do anything that would have been more effective. Maybe nobody could have. I don't know. I certainly couldn't.

BILL: If I had met Bonnie in some other city and gotten into some other line of work, I would have been married to her until today. I know it for a fact. How do I know it? Because in my life, I have never met anyone else like her. I was right about Bonnie. But obviously something went wrong. She was not a once-in-a-while woman. Which was all I had room for then.

DAVID GRAHAM: It amazes me to this day how they were ever attracted to each other. They are just polar opposites in so many ways. Speed. My mom is mellow and slow. My dad goes a mile a minute. I think sexually, they work on different wavelengths. My dad's a very sexual person. A driving force that way. My mom's just old-fashioned in that regard. The way they use their intellect. My mother is much more knowledgeable in a literary way.

Just the way they carry themselves. The way they speak to people. There must have obviously been something very mystic between them that I think very few people ever understood. Some kind of mystic attraction that brought them together. Because I sure as hell can't figure it out. Definitely *not*.

Chapter Eight

Street Life

1.

BILL: In the early years at Fillmore East, I always got along just fine with Sandy Alexander, who was president of the local Hell's Angels' chapter at the time. Because we were dealing with a sitdown situation there, it wasn't as revered to the Angels as the original Fillmore and Fillmore West. Because in those places, they could *strut*.

We did have one scene with them at a Dead show. A group of Angels came into the outer lobby and asked if they could get in. I was standing outside the doors that led into the inner lobby and there must have been a hundred people out there, thirty to forty of them bikers. We were going through the same kind of rap I would always do with them, me explaining that we were sold out and there were no seats. That even if we weren't, they would *still* have to buy tickets to get in. They said, "Open the fucking doors!" I said, "You can't come in here this way, and that's the way it is."

There was a yell and from at the very back of the crowd, this guy threw a chain at me. A tow chain. It hit me right above my nose and there was some blood, which scared me. But I just stood there, wiped the blood off with my hand, and stared right back at them without saying a word. At that point, they could have either stampeded right toward me and put me through those glass doors or the reverse could have happened. Thank God, it was the second. There was almost no sound. They just left. From that point on, there were really no problems with the Angels in New York. It was as if we had been challenged. We had stood our ground so they figured, "Let's try somewhere else."

The real problems on the streets in New York came from the Mother-

253

fuckers. My first contact with them was through the *East Village Other*. When I moved into Fillmore East, they were my tenants. They had an office upstairs in the building, above the theater. They did their articles favorable or unfavorable, they said certain things about me that were not too positive, I left them alone. Then they wrote an article in which they said, "We hear Bill Graham lost his parents in the concentration camps during the war. It's a shame he didn't go with them." At which point, I stormed up there and turned over the editor's desk. Then I evicted them from the building. They were paying no rent as it was.

I said, "You want me dead? What did I ever do to you? Make money? Is that the problem?"

That was it all right. But what was I supposed to do? If I was losing money, would they have paid me? My argument with them was always, "Why do people have to pay for your paper? How do you pay *your* people?" They would say, "Our *goal* is to be free. Your music *should* be free."

"You want *mine* to be free? Okay. I want *yours* to be free."

I wanted to be allowed to run my business. But they didn't want capitalism to rule that part of our society. What they didn't realize was that their heroes were capitalists. I was the antihero. The businessman. But the artist on stage always dictated the price of the ticket by his financial demands. That particular part of society could not accept that. They refused to piss on their own gods. Jann Wenner started it and the *East Village Other* continued it on beyond. That Graham. If not for him, the ticket price would *still* be two-fifty. It would probably be *free* because the artists love us. Sure they did.

On Tuesday nights in New York, we would do three new local acts for two dollars. Some people came in one Tuesday night and asked if they could speak to me about a project involving the street merchants and representatives of all the different Lower East Side organizations. One of them was called the Motherfuckers, a sociopolitical street gang. They wanted their own night at the Fillmore to "express themselves." They said, "You know, Bill, you always say you're part of the community, man. *Prove it*."

I said, "Fine. Every Wednesday night is yours. You respect the building and we'll operate it. You can use it that night but only under our jurisdiction."

The first Wednesday night, people came in and brought their babies. They messed up the floor and peed on the walls and put their feet on the chairs and brought in their cooking utensils so it became like an overnight shelter for the homeless. I said, "This can't happen to me. So it's not happening."

On stage, there was political dialogue. Rallies and music and speeches. Revolutionary documentary art films being shown about grape picking and Cuba. There were four or five hundred people in the house. Who were there just to be in the theater for free. It cost me seven or eight hundred dollars just to keep the place open. But every week, they'd come.

Nothing was progressing at these meetings. There was more and more damage to the house. It was *free*. So people would come in and mess around just for the sake of messing around. Finally, somebody broke the whole display case in the concession upstairs and I said, *"Enough. No more."* It went for maybe two months. It was utter chaos. I was only at two or three of the nights and I kept on saying to my people on the staff, "Give them a chance. Let's help them and guide them. We can't supply them with acts but let's see if anything positive develops." It didn't.

Six months after the free Wednesday nights stopped, we did a benefit for the Living Theater, which Julian Beck and Judith Malina had founded. We gave them the theater but we knew the Motherfuckers were going to come in and try to take it over that night. Halfway through the show, Louis Abolafia, the Naked candidate for president whose slogan was "I Have Nothing to Hide," came in with that element and they went on stage and said, "This is now the theater of the people."

They liberated the theater and they asked me to come up on stage. They said, "We want to work with Bill Graham. We know he's a hard worker but capitalism must understand that the people will always rule." People with berets positioned themselves everywhere and down the center aisle came a mimeograph machine. For the rest of the night, they would write things down and stick them in the machine and run off copies and then distribute them into the street. Letting the people know what was going on inside the theater in blow-by-blow detail. They opened the front doors and said that *anybody* could come in. By this point, all the actors and performers knew that it was out of control and that they had lost it.

JOSHUA WHITE: Basically, the thing I remember most about Living Theater night is that Bill did two things that were brilliant. One, he stood up there and said to them, "No, it's *my* theater." Which anybody else would not have had the nerve to do. Just stand up there and play the role of capitalist pig. The other was that he kept us all together all evening to protect the theater. Because we loved the place and had a great interest in it and were not about to let people fuck with it.

First of all, you have to imagine what it was like while the Living Theater was still performing that night. Julian Beck coming up to you naked, speaking to you with breath that was like speed breath, saying,

"I can't travel without my passport. I can't take off my clothes. I can't smoke dope." He would be *spitting* on you. Not meaning to do it. But he was so wrapped up in the role that his mouth was foaming.

Then they came to liberate the theater and Bill was saying, "Go liberate the Metropolitan Opera House. What are you doing *here?*" I think among other things, these people were essentially a little cowardly. They knew if they did this at the Fillmore, they were not about to get their heads busted open. If they did it at the Metropolitan Opera, that would have been a whole other story.

BILL: Some kid started tearing his seat out. I said, "Hold it. Hold it. There's going to be *no* dialogue unless that stops. That's *not* what this is about. You want to take over this theater, let's talk about that. Until we decide what's going to happen, that's one of your people, *you* control him."

I talked slowly. I was up against something that was forty feet tall. What else could I do but say, "Hello. How are you?" Basically, we got back into the same debate. Let's talk about the definition of what is free. *Music should be free.*

I said, "Then the airlines should be free to transport The Who from London to here. And electricity should be free and telephones. What you're really saying is, 'What should be charged if *something* has to be charged?' In our society, what we use for barter is money."

Why are the tickets this much? And why are the prices that much?

Finally, they said, "Will you give us the theater?"

"I gave you the theater every Wednesday night," I told them. "If I didn't have a profit on the capitalist nights, you couldn't have had it then. Because this theater lives in the *real* world."

This dialogue went on until three o'clock in the morning. By then, the place stunk. People pissed in the aisles, just for the experience of doing it. People ate up all the food and walked around naked. "Why is that exciting?" I said. "Why is that progressive?"

They kept saying, "This is the mandate of the people. What is your answer?"

I said, "It's not going to happen this way."

They would then reply, "He says, 'It's not going to happen this way.' " They would write it down, put it into the mimeograph machine, and run copies of it out into the street. They were going to take out all the seats. Finally, I said, "Look, you made your point. I think I'm going to have to make mine. I want you to understand that when I say this, I mean it. I'm going to ask you to act upon what I am about to say one way or the other. I work and I bought this theater and I have my rights.

"The only way you're going to take this theater is by killing me. I wish you wouldn't. It's not the way it should go. But you can't take the theater and have *me* be part of the operation. It doesn't go that way."

Slowly, the troops started to leave. I had told all my security people to back off. Nothing physical. Don't try to defend the building. Thank God, they did not go into the offices and start tearing them apart. It was not pillage. In the end, they just walked out. By three or four in the morning, it was over.

WAVY GRAVY: I remember trying to mediate the scene between the Motherfuckers and Bill. I mean, it was a *heavy* scene. Eventually, I talked them into going to New Mexico. I showed them slides of the place on an ice cream freezer in this café on Second Avenue and they just lit up for it. They came out to Aspen Meadow for the Summer Solstice and I don't think they had ever seen trees before. They took some psychedelics and some of them are *still* living there. The guy who was their leader is now an elder in the Native American Church and is very highly regarded by Native Americans.

BILL: A month later, the MC5 came to play the Fillmore East. They burned the American flag on stage. They had started back in Michigan with John Sinclair and the Rainbow Coalition and they were being merchandised as the "people's revolutionary band." "Kick Out the Jams, Motherfuckers!" was their big song. I remember they had all their equipment stolen out of a van in the alley. The people's band had all their equipment stolen. By the *other* people, I guess.

2.

BILL: Before we even opened the doors at Fillmore East, I had a guy from the union come in and say they wanted to represent everyone in the building. I said, "There's no union here now and we're not going to have one unless people are dissatisfied. *Then* they have a right to go to the union." We talked this way back and forth a couple of times until he saw that I meant it and then he backed off and never came around again.

Then the city building inspector came around and it was the same old problem. He walked through the building with Kip rubbing his hands and saying, "This building's got some infractions." All the while, he just kept rubbing his hands together, looking for a *schmeer*. Finally I had to tell him, "I don't know what your skin problem is, but I'm not the healer."

I never understood paying people off so they would leave us alone. The building inspector also went away and never came back. The cops were a different problem. I didn't want them to be the enemy. I didn't want them to think that I disrespected them. Because if anything ever happened, I wanted them to come inside the place and help. I went down to the Ninth Precinct station house and introduced myself. The Hell's Angels' club-house was on the same block. The captain wasn't there so I talked to the lieutenant, telling him what I was going to be doing in the neighborhood.

A couple of shows after we opened, Kip called me in San Francisco. He said, "Bill, the cops are coming inside and hanging around in the lobby."

I didn't mind that. But they had their guns on. I do have a thing about that. People cannot get into the right frame of mind to enjoy a show when there is a guy with a piece standing there. Kip said he had asked them to leave but they wouldn't. So the next time I was in New York, I went to see the captain. We got to talking about the neighborhood and one thing led to another. It turned out that he was a jock. So we set up this whole thing. A touch football game in Central Park between the cops and the guys from Fillmore East. Seven men on a team, everyone but the center eligible.

One of the toughest and most brutal games I ever saw. Lower East Side cops and the ushers and street security guys and neighborhood kids who worked at Fillmore East. We started at about one in the afternoon with a keg of beer and played until it was dark. One of the toughest street kids from the neighborhood did something that day that made him a legend. He and the cops already knew and hated one another. We were on offense and he lined up opposite this sergeant he had never gotten along with.

Just before we snapped the ball, he said, "Hold it. *Time out!*" Once he got the timeout, he yelled, *"Fuck you, cop! Time in."* He told me later that he just had to go for it. It was great. Time out. Fuck off, cop. Time in.

End of the game, the score was tied, six to six. It was November so it had started getting dark early. They had the ball, they went back to pass, this guy Pete and I blitzed. We got the guy in their end zone. Two points. A safety. We win. They said, "It's *not* two points." We said, "We win. Eight to six." "You *don't fuckin'* win," they said. "There's no points after touchdowns in this game. There's no field goals. How the fuck can there be a safety? Fuck you, *tie game.*"

"What do you mean, *'Tie game'? Fuck you!*"

The captain came over and said to me, "Want to play another game, Bill?"

By this time, we were packing up our stuff. I said, "Any time. One game down, we won."

"You *didn't* fuckin' win!"

And it started all over again.

The next day, we put the word out on the street. We won. We beat the neighborhood cops in football. That afternoon, a SWAT car came up to the front of the Fillmore East. The cops got out and came inside to my office. They said, "Don't ever fuck with us on the street, Bill."

"Hey," I said, "What's all this about?"

"You *didn't* fuckin' win. What's a *safety?* It wasn't *points*, it was *TDs*."

In the end, these guys called the NFL for a ruling. I said, "I don't give a *fuck who* you call. Ask anybody who plays ball. We got you in the end zone, that's *it*. We *win!*"

This went on for a year. But from then on, they treated us differently. Cops with guns *never* came into the building again. They never busted anyone inside Fillmore East for smoking weed or out on the street for holding dope.

3.

BILL: Joshua White added a visual element at Fillmore East far beyond what was available to me on the West Coast at that time. Beneath that calm exterior lurked a true creative genius. The West Coast light shows were beautiful slides and liquid projection. Joshua choreographed light shows to reflect the complexity of the music and the times we were living in. And he had a truly sardonic sense of humor.

JOSHUA WHITE: Kip Cohen always said that the reason the light show worked so well was that musicians didn't realize that people had eyes as well as ears. They would just play. The Jefferson Airplane would do twenty-minute songs in the darkness in their street clothes with their backs to the audience. There was a lot of tuning and a lot of breakdowns of equipment and the light show was always there to provide a visual. In the theater, the audience *had* to be focused. In the ballroom, they would wander around and relate to one another but in a theater, they were always looking toward the stage.

I could entertain that audience with slides. If the band was tuning, or something. We had visual tricks and gags. We had routines we would do. We would play the music "Also Sprach Zarathustra" and the people would see a field of stars on a blue screen and a rocket ship going up, which was just a slide with one of the guys in the light show providing a fire underneath, and it would sort of go up and up and then it would start to fall down and then it would go up and up and then it would come crashing down and they would see a sun rising and then the sun would dissolve and it would be Richard Nixon with his eyes crossed. People went *nuts* for that stuff.

People began to look at the light show as sort of the emcee. Because except when Bill was introducing the act, there was no one in charge of the stage. The light show was an oleo. An oleo is the old vaudeville curtain that came down with the advertisements on it and people would rent space on it so the audience could read their ads.

What we were was a magnificent color array of things just happening and flowing and oozing and the audience simply made their own images up. It was not unlike if you ever in your life put music on with a silent movie and you were amazed at how synchronous it was. Same thing. The light show was *never* synchronized by the music. We were motivated by the music but never programmed. Other light shows, when the singer said "dog," they put a dog on the screen. Not us.

I was the mixer. It was a lot like being the conductor of a symphony orchestra. The light show was divided up into three areas. Liquid effects, which were in an overhead projector, originally store bought, but finally like the Tin Man, a creature of our own creation. The basic effect everyone remembers was oil and water. We took an industrial clock face and we put oil and water in it and we colored the oil and we colored the water. We took another clock face and put it over the first and pressed down. It squeezed the oil and water out toward the edges. When you lifted up the clock face on top, the oil and water fell into the center. Oil and water never mix. So what you got were different colored bubbles. On the screen, the audience could not see the clock faces. All they saw were the bubbles keeping the rhythm of the music either by doing it very fast or very slowly. The liquid projections soon went from being exploding amoebas to a very slow pouring of mineral oil through those projectors into troughs.

By the time we got through at Fillmore East, we were working with *ten* different grades of mineral oil. We were mixing colors from pure aniline dyes and if we didn't like this shade of purple, we would send to Japan for the right one. We trouped a dishwasher with us when we worked, to clean the clock faces. We had a road boy for the dishwashing machine. We even wore one out. We had two. So that was the liquid part of the show.

Then we began to do the things that made us distinctive. We had a thing called "lumia." Named after a thing called "Lumia" by Thomas Wilfred, an artist from the early 1900s who still has pieces at the Museum of Modern Art. Lovely aurora borealis effects. They began simply by having a fellow on the platform above our heads sitting there with a piece of flexible mirror. The light would hit him, bounce off the mirror, and he twisted around on the screen. Then it became a concrete image hitting the mirror. Birds flying on the screen or a golden butterfly. Like everything else, this also eventually grew.

The fellow built projectors for the top platform. He would have multiple light sources, multiple condensing lenses, multiple software, and multiple mirrors to bounce them on the screen. He would sit there with all these chess pieces moving. They were all motorized on heavy metal laboratory stands. I would be on an intercom and I would say, "Okay, Tom. It's yours." The audience would see a little thing appear on the screen and it would get bigger and it would twist and he would work with it for hours. That was lumia.

The liquid effects took three people to run, plus the dishwasher. Then there was me. I ran everything else. I ran all the slide projectors. We had eight, a thousand watts apiece. I did all the film loops and the concrete images. I ran the strobes and I ran what was one of our strongest things, which was pure color. We had strips that were little small light bulbs instead of one big one. So I could turn a knob and the screen would go red-green-blue so fast that you were seeing white.

A lot of color theory figured into this. Except for the lumia, I turned everything on and off. I would bring one thing on and fade another off. Once I knew one of my people was ready, I would wait for the right point in the music. Then *boom*, there might be an explosion of light and color. The person I had just given it to had the responsibility to react to the music and develop his own ideas within the time period.

Like a conductor, I would then take him out and shift to something else. I was the one person who wasn't holding any equipment. It was all in front of me. So if something went wrong, I could slip up and down the platform and focus and make adjustments. We could look at the band on a closed-circuit black and white television. We had our own monitor for the sound.

Every week, there'd be something new and the combinations were infinite. The great year for me was from when we reopened in 1968 until the summer of Woodstock. For me, that was one brilliant year. After Woodstock, all the famous things happened and then it went downhill.

Chapter Nine

1969

1.

BILL: New York never became home again. Even with Fillmore East rolling, I would only go back there every two or three weeks. I was booking primarily from the West Coast. By now, I had help. But it was like, somebody might bring the ball up the court for me. Within scoring range, *I* took the shot. Nobody else. Other people would see who was available. Or tell me that this act would go well with that act. Not only would they look around, they would help me create by saying, "Who can we put with them to make a better show?"

In San Francisco, I'd moved out of the house and gone to an apartment on Clay Street. I was unhappy about the end of my marriage so I just kept on working. For years, I never made it my primary objective to find someone to replace Bonnie. It was never even close. The only thing that mattered to me was work. I didn't stop working long enough to realize that the imbalance was suicide. Because unless you have love and friendship on a regular basis in your life, there is a lack of completion. Things can be okay no matter how bad they are. But they're not what they should be.

At this time, I had offices across the street from Fillmore West with Brian Rohan and David Rubinson. Along with Michael Stepanian, Brian Rohan was one of the first hip lawyers in San Francisco. David Rubinson, Brian Rohan, and I formed Fillmore Records.

DAVID RUBINSON: The Fillmore Corporation. We had management, records, publishing, recording studios, *everything*. There were two record labels. Fillmore Records and San Francisco Records. There was the

Millard Agency. And Shady Management. The record deal was with CBS and Atlantic. We had one label with each. Elvin Bishop and Tower of Power were on Atlantic, which was San Francisco Records. So was Cold Blood, with Lydia Pence.

AHMET ERTEGUN: Then we started a label with Bill Graham called San Francisco Records. He had a label with CBS called I believe Fillmore. Anyway, it was all right. We had a couple of bands. Tower of Power and Cold Blood. Cold Blood I had originally signed myself. But then I said, "We'll put them on *that* label."

One day, Bill Graham called me up because something had gone wrong. I guess the band Cold Blood had played somewhere and there were no records in the shop windows or there were not enough records in the shop windows, or there were no *windows* in the record shops, or something hadn't happened. I mean, there's always a gripe of some kind. Mistakes, and so forth.

It was a Friday around noon or one o'clock in New York when Bill called from California and he was very, very upset. He started screaming, "What the *hell* is going on with this *fucking* company? Why does the record sit there when we've got this thing . . ." And he was *screaming* at me on the phone.

I said, "Bill, I want to hear exactly what's gone wrong and I'll do whatever I can to repair it. Maybe it isn't as bad as you think. But would you mind? My secretary's going away for the weekend and I've got to dictate two very short letters. Could you hold on for a second?"

He said, "*Okay, okay.*" You know, like that?

I had no secretary there, or anything. I mean, I was just sitting in the office by myself. So I said, "Jane, would you mind taking these two letters before you go? They're urgent."

I said, "First one goes to the publisher of *Billboard* magazine. 'Gentlemen,'" I said, "'I have just received your invitation to renew my subscription and I want to tell you that it is with great pleasure that I am enclosing a check for another year's subscription and another check for the special delivery edition, which I must tell you has been coming religiously on Sunday morning. Furthermore, gentlemen, I must also commend you on the regular delivery, which arrives on Monday. Your reviews have been very good to us and we really enjoy the magazine and I hope we'll have many more years together. With kindest regards, Ahmet Ertegun.'

"And the other letter goes to Mr. Schwartz in the drugstore downstairs. 'Dear Mr. Schwartz,'" I said, "'I want to thank you for having changed the quality of the liverwurst. Now that you're getting the braunschweiger which I advised you to buy, we've decided to continue ordering our lunches from your drugstore. The ham is not quite as good as it once was but thank you very much. Warmest regards, Ahmet Ertegun.' "

So then I said, "Okay, Bill. What was it?"

He said, "What *was* it? I don't *remember* what the fuck it was. What are those letters?"

He forgot. He forgot what it was all about.

DAVID RUBINSON: Bill funded it and then he ignored it. Had we signed Santana to Fillmore Records, it would have been a payday for all. I begged for that. But they had signed with Columbia *before* we formed the record company. Or if the management company had managed Santana. But their management didn't end up in the company.

BILL: We had Cold Blood with Lydia Pence on the label with Atlantic and a band called Aum. On San Francisco Records at CBS, we had a band called Lamb with a singer named Barbara Mauritz, who really had a good voice but never found the right spot. Tower of Power was another one on Atlantic. A bunch of good acts but they just didn't break. There was never a work of consequence. It was the first business move I made because someone else had suggested it. It lasted for quite some time but I had no direct involvement with it. David Rubinson pretty much ran the operation.

In terms of making records, I don't think I have the patience. What I do have is Abe Burrows's ears. If you play something, I can tell you what I think is missing and how it might be changed.

The failure of the record labels had very little bearing on my life. To this day, I have never veered away from what I care about most. Nothing for me has ever replaced producing the live event.

2.

BILL: Michael Bloomfield told me about Ronnie Hawkins and this band called the Crackers out of Toronto. So did Jeremy Steig, who was a musician's musician. About this bunch of guys out of Toronto who were playing with Ronnie Hawkins at some club upstairs. By then, I think they were called the Hawks. I think the first time I ever heard them as the Band was in Albert Grossman's office on the fourth floor at 75 East Fifty-fifth Street. Albert probably had the best ears of anybody I knew. He would say to me, "Do you have a second, Bill? Would you like to hear something? You might find this very interesting."

He played me some tracks off *Music from Big Pink* and I was just blown away. The thump of Levon Helm's drums was different than any other thump. Richard Manuel hit those piano keys like a guy playing on the boardwalk. Garth Hudson got a sound out of the organ like no one else. Robbie Robertson was one of the genuinely great players of our time. Magnificent.

When Robbie backed Dylan, it was like a ballet dancer and a partner. You do the lifts? *Fine.* You do the smile? *Great.* My strength? *Okay.* As a band, on a good night, they were the tightest. Richard Manuel and Levon and Rick Danko, who was *such* a good bass player, and also had an amazing voice. Three great voices and then the high notes which only Manuel could hit. Like Ray Charles.

I spoke to Albert and he said, "Bill, they don't play. They don't tour. They don't do this, they don't do that, they don't do *anything*."

"Can I get a chance to talk to them?" I said.

He arranged for me to go up to Woodstock and talk to them.

JON TAPLIN: The Band was very highly acclaimed but nobody knew who these people were. It was a real cult phenomenon. On the *Big Pink* album, you sometimes could not tell who was singing. There was no lyric sheet. Sometimes you could not understand the words. I had heard Albert had gotten some bids for them to play after *Big Pink*. Five thousand or seven thousand a night or something like that. Then all bets were off. With the new album simply called *The Band* coming out, and the word on it that it was really hot, Bill Graham stepped up to the line. I can't remember exactly. But I think he offered us twenty-five thousand dollars a night. And that *really* got everybody's attention.

ROBBIE ROBERTSON: We'd made this album and then we never showed up anywhere. There was this thing out in the world that we had no control over which made the band out to be very mysterious and very reclusive. It wasn't a plan. It was just the way that it worked out.

Bill Graham spoke to Albert Grossman and he came up to Woodstock to talk to me about performing. Because he thought this whole thing was going on. He gave us a talk about, "We *owed* it to the people to play live."

Now, we had nothing against owing it. But I thought, "I'll play it like this. I'll let him do the talking and I'll let him say all those things and I just won't be bothered denying any of this stuff. I'll just let him go on."

He came up and I let him ramble on for hours. He talked and talked and gave speeches and he was up and waving his arms. Finally at the end, I said, "Bill, I'm convinced. You've talked me into it."

BILL: They were all there and we talked about what kind of pleasure folks out there could have by seeing them live. It was only right that people should get to see and hear them play. Robbie was the obvious leader of the band. There never was any question. He was always the spokesman, right from the start.

At the beginning, very few people in this business who are offered big money turn it down. Not if they've never made any before. I don't know whether it was the money, or what. But they agreed to come out to San Francisco for three nights at Winterland. I thought that if I could put their music in front of the people, then the people would want to eat it after just one taste.

ROBBIE ROBERTSON: It got very cold in Woodstock and we were spending most of our time shoveling cars out of the snow instead of recording. So we came out to L.A. and rented Sammy Davis, Jr.'s house and recorded *The Band* album there. The recording for this album was a very intense process for me. I was on to something and I worked just way too hard on the whole thing and by the time we were finished, I was like a puddle on the floor. There was nothing left. Then it was time to go to San Francisco to do this job that we had promised to do.

Bill had done a nice job. There were nice posters and all that stuff was handled very tastefully. He certainly understood concert promotion as well as anybody in the world. So I was tired. So what?

We flew up to San Francisco and I remember there was somebody sitting beside me on the airplane and you know what it's like when you sit beside someone who coughs and sneezes all over you? The whole time going up there, this person was like hacking and coughing and wheezing and it was horrible. It went into my brain so deeply that when we got there and got set up and everything, with our rehearsals supposed to start the next day, I wasn't feeling very good.

I felt like I had the worst case of stomach flu in the world. That thing where all your functions are blowing out of the top of your head. I was in *terrible* shape. But I thought, "Well, I'm just run down. I'll get over this." In the meantime, everybody was saying, "Listen, I know a great doctor. He'll come right over and give you some vitamins and check you out. Why take any chances?"

JON TAPLIN: We showed up and we stayed at the Seal Rock Inn, right by the ocean. Soon as we hit the hotel, Robbie had a fever of a hundred and four degrees. This was on a Wednesday, I believe. The shows were going to be Thursday, Friday, and Saturday nights. Two shows each night. With the Sons of Champlin and the Ace of Cups playing ahead of us.

Robbie said, "I'll stay here. You guys go do the sound check without me."

We went to do the sound check without Robbie and get it all set up. This was just a *vast* hall compared to what they had experienced before. We went back and the doctors were leaving Robbie's room and there was no improvement whatsoever. For reasons I'll never really understand, Albert refused to postpone anything by saying that this guy was just too sick to play. He just kept putting off the decision.

BILL: I got a call from someone who said, "You better come to the hotel. Robbie Robertson is very ill."

I got to the hotel and Albert was there. He said, "We've got a problem, we may have to cancel. I don't want to. But we might have to." By now, there were a lot of people and money involved in this. There was such a buzz in town about the band that I was willing to do anything I could to make it happen.

ROBBIE ROBERTSON: These doctors came over and gave me shots. The rest of the guys were rehearsing because we had never played anywhere except between ourselves. Then someone else said, "I know a *better* doctor." I was desperate. I felt so bad that anything would have been a relief. The other doctor came and he gave me some shots. I was just getting weaker all the time with all these drugs in me. I was in bed feeling helpless and bad about this thing.

By now, we were racing the clock. We had that classic script going. We were down to the day before and I was *worse*. I couldn't make it to the bathroom by myself. I was so weak. It was horrible. I couldn't eat. I couldn't do anything. All the pressure piled on was making it worse.

So now it was the day of the show. I woke up and I felt *terrible*. I felt *worse* than I did on any of the other days. I was eating little health biscuits and it was like, "This isn't going to do it. I'm dying, and you're giving me a *health biscuit?*" So . . . a last resort. Bill Graham said to Albert, "What do you think about getting a hypnotist?" Albert liked that kind of action. He said, "Well, we've got nothing to lose here. We've tried everything else and none of it has worked."

BILL: I got to the hotel and I said to Albert, "What do you want to do?" He said, "I'll tell you what. I have an idea. Can you find me a hypnotist?" I got hold of the Yellow Pages and I looked. Because the doctors had said there was really nothing wrong with Robbie. It might have been psychosomatic because of the performance coming up. We didn't really know but maybe if we put him in a stable mood psychologically, he would be all right.

I looked under "Hypnotist." Then I looked under "Twenty-four-hour-a-day Service." That was where I found him. Under Twenty-four-hour-a-day Service. We got this guy from Oakland to come out to the Seal Rock Inn and he went into the room with Albert.

ROBBIE ROBERTSON: Bill said he would not cancel the thing. The guys in the band were saying, "Why don't we just put it off a few days? Let him get better." Bill said that people had been planning on this for *months*. They had bought their tickets. There was nothing you could say to his story. His story was very strong. I had to agree with him. It would have been horrible to cancel but it would have been twice as horrible if the thing didn't work.

As a last resort, Albert and Bill came in and told me about the hypnotist. I said, "Listen, I feel so bad, I'll try anything." *Anything.*

Two hours later, this guy showed up. His name was Pierre Cleaumont. He was a French hypnotist with silver hair in a black suit, white shirt, and black tie. He looked like he had come to deal with the dead. He came in the room and Albert was there and all the guys. There are photographs of this, actually. Him with his hand on my head and his eyes closed and on the wallpaper behind me in the room, there was a scene with a tree growing. So it looks like the tree is growing out of the top of my head while his hand is on there. *Very* strange.

He started to work on me and do this hocus-pocus stuff and I was thinking, "Oh, my God. I *want* to do this. I'm not fighting it at all. I *want* to buy it. But I *can't*." It was like, "This *can't* be real."

Finally, he got rid of everybody else and he worked on me. He worked on me for hours. *Hours.* And finally he started to get me. He knew it and I knew it and I felt happy that at least I was succeeding in this. Then he just put me deeper under. Deeper under. Deeper under. Until finally he had me standing up. Then he dealt with everything that was bothering me. My head hurt so bad. He dealt with my head. I was aching all over. He dealt with that. I got tired from standing up and he dealt with that. Every little thing, he just kept pecking away at it.

Finally, I was saying, "I don't feel too bad right now." I couldn't remember any of the things that were bothering me. I was well aware of all this and it was enjoyable and it was fine. He said, "Sit down here on the bed." He went over and got a guitar and he said, "I want to see if you can remember how to play the guitar. I want to make sure you haven't forgotten." He gave me a guitar and I started doodling around and I said, "Oh yeah, yeah. No problem here. I know all this stuff."

Everybody came back in and he told them, "This is going to work."

BILL: A bunch of us were just hanging out and waiting in the lobby area of the Seal Rock Inn by the pool. Albert came out and I said, "Albert, how's it going?" He said that the guy was working on Robbie with a faceted crystal ball on a string. "Albert," I said. "I don't want to rush things. What do you think?" "Well," he said. "I think he's got it out of his legs. Now it's up top."

Earlier, Robbie's legs had been shaking. Albert went away and then he came back again an hour later. I didn't want to press him but I had a whole *army* of people coming. It was a historic event, the Band in San Francisco, playing live for the first time *anywhere*. Word got out about what was happening. Rumors on the radio and people talking about it in the hotel. Albert came out and now it was seven o'clock and it was time to start the show. I was looking for a sign and he just made a face and moved his hands around, meaning, "It's coming up. It's churning. It's trying to leave his body. It's looking for an exit somewhere."

That was when I said, *"Albert. You've got to give me an answer now. Yes or no?"*

He said, "Let's go for it."

By now, it was a quarter to nine. Ace of Cups was already off stage, the Sons of Champlin were on. Robbie was still in the room with the guy.

Then the guy came out. He said, "I think we can do this show. He is now under hypnosis. He is hypnotized. He is aware of what he's doing but he's in my control."

"Albert?" I said. "What do you want to do?"

Albert wanted to go. Time was up. I went in a separate car to Winterland. Five minutes later, the stage was ready.

ROBBIE ROBERTSON: Everybody was looking at me like I was an alien. There was just enough time for me to get dressed. It wasn't like,"Well, now relax for a couple of hours." It was down to the wire. I got dressed and we got into his car and he was driving and he was telling me about this experience that I was having. How I would be able to use it later on in life to control things a little bit more than I would have before. He said, "Now, when you are up there playing, there could be times when you won't feel so good. If so, look over at me. I'll be in the wings and I will say to you, *'Grow.'* And you'll come right back up and you'll be fine."

JON TAPLIN: By this time, Bill was *freaking*. He was back at the hall. The Ace of Cups already played. The Sons of Champlin had already played. It was like ten o'clock at night and the audience was chanting and Bill was wholly unnerved and crazed. But he was a phenomenal guy, Bill. I always found he had a real short temper. The reason people kept playing for him after he had abused them or whatever was that he was the most professional guy at what he did. If you wanted a white Bösendorfer piano, he would find one somewhere and it would be there and it would be in tune. In that sense, he was a total pro.

We pulled in in a limo and everybody was freaking out. Bill was mad as hell. We went out on stage.

BILL: I said to Albert, "Let me say something please before they go on stage." I put a chair by the lead mike just in case for Robbie. I put a chair on the side for the hypnotist to sit where Robbie would be able to see him.

I went on stage and I said, "Sorry for the delay. We want to level with you. There was some last-minute illness in the band. The decision was made, since they had come such a long way, and you've been so patient and decent, that we're going to go on with the show. But I've been asked to tell you by the group that when tonight's over, if you feel you've had a pleasurable evening, okay. If you feel it hasn't been exactly what you hoped for, let us know and we'll see what we can do over the next few nights. But please be considerate of the situation."

Meaning I didn't want to give everyone a refund. But I would have let people come back to another show even though we were sold out. I told them, "Be the judge of what tonight's all about and where it's at." Without mentioning that it was Robbie who was sick. And then I said, "Ladies and gentlemen . . . *the Band.*"

ROBBIE ROBERTSON: Looking down into the audience, it was like a very surreal swirl of faces. I thought, "Well, I can't get into these things. I've just got to think about why I'm here and what I have to do."

We started to play and I didn't feel like I had a tremendous amount of strength. I just needed to remember the songs and play them as well as I could. We did three songs and all of a sudden, it hit me. I felt like I was going to fall down. We were in the middle of a song by then and everything was spinning. It dawned on me that the crowd was yelling so loud and the music was so loud that I would *never* hear him. I would *never* hear him say the *word*. So I was panicking.

I looked over at him and he looked at me and he said, *"Grow."*

I could hear it over the crowd and the music. I could hear it so clearly that it reverberated through my body and I felt okay again. It brought me back up. I played another couple of songs and I looked over and he gave me another *"Grow!"* We made it through to the end. At a certain point, I said, "I don't think I can do anymore." We played for a certain period of time and what I didn't want to do was fall down. I wanted to avoid that.

We didn't play long enough. But I said, "I think we should play it safe here. That's all I can do for tonight." Because we had to play for two more nights.

BILL: Robbie played the set sitting down. His voice was good. It just did not have the physical-ness in it. The Band kicked *ass.* Two or three times during the show, Robbie would look over there and the guy would hold up the little crystal ball. The audience *loved* them. A few asked for tickets for the next night. The next night, they were awesome and the night after as well. It was as if nothing had happened.

JON TAPLIN: We played about a forty-minute set, which was what the guy said was about the limits of his ability to hold him up. Robbie played okay. But for a San Francisco audience who had seen the Grateful Dead, it was really a bogus way of doing it. Bill never told them that Robbie was deathly ill and they didn't know what had happened. They just thought these guys were there to take the money and run or something. There was a lot of anger.

The next day, Robbie was fine. He got through the thing and he was okay. The last night, we played a good long set twice. Bill was reasonable and forgiving again. I think on Saturday night, something else happened. Someone was a little late or something and there was another little fight but it was never outrageous. By the time we played Fillmore East for him we really had our sea legs and it was all sold out.

I think Bill liked the Band because they were less assholes than a lot of the groups he had to deal with. They weren't drugged-out and they weren't having twenty-five chicks come in the back door for free. They presented themselves a little more like gentlemen. I mean, they even wore suits and stuff like that.

In a weird way, Bill was like a demanding stepfather. It was *his* gig. He owned the East and West Coasts in rock and roll and he really did control a lot. He clearly earned your respect by getting out there and being willing to take more of a chance early on. Whereas Larry Magid in Philadelphia came in a little bit later. He became a total fan and paid the Band a lot of money over the years. And Don Law in Boston. But nobody was like Bill in terms of wanting to be there first and get his hip card punched.

ROBBIE ROBERTSON: So anyway we finished the set and I went over to the hypnotist, who said to me, "This thing works, you see?" He was telling me about using it in my life and everything and then he said good-bye to everybody. "Good-bye," he said to me. "I'll see you in the stars." He left and I have never seen him again as long as I've lived.

BILL: Three weeks later, they came and worked Fillmore East and they were even better there than they had been in San Francisco. They were truly awesome. People were just blown out. Because the sound on stage was better than on the album *Big Pink*. They just stood and played and sang. They didn't jump around. No one had ever seen anything like them before. They were really one of a kind.

ROBBIE ROBERTSON: We didn't want to come out with pots and pans and smash everybody on the head. I don't like being smashed on the head and I don't like smashing. We just wanted to come right inside your soul and your imagination. It was intense and it was serious to us and it wasn't a party. It *wasn't* a party. It was a joyous experience but we were never going to be smiling at nothing. That was not allowed in this church. We didn't smile for nothing. We only smiled for *something*.

And Bill adapted to this thing. He got it just like *that*. He treated it like this was the way it *should* be. He put emphasis in places and then they figured out the lighting to make it a little bit more dramatic instead of flashy. The idea was, "Let's make it *sound* brilliant." Our whole thing at the time was that if we didn't *sound* good, what was the point of coming to see us?

It was a very enjoyable time. Because then, it was all fresh water to us.

3.

ALAN ARKUSH: It was spring, the day that *Tommy* came out in the United States. I remember coming home from NYU that afternoon and buying it. We had all heard "Pinball Wizard" and we were *so* high on that record. We used to make them play it on the sound system at Fillmore East *all* the time. In fact, I think "Pinball Wizard" was one of the first stereo forty-fives.

I remember I was trying to listen to *Tommy* so I could absorb it *before* I had to go to work. I got to Fillmore East and everyone was really psyched. Because we loved The Who and we had heard "Pinball Wizard" and we knew we were going to see *Tommy*. They launched into it and it was awe-inspiring. Then smoke started coming into the theater. At first, we thought it was part of the show.

BILL: The fire started in the grocery store on the corner. Someone threw a Molotov cocktail in there because the owner refused to pay protection money to whoever had been shaking him down for it. A few months earlier, I had insisted that we all work out what we do in case of a fire. Who we would position on the fire escape and so forth. Then this happened. At the time the fire broke out, I was in the office in back. The next thing I knew somebody came in and said, "Bill, there's a fire next door." It was maybe ten minutes from the end of the show.

I went into the house. It wasn't smoky yet but the smoke was beginning to be noticeable and there was tension there. The person who came into my office said, "The fire department has been called and the police department has been called." Within the next couple of minutes, smoke started coming in very quickly. I was out in the lobby area trying to decide what to do. I said, "Don't say anything, don't do anything. Let's see what happens."

Within two minutes, firemen started streaming in. In full regalia, carrying their picks and sticks and axes, in those black rubber coats with the yellow seams and the funny hats they wear with the brim around in back. They came in and went right down the center aisle to the stage. I was going down the side aisle at the same time but some guy who was a police officer beat me to it. He got up there first.

FRANK BARSALONA: They had all these special policemen down there that night. Ones who looked like hippies with beards and earrings. I was standing in the back and it started smoking up. I didn't know what was going on because they had the smoke things going in the light show and people were smoking anyway. So who knew? Then all these guys who looked like hippies, in tie-dyes and everything, they came running down the aisles. One guy jumped up on stage.

Without missing a lick, Pete Townshend squared off and kicked this guy right off the stage. Now the other ones jumped up on the sides of the stage and the roadies came running out and they all got into it.

ALAN ARKUSH: Something was burning and The Who went into "Summertime Blues." That was when the cop jumped up on the stage and got kicked in the nuts and that drove the audience *wild*. They were standing up by now because it was after "Tommy" and "Summertime Blues." When the guy got kicked off the stage, it was as high as an audience could ever possibly get. They were all standing on the seats, screaming, and we were thinking, "How the *hell* are we going to get all these people out of a building that's on fire?"

BILL: Smoke was coming into the house now and the audience was in hysterics. They were convinced that we had hired these guys as part of the show. After all, this was The *Who*. They had destroyed amplifiers and turned over trucks and what not. So it could have been part of the set. I didn't see whether it was Townshend or Daltrey who pushed the first guy off the stage because the firemen were telling me, "We have to evacuate this building *now!*"

I went into the wings and I waved to the band and I said, "There's a fire next door."

"Is it real?" they asked.

"Yes," I told them. So they finished their song and walked off. I went on stage and I grabbed the mike. I remember thinking how I would react if *I* were sitting in the audience and someone started talking to me about a fire.

So I said, "Will you listen please? *Across* the street. *Across* the street, there is a fire. We're being asked by the Fire Department to please slowly and quietly evacuate the building. For safety reasons. There is no problem." All I kept saying to them was, *"Across* the street." Because I didn't want them to know that it was right next door.

ALAN ARKUSH: These kids had their adrenaline up. Their heart rate must have been like a hundred and eighty or something. I remember one of the ushers saying, "It's just like a fire drill in school. Everyone grab a buddy." Everyone in that theater got quiet. It was like what they had learned from *hundreds* of fire drills in public school. No one said a word. They all went out in double-file like every single fire drill they had ever gone through in junior high school. It was just astonishing.

BILL: All the fire marshal wanted to know was, "Where the *hell* is that guy who threw me off the stage?" The minute the show was over, The Who were sitting in their dressing room. They knew what had gone on. That they had kicked some guy off the stage. I grabbed the group and I took them out the side door. We went around the block all the way down to First Avenue and then around to 71 East Seventh, where I stuck them away in my apartment. The police were already holding Frank Barsalona, who was trying to get hold of their lawyer. There was no second show that night and we refunded all the money. The next afternoon, Daltrey and Townshend surrendered at the police precinct.

FRANK BARSALONA: I was the only one at the police station that night. I don't think Kit Lambert or Chris Stamp was there. I tried to get the police *not* to arrest them. I told them it was a mistake. I mean, how the fuck could they tell these were police? They looked like guys coming out of the audience. I didn't want them arrested. For all the regular reasons, and because it might affect their getting back into the country the next time, if in fact the arrest held up.

So we were talking and the cops were *really* angry. I went and got a lawyer to fight it and I was there all night. They finally arrested Pete and Daltrey, I think.

JANE GERAGHTY: What happened was that the fire was during the early show and of course we had people outside lining up for the late show. We had like twenty-four hundred people waiting to come into the building. We had to get everybody out who was already in and then they cordoned off the street so they could fight the fire.

Then we had to find money to bail Townshend and Daltrey out. We had to take all our little concession money and count our ones and fives and pennies and nickels. Because the fire ruined the weekend, I think Bill called Frank and asked him if at the end of their tour, they would come and replay the date. We advertised it as "The Triumphant Return of The Who." It really broke them. They were *enormous*. From all of that.

BILL: Before they were released, there was an agreement made that no charges would be brought. That it had all been just a misunderstanding. That The Who had thought it was all just part of the show. I told them to say, "We thought Bill hired those guys. All just part of Bill's madness, only good fun, and we apologize." The next day, Townshend and Daltrey were let go at like a quarter to seven at night. At seven-thirty, they walked out on stage at Fillmore East and played.

JOHN FORD NOONAN: By far, Peter Townshend was the most interesting person aside from Bill I ever met at Fillmore East. When Chuck Berry was opening for The Who, we had already put the pinball machine from *Tommy* in the star dressing room. Peter said, "No, no. We can't have that in our dressing room. It must be for Chuck." So we moved the pinball machine upstairs, and Chuck had the star dressing room.

Peter would come in the theater and there was a Spanish or a Puerto Rican or a Cuban guy who washed the stage or worked as a custodian. Peter would say, "Your accent's a lot better, man. You're getting to know a lot more English." He would remember people from one time to the next.

Peter wouldn't let anyone in the band use anything before they went on. I remember one time Keith Moon was really drunk and they sobered him up before they went out to play. Peter was the most focused and professional and I think it showed in his work.

Of course after one show, we had a party for the band at Max's Kansas City and it lasted seventeen minutes. They walked in there, Keith Moon picked up a bottle and smashed the mirror, and they threw them all out. They said, "Hey, we're *The Who.*" And they said, "We don't care who you are. You're fucking *out!*" I was on my way to it but the party was over before I could get there. They were pretty nuts but Townshend was definitely the most interesting guy.

PETE TOWNSHEND: Bill didn't handle it as elegantly in New York as he did on the West Coast. I saw him dealing with fights and stuff and he would get personally involved. I felt that really wasn't necessary in a sense. I'm not being hypocritical. I did the same thing, you know. I used to get involved. I mean, if somebody came on the stage, instead of waiting for the bouncer to get them off, I would kick them off *personally.* That was how I ended up in jail that day. The night of the fire. I ended up kicking a policeman.

But if somebody came in through the roof or something, Bill would take them out personally. As they were going, he would say, "I'm the fucking promoter. This is my theater. My name is Bill Graham. Remember this. Bill Graham has kicked you out of the Fillmore East. Put that in your fucking diary." *Boot.*

In a sense, I thought, "Well, this could build into a wonderful affection from the public. *Bill* threw me out? I'll come back in again next week." But I also thought that one day he might come up against the lunatic who would shoot him. I've been very worried about that in a sense. Because he is so central to the way he operates. He always fights his own battles and he doesn't use armor and he doesn't use strong men around him. His security people are there to protect the artists, not him. In fact, he's quite capable of taking on his own security men if they get out of line. I mean, he's extraordinary in that respect.

4.

BILL: Chet Helms and I never had any bad words with one another until the big light show strike in San Francisco in August 1969. The light show people felt I was monopolizing the scene. So they were going to mutiny. There was a classic meeting held out at Chet's joint by the ocean, the Family Dog Hall on the Great Highway. The light shows were going to picket the Fillmore West and Winterland because I was only giving them seven hundred and fifty dollars a night. They wanted a piece of the door. For the *light show*. That was some tough meeting.

DENNIS MCNALLY: The main point, of course, was that the Light Artists Guild picked on Chet because he was weak. Bill would have just punched them out and then thrown them out. They threw up a picket line on the Grateful Dead. August 1, 1969. Now, Jerry Garcia's grandmother, who raised him, was a co-founder of the Laundry Workers' Union of San Francisco. Jerry *believes* in labor. Jerry couldn't cross the picket line. When I asked him about it, his immediate response was, "My grand-mother."

JERRY GARCIA: The whole thing was stupid. What Jerry Abrams hadn't figured out was that people didn't go to shows because of the light show. They went for the music. It was that simple. There was no economic margin for light shows to make more money than they were making. What they were making was really a matter of largesse from the promoters themselves. It was like a dance *plus* a light show. But it was not *just* a light show. It was an add-on. Nobody was going to pay more money on their ticket just to get a light show. Really, the light shows, which were not exactly thriving up to that point, but at least were existing, created their own doom. That was *it* for them.

I couldn't make any sense of it. But I felt I should take it seriously. Since it was part of my community. I certainly would be involved in mediating it. If possible.

CHET HELMS: The idea I proposed was that of the Boston Common. Basically, we invited the community. Everyone who had some stake in the ballrooms. We would invite all those voices and try to work out a way of salvaging the ship so we could all survive. That following Tuesday, I would say about three hundred people met on the open floor of the Family Dog ballroom at the beach.

Bill came sort of mid-meeting. When he got there, there was this sort of free-form discussion about what was wrong with the scene. Everybody in it was hurting yet everyone realized it was a major nationally market-able thing. So how do we keep the ball rolling? *Time* and *Newsweek* had reporters there and I think so did the *New York Times* and *Rolling Stone*.

The first thing was that people started accusing Bill of being a monopolist. I stood up and I said to Bill, "Bill, do you have a contract with any of these guys?" There were several band managers there. And he said, "No." Then I went around the room and I asked Jerry Garcia and Ron Polte, who managed Quicksilver, if they had a contract with Bill. And they all said, "No." Nobody had a contract with Bill.

I said, "Look, the marketable commodity here is the bands and the music. You are the strength and the power and you have it within your power to give your power to any functional businessman to run your business for you. Whether it's Bill or me. That choice is yours." I said, "I don't want to hear that Bill Graham is a monopolist anymore. I want you to take responsibility for the decisions you've made. That you have *chosen* to work with this man."

The point was well made in that moment. They promptly forgot it. The irony of it was that it came out in either *Time* or *Newsweek* that I had called Bill Graham a monopolist. Which I did not. What I said was absolutely a hundred and eighty degrees away from that.

DENNIS MCNALLY: So Chet being Chet, they set up this community meeting. Stephen Gaskin made his famous comment to Bill about, "You wanted money. You took the money and you didn't take the love. So you can't ask for love now." That's what Gaskin said to Bill and Bill *freaked*. Probably top five in his lifetime. I've heard him freak just for practice on an agent. That the man's nervous system can handle one like that more than once in a lifetime boggles me. I have listened to him scream at the limits of human endurance for fifteen minutes and come out of the room smiling because it was just a maneuver. This one wasn't a performance. I forget what Bill's first line was but it was a quote from a movie. And Gaskin picked up that it was a quote from a movie.

JERRY GARCIA: Steve Gaskin was a weirdo in his own right. Bill came to the meeting and he pulled that line from a movie and Gaskin knew what the movie was. I didn't. But Gaskin was hip to it and he just sort of laughed it off. But Bill was marvelous. I have never seen him perform like that. Everybody said, "Oh, come on, Bill. Come on!"

CHET HELMS: There was a certain amount of sincerity and stuff from Bill and there was also a certain amount of crocodile tears that he was kind of shedding out there. Basically, Gaskin was calling him on it. How he was calling him on it was by calling out specific bits in Eli Wallach movies that the act was coming from. In others, he was accusing Graham of the fact that some of his histrionics were *learned*. He kept needling him by naming movies. "Now, you're doing the bit from so-on-and-so-forth . . ."

At some point, Bill just got rattled and totally flipped out. He just started screaming, "You slimy, slimy, slimy, little, *little* man." And so on and so forth.

BILL THOMPSON: This was quoted. He said things like, "Fuck you, you motherfuckin' fuck-fucks. You fuckin' cocksuckers. I'll fuckin' shit in your fuckin' grave, you fuckin' bigass motherfuckin' assholes. I fuck you." I mean, this was in an article that was printed.

STEPHEN GASKIN: The meeting was going down and there was some kind of rough rules of order about the person getting to finish what they were saying. Other than that, we were just a bunch of guys in a circle. It got to a place where Graham was going to talk. When he stood up, I thought, "Oh, shit. Here it comes." Because he walked out and he marked a little stage around him with his hand and he said, "You know, I used to want to be in show business. I was going to be the next Eli Wallach." This was when Eli Wallach still had hair. He said he had been to some New York acting school. And he just started out with a full showbiz, go-for-broke rhetoric. He was going to come on like Clarence Darrow. Except what he was doing was stuffing it on Jerry Abrams.

BILL: I said, "You know what dictates money? *Draw.* If I present Jefferson Airplane without your light show, what do you think the people will do? Ask for their money back?"

I said, "Let's do it the other way around. What if we presented *you* and the Airplane *didn't* show up? What do you think would happen?"

They said, "Yeah, we're going to picket Fillmore West."

I said, "Fine. I'll cross the picket line. Kill me."

I said, "The reason you're involved in all this is the same reason we have poster artists. Because we think it makes for a *better* show. The minute you tell me that *you're* essential, we've got a problem."

STEPHEN GASKIN: Oh, he went off on me! He went *off* on me. I was called a slimy little man. A slimy motherfucker. It was reported on the front page of *Rolling Stone* that I had been called a slimy motherfucker. That was my entrance into the press. See, Bill was a *lot* tougher dude than most of the rest of us, and a lot of people didn't understand that. Bill put a toughness and a grown-upness into our movement that would not have been there without him.

The funny thing was that just before Bill stomped out, there was this real gentle hippie who used to baby-sit for Janis Joplin who tried to calm Bill down. He walked up and he kind of melted on to his shoulder a little bit and put both hands on Bill's shoulders and said, *"Bill."* And Bill turned around and said, *"Don't touch me!"* He froze the dude in that position and walked away and left a silhouette of himself frozen with this guy. And then he stomped out.

CHET HELMS: Catch this. Totally unrelated to what was going on inside the hall, there was this bunch of wild beach bum surfer-type guys out there going along the beach. Bill was screaming at Gaskin and then he turned around and stalked out and slammed both doors. The minute he was out on the sidewalk, there was this incredible crash and one of the plate-glass windows came caving in. One of those surfer guys threw a brick through it from a moving pickup. It had *nothing* to do with Bill, you know? It was just totally circumstantial.

JERRY GARCIA: It was like, "Oh, God. *Psychic anger.*" It was so *weird.*

CHET HELMS: The end result of all that was that my place was run for three months as a cooperative with my staff staffing it and our salaries coming off the top. A big calendar was put up so people who wanted to produce shows could do so. It was an open calendar. If anyone stood up and said, "Hey, let's do *this!*" and there was enough energy on the floor with people saying, "Well, I'll contribute this and my band will play this" we did it. Still charging admission. I will say that some of the most marvelous things happened in that period. It was absolutely one of the most free-form creative periods.

For that three months, we were open seven days a week. Eighty per cent of what people bit off never came to fruition. It either got canceled before it happened or I would come to the gig and the guys who had agreed to produce it didn't show or they showed up hours later. For three months, I think we conducted a school in show production.

5.

KIP COHEN: Woodstock capitalized on the smarts that our staff had created for themselves in running the Fillmore. John Morris, Chip Monck, and Chris Langhart were the nucleus of people who staged the festival.

JERRY POMPILI: Two days before the festival, the sheriff's department, which was providing security for the gig, walked off. All right? So guess who was left doing the security for Woodstock? Sixty-four people from the Fillmore East who for three fucking days didn't sleep, barely got fed, and lived in fucking mud. *Right? Wonderful.*

At the end of this, John Morris made this wonderful speech to them, telling them what a wonderful job they had done. But he couldn't pay them. All right? *John Morris.* All right? When he got back into town, I almost *killed* him. I said, "These fucking people better get paid in like forty-eight hours or you will leave this town in *pieces*, you know?" He paid them. But they were the people who really held it together.

JANE GERAGHTY: Bill was *not* for Woodstock. He hated it and he didn't want it to happen. He was *virulently* opposed to it. In one sense, he was probably right, in terms of what happened there. Some bands got paid, some didn't. It was a disaster in the sense that they *didn't* sell a lot of tickets. And in the sense that it was *very* poorly run. But Bill went up there. He wanted to see it. So did Frank Barsalona.

I think people made money *before* the event and then not after. They paid themselves nice salaries to organize it for months. That's my impression. They didn't get rich but you could have had a nice job with them for weeks, and then it didn't matter whether the festival happened or not.

BILL: Michael Lang called me and he said, "Bill, we're doing this and we've got this place upstate and a lot of bands are reluctant to come in." The extent of my involvement with Woodstock before the festival happened was on the phone. I was telling them who they should book and on the other end, I was telling agents and managers that this was okay to do. That it *could* work. But I was never involved in any of the negotiations that went on.

It was obvious to me that they were rank amateurs who were in way over their heads. But anybody who would've tried what they were doing would've been a rank amateur. Because it had never been done before. These people however had very little or no experience in either public assemblage or presenting music. They had no reason to be nervous about me or what I might do to their festival but they did come to me. We talked on the phone and then there was a meeting in a loft somewhere in New York.

It was very clear what our relationship would be. I would tell them the bands that I thought would help them whom they hadn't yet thought of themselves. If there were bands they had chosen that they wanted me to comment on, I would. They were having trouble with some bands and they wanted to use my name and say that I was involved.

I said, "Up to the point in the area that I am helping you with you can." I knew they had Chip Monck doing the staging so I could vouch for their personnel. I was not running the operation so I could not guarantee what would happen but I said they could use my name. In return for

Santana being put on the show on Saturday night. During *prime time.* Which was difficult. What I wanted was no seven in the morning or three in the afternoon. Because Santana still had no album. People on the East Coast had heard of them. But never really *seen* them before.

In terms of the Fillmore East staff, they didn't take them. I gave them to them. I didn't want to stop the idea. I just always related to the person who bought a ticket. What were they going to get for their money? I went up there a week before to look at the site. The site looked good. I thought at the time that it couldn't come off smoothly because it was such a huge thing and there were no blueprints. It was a first. I knew there were going to be some faults, namely traffic. Ninety thousand mice trying to get to one hole, there had to be *some* problems.

They expected a hundred thousand. I thought there would be a quarter of a million. I came back to the city and then I went back up the day before. I didn't work the festival. I walked around constantly and it was a sight to behold. Because the previous festival I had been to where there was an attempt by nonprofessional entrepreneurs to put on something like this was Monterey. Monterey in 1967 was the egg for Woodstock in 1969.

But it was very East Coast, Woodstock. In the sense that there is a way that West Coast people greet each other and say, *"Hello, how are you?"* On the East Coast, it was peace and love but also, "Hey, how you doing?" There was a system of checking someone out that did not exist in California. On the East Coast, it was like they were all adversaries calling time-out for the day. Whereas on the West Coast, they were all like angels flying around who decided, "Oh, let's land *here* for a while." It was an entirely different feel.

6.

WAVY GRAVY: I remember when they still had only about fifty thousand people on the field. One of the promoters said to me and Tom Law, "You want to clear these people off? We want to start taking tickets." And I said, "Do you want a good movie or a bad movie?" Because I knew they had sold the movie rights. So they had a conference and Mel Lawrence got on the walkie-talkie and the next thing we knew it was a free festival. Which I thought was very perceptive of them. To see that this was the way to go. If not for the movie, though, they would have cleared that field and tried to collect tickets. They would have *had* to.

CHIP MONCK: Michael Lang turned around and told me at about six in the morning as people were waking up in the field, "Oh, by the way, you are *also* the emcee." I was standing there and my knees were knocking together and I was absolutely scared shitless. We were all knee-deep in the mud, therefore it was all, "Please. Do me a favor. Do the best performances that you can under the circumstances. Everyone is here to support you. We would like you *not* to perform over an hour. As far as a blue backing or a white so-and-so, or anything that you are used to, or anything that you would usually think is necessary, that isn't even in the cards. So don't bother me about it. But please. Anything else I can do for you? I would be delighted."

I've got a wonderful picture. A slide of Graham at Woodstock. A beautiful color shot of him. He was the most respected of all the systems in that chaos. He was there to help. But he never stepped in and made any criticism or anything. All he did was assist. Which I thought was very gracious of him.

JOHN MORRIS: The reason Bill came to Woodstock was that I was still in love with the man. I still had it in there for him. I called Bill and I said, "Bill, I'd like you to come to the Woodstock Festival."

He said, "Nah, you know. I *hate* festivals."

I said, "Bill, I've booked you into the Concord."

I booked him there and I sent a ticket for him and a ticket for Bonnie, and I flew them both out. On stage the first day, Bonnie was cold. I had a very favored yellow cotton Dunhill turtleneck that I gave to Bonnie to put on and all hell was breaking loose. I turned to Bill and I said, "I need your help. I need you to help me. I need you to work on this thing. You've got to stay and work with me."

He looked me in the face and said, "Get me a helicopter and get me out of here."

I said, "Bill, I need your help. You know what to do. You're calm and cool, you don't do drugs. You're one of the major people in this business. There are hundreds of thousands of people out there. This is like a war and we're in it. I need your help."

And he said, "Get me a helicopter and get me out of here."

Bonnie stood there with her mouth open as he walked off the stage. She put her arms around me and said, "I'm sorry, John." I said, "It's okay." And I never ever saw that yellow sweater she had on again. He let me down. It was the only time. He just couldn't deal with it. At all.

BILL: What came out at Woodstock was that they expected the audience to accept whatever shortcomings they had. Oops, I'm sorry. Ooops, sorry. Sorry, sorry, sorry. It was sloppy in the sense of time. Half hours and forty-five minutes between sets. If one guy in a band was late, they had to wait for him.

Hundreds if not thousands of kids pitched their tent somewhere down the road five miles away. So what were they blessed with? The experience of breathing the same air? They had come from somewhere and paid good money to get there and then what did they get? Look at those roads. Look at that access and egress. Once you got past the main area, even with the delay towers, the sound was *awful*.

When Santana went on, I went into the crowd and I talked to some of the movie people about it. My remark is somewhere in the outtakes of the movie which they never used. They asked me what I thought about how Santana was playing and I said, "It sounds like background music in a Tarzan movie." In other words, only the congas carried. All you could hear was a faint buddda-buddda-boom-boom-boom.

CARLOS SANTANA: I remember having a meeting with Bill Graham in Sausalito because he really liked us and he said, "I'm helping the guy putting together this concert at Woodstock. Only on the condition that you guys get on the show."

He did that with Michael Lang. He told him, "I'll help you. *If* you put Santana on here." This was without us having an album out. People didn't know us from Adam. We had done one festival in Texas and then one in Atlanta. We opened for Janis Joplin in Chicago. By the time we played Woodstock, we were pretty much ready as far as seeing how other musicians did their thing. It was kind of scary going out in front of that much of a crowd. But I felt that if Bill believed we could do it, we could do it, man.

It was funny because every time we had some big part in our lives that gave us more latitude, it seemed like Jerry Garcia was always there. We got to Woodstock at like eleven in the morning. It was a disaster area, first of all. They flew us in on a helicopter. We hung around with Jerry Garcia and we found out that we didn't have to go on until eight at night. They told us to just cool out and take it easy.

One thing led to another. I wanted to take some mescaline. Just at the point that I was coming on to it, this guy came over and said, "Look, if you don't go on right *now*, you guys are not going to play."

I went out there and I saw this ocean as far as I could see. An ocean of flesh and hair and teeth and hands. I just played. I just prayed that the Lord would keep me in tune and in time. I went, "You just keep me in tune and in time." I had played loaded before but not to that big of a crowd. Because it was like plugging into a whole bunch of hearts and all those people at the same time. But we managed, you know.

When we got to New York later on, the ladies were already there, ladies who knew Miles, who knew Jimi Hendrix, the cosmic family they called it at the time, they all started hanging around with us, and they said, "Man, Jimi Hendrix *liked* you. He really *loved* your band."

JONATHAN KAPLAN: Marty Scorsese directed the movie. Not to take anything away from Michael Wadleigh, but basically he had the center camera at the stage. Marty was the one saying, "Hey, here, *this*. Get that. I hear this guy's going to do a meditation session. Somebody go shoot that."

JON DAVISON: Of course, the great moment in the movie is when Bill talks about digging trenches and pouring in gasoline and lighting it. Burning trenches to keep them back. Everybody else is talking about peace and love and what a beautiful experience it is and how it's going to change the world and there is Bill explaining it in terms of a military conflict.

Woodstock *the Movie:*
QUESTION: From a practical point of view, how could they limit the crowd? Because they didn't want this many people here really, I don't think.
BILL: So you find a control point at the beginning of the highways and those with tickets are allowed in and those without tickets are not. And you have to have some control. You *have* to have some.
You know, when you have those man-eating *marabunta* ants coming over the hill in South America, if they want to cut 'em off and stop them from coming, they make a ditch. They put oil in the ditch, they make a flame. I'm not saying they should put up flame to stop the people. There has to be *some* way to stop the influx of humanity.

BILL: Once the movie came out, over the next few years that story got me more hatred from people than anything else. Kids would come up to me at shows and say, *"Hey! How could you want to boil me in oil?"* But I said it. So I didn't really object when they left it in. Even if they did so in order to make me look bad. Like I was the enemy opposed to all the wonderful kids coming there to have fun for *free*.

JOHN MORRIS: I think the movie is really close to what happened at the event. It is the most amazing documentary I think I've ever seen. I remember standing with Bill at the opening. The thing with Bill is that for some reason I always sort of forgive him in hopes that he will forgive me. Like God will let you off in the end. We were standing at the back of the theater and Bill was taking notes on the movie. And they got to the sequence where he's in it with the ants and pouring gasoline to keep them out. Because there's Bill Graham on film in his most down, negative way. He saw it and he snapped a pen in half and it shot right into the audience. This was at the premiere.

BILL: About a week before the festival, the word went out that they had finally made a deal with Michael Wadleigh to make a film with Warner Brothers. The deal they were offering to everybody was that whatever the act was paid to perform, they would get half of that amount again when they gave away their film rights. I said, "You mean Santana is going to sign away their film rights for seven hundred and fifty dollars? *No.*"

They said, "Anybody who doesn't sign doesn't play."

Whoever I spoke to, I said, "We'll be there. We're going to play. Don't put anything in front of me to sign."

Finally, they said, "Bill, you've *got* to sign this." But I never did. Santana played and there was a lot of bitching and a lot of bickering. It was ugly the way that it went down. Warner Brothers was going to make *millions* on the movie. Eventually, I went to them and negotiated. I got a rather large figure for Santana. More than thirty-five thousand dollars. But the price was fair because Santana was so good that day. To the best of my knowledge, everyone that played there other than Santana got half of what their earnings were that night.

The footage they had on Santana was *magic.* I said, "You want to use this, there's a price. You know it's going to be a hit. You don't want to pay the price. Don't use it." Eventually it got to a point where I said, "Look, the word out on the street is that I'm mad. You want to believe that I'm going to blow up your building? Fine. But this is not right. I represent only *this* band. Not the others."

Three hundred thousand people had seen Santana at Woodstock. I said to them, "There's only one thing the audience didn't seem that day when Santana was on, and that was *bored.*"

CARLOS SANTANA: You got to understand one thing. Those artists who were not in the movie, they weren't in the movie because they *sucked* that day. I was there and I witnessed it. A lot of people played *really* bad. They got pretty wasted before they got out there and they didn't sound very professional. If you had put them in the movie, they wouldn't be very proud to watch it today. The main peak for me was Sly Stone. Bar none. He took over that night. By the time Jimi Hendrix went on, it was too late. He paid the price for being the big thing and closing the show.

BILL THOMPSON: I was talking to this guy, Michael Lang, and Artie Kornfeld. And they were walking around with their shoes off, talking about love and beauty and peace. I was a little suspicious. In fact, I organized all the managers of the Saturday show along with Wiggy, the road manager of The Who, the guy from Creedence Clearwater, Stan Markham from Santana, and Rock Scully from The Dead. I organized everybody and we said, "Hey, we want to get our money. Because there ain't going to be any money here." And they started talking about peace and love and all that stuff.

We said, "Hey, we got everybody in the motel here. And we're not going to play unless we get the money."

So they opened up a bank on Saturday to pay everybody. *Cash.* We got it *all* in cash. The Airplane got the second highest money there. Which was fifteen thousand dollars. Jimi Hendrix got seventeen-five.

JOHN MORRIS: It was John Roberts and Joel Rosenman who went and got the money out of the bank. The bands were figuring they weren't going to get paid and realized it was no fun. The kids were having a great time. But there was a tremendous difference in what was going on up on the stage.

BILL: The Who were brilliant. I'm just a big Townshend fan and a big Who fan. Townshend is like a locomotive when he gets going. He's like a naked black stallion. When he starts, look out. Sly Stone kicked *ass.* He really did. But there weren't too many others that I liked. Not live. Hendrix was okay. I had heard him better. "The Star-Spangled Banner" was unreal. As creative a two minutes as you can probably find in rock and roll.

PETE TOWNSHEND: Woodstock was horrible. Woodstock was only horrible because it went so wrong. It *could* have been extraordinary. I suppose with the carefully edited view that the public got through Michael Wadleigh's film, it was a great event. But for those involved in it, it was a terrible shambles. Full of the most naive, childlike people. We have a word for them in England. *Twits.*

I imagine some people managed to go through it completely unscathed and have a really good time. I had taken my wife there with our new baby, who was about six months old or something. At university, her favorite thing now is to go up to people and say, "You know, I was at Woodstock."

I was nervous because we didn't go there by helicopter. We went by road. We got as far as the car could go in the mud and it got stuck. It became the hundred and ninety-fifth limo to get stuck. We got out and landed in mud and that was it. There was nowhere to go. There were no dressing rooms because they had all been turned into hospitals. There was nowhere to eat. Somebody came out of the canteen, which was where we had been naturally gravitating toward in order to sit down and eat because we were told that we wouldn't be on for fifteen hours.

To get us there in the first place, the production assistant in the limo had told us we were on in fifteen minutes. Then when we got there, they said, "Oh, sorry. We meant fifteen *hours*." As we were going toward the canteen, somebody came out saying that the tea and coffee had got acid in them and all the water was polluted with acid. I spent a bit of time on the stage but everybody was very freaked. I would find a nice place to sit and listen to somebody like Jefferson Airplane and then some lunatic would come up to me like Abbie Hoffman or some stagehand and go, "*Ahhhhhhh! Aaaaaaah! Buuuuuuuupw!*"

It was very very frightening. Somebody else would come up to me and go, "Isn't this just *fantastic!* Isn't it *wonderful!*" They would go over the hump of their cheap acid and into *dreamland*. People kept talking about America. It was most unfortunate. They kept talking about the American Dream and the New Albion. All kind of hippie-esque stuff was coming out and I kept thinking to myself, "This *can't* be true. This *can't* be what's happening to America. We're just arriving here. We're just about to break big and the whole thing's turning into Raspberry Jell-O. I don't *believe* it."

BILL: By the third day, it had become a survival camp. It was like, "I live in Poland. It's miserable in Poland? I *live* here. It's *my* country." This was their country. Their space. But it wasn't all that pleasant all the time. Sometimes, there were great highs. But by the third day with the mud and the food running out and the discomfort, it became like a camp of people who were in retreat from something. *Another* kind of war.

BARRY MELTON: I can always tell who was *really* there. When they tell me it was great, I know they saw the movie and they weren't at the gig. It really wasn't all that great to be there and it wasn't really all that great to perform there. Except that everyone had an overriding sense that they were taking part in some momentous and historical event. There had never been that many people together to do anything before. Our equipment got rained on. We only got half our money.

We played right after Joe Cocker and in the time we were setting up our equipment, it started raining cats and dogs. That sequence in the movie when somebody's screaming, "*No rain! No rain! No rain!*" I'm doing the screaming. Definitely induced. In the altered state. I tried to convince the audience that if they all put their thoughts together, they could stop the rain. There were enough people there to psychically achieve the result. It *did* stop raining. *Eventually.*

BILL: The single most significant thing about Woodstock was that relative to most countries, if you got four or five hundred thousand people together, you would have had some major problems. There were some deaths at Woodstock. But that there were so few is a miracle. In light of what people did to themselves, and the amounts they used. I don't think there was any malicious attempt on anybody's part on the production side, in terms of lying to the public about who would play, and who wouldn't. There was no false advertising. Did anybody make money at Woodstock? The movie people.

There was the Woodstock gig followed by the Woodstock film followed by the Woodstock album, which was a monster. Woodstock *made* Joe Cocker, Ten Years After, Mountain, Sly Stone, and Santana. Woodstock also triggered the managers of groups to realize, "Why play five gigs for ten dollars a piece? Let's play one gig in a canyon for *fifty thousand dollars.*"

By helicopter, the Concord was ten miles and a couple of minutes away from Woodstock. In every other way, it was three thousand miles. The guests and the staff knew what was going on over there but it was like a big Chinese wedding in the heart of Chinatown, or the seventy-fifth anniversary of the most powerful guy down there. Outside of Chinatown, what more does anyone know about it but that? It was like another planet to them. The only point of connection was, "Hey, my grandson *could* be there. I bet he is. My God, he could get killed with all those kids in one spot."

The people from the festival should've tied in a little more with the community up there. If nothing else, it would've been funnier. The new world of Woodstock and the old world of the mountains.

SAM FREIBERG: Bill came back here to stay during Woodstock and I served him. My kids were out there at the festival. My wife worked there for some organization. From the Concord to there, it's like ten, twelve, fourteen miles at the most. That weekend, all the side highways were blocked. I had a nephew working here at the time with a little foreign car. He was bringing soda into Woodstock and I showed him a back way to get there through the woods. He made a lot of money.

MICHAEL KLENFNER: All these guys, they live in a sheltered world up there. If they ever see a construction site, it's Irving Cohen's house having a wing put on or they're bringing in a bulldozer to clear the field for another addition to the hotel. They don't see the real world. They read a *Daily News* that doesn't have any advertising in it.

They know Bill, or "Billy" as they call him up there, has made it. He escaped. It's like *Escape from Alcatraz*. He got out of there. When I go up there alone, they'll say to me, "Does he *really* do that good?" And I say to them, "He does." And they say, "Do you mean, he's worth a *million* bucks?"

BILL: These days, Sam Freiberg's got bad feet and he shouldn't be working as much as he still does. Stewie the busboy has lived in the men's quarters at the Concord for thirty-six years. Are they a vanishing breed? Oh, yeah. It started to go a long, long time ago. You never see anyone up there in a fancy car now. Sometimes, a son will go with his father out of respect. For me, it is always an awesome experience to go up there for any reason. But I can never go for more than two days because then I see the sadness.

JACK LEVIN: Years ago, the dining room consisted of so many from Pennsylvania. Now it consists of so many from South America. We can't get American help. When the students come in during the summer, we hire seventy instead of thirty because after the first two weeks, they disappear. They can't take it. There's more drugs going on. When I open the dining room in the morning, I got to pray my whole crew is here.

IRVING COHEN: Now, the union is more of a benefit than a hindrance. If it wasn't for the union, where would they get their sick days? They got an insurance policy and they got a pension plan. It's not like in the days of Billy Graham. When this was the *only* place they could work in. If not for the union, they would go from here and work somewhere else.

BILL: They still have the huge jewelry counter when you come out of the dining room. They still have a guy who will do your portrait. Once it was two dollars. Now, it might be forty. The poker room is still downstairs. The gin rummy players by the pool. But so many of those people look like they're just waiting to die. They play cards and eat and sleep and eat.

Is it any different for the *goyim* wherever they go? I don't know. But it really is a shame what's happened up there. Because for me, the mountains was *such* a great school.

7.

BILL: The word was out that the Rolling Stones were coming to tour America. This was right after Woodstock. During that summer, Brian Jones had drowned in his swimming pool and the Stones had replaced him with Mick Taylor from John Mayall's band and then played a free concert in Hyde Park to a quarter of a million people. I wanted very much to be the one who would bring the Stones over for that tour. So I went to see Ronnie Schneider in New York. Ronnie Schneider was Alan Klein's nephew and I don't know really what else. But he was the one in charge of making arrangements for the tour.

I came to his office on time for our appointment but they told me that he was not there. So I sat down in the waiting room and I waited and I waited and then I waited some more. Finally, Ronnie Schneider came in. The reason he had made me wait so long was because he had been out walking his dog. That was what he did in the mornings. He walked his dog. It was something he was really good at and something he actually knew how to do.

Because he was the one who controlled what they would do with their tour, I had to deal with him. I had brought along with me a book of clippings about all the shows I had done at the Fillmores. We started talking about the Stones and I said, "These are some of the things I've done," and I laid the book down on his desk. "I'd like to get a crack at the tour," I told him. He started looking at the book. Now, when somebody makes me wait a long time, I just naturally want to get something back. I want some attention. Quickly, he leafed through all these pages and pages of letters from mayors and chiefs of police dating all the way back to when I was with the Mime Troupe.

There was one letter in there from Mayor John Lindsay of New York of which I was particularly proud. They weren't going to let us do free shows in Central Park because the Parks Department said they did not have enough trash cans to handle all the garbage left there by the crowd. I sent them the money to buy a hundred and sixty trash cans and we put on the Airplane there for free. Lindsay thanked me for the donation and told me he had heard the show was wonderful.

These were the kinds of things I had brought along with me to impress Schneider. He leafed right through it all, tapped the book shut, and said, "Very nice, Bill. But have you ever done anything *big?*"

Eventually, the tour was booked by the William Morris Agency. It was all big halls for big money. The Stones show I put on that year at the Oakland Coliseum was the first one I had ever done in a place that size.

Fifteen thousand seats with eight-fifty as the top ticket price, two shows. It made for a big gross, with a lot of money for the band.

Before they ever came to play for me, the contracts came through the mail. In the contract was the first of what would eventually come to be the standard kind of rider you see now whenever a super group goes out on the road. Forty pages of details about what the Stones wanted in their dressing room to eat and drink.

The white wine had to be from *here*, the cheese and fruit had to come from *there*. I pride myself on the way I feed performers, especially ones I know come to put on the best show they can do for the people. To have Ronnie Schneider and Sam Cutler, an opportunist without much talent who was functioning as their tour manager, tell me in such detail what I *had* to give the Stones to eat and drink got me going right away.

Instead of providing what it said I was supposed to give them in the rider, I sent someone out to Zim's for hot dogs and hamburgers and all kinds of what I guess they would call junk food now. I spread it all out in the dressing room for them to eat. They wanted catered? I gave them catered. I just didn't go to the caterer they would have liked me to.

The problems started right away during the first show. The Stones went on forty-five minutes late. Jagger told the crowd it was because no one had picked them up at the airport but the truth was that Tina Turner had killed the audience to such a degree that the Stones did not want to play right after her.

When they started doing "Satisfaction" during the first show, all the kids who had been dancing in the aisles rushed the stage. I was under the piano when it happened. I got to my feet and I went to the front edge of the stage to keep the kids from coming up or getting hurt in the crush. Sam Cutler tried to have me removed by a tall, black security guard.

"We'd like to know who you are," Cutler said.

"Get your *fucking* hands *off* me!" I screamed at him. "I'd like to know you think *you* are. This is *my* stage."

I went crazy on him. We grabbed one another and started wrestling right on stage as the Stones played "Satisfaction." But they broke it up and nothing really came of it. Between shows, I went back into the dressing room to talk to the Stones. I tried to make them understand. "Look," I said. "We've got *two* shows tonight. Please be ready on time for the second one."

The kids waiting for the second show had been outside forever because of how late the first show had started. It was simply disobedience for the sake of disobedience on the part of the Stones. It was "fuck you" for the sake of "fuck you." I had to spend the whole night dealing with that.

Between sets, I said to Ronnie Schneider and Sam Cutler, "Why don't you just all get the fuck out of here. I'll tell everybody there's *no* second show and I'll pay you off. *Okay?* Then you can just go away. Just get the fuck away from here and out of my sight. Because you're amateurs. You're *amateurs.* The worst ones I've ever seen."

The Stones and I never had any words. It was always through Schneider and Sam Cutler. By the time they finally went on to play the second show, it was past 2 A.M.

KEITH RICHARDS: It was the height of the hippie period, wasn't it? In music circles, the Fillmores had an incredible underground reputation. So we knew who Bill Graham was before we got to Oakland for that show. Our attitude was, "He's a promoter, man. And he's fucking top of the bill here? What the *fuck?* There's Bill Graham *everywhere.* Who is this, you know?"

It wasn't the billing, it was the atmosphere. Where the promoter had a bigger personality in the building than anybody else who was on the show. It was like, *"BACKSTAGE—*Starring *Bill Graham!"*

We had been on the road and we were shagged out and tired and in no mood to take tantrums from this flamboyant character. Bloody Californian, you know? What did he know? He was a Polack, you know? And later on, we found out he *was* a Polack. But at the time, it was our first contact with him. It was quite the clash of titans.

I remember a poster of Bill Graham up in the dressing room. I want to look at Bill Graham in *my* dressing room? With his finger up, giving me the "fuck you" sign. You know, fuck *you.* We threw food at it. We trashed the dressing room. At the time, the deal was, *"Fine.* We won't work for him again." And I really didn't see Bill for a long time after that.

ROCK SCULLY: The discussion about the Rolling Stones having a free concert in America had started in London. Mainly because I brought with me all this bad press about their ticket prices. I said, "Look, you're getting lambasted now. It's going to get worse when you get there." They were genuinely interested in doing it. After Hyde Park, they were all up for it. They also thought they would make a movie of it. With no idea whatever of what was going on in America at that point.

In London, Sam Cutler said, "We'll hire the Hell's Angels." He said, "We used Hell's Angels for security here."

And I went, *"No, no, no, no. No way.* This isn't the same, you know?"

There was a chapter of real Hell's Angels in London. But there were also these other ones, who had just written "Hell's Angels" in chalk and whitewash on the back of their leather jackets or done it in studs. It was just a style. They were riding around on *mopeds.* A lot of this stuff was happening at the time and it was happening with a lot of cocaine and a lot of drugs and everybody was fucked up, including myself.

Chip Monck flew over while I was there in that two-week period and Michael Lang from Woodstock also came. He wanted in on it. Because I was there talking about a free Stones concert in the United States. We made a lot of arrangements then and there. We also had several meetings once they hit the United States about how carefully it had to be done and how there could be no advance word on it. *At all*.

JERRY GARCIA: Originally, it was going to be they were just going to come out and play in Golden Gate Park, unannounced. Then they made the stupid mistake or maybe Ralph Gleason announced that they were going to pay. That was it. That was the end of it right there. They should have just called it off from then. But the Stones were traveling in like a bubble. They couldn't be contacted. We couldn't explain things to them.

In fact, I think it was Emmett Grogan who wrote on the bulletin board up at Alembic where we were rehearsing and a lot of the planning was going on, "First Annual Charlie Manson Death Festival." *Before* it happened. It was in the air that it was *not* a good time to do something. There were too many divisive elements. It was too weird. And that place. God. It was like hell.

ROCK SCULLY: The Stones queered us getting the park. We had already had meetings with the city and they said as long as not one word leaked out, we could have the park. Twenty-four hours ahead of time, we could start saying anything we wanted to.

Two weeks before the concert, Mick Jagger called. The press was getting so bad that they felt they had to rescue their image with a free concert. So he announced it two weeks ahead of time in New York City at a big press conference. That queered it like *that*. That was *it*.

I called him to talk about it but I had to go through all these assholes just to get to him. Crooks. I mean, it was just such a crooked tour. Burning everybody. The rent-a-cars, the hotels in San Francisco. They could have paid for everything. But they were just like bandits. *Plundering*. So they told me to find another place. Sears Point Raceway, which was owned by Filmways. A facility with toilets and water. Everything already there. It was in the North Bay, sort of opposite Novato. Highway 12 to Vallejo.

Somehow, the Stones got into a terrible row with Filmways, who were promoting their shows in Southern California, over money. Almost the same kind of deal that happened to Bill. What promoters call the nuts and bolts. The Stones left them with the nuts and bolts and that was *it*.

You know, *no* profit. You get the prestige, we keep the money. Then we had the movie negotiations come in.

STEPHEN GASKIN: Just before Altamont happened, I felt there was a real bad vibe afoot. A bunch of dealers had gone big time and were going around in leather tuxedos and whatnot. Showing off really fancy with a lot of money and not very spiritual and I felt we were losing the thing in some ways. I wanted to kind of protest that. So I said, "I'm going to take my meetings out on the beach for a while and not meet in the rock hall anymore."

Altamont was just a culmination of the kind of stuff I was complaining about. We started getting big time dopers from New York who were not hippies and were not psychedelic. It began to get that New York flavor. Plus, talented chemists began coming up with early MDA. The thing was that acid was so harsh that it was self-limiting. Nobody was going to get addicted to acid. It would have been like being addicted to having the shit kicked out of you.

ROCK SCULLY: When the Sears Point thing fell through, we were about ready to throw up our hands. We had already built the stage there. That little low stage that ended up at Altamont was sitting up on top of a hill with these bowls opposite so it was perfect. At the bottom of the hill, people just rolled right off the hill and on to the stage, which was what they did.

The Stones came into town. It was really last minute now. Sears Point had been blown off at the literal last minute. They *had* to save face. Everybody wanted a piece of the free concert, and no one was going to let it go. Melvin Belli's office called and said that we now had to do everything through Belli. Then we got a call from them saying they had found this place. Altamont Speedway.

BILL: I didn't want them to do a free concert. Not without planning. I said to them, "As big as you are, you can't do a free show. You *can't*." *Free* was the dangerous word. Anybody and everybody. You can't stop anybody from coming. Doing what? Bringing what? To be part of what? *Free*. I knew what was coming down and I said, "I've got to get away from this." I remember this very clearly. I went to New York so that there would be no way I would be available and no way they could contact me.

A couple of days before the proposed concert, Chip Monck found me. He called and said, "Bill? You were right. We've got a disaster on our hands. The show is two days from now, we can't build the stage, the power lines aren't in, there's no sanitation and no medical, there's no water. We're in a sandpit. It's not good."

I said, "Chip, *cancel*. Just *cancel*."

He said, "Bill, I can't. The Stones want to do the show. We've got the Dead and the Airplane and Crosby, Stills, and Nash."

"Chip," I said, "Don't do it."

"Bill," he said, "I need a favor. I need your team."

This was Jay Drevers and Willie John Cashman, my guys from the shop. I said, "Chip, don't ask me." Then I asked him the ultimate question. I said, "Chip. No theatrics, no dramatics, no bullshit. I'm going to ask you a simple question. You better take a deep breath first because I'm basing what I do on your answer.

"If my saying no about my guys means that you'll drop it, then forget it. If you're saying you're doing the show hell or high water, that you're going on even with a sinking stage, you can have my crew."

"Bill," he said, "That's how we're doing it. Hell *and* high water."

So I gave him my crew.

8.

OWSLEY STANLEY: It was like a moonscape of crushed auto bodies. Like just all crunched and crushed. As we drove along, we looked over to the left and we saw this place that looked like a skull. It was the actual arena in which they had held all these demolition derbies. I thought, "Oh, my God. This place smells of death. Of the energy of people who come here to watch people crash these cars together, hoping they'll die."

I thought, "This is the *worst* possible place to hold something like this." And I realized that if you took acid at this show, you were going to have a trip that you didn't really want.

CHIP MONCK: At Woodstock, people had policed themselves. The elements were so much against them that we were all fighting against the same thing. So there was great unity there. At Altamont, there was no way of fighting against those individuals. The Hell's Angels. I blame them very pointedly. But their payment was a truckload of beer. So they had already been set up. Everything had already been taken out of the realm of any possible reality. It had been removed from anything conscious or logical involving understanding or negotiation. It was just all gone.

JERRY GARCIA: The idea of using the Hell's Angels as cops, that was ridiculous. If you were going to have the Hell's Angels there, they should have given them a corner of the field where they could rape and pillage and murder and do their shit and just hope that everybody stayed away from it. Kind of obvious, you know? But it was that English mentality. That was where Sam Cutler fucked up. The thing of, "Oh well, we'll use the Hell's Angels, you know." It looked facile. It looked possible. But unless you knew what the Hell's Angels were like, man, you did not know what you were dealing with.

KEN KESEY: Hell's Angels weren't supposed to be at the top. They were supposed to be at the bottom. They couldn't handle the top. But they worked really well at the bottom. And that's what Altamont was. They got up on top and it was a horrible scene. I knew Altamont would happen. I just didn't know where or exactly how.

GRACE SLICK: I felt sorry for Jagger. Because the day had been building up to their act. And he dressed in his tour outfit. Which was kind of a devil's sort of suit. And I just thought, "Oh, man, you just stepped into a pile of shit." "Sympathy for the Devil," and the whole aura of the thing was just real yin/yang. Woodstock was a bunch of stupid slobs in the mud and Altamont was a bunch of *angry* slobs in the mud. It was *all* just slobs in the mud. But definitely yin/yang sort of stuff.

BILL THOMPSON: Altamont was the end of the sixties. It was December 1969, and that was the end. Of the whole feeling. We kept on going but it was a different kind of feeling.

I mean, if *we* couldn't get along, and we were all talking about brotherhood and love, how could we make people believe that? Because we really did believe it then. And I don't know what exactly happened. Maybe just the humanness of everybody came out. The Airplane never again had the greatness of the early days. There were sparks, but it was never that creative again.

DENNIS MCNALLY: What it boiled down to was that in front of the stage there was a six-foot-high chain-link fence. The Angels were between the fence and the stage. At some point in the afternoon, Sam Cutler put the press in there and the Angels left. Seeing people there, the audience tore down the fence. It was at that point that all hell broke loose. There were maniacs in the audience who wanted to challenge the Angels.

One of the Grateful Dead's managers got laid out that day. That was when the Grateful Dead decided they weren't going on stage. They flew back to the city where they were supposed to work at Fillmore West. Rock Scully took them to Grison's, a steakhouse that no longer exists.

Either Mickey Hart or Billy Kreutzman said, "I ain't playing tonight," and walked off. The other drummer said, "My brother drummer's not playing, I'm not playing." And *he* walked off. I think John McIntyre had to go down to Fillmore West and explain why the band wasn't showing up that night.

ROCK SCULLY: The next night, we were working at Fillmore West. Bill Graham came barging into the dressing room and called me a murderer. He said that if I hadn't been involved in Altamont, it would *never* have happened. I was sitting on the floor and we were talking about this disaster and I just lost it. He lost it, too. He was all red in the face and screaming at me. I took a hat off a coat hook, and went at him and he fell over backward. The dressing rooms at Fillmore West were up a couple of steps and he went down them on to his ass and went stomping out. I mean, he knew we were trying to stop it, too.

Bill had every reason to be mad at us for pulling out of his show the night before. But in terms of what happened at Altamont, it had all been taken away from us when it was yanked from the park. After that, all we could do was try to salvage the concert because we had all these musicians who wanted to play with the Stones for free. Had the Stones been not so cut-throat on that whole tour, Bill certainly would have been involved in Altamont, and it would have worked out a lot better.

JOSHUA WHITE: Bill was really upset about Altamont. I remember sitting in the office with him and he said, "That *fucking* Chip Monck." And I said, "What do you mean?" He said, "Fucking Chip Monck. That was the problem at Altamont. It was Chip and his fucking soldier-of-fortune attitude that they can do *anything*. *We can* move it. *We can* do the show *here*." They moved the stage to some cow pasture and people died.

Chip used to go out on tour and do a slide show in which he would speak in the most metaphysical terms. But what he was saying basically was that he was the knight errant and Mick Jagger was the philosopher prince and it was his job to support the philosopher prince. If the philosopher prince wanted a concert in the middle of a cow pasture, *done*.

BILL: After it happened, I was quoted at length in *Rolling Stone* about what happened. I said,

"I would offer Mister Jagger fifty thousand dollars to go on coast-to-coast television or radio with me, not stoned, not copping out, but sit down Mister and rap, open, for an hour. I'll ask you what right you, Mister Jagger, had to walk out on stage every night with your Uncle

Sam hat, throw it down with complete disdain, and leave this country
with one point two million dollars? And what right did you have in
going through with this free festival? . . . What right did you have to
leave the way you did, thanking everybody for a wonderful time and
the Angels for helping out?

"He's in his home country now somewhere—what did he leave
behind throughout this country? Every gig, he was late. Every fucking
gig, he made the promoter and the people bleed. What right does this
god have to descend on this country this way? It will give me great
pleasure to tell the public that Mick Jagger is not God, Junior. I am
not trying to blast at someone that is ten thousand miles away. But you
know what is a great tragedy to me? That cunt is a great entertainer.

"Mister Jagger could have realized what he was doing. His ego
wouldn't allow it. Mister Chip Monck is the best stage manager I know.
I respect him as a man. But the man knew what he was doing. I can't
think that anything but his ego got him to do this. He was one of the
engineers of Woodstock. It took him *months* to build Woodstock. How
could he think that he could do this in one *day?*

"But the guiltiest one of all is the law. The law had the greatest
power to avert this. . . . To me, any time the law sees anything like
this coming, which is a holocaust . . . they can stop anything at any
time. They can block a highway or force them by injunction. Sometimes, force is valid.

"They should have taken Mister Jagger, twisted his fucking arms
behind his back, put him in front of a radio, and said, 'Mister Jagger,
if we have to break your arms, call it off.' . . . if there was no stage,
no sounds, no lights, and if there were no Rolling Stones, the kids
wouldn't have left their homes. Once the kids started, once the ants
came down the hill, watch out. Make way. They're going to eat you.
My point being that the law *knew* what was coming."

I was very bitter about it afterward and very unhappy. I made a remark
to the press that went around and I'm sure the Stones were not happy
about. But I said it. I remember I said it and I don't deny it. When the
press asked me about the tragedy out at Altamont, half of them were
saying, "Wasn't that your show, boss?" I said, "No, it wasn't. I wouldn't
have done it that way." They said, "Well, how do you feel about it? What
do you think of the Stones for doing it? Wasn't it their desire to give
something *back* to the people?"

When I heard that, I got really angry. I said, "I'll tell you what it was
like." At the time, 1969, the Ethiopia of that era was Biafra. The word
for starving people was Biafra. I said, "I don't quite see it like that.

Giving something back to the people? If you want an analogy, imagine the Reverend Billy Graham putting on a gold lamé jumpsuit, renting a helicopter, and dropping *one* live chicken over Biafra." That's what the Stones did with their free concert at Altamont. That's how much they gave back.

I remember reading that it was going to be at Sears Point. Then they couldn't get the permit there. When they switched it to Altamont prior to the date, I remember thinking it was *insanity*. Because there was no preparation. A gig of that magnitude in an era when there weren't the production teams and personnel available as they are now, I couldn't figure out *how* they could do it.

Altamont really was a tragedy because it became an adjective for the negative aspect of rock and roll. There was a speed trial one year in Indianapolis at the Speedway before the big Memorial Day race. A car went into the stands, *thirteen* people were killed. The next day, ho-hum. Life went on and they raced. Not so at Altamont, and not so with rock and roll.

Altamont. The word conjures up an event which was more costly to rock and roll than any single day in the history of entertainment. No other leisure-time activity has that dark a cloud over it. We've never been able to wipe that stain from our record. It's tragic. Far beyond the fact that at least one person was killed.

If you showed the movie of it to someone fifteen years old in New York City now, you could not convince them that it all really happened. It was like a concentration camp for a day.

It will always be something for the critics of rock and roll to use. You can't let all these people gather *here* for a concert. They may hurt each other. Look at *Altamont.*

Chapter Ten

The White Man's Apollo

1.

ALAN ARKUSH: Jimi Hendrix was performing with the Band of Gypsies by then and he was preparing for the New Year's Eve show at Fillmore East. They let him rehearse during the afternoon all through the Christmas shows so I saw them jam every day and play all kinds of great blues things. On New Year's Eve, this guy came to the stage entrance and said, "I got a package for Jimi." The word was that *nobody* came backstage to see Jimi. I mean, no one could give him *anything*. But this guy begged and begged. So I said, "Well, I can't let you backstage. But *I* can give it to him, if you want."

The guy got paranoid. He said, "Look, man, it's really valuable. I really want Jimi to have it."

He showed me this beautiful hand-carved wooden box. So I said, "I'll bring it back to him."

He said, "Tell me what he says. Tell me if he likes the box."

I said, "Okay."

I brought it back and Jimi opened the box and it was full of cocaine. The cocaine was glistening. It had sparkles on it. Jimi did some of it and passed it on and I think actually that was the first time I ever tried cocaine. It was *so* strong. Jimi said, "Thank the man. Thank the man." I went back down there and the guy was gone. He had disappeared.

Jimi played the early show and he played the late show and people were screaming for him to do an encore so he came back out and played an encore. People were cheering and he played *another* encore and the audience still wasn't leaving. He had played a monster set.

Bill or Kip said to me, "You've got to go upstairs and get Jimi to come back down."

So I went running up the stairs and I got through the three people guarding the door and I said, "*Jimi, Jimi!* You've got to go back down and play another song!"

He looked at me and went, "We don't know any other songs. We haven't rehearsed any."

Then Jimi turned to Buddy Miles and he said, "Buddy, you know the words to 'Purple Haze'?" They rehearsed "Purple Haze" right there. He showed Buddy the chord changes and they went back down and played "Purple Haze." It was like every garage band in the world. "Hey, you guys know 'Purple Haze'?"

I took a look and the box was *empty*. It was empty and there had been a lot in there. A lot.

BILL: The Voices of East Harlem were on that show along with Jimi and his Band of Gypsies. Billy Cox on bass and Buddy Miles playing drums. I had to be in San Francisco for New Year's Eve itself because we had a big show at Winterland with the Airplane, Quicksilver, and the Sons of Champlin. I flew to New York to see Hendrix's show on New Year's night. They were recording that weekend, looking for a live album, and when I got there, they told me that the recording had gone so-so the night before.

I introduced the band and I walked to the side of the stage and watched a little bit from there. Then I went to the back of the house and I watched a little bit more and I was going to go into the office. But I said, "*Jesus*, I can't *believe* this is happening." I decided to stay out there and watch the whole thing. Maybe I missed ten minutes out of the hour that Jimi did. And he never really played.

He did every one of his moves. *Side. Up. Under. Piercing. Throwing. Kissing. Fire. Fucking. Humping.* He did it *all*. Picking with his teeth. Guitar behind his head. In one ear. Out the other. Thunder and lightning and motion. Every once in a while, he would give them a little real music. The kids went bananas. They went crazy. They thought he was the greatest. And he was. But not during that set.

The show ended and we got all people out. Just before we opened for the second show, I was sitting with Kip Cohen in the back office when Jimi came in. He had *never* before left the dressing room and come into the back room where I had my desk. He said, "Hey, Bill. How was it?" My answer to him was the neutral one. The face that says, "Whatever *you* want it to have been, that's what it was." If he would have said to me, "You know, I didn't feel right out there tonight." I would have said, "I *felt* you didn't feel right out there tonight." In other words, I wanted to leave it open. I was waiting for his lead. "You felt great? You *looked* great. You felt horrible? You *were*."

But he said, "No, Bill. I *really* want to know. I'm asking you a question, man."

I asked Kip Cohen to leave the office. I shut the door. In so many words, I said, "You're Jimi Hendrix. It just surprised me that you would do that."

"Do *what?*"

"Well, you've got to be aware by now of the fact that you're so popular and your fans are so into your work is that they will be happy for *whatever* you give them. But, Jimi. Aren't you also aware of the fact that you've gotten to the point where you did everything out there tonight but remember to *play?*"

He said, "*What* did you say, man?"

I went into it again. I said, "Look at all the moves you made. Think about the songs you played. There *were* sounds coming out of your guitar. But that was really just physical dexterity, wasn't it? Was it really playing? The improvisations in your music are always great because you never play things the same way twice. But I've got to believe that you know the difference between what they cheer and what comes from the heart."

He said, "Did you hear the *ovation*, man? They went fucking *nuts*."

I said, "You could have brought out the guitar and *pissed* on that stage and for them, it would have been a thrill."

He got angry and he started to leave the room. He said, "*Jesus! Fuck!*" But under his breath like he was also mad at himself. He never yelled at me. I think it had finally clicked in with him that *anything* he did on stage was going to be great with the people. Especially in New York City. Because if he could get them by doing that in New York City, then it would work anywhere else.

Before he left, he just looked at me and said, "*Okay*." He didn't say he was sorry. Just "*Okay*." Then he said, "You here for the second show?"

"Yeah," I said.

"Give me your word?"

"I'm here," I told him.

"You gonna to check it out?"

"I told you I'm going to be here. I'll check it out."

"You gonna introduce the second show?"

I told him I would. I did the introduction and then I stepped into the wings. I never left. Aside from Otis Redding, there will never be anything like that show. The man took maybe three steps one way or the other during the whole set. He just *played*. And he just *sang*. He moved his body but it was always in time to the music. He was Fred Astaire. Not

Harpo Marx. There was grace but *no* bullshit. He was a serpent and he was growling at them and the crowd was into it because it was the late show and only the hip crowd ever came to that one.

The beauty of the night was that he did maybe seventy-five minutes of just brilliant playing. The band saw what he was doing and they got into it. Billy Cox and Buddy Miles played on *his* level. Because they could see that Jimi was *possessed*. At the end of the set, he got the kind of applause that only a great bullfighter receives. Take the ears. Take the tail. He came over to the side of the stage with his guitar hanging limp by his side. He got a towel and he was wiping his face.

When he was through, he put his face about a half inch from mine and he said, "Good enough for you, *Jack? Huh?* You gonna leave me go now? You going to give me my *space* now, Bill? *Huh?*"

I said, "Jimi, you were *great.*"

Then he went out and did the entire first show in fifteen minutes. All the *shtick*. The *Fire. Throwing. Kicking. Humping. Grinding*. But what he had given them before, that was the *real* thing.

2.

BILL: Winterland was the first place where I was able to do things a little larger. The feel of Winterland was to some extent what we also achieved at Fillmore East and West. Inside, people could move anywhere they liked. They could sit or stand or dance. It was up to them. When we started at the original Fillmore, we would sometimes do Thursday night there and then Friday and Saturday at Winterland and then back at the Fillmore on Sunday night. We would put all the lights on a steel dolly and at four in the morning, we would *schlep* it all down Geary to Post and Steiner and go into the side door at Winterland. Between four in the morning and noon, we would set up Winterland. Just Jim Haynie, John Walker, and me.

The place held fifty-four hundred people. On the main floor, they used to have basketball games and ice hockey and what not. It had been built as a huge skating arena with seats around the floor and a balcony upstairs that ran all the way around. It looked like a Roman arena. It had the feeling of a small coliseum. In shape, it was a curved rectangle. I believe it had been built in 1919. There was no back side. People sat behind the stage. Musicians played *surrounded* by the public.

PETE TOWNSHEND: What happened at Winterland was that Bill then made another step which was emulated by people like Don Law in Boston and Aaron Russo. They realized the five-thousand level was a *good* level.

It was a good size. From a crowd control point of view. It meant you could use old skating rinks and there would be fire exits and it was safe. It was a good size. The music would sound good. And it wouldn't have to be so loud that it woke everybody up in the fucking neighborhood.

3.

JOHN MORRIS: There were a lot of heavy people who came in and out of that office Bill had at the Fillmore East. It was not a screaming, yelling, howling scene. It was *power*. No question about it. Everybody came to see what was going on. And everybody sat in that office.

PAT LUCE: It was the gathering place for the industry. It was where everyone went when they had nothing else to do on Friday and Saturday night after dinner. *Everybody* came down to the office. Ahmet. Frank Barsalona. People you liked and people you didn't like, depending on the act. The manager, the record company president. Mo and Joe would be there. If the act was Warner Brothers. Mo Ostin and Joe Smith. Johnny Podell. Dee Anthony. People would go out for a few minutes to see the show but none of them ever had seats in the house.

There would be coffee and food and everybody kind of milling around and what was really fun about the office was that you would have ushers in deep conversation with multimillionaire managers. It was such a democratic situation that you couldn't tell the players without a score-board.

Because in that office, there was *no* deferential treatment going on. There would be fifteen or twenty people in there while we were trying to work. The doctors from the Bummer Palace would be in there taking a break. The record company presidents would be trying to look younger. The agents trying to seem unslimy. Although a lot of them weren't.

Always, there was Frank Barsalona. Mainly because he *always* had an act on the bill. For months, I did not know Frank was someone important. I thought he was someone's chauffeur. Because that was what he looked like. And he was *always* talking to the ushers. He would ask them, "*Who* should I listen to? *Why* should I listen to it? *What's* going on?"

Bill loved the scene. It was like a *bar mitzvah* every weekend. *Every* weekend. And there was *always* a crisis. We were having this party and police cars were coming in and it was all part of the routine. For the late show, people came who didn't have an act on. Agents looking to sign *someone else's* act. People after their dates. A guy who had been out to dinner and wanted to impress his girlfriend by taking her into the office at the Fillmore. They always took their life into their hands when they did that because if they were just *futzing* around and Bill was in a bad mood, they were *out*.

People would come simply because it was *the* thing to do. It was *the* place to be seen. For a lot of us who worked there, that office *was* our social life.

FRANK BARSALONA: I would wander around and I would talk to the ushers. Rather than speaking to the record company presidents. Because they were all presold. The ushers were kids. Basically, we were almost all the same age. I would sit and talk to them and Bill would come in and say, "What the *fuck* are you doing here?" He would have Clive Davis or Ahmet Ertegun out there and he would say, "I've been waiting for you and you're in here talking to some fucking usher?"

I used to say, "But, Bill. They're a *lot* more interesting."

4.

ALAN ARKUSH: We didn't know anything about the Allman Brothers. All we knew is that they were opening for Blood, Sweat, and Tears at the end of December 1969. No one had ever heard them. The album wasn't out yet. But the album cover was up in the lobby of Fillmore East. It had a picture of these guys standing naked in a stream, and we thought, "What a bunch of redneck yo-yos." Our cynical New York attitude. Not only that but they were late for the sound check. A cardinal sin.

We were waiting and waiting. We didn't realize they were driving up from Georgia. This van pulled up and they piled out of it with all their amps. It must have been their first time in New York. These rednecks with their crummy, beat-up Marshall amps. We were going, "These guys are going to be something else. Hope they don't get naked." John Ford Noonan was going, "You guys going to keep your clothes on while you play tonight?"

They launched into "You Don't Love Me No More" and "One Way Out" during the sound check and people came out of their offices. Everyone stopped working and just sort of stood there and went, "*Oh*. These guys are for real." They played four forty-five minute sets that weekend and we couldn't get enough of them. We thought they were *fabulous*.

Blood, Sweat, and Tears hated them. Because they had all their aunts and uncles and grandmothers in from Queens. I had given the Allmans a bunch of wine because we liked them so much. I blew the whole wine budget on the Allmans because they didn't want beer. I lent Duane Allman money out of my own pocket to eat dinner because these guys literally had no money of their own. But they did drink up all that wine and start chasing naked girls up and down the stairs, showing off their tattoos.

Finally, one of the guys in Blood, Sweat, and Tears pulled me aside and said, "Can't you keep them on the third floor? Because my aunt saw one of them running into the bathroom, chasing some girl." This was not the Al Kooper Blood, Sweat, and Tears. It was the one with David Clayton-Thomas in it.

The crew all voted to have the Allmans back. We just requested it so they brought them back six weeks later to play with the Grateful Dead. It was Love, the Allman Brothers, and the Grateful Dead. The Allman Brothers were still unheard and unknown. But these were *legendary* shows. After that weekend, the Allman Brothers were never the same again. Owsley dosed everyone that weekend. That was the night that Fleetwood Mac came down and got dosed.

I have a cassette somewhere of Duane Allman, Peter Green, and Jerry Garcia jamming together. They played "Dark Star" and the Donovan song, "There Is a Mountain." Which the Allmans turned into "Mountain Jam" because of that night. Mick Fleetwood was so heavily dosed that he was sitting on the stage as the audience was filing out with the microphone in his hand. He kept going, "The *fuckin'* Grateful Dead. The *fuckin'* Grateful Dead." We didn't have the heart to turn off the mike. He was saying it like a mantra. "The *fuckin'* Grateful Dead!"

MICK FLEETWOOD: I remember playing at Fillmore East, not officially, with the Grateful Dead. On acid. They had the two drummers and I didn't actually drum. I had a tom-tom and a snare drum and I was gooning around on the stage. Peter Green and Danny Kirwan were playing as well. That was one of the crazed nights there.

ALAN ARKUSH: The next time they came back to Fillmore East was in September. They played along with Van Morrison and the Byrds for this TV show that WNET made for PBS. By then, they had "Idlewild South" out. Then they came back again in March 1971 to record the live album. I was a member of the light show by then and we weren't booked to work that weekend because Johnny Winter was the headliner and Johnny Winter didn't like a light show. We didn't perform, we just came to see the shows. Duane saw me and he went, "Where's the light show?"

I said, "Well, we're not hired to work this weekend."

"What do you mean? I brought the whole family up here to see the thing."

They were one of the few bands who would *ask* that the stage lights be lowered so people could really see the light show. Duane called Bill in

San Francisco. They had done tapes of their sets for the first two nights and they really didn't like them. So Duane called Bill and Bill said, "Yeah, hire the light show. We'll bring them on for you. If you guys want the light show, we'll do it if it will make you feel more comfortable."

I remember I went into our dressing room and there were big jugs of wine and an envelope full of mescaline tabs from them, along with a note saying, "Here, guys, let's have a good night." That's the album *Live at Fillmore East*, with "Eat a Peach" on it. They were so hot that they tore into the early show like it was Friday night late show. Johnny Winter reversed the order. He said he had to catch an airplane. But I'll tell you. He just couldn't top them.

The Saturday night shows, early and late, were probably the greatest I ever saw the Allman Brothers play. Also, one of the greatest live performances I ever witnessed.

BILL: I had played them before as an opening act at the Fillmores. Back when they were still the Hourglass. When the Dead and the Allman Brothers played together at Fillmore East, it was rock at its very best. I remember the Allman Brothers going on stage at one-thirty or two o'clock in the morning for their second set. They came off somewhere around 4 A.M. and the audience was great. They went out and did their encore and then Duane and Gregg came offstage and they said, "Jeez, Bill, we're always late."

I said, "You want to play, you can play."

They walked back out on stage. I told Michael Ahearn, "Put the spots on fine point, and start the mirror ball turning slow time. Stage lights at floor level and leave it." They did and there were little stars of light everywhere as the Allmans started to play. Every number was forty minutes long. I was sitting and half-snoozing backstage and this was going *on* and *on* and *on* and nobody was leaving. Dicky Betts and Duane and Gregg were doing great riffs and they played and played.

They finished up and the applause was really warm. Like the audience had just eaten this huge meal out there. Somebody hit the side door of the theater and the light started streaming into the house.

ALAN ARKUSH: Snow had fallen and there was snow all over the ground. We had been in that theater so long and now you could see big shafts of light coming through the open doors because the place was full of smoke.

BILL: I was looking at my watch and it was five after seven. Duane turned around and looked at me and he said, "Hey, Bill . . . Just like leavin' church, huh?"

5.

ALAN ARKUSH: Some street group was trying to break into Fillmore East one night and there was a riot going on out there and I was on the back door. One of the outside security guys came in and said, "It's hell out there. Don't let anyone out the back door." Then he grabbed this huge steel pipe and ran out the door. Before he went, he told me, "Bar the door and don't let *anyone* through." I could hear the fighting and the screaming and people running up and down the street. So I took this bar and put it across the handles and I locked the door.

Who walked up but Ike and Tina Turner and the Ikettes. And they were all in these white mink coats. Ike said, "Let me out." I said, "I'd love to, Ike, but . . ." He said, *"Step aside!"* Now, when Ike Turner said *"Step aside"* and he had all the Ikettes behind him, you stepped aside.

I unbarred the door. Ike opened his coat and pulled out a silver revolver with a white pearl handle. He stepped out on to the street and fired two shots into the pavement. People scattered everywhere. Ike turned and said, *"Tina."* Not "Tina, let's go." Just *"Tina."* He motioned to her with his finger. Tina and the Ikettes stepped right out into the street and they had no trouble at all.

JOHN FORD NOONAN: Ike seemed like a bad dude to me. I'd rather tell you my Chuck Berry story. Kip Cohen came over to me, giggling. He said, "John, I want you to go up and get Chuck."

So I went up and got Chuck. Chuck was talking to a guy while eating a sandwich as a girl was going down on him. I said, *"Chuck?"* He said, "Let me finish." I didn't know if he was talking about the sandwich or the girl.

ALAN ARKUSH: When I moved up from the house, my job ended up being supplying food for all these groups. I was like the backstage caterer. I remember once the Incredible String Band asked me if I could get them some *mead.* I said, "What the hell's mead?" And they said, "It's sort of like beer with honey in it." And I said, "I'll get you some beer, I'll get you a jar of honey, you make your own mead."

When Ravi Shankar was there, Kip said, "Get him a big selection of Indian food." So I brought in the Indian food and Ravi Shankar looked at it and said, "Oh, couldn't you get me one of those wonderful Danish from Ratner's?"

BILL: In March of that year, I got Miles Davis to open at Fillmore East for Steve Miller and Neil Young and Crazy Horse. A month later, he played out at Fillmore West with Stone the Crows and the Dead. It was one of those things where I wanted to introduce Dead fans to a different kind of music. Miles was very reluctant. Going to visit him was like going to visit the Dalai Lama.

To get an appointment to see him took fourteen and a half years. Take two turns to the left. Go to a phone booth and call and I'll let you know where you go from there. It was one of these. "He could be." Then, "He might be." Then, "He *should* be there." I finally got together with him on a 127th Street and Lenox Avenue up in Harlem where he lived at the time.

I told Miles that I had started listening to him long before rock and roll. I told him my musical background was Miguelito Valdez and Celia Cruz and Tito Puente and Dizzy Gillespie. I told him about my island idea. The three records I would take with me to a desert island. My first record would be *Sketches of Spain.* My second was Ravel's *Bolero.* The third always changed. He was impressed by the fact I had picked those two.

"*Fuck,*" he said. "*Fuck.*"

He was very distinct in his statements. Then we started to talk about what *his* third might be. He expressed some fears about the audience. Woody Herman had already played at the original Fillmore with The Who and I would soon have Buddy Rich at Fillmore West with Ten Years After. Miles agreed to play for me with the band that did *Bitches' Brew.* Wayne Shorter and Jack DeJohnette and Tony Williams on drums. They were brilliant.

What got me more than anything else was that a good portion of the Dead fans really got into Miles. Some of them even *danced* to his music. The highlight of that night was my seeing John Walker at the top of the steps handing out handbills for the following week. Two guys came out past me. They were out there with the *deer.* I mean, their eyes were *big.* They were *exalted.* As they passed me by, one turned and said to the other, "Hey, man. Are you into . . . *Miles?*"

The way he said it was like, "You and I know but very few other people know about this." *Miles.* "Are you into . . . *Miles?*" Like this was Omar Khayyám. Like he had found the new Prophet book by Kahlil Gibran. Because Miles had touched him.

I also put on Roland Kirk. He *destroyed* me. The first time he ever played for me was back in 1967 at the Fillmore Auditorium. I had Jefferson Airplane. They were the local band that was always a home run. So I could book whoever else I liked. I found the Afro-Haitian Ballet troupe and the opening act was Roland Kirk. Roland got there in the afternoon. He was a very strong personality, blind from birth I think, who wore very bizarre sunglasses and long African robes with a tribal cap. He was very outspoken about black and white injustice, racism, brotherhood, and equality. But angry. Nina Simone-angry.

He came in the afternoon with his manager, who was white. Just to check the sound in the hall. He left and the manager came up to me and said, "There could be a little problem. You better talk to Rahsaan." I didn't know who Rahsaan was. Then Roland Kirk called me. He said, "Bill Graham? *Rahsaan*." So I knew who it was.

I said, "Do we have a problem here? We better solve it. What's the problem?"

He said, "It's my name, man. I changed my name and I want it on the marquee. The name is *Rahsaan* Roland Kirk."

I put up *R-A-H-S-A-A-N*, little space, *R-O-L-A-N-D K-I-R-K*. The problem was that I only had eighteen spaces in each line and three lines. Jefferson Airplane was one line. Afro-Haitian Ballet was the next line. I abbreviated "ballet" to "B-L-T." Rahsaan Roland Kirk was seventeen letters and then there were the two spaces in between. I said, "You can have R. Roland Kirk. Rahsaan R. Kirk. R. R. Kirk. How do you want it?"

He kept saying, "*Rahsaan Roland Kirk*. That's what I want on the marquee. See, that's just my *name*. That ain't the name of my band."

I said, "What's the name of your band?"

He said, "Rahsaan Roland Kirk and his All-Star Vibrations Society."

"Roland," I said.

Now every time I would say, "Roland," he would interrupt me and say, "*Rahsaan*, baby. *Rahsaan*."

I said, "Rahsaan, for the amount I'm paying you, I could invest in a new marquee. You're a great artist and I don't want to insult you but I only have three lines."

He said, "Hey, man. Those rock and roll guys and that dance group don't mean nothin' to me. I want the name of my *group* on that marquee."

We went around and around and he said, "Better find a solution because otherwise, I ain't playin'."

As he was talking, I said, "I guarantee your name will be on the marquee tonight. I give you my word."

I went to Jim Haynie and I said, "Find a long piece of wood. Eight feet by two feet. Write on both sides 'Rahsaan Roland Kirk and his All-Star Vibrations Society.' Paint in the letters. Hang the sign under the middle of the marquee."

When he walked into the Fillmore, the sign was there. Rahsaan was very happy. The manager was very happy. Because when they got to the theater, the marquee, which still had only three lines of eighteen spaces each, read, "JEFFERSON AIRPLANE, AFRO-HAITIAN BALLET, AND SEE BELOW."

JONATHAN KAPLAN: The best show I ever saw at Fillmore East, just from an interest point of view, was Roland Kirk opening for Jethro Tull. Here was Roland Kirk, a *genius*. Without question, the greatest musician that ever set foot inside the Fillmore. Just in terms of sheer technical brilliance. He could play *anything*.

And here was this very white, very nice English guy. Ian Anderson. Very bright and very sardonic, who picked up the flute because he figured that was how he was going to be a rock star. Because there were already too many guitarists. Basically, he copied Roland Kirk. One of his many styles was Ian Anderson's only style.

Roland Kirk was getting paid maybe one eighth of what Jethro Tull was getting. After the first night, Roland Kirk was in a *rage* the whole time. He would get the audience going by saying, "Who's this?" And he would play somebody's style and they would guess. And he would say, "You funky, stupid white-ass motherfuckers!"

And then he would play something else and he would insult them when they guessed right. And then he would break a chair. We would say, *"Here comes the chair."* And he would break the chair. But the music was unbelievable. He played a song called *"Blackness."* Then he said, "You only play it on the *black* keys of the piano, you motherfuckers."

It could have happened to some un-nice guy. Some snot rag. But Ian Anderson happened to be a nice guy. Roland Kirk would say, "Who's this?" And he would play all of Jethro Tull's songs in like two minutes. *Better* than them. And he would say, "That's right. How come I'm getting paid *one eighth* of what those guys are getting?"

The thing is that the guy could just be standing backstage and he would have two saxophones and some new African instrument he had found. Just him warming up would make you cry. The guy had such poetry inside of him. Yet his exterior was so rough. His music was *so* extraordinary. There was nothing like it in that place *ever*.

BILL: I liked Ten Years After very much as a band but one aspect of their show personified a lot of my difficulty with rock and roll. The drum solo. The endless, seemingly nonmusical drum solo. Not that theirs was worse than any other. It was not even really bad drumming. It was just like eating dry Cheerios without milk and fruit. I wanted to set an example for all the bands as to what *real* drumming was all about.

So I flew to Las Vegas. Through a friend, I was introduced to Buddy Rich and we went to have dinner. He was playing there with Frank Sinatra

The "Sultan of Psychedelia," a picture that originally appeared in the June 1968 *Playboy* in a regular column designed to take note of who was new and hip on the scene. [Gene Anthony]

Bill and his wife Bonnie in the office of the Fillmore West, listening for the sound of David's heart. [Jim Marshall]

One of the famous touch football games in Central Park, prior to a free concert in 1968. Jim Haynie is to the right of Bill. [Ken Greenberg]

At Woodstock, explaining how things should work to Michael Lang, one of the "organizers." [Jim Marshall]

Introducing Traffic at Fillmore East, circa 1971. Steve Winwood on guitar. [John Olson]

Bill at the press conference announcing the closing of the Fillmore East, April 1971.
[Amalie R. Rothschild]

The end of an era: Second Avenue and Sixth Street, New York, June 1971.
[Amalie R. Rothschild]

Playing his only instrument during one of the closing shows at Fillmore West. [Michael Zagaris]

Bill, Jo Bergman, and Peter Rudge (with security man Stan Moore behind them) walk the mean streets outside Winterland as the Stones get ready to play within, 1972. [Jim Marshall]

Keith Richards, Alan Dunn, Mick Jagger, and Jerry Pompili in the Winterland dressing room, just before the band goes onstage. [Ken Regan/Camera 5]

With Elliot Roberts and a bearded David Geffen on the Crosby, Stills, Nash, and Young tour, Chicago, 1974. [Ken Regan/Camera 5]

Introducing Bob Dylan at the SNACK concert in the old Kezar stadium, San Francisco. Photographer Joel Bernstein stands in the background. [Ken Regan/Camera 5]

A meeting of the minds: with Francis Coppola and Marlon Brando, backstage at SNACK. [Michael Zagaris]

With Pete Townshend, the late Keith Moon, and Roger Daltrey in October 1976, when The Who and the Grateful Dead played together at Oakland Coliseum. [Michael Zagaris]

With a flower in his favorite hat as he talks to Kris Kristofferson and Barbra Streisand during the filming of *A Star Is Born* in Tempe, Arizona, March 1976. [Gregory Crowder]

at the time. I told him I ran a place called the Fillmore in San Francisco and that on this certain show, I had a headliner from England, a group that was very good but they always did a drum solo I didn't care for. I told Buddy I wanted to introduce his music to these kids. But that I also wanted them all to see what a drummer *really* did. What a real drummer was all about.

He said, "*Fuck* rock and roll! Those fuckin' *kids. Fuck them.* These fuckin' asshole rock drummers can't hold *one* stick *or* my dick." He just went on and on. "Those fucking pieces of shit make all these fucking millions of dollars . . ." Buddy didn't like rock and roll too much.

The regular price for the middle act at that time was thirty-five hundred a night. I said, "I'd like to offer you five thousand a night because you're Buddy Rich and it would be an honor to have you in our room. But I want to let you know that the act before and the act after you will be rock and roll. So it may be tough for you."

"What do you mean? The *audience? Fuck 'em.* You just pay me. We'll play."

The night of the show, Sea Train opened. We set up for Buddy Rich. Little old-fashioned bandstands to hold up the songbooks. Which the kids had never seen before. We set up this little midget drum kit for Buddy. One bass, one little snare, bang bang, that was it. I went into the dressing room to say hello to him and his band was all in cardigan jackets with Hawaiian shirts with big flowers on them. Buddy was wearing a turtleneck. The kids outside were already yelling, "*TEN YEARS AFTER! ALVIN! WE WANT ALVIN!*" He heard this and he said, "The *fuck* are they yelling out there? *Assholes.*" On and on.

I said, "Buddy, you know, I grew up in New York and I used to sneak into the Metropole to see you play so don't take this wrong. But would you let me see your song titles?"

"*What?* Are you *out* of your *fucking* mind?"

I said, "I'm not going to tell you what to do. But if you would consider playing something familiar to them, it would help."

"They don't know *shit* out there."

I said, "Buddy, can I see your book?"

"*Here!*"

I went through the book and he had "Norwegian Wood" in there. The Beatles' song. I said, "Would you consider the possibility of opening with 'Norwegian Wood'? They know the song and it would just *hit* them right off."

"All *right*," he said. "*All right.*"

The band came out and Buddy was standing on the side, waiting to be introduced. I said, "Check this out. Would you welcome please, the very best there is . . . Buddy Rich and his Orchestra." Buddy sat down at the drums. As I was making the introduction, people were screaming, *"ALVIN! TEN YEARS AFTER! ROCK AND ROLL!"* The brass section stood up and played that opening riff from "Norwegian Wood." Then Buddy took off. *Bam bam bam bam boom boom boom whanga whanga whanga boom!* The entire room *swerved.* All the kids going to get something to eat turned around and looked at the stage. Buddy fucking *wailed! Dadah! Bababah! Lahaladam! Mopah!*

The room was *mesmerized.* They were eating something they had never eaten before and they could not believe how good it was. They were just *glued* to the stage. He held that room for an *hour.* And he was great. He went off and the kids went wild. *"MORE! MORE! BUDDY!"* I went into the dressing room. I said, "Buddy, they really . . ."

"Fuck 'em!"

Now some of his musicians had *really* loved it. They'd had the time of their lives. Because they were in "Weed Land." It was *home.* After Vegas, they never thought they'd see anything like this again. I said, "Listen, you *got* to go back out. Buddy, come *on.*"

He said, "Nah nah nah."

But his other musicians were gesturing that I should keep after him. They *wanted* to go back out. I said, "Buddy, I'm going to *take* you out there."

"No, you're not."

I picked him up and carried him out and put him down right next to the drum kit and they went *crazy.*

Now I had prepared myself for what came next. I had rehearsed it eight thousand times. We were now in the break, setting up for Ten Years After. I walked into their dressing room and I said hello to Alvin Lee and Leo Lyons, their bass player, and Chick Churchill, their keyboard guy.

Ric Lee, their drummer, was sitting at his drum pad going *brrrr, brrrrr* with his sticks. Warming up at that black rubber pad.

He said, "Hey, Bill. How you doin'?"

I shook his hand and put my other hand on his shoulder. I said, "Ric, how are you? Hey, *man.* Can't *wait* for your solo tonight, baby!"

He didn't do one. They walked out and played a set of harsh rock and roll and if he took three seconds to go off by himself, that was it. It was *great.*

6.

JONATHAN KAPLAN: There were certain artists who came out and did a different show every show. It was not the same *shtick.* When Crosby,

Stills, Nash, and Young played Fillmore East, there was this moment in the show where it looked like byplay. Steve Stills was playing and there was a stand-up bass and he would pick it up and put it on his lap like a guitar. The other three guys would pretend to be *so* surprised and they would laugh and the audience would love it, saying, "Isn't this *great?*" *Every* fucking night. We would be on the headsets and we would say, "Here comes the bass bit." And there it would be.

I remember Bill coming out at this meeting before CSNY played there. He said, "You know, these are the American Beatles. Crosby, Stills, Nash, and Young. I want this to be *very* special." Because it was like a week. They were doing one show a night for six nights during the first week in June.

Now, everyone liked their music. But Bill was carrying the contract with him. He said, "You see this? This is the rider." It was like the size of the New York phone book. One the one hand, we were supposed to be nice to them. But on the other hand, he was waving the rider at us.

ALAN ARKUSH: Crosby, Stills, Nash, and Young were supposed to play the Fillmore and Bill called a meeting of the whole crew. He said, "Crosby, Stills, Nash, and Young are coming here and I want to tell you, they're a wonderful band. But *they're* what's wrong with the business." He gave this whole talk about how groups thought they were bigger than ever and too big for him and they were demanding an inordinate amount of money. It was like his "State of the Rock Business" speech, and I think that was sort the beginning of his disenchantment.

He said, "There's going to be a huge crush for tickets and they're going to make lots of demands on us as the people who run the theater. Let's not let our personal feelings in." And that was it. He dismissed us.

There was a huge line for tickets and we did all kinds of things to make it easy for the kids. We can cartoons while they waited in the theater to buy tickets. I can't imagine that happening anymore. The kids were given numbers and they were entertained *while* they waited in the theater.

DANNY OPATOSHU: There were pretentious groups that gave you head-aches, like Crosby, Stills, and Nash and Young. We would have to put out the Persian rugs for them on stage and they wouldn't even use our sound system because they had devised a new one in Marin County. That was when we got obnoxious. It was, "Don't tell us what to do because we're pop stars. Don't tell *us* about sound systems."

JONATHAN KAPLAN: The requirement was that each one of them had to have a different cuisine catered in their dressing room every night from a different land. So Stephen had Jewish and Graham had Italian and David had Chinese and Neil had Japanese. Then the next night, it all switched around. They never ate the food anyway. But one only wanted Coors in his cooler and another only wanted Bud. If the right one wasn't in the cooler, they would be out the door.

And the treatment of women. I'm not going to name names, but at a time when I and most people were certainly aware of the position in which women had been placed in a male-dominated society, rock and roll was maybe a step down from football in the way that women were treated.

ALAN ARKUSH: They wanted extra spotlights and they wanted their PA and we had to turn the whole theater upside down. The lighting at Fillmore East was great and the sound was great, and it didn't sound as good with their PA because their PA was not tuned to the walls. We repainted the whole stage. We did *everything* for them. We had their equipment all set up and we were waiting for them to come do the sound check and their road manager said, "Where's the Persian carpet?"

We said, "*What* Persian carpet?"

He said, "We *want* a Persian carpet."

We said, "It's not in the rider."

He said, "Well, it was agreed that there would be a Persian carpet."

A carpet on stage for them to *stand* on. So we said, "Okay, we'll get you the Persian carpet." Luckily, we had gotten one for Ravi Shankar so we went back and got his Persian carpet. We brought it back down and took all the equipment off the stage. We rolled out the carpet and put all the equipment back on it. The road manager looked at the Persian carpet and he said, "It's dirty."

John Ford Noonan *snapped*. He said, "Sir, it's *dirty?* This Persian carpet is *dirty?* I'll fix it, *sir.*" This was typical Noonan. He jumped off the stage and ran the length of the theater to the front closet and got one of these industrial vacuum cleaners. On "Saturday Night Live" once, they did a gag with the two swinging guys from Russia using a *giant* Russian vacuum cleaner and that was what it looked like.

Noonan threw the vacuum cleaner on his shoulders and he ran back down the length of the theater to the stage. He plugged it in, got down on his hands and knees, and started vacuuming *every* square inch of that fucking carpet. I mean, he vacuumed that carpet like his *life* depended on it. Meanwhile, in walked Crosby, Stills, Nash, and Young. Everyone was now really embarrassed because John was going crazy. Their road manager was going, "It's fine, John. It's *fine*."

John was saying, "*No*, it *isn't*, sir. No, it *isn't*. We're going to do this *right*. We're going to do this for the Crosby, Stills, Nash!" He kept calling them "*The* Crosby, Stills, Nash." He finished vacuuming and he took the cable and wound it around the vacuum cleaner and threw it over his shoulders.

"Sir?" he said. "Does *he* like it?"

By now, Bill was there. Everybody was looking down at their shoes. The road manager said, "It's fine, John."

John said, "Thank you, sir."

Then he turned to Crosby, Stills, and Nash and he said, "You know, even if you guys were *good*, this would be too much work."

And he walked off. Bill said, "I've got a phone call," and he got out of there. It was *great*. For the rest of the time they were there, John called them "the Supremes." Like, "Would the Supremes like some more food?"

Noonan always really had it in for David Crosby. Because in an article about Altamont, Crosby had said that if a musician had been killed, *real* dues would have had to have been paid. Noonan took exception to that. It was like a musician was *above* a normal human being. All week long, Noonan just let David Crosby have it.

JOHN FORD NOONAN: The first half of their show was acoustic. They would stand up or sit on stools and play acoustic. They kept making me re-center the rug. I remember them saying, "This is *not* center stage." And they would make me move the rug two inches this way. And then I would have to move it two inches *that* way.

GRAHAM NASH: CSNY in New York at Fillmore East. These were some of the best shows we *ever* did. Bill was very accommodating, I must say. Because we had Leo Makota working for us and Leo wanted holes punched in walls for speakers and special things and stuff. I mean, we were a funky band but we were quite adamant about getting what we wanted to do our show best. And Bill was *very* accommodating.

One of the funniest things I remember was that we would always do encores and then get all the way up into the dressing room and then Bill would always want us to come back and do another one. One night, we had done *three* encores. We felt, "Fuck Bill. You know? We just want to smoke a joint here and relax." We had just done a great show and our shows were long to begin with at that point. So under the dressing room door came a hundred-dollar bill. Followed by another one, followed by another one. We were smoking and looking at these hundred-dollar bills coming under the door.

Neil picked one up. He said, "*More*, Bill." Finally, eight hundred bucks came under the door. For us to do another encore. You know?

Other nights, he'd written the greatest little notes and stuck them under the door. By this point, we were locking the door and hiding from him. Because when you're dead, you're dead. If you made eye contact with Bill, you would do anything he wanted. So it became a game.

What Neil wanted to do was take the eight hundred bucks and go back out and do an encore and throw the eight hundred-dollar bills into the audience. I said, *"Neil!* This is *New York!* People will get *killed!"* In the stampede. So sanity prevailed.

I'm sure there were times when Bill thought we were *schmucks* or too demanding or we asked for too much money. But he liked our band. He understood I think the social importance of the band and always encouraged us to do what we were doing. At that time, it was just happening for us. The superstar stuff. Having been in the Byrds and the Hollies and the Buffalo Springfield and having attained a certain amount of notoriety and stardom before, I don't think that super-group stuff wore on us at all. Not at that point. We were having a good time. A *great* time.

BILL: The first night they played, the audience went *crazy.* It was like, "Hey, wow. They love us? We'll do an encore." They did the encore. By the second night, they said, "We don't want to do any more encores." The third night, one of them told me they were *not* coming out. They locked themselves in the dressing room. I slipped a note under their door that said, "Listen, for the sake of my Swiss bank account, please do an encore." They came out. Then the next night, I put another one under the door that said, "The world will never forgive me if you don't come out to do an encore tonight." Some silly bullshit like that.

Every night because I asked, they did an encore. They came in on the last night and Crosby said, "Bill, we're going to play a long, extended show tonight, with *no* encore."

I said, "David, I've said this to you before. A *thousand* times. You can do a *nineteen*-hour show tonight. Without an encore, they'll be disappointed. That's dessert. That's the extra orgasm."

"Nah. We're not doing it. Bill, we're just *not.*"

"You want to spite the world? *Fine.*"

They did the show. They were really great in those days. Their voices. Elliot Roberts, their manager, came to see me. He said, "Bill. You want my advice? Don't push it tonight."

I let the applause go on after the show for three or four minutes. I knew Fillmore East audiences. When they said, "You're coming out again," *you came out!* They were clapping away like mad and I went up the stairs. Elliot was there and he said, "Bill, they're *not* coming out."

I went back downstairs again. Three flights. I went back up. I did that two or three more times. "Fellas? *Fellas* . . ." One of them said, "Let it go, Bill. Let it go. Don't push it." They were still applauding out there but it had dropped a level. I stuck my hand out from the wings. Just my hand. I waved to the crowd and it went back up again. I went upstairs again and Neil Young said, "Put the house lights up all the way."

I said, "They *are* all the way up and they're *still* applauding. Don't you know what you've done to them? What a great night you've given them? Come on out. It's your last night." I was talking to the door.

Neil said, "Just let it go, Bill. And they'll go away."

I said, "Yeah. But it's fifteen minutes *already.*"

It had been about ten. I went back down the stairs. Michael Ahearn was the stage manager. I said, "Michael, I'm going up again and they're going to say the audience is getting quieter. At the count of ten, gradually lower the lights all the way down, as if they're coming out again." I said, "Just count the time out. One second. Two seconds. Three." I raced up the stairs. I said, "*Fellas,* come *on! Come on!* They're *still* out there. They're *not* getting quieter."

"They *are* . . ."

"They're *not.* They're going *crazier.*" Seven. Eight. Nine. "Open the fuckin' door. Just listen." *Ten.* They opened the door. "YEOOOOOW-EEEEEEE *MORE MORE MORE YEAHHHHH!!*"

I remember David Crosby looking at the other guys. "Oh, *fuck!*" he said. "They *still* want us. Let's go."

They did three encores. One of the great moments in sports.

JOSHUA WHITE: It changed for me. The height for the Joshua Light Show in terms of the music and the theater was when The Who played *Tommy* at Fillmore East for a week. The low point was when Crosby, Stills, Nash, and Young came in with a Chip Monck package. Artistically, Chip and I had fought with each other at Fillmore East. At the time, it was like two egos battling with each other.

We got along and we didn't get along and together we created the Fillmore East. We were sort of the two techs who divvied up the space and we had a begrudging relationship. But there was no room there for him to expand his lighting. So Bill did a smart thing. He took him to San Francisco and had Chip redo the Carousel Ballroom and make it into Fillmore West.

But now Chip had come back from San Francisco with Crosby, Stills, and Nash. With him came a wave that was working against me because Crosby, Stills, Nash, and Young were a *lighting* show. They came out and they were purposely surrounded by black. It was the return of Chip

Monck. I saw James Taylor coming in the bookings and other people like that. The *folkies*. The music was changing. It was the seventies.

I was particularly offended because Crosby, Stills, Nash went from being Crosby, Stills, Nash to Crosby, Stills, Nash, and *Young* to Crosby, Stills, Nash, Young, *Taylor*, and *Reeves*. It was like this expanding-contracting thing. These guys were stoned up the wazoo and they came out and sang flat and the audience *loved* them. Absolutely loved them and that was the end. I couldn't stand the fact they could come out and sing badly in a black space with Chip's lights and nobody missed the light show. I never made the mistake of thinking the light show *was* the theater. But when there were three acts on the bill, there was a place for the light show because it provided a visual connective throughout. Especially when Bill was doing his creative booking. But creative booking was going. He *had* to book Crosby, Stills, and Nash. It was also clear that the next time they came around, they were going to play Madison Square Garden.

I knew I got out at the right time. I was really happy to be out of it. Because I saw The Who do a lousy show at the Metropolitan Opera House and the audience went *nuts*. I went to Fillmore East and Crosby, Stills, and Nash were stoned and sang flat and the audience went *nuts*. To me, that indicated that times were changing. We were now applauding the *presence* of the artist. Rather than the performance.

BILL:	You put four big talents like that together, what do you expect? Peaceful snakes? These men were stars *before* they formed the group. They were the first ones to do it that way. The first stars who joined together to become even bigger as a group than they had been before.

It was difficult because these four stars did individual pieces within the framework of the show. Each had their solo set. And the maneuvering never stopped. "Well, *I* don't want to go after *him*. *He* went over well last night. He didn't go over *too* well so *he* doesn't set them up for me *right*. Does *Graham* go first? *Neil* goes second. *Who* goes first? Then how about *Stills*? *Who goes where when?*" There was a lot of that.

Everybody came to these shows. They were the group that brought *everybody* in to see them. They were the El Dorado guys from Southern California. Crosby, Stills, Nash, and Young. I remember Pete Townshend even came down the last night. Back then, Pete never went *anywhere*.

GRAHAM NASH:	I remember one night that week when Dylan came to see us there at Fillmore East and we all knew "The Big D" was out there. So we said, "Listen. Let's not get carried away. Let's just play. Let's just do the one song that each of us has been doing."

What we did was an acoustic set, then one individual song each, and then an electric set. Because Dylan was there, Stephen did *four* songs. I don't know how David and Neil felt but I was *outraged*. We had a game plan. Follow the game plan and we'll be in Fat City, right? But Stephen wouldn't follow the plan.

So I was arguing like fuck with him. This was during intermission. Bill was standing there. Me and Stephen were fucking *screaming* at each other. Stephen had a Budweiser can in his hand and he was slowly crushing it to a flat thing. It was all foaming and dripping over and Bill was looking at us and he was going, "Oh, *God*." And we went back out and did the best electric set we had ever done. I think that was the Tuesday night.

With us, it was always that way. Stephen has always been crazy. I have never ceased to be amazed by the man. I think if Stephen was not Stephen Stills, he would have been committed long ago. I really do. I think his fame and his notoriety and his talent have shielded him from being out there on the street. I really do.

7.

PETER RUDGE: It was 1970. The Who had just made *Tommy*. Kit Lambert, another great genius, another of my true idols, sent me over to New York for reasons known only to himself. He said, "The Who have made this rock opera. Go there and find somewhere for The Who to play. Why don't you get the Metropolitan Opera House?"

So I walked into the Metropolitan Opera House. Sir Rudolf Bing, a countryman of mine, was there. For some reason, I got an appointment with him. It may have been the beginning of him completely flipping. But to cut a long story short, he agreed to let us have the hall.

Bill sensed something historical was about to take place. He said, "You need the Fillmore East family." Right? You *need*.

I went for it. I said, "Nice touch." The Who at the Met with the Fillmore East. Everyone was happy. Only Bill wanted his name in bigger letters than anyone else on the poster. Basically, Bill did it because he wanted to help. Not for money.

Then we took the *Tommy* show out to San Francisco. I said, "Right, Bill. Now it's your *turn*. Find us somewhere to play in San Francisco." We played in the Berkeley Community Theater with the Jefferson Airplane sitting in the fourth row. It was Bill's idea to put these big spotlights up behind The Who and shine them into the house. We paid for it but it was Bill's idea and The Who took it with them when they left.

But the deal was worse than any other deal on the tour. Because it was Bill Graham.

As it all went along, me and Bill began a relationship. We used to spar and we used to fight and it was egos. Every time The Who would come around for the next two years, I would be thinking, "Do I have to go through this aggravation with Bill Graham?" Because whenever I think of Bill Graham, I think of aggravation. It had to be. Even if it was not there, it was created. It may have been created by me at times. But it was not there with other promoters. With Bill, the acts were almost inconsequential.

The great thing about Graham was that he always managed to convince or con the artist and the manager that the place was more important than the act. And he did that brilliantly. For *him*. Whatever venue Bill Graham had was the attraction. And you were lucky to be playing there. To play there, you should take 10 percent less than any other promoter was offering. Because that 10 percent would, as Bill Graham knew, allow him to buy bigger apples, more dartboards, nicer sofas, and all the acts would go back and say, "*Good*. When you go see Bill Graham, you get treated like a *king*." What the acts didn't realize was that *they* were paying for it. For the *privilege* of playing at Bill Graham's place. I could accept that. What rankled me was that Bill never accepted that anyone else understood what he was doing.

The acts would say, "We *must* play for Bill Graham. Last time we played for Bill Graham, we got *two* billiard tables, *three* dartboards, fifteen palm trees, all from Bill's own company, and three leather couches, all also from his own company. Fourteen security guys. The offer of a security guy in our hotel as well. We *want* to play for Bill." So you played for 50 percent as opposed to 60 percent. Bill got on to that very quickly and he didn't ever think that people really knew what he was doing.

But it didn't matter with the acts. It was very hard to convince the acts *not* to play for Bill Graham. Because Bill always got good people. He got attractive people for the acts, be it Jerry Pompili or anyone else. They took a little bit of Bill Graham. You always knew one of these people would be there to take you out to the clubs and Bill would have an in at those clubs. He understood that playing a gig was not just those ninety minutes the act spent on stage. It was based on the twelve hours before and the twenty-four after. They were just as important. And Bill had his town *wired*.

Bill would go to great pains to make sure he did a lot of it himself. As opposed to every other promoter who would say, "Oh, *Gary*. Oh, *Jim*. Oh, *Cindy*, take care of that." Bill would get on the phone and he could turn

an innocent reservation at a little dingy blues club into one of the greatest
performances since Kennedy got Khrushchev to back down.

He played it like the conductor of a symphony orchestra. He was a
virtuoso. Because of that, Bill Graham became even bigger than San
Francisco for the acts. They would say, "Are we playing for Bill Graham?"
Not, "Are we playing San Francisco?" *"Are we playing for Bill Graham?"*

PETE TOWNSHEND: Bill did that thing with the Super Troopers for
Tommy when we played for him in the Berkeley Community Theater.
Fucking great sounding hall. It's very interesting from my point of view.
I remember three details of that evening. One of which was that backstage, I got my fresh supply of Dr. Wong Tea. Bill got one of his guys to
pick it up for me. 'Cause I used to get the concentrate which was never
as good as the straight stuff from Dr. Wong. It was an herbal remedy. Dr.
Wong had more Mercedes than I'll ever own. He was a rich man. The
stuff cost two hundred dollars a month and he had half of the San
Francisco Sufi movement drinking this tea. Powerful stuff. Extraordinary
stuff. Among other things, it had ginseng in it.

The second thing was that I remember that somehow Bill had sorted
out all the important people. I had left no list at all on the back gate.
Absolutely true. *Nothing.* And he had let in all the people that I wanted
to see and none of the people that I didn't want to see.

The third thing was that he had *two* dressing rooms. That was quite
unique at the time. It was the first hospitality room I had ever come
across outside of a festival. In which there were fondues. There was a
meat fondue and a cheese one. What's great before you go on to give a
concert is to have some very quick-acting protein. Raw steak or pasta is
good and they were both *there.*

These three details were more important to me than when we went out
and suddenly the curtain rose and there was four thousand watts of light
on the band. Of course, we picked up that technique and we've used it
ever since.

8.

PETER WOLF: One of the things Frank Barsalona did was mention to
Bill Graham that he was going to sign the J. Geils Band. Through that
word-of-mouth thing and subculture information, Bill had heard about
us. He told Frank, "I've heard great things about the band. Sight unseen,
I'll premiere them at Fillmore East."

Now, to play New York in those days was like you see in the movies
and vaudeville where the guy goes, "Hey, honey! We got the *Palace*." It

was like "Hey, man. I just got off the phone with Frank. We got the *Fillmore*." It was like, "*Wow!* This is *it*, man." It was amazing because we knew all it would take was one good night playing to the right crowd in that milieu. Since there wasn't Kurt Loder every five minutes with the rock and roll news on MTV, it was all word-of-mouth. So if we got a good buzz going or created a good first impression, we would have the possibility of having a career in front of us. We would be able to do exciting things. Which was all we wanted. To play in places that had integrity and to be considered a band with integrity. To be *artists*. That was what our whole thing was about.

We rented this Ryder van and we had a station wagon. Everybody drove down to New York and we got these guys to act like our crew. Previous to this, we had just set up our own stuff. The first thing was "Where are we going to stay?" This was the *Fillmore* and real important. The most important show *ever*. So we ended up deciding we were all going to stay at the Holiday Inn on Fifty-seventh Street. Because we had finally made *it*, man. We were even getting *paid* for this. So it was like eight, nine guys—three rooms.

Now, if memory serves me wrong, which I'm sure it doesn't, we checked into the hotel. Even that was bizarre. We had never really checked into a hotel before. The band never had stayed in a *hotel*. We had stayed in floppy little motels out in New England. But to actually be in New York where there was a bellman to take your *suitcase!* I mean, this was all very *strange*. It was like *New York!*

We were in a hotel and we were going to do a sound check. We went down to Fillmore East and I remember on the wall were the times for the set changes. Three acts doing two acts a night. "Here's your dressing room, here's the stage manager, here is the light guy *and* the sound guy, so . . ." This was *big* time for the band. We were the middle act. Sir Lord Baltimore was the opening act. We played just before Black Sabbath.

DEE ANTHONY: I made one major mistake with Bill. I got involved with some people in New Jersey who were producing this group from Brooklyn called Sir Lord Baltimore. Loud, horrible, I mean I can't tell you. My friend was like forty-five thousand dollars into the band and I said I would help him with it and I went in for like twenty thousand. We had a lead guitarist who said he was going to out-Page Jimmy Page and out-Clap Clapton. When he got out in front of an audience, his right hand froze. Behind his amplifier, he had a mirror. He would fix his hair and get everything all primped up and go out and everything would go wrong. It was like pots and pans.

ALAN ARKUSH: Dee Anthony had a group called Sir Lord Baltimore that Frank Barsalona booked into the Fillmore East. They were *so* awful. As we were moving their equipment, John Ford Noonan found a book on how to play guitar on the guitar player's amplifier. For the rest of the weekend, Noonan kept asking him what page he was on.

DEE ANTHONY: Now, Bill would put on *anything* I wanted in there. He gave every band a chance. They would open, go in the pocket, and headline. If they progressed, within a year they would have a hit album. Bill was responsible for all that. After Sir Lord Baltimore played their first set, I didn't know if I should go back to Bill's office, or what. Frank called backstage and told me to come there. I walked in and Frank was sitting at Bill's desk. The band had just played and they were *awful*. I didn't know *what* to say. Remember, I had given Bill Ten Years After, Jethro Tull, Traffic, you name it. Frank had given him the biggest bands *ever*. Every band we had, we had broken with Bill.

It was dead quiet in there. Bill was standing behind Frank and walking back and forth. I sat down and Frank was snickering and we didn't know what was going to come out of it.

Bill turned around and he said, *"Pus! Pus! Pus!* I was trying to think of one word to describe that band. *PUS!"*

We fell on the floor. They were doing body music or something that you could feel on your skin. I said, "I don't feel nothin'. What did I get myself into here?"

PETER WOLF: We were coming back from the sound check and Seth Justman was feeling a little bit ill and nauseous. I had heard about this doctor on Forty-second Street who was one of those Dr. Feelgoods who were around at the time. Now, I didn't know this guy was one of the *injecting* doctors. He was very famous. All the Borscht Belt comedians, you would see their pictures on his wall. All the guys who were amphetamine addicts.

We were just two guys in town and Seth was not feeling well. Seth went into the inner office and I didn't know that the guy gave Seth a shot. Of something. A shot of something. Seth and I went out and he was feeling better. I said, "Man, we're going to play, I got to do something *real* special. I'm going to gold-leaf and gold spray-paint my shoes. *Got* to have gold shoes, you know?"

We were on Fifty-seventh Street now, like a block from the hotel and Seth was going to get some pills with a prescription the doctor gave him. I went in with him and I said, "Let's see if this drugstore has gold spray paint." They told me the shoe store next door did. "Great. I'll go next door. Be right back."

I was standing in the shop getting the paint when this woman came running in. "Are you with that fellow with the long hair?" she asked me. I said, *"Yeah."* She said, *"Quick, quick."* I ran next door. Seth had passed out. He fell face-first smack onto this counter. We were playing the Fillmore and Seth was in Roosevelt Hospital and they had to stitch up his head where he cracked it.

Bill may have come to the sound check but I don't remember meeting him until he came into the dressing room just before we went on that night. It was a real important buzz. He said, "Hey, guys, you know, I've heard a lot about you and I'm real excited to have you here." We all introduced ourselves and there he was. You know? *Bill Graham.*

It was that he took the time. It was like we had really made it because he said to us that tonight was real important to *him* and that he was really looking forward to hearing us play. He had heard good things about the sound check. But he came to our dressing room. Which became an important formality for me. Throughout the whole J. Geils Band time, I wouldn't go out until Bill came in. And he always did.

Because we were *so* nervous. All our relatives were around and old friends from The Bronx that I grew up with in high school. There was this *buzz.* Frank Barsalona was going to be there along with people from the record company and basically, we were still unheard in New York. Sir Lord Baltimore did their set and I remember coming down the stairs and getting ready to start up and the audience was screaming for Black Sabbath. *"Black Sabbath!* Black . . . *Sabbath!* Black . . . *Sabbath!"* Everybody was shouting "Oz-*zee!"* and this, that, and the other. They were going *nuts.*

Bill had come down the stairs with us. He knew how nervous we were. He got up to the microphone and he said, "Ladies and Gentlemen, for the first time in New York, the J. Geils Band. Please give them a warm welcome."

The place just kept going, *"BLACK* SABBATH! BLACK *SABBATH! BLACK SABBATH!"*

Bill got furious. He went back up to the microphone and he said, "Listen, I *personally* invited this band down. I've never heard 'em play, but I've been told only good things about them. It seems that some people here are just interested in seeing Black Sabbath. If you are interested only in seeing Black Sabbath and don't have the patience to spend the time to give this band an opportunity, will you please leave the theater? We'll refund your money or give you a stub so you can come back for

Black Sabbath. But would you please shut the fuck up and give this band a chance?"

You know, it quieted down. We opened with "Snowcone," an Albert Collins song. Either that or "Icebreaker." They were both instrumentals. We would always open by doing one or two Chicago-style instrumentals. Then Magic Dick, our harmonica player, would sing a song. Then the band would do a little fanfare and out I would come.

It was funny because one time we were playing with Janis Joplin in Worcester and the band was really cooking on the opening instrumental. She came downstairs because she heard the band. She looked at me and here was this guy standing on the side of the stage dressed in patent leather shoes and a ruffled shirt and she said, "Man, who *are* these guys?"

I said, "Oh, they're a good band. J. Geils Band."

She said, "*Shit,* man. They can *really* cook."

I said, "Yeah."

She said, "Man, I *dig* this band."

Just at that moment, there was the introduction for myself. I said, "See you later, honey." And *boom!* I went on stage and started to do this old Chicago blues number called "Love Me." She left the stage and went out into the auditorium. She sat right in front of the stage and watched the whole show.

I remember that first night at Fillmore East, on the third encore, Bill came rushing up to us yelling, *"Go back out! Go back out!"* He became like our coach. After that night, we played Fillmore West and Fillmore East more times in a shorter space than any other band. For a while there, we almost became like the house band.

FRANK BARSALONA: They really did sensationally that first night. I went into Bill's office and we were talking and everybody else was in there. Fred Lewis, their manager, was in there and like sort of timid. I said, "Fred, come over here and say hello to Bill." As we were talking, Ahmet Ertegun came in. He said, "Hello, how's everything? Is everybody happy? So? So? How did they do?" I was trying to introduce Fred Lewis but Ahmet was doing *shtick* to Bill and me and the assembled group.

BILL: Ahmet to me was the greatest raconteur. A genuinely great storyteller. With great style and great humanity. He came in that night with his entourage. Blue suit, white-on-white shirt, blue-on-blue tie, shoes polished. He looked like he had just won the dance contest somewhere. He came in and said, "Ah, *Bill!*" He knew J. Geils had just come off but he didn't know that their manager was standing right there. He said, "So Bill? What did you think? J. Geils Band, huh?"

Sonja, one of my sisters, taught me that in Hungarian, the top exclamation for anything positive or negative is to repeat the words. So I said, "Ahmet. The *J. Geils Band!* The *J. Geils Band!*"

On the second "*J. Geils Band!*" he cut in and said, "I *knew* it! They *sucked!* I knew I shouldn't have signed them. *Terrible,* huh? That Jerry Wexler . . ."

I said, "Ahmet, may I introduce you to the *manager* of the J. Geils Band?"

FRANK BARSALONA: I was trying to stop him. Bill was trying to stop him. Bill finally got up and went around the desk and said, "Ahmet, I'd like you to meet their manager, Fred Lewis." Without missing a thing, Ahmet turned and said, "But I *knew* this. *Fred,* how *are* you? I knew this was Fred. You see, Fred, this is our *shtick.* This is the game we play."

BILL: Ahmet did not lose a beat. He walked over to Fred, grabbed him by both shoulders, and gave him a hug. He slapped him lovingly on the cheek and said, "They were *great!*"

Fred said, "Did you *see* the set?"

"I would miss their set?" Ahmet said. "I wouldn't miss the *J. Geils* set."

In twelve seconds, Ahmet made this kid feel guilty about having even accused him of the crime. He convinced him that he had been kidding, that the whole thing he had said was a parody. Frank had to leave the room. Kip Cohen had to leave the room. They were both laughing so hard that they had to leave the room.

Chapter Eleven

Closing the Sacred Store

1.

BILL: I had gotten a call in the San Francisco office from Sol Hurok's secretary. Some people look up to heroes like Joe Namath or Joe DiMaggio. In those days, my hero was Sol Hurok. I had never met the man but I knew he was a Russian immigrant who had put on everything from the circus to the opera to the ballet. He was *the* guy. The secretary said, "Could Mr. Graham, when he has some time in New York, come see Mr. Hurok?" This was in the spring of 1971.

I went to New York on business and made an appointment to see Mr. Hurok. He was eighty-three at the time but still very active. I went to his office in midtown Manhattan with Kip Cohen and the assistant took us into Mr. Hurok's office. He said, "Mr. Graham, this is Mr. Hurok." Formal introductions, like an ambassadorial kind of thing, and then he left.

Mr. Hurok did not look up from his desk. He had a bunch of newspaper clippings there. Being a notorious upside-down reader, I saw the clippings were about me. Before he even looked up, Mr. Hurok pointed at the paper. Then he said, "It says here, you got lots guts and balls. S'true?"

That was his line. "It says here, you got lots guts and balls. S'true?"

To make a long story short, we started talking. He said, "I'll tell you what the problem is, Mr. Graham."

I said, "Please call me Bill."

He said, "Anyway, Mr. Graham . . ."

He had scheduled the ballet for later that spring in the Metropolitan Opera House. Because of a situation where a Soviet sailor had defected

329

from some ship off the coast of New England and what the American government had then done in terms of offering him political asylum, the ballet had canceled. He was stuck with a month's rent on the building, which came to something like two hundred thousand dollars. He said, "I need to fill it up and I had this idea. I read so much about your success at the Fillmore. I don't know anything about rock and roll but my associate said if we only took the best acts, the highest quality, that maybe we could do something together, you and me."

I said, "That would be *fantastic!*"

We started talking about the possibilities. With no disrespect intended, I explained to him that we lived in two separate worlds. When he asked for more time to make a decision about whether to do this, I explained to him, "Time is of the essence, because these groups are already making their plans for the summer and they make *big, big* money." When I told him that they would expect forty or fifty thousand dollars for a week at the opera house, it was hard for him to believe.

I said to him, "Isaac Stern or Nureyev may earn five to six thousand dollars a night and people think they are incredibly wealthy. But it's nothing compared to the earnings of the super rock groups." He didn't understand that because it was not his business.

FRANK BARSALONA: It was very interesting to see the interplay between Hurok and Graham because it was almost like the student looking up to the teacher. Which was a very funny thing. Hurok was a great promoter but he knew fuck-all about the rock business. Yet Bill was so impressed by Sol Hurok saying maybe his office should do more of these things. Like Bill really needed Sol Hurok.

I'm not putting down the old man because he was a wonderful guy. But Bill was considering going into business with Sol Hurok for no reason. I mean, what the fuck was Sol Hurok going to do for him?

The other thing was they couldn't decide about billing.

PATRICK STANSFIELD: Bill went into Sol Hurok's office. Here was this little man behind this enormous desk. And he looked at Bill and said, "So! I hear you got lots guts and balls!"

Bill said, "Mr. Hurok, all my life, you've been one of my idols. It's more than an honor to work with you as an associate. You are history and I'm just a kid." You know how Bill does that.

He said, "Never in the longest day of my life would I ever presume that my name would ever in any way eclipse yours on the billing. But on the poster, mine will not be one iota smaller than yours."

BILL: We got into a dialogue about billing for the producers. Out of respect for this man, I felt he should certainly be the number-one name and I should get secondary credit, as in "Sol Hurok *and* Bill Graham Present . . ." We had difficulties negotiating that. I waited and waited. I waited for three or four weeks. Finally, there was a decision made on their part that they would go along with the combination of his name and my name side-by-side with my name being second, which was certainly fine by me. I thought that since I would be choosing the acts, booking, negotiating, and *presenting* the acts, it would be nice for me to have my name on the poster and the ads.

I lost three valuable weeks because of his indecisiveness. I had already started contacting groups to tell them about the Met and how important it would be to have rock there for a month, in terms of the opera houses in Los Angeles and Chicago and Detroit. Places they could play in the future instead of the cement factories that passed for arenas in those cities.

When I started contacting the groups again, they said, "Well, we'll see and we'll try . . ." I tried to explain the importance of the month-long event but I had great difficulty convincing them. Over the years, a lot of them had said to me, "Gee, Bill. Let's do something *different*. Let's not just get on stage and blast away. Let's do something unique." But now that I was offering it to them, no one seemed eager to jump right in.

I came to New York and I decided to do nothing for two weeks but try to book the Met. I was going down the list of quality acts I had drawn up to bring in there. Frank Zappa. The Byrds. And of course I wanted the Band. I remember the next part like it was yesterday. I was in my office upstairs at Fillmore East. It was two o'clock in the morning on a Saturday night. I had asked Jon Taplin, the manager of the Band, to call me back. I was so thrilled. I was going to book the Metropolitan Opera House for a month and it was going to be a break for rock and roll and the acceptance of rock and roll in major buildings throughout the country.

Jon Taplin called me back at three in the morning and I said, "This is the gig. It's the Metropolitan Opera House. Eight shows a week, Monday through Saturday, with two audiences on Wednesday and Saturday. It's a highly unionized house with strong costs, security, rental, and what not. But it's the *Met*. Do you realize what a break it is that we can get rock and roll in there, with Sol Hurok and myself putting on the shows?"

Finally, he said, "What's the pay?"

I said, "The most you can make there is fifty grand a week for eight shows."

He said, "*Bill*. Do you expect my boys to work for a lousy fifty grand a week?"

That was his line. I said, "Thank you" to him and I put down the phone. Then I blew up. Kip was in the office. I said to him, "That's *it*." Then I went bananas. "Who the fuck does this lowlife scumbag think he is? That piece of shit. That strutting asshole. That *peacock!* He and Robbie Robertson have the same attitude! Holier-than-thou. He knows *nothing* about the business. I mean, *zero!*"

That was it for me. That was when I snapped. *Out.*

JON TAPLIN: It totally freaks me out that Bill thinks I pushed him into closing Fillmore East. I remember the Metropolitan Opera deal. If I recall, just say he did offer fifty thousand for a week. That was the equivalent of ten thousand dollars a night, or less. The Band hadn't played for ten thousand a night *ever*. We were playing for twenty-five thousand a night when we first went out.

I don't think I rejected it out of hand. I'm sure I passed it by somebody before. But I'm sure I also said, "Bill, I don't think that's enough." It was late at night and he flew off the handle. I never before heard that *I* was the one responsible for Bill closing Fillmore East. I wish he hadn't taken it so seriously. It was just a negotiating ploy. I would have *loved* to play the Metropolitan Opera. But if we couldn't make any money on it, what would we have been doing it for? For prestige? So what?

We had done these kinds of gigs before and the sound was always horrendous. These kind of venues were made to liven up acoustic music. When you played rock and roll in these venues, it was *atrocious*.

Anyway, this is all very sad to hear. Because the Fillmore certainly had a place in the world. I can't believe it. I mean, Bill can say that but there were a lot more voracious people than us. Really. In the world of touring bands, we didn't extract our pound of flesh. We didn't ask for *all* yellow M and M's. We were pretty reasonable in terms of our demands.

BILL: That night after the phone call with Taplin, I took out a pad and I drew a line down the middle. On one side, it said, *"Negatives."* On the other, *"Positives."* I listed all the negatives and I listed all the positives. The only constant positive I came up with was dollars. I can't say that if I had been penniless at the time, I would have made the same move. I hope to God that I would've. But I was far from penniless. The business had been good to me financially.

Kip came into the office and I said to him, "My friend, I've got to tell you something. I can't take this anymore. We've got to think about getting out." I knew I had to do *something*. It could not stay the way it was. I made a decision that was purely emotional. Then I went back to San

Francisco and I thought about it. Soon after, the decision was made to start by closing Fillmore East first.

FRANK BARSALONA: Bill called me up and he said, "I can't take the business anymore. It's not the business that I got into. With Alice Cooper headlining, and all."

Basically, I knew this was coming from Kip Cohen. Because I used to listen to Kip say exactly this. "Look at this, they're puking in the toilets," and all of that. Bill said, "I don't think this business is good for another two years. I want to get out before it goes down the tubes. I want *out*."

I said, "Bill, you're wrong. It's only going to get bigger. From here, it's going to go into the arenas and from the arenas, it'll probably go to the stadiums. I hate to think of the day. But it's going to go into stadiums."

He said, "I will never play Madison Square Garden. I will never do those shows."

I said, "All right. Then you're going to get out of the business *totally?*"

He said, "Oh, if I have to, I will. Because I will *never* do those kind of shows."

We talked for weeks about it. Every time he would come to New York, we would talk. I would go down to his apartment or he would come up to the office or the apartment or the house and we would talk about it and I would convince him that it was wrong. And then he would go back and talk to Kip and they would discuss it and he would go back to saying, "No, I've *got* to get out. All right?"

My thing to him was, "I'll bring in another promoter. And once I do that, Bill, I will give you one month to change your mind." I was going to start working with other people and everything he had done would be washed out.

"Okay?" I said. He said, "That's fair. Absolutely."

PAT LUCE: "Go out on top. It's finished. It's over. It's the end of an era. End it now! End it clean. Go out on top." That was what I was listening to all day long in my office at Fillmore East. That the whole world would notice. That we would really be making a statement about how awful the business had gotten. How terrible it all was. Now, I did not then nor do I now think it was an awful business. It was a *business*. In that business, there were as many wonderful people as in other businesses. I don't remember specifically what it was about the music business that was as awful to them. But it was *dead*.

KIP COHEN: All of the altruistic reasons for closing were 100-percent true. Concurrent to the altruism and the emotional reasons, all valid for closing, it was a *very* smart move. Put in the very simplest terms, you can get out when it's too late, in which case it's a disaster, or you can get out when it's just right and you're right at the top.

I remember playing a substantial role in written statements that were released at the time and I remember feeling in my heart, "This is necessary and this is true." I also thought it was one of the cleverest, most well-timed public moves that had ever been thought of. You created this diamond and then you also decided when it would end.

JOSHUA WHITE: By the end of the Fillmore East, people were coming to *any* show. *Everything* was selling out.

BILL: We were making a fortune by the end. Between the tickets and the concessions. We could have gone on for another *five* years. At the time of closing Fillmore East, it was riding at its best level. So money had nothing to do with my decision. Money *never* was a factor.

A year later, I got my accounting guy to give me some idea of how many trips I made from San Francisco to New York during the final year of the Fillmores. From July 1970 to June 1971, I made *thirty-nine* trips. So it was almost once a week. Always the red-eye so I could get right off the plane and be working in the city that morning.

Sometimes I'd go on a Thursday because some act said, "Bill, come see us in Fillmore East." I'd get in on Friday morning, work all day long, catch the shows Friday and Saturday night, and fly back to San Francisco on Sunday and be in the office on Monday morning. It got to be a tough period. Also, remember that starting back with the Mime Troupe, I'd been going this way for seven years. There was only so much air in the balloon.

ALAN ARKUSH: I remember the day he gathered us all together and gave us one of his speeches. He broke down and he was all upset and he said he was closing the theater and we were *devastated*. Everyone was. I mean, we just thought it was going to go on like that forever. Because we *loved* it, you know? I mean, I looked forward to going to work. I'd show up at one in the afternoon just to hang out and talk. I'd go order sandwiches at B&H and soup from Ratner's and macrobiotic food from the Cauldron and we'd go home at five in the morning.

JOHN FORD NOONAN: I was standing with Bill and we were sort of talking and I said, "You know, it's starting to repeat itself. We've *got* to do something here." There were *no* new groups. It was not like when the Allman Brothers or Santana came for the first time and they did not even have albums out yet and they would rehearse all day and we would hear this music that no one yet knew.

At night, we would be like on a mission. We couldn't *wait* till the fuckin' audience heard them. It was like that shot of Mama Cass in *Monterey Pop* when she sees Janis Joplin. That open-mouth shot? That's what it was like at Fillmore East at the start.

Then the agencies started to package shows and build in acts and the same groups kept coming in. At the end, I think one of the things that affected Bill was that it was always unpleasant outside the theater at night, especially during the late show. There were bigger guys than me outside. I mean, *huge* guys were now the security. Several times, people were thrown through the plate-glass doors in front. Somehow, the spirit of the place changed. It became reds and wine and Grand Funk Railroad. Everyone was *mean*.

Now, I didn't understand money or culture or art but I understood we were starting to repeat ourselves and I said to Bill, "We've *got* to find a way to break out." The next thing I knew, Bill closed it. They got bigger venues and a theater that size has never succeeded again. Has it?

JANE GERAGHTY: I think he was angry at the business. It was becoming greedier, first of all. I think Bill was also going through a very turbulent time in his life. He was getting a divorce. He decided he would rather close than change. It was very upsetting for most people. No one wanted him to close the Fillmore. Frank especially said he was making a big mistake doing that. Bill was just in a state of great agitation and very upset. We were all very sad. Because we had spent a lot of time with each other and gotten to know everybody well, and now everybody would be moving on.

BILL: A few acts had started to play Madison Square Garden and I had been asked by them to do shows there. I said, "You've got to support Fillmore East in New York." They said, "Bill, we love you. But take us to the Garden." And I said, "Well, there's nothing for me to do up there. There's nothing creative." They could make as much doing one show at the Garden as four at Fillmore East. I would say to them, "Do it *here*. It's only one more night. Two shows a night and it's more challenging than the Garden."

I *hated* the idea of rock in Madison Square Garden back then. I thought that was the biggest fucking ripoff in the city. I said it should be just for chariot races and Roller Derby and boxing. Not for someone to play acoustic guitar in. Guilty as the Garden was, it still took two to tango. The Garden could not have had an artist play there unless the artist said they wanted to. They were the finger that pulled the trigger and the audience got the bullet. All the pop festivals had a lot to do with it. The bands got too much money and people got accustomed to seeing them in a huge setting.

Just before I closed Fillmore East, Mike Quatro came to see me. He was Suzie Quatro's brother and Kip Cohen once described him wonderfully as looking like the little guy on top of wedding cakes. Mike Quatro said we were the only ones who could help because he wanted to do something for mankind. A festival of peace and love. He said he had all the contacts and now it was up to me. Union Carbide and Kodak and Xerox were putting up millions of dollars and he had *all* the groups. The Beatles, the Rolling Stones, Bob Dylan, God, Ed Sullivan. He had them *all*. For a *free* festival of peace and love.

I said, "My *God*. How many people do you expect to attract to this thing? Especially if it's free?"

He said, "Oh, between two and three million."

I said, "Where do you expect to put two or three million people?"

He didn't bat an eyelash. He just looked right back at me and said, "We have Wyoming."

I said, "The campus of the University of Wyoming? Or the Wyoming Recreation Center, or what?"

He just looked at me and said, "*Wyoming*."

I said, "You *got* to do me a favor."

"What is it?" he asked.

I said, "Get the fuck out of my office."

You know what he said? "All right."

But that was the way a lot of people were thinking then. What did they need with the Fillmores? When they could get *Wyoming*. For a free festival of peace and love.

2.

BILL: The audience at Fillmore East was also changing. They were becoming demanding rather than appreciative. I remember early Fillmore East audiences for the Allman Brothers and then the later ones. The attitude was completely different.

I was frustrated by people in the business not dealing with their newfound power in the way I felt they should. But it had been coming on for a long while with the rise of the roadie. The snapping of the fingers. First, it was the agent and the manager representing the artist. Then it became the agent and the manager and *all* offshoots of the manager. My question always was, "Who represents the person who buys a ticket?"

The producer. Anybody who had anything to do with the act only wanted to see them become a headliner. They were for the *act*, not the people. It used to be a Sol Hurok or P. T. Barnum or Mike Todd was the biggest star because he was putting on the show for people to enjoy. But in our world, the final decision is always made by the source of the power.

My goal when I first came to New York City had been that Fillmore East would become the white man's Apollo. In that the Apollo always said, "You got the stuff? You got something to say? Walk out on that stage and *do it!*" When you walked out on the stage at Fillmore East, you *knew*. Sound, lights, special effects, light show. You want to show the world your stuff? Do it *here*. The Fillmore East became what I had hoped it would be. But the price was unbearable.

At the end, the biggest acts would no longer support the place. The Doors were playing Madison Square Garden. The acts were saying, "Our careers are more important than the scene." They said to me, "If you don't take us to the stadiums, we'll go with someone else."

FRANK BARSALONA: The night before the press conference, Bill and I talked. Again, I had him convinced. He was going to forget about the press conference and keep Fillmore East going. Now came the morning that he was supposed to do the press conference. I got a call at the apartment from Bill. He said, "Frank, you've got to come down. I'm going to do the press conference."

I said, "I don't want to be down there for that."

He said, "No. You've *got* to come down, all right?"

Finally, I said, "Okay. *Fine*."

I went down there and he had the press conference.

After the press conference was over he said, "Let's take a walk." We walked around the Village for two or three hours. By the end of that thing, we were talking about what an asshole he was and plotting how he could credibly open up Fillmore East again.

We were going to get the kids to send letters to Mayor John Lindsay saying, "We want Fillmore East open again, we need Fillmore East *back*." We would have the parents and kids send letters and then Bill would come in and say, "I've had stacks of letters. By public demand, we're opening Fillmore East again."

We had that all planned. Once Bill did the closing, it just never happened. He couldn't quite get himself to do it.

BILL: At the press conference to announce the closing of the Fillmore East, the only thing I really told them that day was that I was not going to run the Fillmores anymore. But the newspapers made it into, "GRAHAM

SAYS, 'ROCK 'N' ROLL IS DEAD.' " I *never* said that. I said, "I'm not getting back what I'm putting in." To me, this was theater. It was my life. Why did I have to *beg* somebody to do an encore? Because he got 90 percent of the money?

The streets were tough, the bikers were tough, the drug scene was tough. I could have tolerated it for a while longer because Fillmore East worked so well. The building was used for a lot of benefits and it had a role within the community as well. But the artists and their managers didn't see what I saw. Or they didn't want to deal with what I saw. I was forty-one years old at the time. For me, the dues I had to pay were no longer worth the gain.

PETER WOLF: We played closing at Fillmore East. We were on the last show. It was broadcast over the radio and it was us and the Beach Boys and Albert King and Mountain and the Allman Brothers and it went on till like five or six in the morning. Again, we were staying at the Fifty-seventh Street Holiday Inn and I remember all these cabdrivers listening to the show on WNEW-FM in their cabs and it just went on all *night*. I mean, the Allman Brothers started around four in the morning. At dawn, they were still playing "Crossroads," or something like that.

BILL: Over the years, fifty-eight albums were released that had been recorded at one of the Fillmores. *Seventeen* went gold. At the start, musicians would say, "We don't care how many we sell. We just want to make good records." Then they learned the words that were tattooed on their tongues. "We got a bullet? *Do* we have the bullet? We're thirty-five in *Cashbox* and we're going to break through in *Billboard*."

No matter how they were at the start, the business would always take them over before too long.

FRANK BARSALONA: In retrospect, he made a terrible mistake. I think after Bill made that decision, it was a little hard for him to do an about-face and come back in. But I know it's always been a problem with him. That he really missed the most lucrative and prestigious market in America. New York. It was a monumental mistake. A monumental mistake.

To this day, I don't understand the purpose of it. Kip Cohen was *so* wrong. It seemed so clear to me that it wasn't the beginning of the end at all. It really cost Bill. He even went and sold the building. Another silly thing.

PETER WOLF: After he closed Fillmore East, the club scene in New York basically died. That was *it*, really. It has never since been the way it was then. In the era where just word-of-mouth could do it. With no hype or advertisement, a band could make it just by people asking, "How did they do at Fillmore West? How did they go down?" "They were great, man. You *got* to see them."

By playing Carnegie Hall or being on the Ed Sullivan show once upon a time, you knew you were on your way to stardom. Being endorsed by Bill Graham when he booked you to play the Fillmore gave you the same kind of credibility in that era.

JOSHUA WHITE: Nobody seemed to miss Fillmore East then. Now, they miss it *terribly*. But not then. Now, Fillmore East is like a piece of the true ark.

Fillmore East eventually became the Saint. The Saint was the largest gay disco in New York at the height of gay liberation. Pre-AIDS. It was open one night a week, Saturday night, for twenty-four hours. It was a private club which people had to join. Then the whole AIDS thing hit and the Saint's business fell off completely.

Then the Saint was gutted and turned into an eight-theater complex. Eight small movie theaters. Because the neighborhood has come around again. It's become a very nice place to live and they don't have a good movie theater in that neighborhood. It was the Loew's Commodore and then it was the Village Theater and then it was the Fillmore East and then it was the Saint and then it became the Loew's Octoplex. The Anderson is still across the street. I think it's closed.

It was just a remarkable time. Part of the fun of it for me was that I was never angry when I was there. I loved it. I *loved* it. I loved the women and I loved the life and I loved that between shows, there was an appetizing store right next door. I would walk across Sixth Street and go into one of those old Lower East Side appetizing stores. We got to know the people in there and I would send the kid in the light show out for cream cheese and caviar sandwiches on black bread. We would sit in our dressing room and we would have these big chopped liver sandwiches. It was wonderful. We thought we could do *anything*.

I could easily have been just ordinary. By being at Fillmore East, I wasn't ordinary anymore. I had this experience that is a part of my life. Everything I do to this day is always registered to some degree against the fact that for a brief moment, I was in a place where wonderful things happened.

It's the same thing with Alan Arkush and John Ford Noonan and all those people. Whatever ultimately happened in their lives, they were in that one place. That one fragile, fragile place. And it was really great.

And that place was Bill. Without Bill, there wouldn't have been anything like it.

I have worked in many places since with uncharismatic people or less charismatic people. People who were flawed in a different way than Bill. Because all of Bill's flaws, and believe me, he's got plenty, are not flaws of character. They're flaws of judgment or the choices he makes within his life.

Bill never made the mistake that I saw so many people make. Bill *never* thought *he* was the music. Bill always was the *scene*. There are publishers I know who think *they* are the magazine. Bill *never* did that. He knew he was never the music. He never stopped loving the artists. He loved them and he loved hating them.

But it was always a strong emotional tie. He knew how to treat them like children and he knew how to treat them like adults. He knew how to give them gifts. They would sell out for a week and he would give them engraved gold pocket watches instead of a case of champagne.

Very tasty. Hey, Bill, that's *nice*. You could have done anything, Bill, but you did *that*. Hey, *Bill!* Very tasty guy.

3.

ROBERT GREENFIELD: Bill closed Fillmore East. Then he went to San Francisco and closed Fillmore West as well. During the week of closing shows, Bill allowed a camera crew to come in and shoot him cinema verité-style in his office as he talked on the phone to the acts who played the final shows.

The resulting documentary, entitled *Last Days of the Fillmore*, was released in May 1972 along with a boxed, three-record set of the shows featuring such performers as the Grateful Dead, Hot Tuna, Malo, Tower of Power, New Riders of the Purple Sage, Quicksilver, It's a Beautiful Day, Taj Mahal, Boz Skaags, Cold Blood, Stoneground, the Elvin Bishop Band, Lamb, and the Sons of Champlin. Along with the music came a thirty-two-page booklet filled with photos from the shows, a reproduction of both a Fillmore poster and a ticket for a show at the Fillmore. There was also a seven-inch, long-playing disk on which Bill himself was interviewed for seventeen minutes.

DAVID RUBINSON: The *Last Days of the Fillmore* album was all live performances. But on the record, the bands had to be announced. Bill came into the studio and he went, "Okay, okay. Let me try this. No . . . no . . . no. One more time. One more time."

And he did intros to the different bands. He was overdubbing. Like an artist. He could have been Grace Slick. He would listen to the playback and say, "Wait a minute. I can do it better." He was unbelievable. He gave a *fabulous* performance.

ROBERT GREENFIELD: If for nothing else, the documentary is still worth seeing for the classic scene in which Michael Wilhelm, a former member of the Charlatans comes to ask Bill to put his current band on one of the closing shows. Bill tells him there is no room. Wilhelm and Bill kick it back and forth for a little while, Bill making it plain that as the producer, he has the right to put on groups he has already seen and liked and that he thinks the public will like as well. Not that Wilhelm's band won't give the people pleasure. It's only that Bill has never seen them play.

Wilhelm says, "Yeah. Well. Well, I'd just like to say, 'Fuck you and thanks for the memories, man,' you know?"

Bill escorts Wilhelm out the door to the stairs, saying, "The next time you say 'Fuck you' to me, I hope it's out *there* somewhere with no camera around. I'll take your teeth out of your mouth and *SHOVE* 'em through your nose . . . Fucking animal!"

Wilhelm says, "I don't hate you at all."

Bill says, "If you give me, I love you. But if I don't give you, I'm a 'Fuck you!' right? . . . Get out of here! *GET OUTTA HERE!* Go *down* the stairs. Go *out* of the building. Go *out* of this building."

In the *New York Times*, Don Heckman gave the movie a very favorable review, stating that ". . . for anyone who spent any time at the Fillmores—East or West or both—the picture rang true. Bill Graham really was a blustering King Kong with a telephone line for an umbilical cord and a telephone receiver permanently fastened to his ear." Heckman went on to compare Bill's role as a producer of rock shows to that of a good supporting actor, working always to never upstage the star and create a certain ambience in which the leading players could do their thing.

Bill himself liked the film. Concerning the argument with Wilhelm, he said, "Hollywood could *never* have staged that scene. It was too real."

BILL: After Fillmore West closed, I went to the Mediterranean with a friend of mine from The Bronx, Stanley Turnower. We bought motorcycles in Lisbon and headed through Spain for North Africa. Remember the opening scene of *Lawrence of Arabia*? Peter O'Toole on that motorcycle? That was the kind of freedom I felt on that trip whenever we were moving. I didn't want *anything* sticking to me. I felt like a child on that trip. We traveled for two months. I went to Fez and Casablanca in Morocco and then back up through southern France into Switzerland to see my sister.

Once I got back, things in the business hadn't changed. There were still so many punches below the waist. Kidney shots. People forcing me to lie about what food cost for the act in order to make my two cents from the dollar. Being forced to not work straight. I always *wanted* to deal straight. Even though people would say, "Well, aren't *you* one of the masters of the game?" Defensively, yeah. I had to get real good at it or go down the drain as a businessman.

The only difference once I got back was that I didn't have to fill a room where I was paying rent. The Fillmores were gone. At Berkeley Community Theater, I only had to pay for the use of the hall when I *actually* used it. I wasn't fixing lightbulbs and worrying about insurance or making the toilets work. I didn't have to deal with nights when the place was dark because the place didn't belong to me.

With the Fillmores closed, I was free to book any act I wanted. Not that this was the reason I had closed them. That was purely emotional.

JERRY POMPILI: Bill closed the Fillmores and we were doing more shows than ever. At Berkeley Community Theater and then Winterland.

Part Three

Making It
a Business

Chapter Twelve

Touring

1.

BILL: The word was out that the Stones were going to tour America in the summer of 1972. They had done a short English tour the previous spring with Jo Bergman, Alan Dunn, and Marshall Chess, who was president of their new record label on Atlantic, Rolling Stones Records, in charge. In England, they could get away with that. But to come to America for five or six weeks and play forty shows, they needed someone to run the tour.

The last time they had come through was 1969 with Ronnie Schneider. The Stones never wanted to have anyone from the business world or straight society running their affairs and so they had gotten themselves in trouble with the people they trusted more than once. The Who were extremely talented and great but they had also Kit Lambert to look out for their careers, both in a business and a creative way. Lambert then found Bill Curbishley to do that for them and Peter Rudge as well.

With all his shortcomings, Rudge was a very bright man. Extremely bright. He knew right from wrong. His personality got the best of him at times and his ego and his Napoleonic approach to rock and roll and control. When he got to a gig, he had to show he was the master of the universe at that show. To him, you *had* to prove it every day. My first real day-to-day encounters with him were not with The Who but when the Stones came over to tour in 1972.

Rudge was obsessed with detail. More than anything, he was obsessed with putting you instantly on guard and creating havoc if something went wrong. He was obsessed about the Hell's Angels showing up if and when the Stones ever played in San Francisco again.

345

On the phone, he would say to me, "Think it over, Bill. It's *your* responsibility, Bill. *You* must straighten this out and it *must* be peaceful. If not, it'll be *your* fault, Bill." In a sense, he was like a drill sergeant. His job was to break your will. He *made* it his job.

PETER RUDGE: On the 1972 tour, Bill got all these Stones' dates. But let's have a think about *how* he got all those dates. I knew there were problems between the Stones and Bill Graham. To be quite honest, I didn't really get involved in the politics of it. I didn't go to Mick and say, "What did he do? What did he say?" I knew Bill Graham was the best promoter in San Francisco. I *knew* he was. I said to Mick, "He's the best." I have got to say that Mick and the Stones said, "You're right. He *is* the best." Mick said, "I don't have to talk to him. Okay? Let's get a good deal." Mick wanted to come in and *not* talk to Bill. That was really what it was all about.

Mick was always bright. All the Stones knew to a certain extent that you don't go into San Francisco without Bill Graham. Not unless you want trouble. Not that Bill would go out of his way to fight the Stones. The Stones were bigger than Bill. Bill knew that. At that point, I knew how enormous Bill's ego was. Bill didn't do it for money. He did it for the glory and the money and the ego. The *buzz*. Even then. So there was never any argument about Bill doing San Francisco. But Bill also wanted to do L.A.

BILL: I never related to what they did in the rest of the country. I cut my own deals and ended up with my own figures that I thought were fair. Negotiations in those days were never what they became later on. The numbers weren't that big. I had them do four shows at Winterland, two on Tuesday and two on Thursday, with Wednesday as an off-day in between. Stevie Wonder opened. Robert Shields the mime performed as well.

PETER RUDGE: The idea of the Stones doing Winterland was great for Bill. In 1969, the Stones had had problems with Bill in San Francisco. But they had also had problems in Los Angeles with Steve Wolf and Jim Rismiller. They had played the Forum and something had gone wrong. I don't know what it was. Basically, we had no promoter in California. Steve Wolf couldn't get back in the ring with Jagger. None of the other promoters down there meant shit to Mick Jagger or the Rolling Stones or Rupert Lowenstein. By standing up and saying those things back then, Bill Graham had at least impregnated their conscience. So we ended up doing the Forum in L.A. and the Long Beach Arena and San Diego and Tucson as well with Bill.

BILL: I don't know if Rudge was worried and suspicious but I knew from other promoters that when there was nothing wrong, he could *find* things wrong. His was one of the attitudes I had to deal with. That there already was a reputation people had built up for me. As to what I was to them. I was the adversary. He wasn't just coming in to see me, promoter to manager. It was, "I hear you got a fast draw. I hear you're Billy the Kid. Well, I'm *so-and-so!*" Rudge always had that jousting attitude. But it was very, very condescending. That reverse criticism. "Ready for combat, are you? *Are* you, *Bill?*" That was always the attitude he had about him. Instead of one big date at the Oakland Coliseum, I talked him into playing those four concerts at Winterland so people could see the Stones and dance.

PETER RUDGE: It was then for the first time that we got to the point with Bill where you so often get, the one I love and was a sucker for, which was when Bill said, *"I'm going to pass."* On his tombstone, the epitaph will say, "I'll pass. I *can* pass." The response to that being, *"Pass,* Bill. *Pass."* Then I would get into the thing with Bill which I would get into with no other promoter. That kind of chicken game. Who could take it to the farthest? Basically, we'd got it that far and we'd negotiated and we were talking and Bill would like to orchestrate it as *principle.*

There was no such thing as principle. When you're negotiating so finite a thing so if you agree to take the act and you've agreed on where to play, you're talking a *deal.* It's *money.* Bill was the best I ever met at turning money into *principle.* Suddenly, instead of *hondling* over what in essence was 5 percent of the net, which, depending on the number of dates and the stature of the artist and the size of the venue, could be anything from ten to a hundred thousand dollars, it was *principle.*

"I'm *passing,*" he would say.

"Pass, Bill. *Pass."*

But I would get to the point where I knew I had to put a tour on and I had everything ready and was talking to the act and saying everything was in place. Except ". . . still haven't *quite* got the deal done with Graham yet." I could say it for *months.*

In San Francisco, Bill was very good as a promoter. Out of San Francisco, in my opinion he was really a production manager. When Bill went out of town, Bill should have been damn lucky he was getting that consideration. Because Bill's forte was to turn chopped liver into chicken salad. It was the *show* and everything the act saw. The act did not see the contract or whether the deposit was in. They did not see the expenses. They saw the limo, the way they got to the hotel, and the flowers on the table when they walked into the hotel room. He was *great* at getting to the acts. The production he put on in San Francisco for the Stones in 1972 was *stupendous*.

BILL: I did a whole campaign about the shows at Winterland. I went on the radio and talked to the newspapers and told people that if they did not have tickets, they should just stay at home because we were going to block off the entire neighborhood. The police cordoned off that whole area around Winterland. People with tickets could come to the building, those without never even got close. I had seventy-five special private cops on the streets.

Concerning the Stones themselves, we didn't leave each other with good feelings at the end of the '69 tour. I was very happy and elated to be doing eleven of their shows on the '72 tour. The thing in '69 was that they had not been to America in a number of years. The previous time they had toured, the thing to do was get there *late*. Get the kids *screaming*. Don't feed the fish for a long time so they would get enraged and be screaming for them when they came out.

Before Mick Jagger came to San Francisco for their first show at Winterland in '72, I had mixed emotions about how we were going to get along. But when the Stones got off the plane, we shook hands and the minute that happened, I could see they were different people. I had my son David there with me and Mick said, *"Hello, Bill!"* And there was no condescension in it. I put them up at the Miyako Hotel. Although they didn't like it at first, they decided to stay there anyway.

PETER RUDGE: Bill suggested that we all stay at the Miyako Hotel. So we turned up there and there was a row of suites *behind* the building and there were like five of them. Bill had forgotten that what the Stones called "suites" were not always what he called them. We got there and they *hated* the rooms. In for a penny, in for a pound. Bill came over to the hotel as soon as we checked in. He was in my room. The sixth suite, or something. I had one and the guys had the other five. And they *hated* them, right?

Jagger walked into the room and Bill was there. *Silence.* Jagger ignored him. Bill was really uncomfortable. I had never seen Bill *that* uncomfortable. Bill knew that he was going to be made to suffer. There and then, he knew this wasn't going to be fun. He had gotten them to do Winterland but he knew this was going to be difficult.

Bill had come in with a list of restaurants. He had come in with this and that. And Jagger didn't fucking want to know. Jagger *hated* the room. "*Whose* idea was this?" he asked. He *knew* it was Graham's. "Who put us in this fucking place?" And Bill was sitting there. I had never seen Bill so uncomfortable in all my life. We were there, it must have been about an hour. Jagger never looked at Bill the entire time. And Bill was trying to strike up a conversation. For Bill, it was very, very demeaning.

In the end, it was like Jagger said, "Why don't we have a fuckin' party, or something? I want to get *out* of this hotel. I *hate* it."

That was the night we went to the Trident. Where all hell broke loose.

BILL: It was a Monday night with not that much doing in town. So I had Frank Werber open up the Trident, his restaurant over in Sausalito, special for us. Frank got his finest waitresses out there and we had this long table by the window with the finest joints rolled up in little boxes on the table. We had a candlelight dinner there and it was just the Rolling Stones having a party. The shows at Winterland were terrific and on Wednesday night I took them all to dinner at Fleur De Lys. During the day, I took the Stones out on a yacht in harbor for a little tour of the bay.

PETER RUDGE: The whole time, there was never any great friendliness between them and Bill. I don't believe that Mick was particularly fond of Bill then. Keith was not fond of him. Charlie was not fond of him. They saw through him. Certain acts *did* see through Bill. Yet they also understood and appreciated how good he was. When he came after them after the '72 tour to do other things, Bill was the perfect guy. The Stones knew they could snap their fingers and Bill would be on the plane. Because when something was important enough in Bill's mind, he would do *anything*. The Stones would say, "Let's call Bill. It'll be all right." Because the Stones *never* had to worry about selling tickets. Bill is great on the big bands where the tickets sell themselves and he's left to make it unique and different and kind of play up to the artists' egos. After '72, the Stones tended to use him.

BOB BARSOTTI: The first show I ever worked in Winterland was the Stones in '72. The streets were so barricaded that you had to show proof of residence or a ticket even to get close. But that was Winterland. It operated under a different set of rules. Those four shows in two days convinced me this was the business I wanted to be in. I was standing below the front of the stage doing security with twenty other guys. There were no barricades and we were in the crowd and I had never experienced anything like that before. I had never experienced the kind of energy that happened then. Coming from the house to the stage and then from the stage back into the house. I had never imagined that something like that was possible. Not only that but there was a crowd of people waiting two blocks away for the *next* show!

I quit going to school and I worked at Winterland for the next four years.

BILL: The day of the first Stones' show at Winterland, I was standing on the side of the street when this limo came around the corner with Jagger sitting in the back. Jagger waved at me and then the limo went down the runway into the garage underneath Winterland. I thought, "Strange. Jagger never comes *this* early. And he would never wave at me." I ran down the ramp inside. This guy got out of the back of the limo dressed exactly like Jagger. He had a lady with him. The guy had spent a couple hundred bucks on the limo and the outfit just so he could get in to see the show. He did it so well I couldn't throw him out. I said, "Go upstairs and watch the show. But backstage? *Forget it.*"

PETER RUDGE: Now, we had a good deal for those shows in San Francisco. Bill got the same deal as everyone else. He didn't get a better one. It killed him. It *killed* him! It killed him. To the extent that he asked for two sets of contracts so that he could show the other one to his staff. It was a question of face. So he could say something to his people and the world. There was the *real* deal, where we had the same deal as everybody else, and there was the deal where Bill's contract cosmetically, on the surface, was better than anyone else's. And that was how we solved the deal.

It was *very* important for him to get those other dates. Because of the boat rides and the Trident and everything else in San Francisco. He made his money in L.A. where there wasn't *any* of that. That he did straight. The dressing rooms were nice and everything else. But he managed to come out well on the other dates. Therefore he could make San Francisco, which was his home town and where he had to live, the place where he wanted people to know that he was the greatest.

It was a game. Bill would do all those things and it would always come back. "I took you to dinner, the boat trip . . ." It sharpened the box office statement. Bill would always try and put those things in. With Bill, we would get charged. For every penny Bill had spent to let us enjoy our stay, I basically had to assume that he was going to try and charge us.

As far as the artists were concerned, all this worked. Because Bill was a nice guy and they were far less concerned than Bill about the final result. Bill preyed on them. He did a wonderful job in the production and everything else. That was why Bill always wanted a better deal. Because Bill would give us a better show.

BILL: It always seemed that Rudge wanted to go with me into a confrontation. I could never understand why he needed that because I always thought he was highly intelligent. I kind of liked him. Because he was very witty. He wasn't part of the Stones' inner circle. He would ask the group questions but with all English musicians and the Stones in particular, they had one kind of social dialogue among themselves and a different kind of dialogue with anybody that was outside the circle. He didn't seem to fit inside. But he loved to have that thought of him.

When it came to settling the show, he did a lot of *hondling* and he could be a *chazzar*. That was what I was told. Myself, I was never involved in settlements with him. I always had other people do it for me.

KEITH RICHARDS: Bill wooed us. And you know what Bill can be like when he is wooing you. It was all stops out. And he put on a very impressive show. We played small places like Winterland and then the Palladium down in L.A., really from choice, you know. It was almost like all the antagonism the last time we had come through was Bill's way of introducing himself. Like a dog, you know?

The fascinating thing about Bill was that I always wanted to be there when he was *not* around me. Because I wanted to see what went down *then*. You never got the whole picture with him, you know. I can only *imagine* the things he had to do and went through in order to do what he did.

Peter Rudge was another extraordinary character. In a way, Rudge was very similar to Bill. They both thrived off getting out of those mad problems that would come zooming around the corner. Just when you thought you couldn't handle another thing, you know? Their biggest moments of stress came when there was absolutely nothing happening. It was like, "Something's wrong. There are *no* problems."

BILL: Then we did L.A. The Forum. The Stones were on time for every gig, which certainly was a change from the way they had done things in 1969. What I knew from my years of experience was the value of an encore.

The Stones had a history of *never* doing encores. Mick was pretty much his own man when it came to making those kinds of decisions. In L.A., the first show they did at the Forum was great. We had twenty thousand more people outside waiting to come in. The kids inside were going crazy when the Stones came off. Mick said, "Bill, I don't feel up to doin' an encore today." I said, "Mick, it's up to you. If you don't do one, it'll take us forty-five minutes to get them out and clear the house. Because they *want* one. If you go out and do something short, may I suggest 'Honky Tonk Women,' which is around two and a half minutes, I think they'll leave and they'll be very pleased."

He looked at me and said, "You may be right."

They went out, did "Honky Tonk Women." The house emptied in eight minutes.

The biggest difference between 1969 and 1972 in terms of the Stones was Mick Jagger's ability to control an audience. He was a marked man. He was always on and in the spotlights. He drew a very physical audience. All it would have taken was one maniac. Yet Jagger performed with a kind of open looseness without ever giving up control. He knew just how far toward the edge of the stage he could go. He knew just how to throw those rose petals into the house each night.

As far as I was concerned, the previous tour had left a *lot* to be desired. On this one, they came as professionals and they really entertained. It was what rock and roll really needed at the time. To show everyone that we were in the business of entertaining people.

After the tour, I got a letter from someone that absolutely has to be the greatest letter I ever got from a fan. In terms of the Stones at that time and rock and roll in general, the letter says it all. It reads:

"Dear Bill,

"On June 6th, 1972 at Winterland, I saw the best rock and roll band and probably the best-produced rock concert in the world. I also got very drunk and fell in love. Thank you."

2.

ROBERT GREENFIELD: In August 1972, Bill put on Groucho Marx at the Masonic Auditorium in San Francisco. As with Lenny Bruce, it was Groucho's last live performance. In October, Bill spent sixty hours on the air being interviewed live on KSAN. At one point, he reacted strongly to a very negative story told by Nick Gravenites of Big Brother and the Holding Company, among other bands, about how Bill had *really* treated Janis Joplin back at the original Fillmore.

In November, Nick Gravenites was quoted in the "Random Notes" column of *Rolling Stone* magazine as saying, "Graham will not cop to the fact that he did some ugly shit in his life. His memoirs are going to be like the history books about the Americans and Indians written by the Americans. He won't accept the fact that he's been an asshole too."

At the end of December, Bill finally got to present one of his real idols in concert. Tito Puente at Winterland. For him, it was like a dream come true.

BILL: By this time, New Year's Eve was becoming a ritual for Dead Heads. That year, we had the Dead and the New Riders of the Purple Sage and the Sons of Champlin at Winterland and I think we served everyone breakfast at the end of the evening. At midnight, I came out of some kind of capsule in some kind of shape. It became a ritual for me that after everyone left and my sister had taken my son David, who never missed a single New Year's Eve show in his entire life, home, I would be in Winterland by myself. We finished the show at maybe three or four in the morning and served five thousand people breakfast and the trucks had pulled in and everyone had left and it would be getting light outside.

It became a big thing with me that I would stay until I was the last one in the building. I would just sort of walk around because it was the end of the year. I would check myself out and I would get very ponderous in my thoughts. The floor would be covered by the remnants of the party and it would be the end of my year.

ROBERT GREENFIELD: Nineteen seventy-three began for Bill in court where he waged a bitter legal battle for full custody of his son David, then four years old. The judge decreed that David would continue to spend the school year with his mother back in Pennsylvania. For two weeks at Christmas and then during the summer, David would live with Bill.

3.

BILL: When they asked me about Woodstock at the time it happened, I said, "Music festivals are picnics that cost too much money." As the business changed and the acts kept demanding more and more money, we started doing one-day outdoor shows with one big headliner and several support acts. The first one was at Kezar Stadium right near Golden Gate Park at the end of May 1973. The Grateful Dead, the New Riders of the Purple Sage, and Waylon Jennings.

My desire was never to go to larger and larger facilities. As far as I was concerned, Winterland at five thousand was large enough. But it had gotten to the point where the demand was greater than the supply. More and more people wanted to see these acts. Unless the band was willing to give us three dates, we could not satisfy the demand. Bands began to realize that if they could make as much in one date as they could in three, they wouldn't have to stay out on the road as long.

Rock and roll had started in the clubs and the streets and the parks. Then it became a game of supply and demand. As the market price went up, the negotiations got heavier. It wasn't just who had the better amps or piano or stage crew. It got to the point where bands were earning money far beyond their wildest dreams. Musicians realized, "God, I can have a *second* car. I can have a home in the *country*. I can have a *sailboat*. I can have *everything* I want." What else did they need? The *time* to enjoy all these things. Because the road was always the same, the conclusion they reached was, "I want to make more money in *less* time." Result? *Stadiums.*

If we hadn't done it, someone else would have. That was the bottom line. That was the only reason. Once we were going to do it, we wanted to do it *right*. What *we* thought right was. *Our* approach. They had already started doing outdoor shows in Philadelphia and Texas and Chicago and Georgia. But in San Francisco, there was a long history of free shows in the park and an honorable, nonmoney relationship between the people and the bands.

That was why I came up with the name. "Day on the Green." I wanted to make these events *special*. I wanted to create giant outdoor sets so the bands would be going into a space that was like a theater piece. I wanted to keep the posters and the balloons and make the backstage area special for the artists who were coming in. We began at Kezar Stadium and then soon moved to the Oakland Coliseum.

We started hiring people from the Haight-Ashbury Medical Clinic run by Dr. David Smith, to take care of the kids. We used the third-base dugout for a clinic. The concerts were very successful right from the start. We began doing seven or eight a year, mostly in spring and summer.

It was a time when there was an ongoing extension of the sixties into the seventies. The concert-goer was living in the *real* world now, not the world that had existed in the Haight-Ashbury when the original Fillmore was still going. It was beginning to change with the coming of some of the heavier metal rock and roll acts. But there was still an element of the society that wanted to come together to enjoy one another. It was not yet so centered on what it has since become: "Who's playing?" Back then, people still went to shows in pairs. Now, they go in packs. And the feeling was different. After a "Day on the Green" show then, how many empty beer cans would I have found? Not that many. Not like now. Now that drinking has once again become an initiation rite for the young.

4.

BILL: The day that Led Zeppelin played at Kezar, they were flying in from Los Angeles and they had a private plane. One of my guys had a phone on stage and he said, "Bill, you won't believe this." Then he told me that nearly everyone in the group was on the plane and the plane was about to land. But at the last minute, Jimmy Page had decided that he had gotten bored with flying on the private plane. He wanted to be with just regular people. So he was coming in separately on United Airlines.

They all came in one car, Peter Grant and all the bodyguards. They were about two hours late. No Jimmy Page. I went back onstage and the fans were chanting, "We want Led Zeppelin! We *want* Led Zeppelin!" I was playing music over the PA. We began playing it a little louder. Then we played it a little *louder.*

The United plane was landing. Then it was late. Then it had to go make some turns around San Francisco. We were in *agony.* I realized that I had to say *something* that would be pleasing to the crowd. Something they would understand. It had been at least an hour since the last act left the stage. What *could* I say to them that was true that was going to help?

I went up to the microphone and I said, *"Excuse me."* By this time, they just didn't want to hear anymore. I said, "I'm sorry for the delay. We're almost set. But I want to *level* with you. Jimmy's having a little trouble with his double-neck guitar . . ." They all started applauding. ". . . and he wants to get it just right for you. He *really* wants to rock and roll today but he's got a problem with the double-neck." Because the aura of all auras was that he played a double-neck guitar.

This *deep* applause came out. They *loved* that. If Jimmy wanted them to hang for him, they were happy to go on hanging for Jimmy. He was not even around. He was circling somewhere over San Francisco. But he wanted to get that double-neck *just right* for them.

Eventually, he got there and went on stage. I was livid all day long. But I did not raise my voice once. Not that day. What I did have was this fantasy of what would have happened if Page had not shown up and the band could not play and I was the only one who knew it. I got into it as if someone had dosed me.

My fantasy was that when I went out on stage to announce that Led Zeppelin was not there and in fact would not be playing, I had already made a decision not to do this kind of work anymore and also to entirely eliminate this disease from the planet. Up to the microphone I walked, carrying a sack filled with the day's receipts. In my mind, I knew all this *had* to be gotten rid of. What this represented. Peter Grant sitting backstage with twelve bodyguards. Jimmy Page flying *United* so he could be with the *regular* people. Everybody frozen out front. Everyone going *"Uuuuaaaahaaaah!"*

I didn't want to be part of this anymore. As I began to address the audience in my fantasy, a helicopter appeared, hovering over the stage. A ladder was lowered toward me. As I was speaking, I put my foot into the bottom of the ladder and sort of just hung on to it with the sack under one arm. I said, "I want to apologize for the delay. I'm really sorry to inform you that due to a situation beyond our control, our friends Led Zeppelin cannot be with us this afternoon." I could hear it coming from the crowd. The *groan*. Without skipping a beat, I said, "However, would you welcome instead please, your local favorites, the Flamin' Groovies."

Then I threw the sack on board. Up I went. The chopper began to move. Swinging over the stadium, I saw the crowd below. Mass hysteria. This part was always in slow motion. Just as I went over the edge of the stadium wall, I gave them *all* the finger. Then it exploded. It all turned into fire down below. The *end* of the universe. The entire stadium became one big charcoal pit.

In the next scene, I was James Mason at the end of *Five Fingers*. Sitting on the deck of this magnificent villa overlooking Rio de Janeiro, in a white dinner jacket. I was James Mason sitting on a balcony overlooking a magnificent bay. A servant began to pour my wine. I was out of rock and roll for good and I had never felt better in my life.

My valet came over and said, "Excuse me, sir. There are two gentlemen from the bank to see you."

"Send them in."

They came in and said, "The eighty-seven zillion dollars you deposited in our bank from that concert, sir? The cash is all *counterfeit*."

Just like James Mason, I stood up. I took some of the money, threw it in the air, and went into an insane fit of sick laughter.

End of movie.

5.

ROBERT GREENFIELD: That summer, Bill was hired by Shelley Finkel and Jim Koplik to put on an outdoor concert at the Watkins Glen racetrack in upstate New York. There were only three bands on the bill. The Grateful Dead, the Band, and the Allman Brothers. Six hundred thousand people showed up.

BILL: The kids just came in by the thousands and thousands. This was the day *before* the show. All the bands had said they wanted to do a sound check. That morning, I called them all up and said, "Sound check? You got to be here *today*." Because I wanted a show that day. I wanted to give the crowd *something*. I didn't want them to just sit there.

When the Band got there, they said, "We'd like to tune up and rehearse and run through a couple of numbers but there are all those *people* out there."

I said, "You want me to move them?"

Musicians aren't used to doing run-throughs in front of an audience. Usually, it takes them hours to find the right keys and do the tuning. It takes them *forever*. That day, it all got done within one song. The kids went ape.

The Allman Brothers were next. Their guy said, "Look how long the Band was out there. We'd like to play at least half an hour. Maybe forty minutes."

I said, "You want to do a sound check for forty minutes? I got the Dead waiting here."

So the Allmans went out and played for an hour. The audience went bonkers. I mean, they went wild.

Then came the natural move. The Dead roadies were saying, "You really fucked us. How much do *we* get for a sound check?"

The Dead played for an hour and a half. By seven o'clock that night, the kids had seen a great, great show.

I loved all three bands and they all were right for that kind of outdoors gig. The next day, we had an outdoor show for the first time at the Ontario Motor Speedway in Southern California with Leon Russell and Loggins and Messina. I rented a Lear jet, flew cross-country, and worked that show. But there were only about thirty thousand people there.

6.

JON TAPLIN: David Geffen started calling me up and trying to get me to put him together with Robbie Robertson. Because he saw Robbie as the way to get to Bob Dylan. Which was totally right. Robbie came out and I introduced them and David put a push on Robbie that was astonishing. He took him to Paris with Joni Mitchell. Just "Let's go to Paris for a week and do *everything*." Joni wrote "Free Man in Paris" on that trip. David bought his first big painting and for Robbie, it was like, "*Wow*, this is another way of enjoying yourself." He said, "This guy is as good as Albert Grossman. Only he's more *there*. He's more *driven*." Whereas Albert had gotten to the point where he wanted to be up on the farm.

So Robbie said, "Shit, let's see what this guy's got to do." Robbie introduced David to Bob and David just put on this push. Part of the push was, "We'll get Bill Graham to do a tour and it'll be a tour like nobody has ever seen." Bill would work *for them*, so to speak. Bill would promote it and make sure that all the things they wanted to know about would be really together. They would get the *Starship* as their tour plane. All the perks would be there but Bill would still only take a piece. Bob would get to keep most of the revenue.

Bob really liked that. The last time Bob had been out on tour, the promoter had paid him and kept all the rest. Now, he would have the promoter working for *him*, so to speak.

BILL: When word got out that Dylan might tour and that he wasn't going to do it through the usual agency-manager system, I was *very* interested. David Geffen called me. I think David liked me and respected my work and it was through him that my meeting with Dylan was set up.

Dylan himself was very noncommittal. He just wanted to hear what we had to say and what I thought he could do in terms of shows across the country. Bob only wanted to go out for a few dates. Eight or ten or twelve. Which was silly because the *whole* country wanted to see him perform. At the time, he was the single biggest star. If you removed Elvis Presley. Dylan was the most powerful writer-performer in rock and roll.

I think Robbie Robertson and the guys from the Band had spoken favorably about me to Dylan. But there was still a gap between us. All my life, I've felt that musicians and artists have looked at me with an attitude. Which is that they get up every day and create and I am not like them. I am someone who *uses* creative people to my own ends. Whereas all I am ever trying to do is create on my own by putting what they have created out there for others to hear and see and enjoy.

There was also another problem. Who was going to be the star of this show? Bob Dylan or Bill Graham? I always made sure that on that tour, Bob and the Band were the stars. Even though it said, "Bill Graham Presents."

DAVE FURANO: I remember Bill playing basketball with Dylan during dress rehearsals before the tour started. We were at the Forum in Los Angeles. David Geffen and the Band were there. Bill threw Dylan the basketball and said, "I'll shoot you for the tour."

And Dylan said, "*What* tour?"

Here we were, all ready to go. Bill had put up *hundreds* of thousands of dollars. He just gritted his teeth.

PAUL WASSERMAN: The Dylan tour that year was like Jesus coming back. Even I was aware of that. I don't know if it was Bill's doing or David Geffen but I was put in a separate hotel from the group so that when the press would try to find me, they wouldn't find Dylan. *If* they came to the hotel. My job as tour publicist was to keep them *away* from Dylan.

Bill's greatest line, which I will never forget, was when I came in with an early edition of *Newsweek*. Dylan was on the cover. Everyone was looking at it. Bill looked at me and said, "What about *Time*?"

LOU KEMP: I was there hanging out with Bob. He invited me to come and I did. It was like going into a vacuum or a bubble. What happened was that they did *everything* for us. They isolated us from the whole world. Everything was totally outside us. So we didn't even know what was going on. They would just pick us up and put us down and bring us everything and take us every place we needed to go. It was not a normal life at all.

Because when you are on a Bill Graham tour, it's overkill. When Bill has a star, he treats him appropriately. I guarantee that nobody's wife ever treated them as good as Bill treated Bob on the road.

BILL: Being a good tour manager means that you can feel what your artist is comfortable with. Then you build an entire traveling world around him. Like a living room that moves. A lot of it had to do with the people I hired to work that tour. Arthur Rosato and Patrick Stansfield. Low-keyed. No yelling, "*All right!* Move that over *there!* Raise that *steel!*" That would be so *un*-Dylan.

Before we went out, I got the whole tour staff together in San Francisco and I said, "You know, this is *Bob Dylan*. I don't think he's the kind of guy who wants you to say to him every day, '*Hi, Bob!* How you *doin'?* What's goin' on?' Please try to understand that and give him some respect for his privacy."

The tour started. In the third or fourth city in the middle of the night, someone knocked on the door of my hotel room. I opened the door and it was Bob. He came in. I could see he had a problem. I said, "Is everything okay, Bob? Something's wrong?"

He said, "*Bill.* Why isn't anybody talking to me?"

ROBBIE ROBERTSON: We were getting ready to put this whole thing together and we were talking to the people involved in it and David Geffen was helping us out. They were saying, "Well, who should we get to do this?" And David said, "Have you worked with Bill Graham before?" I said, "Yeah, I've worked with Bill Graham." Bob didn't know Bill Graham. So Bob was saying, "What's the scoop with this guy?"

I was saying, "Jeez, you know. He's like the best in the world at doing this. But a *lot* comes with the dinner."

He said, "How do we handle this? Because I don't want to have to deal with this guy."

I said, "We'll do the tour. But he'll travel separately from us." They said, *"Great."* So that was how we did it.

I already knew Bill Graham because I had worked with him and I had a relationship with him. Since I was bringing him to the party, I felt I had to make it work. Make it work for Bill as well. I was being protective of Bill *and* being protective of Bob at the same time. Just by saying, "Maybe these people *don't* belong together. You just stay on that side of the fence and you stay on the other and we'll be fine. Let's go."

We had this plane and we would travel around to all the jobs on it while Bill and some other people traveled separately. During the tour, Bill was *so* reserved. He was on such good behavior. Toward the end of the tour, I started to feel guilty about this thing. I finally said to the guys, "Listen. I want to invite Bill to fly with us. I think he's been punished long enough. He should be allowed to ride on the airplane because he's done an excellent job all along. Anybody got any complaints?"

They said, "No, *no.*"

So I told Bill to come with us. I mean, it was like having a priest on the tour. The only thing was a couple of occasions when we were setting up or doing sound checks. It was the way Bill was dealing with some of the crew. Bill was trying to show how hard he was trying to do a good job. But in such a vulgar, hostile manner that it was hard to appreciate. Unless we were hiring this person as a bodyguard. I 50-percent appreciated it and 50-percent wished that he had another kind of tact so people wouldn't say, *"God.* This guy can be an *animal,* can't he?"

BILL: There is a thing that happens between an artist and his fans when they *really* lock in. The person involved with the artist during the show is so in line that they are not really with anybody else for the moment. Not with the person they came with, whether it be their husband or wife or brother or old man or old lady. Dylan had written most of those songs years earlier. The kids were now in the thirty-year-old world listening to songs they had first heard when they were fifteen and sixteen. It was a soulful experience because there was soulful remembrance going on.

I don't think it could have been much different if it had been a swami there. What they really wanted to hear were words of wisdom. They were saying, "I'm not here to hear you for the first time. I want to check back and relate to when I first had these teachings." Because the poet is always an involuntary teacher. Wouldn't you have paid admission to walk into a studio where Matisse or Van Gogh was painting? That was what it was like with Dylan on that tour.

I have great respect for Springsteen. I have great respect for Jagger. But I have always thought Dylan was the ultimate performer of the ethereal kind. Different from Otis Redding. He just had such a profound effect on everybody. He communicated on as strong a level as I have ever seen an artist communicate with his fans.

A lot of people talk to me about this or that Rolling Stones tour or the first time they saw Springsteen or Prince or Michael Jackson. But in terms of an artist changing people's lives, I think more than any other tour, it was those people who saw Dylan in 1974, playing songs from years before. An entire generation had their minds blown during those nights.

7.

ROBERT GREENFIELD: Bill was living in a comfortable house by a small stream under the redwoods outside Mill Valley in Marin County. Just as it had been during the sixties, Marin itself continued to be a whole other world from San Francisco, the far busier and much more uptight city across the bridge. Marin was just a lot more laid back, man. Friendlier, and well . . . just *Marin*.

Marcia Sult had grown up there, hanging out as a high school girl in the boho coffeehouses and funky Sausalito houseboats where folk musicians like David Freiberg, David Crosby, and Dino Valenti lived long before the rock scene ever got underway. By 1974, she was working as a bookkeeper, cashier, and waitress at that most Marin of restaurants, the Trident. Right on the water in Sausalito, the Trident was not so much somewhere to eat as a state of mind. A place where everyone was family and on a given evening, anything was possible, depending as always of course on the vibes.

Right around closing time one night, Bill came into the Trident after a Grateful Dead show. Marcia Sult saw that he was really out of it. Totally zoned, in every way. Although the kitchen was already closed, she brought him bread and soup to eat. Bill asked her if she would drive him home. Concerned that he might not get there any other way, Marcia agreed to do him this small favor.

MARCIA SULT GODINEZ: We were in the kitchen of Bill's house and Bill came up to me. He stood real close. I turned around and I looked at him and he got down on his knees in front of me in the kitchen. It was one of the most powerful experiences in my life. He was on his knees and he had his head bowed. I don't know what it did to me but it really did something.

It was like this statement of "I'm lonely" or "I need something" or "I'm really suffering." But it was *so* powerful. He didn't say anything. It was like I couldn't *not* do something. I just reached down and embraced him.

We ended up living together very rapidly. Like within three months. I was twenty-four at the time. And still young. Still very naive and inexperienced on many levels.

BILL: After I did the Dylan tour, we started talking about Crosby, Stills, Nash, and Young going out in the summer. Based on the kind of act they had become, it was obvious that the indoor arenas where Dylan had played would be too small. So the entire tour was booked in outdoor stadiums. Up to that point, I would say it was the single biggest tour in the history of rock and roll.

ELLIOT ROBERTS: I gave Bill the 1974 CSNY tour. It was the first pure stadium tour and we played thirty-five stadiums. Bill was the best production-oriented guy. He already had FM Productions and he had his own shop for building sets. There had been other tours with outdoor shows but none that was *all* stadiums. It was real big and we wanted to make sure that the production values would be the best. So we hired Bill.

Of course there was a lot of wrangling. When you were talking thirty-five stadiums and Bill's ludicrous production costs. There was a lot of going back and forth and it wasn't always pleasant. My obligation was to make the best deal for my client that I could make. To make them the most net. The most money under the best and most optimum conditions. My job was to get them the best conditions to play in for the best bread they could make. And Bill's job was to get them for the cheapest he could.

BILL: Before we went out, David Geffen said to me, "Bill, you know, you're going to take these guys out and I want to hear from you *every* day. Call back and let me know how things are going. I want us to stay in touch. If Graham Nash gets more applause on his piano solo than Neil Young does on the guitar, then we have to switch it around."

Okay. I called him the first day. I called him the second. I called and I called. Finally I got tired and I didn't call him. My phone rang in Kansas City, which was like the fifth place we went. It was David Geffen.

"Hello, Bill. How are you? How's everything?"

I said, "Fine."

"Well, how are things going?" he asked.

I said, "They're getting along. No particular problems."

The little battles these guys were having with one another I was not going to tell him about. I finally said, "David, I'm telling you the truth. I know you're concerned and I appreciate the shot you're giving me with the band. But we're all getting along and everything's fine. To tell you the truth, I think they *like* me."

There was a pause on the phone. The way only David Geffen can, he said, "I'll tell you this, Bill. They may like you. But they *love* me. All right?"

GRAHAM NASH: By 1974, it was all getting gigantic. But we wanted to go out and play. Where were we going to play? We were like legendary at this point and we still didn't know why. So when we decided to go out, Elliot Roberts said, "Well. Let's play baseball stadiums."

"*Baseball* stadiums?" we said. "What?"

He said, "Yeah. We're big enough. Baseball stadiums. Fifty, sixty thousand a night. Let's do it. Let me talk to Bill."

BILL: The logistics were a challenge. Sound and lights and traveling and personnel and these four *nudniks* on the road. Crosby, Stills, Nash, and Young. All I heard from them was "*I* don't talk to him. He don't talk to me. In the second half, *I* do the piano solo first. But he does *two* solos! I only do *one* solo. I'm not going to follow that with my acoustic guitar." He's too tall. He's too short. He's too fat. It was a very difficult tour. It was *insane*.

This was during the Watergate era when Nixon was getting ready to either leave or be impeached. Stephen Stills had a tendency to get on stage and pontificate quite a bit. Three of the four *loved* to pontificate. David Crosby was like a wind-up bear. But I liked those guys. Loonies. But I liked them. Stephen always thought he was one of the few Caucasian people on the planet who understood Latin music, Latin people, and Latin percussion. I think he even spoke a little Spanish. He considered himself a real *congero*. Meaning someone who plays the congas and bongos.

We were in Tempe, Arizona, on the fourth night of the tour and that particular night, Stephen really expressed himself playing the congas. I had to go from there to Kansas City to set up the next gig. My phone rang in the middle of the night and it was Stephen and in so many words, he said, "Bill, I really wailed tonight. I lost myself emotionally and physically. And I *really* hurt my thumb. Because I was hitting the congas so hard. I must have broken a blood vessel or something because my thumb is all puffed up. It hurts *so* bad. I don't know if it's going to get better. But I wanted to tell you. Not just because you're the promoter but because you're my *friend*. I wanted to tell you . . . that I'm probably not going to be able to play tomorrow night."

I said, "Should I get a doctor, Stephen?"

He said, "No. Let me see if I can get through the night. Then let's see what happens in the morning."

I said, "I'm *very* concerned, Stephen. Let me call you right back because the first thing I want to do is call Kansas City."

"Why would you want to do that?"

I said, "I'm going to have the show canceled. I want to play it safe so people are forewarned that you won't be playing."

"Why would you do that?"

I said, "I've *got* to make sure your hand is okay. There's no show unless all of you can play. It's not the other way around."

"*You* would do that?"

"Of course. *No* problem."

"Why don't you wait till morning?"

"I'll wait, Stephen. But I'm prepared to cancel and we'll just make it up somewhere else."

"Why don't you just wait, man?" he said. "But I *really* appreciate you're taking that attitude. I really appreciate that you feel that way."

I said, "Stephen, it's *you*. How else could I feel?"

The next morning, I was crossing behind the hotel, going somewhere from my room. There was a swimming pool and next to it was a badminton court. There was Stephen Stills in a game of badminton. He was playing a rather good game. I didn't say anything. I just said, "Morning." And he said, "Morning, Bill."

We went ahead and got on the bus. We went to the next gig and he did his set and he pounded away on the bongos and the congas. Afterward, I said, "Stephen, I'd like to talk to you, please. I'd like to take a minute and thank you and show you my appreciation for your staying in there and pulling it all together."

He said, "Yeah, man. You know. After I talked to you, the swelling went down and everything seemed to work out okay. Hey, but Bill. I really appreciate that you were concerned. It was good to know, man."

I said, "Stephen. I've got to level with you. I was glad to get up this morning and see that you were still able to hold the racket. That you were able to pull through your agony of last evening. But I *got* to level with you. Had you told me tonight that you were *not* going to play, I would've broken every fucking bone in your body."

At that point, he stuck his hands up into his armpits like he was afraid I would break all his fingers and he ran *screaming* from the room. It was one of the great moments.

When we got to Kansas City, there were big problems about covering the field. I think it was one of the first rock shows in an Astroturf stadium and we had to cover it with canvas. The truck was late and they had an expert there who said that if it was not covered by such and such a time, we were not going to have a show. The crew was sort of down anyway and it was very hot. It was in the afternoon and I said to Patrick Stansfield, who was like the *majordomo* on that tour, "You want to get the guys together? Why don't we just talk to everybody?"

They got the whole gang together. I was talking about the fact that we were on the road and that this was not just rock and roll but *Crosby, Stills, Nash, and Young.* I said, "We've got to get the sound up and the lights up and it's going to be tough from here on. Sometimes, no rest. Some days, a little rest. But we really got to get out there and *do* it in every town. Because it's *Crosby, Stills, Nash, and Young.* You've got to be proud of your gig and the fact that you're affecting positive change in this society."

I said, "Sometimes, you've got to lean into the wall and put your shoulder down and bend into the wind and buckle up. Sometimes, you've got to do it for the *Gipper.* You got to get out there and take that ball and run to that line and *kick ass.* And you have to get *down* and *dirty* to do it. Like the *Gipper.* You've got to do it for *the Gipper.*"

Patrick Stansfield stepped into the middle of this circle of workers in the middle of the scorching hot field and he grabbed hold of his nuts. He said, "Yeah. I got the Gipper. Here's your Gipper for you." It was like he was saying, "Cut the shit. You want us to do the fucking job? *Enough.*" I can't ever recall being cut down like that. But he was right.

ELLIOT ROBERTS: We traveled, we played. We traveled, we played. And that was it every day for six or seven weeks. The crew was underpaid. We were all overworked. There were some dates that were just too close to other dates. Everybody was flipping out. It wasn't a very pleasant tour. It was pleasant for two hours the band played and that was *it.* Everything else was a horror.

It was the largest-grossing tour ever to that point. But it was a very low *netting* tour. Because the expenses were *astronomical.* Because of the mistakes made, we ended up having to hire double crews. We had extra people in every hall to set up. Extra union people. So the expenses got outrageous.

GRAHAM NASH: It was a bad experience to us. Financially, we made money. Everyone I talked to that saw those shows loved them. We did play good but there was something missing, you know. We had taken away part of our music. Not musically. But part of the atmosphere and the ambience by not being able to make eye contact with our audience.

It particularly pissed David off, who was always wanting to *feel* the audience.

BILL: They'd always start the second act with each guy doing a little bit of acoustic. Graham would play the piano. Stephen would play acoustic guitar. David would play acoustic. Neil would play acoustic. And then they would all get together to play. But what was the order? Who played first? Who played second? It got to a point where nobody wanted to follow Neil. So Neil went last.

And phone calls. I always figured David Geffen was sitting on his couch in his house in Beverly Hills with the phone to his ear. "Yes. Hello, David. Yes. Neil, *yes*. Has the other guy called? *No?* Stephen *may* call you. He *would* have called. He *should* have called. *David?* David's *good*. Why *should* he say anything better about *you?*"

I always imagined these conversations going on. David Geffen feeling these guys out. And then David getting on the phone with me later to check on everything.

DAVE FURANO: Somehow, we made it to New York. Roosevelt Raceway. I was really frightened. We had let all the people in the night before. They got in and started tearing the boards off the perimeter of the track where the horses race. The rail. They were burning the boards to keep warm. I looked out from the stage at a crowd of humanity that was a hundred thousand people or so, and it looked like all these tribes huddled around their fires. There was Queens, there was The Bronx, there were all the villages of New York with the people out and the fires burning.

I went to bed. It was two in the morning and I knew I was going to have to get up in three hours. Because the sun would come up and Bill would get to play "Here Comes the Sun" and go through that whole ceremony. Just as I was getting to sleep, I was awakened inside my trailer or motor home.

Bill was dressed up in a bunny outfit, skating up and down inside the trailer. I could not believe this. I mean, what was happening. He had on a full-on bunny outfit with ears on it and *everything*. The only thing sticking out was his face and he had roller skates on *inside* the motor home.

ELLIOT ROBERTS: Did Crosby, Stills, Nash, and Young learn something from this? Not to do a big tour with Bill again. That was what they learned. That was what we *all* learned. It wasn't so much Bill. We realized that what we should have done was use a number of promoters, each responsible for their own city. What Bill ended up doing was getting a subcontractor in each city for a low figure. Bill was making 5-percent deals with them and they had so little money that they had to cut everything to try and save here and there so they could pad their bills.

ROBERT GREENFIELD: Following the CSNY tour, Bill and his company took George Harrison out on the road for a national tour. It was less than a complete critical or commercial success.

BILL: We did the national Dylan tour followed by the Crosby, Stills, Nash, and Young tour followed by the George Harrison tour right at the very end of the year. One right after another, and it took me and the company into a different realm, creating what eventually became a very problematic situation. In each instance, the artist did not go to an agency which then contacted the local promoters about shows.

We booked the tour directly with those promoters in each town or with the facility in that town. We were not agents, and we did not use agents to do the work. This was a *big* break from the standard format of a promoter buying talent *through* an agency. Which led to the agencies getting nervous that I was trying to put them out of business by doing their jobs for them. Eventually, there was a showdown with the agents and managers on Long Island.

I was invited to this open forum. A group of mainly agents but managers as well. There had never before been anything of its kind. I mean, a meeting of the *boys*. Somebody had rented an estate in Long Island that was huge. Although they had asked me to come, I had gotten word that it was, "Hey, Bill. *Meeting*." Like I *had* to be there.

They were angry with me for cutting tough deals and coming into their cities with the acts I had taken on national tours. The major agencies thought this could be the start of a trend. Major artists bypassing the agency system. All I kept saying to them was, "This was a one-of-a-kind situation. I felt like doing this, and that's the way it's going to be."

If I *had* to be there, then at least I was going to get some enjoyment out of it. Because *everybody* was there. Frank Barsalona and people from William Morris and ICM and MCA. Managers, agents, and promoters. I felt like I was being made to stand up in front of the union, even though there was no union. There were no rules of any kind in the business at that time. Yet I was being called on the carpet for what I had done.

I knew the meeting on Long Island was going to be held in this huge round room with all these limos and fancy cars outside. So I got a hold of someone at Central Casting in New York. The meeting was called for in the morning from nine-thirty to noon and then there was a break for

lunch. At one, we would all go back to the meeting table. The morning
was pretty much sparring and feeling each other out. The killing was
going to be done in the afternoon.

Before lunch, it was all still dancing. *"Bill,* you're bringing *that* tour
to *my city?* I'm *excited.* I'm *exalted.* You're bringing *that* show to
Cleveland!"

They were sharpening the guillotine. This was appetizer conversation
before the trial by fire. I was the piano player they wanted to shoot. After
lunch, I sat down and I did something I'd never done before. I lit a cigar.
My back was to the big windows facing the room. The shades were open.
As a sign to my guys.

Just then, six limousines pulled up. Out of each one of these six limos
came five *bulyoks.* Guys dressed like "The Untouchables," Elliot Ness-
style. Spats, boutonnieres, top hats, dapper collars. East Coast movie
gangsters. Each carrying a musical instrument case. They all got out of
their cars and came through the front door. The first guy was the biggest
toughest meanest guy.

All he said was, *"Awrite!* Everybody *siddown!* Nobody *moves!"*

I saw some people in the room going, "Ha, ha, ha!" Some froze right
away. The guys started going along the wall around this room until they
were in position five feet apart all around the people. Serious and in dead
silence. Nobody really understood what was going on.

The first guy put his cello case down on the table and leaned toward
me and said, "Excuse me, boss? Is everything *satisfactory?"*

I took my cigar out of my mouth, flicked my ashes into the ashtray,
put on my best Al Capone face, and nodded approval. That was the next
signal. All the guys put their cases down on the table and opened them
up. They took off their jackets. They were all wearing suspenders. They
folded their jackets neatly inside the cases. As they went out the door, in
big letters on the back of every guy's shirt, it said, "BILL GRAHAM
PRESENTS."

It definitely unnerved a lot of the people in that room. It was my way
of saying to them that I knew who they *thought* I was. In terms of what
was discussed afterward, I myself would not have wanted someone else to
bring an act into the Bay Area when I was the one who had built the act
there. By day's end, I'd agreed to forego national touring in the best
interests of the industry. Not that I was that generous. I knew full well
that the major agencies, at their whim, could freeze me out of business
in the Bay Area by not selling me talent. So much for national touring.

PATRICK STANSFIELD: After that meeting in Long Island, Bill agreed to
back down and not force this shit down other people's throats. The

meeting was significant because in most of these promoters' offices now, you can find a picture of the meeting.

It's like the little sign you used to see in every barbershop. *"THIS IS A UNION SHOP."* That little picture shows that these people are part of the system.

8.

MARCIA SULT GODINEZ: I took my son Thomas to Paris to live. Thomas went to school and I worked as a model and we had a little apartment. Bill was calling me constantly. He came over to visit a couple of times and he really really wanted to get married. What I had wanted with Bill from day one was get married and do a family. Be healthy and go through life together and be normal. A little whacky maybe but basically normal and healthy human beings.

Because Bill wanted to get married, I moved back and he just couldn't deal with it. It's hard to describe how it really was. It was a real madness. A real level of subtle insanity going on between Bill and I. Ken Regan, the photographer who took all these pictures of us that appeared in *People* magazine, was a good friend. One time he and his girlfriend came over for dinner. What Bill did at the table was that he wanted Ken and his girlfriend to judge me. It was like a trial. He said, "She went away and she knew I loved her. She went away and she was with this guy and then she came back here."

Nothing that Bill had done during the same time mattered because *I* was really the culprit. Ken and his girlfriend ended up leaving. I don't think we ever ate. They had to get up and leave because it was so intense. Then Bill got up and took some mescaline. Or he announced that he had taken some. I thought, "Okay, I'm going to *really* get into this." So I took some, too. I thought, "I want to deal with this. If he wants to be on a psychedelic level, I'll do it too."

We called Ken Regan at five o'clock in the morning and asked him if he wanted to come over for dessert. We were both just laughing uproariously. It was great fun. And Ken just couldn't believe it. It was total madness. *Total madness.*

BILL: I went from one national tour to another. It was a big logistics year. The other thing going on for me in business was the delegation of responsibility. This was new for me. I had lived one kind of life to this point and now I was trying to learn how to live another. Now, when I say delegating, you have to understand that I was dealing with street people, both in and out of my own business. People who had not gone through the normal chain of command to get where they were. People who did not get a college education and then start as a clerk and become a junior lawyer and then a full-fledged lawyer and then a partner in a firm.

In my business, there were no vice presidents or CEO's. There were no gold bars on the shoulder to show your rank. It was just, "You're in charge of this tour. You go hire some guys and get somebody to check them into hotels. Get someone to drive the bus and get in touch with the local promoter."

For so many people, it was an instantaneous switch in the cornerstone of their life. They went from taking orders to *giving* them. The biggest step that a man can take is when he changes over.

ROBERT GREENFIELD: Inside his company, Bill had serious problems with the people he had hired to insulate him from the day-to-day routine so he could be free to be Bill Graham the showman and promoter all the time. Simply, things did not add up. People had claimed expenses which made no sense. The books were crooked. Between Bill and those who did not just work for him but also considered themselves his closest friends, it was a breach of trust of major proportions.

Within the industry Bill helped create, a certain amount of larceny was factored into every deal. It was just the cost of doing business all over town. But stealing *within* the family was something else again. A year after one of his people had been let go, Bill discovered that his house in Marin County was not in his name. He did not legally own it. In order to get the house back, he had to go to court. *Twice.*

Looking to set his financial house in order, Bill handed the company over to Dave Furano, an essentially very straight businessman who had managed the building at Winterland for the Ice Follies. Through Dave and his younger brother Dell, Bill got into the T-shirt business. The company they formed was called Winterland Productions. In time, it would become the largest purveyor of rock and roll-related merchandise in the world.

9.

BILL: In January 1975, I was flying back from Los Angeles when I read in the *San Francisco Examiner* that a budget cut was going to mean the end of all extracurricular activities in San Francisco city schools. Music and cheerleading and sports. Teachers would no longer be paid for coaching or tutoring or giving any kind of instruction once the regular school day was done. Through the years, I had pretty much taken on a policy of responding to anyone who said, "I want to raise money for something." If I believed the cause was justifiable and that something good could come out of the money that was raised. If they could get the artist to do the show, I would put on the show free of charge, except for my expenses.

This time, no one had to ask me. Because the news made no sense to me. If no one was coming to read books and they had closed the libraries, that would have been one thing. But this was something that money *could* fix.

It was like the yellow school bus. Back at the original Fillmore, a woman came to me and said, "Bill, we don't know where to turn. We're mothers involved with an alternative school in Berkeley. We have a bus that goes around the neighborhood. We've been at it for four years now but the bus has broken down. The engine is shot. We need a new bus but we don't have the money to buy one."

I got together Quicksilver and the Dead and Big Brother. A couple of weeks later, we did the benefit. Two of the ladies and Willie John Cashman, one of my guys, went to Daly City and bought a bus for fourteen thousand dollars. They went to another shop and had it painted yellow and put a sign on the side. For years, whenever I'd go to Berkeley to put up my posters, there was the bus.

Instant solution to the problem. *Toothache? Dentist.* That was what SNACK was. Enough money to keep extracurricular activities going for a year. And then let's see what the city could do.

I went to see Joseph Alioto, the mayor of San Francisco. He said that they needed six hundred thousand dollars to carry on the extracurricular activities program for another year. I told him I wanted to try to put a show together for the community. I asked the Park and Recreation Department to give us Kezar Stadium near Golden Gate Park where we were no longer allowed to do our Day on the Green shows because of noise. I wanted to have the show *within* the city so it would be a communal focal point.

The mayor didn't go for it right away. We met again. I told him I also wanted the fifty-cent tax on tickets for that facility waived. He agreed. It was one of the few times that I *personally* approached all the artists. The Grateful Dead, Graham Central Station, Bob Dylan and the Band, who were unannounced, Jefferson Starship, Tower of Power, the Doobie Brothers, Santana, Mimi Farina, and Neil Young.

I put aside everything to concentrate on this show. Anybody who meant anything at all in the Bay Area, I was going to try to get on that stage. I told them all, "The children will not have musical instruments. There will be no football practices. There will be no cheerleaders. No after-school tutoring. Here is the instant solution. We just need money to retain the services of people who can already teach." I came up with the name SNACK. San Francisco Needs Athletics, Culture, and Kicks. I talked to every band and asked them to give me three or four dates when they could do it. When the dates of the bands crossed, that was when I scheduled the show.

I decided that it would be great if we could have folks on stage whom young people looked up to as role models. People who I thought were valid heroes. In between the acts as we did the set changes, I wanted them to come out and rap. So I contacted Willie Mays and John Brodie and Gene Washington. Joan Baez. Jesse Owens.

I called Marlon Brando, to whom I had spoken many times before. He'd wanted to do benefits on behalf of the American Indians. I'd said to him then, "*You* get the artists and *I'll* do it." I had the same understanding with him that I had with many other people concerning fund-raising events. Over the phone, Marlon agreed to come up for the show.

It rained for a solid week before the date. The night before, I walked that field all night long, cursing the skies. At 5 A.M., it stopped raining. It was beautiful all day long. The show ended at six in the evening. At 6:05, it started raining again. People in the company looked at me in a strange way. They said, "What did you do?"

Willie Mays spoke. John Brodie spoke. Brando arrived backstage. At that time, he was bearded and heavy-set, with his hair just beginning to go gray. A great face, that all-powerful presence. Francis Coppola was also there. It was a nice gathering backstage in an area with lawn tables and umbrellas. After one of the sets, I walked out on stage and I said, "Would you please welcome another friend of ours, and certainly a friend of yours. *Marlon Brando*."

I never heard before what I heard then. The mass was being told something that it was not prepared to hear. It was like they had all just seen a spaceship go by the window. It was like Zeus had just walked out on that stage. *Royalty. True* royalty, on the highest level. *Brando. On the Waterfront. The Wild One. A Streetcar Named Desire. Viva Zapata.* It was *awesome.*

He rapped to the kids. He said that his generation had made a lot of mistakes and left behind a lot of stuff for them to clean up. He said, "Be strong but listen to the people who can teach you. The American Indians were here before us and we have to respect them as we respect one another." There was no put-on. No guru could have done it so well.

He finished speaking and walked to the side of the stage. He stood there with Francis Coppola and some other friends and seemed to be in a trance, totally isolated in this public arena. He was wearing one of those Fidel Castro military bush jackets with big pockets to cover up some of his girth. I went over to him and I grabbed him and I said, "Are you all right?" He just sort of shook his head. I asked him, "Would you like some water?" He shook his head yes. So I went and got him some water.

A few minutes later, he was sitting down at the table but still not speaking. A lot of people were speaking to him but he still had not said anything. People were saying, "That was *wonderful*, Marlon." I went over to him for like the third time. I said, "Sure I can't do anything for you? You're cool? You're okay?"

Very gently, he grabbed both my arms and looked into my eyes. This was not in the movie house in The Bronx where I had gone every Saturday as a kid. I was backstage at SNACK. He turned me around and we were face-to-face in these folding chairs. He said, "You know something? Those weren't *extras* out there."

What a *line*. With him, it had been a lifetime of making movies where everything was rehearsed and scheduled and shot over and over again. He hadn't encountered anything like this since he had started out on Broadway. For the first time in a long time, he wasn't playing a character. He was being Marlon Brando. And it blew his cork.

It was a magnificent day of great music and social awareness. There was a true sense of camaraderie among the fifty thousand people there that day. We even had parents with children. Family time.

SNACK really was the first big rock benefit concert ever done. The Bay Area musicians were called to arms and they responded to the call. For me, it represented the use of the drawing power of our artists to address and attempt to solve a social problem.

10.

BILL: We'd sold a million dollars' worth of tickets for two Led Zeppelin shows at Oakland Coliseum in August 1975. I took one of my rare vacations with Marcia and her son Thomas and my son David and Ken Regan, the photographer. We all went white-water rafting. Down a river in Utah that ended in Lake Powell. We were drifting along in this raft and I looked up in the sky and I saw skywriting. I think my son David saw it first. The plane was just doing an "I." It said, "B-I." Then it said, "B-I-L-L C-A-L-L."

I said, "Who the fuck are they talking to? It *must* be me."

We turned around and went back to Moab to a phone. I called Jerry Pompili back at the office. I had always told him never to cancel a show without my approval. I said, "It's *Led Zeppelin*, right?" He said, "Yeah. How did you know? We just got word that Robert Plant broke his leg hitting a tree on the island of Rhodes and he can't do the tour. It's going to come out in the news tomorrow. What should we do? Refund now, or hold the tickets? Wait for a makeup date? I'm sorry I did this to you but . . ."

I said, "I'm glad you called me. I'll be right home." Jerry had hired a skywriter from some place in Utah to find me.

I went back and returned a hundred and twenty thousand tickets. That alone cost me a hundred and thirty thousand dollars in ticket service charges. We had already put a deposit down on the stadium. We'd done a lot of promotion and advertising. We'd done a poster. We lost it *all*.

In good faith, we had not collected any money from the band. The fact that they said they were going to play these dates made us spend the money. I couldn't sue them. Because the deal was that *when* they played they would receive their money. In legalese, they were saying, "Why charge us? We didn't do anything wrong."

That is the risk that the promoter always takes. Which people may not be aware of. Led Zeppelin said they were going to reschedule and come back. Led Zeppelin management refused to pick up *any* of the cancellation costs. To them, it was an act of God. They could have offered us *something* to help make up for that loss.

But they didn't. And it hurt.

11.

BILL: Jon Peters called me. He was producing the third remake of the old classic *A Star Is Born*, this time set in rock with Kris Kristofferson and Barbra Streisand. They had tried shooting a concert scene for the movie twice before but it hadn't worked. They wanted authentic-looking bikers and a big crowd in an outdoor venue and they asked if we would help them stage it somewhere live as opposed to doing it in a studio setting.

Jon Peters knew very little about rock and roll. But he was from South Philly. So there was very little he *didn't* know about. He wanted fifty thousand people in a stadium from seven in the morning until dark as extras for the live concert scenes. I lined up Peter Frampton, Santana, Graham Central Station, and Ronnie Montrose to perform. The plan was very simple. A live performance by a band and then some movie action on stage and then another band and so on. The intent was to keep the fans entertained throughout the long ordeal.

The real movie for me was backstage. In the beginning, Barbra Streisand would not even talk directly to me. She would talk to the person *next* to me or next to *her*, saying something like, "Well, I don't know if that's right," or "You know, that *might* work." There was no eye contact. No face-to-face.

I would say something, she would say something back, and her manager, Marty Erlichman would interpret the English language she had just used. Before the show, I said, "You're going to be using nearly fifty thousand people as extras in your movie. You're not feeding them, we're charging them three and a half dollars to get in, and they *know* they're here to be used in a movie. You have to give them a hit."

"What do you mean by a hit?" Marty Erlichman asked.

"Barbra Streisand should come out first in the morning and be the greeter and do a few songs."

"How can we do that?" he said. "She *hates* crowds. She's *terrified* of live performances."

"Get Phil Ramone's loops of the tracks from her last album. She can sing three or four songs live to that background."

Finally, Barbra herself spoke. She said, "These are rock and roll kids. They'll *hate* me. They'll boo me off the stage. What do they know about what I do?"

"Look," I said. "You've *got* to listen to me. This is what I do for a living. If you don't want to listen, there's no sense paying me fifty thousand dollars to put this thing on."

It got a little out of hand. Finally, Barbra said, "Who are you talking to?"

I leaned over the table between us and I said, "I'm talking to *you*, lady. Come *on!*"

It was Brooklyn and The Bronx, eye-to-eye at last. It all finally broke down between us. She said, "All right. *All right.* You want it this way? We'll do it this way."

The day of the concert, I walked on stage at seven in the morning and said, "Would you please welcome a friend of yours, Ms. Barbra Streisand." She walked out and got that Brando applause. The bigger-than-life kind of thing. Then she said the two magic words. The ones she hadn't planned on using. She looked at the crowd and said, *"Holy shit!"* They went crazy. *Crazy.* She *owned* them from that point on. Then she went into "People" and nobody moved. It was magic.

The best story happened before the show. Jon Peters had hired fifty or sixty Hell's Angels from Southern California. I'd told him that these guys were not easy to deal with. I'd told him that he had to be strict with them. He went into this whole long rap about, *"Hey.* I'm from South Philly. I been at this all my life. I know how to deal with bikers. I appreciate what you're tellin' me, Billy. But you do your thing and I'll do mine and it'll all be cool."

I didn't say anything except, "If you need me, I've dealt with these situations before. I'll be glad to help."

Then I left to do some work. I got back about ten in the morning the day before the show and Dave Furano met me at the backstage gate and he was freaking out. One of the Angels had a forty-five Magnum on him. During the course of the morning, Jon Peters had gone over to him and said, "Hey, you can't wear that piece around here. *Take it off.*" The word was that the Angel had taken out the gun and pointed it at Peters and said, "You fuck with me, I'll blow your fuckin' brains out."

Peters had freaked and gone into his trailer. I went into his trailer and Peters said, "Guy pulled this gun on me, he was out of his fuckin' mind. I haven't called the police, I haven't done anything. I been waitin' for you. We've got to do something about this."

I said, "Let me deal with it."

He said, "But you can't deal with these guys. They're *crazy.*"

I said, "Let me talk to the guy."

I left the trailer and went across the backstage area to where the Angels were hanging out. I knew a lot of them from Dead shows. I found the one with the gun in the back of a pickup truck along with a buddy and they were having beers. Ten o'clock in the morning and they were having *beers.* I said, "Excuse me. I don't want to bother you but I wonder if I could talk to you for a minute?"

He said, *"Yeah?"*

I said, "I work for the film company. My name is Bill. You got a minute?"

Every other word I said to him was an apology for imposing on him. He said, "Is it private?"

I said, "No." But he told the other guy to leave anyway. He said, "Want a beer?" I climbed into the pickup truck and took the beer and thanked him for it. Then I started to explain that I worked backstage for Miss Streisand and my job was to sort of keep the peace and I had heard there was a slight problem. I didn't want to bother him now but if he had some time later on, maybe we could talk about it then.

"Nah. It's okay. Do it now."

"I heard there was a misunderstanding here."

"Misunderstanding? Fuckin' guy! I'm gonna *blow* his fuckin' brains *out.*"

He was sitting there like something out of *Waiting for Godot.* I said, "I heard the problem was that he asked you to take your piece off. I've got to tell you the truth. I don't like anybody fucking with my piece either. Know what I mean?"

He said, *"Fuckin' guy.* He couldn't talk to me *straight.* Don't tell *me* to take *my* piece *off.* Know what I mean?"

I said, "I feel the same way. You got some time now? Or should I come back later? Because I have a major problem."

I have no idea where it came from but I went into this story. I told the guy that my job was to make sure everything backstage stayed okay for Ms. Streisand because she was the star of the picture. She was a wonderful and decent person. But she'd heard about the situation with his piece. He said, *"She did, huh?"* All of a sudden, he swelled up right before my eyes. He became the Road Warrior.

I said, "I hope you'll give her the respect she's due. Many years ago, she visited an uncle of hers who was a veteran of World War II. He was cleaning this revolver he'd captured from the Germans when all of a sudden it discharged in his abdomen." When I got to the word *"abdomen,"* I lost the guy.

So I said, "In his *stomach.* It was a minor wound and he recovered but ever since when Miss Streisand sees a piece or even *hears* about a piece, she doesn't move. She gets *immobile.* She freaks. The memory has *never* left her mind. She can't function if there is a real piece around.

"So I came to ask you for a solid. Could you *think* of the possibility of perhaps putting the piece away for just a few hours? It's your piece and I ain't tellin' you what to do with your piece. But I could *really* use this favor, man."

Finally, I stopped talking. I looked at the guy and he was staring up at the sky. His level of intensity at that moment was equal to that of General Dwight D. Eisenhower deciding whether it would be Sicily or Normandy he invaded to start the end of World War II.

A good fifteen or twenty seconds passed. Then he said, "Yeah, *right.* I see where that's at. I'll give you one thing, Billy." And he started to undo his holster. "You came to me *straight.* You talked to me like a *man.* People make up stories about us all the time. But, *hey.* I'll do it for *you.* But I'll tell you one thing. That other guy? I'll *blow* his fuckin' brains *out.*"

I said, "I owe you, man. If you need something, I'm *here.*"

I left the pickup truck and went back to Peters's trailer and I knocked on the door. Jon Peters said, *"Yeah. What is it?"* I couldn't tell him what I had gone through or just tell him, "I did it." So I said, "I want to go over the schedule for this afternoon with you."

He said, "Bill, what happened with the biker?"

"Oh, that? Done deal. Anyway . . ."

I wanted to undercut the whole thing. "But what *happened?* Did the guy put the gun away? Tell me about it."

So I proceeded to tell him the entire story that I had told the biker. Jon Peters looked at me and said, "Wait a minute! How the hell did you know about Barbra's uncle?"

Chapter Thirteen

The Last Waltz

1.

ROBBIE ROBERTSON: I had become superstitiously suspicious of the road. Look at what happened to this guy. Look at what happened to *them*. Look at *this* plane. These people who got crazy when they got on the road. This was not a healthy thing. So I was telling the guys in the Band, "I like the music we make together. But I don't want to go out there with it anymore. Because it's becoming more and more difficult and we're not learning from it. We're not growing from it. We're just going back to Milwaukee again. And we *already* know what made Milwaukee famous. So we don't need to go back *again*."

It was just a business and it was not experimental and we were not inventive at this point in doing it. So I didn't want to do it anymore. To bring this to a real strong musical and a very thankful conclusion, I said, "Let's do this on Thanksgiving in San Francisco where we started with Bill Graham. Let's invite these people who have been a strong influence on different spoke wheels of what makes up this music. Everybody representing New Orleans rock and roll, English blues, Chicago blues . . ."

I called Bill Graham and I told him what we were going to do and he was like, "Oh, my *God*." He was *so* solemn about it. And I said, "Bill, you can't take that attitude toward it. Because this is meant to be a *celebrating*. This is *not* a funeral. This is like the end of a chapter."

I didn't realize at the time that it really was like the end of an *era*.

BILL: I went to Malibu to see Robbie Robertson. Robbie had always been the leader of the Band. The spokesperson. Lead guitarist, singer, writer. Due to the nature of his character, he was the one who always said, "What do you think? Levon, Richard, Danko? What's it going to be, Garth?"

We had a long discussion about whom they should invite. They had great taste in music. Most of the suggestions for guest artists came from them. Some came from me.

ROBBIE ROBERTSON: I called Eric Clapton. Because I had seen him when he did the Concert for Bangladesh in Madison Square Garden and he was just fine. We thought Muddy best represented the Chicago blues thing, which had been an influence on so many people and everything. Levon had been to visit there a couple of times. But *we* called all the different people. It wasn't Albert Grossman or Bill Graham calling them.

The only person that called anybody else was Emmett Grogan. He called the poets of San Francisco. Michael McClure and Lawrence Ferlinghetti and Sweet William, Billy Fritsch.

BILL: The name "The Last Waltz" came from Robbie, and it was a great one. The whole idea of serving people food was basically mine. Simply because it was Thanksgiving time. Robbie wasn't too happy about that at the start but we fought for it and won. Also, the idea of decorating Winterland for the occasion by bringing in the sets from *La Traviata* was ours. From the company. Jerry Pompili, Dave Furano, Mick Brigden, Jay Drevers, and the people in the shop.

ROBBIE ROBERTSON: The idea was just to do this show. Then it was like, "Well, if we're going to do this, we should document it somehow. For the archives. Maybe we'll have a video running of it." Then someone said, "I've got a friend with a sixteen-millimeter camera." It was slow coming. It was like, "Well, if you're going to do this thing, you might as well do it *right*." It just gradually grew into what it became. I was the one who got Marty Scorsese to direct the movie. I knew him from when he had worked on the Woodstock film.

Actually, I was making up my list of directors. I wrote down his name and I was thinking, "Who else would get this? Who else could work under this kind of fury and take all this kind of stuff?" Because it was all going to be one-take. I wrote Marty's name down and I couldn't think of anybody else. That was my entire list. I was planning on writing down fifteen names. I wrote his name down and I couldn't think of anyone else.

I met with Marty and I told him what we were going to do. It was a terrible time in his life but he said, "I *have* to do it. I don't have a choice. *Van Morrison?* Are you *kidding? I must* do it." So he jumped in and we didn't have a lot of time to prepare. By the time I talked to Marty, there was less than six weeks left before the show.

I told Bill what we wanted to do, who the people I was thinking about having there were, and that I wanted to handle it in a very low-key, very tasty kind of way. I didn't want it to be a goofy thing. We didn't want a bunch of people that couldn't get in to be waiting outside in the cold and stuff like that. We wanted it to be very, very *tasty*.

Bill said, "I'm trying to get a feeling for the mood and everything." I told him the names of certain films to look at. He had all of his people at Winterland look at Cocteau's *Blood of a Poet*. Trying to understand the realness and the surrealness of it. Just trying to find a place where all this fit in. A world that this fit into. Not so much that we're going to try to fit into it but that we had to build our own world around this. It had to be a *complete* environment.

BILL: This was the era of overindulgence with cocaine. So I took one of the backstage rooms and we painted all the walls white and put a white rug on the floor. The only piece of furniture was in the middle. A glass settee table with black edges. I had a few razor blades lying on top. I bought all these Groucho Marx glasses with the nose attached. We cut away the glasses and I took just the noses and stuck them all over the walls. I cut a hole in the wall and put a cassette machine inside the hole and had it connected to the door. So when you opened the door, it started a tape rolling. When you walked in, all you heard was this sniffing noise, over and over. It was the "Cocteau Room."

ROBBIE ROBERTSON: He was a tremendous help in the organization factor of it. The place being set up right. We had no money. I mean, there was *no* money. We were just doing things. Mo Ostin loaned us money and we weren't even on Warner Brothers Records. Everybody thought, "This is such a nice thing. It's all really in the name of music. There is nothing tricky here. There are no cards at the bottom of the deck. It is just in the name of music and we are trying to do it as good as it can possibly be done under these circumstances." Everybody seemed to get right in tune with that.

BILL: The film guys came in from L.A. They brought in Marty Scorsese, who at the time was not very intelligible. He talked very fast and he was hard to understand because he was so wired all the time.

First, I concerned myself with serving all these people food. A buffet for fifty-four hundred people. We had two hundred and twenty turkeys weighing almost six thousand pounds. Five hundred *extra* turkey legs that weighed six hundred pounds. Stuffing made from seventy bunches of parsley, five hundred pounds of onions, and five hundred pounds of celery sautéed in a hundred pounds of butter mixed with three hundred and fifty pounds of croutons, five quarts of garlic, ten quarts of sage, and one quart of thyme. Ninety gallons of sauce made from drippings. Forty crates of lettuce for the salad. Twenty gallons of salad dressing. Eighteen cases of cranberries. Two thousand pounds of peeled yams. Three hundred pounds of Nova Scotia salmon donated by Louis Kemp and Bob Dylan. Six thousand bread rolls. A hundred pounds of butter patties. For dessert, four hundred pounds of pumpkin pie as well as four hundred pounds of mincemeat. Rock and Roll's last supper.

Up to that time, this was logistically the ultimate exercise in which we as a company had ever engaged. Feeding all these people and promoting that show. We were testing the waters as to see how much people would trust us. Because the ads said only, "Bill Graham Presents, 'The Last Waltz, the Band and Friends.'" There was some disagreement as to whether we should mention who was going to appear on stage with the Band.

I said, "Let's not mention anybody. If we're going to charge them twenty-five dollars a ticket with dinner, they have to believe they're going to get something special." At the time, this was more than double the price of a regular ticket.

We sold out in one day. I refused to list the names of any of the guest artists. That way, I could let the rumors fly. Is Dylan playing? We had already lined up Neil Diamond, Neil Young, Joni Mitchell, Van Morrison, Muddy Waters, Paul Butterfield, Eric Clapton.

Twenty-five dollars times fifty-four hundred people came to a hundred and thirty-five thousand dollars. But all the artists coming to play had expenses that had to be covered. Then Warner Brothers came in for the film because Dylan was going to appear. Dylan was at the heart of the filming. They had no weight for the film without him. They brought in one of the great cinematographers. Laszlo Kovacs. They had David Myers and Michael Chapman, who is now a director. *Major* guys. And Boris Leven was their designer.

ROBBIE ROBERTSON: We had this guy Boris Leven and Marty said, "What are we going to do here, Boris?" Boris was an old man by then who didn't really know from rock and roll but he was smart and he got it because Marty was such a funnel to the music and what we were trying to do. I had such a strong film background myself. Not having done films but in the way I would talk and write and see things. The songs that I wrote were like movies. All the cinematographers seemed to get this.

Leven came and he said, "We're going to have all these long white tables set up in Winterland, right? I want to get amber-orange lights that will hang down, hundreds of them. That will not spread. There will be like a ribbon of light coming down on these white tables."

People were going, "*Hoh!* This is *beautiful*. This is *wonderful*, Boris." Someone was writing all this down and telling us, "We can't afford it." Boris was like, "It *would* have been nice. *Okay. Next.*"

Finally, it was down to like, "We're *not* making a movie. This isn't *Giant*. This isn't *Breakfast at Tiffany's*. What we have in the budget for this is *nothing*." In Boris's mind, he was dressing the set for a movie. So he thought, "*San Francisco Opera House*. Let's go over there and see what they've got in the back room." And that was what they did. They got these chandeliers and various things from operas and Boris put these pieces together and then eliminated things.

BILL: The sets, the lights, and all that, those were our ideas. The food was also us because we continued something we had done for years. Every year at Thanksgiving back at the Fillmore, we'd print up invitation cards and I'd give out three thousand of them to people like Cynthia Sagittarius, who used to panhandle outside Fillmore East. Musicians and people in the business would come and we'd have silent films and chamber music and a big Thanksgiving meal with all the staff there at tables we'd set up in the lobby.

This time it was fifty-four hundred people. So the plan was to have the forty-five piece Berkeley Promenade Orchestra, play dinner music in front of the main stage as the people came in. We even had vegetarian food for people who didn't eat meat.

We had a shirt made up for our staff with a bow tie and a tuxedo painted on the front. I got the staff all together and made a very heartfelt speech to them. I said, "You know, we've taken this building and converted it into a beautiful ballroom with a great show and it's going to be a great evening. But there are two things we need to address.

"There are three hundred of us working tonight at Winterland. A lot of volunteers to serve all those people food. Then we're going to remove the dining room. I want to tell you *how* we're going to do it."

Professional dancers were going to lead the waltzing. Then they would go into the audience and ask people to dance. Nothing was to be forced. As people ate, we would bus the tables. People could sit or dance or move around or *schmooze*. I had shrubs and little trees around the dance floor to separate it from the dining tables. For a couple of hours, we would just bus and clean all those tables.

I told the staff beforehand, "Now, when the meal starts to wind down, and people are no longer coming to eat, you very casually go over to a table and fold it and remove it and make the chairs disappear. The key to the night? I'm gonna give you two things to remember and you *have* to hold on to this, no matter what happens. *Nobody yells. Nobody runs. Nobody yells. Nobody runs.*"

That night, our dining room just *became* a ballroom. One table at a time disappeared. It was absolute magic.

To see the people coming in was fabulous. Some hippie with his old lady in threads that were not worth a dollar but she came in like the Queen of Sheba. They were clean. They didn't have the clothes in which to dress up. It might have been dungarees and a plaid shirt but they were *stepping out.* Don't forget. Twenty-five dollars for the Band and Friends. That would be like seventy-five bucks a show today.

The dinner itself, the food alone, cost forty-two thousand dollars. I staged the show for a 10-percent administrative fee that was consumed by cost overruns. When we finished up, I was left about forty thousand dollars short. I knew all along that my costs were going higher and higher and that my expenses would exceed the limit. I knew I wasn't going to make anything and that in fact, I was going to *lose* money on this. But I never asked for a piece of the movie. I never asked them for anything.

ROBBIE ROBERTSON: When it came movie time, Bill Graham, he got bent all of a sudden. It was like, "I don't want this movie interfering with the people." I was saying, "The movie *isn't* going to interfere with the people. We're going to do everything we can to make it so the people are *part* of this thing. The camera's here and I'm here and we're all here together for this thing. This is only going to happen once in our lives."

I said, "We have to split the difference here. We have to make it so we can get this thing on film and it's shot like no music film has ever been done before with that kind of classiness so that for once it becomes a *film* experience." Because I *hate* music films. I just *hate* them. I go and see them and they're awful and they're boring. I said, "We have to overcome this thing and to overcome it, we have to be able to do certain things."

We were in there and guys were saying, "When people walk the floor, the cameras are going to go like this. We have to drill *through* the floor." Bill Graham was having a fit and there was constantly, "We need more money for this. We need more money for that. We can't do this because we don't have enough money." Bill was trying to make Winterland look as nice as us. He was spending money out of the budget on things for Winterland that he thought were right.

This big issue came up. The balconies were ugly and dirty. He was saying, "We *got* to clean that up back there." And I was saying, "*What,* up *back there?*" He was saying, "See how it's dirty?" But it was like the *last* thing on my mind. Like, who was looking at the balcony? I said, "Well, wash it." Bill said, "No. We need to get a facade for it." A *facade*. I said, "Oh. A *facade*." It turned out we were down to nickel-ing and dime-ing trying to afford this show and we needed more money but the money was gone.

I was saying, "Where has this money gone? We had twenty thousand dollars. Now we have fifteen. Now we have five. What happened to this?"

And he said, "It was for the facade."

I said, "The *fucking facade?*"

From then on, we referred to this as "the *fucking* facade." It covered up the balcony. But it cost fifteen thousand dollars and we were trying to get this thing on film and get everybody there and pay for their wages and do all this stuff we were trying to do. The big issue of the fucking facade became a joke actually. It was like, "Bill, the Winterland balcony will look nice from now on, thanks to the fucking facade. *We* can't fly Eric Clapton in but the fucking facade will be *fine*."

We laughed and we figured out some other way to scrounge up some money that we needed. This was the first experience of like, "You don't know somebody until you sleep with them." This was when I felt like I knew Bill Graham because people kept coming to me and saying, "*Jesus. This guy.* He's screaming at me and throwing things and saying he's going to throw me out of here on my ass."

Marty was saying, "Hey. I'm trying to do a good job here. I know how to do a good job. But I can't do a good job with everything I come up with when this guy throws me a block. I can't do it."

So it became a big job for me in the middle, just saying, "Bill, *please*. Don't make this impossible." He was always, "The *people*. But the *people*." And I was saying, "The people are fine. The people are all fine. What about the people at Watkins Glen, Bill?"

At Watkins Glen, people were climbing on stage during our set and Bill was stomping on their fingers and throwing them back. I said, "Bill. *Bill!* Don't do this during our set." I will never forget his words as long as I live. He said to me, "Robbie, you can't smother them with love *all* the time."

I told him, "So don't give me the 'people' bullshit now. The people will be fine here. They will sense the vibe of those cameras. They're going to know."

BILL: They had seven cameras trained on the stage. I told them, "Look, you can't be in front of the stage with your cameras in the way of the people. You've got to be on the sides." They wanted the master camera position to be in the middle. So we built them this little platform that was like a merry-go-round in the middle of the hall toward the back. I could have done without the attitude of the film people, you know? It was like, "We're here and the people who come in will be just our guinea pigs. They're extras in *our* movie." I told them, "This is a *live* show you're going to try to capture. This is *not* a movie and we are *not* the extras."

ROBBIE ROBERTSON: Every step of the way was *war*. Bill would be screaming in somebody's face with spit flying and then come into the next room and sit down with me and talk to me and it would be Bill the priest again. Then someone would come running in and say, "I can't deal with this animal." And I would say, "What are you talking about? He was just here and he was wonderful. I asked him and he said, 'Anything to make you happy. Anything to make this special.' He said there would be no problem with anything." People would be crying from dealing with this guy through the whole thing.

In terms of the movie, Marty was thinking, "We are not going to shoot this with a bunch of cameras and hopefully, it'll cut together in the end." He was not interested in that. He had every shot drawn up by the lyric in the song. We were not going to have cameras shooting the people chewing gum and clapping their hands. That was not what I wanted. I said, "I don't want to watch people picking apart turkeys. But I do want to get the feeling of 'The Last Waltz' and setting it up. I want to get the orchestra playing Vienna waltz music and people all having dinner and dancing to these waltzes. But I want to get it *mysteriously*."

I wanted it to be romantic. I wanted it to be elegant. All along, Marty was saying, "I want something to be perfectly clear. This is *not* a film about an audience. This is a film about what's going on up on that stage. It's the interaction between people who are all saying good-bye. This is a big good-bye."

We wanted it to be like a ritualistic experience where you would see the shot from the back of the stage out on to the audience and you would see them *mesmerized*. That it was like a ritual, and not a goofy rock show. It was not that vibe. It did not have to do with a girl nudging another girl in the audience and pointing to the stage and then we cut to a shot of Rick Danko up there looking handsome. We didn't want that. It wasn't part of the plan.

2.

ROBBIE ROBERTSON: There were shots which I made them do outside of Winterland at the beginning. The crowd coming in to see this very elegant thing going on in the middle of this sleazy neighborhood with this broken sign out front. All of it somehow made it very soulful to us.

BOB BARSOTTI: People were standing in line in front. As they came down the street, there were potted plants and Astroturf and speakers blaring waltz music. We had the balloon lady in her outrageous costume handing out balloons and flowers to the ladies. We had one of our guys, the Peanut Man, in a tuxedo with a big barrel on wheels filled with peanuts going up and down the line giving out peanuts. So that even before you entered, you knew it was special.

BILL: Before they even got inside, they had been given stuff and there was this whole scene going on in the street. Inside, Winterland looked like a Viennese opera house decked out with velvet everywhere and crystal chandeliers. Tables on two thirds of the floor, the Berkeley Promenade Orchestra playing slowly. As people finished eating, we would ask them to please make room for another person so there was never a time when someone couldn't find a place to sit down and eat. As the eaters diminished and the dancers increased, we slowly took away the tables until the whole thing was transformed. It was just magic. And the show itself was one of the great shows of all time.

ROBBIE ROBERTSON: There were *tons* of sound problems. When a new person came out, how did we do that? Marty was extremely preoccupied with whether this was even *possible* to do. And backups. We couldn't get halfway through it and say, "It didn't work." This was all one-take. You got it, or you didn't. If the cameras started to break down and melt, what did we do? How did we deal with that?

In this song, Marty had to have *this* shot and then *this* spotlight and then everything went out and *this* came up and the footlights. Marty was preoccupied with that. On the night of the show, the gods were with us. A lot of things went wrong but they happened in our favor. Lights blew and it made it look *twice* as dramatic. It was intense and everybody was on edge.

BILL: The Band came out first and did their opening set. Then they brought out Ronnie Hawkins, a huge man with a cowboy hat, who they had backed up way back when they were still the Hawks. They brought out Doctor John and a friend of theirs from New Orleans, Bobby Charles, who wrote "See You Later, Alligator." Then Paul Butterfield. Then Muddy Waters. Eric Clapton. Neil Young. Joni Mitchell. Neil Diamond. Then Van Morrison.

Van did "Caravan." He is the kind of performer that if you catch him on a good night, there is nobody like him. "Turn it up. *Radio*. Little bit louder. *Turn it up!*" The purest kind of performer in that with him you are always getting *one* of a kind. From him, you *never* get the same painting twice. And he was *on* that night.

The night before, at rehearsals, I heard some of the greatest performances of all time. Muddy Waters, Van, Doctor John, and Joni were *awesome*. The place was still empty then. We were running around putting up chandeliers, fixing tables and chairs at three in the morning, while listening to these *awesome* sounds. Dylan was not there. He did not rehearse.

I must say that Robbie and the Band were the greatest house band I ever heard. They backed *everybody*. They played with everybody and switched off on each other's instruments and musically, they were brilliant. With all my *tsouris* with Robbie Robertson, he was the ultimate conductor-composer, the only guy who could have pulled it off.

ROBBIE ROBERTSON: I was on a *mission*. I had something to accomplish there and this was my whole idea and my dream. I had to make sure it worked and that we got it on tape for the album and on film for the movie, and that we played an incredible show for this audience. We proceeded to do this. We did the show and it went on for hours and hours and hours. While we were going, we were changing things. We were taking this out and putting that in and saying, "Why don't we try this?"

It all changed and they were pulling their hair out and Marty was screaming into his headphones but they couldn't hear what he was saying for the cues. It was driving Laszlo Kovacs crazy so finally he ripped off the headphone. Marty got a miscue and he told all the cameras to shut down. But Laszlo didn't hear that. He kept on shooting.

In the movie, that's Muddy Waters singing "Mannish Boy." It's all one shot. Marty thought it was supposed to be the other song and it was just miscommunication. So the gods really were with us.

JON TAPLIN: Bill did the greatest thing that night. In a sense he really saved the day for us. Whatever he thinks of me, I will always be grateful to him because he really took a stand. Bob Dylan was always a little tenuous about the filming of his part of the concert. Because he had this *Renaldo and Clara* thing going on. Howard Aulk, who was Bob's film guy, was *totally* defensive about our thing. He was saying, "Oh, it'll just wreck the value of *Renaldo and Clara* if we let this other movie come out." We went at it all week and typical Bob, he put off the decision till the last minute.

BILL: Dylan was going to start the second half of the show. During the intermission, Robbie and David Braun, Dylan's attorney, came to me. There was this big commotion. Bob had changed his mind. He decided that he *wasn't* going to appear in the film. This concept came to him *during* the intermission. They said, "He's not going to film. He's not into it."

I said, "Isn't that part of the deal?"

They said, "The only way we got Warner Brothers to put up money to make this film, was because of Bob. Without Bob, we don't *have* a film. He has to let us shoot."

Albert Grossman was there but he was no longer a major player in the big Bob Dylan picture. Jerry Weintraub was there managing Neil Diamond. In time, he would be Bob's manager. But not yet. Jon Taplin was beside himself, but he knew Bob wouldn't listen to him. He may have been the Band's manager but that carried no weight with Dylan. Finally, David Braun and Robbie and Scorsese said to me, "*Bill.* You're going to have to go and talk to Bob."

JON TAPLIN: We had a lot of money invested in this thing. Without Bob in the film, it was certainly a lot *less* valuable than with Bob. So it was *very* important to get Bob to do it. Finally, we were getting down and it was getting closer and the intermission was expiring and he *still* hadn't said okay. Finally, it was about five minutes before he had to go on and he said, "Okay, you can film me for the last two numbers." He was doing four.

PAUL WASSERMAN: With Dylan's Socratic way of existing, he claimed he knew *nothing* about the show being filmed. That was not exactly a Pentagon-Chernobyl secret. He *knew* there was a movie. I had discussed it with him. I told him there might be photographers. For the movie, there would be a still photographer but he would be *our* still photographer. Nothing would go out without him. He *knew*. He was *told* there would be a movie. If he didn't retain it, he didn't retain it.

BILL: I walked into the dressing room and Bob was very nice. He just said that he didn't want to be filmed. I went outside and everybody made me aware all over again that we *had* to film him. I made the decision without thinking. I said, "Let's just shoot. I'll *make* it happen."

New instructions arrived from the Dylan camp. "*Don't* let there be any filming." So now the word was officially out. *No* filming Bob. One of his people was assigned to one side of the stage to stand next to the cameraman to make *sure* he didn't film. Everybody else, yes, but not Dylan.

Bob came out of the dressing room. No words, no problems. I walked out and I introduced him. *Bob Dylan.* Not that you can see me do it in the film. But it *did* happen that night. In real life.

JON TAPLIN: We had to turn the cameras away from Bob to prove that we weren't secretly filming him and the guys had to get down from all their stands for the first two numbers. Lou Kemp was standing right there stage left next to Bill Graham. Near the end of the second song, we said, "Okay. Everybody get ready. Put your headphones back on." He went into the third song and we started filming. And it was going great. He went into his fourth song, and that was going great too.

All of a sudden, Bob just clicked back into one of the first songs he was doing, kind of reprising it. I think he was having so much fun that he thought, "Gee. Let's get *that* one on film, *too*. It was *so* good." The Band kicked in right with him and they started going. Everyone was still filming and Lou Kemp was freaking out.

He said, *"Wait a minute.* I don't think you're supposed to film *this* song. I want you to stop."

To Marty, he was saying, *"Stop!"* Marty was just pretending he did not hear.

Bill Graham grabbed Lou Kemp and said, "You *don't* stop! You motherfucker, get *off* the stage. *Don't stop!"*

He was just screaming at him and Lou Kemp backed down. It was like, "This is *history*, motherfucker. Don't *mess* with it." It was so strong that Lou Kemp backed off.

Of course, it turned out later that this was what Bob wanted. For us to keep going to get that one because he thought it was his best tune. It was a nice, fine moment in which Bill was standing up for right, and all that.

LOU KEMP: Bob told me, "I only want *this* much to be shot. Just make sure they don't shoot me any *more*." And I said, "Okay." I was right on the side of the stage where the cameras were. I remember screaming at Bill, "Those guys aren't supposed to be shooting!" And he was screaming back, "This is *history*! And this is *my* show!" Bob was looking over at the side at me, giving me looks like, "What's going on?" Scorsese was going bonkers. This was their big production and he was going *crazy*. I said, "Bill, that's not the point. He doesn't want to be shot. That's *his* call, you know? You've got to respect his wishes, for whatever reasons."

Bill had fifty other reasons. It got pretty intense there. Even some pushing and shoving. We were in different camps, you know? I was there as Bob's friend and looking out for Bob's interests. Bill and I were on separate sides of the line on that one, and it got a little heavy. He pushed and shoved and I pushed and shoved and screamed a little bit. He screamed a *lot* of course. I just raised my voice a little bit and that was how it went down.

More or less, Bob got his way. I think they shot a little more than he wanted but they didn't shoot as much as *they* wanted. As it ended up, everybody came out of it whole.

ROBBIE ROBERTSON: Louie was supposed to make sure the cameras weren't going to shoot him. I remember Bill said, *"Shoot it!"* For some reason, in my mind, I never thought we were *not* going to shoot Bob. I thought, "Oh, we'll go through all this bullshit and in the end, we'll shoot it." I knew the game very well. Thank God for Bill Graham. In the end, it *was* shot. And it looked staggering. He looked amazing in the film, Bobby Dylan. Almost like a Christ figure. A Christ in a white hat. I mean, what *more* could you ask for?

BILL: I stuck my finger in his face and I said, *"Back off.* You *roll* that fucking camera. Just *roll!"* I went to the other side of the stage and yelled the same thing at the top of my voice. Dylan had agreed to do it beforehand and then at intermission, he disagreed. For whatever the reasons were. The *wind.* I don't know why. The *vibes.*

By then, the concert was pretty much over but Ringo Starr hadn't played yet. So I picked him up and carried him out to the drum kit. Clapton also. He was just standing there like a guest. I said, "You guys *have* to play." But nobody had asked them to go out for the jam. So I walked Clapton out. What a *night!*

ROBBIE ROBERTSON: After the show, it was such a relief. I remember saying to the people involved, "Thank God, we got through it." All the cameramen were hugging one another and I remember seeing Bill and I was thinking, "God, you did it, Bill." I couldn't help but feel like, "Well, *everybody* did it." But Bill did it. We did it in his home. Like, "Whose house are we going to shoot at? *Bill's* house." Because it *was* his house, I felt in my heart like he had really done this thing. And he was elated. After having gotten through this thing alive, it was a real high that night. He was proud of it. And I was proud of him for being proud of it.

BILL: I felt so good about the accomplishment. We had such a large staff and we all worked very hard. There was no money. They had asked us to do this, and we did. There was no business deal. There really wasn't. We just did it.

Of course, the Band got paid. We also bonused the Band. I brought their road manager into my office before the show ended that night and I said, "*Here.* Give a couple of grand to each guy." I think it was two grand apiece. I was just *so* elated.

3.

BILL: A week later, their road manager called me and said, "Robbie Robertson wants to talk to you." I said, "Fine. Have him call me." He said, "Don't you want to call him?" I said, "Let him call me." Robbie's ego always bothered me more than anybody else's. He was a great talent and a very handsome, attractive man who later on tried to have a career as an actor in movies. But his ego was too big. He called me and this was one of those conversations that wasn't too pleasant.

He said, "Hello, Bill. How's everything?" Just the tone of his voice got me started.

I said, "Fine."

He said, "How's your family?"

That *really* got to me. I said, "What did you say?"

He said, "How's your family? How are your sisters?"

He had been up in San Francisco for a while before the show and we had talked about our families. I said, "How many?"

He said, "Huh?"

I said, "You asked me how my sisters were? How many do I have?"

"Bill," he said. "What are you talking about? This is Robbie and I'm just calling to say hello." He was calling because somebody had told him I was very angry at him.

He said, "We're going to do some studio stuff for the film and we'd like to interview you and talk about the making of the film and how we first got started playing for you. Man, the show was *great.*"

I said, "Yeah, it was. What do you want to ask me about my family? Do you know who's *in* my family?"

He said, "Bill, what's wrong with you?

I said, "Nothing. Do you know who's in my family? Do you know what I do for a living?"

He said, "*Bill.* What *are* you talking about?"

Then I totally lost it. I said, "Don't you know what you forgot to do while you were up here?

"YOU FORGOT TO SAY *THANK YOU,* YOU MOTHERFUCKER! WE WORKED OUR *BALLS* OFF FOR YOU! YOU STOOD UP AND TOOK

YOUR FUCKING BOWS BECAUSE YOU'RE THE ENTERTAINER. BUT THEN YOU HAVE THE NERVE TO LEAVE THE BUILDING WITHOUT SAYING A FUCKING WORD TO *ANYONE?* WE GAVE YOU EVERYTHING FOR FREE. *EVERYTHING.* AND YOU COULDN'T FIND IT IN YOUR HEART TO THANK US? FUCK *YOU!*"

I hung up the phone and that was it. It was the last time I ever talked to him.

ROBBIE ROBERTSON: I am going to tell you exactly where this comes from. Like all of us, Bill is also famous for the editor in his memory. A lot of people have this thing. As soon as he saw the movie, he said that nobody thanked him. Up to that point, it had never been mentioned. After the show, I thanked him. At the party after, I thanked him. I got drunk and I thanked him too many times. He had given all the guys in the Band a gift. After the show. I didn't know why he would do this. He saved money out of the budget that we said we had spent and gave it to just the five guys in the Band.

I thought, "What a *sweet* thing to do."

But what was this guy? Don King? What was this? After a win, he puts like a thousand-dollar bill in your hand and gives you a little nudge.

I thought, "It's a very sweet gesture but it isn't in context with the whole thing somehow." I thanked him for the money, which I didn't even like. I liked that he wanted to do *something*. But I didn't like that he gave everybody a thousand dollars.

Maybe what I didn't do and I would have to ask Jon Taplin or somebody is take out an ad thanking him in the trades. Because I know how important that can be to certain people. Would I need to be thanked like that? *No.* The personal thing is what means something to me. Bill isn't like that. If I had put a Bill Graham billboard up, it would have been thanking him in front of everybody. Maybe that's what I should have done.

BOB BARSOTTI: The show itself was one of the great shows of all time. You felt like you had this complete experience. It wasn't *just* a show. It was "The Last Waltz," you know? Then when the movie came out, I saw it and it was like some *other* event. It had nothing of the evening. The only thing that was there was the stage. Which was really only part of that evening. It really was. More so than any gig I've ever seen.

PETER COYOTE: To me, you can hear the drug use in the music. Everybody made such a big deal about the music. But the difference between the way Robbie Robertson was playing and Muddy Waters was playing was the whole story. All the white boys were amping up all this synthetic kind of fucking passion and just showing how into it they were. Muddy just came out. He was just fucking being there and doing it and I was embarrassed by the music. I thought, "Is this the fucking best we can do?"

Rock and roll is not for rocket scientists anyway. But even so, don't *fake* it. Go out there, have a good time. Don't *act* out your passion for the audience. Put it in the fucking music. Don't mistake the amplification of the instruments for the emotion that's coming through it. I thought the Band was great. They were the best of the white guys. But even so. Next to Muddy, it was just hype. It wasn't real. I thought so that night and I really saw it when I saw the movie.

ROBBIE ROBERTSON: We shot what we wanted to get. That was the concept. Because the other thing had been done to death in *Woodstock*. People out in the mud, rolling around naked. I mean, how do you compare with that?

JON TAPLIN: Bill was basically ignored in the credits. It said, "Live Event Staged by Bill Graham." I really disliked that. We were going to film Bill as part of the interview section and Bill said no. Maybe that was why Robbie didn't want him to be a major feature in the credits.

BILL: People who live in Milwaukee can see the film and say, "What a *great* film!" But they did not see what else happened that night. He lost the attitude of all those who came. The average guy who had the night of his life. For him, it was a night to remember. The kind of event that dollars alone could never buy. If you said to someone today, "Remember 'The Last Waltz'? Would you pay twenty-five dollars to go to it again?" They would say, *"Twenty-five?* I'll give you *five hundred."* It was a once-in-a-lifetime thing.

When that audience walked into that hall that night, they had white gloves on their *brains*. They *knew* they were flying first class. We did it all from the front door on *in*. What they put up on the screen was a concert film. "The Last Waltz" wasn't a concert. It was a night to remember. Robbie missed it. Scorsese missed it. I tried to tell them about it that night but I saw that I was talking to a wall. What was I supposed to do? Make an appointment with the guy?

Enough. I'm finished yelling about it.

Chapter
Fourteen

Stranded
in the Jungle

1.

ROBERT GREENFIELD: It was not a great time for rock and roll. Not as an art form or a business. At Winterland, the house manager would barricade himself inside his office each night during the show so he did not have to listen to the music that the "kids" in the hall outside seemed to love beyond all bounds, especially in terms of the quality of what they were being offered from the stage.

At two or three or four in the morning, depending on just how long the show had gone on, he would collect the night's receipts, make sure his gun was in the inside pocket of his jacket, and then go home, taking a different route each night so no one would be lying in wait for him on the very tough streets outside. It was a time when people in the business were using as much coke as they could. If only to insulate themselves from what the business itself somehow had become.

When Francis Coppola offered Bill a part in *Apocalypse Now*, then filming in the Philippines, he jumped at the chance. For him, it was an opportunity to get away from the daily grind that work in the office had become as well as a return to his first love, acting. At long last, Bill was going to be in a *real* movie, playing the role of a sleazy Hollywood agent. It was a part Bill knew he could handle in his sleep.

BILL: Ilangpo was in the jungle. But there was a hotel there and that was where we all stayed. A few days after we got there, the hotel got flooded. We had to go stay with the native people in their huts. Salamanders climbing on the walls. Roofs made of World War II corrugated sheet metal. The rain was like a machine gun all day and all night long. I was sleeping on a mat on the floor. The mat was made of hay. The floor was made of dirt. The people cooked outside on an outdoor stove. I spent seven days in the hut.

There were no newspapers. No TV. No women. No drugs. No decent food. There was no relief from the rain. And I began to wonder. Is this *it?* I knew I was not dying but maybe this was where everything ended. My deal with Francis went right out the window. In my contract, it said I got two dollars a day in salary and every other day his pilot had to get me to a phone somewhere by helicopter. He owed me the chopper every other day.

I would go to these little towns and wait for the phone. There would be one public phone and I would put down my booking sheets and go to work. The natives behind me would be squatting in the dirt while I was on the phone for an hour saying, "I'm not paying three with a fifty-fifty split over ninety. It don't go that way."

Once the rains came, I could not even do that. In the valleys, people were living on their roofs. Some were stranded in the middle of rice paddies on a stone, waiting for a helicopter to pull them out. It rained so hard that they couldn't shoot. People working on the film had all kinds of revelations about their lives. Who are we? What are we doing here?

The only other time I had ever done anything like that was when I was in the château in France and the air raids would start. In the ditches, the kids would tell their inner secrets to one another. Because we had nothing else to do but kill time. When it is not your choice to be in a space, you reveal things about yourself. Lynda Carter and Marty Sheen and Cindy Woods, the Playmate of the Year who was in the scene with me. We were all waiting to serve a role in Francis's play. We were all hanging out and treading water.

I was forty-four at that point. During those days and nights, I went through the whole thing of, "Who am I? What am I doing here? What's in my future?" I was not a kid anymore. I realized that part of my drive had been to make it in the sense of financial security. Not just for the want of money. But the need to live better. I was always aware that there was a balance where I had to put back in and not just do things to have more and more.

Who am I and how do I deal with life? What am I and what am I looking forward to tomorrow? There was a part of my job that I did not like. Like what I went through with "The Last Waltz." Sometimes on a daily basis, someone would say "Fuck you" to me and I would say, "Get the fuck away from me or I'll kill you." I didn't like that.

I couldn't sleep at all. I could not get used to the sounds and movements of small animals and the salamanders that were all over the place. I thought about what I wanted to do. What I wanted to do was *not* expand and become a big company. I wanted to stay with what I was doing. When I left Allis-Chalmers to go to the Mime Troupe, I was saying, "I don't really care about having a car. I really don't. If I don't have one, that's okay."

In the Philippines, I realized I was beginning to work at becoming successful in business in ways I had not chosen and did not like. One of the problems was how to go on dealing with talent while making what I thought was fair. I had spent so much time in that war. Fighting with agents and managers who only wanted to get as much from me as they could for their clients. I realized I didn't want to do battle all the time just to make more money.

When I got back home, I made it known that I did not want the company to be involved in expansion for the sake of expansion. I could have done what people wanted me to do and gone into L.A. and Denver and Seattle. But that would have meant the end of all special projects like "The Last Waltz." I didn't want to pay the price. Because the price would have been *more* agents and managers. They would have made me go back to what I had really left when I left Allis-Chalmers. *Work.* Dealing with things I didn't want to deal with. People trying to beat me. That warrior thing.

When I got back, I discussed all this at a meeting in the office. I told everyone, "What it is that I can do, I'll do. Not what I *have* to do but what I *want* to do." Things other than the business. In my and for my life. And for society too. As in what causes or beliefs do we have that we can help?

2.

ROBERT GREENFIELD: By phone from the Philippines, Bill began a long distance courtship of Regina Cartwright, then working as the receptionist in his San Francisco office. In the fourth year of their relationship, Bill and Marcia Sult were going through yet another of their separations.

REGINA CARTWRIGHT: They went through a really difficult long protracted breakup. It went on for eighteen months. I was very shocked that he had problems with her. Later, he told me what they were.

Bill is the most sensitive human being I've ever met. Especially in his private life. He would like people to be mind readers. Bill expects the closer you get to him, the more sensitive to him you will be. He always feels that if he has to ask you for something, then it is not worth anything.

I would say to him, "What's wrong with Marcia? She's a very pretty and unique-looking woman. What's wrong with her?"

He would say, "I have that garden at the house. I have *tons* of flowers in it. I *love* fresh flowers in my house. Marcia won't put fresh flowers on the table."

That meant she didn't care and she wasn't looking out for his best interests. Then she would and it wasn't any good because he had to tell her first.

ROBERT GREENFIELD: When finally Bill and Marcia Sult split up for the final time, Marcia was pregnant. She moved to Maui along with her son Thomas, whom Bill had taken into the family as another son, in order to have her child. Bill flew there for the birth but the child was late so he went back home again. It was Zohn Artman, then Bill's "resident wizard" and special assistant in charge of everything that no one else wanted to do, who helped bring Bill's son, Alex, into the world.

Chapter
Fifteen

Led Zeppelin

1.

BILL: Led Zeppelin always drew a difficult element. That was their initial problem. A lot of male aggression came along with their shows. This was during the warp of the seventies, which was a very strange era. It was anarchy *without* a cause. And there were a lot of rebels without causes. Out there in the audience whenever Led Zeppelin performed.

I thought they were a great rock and roll band with a good white blues singer and a very soaring guitar player. Very melodic and very crafty. Take nothing away from them. *And* they had a very powerful percussionist. They were a good performing band and they created for those people who came to see them the aura of Satan. It was a dark, eerie Satanistic experience. There were always rumors. "Jimmy Page goes to Switzerland once a year to have his blood changed." "Page has read all those books by Aleister Crowley." By 1977, they had become *the* initiation band.

By that I mean, kids saying to one another, "Hey, you into Led Zep?"

"Hey, man. *Of course.*" They were the "*of course*" band.

To give you another example of what I mean. Some months before they came over in 1977, our company softball team was playing against the Dead's roadies in Fairfax. This fifteen- or sixteen-year-old kid said, "*Hey, Mr. Graham! Hey!* When's Led Zeppelin coming? I want tickets, man."

I said, "Are you *really* into the band?"

He said, "*Yeah!* When are the tickets going on sale, man? I want to get the best."

I asked which of their albums he liked the most. He said, "*All of them, man.*"

I said, "Do you like any of their songs better than others?"

He said, "Come on, man. When are they going on sale?"

I looked at him and I said, "You dig the chick?"

He said, "She's *out of sight,* man. When they going on sale?"

He had *no* idea who Led Zeppelin was. It was just out on the block. For the gang that he wanted to get into, the reigning sound was Led Zeppelin.

In terms of the band, I had played them for years before this show. They had played both Fillmore East and West and they had come up through the ranks. Their manager had always been Peter Grant. At the time of this show, he weighed maybe three hundred pounds. He was also tall, maybe six three or six four, and bull-necked. He wore huge satin shirts with ruffled collars. His Levi's and denims were specially made for an oversized man. He had long stringy hair and a scrubby beard. But he was *so* very large. A former professional wrestler who wore big rings on his fingers. His hands were huge and all the jewelry on them was silver and black.

It all started on the Friday afternoon before the weekend of the shows. I got a call from their road manager who said, "We need some money."

I said, "Jeez. This late in the day, I'd have to go to the bank and I don't know if I can get you enough."

"We *need* some money, Bill."

"Okay. How much?"

"We need twenty-five thousand dollars."

They were making hundreds of thousands of dollars for these two shows. Oakland Coliseum was sold out for both Saturday and Sunday. On the night before the first show, without notice, they wanted an advance on their earnings, in cash.

To make a long story short, I went around the city for hours. Somehow, I got up twenty-five grand in cash. Usually, when you're dealing with that much money, you don't deal with singles. I was dealing with singles here. I had a large shopping bag with maybe two or three shoe boxes inside holding hundreds and singles and tens. The most I got from any one person was three or four grand. I put in eight thousand of my own.

I went to the hotel where the band was staying. They had a security guard outside the suite. They announced me and I walked into this anteroom. There sat the dealer. Then it hit me for the first time. This was *drug* money. I said to myself, "Well, it's *their* money. They got a right to it."

I came with the money because I had told them I would. Nobody said anything when I got there. The dealer did not say why he was there. But I knew him and he knew me. What I should have done was walked right out of there with the money and not gone back. But I didn't.

There are some things in my life that I don't feel good about and the scene in that hotel room is one of them.

Next day was Saturday. They were going to leave the hotel in plenty of time to get to the Oakland Coliseum for their set. Instead, they didn't leave until the stage was ready for them to play. *Late.* They were late as usual. Once again, I had to do one of those raps to the crowd. "Sorry about the delay . . ." In fact, I think I may have said the same thing about Jimmy Page having some problems with his guitar and he wants to get it just right so please bear with us. They started twenty minutes late and someone wrote that it was the earliest they had started any show in America on that tour. But they were still late.

They got on stage and there were no problems. Robert Plant was very nice, the way he always was. Every time I talked to him, he was never like a member of Led Zeppelin. He was just himself. John Paul Jones never talked. He was almost nonexistent. But Plant and I always talked about family and kids and he liked my son David very much.

What I didn't like about Led Zeppelin was that they came with force. I had heard stories from other cities about how they had muscled promoters to get better deals. How they had shaken them down for money. And then what they had done with the money. I had heard about the ugliness of their security. How they were just waiting to kill. They had these bodyguards who were *immense.* A couple had police records over in England. They were thugs.

I didn't care for their image and I didn't care for what came back toward the stage while Led Zeppelin was playing. Pushing, shoving, climbing over one another with complete disregard for personal safety. Naked aggression.

PETER BARSOTTI: They had their doctors backstage and they had a table filled with pills and they would all come back and take all these pills. It was horrible. On stage, John Bindon, their bodyguard, crawled out and licked Jimmy Page's boots during the performance. When Page first got out of the limousine, he walked the wrong way. He was so loaded that they had to lead him up on the stage. They brought him up there and he was out there performing and this guy crawled out and licked his boots. They got a girl up on stage and they had her up on the piano.

They would do things after the show. The traditional "Go get chicks out of the audience for the band." I remember standing by the ramp and seeing their guys get girls to come over. It was like no other feeling I'd ever experienced. It was like these girls were going to be *sacrificed.* I wanted to go out and grab these girls and say, "Don't do it, honey. Don't do it." I'm as hard-core as the next guy. But I was afraid for these girls.

These were the kind of guys that would hurt you. Evil people. It was just the *worst*.

BONNIE SIMMONS: I remember sitting backstage and I was watching them have their roadies bring them a procession of fifteen-year-old girls from the audience. The roadies would go out and find the most willing-looking pretty girls and the way they were just verbally abusing these women and sort of throwing them around, not really in a bad physical way, was something you just didn't want to see. Particularly when the girls were *so* young. Obviously, they were being given an audience in front of their heroes. They were getting to see their heroes be these sort of slime buckets.

JIM DOWNEY: Me and the guys, the stage crew, we were standing on the ramp minding our own business. We were pretty happy with ourselves because everything had gone well. These two guys came walking by. If you've ever walked up the ramp in Oakland, you know how steep it is. As they walked by, I said, "Jeez. It's a long way up that ramp."

For some reason, they took offense at it. I guess one of the guys was a bodyguard or something. The other guy put the bodyguard on me and I was standing there, apologizing. I didn't know what I had done. I said, *"Hey! Sorry.* Jack. *Stop!"* They were yelling and I was talking. And then the guy caught the Sunday on me. The next thing I remember is I woke up on the ramp. He knocked me out. I never saw it coming.

When I woke up on the ramp, the head of the Oakland stagehands was standing over me with a bar stool telling the guy he was going to kill him if he came any closer. There were about fifteen stagehands behind him, all ready to go too. I'm six feet tall and I weigh about two fifty. But these two guys were *both* bigger than me.

The guys scared them off and they just took off and kept going up the ramp. Then the deal with Barsotti and Matzorkis happened, to which I was not a party. I was just going, "What happened? The fuck did I do?"

JIM MATZORKIS: After the show on Saturday, I noticed this young kid was pulling these wooden plaques off the trailer doors which the bands were using for dressing rooms. Plaques with the names of the acts on them. Being that it was a two-show weekend, we still had another show. So we really didn't want the signs stolen. I noticed he had a stack of signs and I told him in a manner which I thought was courteous that he couldn't have the signs.

He said, "I want them."

I said, "No. You can't have them."

He said, "I'm taking them."

I said, "No, you're not."

He was just a young kid. Seven, or something like that. So I took the signs from him. It wasn't a violent act of any kind. I just took them away, and I didn't think anything of it. It really was not a major incident. I did not think there would be any repercussions or that I would even ever have a reason to refer back to it again. I took them into our storage trailer so I could then hang them back up later.

I was still in that trailer some minutes after when John Bonham, the drummer in the band, came to the trailer. There was like three or four stairs, like a little portable stairway outside the trailer. He was standing at the bottom of the stairs and he called up to get our attention. I came out to the landing of the stairs and Peter Grant was with him. He kept saying, "You don't talk to *my* kid that way." Bonham was kind of backing him up. But Grant was the one saying, "You don't talk to *my* kid that way. *Nobody does.* I can have your job."

I remember saying to him, "No. You can't have my job."

In the back of my mind, I remember thinking, "I work for Bill Graham. Bill will back me up." As if he could go to Bill and get me fired just because he was the manager of Led Zeppelin. I was thinking, "I don't care if you're the manager of *God*. No one goes and tells Bill Graham to fire somebody. I work for him and he will *always* back me up."

Grant made this comment about, "Who do you think you are? Roughing this kid up? I heard you hit this child."

I said, "No, no. This is a misunderstanding. I only told the kid he couldn't have the signs."

Bonham said, "You know who he is? You don't talk to *that* kid this way."

It was all happening very fast. As he said this, Bonham came up the little stairway to the landing. I was standing there and he kicked me right in the crotch. He gave me a good, unobstructed shot. I keeled over and fell back into the trailer. He wasn't alone. He had a couple of the bodyguards right behind him. All of this was happening fast and I realized, "This isn't good."

They backed me up in the trailer and Bonham was still ranting and raving at this point. I just wanted to get away because here was one of the stars of the band with his bodyguards. The bodyguards were trying to cool him off, actually. At that point, they were trying to break it up a little bit. They got between me and him and told me, "Get the hell out of here."

There was a back door so I managed to get away from there. I took off back through the backstage area where the trailers were out a back gate.

We had another mobile home outside the gate. I went there because I was hurt physically and I was upset and disoriented. The whole bit. I went there to recover and to catch my breath. A couple of people had seen it happen. Bob Barsotti came back and told me he was going to go get Bill and get it straightened out.

BILL: I was in the trailer. Someone came and said to me, "Bill, there's a problem backstage. Some of their guys are chasing Bob Barsotti. They pushed Bob because they claim Jim Matzorkis was offensive to Peter Grant's son." I was told by other people what had happened with the wooden signs and Jim Matzorkis. Now, I knew Jim and he was a pussycat. I went to Peter Grant and he was sitting there fuming. He said, "Bill, I'm very disappointed." And he proceeded to explain to me what had happened. I said, "Wait a minute. Jim is a sweet, gentle guy."

Grant said, "My son *wouldn't* lie." He brought his son in the trailer to tell me what had happened.

The kid said, "The man pushed me and took the signs away from me."

Grant said, "Your man put his hands on *my* people. On my *son*. How could you let this happen? How could you hire these people? I'm very disappointed in you."

I said, *"Peter.* At the worst, this *might* be true. I don't think it happened. I have children. Do you think I would hire people to hurt children?"

I spent twenty minutes with him and he kept saying, "Let me speak to this man. Does this man have children?"

I said, "No. I don't think so. He's too young. But he's a nice man and a good man."

I left the trailer and then I went back and Grant had a couple of people outside. It was like a little army. He was a dictator with this little army. It got to the point where I said, "Peter, I have a son who's also here today. He's also a child. He also wants things. Your child wanted those signs. There might have been a tug-of-war, and Jim Matzorkis tugged a little harder."

Grant said, "I understand. I just want to make sure that this man didn't take advantage of the fact that he's bigger than my son. That he treated him with respect. I want to meet this man."

I went into this long, long speech. I said, "Peter, remember, you're a very big man. Understand that your people have been out there looking to beat up on other people. You have a lot of security with you and they're big. That's your way of showing everyone that you want them to avoid confronting your artists. I don't think you need them but that's the way you approach it. I don't want anyone to get hurt. I can't have that."

He said, "Bill, trust me. I want to meet this man."

I said, "Let's just leave it go at this. Let's drop it. Let us all do our jobs. Let's just forget this and have a good show tomorrow."

He kept on saying, "I agree with you. I agree with you. But I want to meet with this man and I want to make my peace with him and settle this."

Reluctantly, after much bickering, I said, "Peter, let me put it this way. Do I have your word? Do we have your word as a gentleman that this is all it will be?"

He said, "Yes."

I said, "Peter, I'm trusting you. I think I know where he is. Come with me."

JIM MATZORKIS: Bill came to me and said, "Hey, I'm going to work all this out. I'm sorry it happened. He's apologizing. I'll get it straightened out. You don't have to worry." I trusted Bill. I really didn't have any other choice. I also didn't know how crazy these people were. Several minutes later, Bill came back with Peter Grant. Bill said, "Hey. Jim. Here's Peter Grant. I know it was a misunderstanding and I want you guys to get together.

BILL: I opened the trailer and went in first. Jim was sitting in the cubbyhole. Peter Grant went in. I said, "Peter, after you." Jim got up to say hello. I said, "Jim, Peter is the father of the young man." In one move, I was behind Grant. He just grabbed Jim's hand, pulled him toward him, and took his fist with the fingers all covered with rings and smashed Jim in the face, knocking him back into his seat. I lunged at Grant. He picked me up like I was a fly and handed me to the guy by the steps. That guy shoved me out. He threw me down the steps and shut the door. I was now outside the camper. Grant and one of his guys were inside with Jim. Their other guy was stopping me, I couldn't open the door. There was no way to get in the camper.

I heard Jim saying, *"Bill! Help me! Bill!"* And a lot of noise.

JIM MATZORKIS: They threw Bill out. They literally, physically, threw him out of the trailer. Grant said, "Hold him." And Bindon held me. Grant just started working me all over, punching me in the face with his fists and kicking me in the balls. He knocked a tooth out. I remember working my way to the back. You know how narrow those Winnebagos are. There's really not much room in there. It was really horrifying because there was no way out and here was this three-hundred-pound guy just having his way with me. Just beating the crap out of me.

I was protecting my balls and protecting my face. Bindon had me in a full Nelson from behind. But I was strong enough to break away and work my way to the back of the trailer. Then they had me trapped back there again. All this happened in a matter of a couple of minutes. Somehow, I managed to break away and work toward the front door. They caught me there. I remember them having me pinned under the table. The little table they have in a Winnebago. Grant sort of half-pounced on me and Bindon reached down and was trying to rip my eyeballs out of their sockets. I think the lawyers found out later that there was some incident where he *did* rip somebody's eyes out. That scared the hell out of me.

When he went for my eyeballs, that got every bit of my adrenaline going and I somehow got to the door. There were these guys outside holding the door. So I was fighting at the door and yelling for help. Out of the corner of my eye, I'll never forget seeing Bill a couple of times. He was running back and forth along the trailer. He really wanted to get in there but he was helpless.

BOB BARSOTTI: Once they pushed Bill out the door, the trailer started rocking. Bill and I were standing there going, "Oh, *fuck!*" We had another security guard there who ran immediately to get help. I was standing in front of the RV and Bill was trying to get in the door. At that point, Richard Cole, their road manager, came running toward the van. He had this aluminum pipe from one of those tables with umbrellas. He wanted to go in there with this pipe. I said, "That's the last thing I'm going to let happen." I had been seeing this guy doing drugs all day long and he was completely whacked out.

He would try to go one way and I would just step that way. Finally, he realized what I was doing and he went wild. He stepped back and took this big swing at me and I just easily jumped out of the way because the guy was so completely out of it. I said, "I've got to get this guy away from here." So I got right in his face and I said, *"You limey cocksucking sonofabitch!"* He went wild. I turned around and I ran down into the parking lot and he chased me. I got him way down there and then I turned around and I ran back and he was all fagged out in the parking lot. I went back to the trailer.

JIM MATZORKIS: I don't know how I did it but I squeezed the hell out of there. And ran. By now I was bleeding from my mouth and my face. I'd had a tooth knocked out. I had been hit in the crotch, I don't know how many times. I squeezed out and I ran. Some people had started gathering out there by then. Our security guys were just showing up when I got out. Bill and them were trying to decide whether they were going to shoot their way in, or what. Our security guys never carried guns but they all had them in their cars. They had gone to get their pieces out of the trunk.

Because for all they knew, they were killing me in there. If I hadn't been able to get out, they might have.

BILL: Our most experienced backstage commando said, "Bill, we have to do something about this." And he was very serious. He was a peaceful man but strong and highly principled. I said, "The big problem is that they have to play tomorrow. Forget the finances. If sixty thousand kids show up here and there's no show, there's going to be a major riot. The show *has* to go on."

He said, "Bill, this is your company. You're the boss. But I'm representing a lot of people here. We want 'em." He said, "This is Oakland. Not San Francisco." This was not James Coburn talking to Burt Lancaster. This was not a Jim Brown movie. It was the real world. And the security guards with Led Zeppelin were vicious fucking wild animals.

He said, "*Bill*. We're tellin' you up front. Before the show tomorrow. After the show tomorrow. We're gonna do somethin' about it. We gonna *do* these guys."

I said, "First, we got to make sure Jim is okay. Then let's see what's what. Let me think about it overnight."

I said, "If you don't think what I do is fair, if I can't convince you that I've come up with a better way, you can do one of two things, and I'm not going to try to stop you. You can do it here or I'll fly twenty-five guys of your choice to New Orleans, the next stop on their tour, and you can do them there."

That was the deal I made that night before I left to see Jim in the hospital.

2.

BILL: Jim was a bloody pulp. They took him to a hospital and he got stitched up. I went to visit him there and he came to stay at my house. Because I didn't want them to find him. I just didn't want them near him.

That night, their lawyer called me. "Bill, we need to talk about something. We're looking for this young man, Matzorkis. We need him to sign a waiver. An indemnity paper. As well as the other gentleman involved in that minor altercation."

I said, "What minor altercation?"

"What happened earlier this evening. I've been instructed by the band to contact you and say to you that they would find it difficult to play tomorrow unless a waiver is signed indemnifying them against all lawsuits as a result of that altercation."

I told him I would call him back. Then I called Nick Clainos.

NICHOLAS CLAINOS: What I was doing most of Saturday night was talking to their limo driver to make sure those guys stayed in town. Which they were supposed to do but you never knew. Once they said that they expected a release, the implication was that if they didn't get it, they wouldn't do the show the next day. I told the limo driver that if those guys went to the airport, I wanted to know.

I also wanted to know what they were doing generally. Boy, some of the stories that came out from the limo driver. He described things like them going into a pharmacy on Union Street with an English doctor who was on the road with them. He said, "Fill this prescription."

The guy said, "You're not even an American doctor. I can't fill this prescription."

The bodyguards went behind the counter and began knocking stuff off the pharmacist's shelves, saying, "Would you *please* fill this prescription?"

Once they got the prescription filled, they walked out the door, peeled off ten one-hundred-dollar bills and threw them on the floor of the pharmacy.

BILL: I called their lawyer back. I said, "Look. You know what happened. It's not right."

He said, "Bill, I'm instructed not to discuss that."

I said, "I was there. You don't understand. You're lucky that you guys aren't dead. I'll tell you the truth. If there wasn't a show tomorrow, I don't know what would be happening to you."

Now, they were demanding his home address. They wanted to know where Jim Matzorkis lived so they could go find him to sign this paper. Nick came up and God bless him, he was like my brother Roy when I was growing up in New York. Like when Roy and I would get together and talk about the heavy stuff. At a very difficult time in my life, Nick made some big moves.

There we were at three in the morning and it had gotten to the point where their lawyer was saying, "Please understand. If that document is not signed, there may well be no performance." This was a waiver saying that they could not be sued for more than two thousand dollars for what they had done. They never came out and actually said that they would not play but it was obvious that this was the threat. They could come up with any kind of reason to cancel. Someone had strep throat. Their vocal cords were shot.

We could have told them to fuck off altogether or we could sign the agreement. Right from the beginning, we were also in touch with Stan Damas. Nick came right in on that. Because backstage I had said to Stan, "Whoever is involved here, starting with Peter Grant, I want them busted."

Stan didn't want my security guys coming after the Led Zeppelin security guys. Stan had been a sergeant on the San Francisco police force. He retired and then came to work with us.

During the night, Stan called with the information that Grant and Bindon could be arrested under charges of inciting assault. In the case of Richie Cole attacking Bob Barsotti with the pipe, it was assault with a deadly weapon. Then we found out the bodyguard was a professional wrestler so we could also charge him with the use of his fists as a deadly weapon. But we didn't want to do it before the show. Because then there would be *no* show.

NICHOLAS CLAINOS: That night, I remember calling two or three civil lawyers and saying, "What if somebody asks us to sign a piece of paper, saying that unless we sign it, unless we release them from something that we otherwise would not release them from, they won't fulfill their obligation? The law can't allow that, can it? Tell me specifically. *Now.* Not after the fact. Why can't the law allow that?"

They had guys go to law libraries *that* night and come back and say, "It's economic duress." The exact words I got from the lawyer I was using was that, "The signature's not worth the paper it's signed on."

BILL: The decision I made during the night with Nick was that I would sign the paper with my left hand because with my left hand, I still write like an eleven-year-old child. That would prove that I had signed it under duress and that I really didn't want to do it. Nick told me that the paper would not be binding. But it was in our interest that they think it was.

PETER BARSOTTI: There was this whole plot hatched by us whereby I was going to be the guy to steal the document. We were going to wait until it was signed. Then it was going to be handed to the lawyer. He was going to put it in his briefcase and be walking out. He was going to be grabbed by three people. I was going to grab the briefcase, jump in the car, and be gone. That was what we were going to do. I was *so* nervous about it for about half the day. Eventually, we didn't do it because our lawyers found out that it was signed under duress so it didn't matter anyway.

NICHOLAS CLAINOS: I remember their lawyer coming into a trailer backstage on Sunday with this piece of paper. He said, "Look, the boys got a little bit out of hand yesterday." He called them "the boys." "We hope there are no hard feelings. Of course we'll be happy to pay any hospital bills and I just want to make sure that there are no hard feelings."

Bill was sitting there saying, "Yeah. Right."

It was just me and Bill and the lawyer. We were the only people in the trailer. I was sitting there saying, "You're right. No problem. Nothing to worry about."

He said, "Well, I'm glad. Because the boys are over at the bar at the Hilton and they just couldn't concentrate on playing unless this thing is cleared up."

Those were the words that he used. Showtime was one o'clock and this was twelve-thirty. Their lawyer had waited. He didn't even show up until half an hour before showtime. He said, "The boys are at the bar at the Hilton and they just wouldn't feel comfortable with the animosity. They're artists and they couldn't perform without knowing there were no problems and that it was cleared up."

Bill couldn't bring himself to say, "*Fine*. There are no problems." I was sitting there saying, "No problem."

"The boys asked me to bring back an indication to them that there are no problems. Would you mind signing this piece of paper?"

Either he or another lawyer had gotten it typed out. Our plan was to arrest them. We didn't give a shit about the piece of paper. What it said basically was that we released them from any of the problems that arose as a result of yesterday's activities. I said, "No. I don't mind signing it at all." Bill signed his name to it. He was going to sign with the left hand but it didn't matter so he signed it with the correct hand.

Their lawyer said, "Great. The boys will be very happy to hear this." He went away. He went into their trailer and made a call and forty minutes later, the guys were there. They were late but that was expected. Then they went on to do the show.

BILL: I signed the paper and then I went out with Nick and talked to my security guys. I said, "You all know what happened here last night. It was like Nazi Germany. Where people believed that might made right. I've got a proposition for you. We're going for jail. We're going for financial retribution for the guys who got hurt. We do it the other way, we're taking the law into our own hands. They definitely deserve it but I think we're all best served by doing it this way."

I think they understood that I felt the same way they did. They all promised to cool it that day. When the band finally arrived an hour and twenty minutes late, they were totally behind enemy lines. No one spoke. No one smiled. The only thing moving were people's eyes. I couldn't even make myself go *near* the stage. During that show, I saw everything they stood for. I saw their security guys, who thought that they had gotten away with it. As the looks we were giving them got heavier and heavier, they realized that once the show was over, what did I owe them?

When the show ended, they were all lined up at the top of the runway in their cars. Peter Grant was already inside one of them. He had his guys around the ramp. The entire entourage was there to funnel the band into the cars and out of the stadium. Richie Cole and their lawyer and the security guards were there. In front of the lead limo, there were two Oakland cops on motorcycles. I stood right next to them and looked into the car at Peter Grant. I just stared at him through the glass and he went *off*. He was a guy who, in so many words, was saying, "See who I am? I can do *anything* I want." But I knew that within the next twelve hours, he was going to be popped. Stan Damas had told me that the Oakland DA was going to do it.

NICHOLAS CLAINOS: The Oakland police would not file it as a felony. In Burlingame or anywhere in San Mateo County, this clearly would have been filed as a felony. But in Oakland, they didn't consider it serious enough. They couldn't serve a misdemeanor warrant on a Sunday. They said, "We think the elements are there. We'll take your word for it. We'll have to arrest them on Monday."

I said, "You can't. They will have left the jurisdiction by Monday."

They said, "That doesn't matter. We'll just issue a warrant for them."

But it mattered to *us*. It was pretty clear that on a misdemeanor warrant, they wouldn't have to come back into the jurisdiction. They would have just thrown some thousand-dollar bills on the floor and that would have been the end of that. It completely pulled the rug out from under Bill's intentions. But there was nothing we could do. They wouldn't change their plans.

So then the question became, "What *are* Led Zeppelin's plans?"

Everybody was instructed to go and hang out with people and find out what they could. It became pretty clear that they were going to stay on in San Francisco on Sunday night. The limo drivers again were on call and we said, "If anybody makes a move to the airport, let us know." I don't know what we would have done if they had made that move. The only idea I had in my head was that they would be fleeing the jurisdiction and maybe the San Mateo police would arrest them.

But they didn't leave. The next morning, I was down at the Hilton. I passed Stan Damas in the hall and we could not let on that we knew each other. Damas was our guy but they thought he was theirs. I was standing there with two detectives in the lobby and it was not more than a minute before a guy walked up to me. It turned out that all of their underling security people were off-duty policemen from Dallas. That must have been the first city on their tour or something. They had guys spread out all through the lobby. Anybody who looked suspicious or didn't fit in with what was going on, they would walk up to them to see what was going on. They were checking us out.

The detective I was with looked at the security guy. They flashed each other their badges and started to talk. The detective said, "Let me tell you what's going on. The first thing you got to understand is that we're going to arrest your client. Okay? It's *going* to happen. I'm not asking you to do anything. I don't want to jeopardize your job. Just understand that they're *not* leaving this hotel. These guys *are* going to be arrested.

"How we do it is up to you. Why don't you be the guy who lets them know that you can have it done any way they want. We'll do it privately, we'll do it with or without handcuffs. It doesn't make any difference *how* we do it. You tell us how. But these guys are going to leave this hotel and go over and be booked in Oakland."

Their security guy went to bring the word up. In the meantime, their off-duty police guys made a commitment that nobody would leave the hotel. And they didn't. It was surprising. But they didn't.

BOB BARSOTTI: Nobody could find anybody. We finally negotiated it so they came down and surrendered themselves. It got to the point where we realized they were renting fifty rooms in the hotel. And we were looking for four guys. There was no way to find them if they didn't want to be found. So they came walking down. That was a pretty sight, watching them come walking in.

I followed them over to Oakland where they were being processed and jailed. I watched those guys walk though it all with their hands cuffed behind their backs. That was worth everything. I saw them with their heads bowed down and their tails between their legs and I went back and I told that to all the security guys. To them, it meant a lot. It was Bonham and Grant and Bindon and Cole.

As far as I was concerned, every one of those guys in the band was absolutely 100-percent accountable for that shit. Because they allowed it to go on. And we weren't the only ones it happened to. We were just the *last* ones. We were the only ones who stood up and said something. When we started looking into it, there were incidents like that all across the country on that tour. Trashed hotel rooms. Trashed restaurants. Literally like twenty thousand dollars' worth of damages at some restaurant in Pennsylvania. Really outrageous stuff. Like where they physically abused waiters and people in the restaurant and then just bought them off. The accountant would open up the valise as the guys were zooming off in their limousines and say, "Okay. *How much?*"

NICHOLAS CLAINOS: They got into a police car and the TV cameras didn't pick it up until they arrived in Oakland. Of course, the first thing we did was call all the TV stations. They were released immediately. But the damage was done. They were on TV. A member of the group, the manager, their road manager, and their security guy were all on TV as they were led into the station.

BILL: They got bailed out and they went back to England. Then a suit was filed for two million dollars in damages. I kept saying to the three guys, "I'll go all the way with this. But if along the way, you guys want to settle, fine." The Led Zeppelin people kept on upping the offer and saying that if the guys did not settle now, they would drag it out in court. Some of the guys needed the money. So everybody settled.

JIM MATZORKIS: The day before the criminal trial was supposed to start, they pleaded *nolo contendere*. They cut a deal with the judge. The civil case went for a year and a half. They settled for fifty thousand or something like that. The lawyer got a third of that. I had several thousands of dollars in medical bills that were supposed to be paid without coming out of the settlement but they weren't. I learned not to believe anything a lawyer tells you unless he puts it in writing.

NICHOLAS CLAINOS: Before the thing settled, Bill got a phone call one day. He said, "Nick. Come here." Bill's secretary said, "There's a guy on the phone who says he's Peter Grant."
    Bill and I picked up the phone. Bill said, "Hello."
    The guy was speaking real low. He said, "I hope you're happy." Those were his exact words.
    Bill said, "What are you talking about?"
    He said, "Thanks to you, Robert Plant's kid died today."
    And he hung up on the phone. We found out later that Robert Plant's son had died. They had to go home. They canceled New Orleans and they never played again in America as the original Led Zeppelin. In their

eyes, it was all karma and all tied together. Whether Robert Plant ever thought that or only Peter Grant, I don't know. Since then, we have played Robert Plant many times.

PETER BARSOTTI: Plant seemed like the only decent human being there. Although there were no innocents. There *were no innocents*. If his guys did something to me, then he was responsible. He wanted to change it? Change it. I will never forget Bill sitting up on the forklift when they came off before the encore the second day and Robert Plant went over to him and said, "Bill, *please. Please*, you *know?*" They were *this* far apart. Bill just turned his head. He wouldn't talk to him and Plant went back down the runway and did his encore.

Look what happened to that guy. Tough stuff. Anybody that has children can only break out into tears thinking about it. You're such a fuckin' tough guy? You're the fuckin' baddest-ass motherfuckers on earth? Oh yeah? You guys are human. You have families. Things can happen to you. When something like that happens to you, you're just not going to be the same. You're not going to treat people like you did before. After that, you can *never* be that way again, I don't think.

ROBERT PLANT: It was one empire-builder and marauder moving into an area where there was already an empire with some kind of Tartar head. Peter Grant moving into Bill Graham. Bill Graham would always give us this kind of placating, sugary pleasantness. This *veneer*, you know? Dependent upon the mood of the man.

I got no truck with the guy now. But I do remember when we first arrived to play the Fillmore, we came to get the gear in and he told us all to go and fuck off because he was in the middle of playing some handball game on the floor of the Fillmore. And we stood and watched him and said, "Well. Who *is* this asshole?"

By the time we got to that moment all that time ago, it was the whole kind of Peter Grant charade and the Bill Graham beefboys meeting face-to-face. There *was* an altercation. Instead of it being the two big wheels moving away and talking about it quietly and saying, "For God's sake, this is ludicrous," it was just a slagging match.

Finally, all the heavies were released. It was like, "*Ah*. At last, I'm going to earn my money." It was an absolute shambles. I mean, it was so sad to see that I would be expected to go on and sing "Stairway to Heaven." People now know how I feel about that song. I had to sing it in the shadow of the fact that the artillery we carried with us was prowling around backstage with a *hell* of an attitude. I mean it was this coming together of these two dark forces which had nothing to do with the songs that Page and I were trying to churn out.

However, nobody could stop it. I stood at the top of some stairs by one of those mobile cabin things and screamed at Graham and told him that the whole thing was absolutely, totally ludicrous and to calm down. But we were already in the Court of the Crimson King. The last fair deal had gone down. It was *so* unfortunate. However, I had a mouth then just as big as I've got now. It hasn't gotten any bigger or smaller.

But you *are* what you employ. *Really.* And Bill does like a nice, clean ship. That's the way he does it. I don't know whether he does it like that now. All this happened before we went on stage or after or whichever way round it was. It was from out of the tiniest event. Egos and territories and domains and kingdoms and pecking orders and all the kind of crap that is rock and roll came into being. It had nothing to do with money. It just had to do with that kind of intangible thing that hovers somewhere between your feet and the top of your hair. It's that *power*, you know?

BONNIE SIMMONS: In those days at KSAN, if something happened that outraged people and it had anything to do with leftist politics or rock and roll or dope, they called the radio station. People used to call us and say, "My friend is OD'ing. What do I do with him?" And we would be sitting there thinking, *"Schmuck. Don't call a radio station."*

After the first Led Zeppelin show, we were getting *hundreds* of telephone calls. It was all, "That motherfucker, Bill Graham. That *asshole.*" Because there is nothing worse than for people to have to hear that their heroes are the kind of jerks that Led Zeppelin turned out to be. Even when we told them on the air what the story was, nobody wanted to believe that.

It was still, "That *asshole.* That *schmuck*, Bill Graham. He's wielding his power. He's *fuckin'* with *the Zep, man.*" That *really* offended me. Particularly after having seen even what I saw. It always stayed with me. I never again played Led Zeppelin on KSAN after that.

Bill was *crazed* by it all at that point. He had to come on and do an interview. Nick Clainos was sort of like, "No, Bill. No, Bill. *No. Back, boy.*" But he couldn't stop him. Bill was supposed to just read a statement. I remember that Nick said, "Okay. You can say this." Ten minutes later, he was screaming about their abuse of *"powa!"* He was great.

BILL: I wanted to bust their ass on felony charges and see them go to trial. But the county fell down on that and there was nothing we could do about it. It was never close to a total vindication for me. I really was very disappointed at what happened in the end. Far beyond what I have ever told anybody. It was a bitter disappointment. One of the large ones. Because how often do you really get to expose something that *should* be exposed in terms of the abuse of power?

In this case, it was simply brute force. It just wasn't fair. If a child has a problem with an adult, the solution isn't that the child's father who is ten times bigger than the other guy kicks the shit out of him.

Back then, Led Zeppelin was the king of the world. They fucked with promoters by cutting costs and cutting corners. When I think back to that whole incident, I think about that dealer sitting in that hotel room in a cowboy hat, waiting for his twenty-five grand.

It was a time in my life when I had serious personal problems dealing with what I was doing for a living. I didn't like those people. I didn't like their influence on society or their power. I can't say it was Satanistic power. But they thought certain things were cool that definitely weren't.

They surrounded themselves with physical might. The element around them was oppressive. They were ready to kill at the slightest provocation. If they hadn't been that way before, they took on that demeanor because of the power they represented. The sad thing is that I got a lot of hate mail on this from real Led Zeppelin fans. Before John Bonham died, there was still a chance that the band might regroup. People blamed me for the fact that they would not be coming back to the Bay Area. Because I had said that I would never book them again.

Chapter
Sixteen

Closing
Winterland

1.

ROBERT GREENFIELD: Bill's business continued to grow. By 1977, Winterland Productions, the T-shirt concern which had begun in the coatroom of Winterland, was grossing twelve to fourteen million dollars a year in merchandising. Bill did little for the company day-to-day but he was always there to help "carry the football into the end zone from the two-yard line."

Having finally found someone he trusted to run his store, Bill now no longer had to watch the cash register *personally* every day. Nicholas Clainos's very businesslike presence in the San Francisco office freed Bill to do what he liked best. Create. More than anything, Bill wanted to be an artist. His particular art could be experienced only in the moment when it all coalesced for the audience. When the right performer gave all he had in the perfect setting with lights and sound coming together in harmony, thereby causing the whole to somehow be magically greater than the sum of all its parts. It was both a blessing and a curse. You just had to *be* there to know how good Bill really was at putting on a show. It was for that moment only that Bill really lived. But once the moment was over, it was gone for good.

For his forty-sixth birthday that year, the Grateful Dead gave Bill a present he spent the rest of his life trying to return.

BILL: We were doing a show in San Diego and at intermission, someone must have told Bob Weir that it was my birthday. The *schmuck* walked out on stage and said, "We just found out that it's Bill's birthday and we didn't get him anything. So we'd like to give him the name 'Uncle Bobo' as a term of endearment."

I came off the stage and I said, "You dumb fuck, how would you like to be called 'Uncle Bobo'?"

Since that day, I've had to live with that dumb shit. When I'm in the right frame of mind and people say, "Hello, Uncle Bobo," I say, "Do me a favor. Don't call me that. How would *you* like to be called that?"

One time a couple of years ago, I was running through the airport in Denver and a lady was walking the other way and she said, *"Uncle Bobo!"* I was running to catch my plane and she turned and followed me and said, "Uncle *Bobo*. Uncle Bo-*bo*. I think you're the greatest. When are the Dead playing again? Can I talk to you for a second?"

I said, "I'm running to catch my plane right now."

As I was running away from her, she yelled out through the airport, *"UNCLE BO-BO! UNCLE BO-BO!* YOU'RE LIKE THE . . . *GRAND-FATHER* OF ROCK!"

Actually, I was both running *and* hiding at the same time. The *grandfather* of rock. Just what I need. But it happens at every Dead show. At least half a dozen times, I turn to somebody and I say, "Do me a favor. Don't call me that."

I *loathe* the name. It's like Uncle *Shit.* I've asked Bob Weir, "Please, at some birthday, give me *another* present. Give me *my* name back."

2.

ROBERT GREENFIELD: In England in 1978, punk was king. The only problem was that no one in America knew the first thing about it. The reason was simple. There was no MTV.

BILL: The Sex Pistols were the forerunners. They were the kings of punk hill. I had seen either a video or some film on them and I liked the rawness. I liked some of their songs. They really kicked ass. "God Save the Queen." I liked the sound but not the trashing of the places where they played. I had never met Malcolm McLaren, who was their manager. Instead, I dealt with a guy at Warner Brothers, their label over here. He told me they wanted to play a club when they came to San Francisco.

I said, "They're more popular than that. If they play a club, there'll be a riot. There'll be five hundred people inside, and a thousand on the street." He said, "Bill, that's what they want." I said, "I won't do that. I'm not going to set up mania for their sake and have problems in the street."

I said, "Look. They should play Winterland." He said, "They're not going to go from five hundred people to fifty-four hundred." I said, "Trust me. They can fill the place." He said, "You're going to have to convince Malcolm McLaren."

So I called McLaren in London. I had never met the guy before. I said, "Look, you've got to understand, there are *thousands* and *thousands* of Pistols' fans out here." He said, "No. There's an underground rumble but they're not that big." I said, "Do me a favor. Let me do a thing on KSAN. Let me go on the radio and ask, 'How many of you folks out there want to see the Sex Pistols?' Let me see how many postcards that they send in." He said, "Some fan who wants to see them will send twenty cards. That doesn't mean twenty people will come." I said, "Let's just get some indication of what kind of feel there is in town."

KSAN was very cooperative and we did this thing on the weekend with them. I called the guy at Warners' back and he put me on a conference call with McLaren. McLaren said, "Yes, Bill. How are you? What happened?" I said, "Malcolm, what do you want me to do with *eleven thousand* postcards?" He said, "Oh, *my God!* What can we do? Where should we put them?" I said, "Trust me. Put them in Winterland. If only one out of two people who sent in cards shows up, we'll sell out." He said, "My *God!* Go ahead. Go ahead and do it then."

I was looking at four hundred and twelve postcards. That was all we had received. But it figured if four hundred cards came in, five thousand people *could* be interested. This was *my* end of the business. It was not something I needed or wanted to explain to McLaren. As a result, we were the only facility of this size that the Sex Pistols played in America. In every other city, they played a club and they had a riot.

The tickets sold out very quickly. I laid down instructions I had never given before about how I wanted security done around the house. *Heavy* security, using hand-held, two-way radios for the first time. I didn't want anybody to think they could come in and trash the place. I wanted to have a *presence.* I also decided that during the show I would keep the house at quarter light. I wouldn't bring the house lights all the way down. I had extra people stationed in the balcony. I didn't want the fans ripping each other off. Because the attitude in those days was anarchy. We can do anything we want to anybody any time. The punk thing.

The day before, somebody representing a group called "Negative Trend" spray-painted their name on all the walls at Winterland. Negative Trend. Negative Trend. There was nothing I could do about it. The next afternoon, we opened the doors early. Everything was okay. Strange energy. People with nuts and bolts and chains and purple hair. Leather. A *lot* of black leather. A lot of hardware. For this scene, this was *the* major event. They were all there, auditioning for *Ben Hur*. Some pushing and shoving but no major problems at all.

The show started and I was in the box office when a guy came running in and said, "The manager of the Sex Pistols just got here with another band and he asked for you. He said, 'You find the Yank. You tell the Yank I got this band with me and if they can't play before the Pistols do, then we won't play.' " The name of the band was Negative Trend. The nouveau local revolutionary band.

I went backstage and they were all still standing around by the door. I introduced myself to McLaren. He was about five five or five four. A short Peter Asher. Freckles all over his face like out of a cartoon. A beret and a walking stick. Quite bright and musically aware. He knew the times that he lived in. "You're Mr. McLaren," I said. He said, "How are you? You're the Yank?"

I said, "Do me a favor. Don't call me Yank. Call me Bill. Mr. Graham, anything. Don't call me Yank." I said, "I heard there was a problem." He said, "We want these guys to play before us." I said, "I heard you insinuated that if they can't play, *you* won't play." He said, "Well, I'm sure we can straighten that . . ."

I said, "That's not the point. Did you say something like that? *You* don't say that. If you want to ask me for something, ask me. But don't say that if you can't get it, you're going to take away your bonbons. That's not nice. It doesn't work that way here."

"These are friends of ours . . ."

". . . who spray-painted the sides of my building. That's not cute. I have to undo that. Based on what I know about our business, the people out there came to see the Sex Pistols. There were two opening acts. They've been tolerant with both. But if the next band or group of artists on stage is *not* the Sex Pistols, they'll be furious. This band will be received very poorly. Might I suggest that the Sex Pistols go on next and then, when they finish, the stage will be yours for the Negative Trend?"

He had only asked me for fifteen or twenty minutes for the Negative Trend. I said, "You want to play them for half an hour? Take half an hour. Be my guest."

"*You* would allow that?" he said. I said, "After the Sex Pistols, they can have whatever they wish." He said, "That's very considerate of you. That's very nice."

He turned to his boys and they were ecstatic. Everybody was ecstatic. There was a good strong energy buzz in the building waiting for the Sex Pistols. I had three guys working the stage and I made a deal with them. I said, "We're dividing the stage into fourths. Whatever falls into my quarter is mine to keep." I still have a cup somewhere with all the nuts and bolts and pennies and safety pins. Pieces of a garter belt. All kinds of dumb stuff. Because Johnny Rotten told them, "Come on. *Throw* it. Come on."

They came out and the slam dancing started immediately. The place was on the edge of being destroyed but nobody destroyed anything. It was beyond entertainment. It was a statement. Sid Vicious came on without a shirt with cuts all over him, bleeding. Johnny Rotten was bent over the microphone like Charles Laughton in *The Hunchback of Notre Dame*. The drummer and the other guitar player were good. It was pure raw hard core energy. A phenomenon.

They finished their set and then did two or three encores. The Negative Trend hung by the edge of the stage like guys on an aircraft carrier waiting for the plane to land. Once the Sex Pistols finished, we went into our regular routine. I said, "Once again, please, the *Sex Pistols*." And the house went crazy.

At that moment, the Sex Pistols' roadies and Negative Trend's roadies started moving the equipment very quickly. Within ten seconds after the Sex Pistols went off, we put "Greensleeves" on and the Pavlov's dog theory went into effect. For the past thirteen years, we had always ended all our shows the same way. With "Greensleeves." It was our trademark. This was a Bay Area audience. They heard "Greensleeves," everybody left. Two minutes later, the stage was ready. I walked over to McLaren and I said, "It's all yours, Malcolm."

All the people were already outside. The streets were jammed. It was like a Dead concert. People don't just walk away from a Dead concert. They stand there, mesmerized. This was like that, only in a Martian way.

Would I have wanted to earn my living putting on bands like that? *No.* They were an expression of an attitude which I abhor to this day. But as a piece of theater, it was extraordinary. There were no shootings, there were no beatings, there were no deaths. Who am I to set myself up as a censor concerning what the public wants?

It was their last concert. They never worked again in public. They joined the list. Led Zeppelin and Lenny Bruce and Groucho Marx and the Sex Pistols.

3.

ROBERT GREENFIELD: Bill was approached to put on the first rock and roll show in the Soviet Union. He raised three hundred and fifty thousand dollars from Levi Strauss to stage a concert in Leningrad. Bill got commitments from Santana, the Beach Boys, and Joan Baez. At the very last moment, the Soviets changed their minds. Levi Strauss was out three hundred and fifty thousand dollars. The people who had worked for months on the project were crushed.

In the persons of Mickey Hart and Phil Lesh, the Grateful Dead approached Bill about taking them to Egypt so they could perform before the Great Pyramids. Bill said, "There's a fucking war going on over there." So the Dead did it themselves with Bill in attendance strictly as a guest. In Egypt, the Dead played for their smallest audience since the Acid Test. Six hundred and ninety some odd people who had paid. While out in the desert behind them, thousands of Bedouins on camels watched for free.

After the last show, Bill rented horses and camels for a midnight ride out to an oasis in the middle of nowhere. Bill and Mickey Hart, who had once both worked at El Patio out in Long Island, a legendary club where Latin bands played, raced to see who could circumnavigate the oasis first with a tray on one shoulder without spilling a thing. As Mickey Hart says, "To this day, the event stirs deep emotion and is steeped in controversy."

At the end of the year, Bill shut down the last of his great halls.

BILL: Closing Winterland was a hard decision to make. But it would have taken three hundred and fifty thousand dollars in repairs to keep it open and the owner refused to allow any of that to be applied toward my rent. After the Fillmores, Winterland was my ongoing, free-form space. I *loved* that place. People loved it because when they got in there, it was like their bowling alley or their *shvitz*. It was their *joint*. They loved that they could sit all the way around the stage.

It was a great house. One that was as good to me, if not better, than the original Fillmore. I can probably count more great shows there than at the Fillmores because they ended in 1971 and Winterland went on for another seven years. All the great New Year's Eve shows with the Grateful Dead were there.

But every time we had a major show there, plaster of Paris would start falling from the ceiling. If I'd wanted to stay, I would have had to commit to being there for another ten years in order to make back the money I would have had to spend for repairs.

It was a time in my life when I was thinking a lot about having to do things whether or not I wanted to. Being forced to work at jobs I did not like. I had always had problems with that. "You *will* get up today and do *this*."

Before the closing show, I wrote a letter to the Dead. Basically, I asked them to please rehearse for this gig. I told them that there were certain songs people wanted to hear that they had not played in a long time. The Dead had a history of never making a set list for any show. But I felt that this was a special situation.

That night, I put a billboard outside. It said, "They're not the best at what they do. They're the *only* ones that do what they do." Which was something I had said about them to an interviewer and the way I still feel about them to this day. Underneath the billboard on the night of the show, some kid was standing with a sign that said, "One Thousand Five Hundred and Sixty-Five Days Since Last SF 'Dark Star.' " So I wasn't wrong about the crowd wanting to hear certain songs.

It was a great night. For some reason, I always remember the bad stuff. The Dead invited too many bikers. When that happens, an element of fear comes in and I couldn't just let it all hang out. I had some problems backstage. I remember the night primarily because I had a hard time controlling my anger and disappointment at how many bikers were there. Instead of enjoying myself, I had to spend most of the night dealing with that. To some extent, that rained on the parade for me. But Ken Kesey was there that night and Chet Helms and Bill Walton and the Dead played for six hours. The Blues Brothers were great.

What the Catskills were for me, first the Fillmores and then Winterland were for other people. A few weeks ago, some guy in the street came up to talk to me. It turned out he was now a stockbroker, one of those guys who get up every day at 5 A.M. He said, "Bill, you know what was great about Winterland? Not too many people knew but upstairs, on the top level in back of the stage, there was a flat area about six feet wide. Room enough to dance.

"A bunch of us would get wasted and go up there and have our own party. There was the Dead, playing down there in the pit, and when I was dancing up there, I could feel the energy of the whole room coming my way. There were the Dead and we were dancing and I felt like I was part of the show." For people like him, it was living theater. *His* living theater. In that space, he and others were able to satisfy their needs and desires.

After Winterland closed, we did shows at the Kabuki Theater and the Old Waldorf and the Warfield Theater. We got into clubs. But nothing ever replaced Winterland. After Winterland, San Francisco changed. The communal aspect of going to shows disappeared.

BOB BARSOTTI: Back in the sixties when it started, Winterland was the *big* place that nobody liked to go to. But when it closed, it was *small*. It felt like my living room compared to anyplace else. It really felt so intimate there. Winterland was just one big room with an open floor and the stands stacked on top of each other. All wood. It didn't sound like anywhere else either.

In the beginning, it was really part of the ghetto there. By the end, the Victorian flats around there were all going for two hundred thousand instead of thirty thousand. The whole tone of the neighborhood had started to change. They didn't want to see rock and roll happening every Saturday night and kids bursting out at two in the morning making a bunch of noise and throwing bottles in the gutter. There are a bunch of condos now where Winterland used to be.

I never saw the kind of violence anywhere else that could happen in front of that building on a regular basis. It was all centered on what was going on there. People from all over the Bay Area would cruise Winterland on a Saturday night. "Let's go see what's happening at Winterland." Never checking on whether there were tickets available. So it would be a total fluke if they could get in.

There was always this scene outside. We would sell *two thousand* tickets a night at the door. People would just show up to see what was going on. There were probably a hundred fifty to two hundred people who went to every single show. Didn't matter who it was or when it was. Weeknight. Weekend. Four in a row. They were there. *Every night.* That doesn't happen in *any* of our places anymore. It just *doesn't.* It was a scene. Winterland was my college and my graduate school. I got my master's in rock and roll there.

The ideals that made Winterland work don't exist anymore. The camaraderie at the concerts. It's entertainment now and a business and a commodity that people pay for. When they do, they expect certain things in return. It's not like they're all joining in on something anymore. You know?

Chapter
Seventeen

Stones

1.

PETER RUDGE: We were in Barbados. We didn't have a falling out, Jagger and I. We talked and basically, I was full of myself. I was very stupid. I said, "Well, I don't really give a fuck if I rock and roll anymore. I want to open a restaurant." I was going through my whole thing then. I wanted to make movies. I wanted to open restaurants. I wanted to run sports teams. I was really sick of rock and roll.

Jagger said, "Well, I'll call you." And I just took it for granted that I would have the Stones. He may have made his decision before. I still tend to think he decided before. Because he was talking to Jerry Weintraub. In retrospect, I wouldn't have gone with me. You know? I had really become an asshole. Absolutely.

Of all the people who were after it, and I know this through Frank Barsalona, Bill was the one person who said, "Why don't you go with Pete Rudge?" There *is* a code of honor with Bill. He wanted them but *not* at any price. Other guys bad-mouthed me. This and that. I never heard one thing bad from Bill Graham about me. When Bill got them, he called me and said, "Hey . . . *Pete.*" You know?

I said to Jagger on the phone and I said to him by letter, "If anyone else gets the Stones, I think Bill Graham should." So it all evens out in the end. But the other guys I would have killed.

BILL: I think it started with Alan Dunn calling me to make me aware that they were thinking of going out. It must have been in 1980 when we started talking about it. Peter Rudge had made some mistakes with them. He went down to the islands on vacation with Mick and he assumed that he had the tour. The next thing I knew, word got out that they were going to be speaking to other people. Jerry Weintraub, Barry Fey, and John Scher, I think.

It was set up that I would go to New York to meet with Mick. The first meeting, we talked about all the old, funny strange things that had happened through the years with me and the band. It was in his home and he was very, very nice. We didn't finish because he had something else to do. He said, "Let's meet again, Bill. Let's go out and have some Japanese food."

I stayed in New York for two weeks that time and every day we kept going out in the West Side for Japanese food. He *loved* Japanese food. Different restaurants all the time. We had wonderful long conversations. Not about the business. His stories, my stories. We just got talking to each other.

Then we also talked about business. My concept of how I saw them touring. The basic difference between me and the others was that I was not trying to prove to him that I knew Chicago better than the guy in Chicago or Buffalo better than the guy who promoted there. For overall coordination, I thought I was more qualified than the other guys. They wanted to promote the *whole* country by themselves. I wanted to be the tour *coordinator.*

We kept having meetings. I would say, "Do you want to go out again?" And he would say, "Yeah, but I can't tomorrow. Can you meet me the day after?" I would say, "Well, I wanted to go back to San Francisco." But I stayed in New York. We went to a reggae festival together. We kept having meetings. He was always respectful. Very cordial and pleasant. It was easy. I took him to a Latin club. He took me to Japanese restaurants.

Mick said that he and Charlie and Keith would be very much involved in the staging, the lighting, and the design. They already had things in mind for the tour. I told Mick I thought that some changes needed to be made. Over the years, they had always done a straight set about an hour long with no encores.

I said, "I think you should do a long retrospective of the past twenty years and not just the last couple of albums. Give them the Rolling Stones *throughout* the years and *build* the day." He agreed with all of that. We got a little bit into the personalities of the band and what the problems might be. I really felt comfortable and secure about our relationship.

It was a very special time for me. Not just because the Rolling Stones were so popular. But because on a given night, they were the very best rock and roll band in the world. The thought of entering into an extended creative relationship with them was something that meant *everything* to me. It was something that made me wake up every day feeling more alive than I had ever been before. So I pursued their tour with total, wild abandon. Basically, I did nothing else. To put it bluntly, I turned the company over to other people. Because I really wanted to bring this tour home.

Still, between Mick and I, there always seemed to be a question that wasn't being asked. If it couldn't be answered, I didn't think I was going to get the tour. After six or seven meetings, I said to him, "I have the feeling that there's something on your mind that you haven't asked me. I hope you don't think that this is a 'Bill Graham Presents' tour. It's the *Rolling Stones*. The name of my company may be relatively well known but on this tour, the Rolling Stones are the *stars*." He never said anything but I think that was the one thing that needed to be clarified.

This was at the last meal we had together. He said, "Listen, Bill. Where are you going now?" I went back to California and he went down to the islands. I was a wreck by then because I *really* wanted to do it.

KEITH RICHARDS: In the period since we had been on the road in 1978, Rudge had gone under. Everything had collapsed. There wasn't really anybody else capable of taking us out. That we knew. Before that to me, Bill was a straight promoter more than entrepreneur or a tour manager.

When we wanted to go out again in 1981 and Peter was not there, who else sprang to mind? It was immediately Bill Graham. Even though up to that point, I'd never particularly thought of Bill as doing the same thing that Rudge did. I didn't know if he'd have the patience to deal with all of us. But he certainly drew on huge reserves of it to deal with it. He was amazing.

Even though it was a more organized period, we still had a lot of problems. Different kinds of problems. Much more ramshackle in a way, you know? We had just gotten Ronnie Wood in to replace Mick Taylor, who had left the band. So we had changing personnel.

We were umm-ing and ohh-ing about going on the road in 1981 and this was already May or June. I mean, if you want to go on the road by August, you're already late. That was the other thing. Bill put it together like *voom*. He had like six weeks to nail a tour together and the band hadn't played for years. It's always stop and start with the Rolling Stones. You get that big, you record once every two years or once a year and tour every two or three years. The band gets rusty.

Charlie's father had just died. He was really depressed. He really didn't feel like doing anything. So I said, "That's why you've *got* to work. You've just got to get *in*. A tour would be a perfect thing." So I convinced Charlie to do it.

They were worried about whether Ronnie Wood would stand up to it.

Whether his health was good enough. Ronnie's tough as old nails, you know. He's kind of like me in that respect.

In order to get them on the road, I said, "Look, I'll take *personal* responsibility for Ronnie. Just to get this thing moving." Then I had to have a few words with Ronnie. I said, "*Listen*. You better *not* screw up."

In 1969, it had been just pure *anarchy*. Nobody was in control anywhere. It was just this huge, bewildering moving of tribes. By 1981, the country was fairly smoothed out. It was all that Ronnie Reagan complacency.

It was also so much a bigger deal by 1981. The money. Things like corporate sponsorship were coming to it. The figures were bigger. The fact that it was taking place in a sort of more ordered environment did let us put on a better show. With sponsorship, we could use the money they put up to keep ticket prices down.

The idea was that it could be used. Obviously it could also be abused. Like watching tennis players who put their shirts up for sale with corporate logos everywhere. I've often thought of doing that with the record cover. *No* record cover. It will just say, "*This Space For Hire*." I could rent out the space on my record cover and I'll make some money for my old age.

BILL: A couple of days later, I was in San Francisco in my house and the phone rang and the first thing the voice at the other end said was, "Well, you ready to go to work, Yank?" It was Jagger and we started putting things together. My pay was going to be based on what they earned. I got a percentage of the net.

So then we had to say, "Does the cost of the limo come out? Do the telephone calls come out?" But my dealings with them were very fair and generous. Not only was I the tour director but we also produced the West Coast dates. Winterland Productions got the merchandising deal, and that was huge. FM Productions did the design and the construction of the staging. So it involved every aspect of my business then.

We were dancing with Big Bertha. I mean, this was the *Rolling Stones*. We knew that if they felt like playing and their attitude was right, we were going to turn on every city we went to.

MICHAEL AHERN: The difference between the Stones 1972 tour and the one they did in 1981 was *mega*. This was an all-stadium tour. We were operating with thirty-five semi-trucks and three or four different staging systems. We had site coordinators either off building or taking down a stage while the production moved among them with sound overlapping. You needed a calendar to do it. There would be four staging systems, A,

B, C, and D, and Sound 1 and Sound 2 and Lights 1 and Lights 2. Because of how long it took to break it all down, we had to have backup units matched up.

BILL: Peter Wolf from the J. Geils Band found us Longview Farm up in Massachusetts. That was where the Stones rehearsed. It was in the middle of nowhere. Beautiful rolling countryside. I would walk into this barn where they had set up and there was that *sound*. They worked very hard. They rehearsed for hours and hours. I knew then I was going to have the same experience I'd had with Dylan in 1974. I knew if the band stayed healthy and we eliminated the bullshit on the road, no heavy-handedness, no yelling and screaming, it was going to be *great*.

Understand. Bill Wyman and Keith Richards were not normal guys. They were *Rolling Stones*. They'd been royalty for twenty years. They knew we were going to have a private plane but we were going to stay at hotels with a *huge* entourage. Sisters and mothers and brothers and children and friends and wives.

But Keith was in a good frame of mind and the rest of the band wanted it to happen. There was a warm communal familial spirit up there which a lot of people said was new. I didn't push my relationship. No backslapping. We all had a job to do.

In terms of the Stones themselves, I was still a hired hand. I didn't assume I was on the inside. I carried my charts and my plans and my maps around and whenever I saw a free moment, I would get to know them a little better. The key person was Mick. When Mick so chose, it was Mick *and* Keith. When they both so chose, it was Mick, Keith, *and* Charlie. They both loved Charlie very much.

Every couple of days, I would go out for a run with Mick. The once-in-a-lifetime experience for me was that I was dealing with a major artist creatively and conceptually. They were in full control. They could veto anything I said. But it was all one-on-one. I didn't have to go through anybody else. They painted. I could tell them what I thought of the painting. They could tell me what they thought about it.

PAUL WASSERMAN: In those days, everyone treated Mick Jagger like Prince Charles and Keith Richards like the *other* son. Bill and everybody from the company just dealt with Mick and then they realized they had to deal with Keith too. In 1981, Keith wasn't on smack. He wasn't doing smack. But he always had this cold, let-me-alone look on him. Not that Mick's exactly warm. Mick at least knows what he has to do for the money. Keith doesn't want to deal with worldly things. Everyone dealt with Mick to begin with and *then* they would get to Keith so he wouldn't feel left out. There was that little tension in it.

KEITH RICHARDS: Bill was *incredibly* diplomatic. Because there were several conflicts on the tour. By this time, the division between Mick and myself had started to show itself. For whatever reason. The fact is that it existed. Like all those sort of things, the causes were slow, tenuous, and mysterious. I don't know myself how it started, really. But the fact is that by 1981, it started to show itself on that tour and Bill really had a problem on his hands.

I had the guys in the band coming to me saying, "Mick's got a million-dollar stage. With *our* money." They were complaining to me. And I said, "This is ridiculous. I mean, it's *your* money. You should be asked."

So then I went and saw Bill and I said, "What the fuck's this million-dollar stage? The boys are moaning to me. Now I've got to look like the asshole who's fightin' Mick for his stage." I just put it on Bill and that was one example of things that were going on all the time. It was a hydraulic stage. I don't know if it was *really* a million. Say six hundred thousand. Three quarters of a million maybe.

Bill had to deal with what became my litany. "Look, I'm talkin' for the band. Not necessarily for myself. Although yeah, I happen to agree with 'em this time." He had to listen to that from me and then Mick saying, "Oh. *He's* speaking for the band," and it just became like a cracked record. Really, it was up to the other guys but they didn't want to get into that shit. So that was the situation Bill really had to work in on that tour.

BILL: At the farm during the rehearsal period, there was a discussion about having certain things on the stage and what it would cost. Keith finally walked outside to talk to me and he said, "You know, I want to play on a stage. *Not* a fucking *toy.*" Those were his exact words. The suggestion had been to have the stage built inside a track so the amps could move from one side to the other. It would also turn the stage so the people on the sides for one song would then be in back and in front. Keith said, "I don't want to play on that fucking track."

I said, "Let's see if we can't find a way to make it work." We went back inside. Keith said, "What will this thing cost?" I said, "Well, in the budget, it looks like eighty grand." Keith said, *"Eighty grand? Eighty grand?* I'm not paying *eighty grand* for a fucking *toy.* Especially if it doesn't work."

All of a sudden, Mick went to his aid. It had all been his idea from the start. But now he said, *"Yeah.* What if it *doesn't* work, Bill?"

Now, they were on the same team. Neither of them wanted this stage if it didn't work. I said, "Hold it. *Hold it!* If the fucking thing doesn't work, you don't fucking pay for it."

And they both said, "We'll take it. That's a deal. If it works, we're paying. If not, it's on you, Graham."

Now they were allies and I was the bad boy. When we tried the stage out for the first time, I nearly shit in my pants. I'd had to guarantee that I would pay for it if it didn't work. Thank God, it did.

At the very beginning of the tour there was a little misunderstanding. The late Ian Stewart found them a club to play in Worcester, Massachusetts called Sir Morgan's Cove. I went there in the afternoon and there were already thousands of kids around the place. It was steaming hot and the cops brought in the riot squad and surrounded the club. I said, "Let's open the doors. Don't expect the people across the street to leave. We'll open the doors and windows to let them hear the music."

One kid tried to break through the line of police and a cop lifted his riot baton in the air but didn't really touch him. They snapped a picture that appeared on the cover of the *New York Post* the next day with a headline saying *"RIOTS."* Facilities all over the country wanted to double their security and triple their insurance. That gig caused me a tremendous amount of problems. The Stones also wanted to play the Orpheum Theater in Boston but Kevin White, the mayor, wouldn't let it happen. So we never even got to play Boston at all.

The biggest pretour questions were: *"Where* do we start?" *"How* do we start?" "How do we announce it to the public?" Mick liked the idea of announcing the show in Veterans' Stadium in Philadelphia on the fifty-yard line. The buzz was already getting out that the Stones were rehearsing. I said, "Mick, they're going to ask you when tickets are going on sale when you sit down that day to talk to the press. You say, 'I do believe we're going on sale now. Is that right, Bill? Are we on sale now?' "

When the press conference went out live on the radio that day, people in the city of Philadelphia ran out of buildings. They did U-turns in the street. Kids left school. They were going *crazy* to buy tickets. I wanted that to happen. It all started when Jagger walked into the stadium. He was *way* over on the other side from the kids in the stands, stuck behind this steel mesh fence. I said, *"Mick,"* and he just veered. He never even looked at the press table. He veered and ran across the field and worked that fence for half an hour and it was in all the papers the next day. He kissed fingers through the fence and signed thumbs and little pieces of paper.

At that kind of stuff, he was the *best*. The best PR man in the known universe. The next day, the press wanted to know, "How many tickets have you sold?" We were at ninety thousand, I knew we were going to be sold out by the following morning. I told the press we had sold out already. "How fast?" they wanted to know. "Four hours and twelve minutes," I told them. I made up a figure.

The disc jockeys began asking, "Is there going to be *another* show?" I said, "I don't know. We've got to think about it." The third morning, we put the *second* show on sale. It sold out. Ninety-four thousand *more* tickets. I wanted the industry to know that the Rolling Stones had sold out Philadelphia, ninety-four thousand times *two*. The first one was four hours and twelve minutes? The second went in three hours and eight minutes. I made up another number. Just to let them all know.

Every promoter in the country was saying, "Bill, can we get the band?" By then, I had pretty much made up my mind that the goal for the tour was that we would fill in between the dates. We would do a coliseum on a Tuesday night somewhere or an indoor date. We would also do dates like the Fox Theater in Atlanta with the Stray Cats. A three-thousand seater. That was Keith's thing. To go from small to big.

Right before the tour started, a disc jockey sent a box to the tour office on Fifty-seventh Street. It had a petition with thirty-six thousand names on it. Signatures from kids. "We would like the Rolling Stones to come to Rockford, Illinois." I showed it to Mick and the group and I said, "I think we should do this. It's an eight-thousand seater. We're going to hit Chicago later on our swing back. We could do Rockford on our way from Buffalo to Boulder." They agreed. The press we got out of that was *awesome*. I put the Go-Gos on that date.

They played with different people everywhere that we liked. Etta James. The Neville Brothers. The key was that whenever possible, we did doubles. Outdoors in the major cities, we did *two* dates in the same stadium. It was unheard of in that era. In 1978 in Seattle, the Stones had done thirteen thousand people in the Seattle Coliseum. In 1981, they did the King Dome times *two*. Seventy-two thousand people times two. A hundred and forty-four thousand people.

Just before the first show of the tour, I was going from dressing room to dressing room like the coach. "Here we go. *Twenty*. Twenty minutes. *Fifteen*. Fifteen minutes." I got to the next dressing room and I swung the door open. I didn't really know Keith yet. Not like I could say to him, "Hey, *schmuck!*" It was still *Keith*. I swung open the door and as I did, I said, "Fifteen, Keith."

He had his head down and he was putting *lime juice* in his hair. He had this lime and he was squeezing it, trying to get out one more drop. As I was moving away, I said, *"Fifteen, Keith."* I heard this voice saying, *"What'd you say?"* Without missing a beat, I turned around and put out my hands to him and said, "Whenever *you're* ready, baby." He fell down. He just *dropped*. It was great.

KEITH RICHARDS: I think it was in San Francisco where I suddenly got a call. Because Ronnie Wood was supposed to come over and see me and he didn't come. I was waiting and I was waiting. He was in this room all the way down at the other end of the hotel, which had two wings. He had a pipe going with some guys and I was pissed. I stormed down through the lobby from one wing to the other. Patti Hansen, who is now my wife, was behind me and she was going, "No, don't. *Don't.*" She was clawing at my shirt and trying to keep me back. She's a tough bitch too. My shirt was in shreds in the middle and I was still marching across the lobby.

I got up to Ronnie's room and he opened the door and I smelled this shit coming out and *bang!* I hit him. It was the only way to deal with it. Because he was in the Stones. If it had gotten any further, they would have held it against him. I mean, I just had to deal with it. It was the only time I ever popped Ronnie one. Otherwise, it would have just dragged on and on and on.

I'm sure Bill knew about it. Although I don't think we ever talked about it, as *such*. The next day, Ronnie and I had a bit of a ha-ha-ha, and it was over. I think Bill just breathed a sigh of relief and turned a blind eye.

See, by that point, I had sort of come to an agreement with my body. I was in good shape. Mick was running like five miles a day. Which was fair enough. For me, there was enough exercise on stage. Running around up there. Especially with the guitar on my neck as well. Some of them are *heavy*, man.

BILL: Keith had these boots. Every gig, he drove me out of my mind. He wouldn't walk on stage unless it was in those boots. The heel broke off in Candlestick and he wouldn't go on stage without them. So I took the boot and the heel and I ran through the backstage area. I just went up to every guy I saw and I said, "Excuse me. Excuse me. Excuse me. Can I look at your *shoe?*" To find the right size heel. Finally I found a guy sitting backstage and I took his shoe and I said, *"Thank you."* He said, "Wait a minute. That's my shoe." I gave him a hundred dollars. I went into a room and I took the heel off and I put it on Keith's boot with a hammer and a nail. You know how good I am at that? The *worst*. I'm surprised he didn't bleed to death.

There were stagehands who could have done it for me but I wouldn't let anybody else touch it. Keith said, "Bill, you fixing it?" I said, "Yeah, I'm fixing it." He said, "Is it going to stick? Because it's your ass if it doesn't, man." This all happened about twenty minutes before the show. But it took me thirty minutes to do it. So we were ten minutes late.

PETER WOLF: The Stones were late, the place was going nuts. But Keith lived and slept in this one pair of boots. He wouldn't take them off and he just *had* to play in them. The heel fell off. "Hey, man! What size shoe you wear?" "I wear an eight." "Hey, man, those boots are an *eight*." "No, *no!*" "*Got* to have those *boots*, man." There was Bill Graham sitting there with a hammer and nails and tape, getting this fucking heel, running back and forth, forth and back.
    "What's the matter, Bill?"
    "Keith's *boot*. Stay out of the fucking way. I got his *boots*."
    He loved it and he loved them. He loved the insanity of the artists and understood it. Because I think he himself wanted and desired so much to be one. Which in a sense he became anyway. Through the presentation and the artistry of the presentation.

                                    2.

BILL: Mick had said, "Bill, I don't want to go higher than fifteen dollars a ticket anywhere." I was *possessed* to play as many doubles as possible for several reasons. Most important of all, it allowed the hundred and twenty people on the tour to spend an extra day in one place. In every stadium we played, it cost us forty to fifty grand just to put up the stage. So much of what we would now make from a second show would be *gravy*.
    If you wanted to know how strong the Stones were on the tour, they sold a hundred and twenty thousand tickets in Boulder, Colorado. Another for instance. Houston and Dallas were only about four hundred miles apart. But I wanted to do a double in *each*. I just wasn't sure it *could* be done.
    The time before when they had done Dallas-Fort Worth, it was ten thousand seats. Now I wanted to go two times *eighty thousand*. The Cotton Bowl in Dallas and the Astrodome in Houston. I wanted to do a hundred and sixty and a hundred and twenty. Two hundred and eighty thousand tickets.
    I had an idea that I felt would ensure four sellout dates in Texas and I mentioned it to Mick. We'd been charging fifteen dollars a ticket but I said, "I want to go seventeen-fifty a ticket here." Mick said, "No, no, no." I said, "Hear me out. We'll still be getting fifteen dollars of the net. With the extra two-fifty a ticket, we should be able to buy the biggest band in Texas and they will *guarantee* us four sellouts. But I know they'd want a lot of money. ZZ Top."

I called Bill Hamm, the manager of ZZ Top and I explained to him what I wanted to do. They would be the middle act on a three-act show. I said, "I know you're huge. But this is what you can make. Two hundred and eighty thousand tickets. Two dollars and fifty cents a ticket. *Seven hundred thousand* dollars. For four shows."

I proposed it to Bill Hamm and he gave me one of the great ego-gratification lines in terms of letting me know who he was and who they were. He said, "Bill, I sure like that idea. That's a nice package. But I'll tell you. We're *big* down here."

I said, "I know you're big. That's why I'm giving you that kind of money. Because I want to sell out two shows in each place."

He said, "Bill, tell you what we'll do. I got it. I got the whole picture. We'll put out posters and T-shirts and really make it the biggest event in the history of Texas. Bill, we're going to call this the *'ZZ TOP WEL-COMES THE ROLLING STONES TO TEXAS'* show."

I said, "Bill. Hold it. *Hold it*. Rolling Stones, ZZ Top, *and* an opening band."

Finally, we worked it out. How many T-shirts he could hang up in the merchandising area, how many *we* could hang up. How long *they* could play. Your lights, our lights. We worked it out. Agents were calling and *begging* me for favors. I put Mollie Hatchett on as the opening band. Bill Hamm's agent called me back. "Bill Hamm *hates* Mollie Hatchett. He doesn't want them on the show. Put someone else on."

I said, "Look. It's the Rolling Stones' show. But out of respect for Bill, I'll put someone else on."

I told the Mollie Hatchett's agent that I'd put them on with the Stones somewhere else. I asked Bill Hamm's agent, "Is there anyone else Bill *doesn't* want?" The agent said, "He doesn't want some long-haired hippy dippy band up there. Just a nice, easy band." I checked with our Texas promoter. "Give me some insights," I said. He told me, "Billy Gibbons, the lead guitarist in ZZ Top, his favorite band is the Fabulous Thunderbirds. Four guys from Texas. From *Austin*." I said, "Boy, that's a nice fit. Okay."

I called Danny Weiner out in California. I said, "Danny, where are the Fabulous Thunderbirds on such and such a day?" He said, "They're playing a few college gigs in California at a thousand dollars a show." I said, "I've got some money to play with. I'll give them ten tousand dollars for four shows."

Danny was beside himself. He said, "You've *got* to be kidding." He got them out of their college dates because they were dying to work with the Stones and also, it made for a great show. The Stones. ZZ Top. The Fabulous Thunderbirds.

Once the show was set, Dell Furano, the head of Winterland Productions, printed up thousands of T-shirts that read, "Rolling Stones, ZZ Top, the Fabulous Thunderbirds." The shows sold out, boom, boom. Four shows. Going, going, *gone*. Two hundred and eighty thousand tickets. ZZ Top was off in Europe on tour. They came back two days before the date. I was on my way to Texas from another city on the tour.

I got a frantic call from Bill Hamm's agent. He said, "Bill, we got a big problem. Bill Hamm doesn't want the Fabulous Thunderbirds on the dates." I said, "Come on. You *got* to be kidding. They were handpicked because they're Billy Gibbons's favorite band."

He said, "Bill Hamm wants ZZ Top to be the only Texas band on the show." I said, "He never told me that. Tell Bill it's too late now. We sold the tickets. We printed the T-shirts. It's all done." The agent called me back and said, "Bill, it's a very serious issue." I said, "I went through this once already with Mollie Hatchett. The *Rolling Stones* are the headliners. You really should have *no* say about who else plays with them. Out of respect, I took Mollie Hatchett off the bill. I put the Fabulous Thunderbirds on for ZZ Top. I'm not going to fuck these guys now."

He called me back again. "I hate to say this to you," he said. "But this is the message. Direct from Bill Hamm. Unless the Fabulous Thunderbirds are off the show, ZZ Top won't play."

I finally said, "Let me put it this way. I have no problem with ZZ Top not playing these dates. As long as your boss Bill Hamm understands that when I'm asked by the press for the reason, I will tell them the truth."

ZZ Top played *all* the dates. For calling his bluff, Bill Hamm has never allowed ZZ Top to play for me again. He brings in another promoter whenever they do San Francisco. That the lead guitar player never stood up to his manager *astounds* me. On the other hand, they may not even know what went on. They may not even care.

To me, ZZ Top, but mainly Bill Hamm, personify the abuse of power as it exists in the upper echelon of rock and roll. ZZ Top remains the only artist in rock and roll we are not allowed to present. *Still*. To this very day.

KEITH RICHARDS: We played the Superdomes and the Astrodomes and all of the big football bowls. In a small place, it's more spiritual really. You don't have that much room to cover. In those football stadiums, the stage that we had designed ran a third of the way around, and we had to *work* them. They were not there for fun. We had to *move*. We were doing three or four miles a show, at least. Maybe more, I don't know.

Physically, it was more demanding. But so long as it wasn't too humid. At least we had fresh air.

BILL: Dallas, Texas, the first show. One of those crazy Texas afternoons. I was standing behind the amps like always. Right behind Keith because I loved to listen to him. It was hot and sunny and humid and I was facing the back of the stage for a second and when I turned around again, it was pouring rain. Torrential downpour. On every outdoor date that we did, we had a large stage with a lip over it so the stage would stay relatively dry if it rained. Everybody always thought I was crazy but I always had two three-wheeled carts filled with sand on both sides of the stage.

Everybody would say, "Bill. We don't need this today." And I would say, "Put it there." Sure enough, it started pouring buckets that day. They were all under this canopy and the band would be protected if they stayed under it. As I turned around, I saw Keith looking at Woodie and then he looked at Mick and then all of a sudden, he just started moving forward.

It was like in *The Magnificent Seven* when all seven of them come down the center of that little town. He went out front from underneath the canopy as if to say *"Fuck you!"* They were all playing wireless guitars so they could do it. He went out front and so did Wyman and Woodie and Mick and they never came back in.

They were working on the ramps in the pouring rain. We always traveled with spools of clear vinyl to cover the equipment. I got Michael Ahern to start cutting it up into fifteen- and twenty-yard lengths which we threw into the crowd, creating long umbrellas for the kids to huddle under.

Still, the water was collecting on stage and I wanted to get rid of it so I could spread the sand I had been saving for use all throughout the tour. I got some towels and a cloth and started creeping out on stage to mop up the water. Keith looked down at me like he could not believe that I would actually do this during the show. Like in some ways I was crazier than he would ever be.

At the Meadowlands in New Jersey, we put Tina Turner on as the opening act and she came out and did "Honky Tonk Women" with the Stones and it was just great. Her price doubled after that date.

Any band that *ever* opened for the Stones, it always did *great* things for them. It crossed them over into brand-new markets. Stevie Wonder back in 1972. Muddy Waters and B. B. King and Ike and Tina Turner even before that in 1969. The Neville Brothers and Tina in '81.

In Pontiac, Michigan, they played the Silverdome. Because we were so near Detroit, we had Iggy Pop open. He was a favorite of Keith's. He came out wearing ladies' sheer stockings and a very, very short brown leather miniskirt. Long, long stockings and a short skirt and a shirt which he eventually took off. He was just *Iggy*, you know?

There were eighty thousand fans there. Never in the history of rock and roll have more material objects been thrown at *any* artist. Hair brushes, combs, lots of Bic lighters, shoes, sandals, bras, sweaters, hats. *Tons* of shit. I had never seen anything like it. I thought the Sex Pistols had set the record at Winterland. But now we were in the *Silverdome*. Eighty thousand people throwing shit. Like it was warm-up time.

When it was over, we cleared the stage. I had the guys with brooms put everything into these boxes. At my request, one guy itemized everything. He gave me the written list. Seventeen Bic lighters, six hair brushes, nine sneakers, three hats, nine bras, four corsets, and on and on.

I went to Iggy's dressing room and said, "Ig, I got to tell you. You broke every fuckin' record in *existence*." I said, "You want to have some fun? Let's go back out on stage and thank the audience for bestowing all these gifts on you."

I took the box up on stage for him and he went to the microphone with the list and he said, "I want to thank you very much for the following donations." And he began to read the list. At first, they didn't understand. "Six combs." *YAY!* "Nine unmatched sneakers." *YAY!* He read the *whole* list. They went *crazy*. Then he said, "Thank you very much. I really appreciate this."

New Orleans was a tough one because I had to make a decision as to whether we should play there or go to Baton Rouge to the university stadium. The history of rock and roll shows in New Orleans was not all that great. I decided to go for it and do the Superdome. They became the first and only rock act in history to sell it out. Ninety-two thousand seats and we put the Neville Brothers on the show with them. We also went into the record books for doing the biggest balloon drop in the history of an indoor closed stadium. We dropped sixty thousand balloons at the start of the show.

Since we had a few days off, I decided New Orleans was the ideal spot to throw a middle-of-the-tour crew party. We got Paul Prudhomme, the great Cajun chef, to cater a party for us on this beautiful paddlewheel steamer. I invited all the local musicians. The Meters and Alan Toussaint and Professor Longhair and a lot of local Cajun musicians. Nine hundred people on the boat and we danced all night and it was a great party.

On most of the other days off, I worked. Like Rommel, I would go from city to city, putting my maps on the walls. It was a war with no casualties.

Meeting with the local promoters and police chiefs in every town so there would be no muscle and nothing heavy-handed.

Wherever they went was the rock and roll capital of the world for that day. They were the major event in that city. Because how could anyone have two better foils than Keith Richards and Mick Jagger? Keith Richards could take a towel and throw it over his shoulder and he became Errol Flynn in *Captain Blood*. And Mick was Mick.

KEITH RICHARDS: As long as I knew what was going on, I'd usually say "Yeah" to everything. It was very rarely that I'd say no. Mick and I used to think very much down the same lines. Wherever we were, South Pole or North Pole, you asked one of us, and we would both say the same thing. Then that disappeared. I don't know where. I presume the problem then between Mick and I was that I got out of it. The more I got out of it, the more he got to run the show.

When I came back, sort of like to take the weight off your shoulders, old buddy, instead of welcoming me with open arms, he resented it. That's very broadly speaking. I have the feeling that was when the rift started between us. I was no longer sort of the silent, supplicant partner. It took me a long time to figure that out. I just wanted to say, "Hey, I can help you out now. I'm not looking for the man everyday. I can get back in and help you out."

But he just couldn't give it up. Inevitably, once somebody starts to fight you, you've got to fight back. You've got to react in some way. Whether you like it or not. You've got a fight on your hands. Then I started to get into it.

In the last year or so, I've been really happy. Because I don't have to wake up every day thinking of like three different triple crosses that can go down on a certain decision. I mean, it got like that at the end. But Bill would always come to me with the things he thought I needed to know.

On that tour, nobody in the band knew we were producing a movie until the cameras started rolling. Again, it was Mick's idea. Unfortunately, the band hadn't been informed. I found out about it a day before. Through the grapevine. Everything was hired and signed but the Stones didn't know that we were producing it.

After the inevitable clash when I found out about that, Bill started to come to me occasionally if there was something he thought I ought to know. Which was diplomacy of the highest order. Him just working with Mick would have made it worse. He did it absolutely right. He let me know what was going on so we could avoid more problems.

It was very strange. Although the problem had been there earlier, that was the only tour where suddenly it really became silly. Mick had his own car, where nobody else could go. The rest of the guys were not like that. It was just surprising. To suddenly find him like that. This kind of internal tension was pretty much unknown to the Rolling Stones. It was the first time we had to work with it being there.

Rudge probably couldn't have handled it. That was the difference between him and Bill. That would really have driven him over the brink. The way that Bill handled it was amazing. Because usually people caught in the pincer go bye-bye. Not that it would have ended the tour. Mick and I were too professional by then to do something like that.

But we could have made the atmosphere more livable for everybody. I mean, Mick and I *chatted*. It wasn't as if we *never* saw each other. But it was very *formal* in a way. Which is a drag with a friend. It was very English, really. Falling back on the formal rules. You know. In order to get the job done, old boy. That's the most frightening thing about Mick. When he's *really* polite to you.

BILL: We had a meeting in Chicago in a conference room. I was there just as a friend and a mediator. The band felt somewhat offended that they weren't aware of everything that was going on. Decisions involving the entire band were being made without everyone's knowledge. I think Mick always had good thoughts in mind. I think he did what he did by rote because they did not have a manager. I was there just to do the tour. In terms of the movie, I didn't really get involved in all that.

When it involved the tour, it was always Mick and Bill with Mick as liaison for the group. In terms of the movie, Mick made the managerial-type decisions. That was where the problem lay. He was making what he thought were decisions in *their* best interest.

They shot the movie *Let's Spend the Night Together* at the outdoor show we did in Tempe, Arizona. They brought all these girls up on stage for "Honky-Tonk Women," which they did only for the movie. Again, that was Mick. Keith was not into that kind of showbiz thing. That was Mick and Hal Ashby, the director. But we did do all the staging for it. We got the ladies and designed that backdrop, off the cuff.

There were times when Mick and Keith didn't want to be bothered. When they wanted *other* people to make the decision. Other times, it was, "*You* don't make that decision for *me!*" With them, everything was timing. You just had to know how to ride the wind.

In every town, they had to live up to the myth of being the Rolling Stones. Most of their shows were tens and elevens. Sometimes, a nine and a half. But they never backed off. Two hours and fifteen minutes. All the old songs and the new plus encores like they had never done before.

Bill with Marcia Sult and his sons on the Larkspur Ferry, New Year's Day, 1977. Left to right: Thomas Sult, Alex, and David. [Marcia Sult Godinez]

The stage at Winterland set for "The Last Waltz." From left to right: Rick Danko, Joni Mitchell, Robbie Robertson, Levon Helm on drums. [Ken Regan/Camera 5]

Closing Winterland, New Year's Eve, 1978.
[Michael Zagaris]

"I wanna play on a stage, not a toy." With Keith Richards at Longview Farm in Massachusetts, September 1981. [Ken Regan/Camera 5]

Backstage with Mick Jagger at Wembley in London, June 1982. Publicist Alvinia Bridges stands in the background. [Ken Regan/Camera 5]

Like Rommel with his maps
and charts on the 1981 Stones tour.
[Ken Regan/Camera 5]

With Bill Kreutzman and Jerry Garcia of the Dead, Frost Amphitheatre, October 1982. [Ken Friedman]

As Father Time, in Oakland, the year he rode in at midnight on a mirror ball. [Ken Friedman]

With Carlos Santana at Slane Castle, Dublin, during the 1984 Dylan-Santana tour of Europe.
[Ken Regan/Camera 5]

To Gary — Where's My Light — Fool   Love Jack Biel 2/1/84

Playing a movie mogul very much like Jack Warner in Francis Coppola's *The Cotton Club*.
[Lorenzo Doumani/Totally Independent Ltd.]

With Jack Nicholson, "true American royalty," backstage at Live Aid, Philadelphia Veterans' Stadium, 1986. [Ken Regan/Camera 5]

Onstage at Live Aid with Stephen Stills, Graham Nash, and David Crosby. [Ken Regan/Camera 5]

With arms around Jack Healey and Mary Daly, in front of the artists who made "A Conspiracy of Hope" a success, backstage at Giants Stadium, 1986. [Ken Regan/Camera 5]

"All the best moments came when I was alone." In Mendoza, Argentina, on the Amnesty International tour of the world, 1989. [Neal Preston]

The entire company gathered onstage at "Laughter, Love, and Music," Polo Field, Golden Gate Park, November 3, 1991. [Ken Friedman]

A crowd estimated at anywhere from 300,000 to half a million. [Scott Sommerdorf/*San Francisco Chronicle*]

Truthfully, they got to me every night. They were *that* strong. Fucking monsters.

The last show was at Hampton Roads, Virginia. Fifteen thousand seats, indoors. They shot it for closed-circuit video. I was against that and I don't think it worked. But it was a great last show. I beat Bill Wyman four out of seven in Ping-Pong backstage. Mick bought me a sweater and said, "It worked out." He was very happy and very pleased.

In fact, he did not wait until then to tell me. In L.A. a couple of weeks before, he had said this to me. That he was happy. That we had done something together as well as it could have possibly been done.

On the plane trip from Hampton Roads to New York, someone said to me, "Bill. If you've got a minute, Keith would like to see you up front." There was a bedroom up there that Keith had made into his own private space on the plane. I went up there and he said, "Would you step into my office?" He took me into the bathroom and "Bill, we've got to celebrate, man. The tour's over and you've taken me through it. We've come out alive and it's really been great. You've been a driving asshole at times but you made it happen. We're not going *anywhere* without you again. By that, I mean the next time."

Then he handed me this package wrapped in newspaper with a rose stuck on it. I opened the package and it was those boots. They had tape and glue and rubber bands and shit all over them. I still have them. In a glass case in my house.

3.

BILL: I organized the Stones' tour of Europe in the summer of 1982 out of London. There were some countries that the band didn't think they could play. Italy and Spain. Everybody said, "You go to Italy, they're going to kill you. You'll die." But I had strong feelings about both these countries. I'd spent a lot of time in them over the years. The passion was there. They were ripe and ready for the Rolling Stones. When I said to the Stones, "Let me try something," they would let me because of the U.S. tour. By now, there was a friendship and trust and respect between myself and the band.

To start the tour and give it a buzz, they wanted to play some break-in dates. So we decided to do two-thousand-seat theaters in Aberdeen, Glasgow, and Edinburgh. We contacted the newspapers in each of these three cities and told them to be across the street from a theater at a quarter to twelve. At twelve o'clock, Michael Ahern was in Aberdeen, Mick Brigden was in Edinburgh, and I was in Glasgow. A guy walked out from the theater with a ladder. He climbed up the ladder and put on the marquee the following: "ROLLING STONES HERE." Then he put up the date. Then he put up *"ON SALE NOW!"* It was like "Candid Camera."

People who were walking past the theaters went wild. Fifty minutes later, *all* the tickets were gone. They played those cities three nights in a row and kicked ass and then we went to Rotterdam.

KEITH RICHARDS: Basically, it was a replay of the American tour. But the amazing thing about it was the audiences were as big. It was the first tour in Europe I think where rock and roll was played in football stadiums. Before that, we'd be playing these five- or eight-thousand-seat festival halls. For a whole tour to be at racetracks like L'Auteuil in Paris or football stadiums was something new.

The tour was things that you wouldn't dream of. *Lap of luxury!* Bill did it so outrageously. From the top to the bottom, he had his eye on *everything*. What really amazed me was the stature of Bill's diplomacy. When I say "diplomacy," I mean with Bill, it was *handled*. The thing with working with Bill on the road is that I wouldn't really know everything that was going on. I would just hear like little filtered bits.

Because I was doing what I do. The *show*. I would only hear about it *indirectly*. Bill needs me to do *this?* Because so-and-so needs *that?* Oh, *really?* I don't *want* to know. I could say, "Bill, *handle it*." And I knew it would be done. Because if things weren't being run smoothly, I'd say, "What do you mean?" And I'd start to take control myself. Instead of doing what I *do*.

PETER WOLF: The Stones decided to have a party for the crew. Bill got this nightclub. I think it was Keith who said, "Come on by this club." We were sitting there and there were the Rolling Stones in Germany and it was the tour of tours and they were playing like this really *schlagen* disco music. Keith said something like, "Hey, man, can't you play some *Motown* or something?" I was sitting there with Mick and we were chatting away and drinking and all of a sudden, Bill came running up to me and went, *"Wolf,* you've *got* to do something! You're a deejay. Get up there and *stop* them."

I went up there and there was Keith with a Bowie knife to the throat of this German guy. I guess this was the second time he had gone up there personally and said, "Listen, man. Can you stop playing this shit?" The guy didn't. He kept on playing it. Out came this fucking knife. Bill was pulling on Keith and Keith was fucking going after the guy and Bill was saying "Get in there, *Wolf*."

So I ran in and said, "Oh no, I'll play some records." I did that for about fifteen or twenty minutes. Then I figured, "Well, *great*. The guy's got the idea now. I'll go sit back down." I guess maybe he didn't. Twenty minutes later, that music was back on and I could see the Bowie knife coming and Graham jumping on Keith, trying to hold him back. Oh, *God*.

KEITH RICHARDS: We were in Madrid, doing an open-air show in a place called "the Cauldron" which is Madrid's famous soccer stadium. It's called "the Cauldron" because the sun beats down on you, it's very steep and it's just like a frying pan, and really unbelievable. This was a show at night. As we went on, there was this bolt of lightning. The thunder rumbled and it just pissed down on this intricate stage and all these balloons and everything they had put out. It all started to shred and rip away and topple over and the water was flooding the stage.

We were still playing because we were on the radio mikes and no longer in danger of being electrocuted. So that was cool. We'll just get wet. And not play very well. Everybody was raving. It was *pissing* with rain. We couldn't even see the first row. It was a just a curtain. Then as it let up, these guys came on with mops. We were playing and I turned around and it was Bill Graham pushing the squeegee. Organizing this army of squeegees. Because we were literally ankle-deep in water on stage. It was amazing.

It's a very rare person who can deal with the paper clips *and* with the boardroom at the same time. Bill is one of those people. Which is why he drives everybody mad. To him, it's all the same job. From the top to the bottom. If he saw something not right, he'd fix it, whether it was a bent nail on the stage or closing a deal for a hundred shows at the Superdome.

BILL: In Spain, they played in Barcelona and Madrid. At four o'clock in the morning in Barcelona, Keith called my room and insisted on having some broiled salmon. Because it was on the hotel menu. I said, "Keith, the kitchen closed at *eleven*."

He said, "It says *broiled salmon*." I went to his room. He'd had a little accident. He'd broken his nose on the ashtray. I said, "How did you do that?" Actually, Patti Hansen had called me first and said, "You better come upstairs. He cut his nose."

I said, "How could he cut his nose?" She told me that the ashtray had slipped and turned over and he hit his nose against it and cracked it.

I got *so* mad at him. I went and found the Yellow Pages and I said, "*You* find me broiled salmon in this book. You find it and I'll go get it for you."

Mick was *such* a professional. He would be at every gig an hour before.

Which was just not Keith. He got there when he got there. He was never late but it began to be taxing on Mick. Sometimes, Keith would get there half an hour or twenty minutes before the show. Mick has always had to live with the fact that Keith is the leader of the band. Whether he likes it or not.

KEITH RICHARDS: I can't remember things between Mick and myself being any worse than at that point. It certainly wasn't better—1981 was the first time we'd been on the road and worked under that sort of atmosphere. By 1982, we'd sort of got it down. So that it was like a little formal science between ourselves. The only difference by 1982 was that people were in blocks. You were either with the boys or with Keith and Mick. It was becoming more and more *me*, and not the band. The lines were hardening. The previous tour, they were just being formed. It was basically just Mick and myself that were involved in it. By 1982, it had been solidified. With *camps*. It was starting to get ridiculous.

ROBERT GREENFIELD: Although Bill could not have possibly known it then, for him this was the top. By taking the Stones out on the road so successfully first in America and then Europe as well, he had finally reached the highest peak on the mountain of rock.

To be sure, the money was astonishing. But for Bill, it was always a mixture of profit and having fun. No one got off like Bill did on the mad, continuing chaos of Mick and Keith, the longest running soap opera in the history of rock. No one better appreciated the ultimate buzz of being the only story in town on whatever day the Stones happened to come into your town.

For Bill of course the best part was that he had done the whole thing *right*. *His* way. The way Bill alone always knew it *should* be done. It was the ultimate dream for someone who lived for control. Bill had done it his way yet both the band *and* the people who had come to see the shows seemed pleased. Bill had given them all a meal no one else could have served in the exact same way.

Mick Jagger now asked Bill Graham for advice. Even for Bill, this was heady stuff. It was the ultimate get-off for someone who no longer had to worry about what things cost or how much money he had in the bank. Bill was able to handle it all because he was happy. Professionally, he felt fulfilled. Personally, his life was something less than perfect. But for Bill, business always came first.

Thanks to him, the Stones had finally worked in the kind of environment he had spent his entire life trying to create for the artist, believing always that if the performer was happy, no matter *what* it took, then the fan would get not only more than he had bargained for but also more than the cost of the ticket he was clutching in his hand.

When it came to his own life, Bill had no distance. To him, the cigarette butt lying on the floor of one of his new venues in the Bay Area was as important as the act about to take the stage. To Bill, there was no real difference between the two. Although he was a very deep thinker who could brood about problems real or imagined with a look on his face only ever seen anywhere else when Klaus Kinski somehow managed to *schlep* that boat over the mountain on the motion picture screen, Bill could never step far enough back from his own life to see the pattern of it all.

It might have helped a great deal if he had. It might have saved him from some of the terrible pain he would suffer during the ensuing decade, much of it self-inflicted by a desperate need to find something as perfect and satisfying as working with the Stones in 1981 and 1982 had been. For no matter what he was doing, Bill was always completely involved. And he was always doing *something*. Bill craved action. It was his most obsessive need.

While on tour with the Stones in Europe, Bill became engaged to his longtime personal assistant, Jan Simmons. All the while, Regina Cartwright continued to figure prominently in his life. After the tour was over, his relationship with Jan Simmons ended not with wedding bells but tears. She moved out of Masada, his home on seven acres on top of the highest hill in Corte Madera in Marin County, not to see him again for months.

Yet not so long after they had reestablished contact, she went back to work for Bill as his personal assistant again, continuing in the job until she began working for the Grateful Dead in 1990. Where Bill and some women were concerned, the relationship never really ended. Instead, it just changed shape over time, becoming something he could more easily manage without having to give up so much of his attention or increasingly precious time.

By now, Bill had structured his company so he could be out on the road for months at a time. He had Gregg Perloff and Sherry Wasserman to book and settle his shows. He had Danny Scher to spearhead the construction of a permanent concert facility called the Shoreline Amphitheater in Mountain View, a bedroom community located between San Francisco and San Jose. There was a nightclub division headed by David Maieri. A management company in which Mick Brigden and Arnie Pistilnick worked. A catering concern called Fillmore Fingers and an in-house agency known as Chutspah Advertising. There were fifty full-time employees at Bill Graham Presents with another two hundred and fifty available to work part-time at shows.

Although Bill had personally trained all these people and many of them had never worked for another boss in their adult lives, the company ran very well without him now. Bill did not need to be there for the day-to-day. And so he went looking for things to do. Projects into which he could throw himself with more intensity than could be handled by those who did not share his passion for the work or his overwhelming need to make everything happen exactly the way he knew it should.

The first U.S. Festival in 1982 was a perfect example. Steve Wozniak, who along with Steven Jobs had brought the Apple computer into the world, and so now really did have more money than he knew what to do with, hired Bill Graham Presents to put on a rock festival to rival Woodstock. In terms of backstage acrimony, it nearly did.

Everything about the U.S. Festival was to be *big*. Two million dollars for landscaping. Twenty-three thousand dollars spent on dry ice to cool amplifiers which sat in the blinding hot sun of the San Bernadino Valley on the biggest stage in the world, built from ten trailers' worth of steel. A giant video screen. The world's biggest sound system, with huge delay towers. The technology of the computer age meeting up with the reborn New Age spirit of a Woodstock to which almost no one working on the project but Bill had actually gone.

Wozniak's people held daily morning "centering sessions" on the site. Standing in a circle while holding hands, they compiled mental lists of all their problems so they could then wipe the slate entirely clean. Bill called them "Stepford wives . . . smiling all the time with that glassy look in their eyes." In every way, it was truly a marriage made in hell.

Although Bill kept adding new acts in order to build interest in the Labor Day weekend shows, tickets sold slowly. The shows began in hundred and ten degree heat. The Kinks were set to play on Saturday night. But they wanted to wait so they could be the first band to appear in darkness. Backstage, Bill had one of his guys drive a forklift over to the Mercedes owned by their manager, raising it into the air until the manager yelled loudly enough for Bill to throw him out of the backstage area. The Kinks then went out to play their set on time.

Paid attendance at the festival was around sixty thousand. By conservative estimates, Wozniak lost from ten to twelve million dollars on the first U.S. Festival. Remarkably, he went right ahead and put on another one the following year. Without Bill or his company.

That fall, Bill was contacted by musicians in England who had performed together in September at a concert put on by British promoter Harvey Goldsmith for the Prince's Trust at Royal Albert Hall. Ronnie

Lane, a former member of the Small Faces, was suffering from multiple sclerosis. Jeff Beck, Eric Clapton, Kenny Jones, Andy Fairweather-Low, Jimmy Page, Paul Rodgers, Charlie Watts, and Bill Wyman all came over to do a short tour of America, raising over a million dollars for their cause. The ARMS tour (Action and Research into Multiple Sclerosis) was the first benefit tour ever.

The year wore on. Bill did a small part in Francis Coppola's *The Cotton Club*. He made a serious bid to take Michael Jackson and his brothers out on tour in a manner that would have first involved and then financially benefited the people in the inner cities who were their greatest fans. Instead, the Jacksons went out with people who knew little about the art or the business of rock. The tour was neither a commercial nor a critical success.

That summer, Bill took Bob Dylan and Santana on a tour of Europe. In Ireland, they played Slane Castle outside Dublin. Van Morrison and Bono of U-2 were there as well. By telling each artist separately just how much the others wanted to play with him, Bill got all three of them to go out on stage together after Dylan had finished his set.

BILL: They walked out and started singing "Blowin' in the Wind." Because supposedly they all knew the words to that song. But the words started getting mumbled and they wound up humming with one another. Then they did "Tupelo Honey," which *blew* Van's mind.

That was *it* for me. That was the part people don't think I really understand. Those magical places where there is pure momentary cessation of negativity. Van Morrison, Bob Dylan, and Bono singing "Tupelo Honey" on the side of a hill by a castle as the sun was going down. In front of sixty thousand people.

Part Four

Out of the Fire

Chapter Eighteen

A Personal Plea

A PERSONAL PLEA

ON MAY 5TH, NINE DAYS FROM TODAY, THE PRESIDENT OF THE UNITED STATES PLANS TO VISIT A MILITARY CEMETERY IN WEST GERMANY WHERE MEMBERS OF HITLER'S NAZI SS CORPS ARE BURIED. THE NAZI SS WERE ALL *VOLUNTEERS*, WHO VOLUNTEERED TO MURDER AT WILL, AND WERE DIRECTLY RESPONSIBLE FOR THE ANNIHILATION OF SIX MILLION MEN, WOMEN AND CHILDREN, PRIMARILY JEWS.

IN THE FACE OF MYRIAD PLEAS RANGING FROM U.S. VETERANS GROUPS, TO SENATORS AND CONGRESSPEOPLE REPRESENTING ALL OF OUR STATES, TO AMERICANS OF ALL FAITHS AND CREEDS, TO THE CITIZENS OF THE STATE OF ISRAEL, TO A DIRECT IN-PERSON PLEA OF ELI WIESEL, CHAIRMAN OF THE U.S. HOLOCAUST MEMORIAL COUNCIL WHO, AT A WHITE HOUSE CEREMONY IN FRONT OF A NATIONAL TV AUDIENCE, IMPLORED THE PRESIDENT TO "DO SOMETHING ELSE, TO FIND A WAY, ANOTHER WAY." PRESIDENT REAGAN, NEVERTHELESS, *HAS DECIDED TO GO TO THAT PARTICULAR CEMETERY.*

WHY? THREE REASONS: FIRST, THE WEST GERMAN GOVERNMENT OF HELMUT KOHL HAS BEEN EXTREMELY SUPPORTIVE OF PRESIDENT REAGAN'S COMMITMENT TO THE DEPLOYMENT OF U.S. MISSILES IN EUROPE AND HAS BACKED THE PRESIDENT ON HIS "STAR WARS" THEORY. THUS, THE PRESIDENT'S STRATEGY OF MINIMIZING THE HOLOCAUST

DURING HIS VISIT TO WEST GERMANY WAS AIMED AT SUP-
PORTING A KEY POLITICAL ALLY.

SECOND, PRESIDENT REAGAN HAD ORIGINALLY AGREED
TO THE VISIT LAST NOVEMBER, IN THE MISTAKEN BELIEF
THAT HE WOULD BE GOING TO A CEMETERY WHERE BOTH
U.S. AND GERMAN SOLDIERS WERE BURIED. AT THE "11TH
HOUR," WHEN THE MEDIA MADE THE PRESIDENT'S PLANS
TO VISIT THAT PARTICULAR CEMETERY PUBLIC KNOWL-
EDGE, MR. REAGAN THEN ADDED A FORMER CONCENTRA-
TION CAMPSITE TO HIS ITINERARY, OSTENSIBLY TO BALANCE
OUT, BUT NOT CANCEL, HIS 5TH VISIT TO THE GRAVES OF
NAZI WAR CRIMINALS.

LAST, PRESIDENT REAGAN REPORTEDLY WAS ADVISED BY
WHITE HOUSE COMMUNICATIONS DIRECTOR PATRICK BU-
CHANANANAN NOT TO CHANGE HIS PLANS BECAUSE THAT
WOULD BE "CAVING IN" TO THE PROTESTERS, WORDS THAT
MR. REAGAN HIMSELF USED. BUCHANAN WAS ALSO RE-
PORTED TO BE THE SOURCE OF THE LANGUAGE MR. REAGAN
USED WHEN HE SAID THE GERMAN SOLDIERS BURIED IN
THE CEMETERY WERE ALSO VICTIMS OF NAZISM, "JUST AS
SURELY AS THE VICTIMS IN THE CONCENTRATION CAMPS."

THE PRESIDENT'S RATIONALE ON THIS ISSUE SUGGESTS A
TRAGIC MENTALITY, FOR IT IMPLIES THAT THE HOLOCAUST
HORRORS ARE PART OF THE PAST, AND SHOULD BE FOR-
GIVEN AND FORGOTTEN. IMPOSSIBLE. MANY OF US FORTU-
NATE ENOUGH TO HAVE COME HERE FROM EUROPE TO LIVE
IN PEACE CANNOT FORGET AND WILL NOT FORGIVE. AS MR.
WIESEL SAID AT THE WHITE HOUSE, "FORGIVE THEM NOT,
FATHER, FOR THEY KNEW WHAT THEY DID . . . THE ISSUE
HERE IS NOT POLITICS, BUT GOOD AND EVIL, AND WE MUST
NEVER CONFUSE THEM."

PLEASE HELP TO PAY RESPECT TO THE SIX MILLION VIC-
TIMS OF NAZI SLAUGHTER, AND THE MILLIONS OF U.S. AND
ALLIED SOLDIERS KILLED IN THE HORROR THAT WAS WORLD
WAR II BY SENDING LETTERS AND TELEGRAMS OF PROTEST
TO OUR PRESIDENT. *AS THE MOST PROMINENT REPRESENTA-
TIVE OF OUR COUNTRY, OUR PRESIDENT HAS NO MORAL RIGHT
TO PAY HIS RESPECTS AT THE GRAVES OF MURDERERS. HE
MUST FIND WAYS OF FULFILLING HIS POLITICAL MISSION
OTHER THAN BY CONDONING GENOCIDE.*

BILL GRAHAM

P.S. THE PLACEMENT DEADLINE FOR THIS AD WAS 5:00 P.M. ON WEDNESDAY, APRIL 24TH. IF, AS YOU READ THIS, PRESIDENT REAGAN HAS NOT ANNOUNCED THE CHANGE IN HIS PLANS TO VISIT BITBURG CEMETERY, THERE WILL BE A RALLY IN *UNION SQUARE IN SAN FRANCISCO FROM 12:00 NOON TO 3:00 P.M. TODAY* FOR THE PURPOSE OF DEMONSTRATING THE EXTENT OF MASS PUBLIC OPPOSITION TO PRESIDENT REAGAN'S PLAN TO VISIT THE GRAVES OF NAZI WAR CRIMI-NALS.

(This ad paid for by Bill Graham, Bill Graham Presents, 201 11th Street, San Francisco, CA 94103.)

1.

BILL: It was early fall when Reagan's people first said he was going to go visit this graveyard in Germany where Nazis supposedly were buried along with American soldiers and other victims of World War II. He was going to lay a wreath on their graves. When I first heard the story, I was certain that there were enough of us to get a campaign together to stop him from going there. I *never* thought the President would actually go through with this. I said, "Come *on*. You *must* be kidding. He wouldn't be *that* stupid. *That* insensitive. To disregard the pleas of *millions* of Jews. He just *wouldn't*."

When the announcement was made that he *was* going to go, there was a lot of heat put upon him by prominent rabbis and clear-thinking senators and congressmen. So I thought there was still a chance that he would get smart and cancel his plans. Finally, I saw his chief of staff Donald Regan on television: he said, "Look, the President is going to Bitburg. *Period*." Those were his exact words and that was what made me write the ad and get into planning the rally.

It was not only Jews who were angry about Reagan's visit. I talked to veterans and they were *incensed*. When I started asking people to come to the rally, no one turned me down. The mayor of San Francisco, Dianne Feinstein. Willie Brown, the Speaker of the state assembly. Five of our city's supervisors. Reverend Cecil Williams from Glide Memorial Church. Tom Lantos, from the U.S. House of Representatives, who himself was a Holocaust survivor.

In retrospect, probably the biggest mistake I made was putting just *my* name at the bottom of the ad. Usually, it's always something like "We, the undersigned . . ." and then a list of a hundred and twenty names. But I never thought about that. Fifteen years earlier, I had taken out ads in the *New York Times*, the *L.A. Times*, and the *San Francisco Chronicle* protesting the killing of four students at Kent State by the National Guard. The ad was like a scorecard that said "Cambodia," along with the number of deaths that had been recorded there. "Vietnam," along with the number who died there. And then "Kent State" with a "4" next to it along with an asterisk. At the bottom of the page, there was another asterisk. Next to it, it said, "Figures subject to change." In huge four-inch letters in the middle of the page, it said *"WHAT NEXT?"*

At the bottom of that ad it said, "Taken out by Bill Graham Presents in New York City, Fillmore East." Somebody sent me the ad. Next to "Figures subject to change" at the bottom, they wrote, "There should be more of you dirty left wing bastard cocksuckers and motherfuckers killed."

But when I took out the Bitburg ad, I didn't think about that. I didn't think there would be any retribution. I mean, I've challenged people to duels all my life.

ESTER CHICHINSKY: I sat on a chair right in back of the stage for the rally. I did not speak. A lot of people that were there, they said, *"Ester, why didn't you stand up and speak?"* Because a lot of people who spoke that day had not been there to see it themselves. For them, it was easy to speak. I get very emotional if I have to speak because when I speak the truth, I can't help it, it takes me.

I was very proud of Bill for doing that. He paid a price. But it was *not* a price. He owed that to himself and to his parents. That was worth a lot more. Because we live in a country where one can stand up and still speak out. If people had had that opportunity in Germany or any of the other fascist countries, maybe some of it would not have happened. What is left behind for us is to speak out. To *tell*. Because there are stories being told and movies being made for television. Which I cannot watch because they are not based on true things.

Bill honored himself by doing what he did. He identified himself not simply as a survivor of the holocaust but as a human being with the right to speak up and make people aware of what can happen.

BILL: The day of the rally was a Friday, I think. April 26, 1985. I went into the office in the morning to make sure we had enough pamphlets to hand out to the public, asking them to send telegrams to the White House. For me, it was like a "Day on the Green." I got up early. Five or six in the morning and my mind was ready. Like a football coach on the day of the game. I might have already been in the office by 8 A.M. that day, carrying my suit for the rally in a plastic bag.

I didn't sit down at my desk that day to write a speech. When I speak, it's off the top of my head. I took a little three-by-five card and made two or three notes. But mainly I was there to introduce the other speakers. Because the issue was so *clear.* I had to hold myself back during the day. I kept thinking to myself, "How can this *putz,* this yo-yo, do this?"

These weren't Resistance fighters who had been killed in the war. These were *Nazis.* By going there, Reagan was saying, "It's okay. You're all forgiven. That was *yesterday.*" Not to mention another point made in the ad. Which was that the SS were always *volunteers.* Who could not say, "We didn't want to do that." Who could not say, "We were forced to stand by those gas chambers." They *wanted* to collect the teeth. They *wanted* to cut the fingers off to get the rings.

When I got up on stage, I welcomed everybody and thanked them for coming and then I brought out the speakers one by one. After every few speakers, I asked people to send telegrams to their congressmen and senators. As it happened, the Senate that day condemned Reagan's visit in a voice vote. He said he was going anyway. I was the last speaker. I read something from the short essays of Thomas Merton. A list of man's rights, simply stated.

What stuck most in my mind were the three or four holocaust survivors who spoke. A lady from down on the Peninsula who stepped to the microphone and stood there for maybe fifteen or twenty seconds without saying a word. Then her arms came up as if to say *"Why?"* As if she was dumbfounded. I should have asked Ester to speak. But I didn't want people to think I had dragged her out there just because she was my sister.

When it was over, I was extremely disappointed that it had not affected more people the way it had me. The reality of the times we live in is that we no longer feel everyone else's tragedy as we do our own. I can't say I feel as deeply involved with what the Turks did to the Armenians at the turn of the century or the plight of the Chinese in California as I did about Bitburg that day. So who was I to say, "Where is everybody?" Forty years ago, if there was rape in The Bronx, it shot through the entire community. Today, the rape is on page twenty-one of the *Daily News.* Right after "ho-hum."

I thought the park should have been *full* that day. *Steaming.* I thought America should have said, "Our President *cannot* condone genocide." Because it *should* have been more important. The Bitburg incident involved the actions of a man who was considered the leader of the free world. He was like a superstar going on television to endorse a product that would *rot* your teeth.

Not that our rally did any good. Reagan went to Bitburg on May 5. By then, I was in Europe. I had gone over there to meet with Bob Geldof concerning Live Aid. I called the office from St.-Jean-Cap-Ferrat in the South of France and the answering service answered. I said, "Jan, please." They said, "Bill Graham is closed today." They didn't even say Bill Graham Presents. I said, "What do you mean, it's *closed* today? It's a *Tuesday*." She said, "Hold on a second." Because she had another call coming through.

When she got back on, I said, "I'm going to call back. Let the phone ring because I want to get through. I have twenty-four lines in the office. Why are you answering the phone for them in the middle of the day?"

She said, "I told you, sir. Bill Graham is *closed* today."

I said, "How can it be closed? It's *Tuesday*."

Her exact words were, "Bill Graham burned down last night." Not Bill Graham Presents. *Bill Graham.*

JAMES OLNESS: The building was a brick warehouse with offices inside it. Basically, one room. So when it burned, the *whole* thing burned. Not the bricks themselves but the entire contents. There weren't any firewalls or anything. It was just like one room, burning. The flames shot up through a skylight and then air rushed in to fuel the fire. It was completely gutted. The ceiling had fallen in.

JAN SIMMONS: My desk had a computer on it and a telephone. The whole computer was melted flat. There wasn't that much left of the phone. There had been hundred-foot-high flames shooting out of the window and it had been a regular inferno inside. Everyone there was crying. We were in shock. I cried several times during the day. As soon as I would stop, it would hit me and I would just fall apart.

SAN FRANCISCO EXAMINER, TUESDAY, MAY 7, 1985:
        FIRE GUTS BILL GRAHAM HQ
     ARSON BLAZE "SUSPICIOUS" PROBERS SAY

"A fire of suspicious origin destroyed the headquarters of rock promoter Bill Graham early this morning. The fire, at Howard and 11th Streets, caused at least one million dollars in damage and went to four alarms. Nobody was injured.

"Investigators found two homemade incendiary devices outside the building. Captain Richard Crispens, Head Arson Investigator, said that two corked gallon jugs containing gasoline were found that look like Molotov cocktails. . . . Left in ruins were the offices, Graham's expensive furnishings, and his collection of rock memorabilia, including posters from Graham's productions dating back to concerts at the Fillmore and Winterland Auditoriums in the 1960's . . ."

JAMES OLNESS: The office was like a little museum that was filled with special things Bill wanted everyone to see. He collected and saved *everything*. There were a lot of Jim Marshall photographs of Jimi Hendrix that had been blown up to twenty by twenty-four. The Bob Dylan pictures varied in sizes. Some were sixteen by twenty with a mat. Some were color, some black and white. There were stacks of photos behind Bill's desk in racks that had never been hung. There were gold records with his name on them. The ones he really liked behind his desk were torched. There was stuff like a pillow from the closing of Winterland up on the wall that said, "Thanks for the Memories."

Over the drinking fountain, there was his Father Time beard from a Grateful Dead New Year's Eve show. It was in a glass case with a hammer and it said, "In case of New Year's, break glass." There was a letter from a fan who snuck into a Fillmore New Year's Eve show along with repayment, five dollars and a fifty-cent piece in a little baggie. We pinned up the letter and the baggie in a wood frame.

In Bill's office, there were the things he collected and that people had given him. The letters he liked best, the pictures people sent him. Pictures of his family and some of the employees and particularly nice shots of some of his favorite artists. He lost the only photograph of his parents but we found that we had a copy of it. Bill once told someone else who worked in the archives that he was a "frame freak." Bill loved to frame things and put them up.

They were all like a moment in time for him. Being able to pull something out from the past and show it to somebody. Like a little mental trigger. Especially since Bill came from a country where all of his history had been worked on to be destroyed. Actually, the Nazis were setting up an archive to a dead race. They were cataloguing things. They would take *everything* from a synagogue and have huge warehouses of stuff with people who were archivists cataloguing everything and keeping track and indexing.

They wanted to create a museum to a dead race after it was all over. Who they killed and what they had confiscated. They saved *everything*. They saved teeth. They saved eyeglasses. They didn't destroy *that* kind of stuff.

BILL: When I made my first call to the office, I was sitting on the edge of the bed in my hotel room holding one of those French telephones. I had to go through the front desk to make international connections. All the lines to America were tied up. After I hung up with the answering service, I couldn't get through to anybody. I kept calling people at their homes but they were all down at the office shoveling stuff out.

I finally found Ray Etzler by phone at home and I said to him, "Can you give me any details?" He said, "Sorry, Bill. God, you know. We can't believe what's happened." I only talked to him briefly. About half an hour later, Nick Clainos called me. I had already started making plans to get to Paris in order to get back home. My reaction was not physical. There was no great outburst. I just couldn't believe it. I was calm. I was all alone in a foreign place and I guess I was in a state of shock. A woman or a man can be raped physically and emotionally. That was how I felt. Like I had been raped emotionally.

What was up on the walls in that office was my life on a day-to-day basis up to that point in time. The life I had found for myself when I was thirty-five. I never put the things I loved in some big vault or a safe. They were up there on the wall for everyone to see. What was in that office was all the art I owned. It was the expression of what everyone there did for a living. If someone wanted to know what that was, I could say, "There it is. Up on the wall." It was an ongoing museum of what we did.

Nick is such a practical person that he first gave me all the facts. He said, "Bill, this is what happened. We don't know for sure but I got a call from Steve Welkom, who got a call from the fire department . . ." Then he said, "Bill, we're all down here. We're waiting for you to come home, boss." When I hung up with him, it was three in the morning. I had a seven o'clock plane from Nice to Paris. I went downstairs and I walked around for a couple of hours in the dark down by the water.

The funny thing was that both Reagan and I were in Europe at the same time. I was actually going to go to the concentration camp Reagan visited before he went to Bitburg. I had been contacted by a rabbi who was going there to protest the visit and I was going to go with him. But I felt like I might have tried to spit at him or to punch him. I would have been like Abbie Hoffman at Woodstock when Pete Townshend kicked him off the stage. If I had gone there, I would not have been able to control myself. So I didn't go. Besides, what good would my violence there have accomplished?

That night, I just left my room and I walked. I walked and I walked up into this little community in the hills. I walked for *hours*. My mind was partly on the fire but it kept coming back to Reagan. I blamed him for what had happened. My love for America was always founded on the feeling that here, I had my rights. In this country, in America, I could take my shots. Obviously, some person had thought I was wrong to declare my feelings in print about the leader of our country condoning genocide.

But what right did that person have to throw a fire bomb into my office? Why didn't they come *talk* to me about it? Why didn't they confront me *personally?* I had been dealing with the public for twenty years. I knew how crazy some people could be. I had seen them on the streets outside the Fillmores. I knew the street wasn't always fair. I had been cold-cocked myself a few times. But this one was *so* cold. I had no chance.

On the phone, I'd said to Nick, "I feel terrible that you people are going through this and I'm not there." I mentioned it to him and to Jan. When I got to Paris, I was on the phone all the time. I flew from Nice to Paris and from there to London and then on to San Francisco. In Paris, I picked up the International Edition of the *Herald Tribune.* I opened the paper as I was giving my ticket to the stewardess and I just froze. Reagan had been to Bitburg on a Sunday and on Monday, they went to Madrid. I was thinking about the fire and when I flipped open the *Herald Tribune,* there in the bottom left corner was a picture of Mrs. Reagan dancing the flamenco at some party in Madrid.

I couldn't understand how that could be. I knew they were in politics but they had only just been to a concentration camp. How could their systems flush all that out so fast? It *staggered* me to see that picture because to me, this was a continuation of her husband's actions. It meant *nothing* to him. If only he had said, "We *need* to do this because of Germany and Chancellor Kohl," that would have been one thing. But he was saying, "I'm doing this *because* I'm doing this. Even if I don't have any reason at all, you can't do *shit* about it." *Power.* And frightening stupidity. What he didn't realize was that we all saw that, too. There were a lot of me's watching what he was doing.

I thought about the time when Walter the cop came at thirty seconds to two o'clock in the morning at a show with the Dead, the Airplane, and Joan Baez. We were having a party to celebrate Pigpen's birthday. He said to me, "You know what time it is?" And he started quoting articles and sections from the penal code, telling me we had to be closed at two. We were in the kitchen of the original Fillmore and I threw open the doors so he could hear them playing "Dancing In the Street." I said, "Who are we bothering? The front doors are closed. We're not letting any more people in. It's a party." But he wouldn't give in.

Finally I screamed, *"KILL ME. SHOOT ME. I DON'T GIVE A FUCK. YOU'RE NOT GOING TO STOP THIS PARTY!"*

He said, "Relax, Bill. What do you need? Half an hour?"

At least I had my shot with him. With Bitburg and Reagan and then the fire, I felt completely powerless. I didn't really get a shot.

I didn't want anyone to pick me up at the airport in San Francisco. So I took a cab to the office. The cabdriver knew who I was. We drove for a while in silence and then he said, "I was really sorry to hear about your fire." It was nice. It was as if we were friends but we just didn't know it.

By the time we got to the corner of Eleventh and Howard, it was eleven o'clock at night. All the brick was up and all the wood was gone. Everything was charred and the roof was gone. A lot of the office staff was there. A couple of policemen and a fire inspector. I hardly knew how to react. I just stood there, stunned.

During the trip back, a kind of guilt had begun to set in. When I got there, it hit me the hardest. When people who were there saw me, they walked over and began to cry. Men and women from the office that I was close to. My guilt while flying back had to do with, "How did the rally affect the lives of all these other people?" Because now the company where they worked had burned down.

I had already started thinking about what was gone. Two letters came immediately to mind. A woman who wrote to me and said, "I'm thirty-nine years old and my name is so-and-so. In 1966 and 1967, I worked in your box office with your wife Bonnie. I became pregnant and my man left, and I didn't know what to do. In the course of nineteen months, I stole $3200.00 from you. I am now a registered nurse in Marin and have gone back to the church. I always knew that you treated me fairly and now I want to make my peace. Please find enclosed $300.00 and I'll send the rest as I can. May God be with you and will you forgive me?"

I covered her name with a piece of paper and put the letter up in my office. Because when I was a kid, I did what she had done. I snuck into movies plenty of times. I needed? I *took*. The other letter was from someone who had snuck in a side door at the Fillmore East and had one of the great experiences of his life. He sent me five singles and the rest in change in a baggie to pay for that ticket. Which cost five-fifty at the time. Two people who had done something they thought was wrong and dealt with it from a good place.

After I looked around at what was left of the office that night, I went to my sister Ester. Ester only ever cries when *she* has a loss. When someone else has a loss, she can be very strong. On this, she stayed with me all the way.

DAVID RUBINSON: This movie of Bill's life, it ends when his office gets burned down and all the visions come back with his sister and the concentration camp. He's got a multimillion-dollar business, he's got a mansion on the hill, he's got a Jaguar, he's got everything that could ever be done. The perfect refugee story. And they wake him up and they say,

"Bill, you better get down here." And he walks in there and sees a swastika on the fucking wall and the building is burning, and it's San Francisco.

I called from Tokyo when I heard. I called up from Tokyo. They said, "He can't be disturbed." I said, "Fucking get him on the phone." I said, "Bill, I'm coming home. We're going to get a hundred thousand dollars and we're going to find those motherfuckers. We're going to go into every bar in the Richmond District. We're going to go everywhere and we're going to put ten grand on the table. You know how to do it. Here's five grand more if anybody can tell me who did this shit."

I said, "Bill, I'm going to fly home. I can't stand this. It's got me *nuts*. I can't *sleep*. I couldn't sleep until I talked to you." I said, "Let's do it *now*. I'll come home right *now*. We'll get three or four people. And we'll get ten or fifteen grand apiece in cash. In *hundreds*. Fuck the *police*. Fuck the *FBI*. Fuck *everybody*. *We'll* do it. We'll do a Haganah number on these bastards, they'll never believe it."

I said, "You know why we've *got* to do it? Because they'll do it *again*. If they think they can do this to you, they're going to do it to some poor *rabbi*. They're going to do it to some poor woman on the *street*. Let's *get* these motherfuckers."

JERRY POMPILI: I was fucking *irate*. I was sure that it was a bunch of suckass right wing assholes from Pinole or Hercules. I knew that we could get these fucking guys and all it would take was money. I designed an ad. I wanted to run this ad in the paper. Promising a ten-thousand-dollar reward for information. Not just mention the reward in some story. But run it as a *full-page ad*. A reward for information leading to arrest and conviction.

I knew that guys like this, their own mothers would fucking turn them in. That was the kind of people they were. They were scumbags and they hung out with scumbags and scumbags will *always* sell each other out.

DAVID RUBINSON: And Bill, with all his rage and his upset, said, "I can't perpetuate this anymore. I can't be part of it. I can't think, 'They got me, I'll get *them*.'"

I said, "I get it. I understand what you're saying. I'm crying for you." I was beside myself and I was crying and Bill was saying, "We can't do that." He said, "I want to do it so bad. Can't do it. It's *over*. I'm not going to go back and do this and perpetuate this kind of thing." It was the most unbelievable thing.

I said, "Okay. But I'm *serious*. If tomorrow morning, you wake up and you *turn around*, let's *go*. We'll *find* the fuckers."

Bill said, "We're *not* going to do this. We're going to forebear. It's got to be quiet. We're just going to let it go and we're not going to perpetuate more of the retribution vengeance number."

I still don't agree with that.

JERRY POMPILI: The excuse was that more violence would come out of it. To me, that was why the Jews were gassed. Because they didn't do enough to stop it from happening. I was going to put my *own* money up. Bill was afraid that more would happen. He was very frightened of this. Was he right? I don't know. I wanted their asses. That was the difference between us. This was like rape and you can't depend on justice from the courts in some of these cases. Because some lawyer will say, "Hey, honey. Didn't you shake your ass at them?" So it was like, "Bring the fucking hammer *down* on them ourselves." But Bill wouldn't let us do it.

BILL: Every day that passed, I thought, "Oh, God. *This* is gone." And I would remember something else. This was signed by Eric Clapton. This was signed by so-and-so. A picture of that person. The things in my office were one of a kind and very special. A couple of weeks after the fire, somebody showed me a copy of the ad that ran concerning Kent State fifteen years before. It had made it through the fire but it was all charred and burned around the sides. It had run on May 7, 1970, fifteen years earlier to the *day*.

JAMES OLNESS: The dance-hall keeper's permit was saved. When we discovered that it had been saved, they cleaned off the frame and brought it to Bill. He looked at it and he said, "Now, I know we're *still* in business."

BILL: Within a day, we had found another office space. I had nothing to do with that. It was the people at the company who did it. If anybody wanted to know the reality of that company, all they had to do was look at the fact that we were functioning again within twenty-four hours of the fire. We had a show that night at the Warfield Theater. Julian Lennon. The company was functioning through it all. This building had burned down yet the birds all went and made another nest. The system put up another tent.

In terms of the fire itself, there was an investigation. There was a letter sent from the grand jury foreman to the fire chief instructing him about how serious a crime this was, especially in terms of the rally. He said it was a kind of political terrorism. He said he knew how difficult arson investigation was but that they wanted this matter pursued.

JAN SIMMONS: Memo to Stan Damas

"On Monday, May 6th, the day before the fire, Bill received two negative letters regarding his *'A Personal Plea.'* First one was handwritten in blue ink on white lined paper, like from a paper tablet, and it said something like the following: 'Eat shit and die, you fucking liberal asshole.' Enclosed was the top part of Bill's newspaper ad reading 'A PERSONAL PLEA' with the rest cut off. No name or address. I looked at the envelope and noticed there was an Oakland, California postmark but didn't look at what date it was mailed. I looked to see if there was a postage meter stamp or a regular stamp. There was a regular stamp.

"When I first mentioned this to Inspector Kennedy of the Arson Task Force on the day of the fire, I think I told him it was something referring to Bill as a 'Jew something or other' but after thinking about it more clearly later in the day, I remember that this particular letter did not say anything about Bill being a Jew. It only referred to him as a liberal.

"The other *did* make reference to Bill as a 'Jewish so-and-so' but the second was not so shocking as the first one and didn't bother me as much. Bill had received approximately ten or so negative letters over the week following the rally and I believe he has all of those early letters. I was disturbed by the first letter described above and I had it sitting on the very top of my mail pile on top of my desk so that I would remember to show it to Nick Clainos the next morning . . . Both letters were burned up in the fire."

BILL: Did they ever get a *serious* lead? No. There were some kids who said they knew who did it. They said it was drug dealers who had something against me. There were policemen involved for maybe a year who would come to the office and say, "We have this lead. We have that."

I got some congratulations on the fire. Four or five letters that said, "Hitler should have taken *you* along with him." We handed those letters over to the police, and there were no leads. Nothing panned out. The mayor put up a reward. Was the investigation as big as it should have been? I don't think so.

A woman walking her dog that night supposedly saw either one or two men, one with a swastika on his jacket. But no height, no weight, no where, no what, no how. There were no fingerprints on the Molotov cocktails that they found. I haven't the slightest doubt that it was connected to Reagan's visit to Bitburg and my ad in the newspaper protesting it. I would stake my life that the two events were related. Look at the timing. What else could it have been?

In terms of insurance, to the best of my knowledge, we were covered the way we should have been. There again, I had nothing to do with it. At this stage of my life, what do I know about insurance coverage? Not that I'm saying, "I have *other* people to do that." If I were to read the policy in jail for a hundred days straight and they were only going to let me out if I understood every word of it, I would *still* be sitting in that cell.

There were *hundreds* of gold and platinum records on those walls. Most of them were in the back. Those records were just symbols of success. Symbols of somebody having made a lot of money with a record. The photos and the letters expressed far more. The letters from all the musicians who had been on the ARMS tour, saying how they felt about it. In terms of Fillmore posters, I had maybe two hundred framed on the walls.

In my office, I had framed a pair of counterfeit tickets from a New Year's Eve at Winterland in the late sixties. Five dollars including breakfast. I remember so clearly when they brought the two people who has passed the counterfeit tickets into my office. A guy in his mid-twenties with a beard and his girlfriend. They had on Goodwill clothing. She had on a cloth she had wrapped around herself. But clean and nice.

I looked at the five-color poster that Bonnie had done for the show. It was a globe with doves flying around it. The guy had reproduced that poster down to ticket size. The fine print on it looked like *Japanese*. I said, "How *long* did it take to paint these tickets?"

He said, "Two weeks, sir." I asked him where he lived and he said, "Eureka." I asked, "How'd you get down here?" He said, "Hitchhiked."

His wife was standing there like a little angel and all they wanted to do was spend the evening with the Dead and Janis and Quicksilver and then have breakfast there with all their friends. Finally, I said, "This is an *incredible* piece of work. *Here.* Enjoy yourself." I gave them backstage passes. I had those tickets framed and they were up on the wall of my office and they burned in the fire.

The fire was the beginning of a stretch of time in my life where it was like my balance was being challenged on a constant basis. I did not know if I was going to make it at times. Every time my head came up and I said, "I think everything's going to be okay," my head got shoved back underwater again. There were times when my head was underwater for *such* a long time, I was gagging. In the ensuing years after the fire, there were *no* intervals. There were no rehab periods. Only madness and new projects and more and more work.

I have to fend off negative traits in myself all the time. A dark voice that says, "No. You have *no* right to do that." I'm twenty pounds overweight right now and I had a bagel and cheese and butter for breakfast. The dark voice. And it fucks with me all the time. The dark voice said to me that in terms of the fire, I was being punished for something I had done. I *still* feel that. The fire was the single closest thing to a physical handicap I will ever have. Like a limp that will never leave me. Not so much the fire itself. But that I must have done *something* to make it happen.

Chapter
Nineteen

Going Global

1.

BOB GELDOF: Nineteen eighty-four came round and I did that Band-Aid record called "Do They Know It's Christmas?" Suddenly, all these other countries started doing them. Literally, *every* other country had a Band-Aid record. Obviously in America, there was "USA for Africa," which was the most famous. But in France, "Chanson Frontière" is more famous. There was a Turkish one. There was "Northern Lights," the Canadian one, and the Italian one. In Italy, they all refused to sing someone else's song so the only thing they could all agree to sing was "Volare" and that was the Italian Band-Aid song.

Yugoslavia had one and Hong Kong had one. All of Europe. I thought, "I wonder, could we link them all up and get them to do it on Christmas Day?" Then I thought, "Well, that's fuckin' boring because actually, they were all shit. All those records were really shit." However, I liked the linking-up idea because it was symbolic, or whatever. So that was the genesis of the idea that became Live Aid. I went to Harvey Goldsmith to do it over here in England, not because he was the only capable one but the one most *likely* to do it. He was used to this sort of thing and I also happen to like him very much as a man.

Harvey didn't get the idea of Live Aid right away. He just looked at me and he actually said, *"Why?"* I said, "Why *what?* He said, "Why are you doing *two* shows?" I said, "It's not *two.* It's *one.* It's on two continents but it's *one* show." He said, *"Why?"* I said, "Because we can sell that as an idea." He said, "Why do we need to go around the world?" I said, "Because of what this is." Then he said, "Why, are you *mad?*"

I felt it *must* be possible. How many satellites were there up by now? I thought it would be *easy*. I can't remember what sparked the idea of two shows. But the time lag thing broke me. Whenever I had gone to see an act, the changeover was the thing that really bugged me. Even if you were on a revolving stage, that wasn't good.

This was going to be a TV show. It wasn't a concert. Never to me. It was a *TV show*, and the TV show was to get at one end. *Money*. It was all a pragmatic exercise. My thing was to have a "Global Jukebox." Fifteen minutes. That was all you would be allowed. You had to do *hits*. You weren't allowed to do anything else.

You would have three lights. When the orange one went off, you better fuckin' come to the last of your parts because when it went red, you were *off!*

HARVEY GOLDSMITH: Bill said, "We've got to do it at Stanford Stadium." I said, "It doesn't work timewise." Anyway London-Stanford didn't sound right. We phoned Jack Boyle and we were going to do it at RFK Stadium in Washington. It was in the middle of nowhere and Bill said the logistics would not work. We talked and talked and talked. Finally, I said, "What about Philadelphia?" He said, "M'well. Mmmmmm. Not really."

BILL: I think Harvey Goldsmith always felt that I had taken his idea for the ARMS tour over and made it work in America. In some ways, he could be like a little Alfred Hitchcock. Still, because the cause was so good, I was determined to do everything I could to work together with both him and Geldof.

I went and looked at the joint in Washington, D.C., and I looked at the Meadowlands, and I decided on Philadelphia. I had used JFK in Philadelphia for the Stones in 1981 and the backstage area was huge and the stadium held a hundred thousand people. I went back there to look at it again and it was good. Because what we needed was room for all the trailers for all those bands.

After running around for weeks, I finally decided to do it there. Larry Magid was the promoter in Philadelphia so we didn't need up-front money. Larry and I had worked together for years. That was one of the other reasons I went there.

BOB GELDOF: Bill wasn't doing things and we flew to America, *freaking*. I mean, freaking *out*. We had huge fights with those people who work in his office. They said, "Hey. Don't tell *Bill Graham* how to put on concerts." You know? Everything had to be uniform on stage so that when we switched, all that told you it was America or London was that the kids would look different.

Bill was only at some of these meetings. He kept coming in there with the girlfriend. He was having some big row with his girlfriend at the time and the girlfriend came in. I remember this woman in a white dress coming in and the next thing that Bill got up and walked out. I mean, really weird stuff was going on. Like there was some big fight and she kept going on and then he would walk out with her.

ROBERT GREENFIELD: Bill and Regina Cartwright were in fact in the midst of what she would later call a "really bad period." Bill was distracted. He did not yet have the focus or attention span to deal solely with Live Aid. Not like Geldof did. It was as though for the moment, the two men had reversed roles. The artist (Geldof) had become the harried promoter while the promoter (Bill) was acting like some artist who was not yet sure whether or not this was a show he really wanted to play. It was the first phase of what was fast becoming a pattern as Bill took on more special projects than any man could ever have reasonably hoped to make work.

BOB GELDOF: We had plans for the stage, which was a tri-stage. Band setting up, band coming off leaving band on stage. They were going with a two-stage, which was going to hold up the whole fucking broadcast. They were saying, "You fuck off and mind your business." I said, "It's the *same* business." I was really going spare.

BILL: As the show grew, Bob Geldof had a certain number of acts which had committed to him. He had no black acts. It was obvious to me right away. Certain major black acts were not available. People could say, "They *should* be available for their brothers and sisters in Ethiopia." That was not for me to say. What I could say was that I contacted every single major black artist. I won't name them because I'm still in the business. But they *all* turned down Live Aid. I also turn things down. That doesn't mean they didn't care. But all the major black artists? *All* the biggest ones? You name them. They *all* turned Live Aid down.

Larry Magid was a great help. Because he was out of Philadelphia, he knew a lot of the black acts. Through Larry, we got the Four Tops, Teddy Pendergrass, Ashford and Simpson, and Patti LaBelle. All Larry. I said, "Larry, I *need* your help." He came through and I am indebted to him.

As it grew, a lot of acts that could not be bothered now *wanted* to be bothered. Heavy metal acts and certain rock and roll bands suddenly wanted to be on the show. I mean, like ten days out. Groups like Yes and Foreigner and Ozzie Osbourne. It was hard for me to say no to them because of the power structure.

Had I not been a promoter on the West Coast, I could have made my decisions without regard for what they might do to me in return. But I could still be damaged by them. Just like I had been by ZZ Top. I would have had to pay the price later on. Over the years, I often paid that price because of decisions I'd made concerning benefit projects.

Ten days before the show, I was in New York and I was getting pressure from every side. Black Sabbath was driving me crazy. Their agent would call and say, "*Bill*, I *got* to get my act on the show." Ironically, the act had been asked to do it a few weeks before but they had said, "We don't wanna do another benefit." I told him, "The show is *so* tight. I've got eleven minutes for this act, twelve for another, fifteen for a third." Then the manager would call. Then the record company president. Heavy pressure. Also they started to squeeze Dell Furano, who was doing their merchandising. Dell could only ask me to try.

I asked one act to do one song, I asked someone else to drop a couple minutes. The show originally started at noon. I had already moved it back to 9 A.M. I had *so* many acts. Finally, I made a slot for Black Sabbath at eleven in the morning. Can you imagine looking at Ozzie Osbourne at eleven in the morning? Following the Four Tops?

The irony of the whole scenario? Six months later, Gregg Perloff, who does most of the booking for me now, walked into my office and said, "Bill, we got a problem with Ozzie Osbourne. He doesn't want to play for us in the Bay Area." *Reason?* "We were not considerate to him at Live Aid. We put him on too early in the day. It was an insult." I flew to Omaha where he was playing and worked that one out myself.

Another example. Bert Block called me for Kris Kristofferson. He said, "You know, Bill. Kris has been an activist all his life. He wants to do something." I said, "Bert, I have no room." He said, "Bill, it's *Kris Kristofferson*." I said, "Bert. It's *Bill Graham*. Tell Kris to come to Philadelphia. *Without* his band. I'll do for him what I'm going to do for Joan Baez. I'll put a slot in. *No band*. Because I don't have room for five more guys." "My star's not going to travel without them." "Bert, I *can't*." He called back and said, "I just called Kris and he *won't* do it."

I said, "I can't believe Kris would say that. I *know* Kris. Politically, he's been a major activist for years."

He said, "Bill. Kris feels highly insulted. He can't believe you're treating him this way after all he did for you. He gave you *A Star Is Born*."

I said, "Bert, he didn't *give* me *A Star Is Born*. I was hired. He happened to be in the movie."

Kris didn't show. Three years later, he was looking for management. We had dinner together and we went over that whole story. He said, "You know, Bill. I felt so bad I couldn't get on that damn thing. I would have done anything. I would have *walked* to Philadelphia."

I said, "Really? Your manager never told you that I invited you?" He said, "*No.* He said you had no room for us." I said, "No. *Kris.* I said over and over again that *you* could come." He said, "My manager *never* told me that." I said, "That's your manager."

Kris was telling the truth. So you *cannot* blame the bands all the time. It doesn't always happen to be their fault.

BOB GELDOF: Paul Simon rang up. He said he was pulling out because of the way Bill Graham was behaving. Bill was very rude to Paul Simon. Paul said Bill had shouted at a lot of people and said, "You'll do what I fuckin' say." That sort of thing. "You'll only have *this* amount of time on. If you don't like it, get the fuck *off.* There's *no* sound check." Without being smarmy, an artist and singer of Paul Simon's stature, I mean *really.* I know that Bill is Bill Graham and Paul Simon is Paul Simon. Paul said, "Really. At this stage in my life, I just don't need that crap. He's a deeply unpleasant man and very insulting. Bob, what the fuck can I tell you?"

I was there on the phone saying, "Paul, *please, please* don't pull out." I was actually begging. I couldn't see what we would do for an end. He said, "I can't work with this guy insulting me." Then Willie Nelson went. ABC were killing me to get MOR acts and in the end I just said, "*Fuck off!*" *They* wanted to determine the bill. In the end, I literally said, "*Fuck off!* Take it. *Don't* take it. I don't *care.*"

2.

BOB GELDOF: Toward the end, it started shaping up. England was really full up. So we had to send some people over to Philadelphia. Chrissie Hynde and the Pretenders and Simple Minds flew to America simply because England was full. There was a lot of fuss about that and the Thompson Twins did the same.

Bill was going fucking ape shit and giving them a bum steer because they weren't the acts he had gotten and they were coming in on his show. An ego as big as his, you have to be very fucking tactful and I am not a tactful person. I'm very blunt and he's as blunt as I am. He and Harvey also were rivals in a certain sense anyway and it was something else I didn't need at the time.

Lionel Richie came in on the last week and Ken Kragen said I had to keep it quiet that Lionel was in and I said, "*Why?*" The obvious reason was that they weren't sure. They were going to see how it panned out.

Right at the last moment, if it was a biggie, they would come in. "Hey. I'm a *special guest.*"

It wasn't everybody. People like Eric Clapton gave up a couple of nights in Caesar's Palace and flew in to do it.

BILL: The hardest thing was how to keep all the real heavies in that frame. Every time a new heavy wanted to come on, not only did they want to be on the show, they wanted to be on during the *last three hours.* The last three hours was Madonna and then Neil Young and Mick Jagger and Tina Turner and Hall and Oates and Bob Dylan with Keith Richards and Ron Wood. And Lionel Ritchie for a little piece.

About a week before the show, I was in Philadelphia at the hotel and the hotel was like the control room of an aircraft carrier. Michael Ahern had his charts and we had this huge stage up and we were working out which trailer would go next to which trailer and how we would get all the cars backstage. The in and the out. It was *beyond* military. The greatest challenge of this show was segueing. When they finished a set over in London, we had to start one in Philadelphia, and vice versa.

My phone rang at the hotel one morning. It was Bob Geldof. He was *ecstatic.* Royalty had committed to being the host and hostess over in Wembley. Prince Charles and Princess Diana.

He was *so* ecstatic that he got them. I put the phone down and then I woke up and I said, "He's got royalty. He's thrilled." I went to breakfast and I said, "We got to get royalty. Then it will be sanctioned. It will be *official.* Then *everyone* will know. Not just the rock and roll world. The *whole* world will be aware of this."

I said to myself, "Who is fucking royalty in this country? It ain't the President or the Vice President. Royalty in our country is baseball stars. Football stars. Movie stars."

I sat there eating breakfast and making a list. I came down to two heroes. Two Marlboro Men in our society. Clint Eastwood and Jack Nicholson. Nicholson had just finished *Prizzi's Honor.* The movie that had that great line in it when he was lying in bed next to Kathleen Turner and she says, "He was such a great man, my husband," and Nicholson says, "If he was so fuckin' great, how come he's so fuckin' *dead?*"

I had met Jack when he was an usher at a benefit we did for McGovern in San Francisco in 1972. So I called Lou Adler and told him my story. I said, *"Lou. I got to talk to you about royalty."* I told Lou the whole idea and he said, "Geez. I don't know. Let me see if he's interested. I'll call him." I didn't ask him for Jack's number. Lou called Jack and then he called me back at the hotel and he said, "Bill, he's on his way out now.

He wants to think about it. Here's his number. Call him tonight. Eight your time, five his time." I said, "Fine."

That night, I had to go to New York because I'd arranged a rehearsal for Tina Turner and Mick Jagger with the Hall and Oates band. I drove from Philadelphia with Mick Brigden and it was pouring buckets. It got to be eight o'clock our time. We couldn't find a phone. We went to this one gas station but there was a guy there on the pay phone for like an *hour*. We drove to the next phone but it wasn't enclosed. I was standing there with the receiver in my hand and it was pouring and I was getting soaked. It was five o'clock on the West Coast and if I didn't call him at *exactly* five, Jack could say, "I was at my phone and you didn't call me." It was already eight minutes past the hour and my mind was working like crazy. "He's on his way to a beach in Maui and I'm keeping him from making his plane."

I called him and I said, "Listen. You got a minute?" He said, "Where are you?" I said, "I'm standing by a pay phone on the Jersey Turnpike." He said, "The *fuck* you doing there?" I told him about Live Aid. He said, "Read about that." I told him about Geldof and his call and how he got royalty. I said, "So, you know, Jack. I'm calling *you*." He said, "So you called me, huh?" I said, "Yeah." Then he said the magic words. "So you want *me* to be fuckin' royalty?"

I told him that he could say hello to the public in the morning and start the concert off. He said, "Well, I don't do that kind of improvisational shit, man." Finally, he said, "It sounds like a righteous cause. It sounds like a good thing to do. If you want me to fuckin' do it, I will. But you got to tell me *exactly* what you want me to do."

By this time, I was completely soaked. I was holding the phone and Mick Brigden was in the car and I was giving him the thumbs-up sign. I said, "Jack, you'll be the greeter. I want you to go backstage and just hang out." And he said, "Hey, man. I'm going to hang out with Bob Dylan and Jagger and Keith Richards and all them guys? It's okay by me, man. It's okay by me."

I asked him if there was anything he wanted at the hotel in Philadelphia and he said, "You think I could have some fresh fruit and Evian water?" I said, "You got it." I said, "Can you be at the show by eight in the morning?" He said, "Eight o'clock. You got it, man. Sounds like it's going to be a *ball*."

When I put down the phone, I was on Cloud Fucking *Eleven*. I ran back through the pouring rain to the car and I said, "We got fuckin' *royalty!* We got *Jack*. Fuck the prince and the princess. We got *Jack!*" I felt great. Then we drove to New York and had this great rehearsal with Mick and Tina. I remember Tommy Mottola was there.

HARVEY GOLDSMITH: The night before Live Aid, Tommy Mottola phoned me up and said he was pulling out Mick Jagger and Hall and Oates unless they got a better slot on the program. I said, "If you want to pull out Mick Jagger, be my guest. I'd like to see you try. And if you want to pull out Hall and Oates, good-bye." This was I think eleven-thirty on the Friday night. That was how bad it was. The difference between America and England. The grind that we went through was *horrible*.

BILL: The first person I put on that morning was a kid who had been living in the parking lot for ten days. I said to the audience, "Someday, this might happen to you. You know, we all have dreams." He sang one song and he's been writing me ever since. Then I said, "Would you welcome please, a friend of yours and certainly a friend of ours, *Mr. Jack Nicholson.*"

They went mad. He was wearing those dark shades and he did that walk of his and he was *brilliant*. He said, "Hey. Hello, world. Say hello to Philadelphia." When he said that, everybody felt like they were in the right place with the only guy they had ever wanted to be there with. It was one of those moments. *Fucking* Jack Nicholson.

I wanted Joan Baez to open the show. Even after all the problems she had given me in Europe on the Dylan-Santana tour about where she should be billed when we played in Paris. I was the one who called her agency and said, "If anybody deserves to be on this show, *she* does." For all her years of social and political action. Early on, I believe that Joan was truly innocent and really exactly what she claimed to be. But in her, the change came quickly. She became a manipulator. In many ways, for good things. But she became shrewd. I still thought she should be there.

In her book, Joan Baez said I put her on the show because I felt I *owed* it to her. Your *ass*. I did it because it was the righteous thing to do. She didn't like the slot. Her manager said, "Bill, how could you put her *there?*" I said, "If you have a nineteen-course meal, how do you remember one from the other? But the *appetizer*."

I said, "*Trust me*. When Jack Nicholson introduces Joan Baez, it will have meaning."

Between Live Aid and Amnesty, my organization has kept Joan's career going. We've plugged her into the next generation of kids. The ones who love U-2. Jack Nicholson introduced Joan Baez as a singer whose voice was always heard when there was a just cause that needed a song. Joan said, "Good morning, children of the eighties, this is your Woodstock and it's long overdue." She sang "Amazing Grace" and we were in business. The day had officially begun.

During the rest of the day, I worried about the schedule and making sure that the next band was there, ready to go on. I changed everything from the night before. I didn't like the TV guys at all. Mike Mitchell and Tony Verna. They wanted to take *all* the credit for everything happening there. I changed their entire script around. I changed who was presenting who. Because they had no feel for the presentations.

I was trying to make up time all day long. If I lost a minute here or there, I would ask an act to drop a song. This got me into problems with the Thompson Twins' manager. I even asked Bob Dylan to drop a song but he wouldn't do it. We had a turntable so the changeover between acts was very fast. Michael Ahern was there but I drove them mercilessly. I was Genghis Khan. "Move the piano. Put the drums *there. Go. Go. Go.*" The main reason I had them put a Porta-John on stage was for me. The acts could go before they came on. But I never left the stage.

KEITH RICHARDS: At Live Aid, Bill was a cartoon. I could see his head and feet and his arms were *rrrrrrrrr*. Like he was "The Road Runner." Exactly right. In this trailer. Boom, *boom*. On the stage. *Boom, boom*. In this continual blur. With this little head on top.

BILL: Some of the artists were very cooperative and congenial and some of them acted like stars. Jimmy Page, Robert Plant, and Eric Clapton were standing in the backstage area when Madonna got out of her limousine with her entourage. They started walking through and her advance guys were saying "Move, *please. Move*, please. *Madonna's coming.*" One of them touched Eric's arm and told him to move over. Eric said, "What's this?" The guy said, "You *got* to look out. Madonna's *coming.*" And Eric said, "You *must* be jeowking!"

For the finale, we had the following people on stage: Lionel Ritchie, Harry Belafonte, Mick Jagger, Joan Baez, Chrissie Hynde, Sheena Easton, Dionne Warwick, Melissa Manchester, Patti LaBelle, Peter, Paul, and Mary, as well as assorted other actors and musicians. It was chaos because Lionel Ritchie came in at the last minute to join the show. Before that, I had Dylan as the closer. I didn't want "We Are the World" as the last song. I wanted "Blowin' in the Wind."

I didn't mind the fact that there weren't enough microphones on stage for all the people and some of the singing could not be heard. I minded the *song*. Certain songs are like postage stamps. You know what story they are supposed to tell. "We Are the World," "We Shall Overcome," and "Let It Be" are all great and I respect them but they are *too* automatic. "All right. Get the doves. Let's show the peace slides now."

Everybody knows "Blowin' in the Wind," but the verses are *so* strong. Everybody could have sung "The answer, my friend, is blowin' in the wind. The answer is blowin' in the wind." I felt that using "We Are the World" was a retread. Also, Lionel Richie represented to me a slicker side of the business.

After it was over, everyone was very complimentary. Mick Jagger and Keith, separately, were nice to me, saying, "God, what a *great* day." It was about two in the morning and I was still on stage. It was all over and I saw Jack Nicholson getting ready to go. He said, "Hey, Bill, what a *great* experience. I can't thank you enough. This was really something."

I said, "Good. Now, I want something."

He said, "What?"

I took him into a corner of the backstage area and said, "You've got to give me that line from *Prizzi's Honor*." He did it. For me, it was like my own *personal* finale.

3.

BILL: Two days later, I saw the tapes. The people at home were *raped* by television. The consciousness of MTV was completely out of keeping with what Live Aid was all about. Sharing and letting go of the profit motive for one day. They were no different than the T-shirt bootleggers who worked on the streets outside of JFK Stadium. ABC butchered some of the acts because it was time for them to cut away for commercials.

Because of the nature of the show, I couldn't believe that the sponsors did not say, "The next three hours brought to you courtesy of . . ." Like on public broadcasting. ABC cut away from artists in the middle of songs. They didn't show the Crosby, Stills, Nash, and Young reunion or the Led Zeppelin set. In defense of themselves, ABC said, "We have a business to run. We have electric bills to pay." They were actually quoted as saying that in the *New York Times*.

MTV were a bunch of pricks. I said to them, "Don't lose the essence of the event. Don't push *your* thing. Do documentary. Come backstage and talk to the artist. Talk to the people in the audience." I talked to them until I was blue in the face. Instead, they put a booth on stage facing the audience and it was like Popeye and Mr. Magoo.

They would say, "*Hey*, now here we are *backstage* at Live Aid and *gee*, I wonder who's behind *that* wall?" They trivialized everything. They went for the fifteen-year-olds. Unfortunately, that day, not *only* fifteen-year-olds were watching.

I thought Martha Quinn was the only sane one. The rest of them were in *heat*. They were so "blown out" by the stars. That was all they could talk about. Whatever industry we're in, it's forever young.

ROBERT GREENFIELD: Bill had just played a leading role in producing
a concert which not only raised millions of dollars for famine relief in
Africa but was also seen live on television around the globe. In a scruffy
T-shirt, ridiculous shorts, heavy boots, and a two-day growth of beard,
he had clumped back and forth across the stage all day long in full view
of the entire world, many of whom had never before seen him in action.
Considering what a great success Live Aid was, by all rights Bill should
have been a happy man.

On the day after the show, I found myself standing in the small room
at the front of the apartment just off Madison Avenue in Manhattan which
had been converted into his company's New York office. In what had once
been the living room, Bill sat on a sofa raging about what the television
people had done to Live Aid. One by one, like lambs being led to the
slaughter, media representatives from the *Washington Post* and CNN
slowly moved past me, heading into the inner sanctum for their fair share
of abuse.

Those who had seen Bill like this before might have said it was just an
act. But his voice was raw and rasping. His eyes were bloodshot and set
all the way back in deep hollows in his face. To me, he truly seemed
beside himself. So possessed by anger that I did not want to stick my
head in there to say hello. Instead, I stood there in that little room
outside the lion's den for a very long time, listening to the awful roar.

BILL: Is the backstage at a Broadway play always that serene? Do the
two stars always get along? Walk into the kitchen of a great restaurant
sometime. See what you find. Despite the aims of Live Aid, there was
still infighting. Bob Geldof and I never had harsh words, ever. He's a
decent man. A bright fellow. To the artists, Geldof was an artist as well.
So he was able to pull in people in a way that was not open for me. He
took the thing as far as he could. For that, I have great respect.

In terms of the forty-five million dollars raised by Live Aid, I don't
really know how much good it did. If they had used it to build a dam to
get water into those desert lands, fine. But bringing in truckloads of food
was like putting a Band-Aid on for a blood clot. In that situation, they
were dealing with terminal cancer. We could have done a benefit every
other day and raised ten million dollars. Until they learned how to do
something with the land over there, until whatever dictator happened to
be in charge allowed something to be done with it, Live Aid remains at
best a righteous gesture by a lot of people toward other people.

What it did prove was that rock and roll is *the* international means of
communications. By far, it is the most powerful tool. It made all of us
aware of the awesome influential communicative weight of rock and roll.

It reminded the straight world again that rock is big biz. The first time was Woodstock.

In terms of the artists who volunteered their time that day, I doubt that very many of them really understood the situation in Ethiopia. I know I didn't. We all just wanted to do *something* worthwhile. Even if they *did* understand it, how many of them would have said, "Before I do this benefit, I want to make *sure* this grain reaches that village?"

With Live Aid, the money was raised and *then* they had to determine what to do with it. The most effective benefit is the one where the cause comes first. The more specific the cause, the better. Back to the bus in Berkeley. We need a bus. You need a bus? Do a benefit. Go to South Dale City. *Buy* the bus. *Paint* the bus. *There's* the bus. I can see it every time I go there.

Chapter
Twenty

A Conspiracy
of Hope

1.

ROBERT GREENFIELD: Bill was approached by Jack Healey, the head of Amnesty International in America, to produce a tour which would raise people's consciousness concerning the work Amnesty had been doing world-wide for the past twenty-five years. Bill told both Jack Healey and Mary Daly of Amnesty what he told anyone who came to him about raising money for some worthy cause by getting rock stars to put on a show. You get me the talent and I'll do the rest.

In Dublin, Jack Healey met with Bono, the lead singer of U-2, and Paul McGuinness, the manager of the band. They gave him a letter stating that they would tour for two weeks anywhere he wanted in order to celebrate Amnesty's twenty-fifth anniversary. Thanks to U-2, the tour now had credibility. In terms of finding other acts, the hunt was on.

MARY DALY: While Jack was away, I called Gil Friesen of A&M Records and I mentioned to him that we had a two-week commitment from U-2. We just didn't know U-2's relative power. Gil called back in two days and said, "I talked to Sting. And Sting's *in*."

JACK HEALEY: A lot of people said, "U-2 *who?*" They didn't know. But Bill loved them as a band. He loved Paul McGuinness and all that. He said, "You need a *lot* more talent." And I said, "But are *you* going to do this?" What I did essentially was gore him a bit. I told him he *had* to do this. I really sort of tore into Bill because I thought he wasn't movement enough.

I kept saying to him, "You are not *emotionally* attached to this event."

I kept repeating that line. Eventually, he sort of exploded. He said, "What do you mean? What are you saying to me? *I'm* not emotionally attached to this?" He yelled for forty-five minutes. I thought, "Oh, *good*. I gored him. I got him. I got him!" When I left, I *knew* I had him.

BILL: From that point on, I had ideas. To max out the consciousness-raising, I wanted to play in large places wherever we could. I wanted to use the media by having press conferences at all the airports when we landed. I wanted to have people fill in applications to join Amnesty at the shows.

There *were* some major problems. Primarily pertaining to one act. The Police, who were managed by Miles Copeland.

JACK HEALEY: We had a lot of trouble getting talent. Paul McGuinness came over and stayed with Bill for a while to start calling too. None of it really worked too well. I think eventually Bono called Peter Gabriel. I think Lou Reed called U-2 in Ireland and asked to be on it. Jackson Browne came on because Jackson had been with us for years. That was easy. Joan Baez was easy. I think the Neville Brothers came from Bill. Where Bill was the most responsive was in the coordinating and the nurturing of the talent. They knew he was there so they were secure. If Bill was there, they would come aboard. I mean, who were Jack Healey and Mary Daly?

Then we had some meetings with MTV. Bill was in the MTV meetings because he was incensed with what MTV had done to Live Aid. And so was McGuinness. We sat in and pretended to run the meeting but Bill ran the meeting. Bill told them, "I'll pull the cord on you." And they knew he meant it.

Then Bill would explain the hand. The famous hand. The customer was here. Pinky finger. Then the manager. Next finger. The agent. Next finger. The act. And Bill, the promoter, was the *thumb*. I heard that speech *seven* hundred times. Of course, with all these fingers, he could also be the *fist*.

BILL: I had seen a number of the videos they had gotten actors and actresses to do about what Amnesty meant to them. They went to see John Huston, the great director, at his home. He was very ill with emphysema. The last things he said in the video was, "Amnesty International is a conspiracy of *hope*." That hit me. The name of the tour became "Conspiracy of Hope," with the logo being a candle with barbed wire around it.

JACK HEALEY: The night we started at the Cow Palace in San Francisco, Bill walked up to me. He was in the middle of two million three hundred thousand things and he said, "Oh, *Jack*. I forgot to give you this." It was just an envelope and he had to go off someplace else as usual. I opened it up and in there was everything we had tried to offer him. A series of checks. We didn't pay any of the artists but we paid the working grunts their going rate. We didn't want the working person to be suffering. He gave it all back. He donated his whole organization's time.

ROBERT GREENFIELD: The tour began in San Francisco and then moved to L.A. for a show at The Forum, which lasted six hours. Bob Dylan played that night wearing a short-fingered glove on one hand. He was backed up by Tom Petty and the Heartbreakers, with whom he was about to tour. Dave Stewart of the Eurythmics and Bob Geldof did "Get Up, Stand Up," the Bob Marley song. Bono and U-2 did "Maggie's Farm." Then all the performers came back on stage to sing "I Shall Be Released." People like Jamie Lee Curtis, Rosanna Arquette, Madonna, and Sean Penn introduced the acts. Jack Nicholson was backstage. John Huston was there too. Unlike San Francisco, it was star time all the way.

JACK HEALEY: Then we went to Denver. I had to go speak at my annual meeting in Washington and Bill had to go to Philadelphia for his son David's high school graduation. So we both missed the press conference in Denver and we both came back that night to see the show and it was half-filled. We lost a *lot* of money. About a half a million dollars. We lost money but it was all right. We were on the move and Atlanta was sold out and we were moving.

Now, do I *have* to tell this? Does Bill want this told? Because then we started the battles.

ROBERT GREENFIELD: The battles began over who would close the show. U-2 had been the final act on stage up to that point with Sting preceding them. Miles Copeland, founder of IRS Records and Sting's longtime manager as well as the manager of the Police, wanted the Police reunion to be foremost in everyone's mind. He wanted them to close the show.

BILL: This would be under the heading of what I had to go through at gigs where no money was involved. Part of Amnesty's deal, on an international basis, was a radio broadcast of the final concert in Giants' Stadium to Japan, and a syndication of it to television stations nationwide through Viacom. In Atlanta, Miles Copeland decided to tell the Amnesty people that he didn't want Japan or Viacom to be part of the deal. He was soon releasing a Police video and it would conflict with his business. He threatened to pull the Police altogether from the show.

I had to hold a meeting after the Atlanta show just to calm them all down. This man was just inhuman. He didn't give a flying fuck about his fellow man. The only reason Miles Copeland was tolerating it at all was because Sting was *really* involved. I wish I had a tape of that meeting. If the essence of that meeting could go into this book, it could *replace* most of the book.

MARY DALY: Miles Copeland, their manager, and Bruce Allen, Bryan Adams's manager, and Gail Colson, Peter Gabriel's manager, had all indicated that the live television broadcast on MTV from Giants' Stadium was *off*. For us, this was to be a source of revenue. Since the whole thing was an awareness campaign, how could we do it without building to Giants' Stadium and a national television audience? We would have lost the momentum of the event.

Basically, the artists didn't know *anything* about this at that point. At our regular morning meeting, Bill said, "We're going to do this *other* meeting and I'll chair it. Miles is going to attack and you just have to respond very straightforwardly. Let *him* lose *his* cool. You keep *yours*."

Bill was stage managing the meeting. But he seemed much more worried about it than I felt. I felt asking for the television rights was not only vital but it was all up-front. It had all been in the original deal.

Jack and I didn't understand what Miles had done with the other managers. U-2's management came to me during the show and said, "You know, this is going to be *very*, *very* rough, this meeting after the show. You better understand this and *know* it. You have *no* friends in this meeting."

Which seemed unbelievable to me. Because here was this family of people traveling together. The moments of intense experience had all been there. Everybody was certainly wonderful to Jack and me. That was on the artists' level. Bryan Adams, I think, came to me one morning at breakfast and said, "Why aren't you guys doing a movie? This should be *recorded*, you know." It was totally mixed signals all over the place.

The meeting took place in a large room backstage at the Omni. It was a long show and the meeting started fifteen or twenty minutes after. It was very late at night and people were tired. Also, there was tension. It was like a prayer meeting, in that it was a semicircle of folding chairs in this big empty room. Joan Baez's management, and the management of the Neville Brothers, and Lou Reed's management were out of it at that point. They weren't invited to the meeting because they had nothing to do with the television or the three hours of syndication.

The problem was the three hours of syndication that Viacom was doing. All of a sudden, it had become a national TV event. It was sort of clicking in my mind when I saw the Police perform. Although it didn't occur to me until *after* the meeting that the final performance of the Police *ever* on TV was worth something. And that money *wasn't* going to be going to the Police.

So it was a dual thing for Copeland. It was the emotion *and* the money. That was true with his whole thing. He didn't want the band being seen as no good. Plus, the reunion with Sting had great *commercial* value.

Sting came over to me and said, "Don't take this personally." Sting said, "This is *business*. There's no way I want my management to hurt what you're trying to do. There are some business things that have to be worked out." He said, "You stay away from Miles. Let Miles and Bill meet. That's what Bill does." In Sting's mind, it was "The Miles/Bill *Gladiator* Show."

JACK HEALEY: Earlier in the day, Bill said, "Jack, I'll tell you what. I've got to stay in this business but we've got a very important battle tonight. And the battle has to be won by the promoter because this is the nature of this business."

I said, "Oh, Bill. Don't worry about me supporting you."

He said, "Oh, Jack. I'm not worried about you supporting me. I'm only worried about *winning*."

I said, "Yeah. Me, too. You kidding? I'll *kill* him."

Bill said, "No, no, Jack. I don't want *you* to kill him. What I want you to do is be the best blocking back you've ever been. You hit him, and I'll take him out."

I said, "Okay. That sounds great."

He said, "The key is . . . toward the end of the evening you let *me* handle it. I'll take it."

MARY DALY: Everybody sat down and there was no kidding around anymore and it was very tense and quiet. Bill opened the meeting by saying, "We have issues to talk about here. Calmly." He was clear and straightforward and direct. A different Bill than I had seen before. Which threw us a little bit. There was a neutrality and justice there.

Bill pulled out the letter that had gone out on April 1. Clearly, it talked about the television broadcast. He read the letter and then he opened the floor for conversation and Miles jumped in, saying, "These people . . ." He said, meaning us, meaning any charity, "They want *everything*. They're going to *take* everything. You give them something, they take *more*. They take it *all*." He went on and on about how the managers had been ignored in this project.

I was dumbfounded. He said, "We've *never* agreed to do this and we're *not* going to do this. This is *out of the question*."

Miles, at this point, was yelling. His voice was raised and he was shaking his fist. He started from a position of "Let me kick you in the gut and *then* tell you what I think." Nobody really responded. Bruce Allen spoke next. He was Bryan Adams's manager. He said this was too much and they hadn't been consulted. They were all saying, "*No* Viacom TV. *Maybe* MTV."

The Japanese radio broadcast would have been about six hundred thousand dollars of income. Which was almost exactly as much as we had lost in Denver. From our point of view, we were not used to losing that amount of money on a speculative thing, we *needed* it. Because you can't put Amnesty's money at risk *at all*. Doing that broadcast was important to "X" out Denver.

Everybody kept talking and then Sting and U-2 talked. Sting said, "I'm very torn about this. My point of view is that we're all geese who can only lay so many golden eggs. My commitment to Amnesty is personal. I want to be useful to them for a long time. I'm in a situation now, through no fault of anyone's, of some overexposure questions. There are career decisions here. I want my career to continue, both for myself and so I can continue to be useful to Amnesty."

Sting wanted to be there because Sting wanted to make sure they were doing the right thing. Miles, at that point, had Sting split. He had said to Sting in so many words, "This will *hurt* your career. If they see you with the Police, you're finished as a solo act." That was what was going on. Miles had all of Sting's insecurities working.

I didn't understand why *all* the artists weren't there. I even said so to Bill before the meeting, "Shouldn't the artists be here?" And Bill said, "*No*." Because I was ready to go get them. I was tired of being in the situation of getting two different stories from everybody. This was a community of interest. Let's get everybody in on it.

Then Jack talked. He said, "We're not here to steal anything from anybody. We've talked to all of you. We've had agreements." He sort of focused on Bruce Allen and said, "I had dinner with you. I talked to you. I can't believe I wouldn't have brought up the reason I went there to talk to you. But I don't remember word-for-word our meeting."

Then I started talking to Miles. I said, "Miles. Are you calling me a liar?" I said, "I sat with you. I told you about the shows. The six concert shows. The MTV broadcast. The syndicated broadcast. You didn't object to any of that, verbally *or* in writing. You had *months* to do that."

I was very emotional and I said, "Miles, I feel like we're in a deadlock here and I don't understand how to go forward. You're saying you're in a difficult situation. That we're holding a moral obligation over your heads. We're at total cross-purposes. Amnesty *needs* awareness. You don't want *any*."

I said, "We need awareness because the publicity from this can make it easier for us to pressure governments to free prisoners, stop torture, stop executions. This same awareness affects your bottom line. We're dealing with the bottom line of people's *lives*."

Then Miles attacked back at me. "You *didn't* say that. You *didn't* say that. You *didn't* say that."

I said, "Miles, I never, never, ever told you specifically about plans for the movie. I told you everything else. You *can't* do this."

And then I started to cry. Which I had never done before. Never *ever*.

Bill said to everybody, "Let's remember who these people are. These are *good* people. Maybe they've made some mistakes. They don't know our industry. They have no understanding of the business part of our industry. But these are *good* people. These people don't hurt people."

BILL: I tried to explain to Miles Copeland why we were doing all this. I said, "Your concern is for the career of your artists but what about this event?"

He said, "I think Jack Healey is an opportunist just like Willie Nelson."

I said, "You *dare* put Jack Healey in the same breath as Willie Nelson? You've gone too far."

JACK HEALEY: Copeland's remark about me being like Willie Nelson was a way of writing me off. Like I was just another shit. What Bill really meant when he answered him back was, "Jack Healey is a *human rights leader* and we're going to respect him in this meeting. Knock that off."

Copeland had to take it because Bill had the authority of everybody in the room Bill did not play around with Amensty. He respected and protected it. He knew that was his job and that was what he did for me.

Earlier in the night, Copeland had asked me to come in the room to talk to him. I had just heard about this thing that the Police were going to close in Chicago as well. Miles pointed to a chair and somewhat rudely he said, "Sit down."

I said, "Miles, you take this chair and shove it up your *ass*. I'm throwing you *and* the Police off this tour. You are *going*."

And I left the room. I slammed the door behind me. That threw him into a total catatonic response. They never expected that from me. But he kept trying to do that to me. That was what he did in the meeting again. I hate to use Willie Nelson's name in this way because he's such a fine person. But it was like Copeland kept relegating me. Like I had *nothing* to say about this tour.

MARY DALY: At this point, Gail Colson, Peter Gabriel's manager, said, "I'd forgotten about the letter. Clearly, it was in the letter. We *will* do the syndicated broadcast." She broke it at the point. Bruce Allen said, "We don't like it. We're not happy. We don't like this. But we could live with the syndicated broadcast." Miles still had to get in a few more shots. He kept snapping at Bill. What Bill was really saying to the managers was, "This may not make any sense at all from a business point of view but you made obligations to these people and it's not the same as making a promise to a promoter."

Miles was finished then. It was clear that he was by himself. Miles said, "All right. We'll do this. But *no* Japan." We lost the radio broadcast for Japan. The radio meant nothing. He just had to get something back.

When it was over, there was just this feeling of embarrassment in the room. Clearly, we had won. But to me, we had lost so much by having that meeting. Just in terms of the way we felt. That it *was* a different world.

I went back in the van with Jan Simmons and Bill. Bill just put his arms on my shoulder and hugged me for a long time and said, "Don't talk. Don't talk. Don't talk."

MICHAEL AHERN: In terms of Miles Copeland appearing to be a contradictory force in this, he was actually representing his artist as a manager ordinarily would in the context of negotiations. The artist is not and certainly never wants to be the person to sit there and say no to *anything*. The artist will say yes to *everything*, go behind the door, and say, "Miles, *listen*. I'm a nice guy. I'm doing this because I love peace, light, freedom, and all that kind of stuff. Would you please go tell these people the answer is *no?* It can't be me saying it because how can I be an asshole?"

So people who think they are talking directly to the artist at his most heartfelt and sincere do so because they have never done it before. They only have the perception of the manager as being a big "bah humbugger." Whereas in actual fact, asking for a movie on *top* of the television, on *top* of the tour itself, is actually maybe going a little further than the artist wanted to do.

I have a more balanced view of these things because I heard and saw it from all the sides. At the time, Sting was setting up a TV deal in Japan. That was what no one knew. That was why the broadcast out of

Giants' Stadium couldn't go to Japan. Your point of origin determines your point of view about things. Somebody from Amnesty looking at it says, "That was just awful of old Miles to do *that*." Yet if you're Miles, it was like these people had a lot of gall going directly to the artist.

ROBERT GREENFIELD: In nearly all respects, the "Conspiracy of Hope" tour was a success. It ended in Giants' Stadium in New York with a day-long concert to which Bill added Carlos Santana, Miles Davis, and Ruben Blades in order to bring some Third World flavor to the show. MTV managed to cover the event in a manner which Bill somehow managed to control.

By then, Bill himself was hyper, speeding on natural energy and the obsessive need to get things done *right*. On a walk through an empty Giants' Stadium the night before the show, Bill discovered that the local promoter, never one of his great favorites to begin with, was nowhere to be found. The following Sunday being Father's Day, the local promoter had left the venue to take his father out to dinner.

Bill was totally outraged. In his eyes, this was a capital crime. To one of the local promoter's people, Bill screamed, "I want him *arrested!*"

The "Conspiracy of Hope" tour accomplished many things. It served to introduce Amnesty International to a generation which before had never really been exposed in any great degree to its good works. During the final show, forty thousand people joined up as brand-new members. Within the next nine months, another hundred thousand did the same. The tour raised two point five million dollars, all of which went to Amnesty.

Although as a band, U-2's motives in doing this tour were as pure as could be, the two weeks they spent doing shows across the U.S.A. served to expose them to a far wider audience in America than had ever seen them play live before. Both Live Aid and then the Amnesty U.S.A. tour made it plain to far less altruistic acts and more narrow-minded managers just how much good charity work could do for a career.

For the grand finale of the final show of the tour in Giants' Stadium, Bill brought out on stage several prisoners of conscience. Men and women who, much like his sister Ester, had been tortured and imprisoned for their political or religious beliefs. Many were still alive only because Amnesty had interceded for them. From Bill's point of view, the only problem was that none of them had ever before appeared before sixty thousand rock fans. Stunned by the power of the moment, the ex-prisoners of conscience began to reach out to one another, walking in *front* of the performers everyone else had come there to see.

The lasting visual image I have of Bill that day is watching on television as he scurried back and forth across that stage, bent over like a stooped, very frantic old man, moving those prisoners of conscience off to the side so all the kids out front could see. It was as if he was saying, "You've been tortured? You're an ex-prisoner of conscience? You want to have a reunion with your fellow man? *Fine.* Just please not *here*. Not in *front* of the band."

2.

BILL: In August of 1986, I went to New York with Santana. They had a gig at the Pier and one at Jones Beach. Every few years, I rent a car or go with a friend and drive up to take a look at my old neighborhood. I go up to The Bronx. University Avenue and 175th Street. I go up to Van Cortlandt Park. I go up the Grand Concourse to where the old Loew's Paradise and Krumb's ice cream store used to be. All my old haunts. The schoolyards that I played in. P.S. 82. P.S. 104.

I was there with Santana so I rented a car and I drove up through Harlem across 125th Street and then past Yankee Stadium. I went up to 175th Street and University Avenue and I parked the car and I walked up the hill to Montgomery Avenue. I hadn't been there in two years and it was really run-down. It was eerie for me to see.

It was a hot summer day and people were sitting on the street. They were waiting. For Godot. For life to go on. I walked across the street on University and two young guys literally offered me anything I wanted. "What are you looking for, man? What do you need? We got the best. You want any *snap?* Any *pop? Luudes?* You want *pussy?*" Whatever you might name.

I told them no and I kept walking up the hill. My apartment house was just a bunch of bricks. There was nothing there. It had been knocked down—1635 Montgomery Avenue was gone. It wasn't that the neighborhood wasn't white anymore. It was what had happened to the people who lived there.

Everyone was hanging on. Any edge they could find, they would take. I wasn't walking through a ghetto somewhere. I was walking through *my neighborhood.* I went over to Sedgwick Avenue and I went back down to University and during the course of maybe two and a half hours, I could have scored a dozen times.

I was down by Tremont Avenue and I saw people getting off a bus. A guy walked over to them. He was standing at the bus stop just checking people as they got off the bus, saying, "What do you need? What do you need? What do you need? We got it. We got it *here.*"

Then I went up to DeWitt Clinton, where I went to high school. People

were standing in the street shooting up. I saw all the various shapes of
the go-betweens. The dealers. Hanging around. They weren't standing
there because they loved to watch the traffic. They were waiting for the
ball to go up so they could do another deal. It was a given. It was an
accepted way of life. That was what life there had become. That was the
way it was. *Those* days had been *my* days. These were *these* days. Maybe
fifty years from now, it would be worse but what could have been worse?
That there would be nothing left there at all?

ROBERT GREENFIELD: Bill got together with David Maldonado, who
managed Ruben Blades. Together, they came up with the idea of doing a
Crack Benefit in New York City. Bill went to see Walter Yetnikoff, then
head of CBS Records, for seed money. Bill held the press conference to
announce the event in the back room of the Carnegie Deli where he loved
to eat because the late Leo Steiner would always make sure that white
linen, rather than ordinary paper napkins, were brought to his table.

Bill wanted to do three separate shows. A rock show, a rap show, and
a Latin show. He wanted to put them on in some armory in The Bronx.
Right in the middle of a drug epidemic which had not yet grown to the
proportions it would soon assume. He thought about doing it in Yankee
Stadium. But he could not get insurance. This was long before rap came
into the mainstream on MTV so white kids could watch it at home after
school. Combining acts like Run-DMC, the Allman Brothers, and the
newly reconstituted Lynyrd Skynyrd band might have brought in a mixture
of fans who would cause problems that no amount of security could solve.

Instead, Bill put on one show in Madison Square Garden. Crosby,
Stills, Nash, and Young, Santana, Olatunji, Run-DMC, Ruben Blades,
and Tito Puente. The next night in the Felt Forum, he did an all-Latin
show. Nothing really worked the way he had hoped it would. What
frustrated Bill the most was that he just could not get others to share his
all-consuming vision of the problem crack would soon become. But then
they had not walked the streets of his old neighborhood.

BILL: New York was *tough*. Things there didn't come together. It was all
separate camps. Factions. Even within the Latin community. Even within
the black. New York City in general is such a Survival City these days. It
is the hippest and saddest place on the planet. I feel sadder about New
York than any city or situation anywhere. I mean, where do they sit on
the roof and play Mah-Jongg now? Where is, not the New York that used
to be, but the New York that *should* be?

3.

ROBERT GREENFIELD: Like an aging fighter who refuses to leave the ring, Bill was starting to take some shots to the body and the head. He had always taken them before but now they seemed to hurt him more. The pain lingered. The anger and the bitterness stayed with him even long after the event was done. The frustration of not being able to get his way when he knew beyond all doubt that his way was the right one drove Bill wild.

A case in point. The fiftieth anniversary of the opening of the Golden Gate Bridge. Despite superhuman efforts by both himself and his company, Bill could not persuade his beloved adopted city of San Francisco to let him shut the bridge down for a day in order to celebrate the event.

I remember running with him one Saturday on a path that led to the sea and then riding still soaked with sweat in the front seat of his big, classic Mercedes convertible on which the top was never up, no matter how cold it got. For a solid hour as I stood beside him, shivering in the wind on a narrow ledge on a very steep slope in the Marin Headlands, Bill talked about how it would all be done.

The bay was as blue as it only ever gets in Northern California on a beautiful, sunny day. Behind us, the bridge hung like a backdrop on a stage. Oblivious to everything but what he was saying, Bill talked. He gestured with his hands and he talked, showing me how the bands would be *there* with the parking *here* and how on the bridge itself, all the people would stand. At that moment nothing else mattered to him. This show was the most important thing in his world.

BILL: The vision I had for it came from when my son, David, was five or six years old. We were in New York City and it was Christmas Eve. I was up very late in the suite in the Park Lane Hotel where I always stayed then. It was 3 A.M. and it started to snow. Snowflakes were coming down like silver dollars. I woke David up and he said, "Dad, I don't want to get up."

I said, "*Try*. I know it's hard for you but this is going to be an experience you'll never forget." You know how kids are. "*No, no, no.*"

I got him up and I got him dressed and we went down on to Fifth Avenue and there it was. *No* traffic. *Nothing* moving. Solid *snow*. A few tracks here and there but maybe ten people out. No more. We walked down the middle of Fifth Avenue from Fifty-Seventh Street to Washington Square. The store lights were on all the way down Fifth. Saks and B. Altman. The Christmas windows. Past the Empire State Building. We walked and we talked and we were alone on this quiet island in the snow. That was what I wanted for the bridge. An open walkway for a day.

Politicians didn't want to do it. They didn't want to celebrate one of the wonders of man the way it should have been done. So it never happened the way it *should* have been done.

ROBERT GREENFIELD: Bill reopened the original Fillmore only to have it closed by the big earthquake that struck Northern California in 1989. He played a part in Francis Coppola's *Gardens of Stone*. He appeared as Father Time at the stroke of midnight as the Grateful Dead played in Oakland Coliseum on New Year's Eve, a moment he described by saying, "There is no space on the planet that, for a period of from five minutes to midnight until ten minutes after, where the energy is any better. *Nowhere* on the planet." Then he went to work bringing rock to Moscow for the very first time.

Chapter
Twenty-One

Rocking
Behind the Curtain

1.

BILL: I never went looking for causes. For more benefits to do. People came to me and I'd say yes. At my company, we had the tools and the talent, free of charge. Now that the word was out, everybody knew about us.

I got a call from a lady I didn't know in L.A., some publicist, who said she was calling on behalf of a guy named Allan Affeldt, who was president of the American Peace Walk Committee. He was heading a team of two hundred Americans who had been given approval by the Russian government to walk on an antinuclear march from Leningrad to Moscow.

She said, "We know you're busy, Mr. Graham, but can you help us at all? Could you guide and advise us with the production of a show to commemorate the end of this walk?" I asked her when it was taking place and I told her to have the guy call me. Allan Affeldt called me and then he came to San Francisco.

Concerning the show itself, the first thing I said was, "If you can possibly change it from June, make the show on the Fourth of July. The symbolism would be great." They said, "Fine." First, I sent Steve Kahn over there. Steve is a twenty-year BGP veteran who was on the road with Santana forever. He now flies the company plane and helicopter. He has been everywhere and knows everyone. He is the ultimate Yellow Pages and totally dedicated to doing things right when it comes to anything short of war. I always send "Killer" first. On my dollars, he went to Moscow to be the liaison with this organization called the Soviet Peace Committee.

491

STEVE "KILLER" KAHN: Bill was working on the bands. He got Santana committed. The Doobie Brothers. They wanted big acts but it was summertime, touring time, and all the big acts were already committed. We were a little bit concerned that if we had an act that was *too* big, they would want to have too much control.

With the Soviets, nothing worked fast. We take for granted that you pick up a telephone and make a call in a matter of five minutes. This could take all day in the Soviet Union. If you were in the U.S. trying to deal with them, they were twelve hours out of synch. Basically, you had to go over there. Because making a call to the Soviet Union took *hours* to book. The same making one out. Sometimes they would answer telexes. Sometimes, it would go three, four, or five days. The way it worked in the Soviet Union was face-to-face.

BILL: I went over there and looked at the stadium and it was beautiful. Dynamo Stadium, pronounced "Dee-na-mo." It would hold about sixty thousand people. I was on one side of the field and I was saying, "We'll put the stage here at one end and we'll have the people *there*. I want to let you folks know that we'll have fifteen or twenty thousand people on the *grass*."

The interpreter said this to about twenty suits and ties. The general director, the assistant general director, the bottle washer, they were *all* there. Very proper and official, with only one guy who spoke English. When the interpreter said there would be twenty thousand people on the field, they all looked at each other like I was crazy. Like, "Oh no. This is *hallowed* ground. Touched only by twenty-two people at a time. The Russian soccer players."

They weren't even nasty. They just said, "It's *unthinkable*. People sit up there. We'll have guards *here*. Anybody comes on the field, they'll be *shot*."

Right next to Dynamo Stadium, they had a little Dynamo Stadium. It held forty thousand people. The next day, I went to look at that. It was a training field. They said they would let us use it. We left. Total time there? A day and a half.

We came back to America and a couple of weeks passed. No money, no stars, no nothing. I called Stanley Sheinbaum to try to get Barbra Streisand but she was busy doing other things. Again, I had my Triple A List, my Double A List, my A List. This guy said no. That guy said maybe. I kept on thinking about Streisand but she had other commitments. We were dead in the water with about three weeks to go.

Santana was going to be off on a European tour but it got canceled. There were rumors about the Doobie Brothers maybe getting together again so I called them. In the end, I wound up getting James Taylor, the Doobies, Santana, and Bonnie Raitt. I had the acts. But *still* no money.

Aeroflot was going to give us the plane at a good price but we still needed some money to pay for it. Our show budget looked like it was going to be between five and six hundred thousand dollars. Because there was nothing in Russia that we could use. No staging, no roofing, no sound, no lights.

There was also no food. I could not find lettuce in Moscow. I could not get fresh fruit. I could not get ice cream. I could not get a decent meal in Moscow unless it was black market. Laszlo Hegedus from Budapest was one of our unsung heroes. He only had two words. *"S'possible." "S'* . . . *possible."* He knew Budapest backward and forward and he knew that we would have to *schlep* everything in from outside Russia. Budapest to Moscow is eight hundred miles. Laszlo sent three air-conditioned trucks filled with fruit and food and rigging and lights and sound.

There was still no money. Out of the blue, I called Steve Wozniak. Steve was a decent guy. A wonderful *nebbish*. All the money he lost on the US Festival was like the price he had to pay for sitting in a room all of his life putting together computers. He knew *nothing* about the street. He had never once played half-court in his life. But I liked him all the same.

Over the phone, I said, "Steve, this is the picture. . . . They're going to do this march from Leningrad to Moscow." I told him the whole story and who was playing. I said, "Steve, I don't know where else to turn. They've tried to get sponsorship but they can't get it. I need half a million dollars."

Steve said, "Can I get four tickets?"

This is the way his mind works. It goes right past the hotels and makes a left turn and doesn't stop for anything. I said, "Can you get four tickets? Steve, you're my guest. Whether you're in for the money, or not." I kept saying to him, "Think about it. I know I've just hit on you, I can't expect you to give me an answer right away."

He kept saying, "No. No, no, no. Tell me a little more."

I told him how we were *schlepping* all this stuff in from outside Russia and the problems we were having. He said, "Could I make it *six* tickets?"

I said, "Steve, if the show happens, you're my guest. No matter *what*." Finally, I said, "If you want to call me back, fine. The only thing is, I've got a time problem, Steve. Forty-eight hours."

He said, "No, no. No, it's okay. Sure. Let's do it."

One conversation. Within a couple of days, I had the check. Five hundred thousand dollars. I called to thank him. He called back and said, "Bill, I know you've got a million things to think about but . . ."

I said, "What's the problem?"
He said, "I'd like to take *ten* people."
"No problem."

STEVE "KILLER" KAHN: We were doing the Grateful Dead in Ventura
during the second week in June. I flew Bill down there and we were really
happy because the show was set to go in Little Dynamo. The people
would be on the grass. We had the bands committed. We were feeling
good. Somebody at the concert dosed Bill. Bill got dosed. He was flying.
It was a *heavy* dosage. Bill was on the phone with Laszlo. He was walking
around with a little wireless phone talking direct-dial on a call to
Budapest, and he was *dosed*.

BILL: They had given me a trailer with a phone in it so I could work. I
was sitting inside the trailer when I realized I'd been dosed. Heavily. I
stood up inside the trailer and it was *moving*. I was standing inside a
castle and the music playing was from *Götterdämmerung*, the last opera
in the *Ring* cycle by Wagner. Only it was the Dead playing "Terrapin
Station." I was William Penn. I was Arthur Penn. I was Sean Penn. I was
a Cossack. *Wuuuuuuuuuuuuuu!*

I said to myself, "I *have* to control myself. I've been dosed. I have to
deal with it." I stayed in the trailer most of the time. At the end of the
show, I went outside onto the empty field. To me, it looked like a bull
ring. Facing the ocean was this line of Porta-Johns. Just dozens of them.
One next to the other. All the waves coming in were *tidal* waves. All the
dimensions of everything were times a hundred.

I was standing in the middle of the field as these *huge* trucks backed
up to the stage to reload the equipment. The guys doing the loading each
looked like Mr. Universe to me. *They* were huge.

There was the ocean and thousands of white Porta-Johns with red roofs
all moving toward me in military precision and they were *huge*. I was on
another planet. Peter Barsotti and his wife, Bettike, came over and stood
by me. I took off my shoes and sat down and we talked. Each one of my
toes looked like a *continent* to me.

We all flew back from Ventura in the company plane. It was like *Star
Wars*. Imagine flying in a small plane along the Pacific Ocean on a clear
summer night and you're *fried*. I was flying in outer space. I said, "Look
at where we are. This is Venus. That's Mars." In terms of being taken
somewhere else, one of the most awesome experiences of my life. Like
being out in public with no clothes on.

STEVE "KILLER" KAHN: We flew back into Novato and Bill could not
drive on his own. We were not going to leave Bill alone. We took him

home and we were sitting at his kitchen table. It was one or two in the morning and his sister Ester was up there with her husand, Manny. They were taking care of Bill's son, Alex, who was staying at the house.

We didn't tell Ester that Bill was a little zoned but it was pretty obvious. Bill mentioned that he wasn't feeling well. The phone rang. I picked it up and it was the woman who worked for the Soviet Peace Committee.

She said, "Hello, this is the Soviet Peace Committee. I've got to report to you that we cannot do the concert on July 4. It has to be on July 6."

I was sitting there in disbelief. I looked over at Bill and I repeated this to him and he gave me that look. *The* look. He came over and picked up the phone and said, "Can you repeat that?" She repeated it. I've seen Bill in tirades before. Bill is one of the few people who uses anger and emotion as a communicative tool. It's very rare that he *actually* goes off the deep end. Where he's *not* in control.

He was right at that edge of being out of control here. He was screaming, *"DO YOU THINK WE ARE ANIMALS IN THE ZOO?* YOU CAN CALL US UP AT YOUR WHIM AND SAY: *'NOT* JULY FOURTH. JULY *SIXTH?'* YOU THINK WE CAN CHANGE EVERYTHING AND TELL THAT TO ALL THESE BANDS? WE *WON'T* DO THE SHOW. THAT'S *IT!"*

It was *so* surreal. It was out of a Fellini movie. Ester, from out of nowhere, went into the refrigerator and got her pot warming up on the stove. Bill said, "Ester. What are you doing?"

Without batting an eye or changing her tone in any way, she said, "Making chicken soup for you."

Bill said, "The *world* is falling apart. The concert is falling apart. Nothing is going right. And *you're* making *chicken soup?"*

I said, "Please, Ester. I'd *love* some." We were there until five in the morning, calling back and forth. The next day, they finally sent us a telex that said the show would go on the fourth. But they didn't tell us that the stadium would have to change to Islamjovjo.

2.

ALLAN AFFELDT: At this point, I had over four hundred people with me. Two hundred and thirty Americans and two hundred Soviets. We were walking from Leningrad to Moscow. Ten to fifteen miles a day. Country roads, highways. We went where people had not seen Americans or foreigners for that matter, maybe since World War II. Little tiny towns. Little farming villages. People came out in unbelievable droves. There was a city called Novogorod. Where there must have been fifty thousand people who came out to see us. It was really unbelievable. Not a single person who was there would not describe it as the high point of their lives.

The last time they had seen us, we had been their great allies in what for them was the great patriotic war, World War II. We had fought side by side with them against the fascists. Then somehow we became the evil empire and they never quite understood. Because they had a visceral understanding of what the Americans were all about and it didn't match up with the political reality.

Here we were, suddenly, from out of nowhere. Two hundred Americans walking down the main road. Everything stopped in the whole city. The roads were lined five-deep with people. They were cheering and crying in a way you can't really imagine and bringing us their most precious heirlooms. Just to give them to us.

Every day, Bill and I were talking on the phone and Bill was saying, "*Where* is the show going to be? I *have* to know." And I was saying, "Bill, I *can't* tell you." All I could tell him was that I trusted Mr. Fedosev of the Soviet Peace Committee to deliver us a venue that would be adequate. And every day, he would say, "How *many* rooms am I going to have?" And I'd say, "I *can't* tell you. But they've guaranteed a hundred. And drivers and vehicles and interpreters for all those people." And he'd say, "How *many* people are going to be there?" I'd say, "I can't tell you. They don't sell tickets here. They don't have Ticketrons. They *distribute* them."

Every day, he was on the borderline of saying, "I *can't* do it. I can't *do* it." Because Santana and James Taylor and the various artists were calling and asking him the same questions he was asking me and he couldn't tell them. We were definitely going nuts. We were not sleeping. I think it was Novogorod where Bill had given me a deadline and said, "*Okay.* By this date, we've *got* to have all this stuff or I simply *can't* do it."

I called him that night from Novogorod and explained what had happened that day. And he just decided to go ahead and do it. He got a sense through the phone that there was something really special happening. Even if nobody could describe it or explain it. There was something really miraculous that had never happened before, and might never happen again. It was never a business thing for Bill. From the very beginning, Bill had a very clear sense of what it was all about. It was never a business transaction. It was a labor of love.

BILL: I left ten days in advance. Jan Simmons was awesome because I left it all to her to get papers and visas and passports together for a hundred people. Nick Clainos took care of the cable television deal, which got us another hundred and some odd thousand dollars. We made a deal with Aeroflot to give us a charter plane. James Taylor, some Doobies, and Bonnie Raitt all converged on Washington. I was already in Moscow with Killer and about fifteen of my staff from San Francisco, headed by Peter and Bob Barsotti.

The trucks started to arrive from Budapest. The food got in but they wouldn't allow us to bring in a photocopy machine or an automatic coffeemaker. Even the hotels didn't have photocopy machines. They were that concerned about government secrets leaving the country.

PETER BARSOTTI: You could talk to a guy for weeks and not really understand who he was or what his real job was. They wanted to have schedules from me for everything. I had no idea. I was totally making it up as I was going along but they wanted everything in writing ahead of time before they would give me anything. I said, "Look, we need to be flexible." Bad word. *Flexible.* No such word.

BILL: Our biggest problem was that we needed *sixty* interpreters. The riggers needed an interpreter. Stage, security, catering, press. The roadies. Interpreters for the guy on the sound board. *Nobody* spoke English. *Except* for the interpreters.

The other main problems were getting transportation and decent food. People said to me, "Bill, how does it feel to be in the mother country of your family?" Nothing. I felt nothing. In the hotel, there were two channels on the TV and no room service. There was a lady on the floor. When I got off the elevator, she gave me my key. When I left the floor, she took the key back. I went in and out of the hotel, I had to show a registration card.

The hardest thing to make them understand was that we wanted a fair shake on the tickets and how they were distributed. The main point I stressed over and over again was that inside the stadium, there would be *no* uniforms and *no* weapons. If I saw guns or uniforms inside the stadium, I would stop the show. *No* security of theirs inside. *We* would control the backstage area. That was the strongest point we had to get across to the Russian authorities.

The day before the show, we had the sound check and the press conference. The Soviets wanted to handle the tickets and they wanted to handle the press. They were giving tickets to *their* press but not ours and I went crazy. Because I threatened to cancel the whole show, they finally gave me back those tickets. They had absconded with three hundred of them. It finally got through into their brains that I was a madman. I acted like a madman. They had never seen that before.

ALLAN AFFELDT: They didn't do any advance PR because behind the stage, there was nothing but big fields in a big park. They were certain that if they did any advance public relations on the show, there would have been a quarter of a million people there, jumping over that fence. It was kept very, very tight. We were told we couldn't have tickets, or very few.

I held a press conference on maybe the second of July. It was the largest press conference the Soviet Peace Committee ever had. Every imaginable bit of foreign press was there. Of course, all they wanted to talk about was the show and Bill kept talking about *why* we were doing the show. They kept hounding him about how much it was costing him and Bill kept talking about *why* it was important.

After, there was this Soviet who was handing out tickets to the press in blocks. Like, "Here's a hundred tickets for you." We, the International Peace Walk, and the walkers, we could not get tickets. Bill got *hysterical* about that. He had a fit in the lobby and was screaming and yelling and taking the tickets away and saying, "If I don't get these tickets now, I cancel the show." I think that was the first time the Peace Committee saw, what's an appropriate word? How *expressive* Bill could be.

BILL: I was working with Mr. Fedosev, who I loved. Mr. Fedosev did not speak English. So we had an interpreter there all the time. But Mr. Fedosev did not use the interpreter to speak to *me*. He always looked right in my eyes and then she would say, "Mr. Fedosev wishes to inform you."

Four or five days before the show, I decided I wanted a little extra *zetz*. The marchers were going to walk in with the American and Russian flags. Russians on one side, Americans on the other, and then they would cross over at the front of the stage and exchange flowers. I wanted this other thing to happen at the finale when all the musicians were up there. I went to Mr. Fedosev and his interpreter and I said, "I need a hundred doves. As the musicians all come out at the end for the finale, I want doves to fly in the air."

She said, "Mr. Fedosev wishes to inform you this is very difficult, to have the doves." For the next few days, it was an ongoing thing. The day before the event, he came into this meeting we were having at the back of the stadium. He always looked very formal with an attaché case and a suit. His interpreter said, "Mr. Fedosev wishes to inform you that he has news of the doves. He has located the doves. Only there is problem. You wish to use doves at particular time—10 P.M. at night. This is when doves are sleeping. They will not fly."

I said, "Please inform Mr. Fedosev that I agree with him. If they were my doves, I would feel the same way. I do not wish to alter the lifestyle to which they have become accustomed."

He liked that. He broke out laughing. I said, "Therefore with his permission and the permission of the trainer, I will use them for the opening."

The show itself was going to have four Russian bands and four American bands. We started with their act and then James Taylor. Their act and then Bonnie Raitt. Their act and the Doobie Brothers. Their act and Santana to close. Their acts weren't nearly up to snuff. There was a band called Aquarium that I really wanted with a singer and songwriter named Boris Grebenshikov but they wouldn't let him on the show because he was underground.

BORIS GREBENSHIKOV: Some information about the show *was* in the newspaper. In Russia but not a lot people are taking newspaper seriously. Because nobody believe in anything official. The outdoor concerts of this caliber we had before usually were restricted to *official* rock and roll.

At that time, there was a huge split between our popularity and our unofficial status. It seemed to the Ministry of Culture that the people should stick to their idea of what was good and accepted for Russian people. They were operating solely from their own idea of what was good.

That meant the people who worked with Bill Graham from the Russian side were trying to push their own friends and relatives. Basically, a chorus. All the people in power, they kind of relate to each other. They know each other, they socialize with each other. And so when it comes to choosing who's going to play, they will invariably pick up the people who are doing all the whoring for them. *"Autograph"* was a band acceptable to them. They were the foremost of Russian rock and roll because the people in charge did not know what rock and roll is. They were not interested in it. They were only interested in the idea of selling to the West. A lot of people in the West would lend their acceptance to this because it confirmed their expectations of Russians as inferior and insincere. It was like a perfect balance.

At that point in time, not a lot of bands would have been able to play in a stadium. Not a lot of people would have had the equipment to do this. In fact, we *were* approached by some people from Peace Committee, asking us to do this gig and we said, "Yes, *gladly!*" To play with Carlos Santana and James Taylor and, basically, to work with Bill Graham was in itself an honor. Because he is a legend. All of these people are legend and it would have been interesting to participate in this.

A couple of days before the concert, we got word that the Ministry of Culture said no. Aquarium cannot appear there because they are not an official band. I think I was told that whoever told Bill Graham, or somebody in charge from America, this said that Aquarium could not appear because they were busy elsewhere. That we were not in Russia at all but in Mongolia or China or whatever. Completely not true. Because we were all there. Sitting in the stadium for the show.

3.

BILL: We distributed twenty-five thousand tickets. All the American press said, "They'll *never* give those tickets to the public. You'll see the *Army* in there. All you're going to see in there will be *Politburo* guys."

BORIS GREBENSHIKOV: The idea was that the tickets will be free. But the people who kept the tickets were the people on the official side that come from all the leaders. They had all the tickets and they had given them away as some kind of reward to a lot of their friends and relatives again. In effect, they had used the tickets as a means of reward for people whom they felt positive toward. All the tickets that were left *then* were finally given away freely. But not before the concert was practically over.

The young people who stood in line all day trying to get in, they were let in at the *end* of the day. When most of *them* had already left. When you stand in a queue for like ten hours, well, you start to feel hopeless. And I think a lot of tickets were really sold. For the underground. The black market.

STEVE "KILLER" KAHN: All this put Bill in the rawest mood possible. He was being *so* belligerent to the staff and to HBO. Finally, Peter Barsotti and I took Bill aside and had a real heart-to-heart talk with him. We said, "Look it. We're *all* here for the same thing."

We said, "We *all* have to enjoy it, Bill. If *you're* not happy, *nobody'll* be happy. We're *so* close to pulling it off. Let's pull it off and leave with a good feeling. Let's not have you make an enemy of people who work for you and people who are here to make this thing work."

He heard it. It wasn't easy. It was very, very emotional while Peter and I spoke with Bill on this. But finally we got things calmed down and got the show going on time.

BILL: They roped off the press box on top. Official-official. They said that only myself and one other person from my organization could go up there. I said, "*Every* one of my people can get into that space or else there's no show. Don't tell me we can't get into a space." I got that straight with Mr. Fedosev. Twenty-eight of my people were allowed in there.

At three o'clock, just before we were ready to open, rows of soldiers trotted in from two sides of the stadium in full battle gear. Helmets and guns. In step. Crisscrossing one another as they came in. *Hundreds* of soldiers. Then they went back out again. I went looking for Mr. Fedosev. I said, "What was that?" His interpreter said, "Mr. Fedosev wishes to inform you that in the case that there is a problem, these soldiers will be on the outside. They were only just going through their maneuvers." I said, "That's not needed. They're going to *stay* outside."

It was now three-fifteen and I wanted to open the doors. I could see the public walking up to the side gates. Just before they came in, hundreds of young men dressed in blue jumpsuits and soft blue baseball caps came into the stadium. They formed a line ninety feet in front of the stage in the middle of the house, creating this moat between the audience and the stage. They sat down cross-legged and every twenty guys, there was an officer with a radio pack on.

The public was coming in and the public was directed to sit behind this phalanx of soldiers in athletic disguise. I went looking for Fedosev and his security but they were nowhere to be found. I was sending people all over the place. The show was supposed to start at four and it was twenty to four. People were just filing in behind the moat and not asking any questions.

I finally found Fedosev upstairs in the press box. I said, "We have to go down on the field." He said, "Yes. Everything is wonderful." I said, "*No*, it's not." We went down on the field. I pointed to all the guards and I said, "What is this?" Through the interpreter, he said, "In case there is a problem, the stage and the artists are protected."

I said, "We built an eight-foot barrier in front of the stage for that. That protects us."

He said, "No. This is for *more* protection."

Very calmly, I said to him, "We cannot have a moat in front of the stage. We will lose exactly what we came for. That is why the show is free. That is why there is no reserved seating. So people can go wherever they want. Now they're cut off from the volleyball and basketball courts we set up at the sides of the stage. We can't have this."

He said, "This is the way we do things here."

I said, "No, it's not. You've never had one of these before. I can't let you do it this way." What I had finally learned after all this time was to look at *him* and not the interpreter when I talked. I said, "Until these men move, there is no show."

He said, "We should not let this small item stand in the way of the show. You asked for no uniforms, you asked for no weapons, you have your doves, it should be done."

I said, "There's no show."

BORIS GREBENSHIKOV: I have never seen as many soldiers in my whole life. There was a lot of military cars around the stadium and there was a lot of people pretending to be, I don't know, young sportsmen standing in line. But knowing *exactly* what to do. They wanted to minimize all the connections between Russians and people from the West. To minimize the risk that something may happen. The concert was good for the official face of Soviet Russia. It was like, "Yes. We are opening up and letting that kind of rock and roll concert happen." But only if they could minimize the risk by only letting in people who would behave safely.

ALLAN AFFELDT: They brought in all these guys with their little soccer suits and their blue hats. And told us they weren't security. And that was just completely unacceptable to Bill. He was screaming from the stage that he was going to cancel the show and that he had to talk to Fedosev right *now*. I don't know if Bill knew what he was talking about when he was saying, "I *must* talk to Fedosev *now* or I leave the show." Because this guy was a member of the Supreme Soviet. This was not a peon you order around in that way. Bill said, "I want you *now. Here.* To talk about people on *my* field at *my* show."

Gendrick Borovik, who was the president of the Peace Committee and more significant in a media sense, kind of a Phil Donahue character in the Soviet Union, with his own television show, was on stage with Bill and they were *screaming* at each other. Borovik is a very dignified gentleman. And Bill was just *screaming* at him. We were fairly certain Bill was going to punch him. And that would have been *it*. That would have been the end of *everything*. Bill would have gone to jail.

BILL: I went back down to the stage. It was five minutes to four. Fedosev was standing there with the security guy who had the walkie-talkie. I must have said this twenty times. I said, "We've come this far. We want to do this *right*. You *never* told us about these fake soldiers in jumpsuits on the field. This is not *right*. . . ."

He said through his interpreter, "But these are *not* soldiers. . . ." I said, "They're dressed in a *kind* of uniform. I don't want to get into that with you now. You've thought about how to protect everything and there's *nothing* to protect. We can't play to a moat. The musicians will *not* play to *nobody* in front of them. We *must* have this contact. This is what democracy is all about."

On and on and on. The interpreter said, "Mr. Fedosev wishes to inform Mr. Graham . . ." I looked right at Mr. Fedosev. I said, "I'm sorry I have to do this." I had already told Peter Barsotti. When I make this move, that's *it*. Just *do* it. Peter was on the other side of the stage. I said, "Tell Mr. Fedosev, that I understand that it is not him. But I'm sorry. *Peter! Strike* the stage."

Peter took his men and started to remove the equipment. Fedosev got on the radio and started talking in Russian. Through the interpreter, he said to me, "We will move the men but now there is bigger problem. If we move the people as well, there will be a *riot*. People will hurt one another by climbing over each other. Earlier, we could have done it. Now, it is too full. There is no way now." I said, "Give me your interpreter and let her come with me."

It was now two minutes to four. I went off the stage into the middle of the field. I sat down in the middle of the line with the toy soldiers and I said to the interpreter, "Tell the officers only to do what I do." There were at least four or five hundred guys in a double line, all seated cross-legged. I sat down and moved up a foot toward the stage. They did what I did. The public people behind us moved as we moved, foot by foot. We were all sitting cross-legged on the ground, sliding along a foot at a time. Imagine fifteen to twenty thousand people wiggling across the grass. We moved the entire stadium right up to the stage. *No* problems.

PETER BARSOTTI: The thing was supposed to open with the marchers doing a circle around the track and the artists coming out on stage. Bill was arguing with this guy. Everything was falling apart. They moved the audience up. All the roses were there but they had thorns in them. The artists were there. We had built this proscenium piece. It was two hands joining and the hands were doves. There was Soviet arm and an American arm, shaking hands. It started ripping down because they didn't put grommets on it and it was falling. I had eight guys trying to tie it back up.

All of a sudden, the final blow was that the marchers started coming in. *Without* a cue. They just started walking in. *No music.* I went, *"Bill. There they are."* I went, *"Bill.* Let's *start* the show." I pressed the music and the tape started and they made it to the front and the little kids came up and planted the flags and the artists came out and threw the roses and all the pigeons and the doves came out and this show started and it was totally, absolutely *wonderful*. The show was really, really everything it was supposed to be in terms of soulfulness and a coming together of the two countries. But it was the hardest time I ever had with Bill.

ALLAN AFFELDT: A lot of people came because they were *supposed* to be there. Because the Peace Committee had invited them to be there: A lot of those people left. By the time we got around to Santana, it was a six-hour show. Which was probably twice as long as any Soviet rock show had ever been. The first time they really woke up was when Bonnie Raitt started jumping around on the stage. Because I'm sure they hadn't seen a woman do something like that before.

STEVE "KILLER" KAHN: It took three or four acts to loosen them up. When the Doobie Brothers were on stage, I was standing there with Bill. Peter and Bill and I and Bob Barsotti, we were all giving each other big hugs. Because we knew we had pulled it off and we were going to make it on time. We were looking out at the crowd and it was getting dark and I said, "You know, Bill. That could be 'Anytown, U.S.A.' out there right now." People were standing and applauding and yelling and we couldn't see the back. The stands were kind of half-empty because the factory workers had left. But the crowd on the field was really ecstatic and they stayed till the end.

BORIS GREBENSHIKOV: Basically, Santana commanded most of the admiration of the crowd. Santana is a name everyone knows in Russia from long years of listening to them. Doobie Brothers band practically were unknown. They were nice. Only that Russians were not familiar with the music. Santana, well, he's closer to Russian consciousness because he kind of presents the spiritual aspects. Doobies are entertainment. Carlos is something spiritual. Russians will usually go for something spiritual. He is so melodic and that is a sign of the spirit.

CARLOS SANTANA: When we finished, they just responded. Their hands were up in the air like they had just received the Holy Spirit or been to a Grateful Dead concert. After the last note was played, after all the bands had played "Give Peace a Chance" and everybody was walking out backstage and all the roses had been thrown, we started hearing all of a sudden, *"San-tan-a! San-tan-a!"* I turned around and looked at Bill and I just started to *cry*. When I heard people who didn't want to go home start chanting *"San-tan-a,"* I broke down. I broke down like a little kid and hid my head and my face in my wife's chest.

BORIS GREBENSHIKOV: I went to the show and I kind of got introduced to Carlos Santana. And in fact, I even talked to Bill Graham for about fifteen seconds. He said, "Yeah, yeah. You should appear on stage singing 'Give Peace a Chance.' " I could not afford to. It would have been a little bit dubious for me to appear as some kind of figure there. It would have seemed to a lot of people that all was as it should have been.

Still, it was the first time I ever saw anything really happen. Real in terms that I'd been listening to all this music for a long, long time and it was the first time I was *seeing* it. I *felt* it in the end.

ALLAN AFFELDT: So we set an important precedent, I think. They learned that the music *isn't* dangerous. That kind of energy isn't really dangerous. It depended on how it was done. They couldn't understand when Bill explained that there were ways of defusing that kind of energy by setting up volleyball courts and things like that, which of course had never been done before.

They really weren't willing to extend in total faith. Even knowing he'd done this thousands of thousands of time all over the world. Because they were convinced that things were different in the Soviet Union and people would behave differently in the Soviet Union. After the show, I think they realized that maybe, just maybe, there isn't any difference.

BILL: At the end of the show, I was standing on the side of the stage. Exhausted. I mean, fucking *drained*. I was hugging my son David, who'd come over to help, and it was very emotional. We had a sign that was a tic-tac-toe board with the words, "OUR CHOICE" above it. There was a globe and a bomb and a globe and a bomb and what was going to be in the last square? A globe or a bomb? At the end of the show, David went across the stage with a globe and patched in the last square. It was something else.

I saw Fedosev coming toward me. He had an American flag in his hand made of cloth on a little stick. And a pen in his other hand. He looked at me, put out his hand, took my hand, and gave me a hug. Now, this was *Mr. Straight*. Then he himself said, without an interpreter, "*Beeel. You wurrrr rriggght. Please sign.*"

Chapter
Twenty-Two

Around the World
for Amnesty

1.

ROBERT GREENFIELD: On less than twenty-four-hour notice, Bill put on
a free concert for U-2 in San Francisco in Justin Herman Plaza down at
the foot of Market Street just across from the Ferry building in the
Embarcadero. The stage was set up at eleven in the morning with the
performance scheduled to begin at noon. With the only notice being an
announcement over the radio, about twenty-five thousand people showed
up.

Everything was going great until Bono decided to spray paint "ROCK
AND ROLL STOPS THE TRAFFIC" on a large piece of art standing in
the square. The city got upset. Bono refused to apologize for what he
considered to be an artistic statement on his part. It was a problem.

There were other problems as well. Bill had demanded that U-2 play
two shows for him on this tour rather than one. The second did not sell
out. There was a lot of discussion about the guarantee and how much
money the band was due. Eventually, it led to a falling out between Bill
and Frank Barsalona. For years, the man who had pioneered the business
of putting on rock shows and the man who had pioneered the business of
being a rock agent had been good friends. Now they were not even talking
to one another.

Winterland Productions, half-owned by CBS Records, was sold for a
huge amount of money to MCA. In San Francisco, Bill helped host a
dazzling benefit for Aid and Comfort, raising nearly half a million dollars
for local AIDS charities. Three months later, Zohn Artman, who for a
while had done everything for Bill, from bringing him racks of suits to

506

select his clothes from to helping him buy his Mercedes and his house, died of AIDS.

As 1987 ended and the New Year began, Bill was wondering whether it was going to be possible for Amnesty International to put on a world tour, journeying to Third World countries where rock had never before been performed. The sheer logistics of such a tour were staggering. And then, of course, there were all the egos involved.

BILL: Money was one problem. The expenses of getting into Third World countries was *so* high. There were the political ramifications. Whether we could do it legally and logistically.

The other problem was the artist commitments. Peter Gabriel and Sting. I had a very tough time convincing the Amnesty people that these two were *not* enough. Because those are *big* names. But when you're talking about sixty- or seventy- or eighty-thousand-seat arenas in Spain or Italy or France, you need a *steak*. Sting had already toured and played around a lot that year. Peter Gabriel had just toured.

I said, "With no disrespect to the artists, you can tell them this to their faces, on the plate, they are veggies. We need a *steak*."

That stayed with us through the entire tour. Peter Gabriel would say, "Ask Bill. I'm just a carrot. Bill wanted a *steak*." We had to get a Michael Jackson. A Springsteen or a Streisand. U-2 said no. They said they weren't going to do it. A lot of time passed but Jack Healey didn't want to believe that.

ROBERT GREENFIELD: It was decided that the tour would be announced in São Paulo, Brazil, on December 10, 1987. Amnesty sent Bill a round-trip ticket so he could attend. Bill flew ten hours from New York to São Paulo. For Bill, it was a great trip. A stewardess who recognized him let him sit upstairs in the 747's first-class lounge. He spent the day in São Paulo, got in a car to the airport, and then flew ten hours back to New York. Upon arrival, he went straight to the office to work.

MARY DALY: We went through the list of the not very many artists who could sell out stadium shows everywhere in the world. It was not a long list. Bruce Springsteen was on the list. As unattainable. Dire Straits. Mark Knopfler was a longtime Amnesty supporter. The problem was that there was *no* Dire Straits at the time. Would they ever work again? Michael Jackson was on the list of course. Write home and weep. A Beatles' reunion would have done it. The Stones. It was a handful. The biggest bands in the world.

BILL: I tried to be very realistic. If we were talking about a plane for the equipment and a plane for the personnel, it was going to be a tremendous sum of money. We were going to go to countries where we could only charge one or two bucks for the people to get in. We were not going to make a lot of money in those places but we *had* to go there.

So we needed to make a *lot* of money in Paris and London in order to balance that out. I said that for every date we did in a place like the Ivory Coast or Zimbabwe, we needed to do one in a city like London to pay for it. They didn't want to hear that.

They said, "*We* don't want to do Japan because *he's* going to release his new album *there. He's* going to release his new video *here.*" I said, "Well, I can't deal with that. We're going to do an *Amnesty* tour. If we're going to do it, let's *really* do it."

I had a long list of things to tell them. All the problems were already there. As rock got bigger, so did the politics. "My greatest hits are being released *there.* I've got *this* video *here.* Wait a minute. *We're* very big *there,* why should *we give* it away?" On and on. I'm not saying this was Sting alone. I don't want to nail him in particular. For now.

I said, "You know what we *really* want to do on this tour? We want to take the human rights issue into countries where people are being deprived of their rights. The only reason to do London is money. New York? *Money.* Philadelphia? *Money.* But unless you go and do shows in New Delhi, Zimbabwe, Costa Rica, and Argentina, I ain't doin' it. I'm not doin' this tour to raise money unless we go into those places."

I sat down with Peter Gabriel and I said, "Peter, the one thing I learned through Bob Geldof is that artist-to-artist is much more successful than me-to-an-artist because I've had to hound these people all my life. It'll be much more effective for you to pursue the 'steak.' " The field had narrowed down to Springsteen, who was scheduled to play for us soon in the Bay Area. Peter, God bless him, came out and talked to Jon Landau.

PETER GABRIEL: I went after Springsteen and didn't manage to get near Bruce. But I hitched a ride back with Jon Landau and bent his ears for an hour. I understood not getting access to Springsteen. Having been in that situation myself. There are so many people wanting to hit on you and Bruce has always had a larger draw. The job in hand is trying to perform for the people and play your music well. You don't want to listen to a hundred hustlers at every show. Even though some of them *may* be your fellow musicians. I was there to hustle.

JON LANDAU: To tell you the truth, my instinct basically from that night was that we *were* going to do it. I mean, I was sold. I was *sold.* I discussed it with Bruce a short time afterward in Seattle. Basically, he was very enthusiastic about it. Although in terms of income for him and the band, it was a *vast* loss. From his point of view, it was not even a blink. He said, "Let's check it out. It sounds really good to me. But let's check it out."

Frank Barsalona has been Bruce's touring agent since 1977. He was very familiar with the last Amnesty tour. So I brought Frank into the picture and I decided to meet with Jack Healey.

JACK HEALEY: Here's where I don't know what to say next. Because the next thing that happened at the end of the meeting was that they would not have Bill run this tour and that was what caused all the problems.

JON LANDAU: That it was going to be an Amnesty tour and not a Bill Graham tour is a summary, or a conclusion that *could* have been drawn. It wasn't expressed that particular way.

BILL: Everything changed. Once Springsteen said yes, everything changed. Because now we had the *steak*. We had the veggies. We had the ticket sales and the media value. I mean, *Springsteen! Sting! Peter Gabriel!* It was like one plus one plus one equaled *eleven!* Springsteen put us on the *big* map. This was now the *World Cup*.

I went to a meeting with Jack Healey and Frank Barsalona in Frank's office. Jon Landau was there for about five seconds then he left. I said, "Let's put *all* our cards on the table. I want to give you people seventy-two hours to think about it. I'll get out. Totally. Landau and Springsteen have been on their own for years and years. They've got their *own* way of doing things. I'll back out."

It was a Friday afternoon and I said, "Take till Monday night, I'll back out. Those guys have another way of running things. I know I've made a commitment that is going to take six months out of my life. I'll only do it if I feel we can all work together."

JON LANDAU: My point of view was, knowing Bruce and believing as they had been telling me that Bruce was the essential element and that they were depending on pulling in Bruce's audience as the cornerstone to being able to play many of these venues, was that we couldn't have artists of this stature, Bruce, Sting, and Peter, come out and do twenty minutes and then have half an hour set change and have somebody else do twenty minutes and have fourteen acts.

Basically, what emerged was a discussion of the idea that instead of trying to put on twenty Live Aids with ten or eleven acts, we should have five artists and the same show and people should be able to play for a good amount of time.

Bruce, Sting, and Peter for more or less an hour and forty-five minutes for Tracy Chapman and Youssou N'Dour. And it was decided that at each country, we should do our best to find some relevant artist of that country. I was absolutely in favor of that.

But we had no problem with Bill being there. *We* never said or did anything or wanted him not to be there. If it had come about that for some reason, Amnesty had contacted us *prior* to hiring Bill, we would have done the tour. We were doing an Amnesty tour. I would not have said, "Well, we better go hire Bill Graham." My attitude was coexistence and professionalism and to communicate when necessary indirectly and resolve issues. In the actual length of the tour, as far as I am concerned from my point of view, Bill and I had not one problem.

JACK HEALEY: Bill didn't really understand what Frank was telling him about the tour. Not a bit. That Amnesty was going to run it. Because how can a little guy like me from a nonprofit run a DC-10, twenty stages in six weeks, and a million people?

MARY DALY: During the "Conspiracy" tour, there was a moment when Paul McGuinness said, "Every ship needs a captain. Bill Graham is the captain of this ship." My understanding is that Landau and Frank Barsalona said, "Every ship needs a captain. Amnesty has to be the captain of the ship."

BILL: I kept insisting on a couple of major points. That in every country, we should get an entertainer who had been active in the human rights movement from that country on the show. There also had to be a balance of Third World and our world dates. Everybody wanted Moscow to be in. I said to Jack over and over again, "I have relationships there with the Soviet Peace Committee." He said, "Bill, the Springsteen people have contacts there. Let *them* work on it." Fine. I kept saying over and over, "Jack, I can get through there." But they wouldn't listen.

We had a promoter chosen in Paris. Springsteen's people wanted to work with a *different* promoter. Jack said, "Bill, we're going with a different promoter there." I said, "Jack, *why?*"

It was the beginning of my realization that whatever *they* said was going to be okay with him.

ROBERT GREENFIELD: The last time Bill had gone out on the road for Amnesty, he had been in total control. The wily shepherd leading a pack of newborn lambs over a very steep and rocky path. Now, a star of epic proportions had entered the mix. Although Bill and Jon Landau never had a harsh word with one another, their methods of doing business could not have been more opposed.

On a day-to-day basis out on the road, Jon Landau preferred all the theatrics to take place *on* stage, preferably while Bruce and the E Street Band were out there tearing it up, rather than in some backstage dressing room where people were too busy arguing to even go out front to watch the show. His management style was designed to ensure that it was Bruce Springsteen who would be the focus of everyone's eye. Not Jon Landau or Bill Graham or anyone else.

There were conflicts over nearly everything. How many shows would be done on the tour, where the shows would be, and how long they would last. Whose stage manager would be in charge. When and where the opening press conference would be held and who would be there. As Elliot Roberts, who was on the tour as Tracy Chapman's manager would say, "Bill had a vision. And every time, it wasn't his vision, Bill took it personally. There was nothing that he *didn't* take personally."

What would have been a difficult tour even under the best of circumstances began for Bill to take on the proportions of a legitimate nightmare.

MARY DALY: It was horrible. The feeling day-to-day was the *meanest*. It was like chalk on the blackboard. It felt like that for about eighty days. There was barely a joyful moment once we got on the road. It was horrible. Only when I was with the artists did I have a good time.

BILL: It's amazing how difficult it is for me to talk about this. Yet at the same time, many of the highest moments of my life were during that tour. In places like Costa Rica, they had never seen a video screen before. To them, production was a guitar in a club. In Costa Rica, we saw people who had *walked* from Guatemala and Honduras. Tickets cost two dollars.

During Springsteen's set, I took a bicycle and rode around the outside of the stadium. That was one of the highlights for me. It was drizzly and cold. I saw maybe fifteen military guys. They had all put their guns against the wall and they were *dancing* arm in arm with each other.

In Barcelona, Peter Gabriel did a twenty-minute version of "In Your Eyes" that was *immense*. I saw a lady and started dancing with her on the side. It was lovely. But none of the good stuff came with the larger group. If I hadn't stood my ground with those people, the shows would never have happened in Costa Rica or New Delhi.

We finished Costa Rica and we were in Montreal after doing a show at Maple Leaf Gardens in Toronto. The only real tour meeting that ever took

place was there in the hotel. All the managers, Jack Healey, and me. Jon
Landau said, "We don't know what's happening in New Delhi. We don't
feel right. We've made a decision among ourselves, Bill, that unless you
go there immediately, we will have to cancel the show."

My one favorite moment on the tour. As Landau said it, I couldn't
resist. Miles Copeland was there. Gail Colson and Jack Healey and Elliot
Roberts as well. I said, *"Fine.* I think the American dates are good
because we have professionals in Philadelphia. I don't have to be in
Oakland or Los Angeles. I'll go to New Delhi tomorrow morning. Under
one condition. If everything works out in New Delhi, it's *my* market."

I said it so seriously that none of them caught on right away. The first
one to break up was Landau. Any shows that went there from now on
would be *mine.* It would be *my* market. I would be the promoter of record
from then on in New Delhi.

I know now they did it to get rid of me. I didn't have a press agent but
the press always liked to talk to me. They didn't want me talking to the
press about what was going on behind the scenes on this tour.

2.

BILL: We were dealing with so many emotional firsts. In every country,
there were various levels of madness. Making sure the police in that
community understood that within the facility, there would be *no* uniforms and *no* weapons. In India, they laughed at me when I first got there
and told them that. They said, "Well, of *course!* What do you mean? How
else do you think we can control that crowd? By a show of force! By *fear!*"

In India, the local branch of Amnesty in New Delhi had made a deal
with the government. They were going to permit the show to come in so
long as it did not push Amnesty. The intermediary was the *Times of
India,* their major newspaper. They were celebrating their hundred and
fiftieth anniversary.

By the time I got to New Delhi, all the street posters and all the
advertising said that these artists were coming there to celebrate the
newspaper's anniversary. There was no human rights message *anywhere.*
The next night on television, I saw a special about the newspaper and the
commentator was sitting there with the logo of the *Times of India* behind
him and he said, "All these great artists are coming here to celebrate
with *us.*" I went insane. I mean, *insane.*

I had Jerry Pompili come from the office in San Francisco to help set
up the media so we could start changing it all around. We held a press
conference and got all the other newspapers together, none of which were
covering the story before. I did interviews with those other newspapers

before the bands got there to let them know this was *not* being done for the *Times of India*.

I had screaming matches with the publishers and editors of the *Times*. It all started out very polite, with everyone saying "Meester Graham. How *are* you?' Three days later, I was saying, *"Rudyard!* I don't give a *fuck* what you think!"

Bob Barsotti came in and he started working with the people out at Nehru Stadium, where they play soccer in New Delhi. It was the only major place that size available to us. Sixty thousand seats. The stadium manager said, "I can't believe we're doing this. Allowing people on the *pitch.* The stage *can't* be on the field. It has to be at the far end."

Not only that but we wanted to let people in three or four hours before the show to get them in off the streets and separate the ticket holders from the nonticket holders. We wanted to put up a couple of volleyball courts. *"Volleyball courts* on the pitch?" He couldn't believe it. We wanted beach balls for the people to throw around and of course they had never heard of that either.

India was incredible for a lot of reasons. We had to bring *everything* in. They did not have stages there. They did not have sound. When the stage was built, there were no power tools. The stage was built without power. They used saws and hammers. No generators. They didn't make them available to us so we didn't have them. Whenever they cut a piece of wood to fit a space, it was two guys with a double-handled saw. *Thousands* of guys, *schlepping.* There were no forklifts. It was all *human* labor.

I was staying on the tenth floor of the Hyatt in New Delhi. When I first got there, I put down my bags and walked over to the window. When I looked straight down, there was a beautiful pool and a hedge of trees maybe fifty feet away. Right on the other side of the hedges—total poverty. Shacks. People pumping water out of a well in the middle of the dry ground.

I watched the male nurse on the tour walk across the street and give away whatever he could. All the soap and shampoo and stuff from his room. A policeman came over and said, "Don't do that." From my room I saw a young man washing his body with the soap. I was convinced that it was the first time he had ever put soap on himself. Maybe it was the second time in his life. Total *poverty.*

All week long, there were meetings. I lowered the ticket price and changed the advertising in the newspapers. On the day of the show, we opened the doors early. The police were outside with these long bamboo sticks they used to hit people just to keep them away. We opened the doors and all these young people came into the stadium and walked onto a pitch for the first time in their lives.

To them, this was *hallowed* ground. I had my guys standing there and they started playing volleyball. It was so far beyond what they thought they would be getting and then we started playing taped music for them. There were ten or fifteen thousand people in there by then and we were getting what we wanted. It was familial and easy. That whole attitude.

At one point, I was walking toward the stage from the back of the field and I couldn't believe my eyes. Four tie-dyed Deadheads were playing Hackey-Sack right in front of the stage. As I walked up, one of them said, "Yo, Bill." They couldn't get into medical school in the States so they were going in New Delhi. It was like being back in Berkeley. "Yo, *Bill!*" In India.

On the day of the show, I wanted Jack Healey to hold a meeting with all the musicians to explain the ruse under which Amnesty had been allowed to come into India. I said, "Jack, you *have* to tell all the musicians about this." He finally agreed to hold a meeting. But he never did.

I saw Jack in the middle of the show that night and I lost it. It was the only time I really lost it on the entire tour. *"You fucking slimy piece of shit!"* I screamed at him. "I want you to *fire* me. I want to *leave*. I gave a commitment to do this thing and I'm not going to *quit*. But I want you to *fire* me. *Fire me*, you *cocksucker!"*

I went crazy and they all saw it. I should have just taken him aside but I didn't. He Jell-O-ed out right in front of me. I said, "Get the fuck out of my sight." Because he *never* stood up to them. Once Bruce came in, he became a groupie.

JACK HEALEY: I just made the decision. The best way to do this was to keep making compromises. To keep it all going and finish it with the team I started. No matter how angry or upset and mad everybody was. Mo matter how hard the schedule was. The best thing I could do was keep everybody on board and let them go to the end. After it was done and a success, let them bitch and moan against the positive framework of the tour.

BILL: Near the end of the show in New Delhi, a guy leaped over the front of the stage and was going to go up the ramp to try to touch Bruce. Jerry Pompili was there and Jerry grabbed the guy. Just as he did, two plainclothes policemen yanked the guy away from him and started dragging him off. I went over as they were taking him out of the stadium and I said, "It's okay. Let *me* deal with it." The guy said, "Please, *meester, meester.* They will *beat* me! They will *beat* me!"

I went with these two guys outside the stadium but they wouldn't let him go. I said, "Excuse me!" The cop just turned and said, "You get *away* from here!" I said, "Don't take him. He was just going on stage." The kid was trembling and begging me, "Don't let them take me to the station. *Please. Please.*"

Finally, I just put my arms around the kid. I said, "If you guys beat him, you're going to have to beat me and I'm the *producer* of this show." It was the only time I ever said that to anyone on that tour. I said, "This is my *passport* and this is *who* I am. This man is *my* responsibility. He didn't do anything to you. All he wanted was to get on stage."

It was written in their faces. They wanted to have the *pleasure* of beating him. When they finally let him go, I took the kid back inside the stadium. He couldn't stop saying, *"Thank you. Thank you.* Thank you." He said, "I just wanted to touch Bruce. You know?"

ROBERT GREENFIELD: After the show in Greece, there was a move by the managers to have the local act in each country removed from the bill. The reason was simple. *Time.* Not since Bruce Springsteen had toured in 1973, opening for Blood, Sweat, and Tears at among other venues, a Bill Graham show at Berkeley Community Theater, had he ever worked on stage with another band. Bruce was accustomed to getting on at eight and finishing somewhere near midnight. In Barcelona, his set began at three-thirty in the morning. Always, he had to be on last because if anybody else followed him, the crowd might leave. It was just as Bill had said before the tour. Bruce was the *steak.* The entire plate belonged to him.

Bill suggested that each musician cut one song from their set to make room for the local artist. After all, for that performer to appear in his own country on such an important show was the event of a lifetime. But there was no compromise offered. In turn, Bill also refused to back down. Instead, he told everyone that if the local act was not permitted to play, as they had been promised they could, with their names already on the posters in each country, he would go to the press and tell them why. It was a threat Bill was fully capable of carrying out.

BILL: I got to Harare in Zimbabwe about two days before the show. I went to the hotel and there was a note there from Allan Affeldt, the guy from the American Peace Walk Committee who had done the Soviet walk. He was there staying with friends. They found this businessman who owned his own two-seater plane and he took me out to Victoria Falls. We flew over herds of deer and gazelles and giraffe. We flew over lakes where there were *millions* of birds. Swans and geese. The numbers were ridiculous.

I looked out and there was Victoria Falls. We flew into the mist and then we caught the sound. The wave of the sound. We were minuscule. For a moment, I was afraid that it would suck us in. Then we went up again the next morning so we could see sunrise over the falls. It was beyond belief. The scope of it. Compared to Victoria, Niagara is *nothing*. It was beyond anything I had ever seen.

It was the only day, the only space of time on the entire tour, when I wasn't miserable. Every other day, I had to see those people. Every other day, I had to deal with their attitudes toward me. Knowing I had to deal with those people every day made it unbearable for me to get up in the morning.

Now, Youssou N'Dour is from Senegal. For Abidjan in the Ivory Coast, he kept saying, "Bill, I'll get the local act. I'll get the local act." For weeks, I said, "Youssou, who's the act?" And he said, "I will get him. I assure you. *Je n'oublie pas.* Don't worry."

We got to the Ivory Coast the day before the show in Abidjan. He *still* hadn't picked the act. I said to Jack Healey, "Jack, you get to the press conference and I'm telling you right now, somebody in the audience is going to say, 'Who's the local act?' " He said, "Ah, Bill. . ." I said, "Jack, I'm telling you. It's going to happen."

We got to the press conference, Sting and Bruce and Peter Gabriel, and Jack and the local Amnesty guy. The first question? "I am from the local independent TV station. Who is the local act?" The press people were all looking at one another, saying, "How can you insult us by not having one in this country?" Sting said, "Where's the local act, Jack? There's no local act? Let's put a local act on." Springsteen said, "Yeah, hey. Let's get somebody, man. We'd like to hear some of *your* great music."

What else were they going to do? It was very embarrassing for them because for the first time on the whole tour, there *was* no local act. When the press conference was over, I spoke with Jules Frutos, the French promoter in Abidjan, and I said, "Get me some tapes of the local acts." During the night, I listened to them. We got in touch with a guy named Isaac Ishmael. Done. He accepted the offer to play. I said to Jules, "Call George Travis and tell him we found the artist." George Travis was Springsteen's stage manager. The one brought in to replace Michael Ahearn as stage manager for the tour.

The show was set to start at two the next afternoon. At one o'clock, I saw George Travis come over to where Jules Frutos was standing. He said to him, "Just make sure to play a lot of *local* tapes in between the acts."

Instead of our regular tapes. That, in his mind, meant that the audience would hear the local act. Without the local act *being* on the show.

I went bonkers. He had no intention of letting Isaac Ishmael play. I went to him and I said, "George, why are you doing this? There's a local act here, ready to play." He said, "Well, I don't know *what* you got us into this time." I said, "George, we're not going to have any words." And we never did. I called the hotel. I asked Gail Colson to find Peter Gabriel and get him down to the show. I said, "We're going to have a riot. We are going to have a riot. You know why? *I'm* going to create one."

Peter Gabriel came down to the facility. I said, "Peter, this is the situation. The act is here. You have to tell Bruce and the other artists that this act *is* going to play." Peter did that. What was Bruce going to say? Of course, he was going to say yes. The guy played and all the musicians went out to watch him. He blew everybody away. Most of all, Bruce. Who watched his *entire* set.

A few days later, we were having this press conference in São Paulo, Brazil, and they said to Springsteen, "How did you like going to each of these countries?" And he said, "Yeah, man. A couple nights ago in Abidjan, I saw this *guy*. I thought it was *Wilson Pickett*, man!"

3.

JON LANDAU: Nobody went on that tour for fun. It was fun in a certain way but it was a brutal, punishing experience. Somebody said to Sting at the first press conference, "Aren't you guys just a bunch of rock stars doing this for publicity?" And Sting said, "Yeah. Me, Bruce Springsteen, and Peter Gabriel, we really need publicity, you know?" Like, there are easier ways to do it.

PETER GABRIEL: There were quite a lot of arguments. I would go and sit by Bill in a lot of the fights and then try and sit by Jack or George Travis. I mean, whoever it was, I was trying to play the role of peacemaker at times. Which was not the easiest task.

I remember Jack actually said to Mary Daly and I, "Can you have a word with Bill, because he looks suicidal." And at times, you know, he did. For all of us, musicians, crew, Amnesty people, there were two driving forces. The cause and the ego. We were continuously driven by both masters. I think all of us. When cause and ego were locked together in the same direction, it was unstoppable.

JACK HEALEY: The goal was to get to Argentina and celebrate the Human Rights Declaration with the Argentineans and we did it. When it was over, I really didn't give a shit in a way about how I felt or any of it. It got done. Everybody was angry. Everybody was depressed. Everybody was mad at me.

But that's okay. Because it ain't all *that* bad. Human rights *is* improved. We signaled the improvement around the world. We were almost a prophet of things getting better. Except for the Chinese, look how much better the world is now.

BILL: The Amnesty Tour was such a compressed version of so many things that have happened over the years that I really can't even talk about it. It's not that I'm afraid of offending anyone. Because if I did say everything, a lot of these people would *never* work with us again.

The way I was treated, the way other people were treated, the people who took the bows and the credit. The way certain people looked to the world and who they *really* were. I never want credit for what I didn't do. And I have never minded getting credit for what I *have* done. People who did nothing got credit for doing things they *never* did. My main concern was to keep my word and make it go. No single project in my life ever saddened me more or exhausted me as much.

Simply because of what happened to so many people when they got into the big ball game. Relative to the way they would stand and talk and relate to other people. I really don't want to always yell at the world that I am right and they are wrong. But in this case, *so* many people were wrong. The abuse of power on a high level was unparalleled. The world out there said, "*Boy!* What a *great* tour!" And they were right. But what a *price*.

Chapter
Twenty-Three

Breakdown

1.

ROBERT GREENFIELD: For Bill, Amnesty International was the single most difficult professional experience of his life. It represented the clearest proof yet that the business he had helped create had somehow gotten away from him. The harder he squeezed down on what had once fit so comfortably into the palm of his hand, the more it seemed to change shape and direction, eluding his grasp like something that from now on would remain forever out of reach, just beyond his control.

JON LANDAU: I see Bill as the inventor. The entrepreneur. That person is always a creative person, which Bill is, with a creative temperament and a creative ego. Okay. But here's what happens when something is invented. Henry Ford invents the automobile. Then the process moves from the entrepreneur-inventor. It moves out into large numbers of people and it becomes a profession. Henry Ford, who started the car business, would fail at the car business if he tried to be in it today.

ROBERT GREENFIELD: Even as Bill suffered through the Amnesty International Tour, he was doing his best to take care of business on the side. Unbeknownst to anyone else, when Bill left the tour in Montreal, he did not go straight to India. Instead, he flew to San Francisco and then to Australia where he joined Mick Jagger, then touring there under the aegis of Bill's company. The two had dinner in Brisbane. Bill then flew from Australia to New Delhi, rejoining the tour in time to go from New Delhi to Athens to Zimbabwe.

When the Amnesty International tour ended, Bill could not fly direct from Buenos Aires to Sydney to rejoin the Mick Jagger tour. So he went charter with Amnesty from Buenos Aires to New York and took a commercial flight from New York to San Francisco, where he went to the office to work for seven hours. He then flew to Maui to see his son Alex. From Maui, Bill flew first to Sydney and then Melbourne in order to join Jagger, who was about to complete his tour by going on to perform in Djakarta, Indonesia, and Auckland, New Zealand.

Essentially, Bill flew for thirty-eight hours nonstop. He was fifty-eight years old at the time. Bill always claimed that he did not suffer from jet lag. Unlike other people, it simply did not affect him. At least that was what he said.

The following summer, The Who were on the road again in America. Six months earlier in England, I had sat across from Pete Townshend in a cold, drafty room outside his recording studio on the river in Twickenham on the day that Roy Orbison died, listening as he told me how he would not be going over with The Who to tour America one last time even if it *was* the twenty-fifth anniversary of the band. Once the tour began, reports indicated that the three original band members would each take home between twenty-five and thirty million dollars each. It seemed reason enough for anyone to change their mind.

Seeing how well The Who had done for themselves in America, Mick Jagger and Keith Richards somehow managed to patch up their differences. Because it was only rock and roll and a business after all, they buried the hatchet and began working together on yet another album. The buzz was that they would soon tour again.

Based on what he had done for the Stones in America and Europe in 1981 and 1982 as well for Mick Jagger as a solo act on tours in both Japan and the South Pacific, Bill figured for certain that he would get the Stones' American tour. How could he not?

Even those in the business who had no great affection left for Bill saw it as a perfect match. The chaos and energy of the last, great sixties band out on the road in America with the man who had more or less invented the form. But for Bill, it did not happen that way at all.

BILL: A few weeks ago, I started to see a psychiatrist three times a week. I wanted to try to understand the extent of the despair and the depression I'd been feeling for months. Before that period, I wasn't feeling well. But when I got the news about losing the Stones' tour, and about how it went down, things got progressively worse. I was already feeling very badly before but I hadn't *cracked*.

What kicked off the problem was my beginning to take sleeping pills in 1985, doubling the dose in 1988, and the effect that had on my thinking. The pills were Halcion, given to me on a doctor's prescription.

Our childhoods affect us all. We don't know how but it affects us. It dictates what happens later on to some extent. In my life, I haven't had that balance of pleasure and joy. I saw a priest on television the other night talking about the difference between pleasure and joy. Pleasure you can get from material things and things you do. Joy you receive out of a relationship. You have a baby, that brings you joy. Twenty years later when the child graduates from college, it gives you joy. Eating ice cream is pleasure. Buying a house is pleasure. In my life, I haven't had that much joy.

I've traced it pretty much to the combination of three things happening. The fire at the office. Then Live Aid. And the final breakup with Regina Cartwright, the longest ongoing relationship I'd ever had with a woman. In the fall of 1984, she asked me to marry her but I said, "Let's go our separate ways." We did and then she began another relationship, which I found out about. It was a very trying time.

The combination of those three things, my problems in that relationship and the guilt I felt about my inability to complete that relationship, the fire, and Live Aid all at the same time, did it. During that time period, what with the ARMS tour in 1984, Live Aid in 1985, Amnesty U.S.A. in 1986, Russia in 1987, during the greatest years of expansion of my company, I busied myself with things that were never financially rewarding. Things that had nothing to do with money. I was looking for a means of escape.

The whole issue of the Rolling Stones going out on tour started when Joe Rascoff called up. Rupert Lowenstein is the financial adviser to the Rolling Stones and has been for years. I like to refer to him as "the Rotund Abacus." He lives in London. Joe Rascoff is their American representative. He and a man named Bill Zysblat were involved with the Stones before and now they're partners. On the 1981 and 1982 tours, Bill "Zee" was pretty much the tour accountant and Joe was the man above him.

Joe Rascoff called and said, "They're going to go on tour. Bill, the situation is that there's another organization bidding to do it." I didn't really know what he was talking about. He said, "You should consider whether or not you want to make a bid to *buy* the tour. Because we already have an offer." Which had never happened before. I have never *bought* a tour. He said, "If you want to bid, go ahead."

I said, "I don't know what you're talking about."

He said, "You have ten days to get a bid together. We'll have a sponsor. I don't think you'll be able to beat these numbers and I'm not telling you what they are. If you buy the tour, you'll have to guarantee ticket sales and merchandise and so on."

In other words, there was an organization somewhere that was willing to put up "X" number of dollars for all the gigs, the merchandising, and the pay-per-view television rights for the final show. They told me they might do between fifty and sixty dates, not starting until September 1.

Joe said, "Bill, Mick and the guys love and respect you and they want to see the extent of your desire to be involved."

The one thing I couldn't put together was *who* we were bidding against. Jerry Weintraub maybe. Or Michael Cohl. There were only four or five names we could come up within the industry. Rascoff wouldn't give us any leads. He kept saying, "You don't know them directly." It was like Jackie Mason. Did we know them *indirectly*? There was never a helping hand.

All this came as a surprise to me because I assumed we'd done such a great job with the Stones in America in '81 and then again more in '82. My company had then taken Mick on his solo tour to Japan. At the time, I didn't realize that my problems with the Stones may have started there. Now, I also realize that I didn't apply a grain of creative thinking to the process of coming up with a bid for the tour. *None.*

People had already begun to tell me about Halcion. But I didn't heed anybody's warning. They said I had to be careful with those pills. But I said, "Then why would a *doctor* allow me to take them?" When things got heavier about a year and a half ago, I doubled up. I would take *two* a night. With the Halcion, I never had trouble sleeping. When I woke up, I didn't know I wasn't clear. But I was lethargic in my thinking. I felt heavy-headed. As time passed over the last few years, I got fewer phone calls at home. Whenever I had any time off, I would just stay home all the time. I didn't go out at all. But I never realized it was because of the pills.

I took them every night. When I had to double up, there was never a challenge from the doctor saying, "You *shouldn't* do that. You *can't* do that." Jan Simmons showed me some articles about Halcion and how it could affect your character. But I felt that I hadn't lost anything to it. What could it do to *me?* It was almost like *Notorious* with Cary Grant and Ingrid Bergman. Until she got very sick from the poisoned coffee, she didn't know anything was wrong.

For me, they were a great solution. Whenever I wanted to go to sleep, I could take those things. Twenty minutes later, I would be asleep. Eight hours later, I'd wake up and I was ready to *burn* again. I was ready to go out there and *work*. Even though once I was out there, I would find myself asking "Why is my life this way? *Why?*" I was depressed all the time but I did not know why.

At the end of the Amnesty International tour, I joined Jagger's solo tour for the last week. While we were in Djakarta, Indonesia, Rupert Lowenstein asked me up to his suite and said, "Bill, we really ought to work together with Mick and Keith." He was warm and friendly and said, "You'll be out there with us when we go." I felt very good about the whole thing.

While I was out with Amnesty when I belonged on Jagger's tour, I never thought, "Oh, Mick will fire me." I called and spoke to him a couple of times and said, "I hope you understand, Mick. I made a commitment to these people and though as it is, I feel that I have to see it through." He said, "Well, then *when* will I see you?" He was very decent about it and I never thought, "Oh, my God, I should be there with him *now*." Mick Brigden and Jan Simmons were there in my place. The Australian promoter was also very efficient, so I never thought of the consequences. But I should have.

When the call from Rascoff came, he said, "We want your bid within ten days. I'm going back down to Barbados where they're starting rehearsals."

I said, "My *God!* How much time did the *other* people have? You're giving me *just* ten days?"

I asked him all kinds of questions and then I called Mick in Barbados. I said, "I just want to let you know what happened here. I was asked to bid on the tour. This is a surprise to me but it's *your* life. When I make my bid, understand, I only have ten days, I want to be able to talk to you *directly*. I was to come down and see you, rather than just put it on a piece of paper."

He said, "Sure, Bill. Let me know when."

I felt very relieved by that. The following week, Rupert and Rascoff went down there. Rascoff called and said, "Can you come down right away?" It turned out the other people had gone down there and made their pitch but it had not gone too well. Mick still wanted to see me.

I got a map and marked off the cities I thought they should play. I got some notes ready as a presentation but it wasn't formal or fancy. I wasn't creative in the sense of what we *could* have done. I never dealt with the one issue that was going to be a roadblock for us all the way.

Before I went down there, we got wind of who the other party was. A promoter. Concert Productions, International, CPI. An outfit based out of Toronto which pretty much controls Canada. They're partially owned by a beer company. The people bidding to buy the tour was this organization and the mother sponsor would be Labatt's Beer.

In time, we got to know that Labatt's was not that heavily distributed in the United States. But a beer called Rolling Rock was sold on the East Coast and that would in fact be the product pushed as the tour sponsor. Rolling Rock. Because of the connection. Rolling *Rock*. Rolling *Stones*.

On the phone, Rascoff said, "Don't worry about the sponsor, Bill. The deal we're getting, you *can't* match. Their numbers are *so* incredible."

I said, "What's the sense of me even going to get one?"

He said, *"Don't."*

I said, "Are you telling me that if my numbers for tickets are good enough, you'll use me for that *only?*"

He said, "Well, Bill, that's the way it is."

I kept on saying, "But I'm the *incumbent*, Joe. We're the ones who did it *before*. If there was any dislike of me, you would not be calling me. You must be getting instructions from Mick and the group saying, 'Get a bid from Bill.' Or, *'Don't* take the other guy's bid.' "

During my first conversations with Joe, I began to get an inkling that something was wrong there. He kept saying, "We didn't approach these people. This thing came out of nowhere, Bill." I said, "Joe, but you *accepted*. When they came to you, why didn't you say, 'You want to bid on our tour? *This* is our team. The Rolling Stones, Rupert, Rascoff, *and* Bill Graham.' "

They could have hired us directly and paid me or the promoters could have paid me to do the tour. I kept saying, "If the Stones don't want to use our services, tell me. But if there's a favorable relationship, why not *maximize* it now?" My preference was that the Stones *not* have a sponsor. Jovan sponsored them in 1981 and I didn't think it was right then. I also did not like the fact that if these people owned the tour and cut all the local guys into their deal, each promoter would make less than in the past because the pie was being cut another time. I began to realize that Rupert and Rascoff were middling me out.

Nick Clainos and I flew to Barbados and I made a presentation. The Stones were in the studio but the only ones down there then were Mick and Keith. Keith's wife came down and he disappeared. For the two and half days I was there, I never saw him. The meeting took place with me, Mick, Nick Clainos, Rupert, Rascoff, and John Branca, their lawyer from L.A.

In Barbados, I told them I thought they didn't need a sponsor but if they wanted to get one, go right ahead. I made a bid based on fifty shows. Later, it turned out they wanted to do sixty. In the conversation, they said, "We're willing to play until December 15." I said, "My *God*. That's *sixty* shows. The numbers could go up to *three* million tickets."

A week before Barbados, I was at the Rock and Roll Hall of Fame awards dinner in New York. Mick and Keith were there and they were decent. But I felt Rupert and Rascoff being *cold. Ice.* I said, "Hello, how are you?" "Mmmm, all right. Thank you, Bill." A very distant attitude.

I came back from Barbados to San Francisco. I thought the meeting down there had gone very well. Charlie Watts showed up on the second day and he was very nice and Mick and I had dinner that night. I came home and I still didn't feel right. Over the phone, I said to Rascoff, "It doesn't feel right. I don't know what I'm doing. Why if I'm bidding against someone else can't I bid on the merchandise? Give me guidance on the number of tickets and the ticket price."

He kept saying, "Well, we're not sure yet, Bill."

Within a day or two, the Grammys were in L.A. It was agreed that Rupert and Rascoff would see me in L.A. and then they would fill Keith in. Rupert has a home in Beverly Hills. I took the limo and went there. Rupert and Rascoff *only* were there. No Keith. They said very clearly, "Bill, the boys care for you. They have great respect for you and fond memories of you. However, the numbers are just too big. There is just no way you can match those numbers."

I kept saying, *"What* are those numbers? What *are* those numbers?" They wouldn't tell me. Rascoff said, "This is what we've decided. They still want to avail themselves of your services." Rupert mentioned the amount. It was fifty thousand dollars a month for ten months. March through December. They said very clearly, "Bill, we're not interested in *anyone* in your company. This will *not* become a Bill Graham tour. The guys want you to be involved in the *creative* areas. We would like you to be involved as a creative consultant."

I said, "Why wouldn't you want me to be involved in the ticket pricing, who the promoters are, where we play, and who else plays?"

They said, "If you have some input, fine. But that's not your responsibility."

I said, "Whose responsibility will it be?"

Rascoff said, "There'll be other people buying the tour and I will be involved."

I said, "Well, Joe. Are *you* going to guide the tour? Is that what you're saying?"

He said, "Bill, here's the offer." But they had great difficulty trying to lay it out. They said, "The guys want you to be available to them as a creative consultant in those areas that need creative decisions." They kept saying over and over, "Please understand what the offer is. There's no disrespect here. We're not hiring your *company.* The offer is for your services as an *individual.*"

I said, "Would you expect me to be on every date?"

Rascoff said, "Bill, that's really up to you. You're a professional. You know when to be there and when *not* to be there."

I said, "I can't believe you're making me this offer."

And Rupert kept on saying, "Bill, there's no way you can match their numbers."

I was blown away. I thought the presentation in Barbados had gone okay. Thirty pages of suggestions that I showed them, which I'd done on a day's notice. I said, "That's not what I was pitching for. If I think the routing is going the wrong way, I don't have any input there. It doesn't make any sense. You wouldn't be offering me a half a million dollars for my personal services if the group didn't want me involved." I said, "I don't think Mick is saying, 'Let's not have Bill involved.' I think you guys are not standing up for me. My guess is after Barbados, you were told, 'See if you can make this happen.' "

I told them that if we could not strike a deal for me to do the whole tour, why not let me be the tour director? Even though it would be my second choice. "Forget the title." I said, "That isn't important. Just let me do what I did that last time under *their* umbrella. Let them put up the money. But let *me* do the tour." My guess was that the Stones would pay me.

The Stones themselves had made me *this* offer. Because the other guy didn't want me involved at all. Rupert and Rascoff must have said to the other guy, "We've got a slight problem here. The Stones want Bill involved." When they could have said, "Bill is on *our* team. Let's work all this out." The truth was that Rupert and Rascoff wanted to run the tour and then said to Mick, "This is a problem. How can we work this out?" Mick turned to them and said, "Can't you work it out somehow?" And they both came up with this idea. "You want Bill? What if we get the best of both worlds? *Their* money *and* Bill's creativity."

The amount of money they offered me was *very* generous. In a sense, it was a good offer. But I never answered them.

I didn't feel like I was connecting. I knew I was losing something but I didn't understand why. If Mick wanted me involved, why all this distance? I was emotionally fried.

I flew to Europe. I said to myself, "I'll go there on some other things." I got to London and I called Mick at his home and I said, "Mick, I happen to be here. I'm just wondering. Are you going back in the next couple of days?"

He said, "Tomorrow night, or the night after, I'm flying back to New York."

I said, "Would you mind if I flew back with you? I'd like some of your time and I know how valuable that is. So, can I fly back with you?"

He said, "Of course."

That was what I wanted to do. I met him at the airport. We sat together and he listened to everything I had to say. I went through my thirty pages of notes. I said, "Tickets are not a problem. You're going to be *so* big. But it's the *way* you do it, Mick. It's the *style*."

The Concorde was delayed, so we sat in the first-class lounge. He said to me, "Bill, you've got to understand, this offer we were given is so huge that I don't think you could match it."

I said, "Whatever it is, let me know the number."

He said, "The other guys in the band haven't been as fortunate as I have. I want to get out and do this for them. I've been told the difference between your number and theirs is *millions*."

I said, "Mick, I don't have a sponsorship number. I don't have a pay-per-view number."

Point blank later on the plane, I said to him, "I don't think you should go out with that kind of a sponsor. It doesn't make sense."

He said, "Well, it's only 'Rolling Rock.' A minor name. So we won't be held under such scrutiny. It'll be a smaller label."

I went through possible support acts. I had started to talk about Guns 'n' Roses in Barbados. I had given them a list. INXS. Living Colour. But make it hip and young and *kick ass*. Let there be an opening act and a second act. Do an hour, take a break, and do another hour. If you can't do two hours straight as the Stones. I talked about the tea party. We would hold a press conference in Boston Harbor to kick off the tour on a ship with all the press there. It would be the rock and roll equivalent of the Boston Tea Party for the press.

At one point on the plane, I said, "I can't tell you to think about the money the way I do. I can't tell you to have the same values I do. You're the Rolling Stones. Yet the numbers will be so big that if you go out with these other people *or* with me, you'll *each* make sixteen or eighteen million. What's the difference?"

He looked at me and he said. "Well, *two* million dollars."

There *is* a difference between sixteen cents and eighteen cents. There *is* a difference between sixteen dollars and eighteen dollars. What's the difference between sixteen million and eighteen *million?* He kept saying, "Bill, it's not me. It's the other guys." Then he finally said, "Bill, you don't understand. I'm only doing this tour for one reason. The *money*. And the numbers will be better the other way."

I kept saying, "Let *me* do the tour. The way we did before. If you do use these other people, let me run it and you'll still make all that money. If you do take a sponsor, I would fight to keep their signs off the stage. Let me do it being involved in all these areas and don't pay me till it's over. Shake my hand. At the end of the tour, you guys pay me whatever you want. I want to prove to you that while I'm not saying it's wrong for you to do it only for the money, *I'm* not doing it for the money. It's only a secondary reason for me."

He made a lot of notes. My first choice was, "Me and you guys." Second choice, "Use those guys and let *me* direct the tour." Third, "If those two didn't work, creative consulting." What I was gambling on was that I would never have to go to that.

We had a very good, warm three and a half hours on the plane. We got off and he said, "I'll let you know, Bill." The biggest point he agreed to on the plane was to do me a favor. He said he would get Rupert and Rascoff to finally tell me the number. I said, "If I can match that number, let me have my shot."

He said, "I don't know why you *can't* have it."

I said, "Tell them. Just give me that number."

Because I was going to raise the money from all the promoters. That was when he hinted, "Well, I think there's a problem with Rupert."

I said, "Can I call Rupert? I'll call him and I'll be glad to talk to him and find out what it is. He may have a problem with me but let's air it out. I have no problem with him."

Mick said he would be staying in New York for a day and then going to Barbados. He said he would call Rascoff and Rupert. He said, "Where will you be, Bill?" I said, "I'll be in New York until I talk to you." He said, "Stay in New York. Rascoff will call you tonight or tomorrow and you'll get the numbers."

When I left the plane, I was totally confident. *Totally.* One way or the other, I was going to get it. On the plane, I'd worked it out that they could do so many more shows and sell so many more tickets that they could gross a *hundred* million dollars. I got home in New York to my apartment. I called Nick Clainos. I was on the phone with Nick when the other phone rang. It was Rascoff. He said, "Bill, I heard you were in London with Mick. I just got off the phone with him. I don't know what you're looking for. I don't know why you don't understand."

I said, "Don't understand *what?*"

He said, "Their numbers are just too big, Bill. It's done."

I said, "It *can't* be done. Mick told me that it's *not* done. The numbers are huge but that he would instruct you to give me the numbers."

He said, "Bill. You know Mick. He has a certain position to maintain. It may have been difficult for him to get out of it on the plane. *Bill.* It's *done.*"

I said, "He told me the deal isn't done. It's not signed."

He said, "It's not signed. But their numbers are too big. Mick wants you involved. We made you an offer in L.A. You didn't answer."

That was when I flew back to San Francisco. When I got back there, Gregg Perloff walked into my office. He had just gotten a phone call. People in Canada were calling stadiums for availabilities. I said, "They must be jumping the gun. Because I know the tour hasn't been awarded yet."

I called Rascoff. I said, "Joe, I don't understand this. Mick tells me the deal hasn't been made. You tell me the money's too big but it's not really done yet and yet they're already calling stadiums. This is an example where by not having me involved, you and I already disagree in how this should be done. Call the *promoters*, not the stadiums, to get the local avails. Let *them* do their jobs. Let them keep their part."

There was a pause. He said, "Bill, you see, here's the first example already of the problems we're going to have."

I let him have it. I said, "What I think is happening Joe, is *you*. And Rupert. You both want a bigger piece of the pie. The more work you guys do, the bigger it will be. You're going to prove that you can do this. These promoters are the reason these stadiums are safe to play in each city. You want to bring in this other promoter who will overshadow them."

That was when I sent the letter. The letter started by saying, "I'm writing to you again because it's hard for me to believe that this is now a closed issue." I said, "I'll do either one. Give me a shot at buying the tour. If not, let me be the guy under their umbrella. Or, I'll do *that* job." Because what I had realized during the agony of doing Amnesty around the world was that I could not be under the thumb of people who did not approach these things the way I would. If I was to have no real say in the Stones tour, I would go through madness. Which I had not understood until Amnesty International.

A few days later, I had an appointment to meet with John Fogerty in my office. We were in the middle of a conversation about old times and I went to the bathroom. On my way back through, I said, "Any calls, Jan?" Jan Simmons said, "Well, I didn't want to show you this until the meeting was over with John." She showed me this *fax*. In so many words, it said, "We're sorry it's taken this long, Bill, and we're sorry that it's not going to end up being the way you hoped that it would be when you came to Barbados. We're sorry it's not going to be the way you would have wanted to do this tour but we have decided to go about our business in a different way. Looking forward to seeing you in San Francisco." It was signed by every member of the group.

When that happened, my bubble burst. I had been burned out to some extent up until then. I had been in an emotional frenzy for the last few years prior to this. I took it for granted that I would be working together with the Stones because I'd done my job so well last time. This was going to be a return to creative work in friendly waters. A chance for the company to express itself and *fun*. Everybody would have won.

From that moment in March until June, I had an experience the likes of which I never had before. I was able to do *nothing*. I became inefficient and incapable. Some days, I couldn't go to the office. Even when I did, I couldn't function. I couldn't read. Anybody who came into my office, I was afraid they would ask me for a decision. I reached the point where I was taking two pills a night and I *still* was not able to sleep. *With* the two.

Then I began to realize, "Why am I this way? What has happened to me? Why was I not able to make these people understand?" Part of it had to be that I wasn't there with Mick in Australia on his tour. I wasn't there for most of the dates. I missed a month. Another part was how Rupert felt about me. Had I thought about it more and not been as lethargic, I would have created a relationship of sorts with Rupert.

Those three months were my first experience ever of not being able to function at all. At *all*. *Totally* dysfunctional. During that period, I went two and three days at a time without sleep. No sleep at all. I would stay up all night watching television. I became an absolute TV junkie. Because I couldn't read. I would read the same line *five* times. I had no attention span.

I began to think, "What got me to being this way?" The crusher was the Stones decision. But then I realized what led up to it. The fire, Live Aid, my relationships with women. It had already begun taking its toll during Amnesty International. My strength has always been confidence in myself and faith in my abilities. But now I felt almost powerless.

During the months after I lost the Stones tour, I thought about suicide many times. For the first time in my life, it seemed like a choice. I realized I'd spent my entire life not facing up to some serious personal problems relating to my childhood. There was obviously guilt that I'd survived while others didn't. Because of that guilt, I always had to do *something*. During those months, my day-to-day life was unbearable. I could not play racquetball. I would get up in the morning and then I would watch TV or go to work. I got into habits I'd never had in my life. Watching TV on a Wednesday afternoon at my house in the dark in my room. I cannot tell you the agony of those months.

I'd go to the office and not do anything. I'd come home and go to no parties. When I was in the office, it was very difficult for me to relate to what people wanted me to do. I was afraid of making any decisions because I felt totally inept. I was not functioning. They had shot me down in public. The public was told that Bill Graham had let a sixty-million-dollar tour slip through his fingers. That was in *Rolling Stone* magazine. And that was not the truth!

For the first time in twenty-four years, the world was being told that in the business sense, I was a loser. My definition of madness is those months. I was ready to be committed to full-time care. I told that to my doctor. If he thought that would be better. Because I could not function out there.

What's wrong? What's wrong? What's wrong? That's what I asked myself all of the time.

The maddest part of those months was not being able to bury the could-have-beens. What I wanted to do was take those people on the road. I could have given my son David a job on the Stones tour. They would probably have been rehearsing in New York and we could have been back there in the summer and my son Alex would have been there and Killer would have had the plane and we would have been able to scout stadiums and have some adventures. When the guys were rehearsing in Massachusetts, I could have said, "Mick? Keith? You want to fly down?" Because of the plane, we would not have been stuck up there. On Friday night, we could have come to New York and gone to Fire Island or wherever we wanted.

Nineteen eighty-one was like a caper. And this would have been another one. I kept thinking about how we would do the opening press conference. *Ideas. Ideas. Ideas.* All those months, they just kept pounding away at me. I imagined how when the dates were put up for sale in the parking lot of Oakland Coliseum, nothing would be said to anybody. People would be driving home at nine o'clock at night and what would appear in the parking lot of Oakland Coliseum would be the hologram of the tongue. The Stones logo. We would tell the media to check it out. The *tongue.*

And that is how we would announce the date. That would be the announcement that the tickets were on sale. Right there—9 P.M. That night. No warning. A sign in the sky. No name. Never use the name. Just the tongue. When the kids came to buy tickets, they could buy a shirt. On the back, it would say the date. For three months, you would have had thousands of walking ads. People wearing that shirt. With the date of the concert. Then we could sell *more* shirts at the show when they came back. Those first shirts would replace the newspaper ads. Not one ad.

The Stones would be *news.* No ads. Maybe a billboard in L.A. with just the tongue. It would say *"COMING SOON"* like a movie. Late one Saturday night in June, before the tour started, at maybe eleven or twelve o'clock, I started writing these things down. I hadn't had a creative moment since that fax came in. When I lost the Stones tour, I even stopped taking my three-by-fives around. I wasn't *seeing* things anymore. That night, I solved all the tour money problems. I solved all the sponsorship problems.

I was going to call them the very next day. I knew they were already totally signed. But I figured out how I could get them out of that deal and make them a *new* deal. Nobody could have come close to the number I was going to offer them then. My number was another 50 percent *higher* than anybody else's. I had thought it all out. The guys in Canada hadn't done any real work yet. They could still promote the shows in Canada to make their money. There was ten million dollars there.

The Stones could have done *eight* Jerseys. *Three* Philadelphias. *Five* L.A.'s. The first call would have been from Nick Clainos to Rascoff. They're being guaranteed sixty-five million dollars? I was going to give them a *hundred and twenty-five million*. *Twice* as much, *guaranteed*.

If I'd done the tour, in each city, we would have found something that needed fixing. We would have landed at the airport for the press conference. The Stones would have said, "We're glad to be in Detroit and the hundred thousand dollars goes to . . ." In each city, they would have given away a hundred thousand dollars, which is six and a half million dollars. *Peanuts*. One of the ways we would have gotten this money is that I had a sponsor idea that *couldn't miss*.

Hyatt Hotels. The Pritzker boys. They would have *died* to do it. They could have given us five million dollars of hotel space. We would have saved three million in hotel bills for two hundred people on the road. In each city, we would have stayed at a Hyatt. They would have gotten off the plane at the airport, the podium at the press conference would have said *"Hyatt."* Classy. Clean. I did it all in one night. That was what the sleeping pills had taken away. In Barbados, I didn't have my *chops*. I was taking two pills a night. I didn't have my *fastball*.

The way I had it worked out, the Rolling Stones would have done all these stadiums in November and December, either in hot areas or under domes. Every day a stadium date. The field festival seating and the stands reserved. *Not* with beer for a sponsor. The Surgeon General had said he did not want famous people to endorse beer or beer consumption. What if a kid on his way home from a Stone's show crashed his car and he was drunk? *Beer! Stones!*

They wanted to do this thing with sponsorship, do it with *Hyatt*. The airline that took them from city to city? *Donald Trump*. Give us five planes that we can use. Two cargo planes, two crew planes, and the Stones plane. Wherever the Stones go, it says on the nose of the plane, *"Trump"* right over the tongue. Or United. *"United"* and the tongue. The entire planet is made up of Stones fans. The guys who are now vice presidents and presidents of companies are fans of the Stones.

The whole tour should have been filmed. Really do a docudrama. Get Chicago and Detroit in there. A live tour album. A tour video. That would have been *millions* of dollars. The final show? Bring in all the greats somewhere. A grand finale in the Meadowlands. Close-circuit it throughout the world. I had the staff. Michael Ahern. Mick Brigden. Jan Simmons. Peter Barsotti backstage. Bob Barsotti, front of the house. Danny Scher, sponsorship. Gregg Perloff, booking. Eleanor, stage designing backstage. Jerry Pompili, security.

At six the next morning, I looked up to see what time it was and realized I'd been writing since midnight. For the first time, I had some slight hope. Because as I told the psychiatrist, "Isn't it strange that if the Stones for some reason decided *not* to tour, I wouldn't feel nearly as bad?" I believed then that I still had a real chance to get that tour. But it did not happen for me.

There was a movie on television that night. At three in the morning. I was writing all these things down and there was a guy on TV talking straight into the camera and you very seldom see that in a movie. A guy talking *into* the camera.

It was Burt Lancaster in a TV movie called *Barnum* about P. T. Barnum. Some of the things he said were *great*. About how he wanted to bring art and culture to the United States. He was the first one who *schlepped* that huge elephant around America. But he also brought opera singers and ballet. He was the *first*. He was Hurok. Barnum, and then Hurok. Looking right into the camera, he said, "Genius is when you invent something. You invent thoughts or ideas. I invented the *audience*."

And he pointed at the camera and he said, "I invented *you!*"

I never looked at P. T. Barnum as any hero of mine. By the time I was born, the audience already existed. But I've been lucky enough in my life to use the combination of the artist and the audience to create an event. That's what I want to be part of. That's what I've always wanted to be part of. And make a difference.

That is why I left the straight job and went to the Mime Troupe and then left the Mime Troupe to do the Fillmore. That was why I spent money when people said I didn't have to. Because I wanted to do something *beyond* the making of money. That's what the Stones tour was for me. It had *nothing* to do with money.

Sure, it was still difficult for me to swallow. But not as difficult as it was before I experienced those twelve hours. I knew then I could still function. I knew then these were new thoughts that were in my head. Despite all I had gone through, I was still *alive*.

Chapter Twenty-Four

Last Word

1.

ROBERT GREENFIELD: Despite how much sense some of the plans he had stayed up all night to diagram on countless sheets of yellow legal paper lined in blue really made, the Stones toured without Bill in 1989. Before they came to play for him at the Oakland Coliseum, Bill went to see the band work in other cities. As soon as the Stones took the stage, the audience leaped up onto their chairs, standing there for the entire show. People who had paid hundreds of dollars for their seats could not see.

In Oakland, Bill had a handbill printed up asking people not to do this. He put one on every seat. He had T-shirts made for all the ushers which on the back said, "PLEASE DON'T STAND ON THE CHAIRS." When the show began, Bill personally worked the aisles, asking people to sit down so that everyone behind them could also see. Bill was so pleased with the result that it was as though he had in fact gotten the entire tour at the very last moment.

Total cost of handbills and T-shirts? Sixty-two hundred dollars. For which the Stones' business manager made it very plain that he did not intend to pay. With thirty-two more cities coming up on the tour, one of Bill's people asked the business manager if he would now be doing this wherever the Stones played.

"What for?" the business manager asked. "We're sold out."

2.

ROBERT GREENFIELD: The Stones were already on tour when the Bay Area was hit by a major earthquake in October 1989. Mick Jagger got in

535

touch with Bill. The Stones wanted to donate money to people whose lives had been devastated by the quake. Jagger wanted to know how much Bill thought they should give. Bill recommended the sum be somewhere between a hundred and fifty thousand and three quarters of a million dollars.

In the end, the Stones gave a quarter of a million dollars to victims of Hurricane Hugo in South Carolina and another two hundred and fifty thousand to victims of the Bay Area quake. Bill flew Jagger down to Watsonville where they both boarded a school bus with the local press to visit a camp for the homeless as well as what little was still left standing of the Pacific Garden Mall in Santa Cruz.

Bill still felt as though he had not done enough. So he organized a twelve-hour telethon on KQED, San Francisco's public TV station, with live concerts from the field at Watsonville High School, in Henry J. Kaiser Auditorium in Oakland, and at the Cow Palace just outside San Francisco. A lot of aging hippie bands from the glory days of the Fillmores like the re-formed Big Brother and the Holding Company performed along with Crosby, Stills, and Nash, Neil Young, Bonnie Raitt, and John Fogerty. The benefit raised a million dollars, a sum which Bill matched through his company for a total of two million dollars.

Had he gotten the Stones tour, Bill himself would not have been in San Francisco when the earthquake struck. He would not have had the time to organize the benefit. With a kind of bitter irony, he himself could not help but note that the two million dollars raised was the difference between what he had offered each of the Stones and what they had received for doing the tour for someone else. When it came to people in need, he said that two million *did* make a difference.

For Bill, the personal highlight of the show was bringing out Bob Hope. Hope received a long, standing ovation from people whom back in the sixties he would probably have tried to send to a small atoll in the South Pacific where nuclear weapons testing was going on. As Graham Nash noted in Oakland, "Hope and Crosby . . . together on the same stage again."

Later that fall, Bill produced the live entertainment segment of a rally put on by the late Mitch Snyder for the homeless in Washington, D.C., to which some two hundred thousand people came. In June, 1990, Nelson Mandela toured the United States in order to raise money for antiapartheid forces in South Africa, where he had been held as a political prisoner for more than twenty-seven years.

With Harry Belafonte as his personal sponsor in the project, Bill worked to organize Mandela's appearance at Yankee Stadium in New York. Right from the start, there was serious political infighting among the local sponsoring organizations as to exactly who would control the event. Everyone seemed to have their own private agenda. Frustrated by the brutal internal politics, Bill felt compelled to withdraw at the very last moment, leaving it to Ron Delsener and Billy Joel's people to pull the event together.

In Oakland, sixty thousand people filled the Coliseum to welcome Mandela to the Bay Area. At five dollars a seat, the audience comprised the biggest cross-section of people ever to come to any show Bill had ever put on. Bill worked on the project with Melissa Gold. Many years before, they had been involved in a brief relationship. The two of them now seemed to come together on a different plane.

BILL: It is now nearly a year since I lost the Stones' tour. I am over the pain. I feel so good now that I really don't want to say how much I grieved. But they changed my life. That's the irony. Now I *love* the fact that I'm alive. A year ago, I didn't know if I was going to live. I couldn't function.

Two months ago, I started sleeping again. Thanks to the Stanford Research Clinic. Now I feel confident again. I understand things I did not understand before. For fifty-nine years of my life, I looked at people when they said they had a cold. I would say, "What do you mean, you have a *cold?* You mean it has you *down?*" When I had a cold, I would say, "Go *away*, cold." I could fly to London or Brazil and I would be up. My body would say it was tired. I would say, "You're *not* tired." But it really was.

The comeback took a long, long time. Besides the depression, I was always exhausted from not sleeping. I took a lot of different things like Prozac and Lithium. But now I am coming down. I only take one Lithium in the morning. Now I am on my way to full recovery. I never thought I was super-human. I just knew I was lucky to have a different metabolism than most people. I had the stamina and the health to work. Through the years, I can count on one hand the number of days I did not go to work. Now I am much more aware of being average. I can be affected by what other people are affected by. I'm human.

In the past, I would always move *past* a disappointment. A relationship with a lady that went bad, a fight with my son, or when I lost an act or some business venture that failed. The fire in my office. I would just spit them out and keep going. Now that I got stopped by something, I try to understand it all in another way.

My mind is back. I feel clear in my thoughts. I have energy. But losing the Stones was like watching my favorite lover become a whore.

3.

ROBERT GREENFIELD: Bill was changing. Losing the Stones' tour was part of it. So was coming off Halcion. So was turning sixty. In January 1991, Bill celebrated his birthday with some friends, Melissa Gold and Steve "Killer" Kahn among them, at his house in Telluride. For years, he had been trying to get a movie made about the Doors. Shooting had just wrapped on Oliver Stone's version of Jim Morrison's life and times. Despite the credit he received as executive producer, Bill was allowed far less input into the movie than he would have liked. He was not pleased with the result.

From Telluride, Bill continued on to Los Angeles. Barry Levinson had first tested and then offered Bill the role of Lucky Luciano in *Bugsy*, a movie starring Warren Beatty as Bugsy Siegel, the gangster whose dream it was to build Las Vegas. Bill was as excited about getting the part as he had ever been about putting on the Stones.

In April, intermediaries arranged for Keith Richards, then in San Francisco to shoot a video with John Lee Hooker and to do some songwriting with Tom Waits, to come see Bill in the office. The two talked for hours, thereby formally burying the hatchet. It was no accident Bill had survived for so long in the business of rock. He was always able to move forward without looking back.

During the summer, Bill did his best to persuade the Stones to do a concert in Moscow to celebrate the rise of democracy in what used to be known as the U.S.S.R. Instead, heavy metal bands performed outdoors, with the kind of result that is often the norm at such shows.

In October, Bill put on the only "Day on the Green" of the year. Fifty thousand people turned out to see a heavy metal show with Soundgarden, Faith No More, and Queensryche opening for Metallica. It had not been a great summer for concert promotion. Ticket revenues everywhere were down. Even Bill was beginning to wonder if his business was in fact as recession-proof as it had always seemed.

Personally, his life was going well. Melissa Gold was essentially living with him up at Masada. The two of them spent nearly all their time together up there or working late at night at the office where Melissa was setting up a long-term project designed to improve the quality of California's public schools. Unlike so many of the women with whom he had been involved before, Melissa seemed to be a calming influence in Bill's life. To many of those who knew him well, it seemed that for the first time as an adult, Bill no longer was alone.

For weeks, Bill had planned on going to the show Huey Lewis and the News did at the Concord Pavilion on the night of Friday, October 25,

1991. The band had actually played there for him six days earlier. But tickets for that performance had sold out so quickly that another date was added, one which the band had to come back to play. In order to both see and thank them, Bill wanted to cover the date himself. It was something he still did on a fairly regular basis, appearing at any show where he had a strong personal connection to the artist or he feared the act might draw a particularly rowdy crowd.

Bill worked a regular day in the office, calling but missing Mick Jagger at the château in France where he was working on a new solo album. At about ten after six, Bill left the office with Melissa Gold. In Bill's big Mercedes with the top down, the two of them drove out to Sausalito. There, Steve "Killer" Kahn came to pick them up in the helicopter Bill had first begun to use after the earthquake caused the partially collapsed Bay Bridge to be shut down for repairs.

The red and white Bell Jet Ranger 206B they boarded that evening is the same, very familiar helicopter seen in countless action and adventure movies as well as the opening footage of "Eyewitness News Team" shows all over America. It is not only the most commonly used commercial helicopter but also the safest, averaging 0.6 deaths per one hundred thousand hours of flying time.

Along with the company plane, the helicopter was kept at the airport in Novato, about twenty miles due north on Highway 101 from where Bill lived. With the Marin County Friday evening rush hour in full swing, Bill beat the traffic by having "Killer" meet him halfway in Sausalito. Someone from Bill's house came to pick up the Mercedes. Later that night, Steve Kahn would drive Bill and Melissa home from Novato in his car.

It was all part of the regular routine designed to make it possible for Bill to go places in the quickest and most efficient way possible. Nothing delighted Bill more than being able to save an hour, especially one wasted in transit.

It had been a warm, clear day. That night, the first big storm of the season hit, dumping four and half inches of rain in some of the wetter sections of Northern California. The ride over to Concord was shaky at best, the helicopter touching down in the parking lot of the Pavilion later than planned because Steve Kahn had altered his route, choosing to fly around San Pablo Bay rather than straight across it.

In a reception room backstage at the show, Melissa Gold told someone how frightened she had been during takeoff. Steve Kahn said the good thing about going anywhere in a helicopter as opposed to a small plane was that you could always turn around and come back.

To Doug Warwick, the assistant general manager of the Concord

Pavilion and an old friend from their days together out on the road with Santana, Steve Kahn confessed that Bill had been scared, saying, "He told me to turn around about six times."

Doug Warwick offered to bring the helicopter inside the Pavilion where it could be literally put on stage for safekeeping overnight. Bill, Steve, and Melissa could then be driven back home. Steve Kahn listened to the offer. Then he went over and sat down at a desk in the Pavilion office, using the phone to check on the weather.

In the inner sanctum where the band was getting ready to go on stage, Bill sat talking about much the same thing. He said the ride over was one of only two trips he had ever taken through the air when he thought that he wasn't going to live through the night. The band joined in on a general discussion of the fear of flying, always a constant theme in the business of rock.

Mario Cippolina, the bass player in Huey Lewis and the News, whose late brother John was the lead guitarist in Quicksilver Messenger Service, told Bill he should stay to watch the show. Then *he* would drive him back home. The offer was half-serious and not one to which Bill replied.

Mario Cippolina had literally grown up around Bill, having gone to his first show at the original Fillmore at the age of nine. He had house-sat Bill's old house in Mill Valley, one which his father had actually sold to Bill. That night, Bill told Mario Cippolina how happy he was feeling. How healthy and content he had been ever since his sixtieth birthday. Bill said he was loving his life now.

Twice that night, Steve Kahn got in touch with the Oakland Flight Service Station at Oakland's International Airport in order to inquire about flying conditions. Like most helicopters, the Bell Jet Ranger was not equipped with instruments designed to make all-weather flying easier. Twice that night, the air controllers told Steve Kahn not to fly.

It was the standard response. Whenever the ceiling is below a thousand feet and visibility limited to less than three miles, Visual Flight Rules recommend that small planes do not fly. The same rules do not apply to helicopters. So long as a helicopter pilot flies at a speed which allows him to see and avoid obstacles, the decision as to whether or not to go is up to him.

Having myself flown with Steve Kahn on a very small plane, I can only say that there never was a more cautious, dedicated pilot. His entire life revolved around flying and Bill. Often, he had flown through weather far worse than what he was looking at that night.

Huey Lewis and the News went on stage at twenty minutes after nine. By then, Bill was sitting upstairs in the Pavilion office where Doug Warwick was about to settle the show with Joe Louis Walker, the opening act, and the accountant for Huey Lewis and the News. Seeing what was going on, Bill looked at Steve Kahn and said, "Time to hit it. Let's get going." Along with Melissa Gold, they boarded the shuttle van for the three-hundred-yard ride to where the helicopter was sitting in the restricted area of the parking lot reserved for those who chose to arrive at shows by air.

Steve Kahn had about ten minutes of prep to do before lifting off. He had to check in with the tower at Buchanan Field, the airport in Concord. When the helicopter took off from the parking lot outside the Concord Pavilion on the final night of their concert season, it was not raining. The weather in Concord was wet and misty but calm, just as it had been on that side of the bay all day long.

A short while later, someone working the show opened a backstage door to run out and get something from his car. Rain was coming down so hard that he turned right around and went back inside, deciding it made more sense to wait out the storm.

Steve Kahn was returning to Marin County along the same route he had used to fly into Concord. High winds, heavy rain, and low clouds may have forced him to fly at a lower altitude than before so he could follow the lights on Highway 37 as it led along the waters of San Pablo Bay back toward Gnoss Field in Novato and home. He may have been trying to set the helicopter down in a field. A sudden downdraft may have struck the craft.

Because a helicopter cannot fly straight into the wind, Steve Kahn may have been "dogging" or rotating the craft so as to maintain a twenty-degree angle into the oncoming storm. Condensation inside the cockpit may have combined with the conditions outside to limit his visibility. No one may ever know for sure.

At about 9:55 P.M., in an area where high winds regularly whip through hills not all that far from the Sears Point Raceway, originally the chosen site for a concert which eventually was put on at Altamont, the helicopter struck a two-hundred-and-twenty-five-foot high Pacific, Gas, and Electric transmission tower carrying a hundred and fifteen thousand volts of power to customers in Fairfield, Vallejo, and Novato.

The helicopter hit the very top of the tower, which was not lit or otherwise marked, in accordance with FAA regulations, bending it over one hundred and eighty degrees. The front of the helicopter exploded. All three occupants were thrown from the cockpit to the ground. Their death was a result of total body trauma. Most likely, there was no prior warning or any recognition on their part of what was about to happen before the accident occurred.

On stage at the Huey Lewis and the News concert in the Concord

Pavilion, there was a momentary surge of power. The lights on the truss on Mario Cippolina's side of the stage went out and stayed black for a song and a half. Out in the house, Doug Warwick noticed that the sound system had dropped to half its previous volume. Heading backstage, he asked, "Did we get a power drop? Did something blow up?" He was told there was a brownout in progress. At the time, no one knew the crash was the cause. The show itself went on.

After the show was over, Mario Cippolina was driving home with his girlfriend and two sleeping kids in his Mercedes. When he reached the bottom of the bridge in Vallejo, there was a roadblock stopping him from getting over to Highway 37. The policeman on duty there would not tell him what was going on.

Using his car phone, Mario Cippolina called the police station in Novato. They told him there had been a helicopter crash. Right away, he had a bad feeling. Even now, long after midnight, the wind was blowing his Mercedes back and forth across the road. In such weather, he felt there was a slim chance that any other helicopter had been flying in the area at that time. Using his car phone, Mario Cippolina called Bill's house, leaving a message in which he made no mention of the crash.

When he got home, Mario Cippolina continued calling, trying to find out if anyone had seen Bill at the gig after 10 P.M. The helicopter had gone down at around 9:55. If anyone had seen Bill backstage at the show after ten, then that would mean he was all right. Finally, Mario Cippolina broke down and called Steve Kahn's wife, Rosann. Doug Warwick had already called her to see if Steve Kahn was home yet. When she asked him why, he told her that Steve had left some things at the hall. It was nothing urgent. Rosann Kahn told Mario Cippolina that she had been paging her husband on his beeper. But he had not called her back. Nothing could have been more unlike him in every way.

Eric Blockie, whom Mario Cippolina had called, got in touch with Nicholas Clainos. He in turn called KCBS, the radio station broadcasting the news. They told him how many people had been killed and their gender, as well as the make and color of the helicopter. When Nicholas Clainos called Rosann Kahn to check on the make and color of the craft, they both knew the awful news was true. Bill's helicopter had in fact never made it back home to Marin County again.

4.

ROBERT GREENFIELD: All day long on Saturday, the story was all over CNN. In many Sunday newspapers, it was front-page news, reflecting a life which for the most part had been led in the public eye for the past twenty-five years. Bill Graham, a man who had never really been sick a day in his life, who at sixty still possessed more energy and stamina than most people one-third his age, was suddenly, inexplicably gone. Those who knew him felt compelled to get on the phone to share the news.

Those who worked for him headed immediately for the office, knowing there were jobs to be done. The media gathered there as well, looking for suitable quotes and sound bites they could send out over the air. Almost no one at BGP that day could speak for long without breaking down in tears. The press actually retreated, leaving Bill's people to tend to the details of his funeral.

The funeral was held on Monday at Temple Emanu-el, a large, imposing cathedral of a synogogue in the very exclusive Presidio Heights section of San Francisco. Two thousand mourners filled every seat. Huey Lewis and the News were there. The Grateful Dead. Neil Young along with his longtime manager, Elliot Roberts. Grace Slick. Paul Kantner. Danny Aykroyd. Ann Getty. Ahmet Ertegun and Jann Wenner flew in from New York. So did Frank Barsalona. All the major promoters with whom Bill had worked were there. Larry Magid, Barry Fey, Jack Boyle, and Ron Delsener. Talent agents and former stage managers. Employees past and present. People whom no one had seen in years. People whom no one knew.

From the podium, people talked in pairs as though to offer one another support. Peter and Bob Barsotti of BGP, two brothers who never in their lives had worked for anyone but Bill, having started at the Berkeley Community Theater while still in high school. Paul Kantner, with whom Bill had so often been at odds, spoke eloquently. So did Mickey Hart, who had always shared Bill's love for Latin music and the pulsing rhythm of the drum. Gregg Perloff of BGP talked. He was followed by Bill's son David and then Bill's sister Ester. "Mother Courage" Bill had always called her. The greatness of her spirit was never more evident than on that day. Row on row, people sat in silence, crying bitter tears.

For the benediction, Carlos Santana played a very raw, gut-wrenching version of "I Love You Much Too Much," the plaintive and very *schmaltzy* song from the forties which Bill had first taught Carlos in the studio by humming the melody on to a tape. When Bill took Santana to play in Israel, he had insisted that Carlos perform the song at every show.

After the speakers were done, the pallbearers slowly escorted the casket out into the street. As the casket disappeared into the hearse, they stood surrounded by photographers who were in turn surrounded by people who had come just to quietly watch. For a moment, no one moved. Then those who had borne the casket grabbed one another in an embrace so fierce that it was painful to watch. Grieving members of a tribe that had only just lost its greatest chief.

Escorted by motorcycle police, more long black limousines than had ever before been seen at a private funeral in the city of San Francisco formed a phalanx for the procession to the cemetery. Bill was to be buried in Colma, the same small town south of San Francisco filled with graveyards where so many years before Bill himself had gone to the funeral of Charles Sullivan, the black man who stood up for him when the Fillmore Auditorium was on the line.

As always at Jewish funerals, mourners stood everywhere among the graves, the living mixed in with the dead. Overwhelmed by grief, Bill's sister Ester embraced the stone marking the grave of her son Avi beside whom Bill was about to be laid to rest cloaked in his *tallis* or prayer shawl, as Jewish law prescribes. A rabbi led the mourners in the *Kaddish,* the traditional prayer for the dead. One by one, people then came forward to put dirt into the open grave. At the back of the crowd, Bill Walton, well-known Deadhead and former All-Star NBA center, stood above it all in a suit and tie, paying his respects. It was the sort of completely incongruous touch Bill himself would have loved.

That afternoon, services were held in the same temple for Steve Kahn. They were followed by services the next day for Melissa Gold. After their third funeral in two days, the emotionally battered employees of Bill's company straggled back into the office looking, as one of them said at the time, like wounded soldiers in a war of death.

The shows themselves never stopped. Bill had always told everyone who worked for him *never* to cancel a show unless they heard from him *personally.* When managers, agents, and musicians asked if perhaps it would not be better to postpone concerts which had been scheduled long before Bill's death, they were told that no one had heard from Bill *personally.* Therefore, the shows would go on as planned.

On the night before the funeral, the Grateful Dead played at the Oakland Coliseum. On the following Saturday, Neil Young, Don Henley, Tracy Chapman, and others performed at the annual benefit concert for the Bridge School at Shoreline Amphitheater. At the end of the show, Neil Young, Willie Nelson, Nils Lofgren, and the Stray Gators played a lovely acoustic version of "Greensleeves," the traditional English folk song Bill had always used to let his audiences know that the show was over, with no more encores to come despite their continuing applause.

Without feeling the need to call a single meeting to discuss what their respective jobs would be, the people at Bill's company went to work organizing a free concert in the park on Sunday in honor of Bill, Steve Kahn, and Melissa Gold called "Laughter, Love, and Music."

Although no announcement was made concerning who would perform, a crowd estimated at anywhere from three hundred and fifty thousand to half a million people filled the Polo Field in Golden Gate Park that day to pay tribute to Bill. It was as though an entire generation had reassembled for one brief moment in the sun to say *Kaddish* for their mythic father. The one person who when everyone else was spinning madly in circles had always been firmly in control.

Jerry Pompili began the day by saying, "Good morning and welcome to the Fillmore Auditorium. Welcome to the Fillmore East and the Fillmore West. Welcome to Winterland and the Berkeley Community Theater." After listing nearly every venue in which Bill had ever put on a show, he ended his greeting by saying, "Welcome to Golden Gate Park. Welcome to Bill's place. This is just another of his dance halls today." Then the show began.

Aaron Neville sang "Ave Maria" as ballerina Evelyn Cisneros danced. Jackson Browne performed followed by Joe Satriani. Carlos Santana played, first with his own band and then Los Lobos as well. Robin Williams did a wild set of manic stand-up comedy before what had to have been the largest live crowd he had ever faced. ("How can it be? Strom Thurmond doesn't even have a cold and Bill is dead?")

Crosby, Stills, Nash, and Young sang eight songs, "Teach Your Children Well" and Neil Young's "Long May You Run" among them. The Grateful Dead and John Fogerty played together. Joan Baez and Kris Kristofferson closed the day by singing "Amazing Grace."

Eight hours after it had begun, Jerry Pompili ended the day by asking everyone to give Bill a standing ovation and one last cheer. Then he looked out over the massive crowd and said to the heavens above as he had so many times before to the man himself, "Hey . . . *Bill! Great show, Bill.*"

In terms of the music business Bill Graham had helped create, it was a historic occasion. For the first time ever, all those many people had turned out for a man who played no instrument. Who could not really sing. Who had not written a single word of any song performed from the stage that day.

At long last, the crowd had finally come for Bill.

Afterword

My father was the ultimate survivor and I have no reason to believe that this quality of his nature has changed. He is still alive within all of those he touched.

Bill used to say that he was born in San Francisco in 1965, three years before my birth. In a strange way, I feel we grew up together surrounded by a culture of art and music that was new to both of us. His adult transformation was parallel to my adolescence, a time I will cherish forever.

In establishing the standards of a new industry, Bill provided a forum for voices to help implement positive change. A man of many contradictions, he fought for what and who he loved, and often loved who and what he fought against. Although my father was forced lifelong to scream for his rights, he never lost the balance in his common sense. He never forgot the important things—truth, love, a healthy environment for our children, and the opportunity for free expression for all.

My father brought many voices to the people. The one that will ring loudest to me, however, is his own. The way he loved was the way I felt after his spirit flew into my heart when he died. I was hungry to love and could only hope to help as many people as he did. May his spirit live on forever.

—David Graham
May 1992

Acknowledgments

For all their help, goodwill, and generosity of spirit during the long haul it took to get this book into print, I would like to thank the following people: Jerry Pompili, Nick Clainos, Jan Simmons, James Olness, Gary Orndorf, Paul Bresnick, Erica Spellman-Silverman, Milton Hare, Edna Gubisch-Chan, and Bruce Tracy.

Speakers

Author's Note: Efforts were made to contact nearly every major figure discussed in this book. For the most part, those who do not speak in their own voices are absent from the text because they refused to be interviewed for this book. I would like to thank those who were kind enough to give me their time but who, for reasons of space, are not represented in this book.

ALLAN AFFELDT—Organizer and founding chair of the group which completed the Great Peace March across America in 1986, he served as president of the American Peace Walk Committee in Russia.

MICHAEL AHERN—One of the first stage managers at Fillmore East, he is now an independent production manager.

ISAAC AMATO—A retired high school librarian, he went to school with Bill in The Bronx.

DEE ANTHONY—The preeminent manager of rock and roll acts during the Fillmore East years, his clients included Humble Pie, Joe Cocker with Mad Dogs and Englishmen, the J. Geils Band, and later, Peter Frampton.

ALAN ARKUSH—A television and movie director, he directed *Get Crazy*, a movie very loosely based on his experiences working at Fillmore East.

KEN BABBS—A former Merry Prankster who now lives in Oregon, he writes and edits *Spit in the Ocean*, "a literary journal published intermittently at no set date."

PAUL BARATTA—Originally an actor, he was hired by Bill to help run the original Fillmore.

FRANK BARSALONA—Along with Bill, the man generally acknowledged to have done the most to make rock into a business. In 1964, after booking the Beatles' first two shows in America, he founded Premier Talent, the first talent agency devoted solely to rock.

BOB BARSOTTI—The last house manager at Winterland, he began working for Bill as a high school student in Berkeley.

PETER BARSOTTI—He has spent his entire professional life producing public events for Bill Graham Presents.

549

PETER BERG—A former member of the Mime Troupe and an original Digger, he is the director of Planet Drum Foundation, which disseminates information on bioregional concerns.

MICK BRIGDEN—A former road manager for Humble Pie, Mountain, and Peter Frampton, he is a vice president of the management division of Bill Graham Presents.

GARY BROOKER—He is the lead singer and one of the founding members of Procol Harum.

ERIC BURDON—He is the former lead singer for the Animals.

REGINA CARTWRIGHT—She and Bill shared a long-term relationship.

ESTER CHICHINSKY—Bill's sister, she lives in Marin County with her husband, Manny.

NICHOLAS CLAINOS—He is the president of Bill Graham Presents.

ERIC CLAPTON—He is the former lead guitarist in Cream and Derek and the Dominoes.

BILL COBLENTZ—An attorney, he has served as both a regent of the University of California and the lawyer for the Jefferson Airplane.

IRVING COHEN—He is the maître d' of long standing at the Concord Hotel in Kiamesha Lake, New York.

KIP COHEN—He served as director of Fillmore East.

PETER COYOTE—A former member of the Mime Troupe and an original Digger, his credits as an actor in movies are extensive.

MARY DALY—She was the Communications Director of Amnesty International.

RONNY DAVIS—The founder of the San Francisco Mime Troupe, he also worked at the Concord Hotel as a teenager.

JON DAVISON—He produced the movie *Robocop*.

JOE DEROSE—An attorney, he helped put himself through school by working summers at the Concord Hotel. He is now in the insurance business in New York.

JIM DOWNEY—A stagehand, he continues to work for FM Productions in San Francisco.

FRANK EHRENREICH—The brother of Bill's foster father, he lives in Florida with his wife.

ROY EHRENREICH—He is Bill's foster brother.

AHMET ERTEGUN—The legendary cofounder of Atlantic Records, he continues to mix high society with low down rock and roll.

RAY ETZLER—Having begun his career in the music business by flipping hamburgers at Fillmore West, he worked along with Bill as the long-term manager of Santana.

SAM FREIBERG—He continues to work as a waiter at the Concord.

DAVE FURANO—He was the first president of Bill Graham Presents.

DELL FURANO—He heads Winterland Productions, the largest merchandiser of rock and roll–related items in the world.

PETER GABRIEL—A founding member of Genesis, he performed on and helped organize both the Amnesty USA and Amnesty International tours.

JERRY GARCIA—He plays lead guitar for the Grateful Dead.

STEPHEN GASKIN—The author of *Monday Night Class*, he still lives on the Farm, the landed commune he founded in rural Tennessee.

BOB GELDOF—Having been knighted for his efforts during Live Aid, he works as a musician in London.

JANE GERAGHTY—The former controller at Fillmore East, she is now vice president at Premier Talent.

MARCIA SULT GODINEZ—She now lives in Maui, where she manages an art gallery.

JUDY GOLDHAFT—A former member of the Mime Troupe and an original Digger, she is a director of Planet Drum Foundation and a rap and movement performer.

HARVEY GOLDSMITH—He is the best-known rock promoter in England.

DAVID GRAHAM—A recent graduate of Columbia College, he manages Blues Traveler.

BORIS GREBENSHIKOV—The former lead singer of Aquarium, he was for years the mainstay of the underground Russian rock scene.

MARUSHKA GREENE—Bill's secretary at the original Fillmore, she now works for the Grateful Dead.

MICKEY HART—He is one of the drummers for the Grateful Dead.

JIM HAYNIE—He is an actor who appears in plays and movies.

JACK HEALEY—He is director of the American branch of Amnesty International.

ROBERT HELLER—He is an actor and director in the theater in New York.

CHET HELMS—He now runs an art gallery in San Francisco.

STEVE "KILLER" KAHN—Having spent years out on the road with Santana, he was Bill's friend, personal advance man, and pilot. He earned his nickname on the 1974 Bob Dylan tour when someone noted that he was a "killer" with the ladies.

PAUL KANTNER—A founding member of the Jefferson Airplane, he continues to perform as a musician.

JONATHAN KAPLAN—He directed *The Accused*, for which Jodie Foster received the Oscar as Best Actress.

LOU KEMP—A boyhood friend of Bob Dylan, he runs a fishery in Minnesota.

KEN KESEY—He is the noted author who once also served as the chief Merry Prankster.

MICHAEL KLENFNER—A longtime friend of Bill's, he began doing outside security at Fillmore East. He now works as an executive consultant in New York.

JON LANDAU—A former editor and rock critic for *Rolling Stone*, he is Bruce Springsteen's manager.

JACK LEVIN—He works as an assistant maître d' at the Concord.

PAT LUCE—She is the former publicist for Fillmore East.

BONNIE MACLEAN—Trained as an artist, she designed several of the early Fillmore posters.

DENNIS MCNALLY—The author of *Desolate Angel*, a biography of Jack Kerouac, he is in charge of publicity for the Grateful Dead.

JIM MATZORKIS—The general manager of an imported automobile port processing company, he has not worked in the rock business since the Led Zeppelin incident.

BARRY MELTON—The former lead guitar player for Country Joe and the Fish, he is now a criminal attorney in San Francisco.

CHIP MONCK—The preeminent lighting designer of his era in rock, he now lives in Australia.

JOHN MORRIS—The first director of Fillmore East, he founded the Rainbow Theatre in London.

MARK NAFATALIN—The organ player in the Paul Butterfield Blues Band, he works in the Bay Area as a blues musician, deejay, and blues festival producer.

GRAHAM NASH—A founding member of the Hollies, he performs and records as a member of Crosby, Stills, and Nash.

JOHN FORD NOONAN—He is an award-winning playwright.

JAMES OLNESS—He works as the archivist for Bill Graham Presents.

DANNY OPATOSHU—He works as a screenwriter in L.A.

GREGG PERLOFF—The executive vice president at Bill Graham Presents, he is in charge of the concert division.

ROBERT PLANT—The former lead singer of Led Zeppelin, he now records and performs as a solo artist.

JERRY POMPILI—From house manager at Fillmore East through running Winterland in the seventies, he has spent the past twenty-four years working for Bill.

HY RANKELL—He continues to work in the dining room at the Concord Hotel.

KEITH RICHARDS—The lead guitar player and co-songwriter for the Rolling Stones, he now also has his own band, the X-Pensive Winos.

ELLIOT ROBERTS—The preeminent manager of L.A.-based folk rock in the seventies, he continues to manage Neil Young and Tracy Chapman. He too worked at the Concord Hotel.

ROBBIE ROBERTSON—The lead guitarist in the Band, he has also worked as an actor. He continues to record solo albums.

RITA ROSEN—Bill's sister, she lives in Los Angeles with her husband, Eric.

DAVID RUBINSON—A record producer, he manages musicians and other producers. As a teenaged musician, he worked extensively in the Catskills.

PETER RUDGE—The tour director for the Rolling Stones and a former manager of The Who and Lynyrd Skynyrd, he has returned to rock as a manager.

CARLOS SANTANA—He continues to record and perform with the band that bears his name.

ROBERT SCHEER—A founder of *Ramparts* magazine and one-time candidate for mayor in Berkeley, he now works as a journalist and college professor.

DANNY SCHER—He is vice president in charge of special events at Bill Graham Presents.

ROCK SCULLY—He is the former manager of the Grateful Dead.

BONNIE SIMMONS—She was the long-term female voice of KSAN, *the* FM rock station in the Bay Area.

JAN SIMMONS—Bill's longtime personal assistant, she now works for the Grateful Dead.

GRACE SLICK—She is the former lead singer for the Jefferson Airplane.

OWSLEY STANLEY—Also known as "Bear," he designs and creates jewelry while remaining part of the Grateful Dead family.

PATRICK STANSFIELD—The first professional stage manager at Winterland, he is now the tour director for Neil Diamond.

MICHAEL STEPANIAN—He continues to practice criminal law in San Francisco.

SONJA SZOBEL—Bill's sister, she lives in Vienna.

JON TAPLIN—The former manager of the Band, he produces movies as well as running his own company in L.A.

DEREK TAYLOR—He is the former publicist for the Beatles.

BILL THOMPSON—He is the former manager of the Jefferson Airplane and the Jefferson Starship.

PETE TOWNSHEND—The former lead guitarist for The Who, he continues to make albums as a solo performer.

ROBIN TROWER—The former and current lead guitarist for Procol Harum, he had an extensive career of his own in the seventies.

EVELYN UDRY—Bill's sister, she lives in Geneva.

PHIL WALDEN—He founded Capricorn Records, the label which first brought Southern-based rock to national prominence in the seventies.

JOHN WALKER—The doorman at the original Fillmore, he died in 1990.

JOHN WASSERMAN—Now deceased, he was the longtime rock columnist for the *San Francisco Chronicle*.

PAUL WASSERMAN—He does publicity in L.A.

WAVY GRAVY—He continues to do what he has always done while also running Camp Winnarainbow for kids in the summer.

DAN WEINER—He is the founder of Monterey Peninsula Artists, a talent agency representing rock and roll acts.

BOB WEIR—He is the rhythm guitarist for the Grateful Dead.

JOSHUA WHITE—He is now a television director.

WES WILSON—He still works as an artist.

PETER WOLF—He is the former lead singer of the J. Geils Band.

Index